# The Life Story
## of Henry Ramsey Jr.

*to*

Dorothy Patterson,
a very special friend,
with respect and admiration

*H R*

a gift from
Carole Kennedy

# The Life Story of Henry Ramsey Jr.

...

AN AUTOBIOGRAPHY

HARDSCRATCH PRESS · 2008

The poems by African American writers that appear in this book (cited in endnotes
with each chapter) are reproduced by permission or are in public domain.
"Dear Lovely Death," "Dinner Guest: Me," "Harlem Sweeties," "Mother to Son,"
"Question (1)," and "Warning" are from *The Collected Poems of Langston Hughes*,
by Langston Hughes, edited by Arnold Rampersad with David Roessel,
associate editor, copyright © 1994 by The Estate of Langston Hughes.
Used by permission of Alfred A. Knopf, a division of Random House, Inc.

Verses from the song "Henry (When Henry Plays His Steel Guitar),"
words and music by Keb' Mo' and John Parker (© 1998 Warner-Tamerlane
Publishing Corp., Keb' Mo' Music and Parker's Pen) are used by permission
from Alfred Publishing Co., Inc. (All rights on behalf of itself and Keb' Mo'
Music; administered by Warner-Tamerlane Publishing Corp., all rights reserved.)

The front cover portrait (and hardcover dust-jacket portrait) of Henry Ramsey Jr.
first appeared on the cover of *The Jurist* alumni publication at Howard University
School of Law. The Summer 1996 edition of the magazine was dedicated
to Dean Ramsey on the occasion of his retirement.


Printed in the United States of America.

First printed December 2008.

Hardscratch Press, 2358 Banbury Place,
Walnut Creek, CA 94598-2347.

www.hardscratchpress.com


Library of Congress Control Number: 2008939050

ISBN: 978-0-9789979-2-2 (hardcover edition)

ISBN: 978-0-9789979-3-9 (soft-cover edition)


9  8  7  6  5  4  3  2  1

In loving memory of
Charles Arthur Tillman and Nellie Watson Tillman,
my father and mother.


And to all the generations of men and women—some famous but most
unsung—whose sacrifice and courage in the face of cruel oppression
have made possible the life recorded in this autobiography.

Contents : *My Story*

*Memorable Events*

# *Preface*

During the writing of this manuscript, people have suggested that I make an effort to publish it commercially. Many people would find my life story interesting, they say, and would find value in my views on contemporary issues, particularly those that concern African Americans. I appreciate their opinions but have decided that I should not seek to commercialize my memoirs.

A document written for the general public—or even for a narrower slice of that audience—would differ greatly from the personal, candid conversations I wish to have with my descendants. I think I have learned a great deal during a lifetime of experiences and personal study. I want to share ideas and observations with my grandchildren, their children, and—I hope—their children's children. It is to them that I am speaking here. I hope that, at some point in their own lifetime, each one of my descendants will have an opportunity to read and reflect on what follows, and that each will find at least some of what I have written to be informative and helpful.

While reflecting on what has happened during my life, I sometimes think how interesting and satisfying it would have been to have had the benefit of the thoughts and ideas of my father Charles Tillman.[1] I wish I had known what my maternal great-grandfather Wesley Williams[2] thought about what was going on in his life during the latter half of the 19th century. How would he have described the struggles he encountered? I wish I knew something about the lives of Charles Tillman's parents and other ancestors, and those of my biological father, Henry Ramsey Sr.[3] But, alas, I have not found a single word.

I feel a strong need to communicate with my progeny across future decades and generations. This book, therefore, is for them. In a separate publication to follow I have attempted to document—to the best of my ability and resources—their relatives and ancestors. To the extent that what I have collected concerning our family's genealogy is incomplete, I hope the start I have made will provide a useful foundation for any historical or genealogical research that my descendants may want to undertake.

## HISTORICAL EVENTS DURING MY LIFETIME

THERE HAVE BEEN EXTRAORDINARY changes in American life—especially for African Americans, other people of color, and women—since my birth on January 22, 1934. My generation has witnessed a great and noble struggle to gain and secure the civil rights of African Americans and other people of color. That struggle has been mostly successful. There has also been an enormous extension of educational opportunities for all Americans. The increase in human knowledge during my lifetime has been amazing. The electrification of rural America and the shift of our national population from agricultural and rural to industrial and urban areas occurred since my birth. I have also seen the development of our national highway system and of commercial passenger airline travel, domestic and international.

Many technological concepts—atomic energy, computers, credit cards, digital cameras, helicopters, intercontinental ballistic missiles, the Internet, jet engine-powered airplanes, mobile telephones, plastic, radar, rocket-powered space vehicles, satellites (communication and surveillance), television, transistors, and Velcro—may have been dreamed of and their development may have been in progress before my birth, but such technical inventions were essentially unknown among the general public in 1934. Today, those creations are commonplace.

Medicines and medical procedures that you, my family, will most likely view as ordinary were first conceived and developed after my birth. Some were considered extraordinary or even miraculous when

first discovered. Important examples include DNA[4] and its role in biological reproduction, penicillin, the human genome, human organ
transplants, human joint replacements (for example, knees and hips),
animal cloning, magnetic resonance imaging (MRI),[5] endoscopes,[6] and
CT scans.[7]

During my lifetime, there have also been extraordinary issues of
war and peace involving the United States: World War II (1938–1945,
but the United States formally joined the fight in 1941); the creation
of the United Nations (1945); the rebuilding of Europe (including Germany) and Japan after World War II; the Korean War (1950–1953);[8]
the Vietnam War (1965–1973), known in Vietnam as the American
War; the Cold War (1947–1989); the collapse of the Soviet Union
(1991); the creation of the North Atlantic Treaty Organization (NATO,
1949);[9] two different wars with Iraq (1991, 2003) under two presidents
named Bush (the father, George H.W. Bush, and the son, George W.
Bush); the development of Japan as one of the world's strongest
economies; the creation of the European Union (EU, 1992); the long
and successful struggle by Africans and other people of color to eliminate most European colonization on the continents of Africa, Asia, and
South America (the 20th century); and the emergence of the People's
Republic of China and India as international economic and military
powers (the late 20th and early 21st centuries).

The United States initiated various small wars against smaller
nations that were incredibly weaker than our country economically and
militarily. Examples include Granada (1983), Panama (1989), and Iraq
(2003). I can think of no legitimate justification for the invasion of any
one of those three countries.[10] I do not mention Afghanistan because I
think the circumstances of that war were materially different from the
other three. In my judgment, even the Afghanistan problem, however,
could have been handled—in terms of American national security—without occupying the country. I also did not mention Bosnia (1992) because that incursion was a NATO operation.

I could go on with the list of changes, conflicts, and differences that
have occurred between my birth and now, but I think the point has

been made: namely, the world in which I now live is phenomenally different from the one into which I was born. You may very well experience comparable cultural, economic, environmental, political, social, and technological changes and issues during your lifetime.

## THE WORLD YOU INHERIT

THE STRUGGLES OF AFRICAN AMERICANS and other people of color for equal rights and fair treatment have advanced dramatically, but those ideals still have not been fully achieved.[11] There remain many issues with which you will likely have to contend. As is often said, we still have a long way to go. Today, we still find an urgent and desperate need to eliminate greed, poverty and ignorance—and the consequences of those evils—in our country and throughout the world. There is no valid reason that anyone in the United States, especially children, should have to go to sleep each night hungry. But millions do. There are no valid reasons that millions of people should be homeless. But millions are. There is no valid reason for any U.S. citizen to be without adequate health care. But millions are. There is no valid reason why any American citizen should be denied reasonable access to a meaningful education. But millions are. There is no valid reason that people who are able and willing to work should be unemployed. Yet millions are.

We have over-fished many, if not most, of the planet's oceans, lakes, and rivers. We have significantly polluted our air, waters, and soils. We are destroying or exhausting natural and, in some instances, nonrenewable resources (e.g., crude oil, trees, medicinal plants, and various animal species) at an incredible rate. We seem unable to adopt meaningful habits and effective practices of conservation and preservation of those precious resources. Far too many of the world's people—including those of us in the United States—seem irresponsibly ignorant of what we are doing to our environment and of the dire potential consequences for future generations. There are ways and means whereby we can reverse at least some of the damage to our environment and can prevent further harm. I commend the following two books to you for your edification:

*An Inconvenient Truth,* by former U.S. Vice-President Al Gore,[12] and *Plan B 2.0: Rescuing a Planet Under Stress and a Civilization in Trouble,* by Lester R. Brown.[13]

My generation faced the Cold War and the specter of nuclear weapons destroying our planet. The threat is still with us under the term "weapons of mass destruction." Such weapons could prove fatal to all of humankind, both in terms of destruction of life itself and of rendering much if not all of the environment unable to sustain life. It is critical that everything possible be done to eliminate every nation's store of nuclear weapons and to prevent the use and proliferation of any such weapons of mass destruction.

Simply put, the appalling and contemptible facts in the immediately preceding paragraphs desperately need to be addressed and replaced with new and positive circumstances. Because I am certain that such changes will not be accomplished in my lifetime, I ask you to do all you can to help bring about the needed corrections during yours. I ask you to add your voice, personal energy, and reasonable financial resources to existing and future efforts to achieve these mandatory objectives.

As to poverty, I urge you to carefully note the following comments by William F. Pepper, written in 2003:[14]

> We have effectively made the masses of poor more invisible than ever. They have limited mobility and resources to travel so they, for the most part, stay where they are in their rural or urban areas. The media rarely visit them to report on their condition and, of course, most Americans do not go where they are. Even if they did live amongst us, there are always the problems of time and personal priorities. Although we do encounter them occasionally whilst we are on holiday in other countries, in America there is also the fact that their condition in a land of plenty makes their fellow Americans uncomfortable. It is easier to avert one's eyes than to look and become aware of the misery in our midst.

Join and actively work with organizations devoted to addressing these issues. You should be involved in the effort to make your world a much safer and better place for everyone. I hope that what I have written will help you to understand why you must do so and will help motivate you to act. Take action for me, for living generations, and for the generations before me who have participated in the struggles to make our country and planet better places than they were when we were born.

So that my comments are available to each of you, I plan to have copies of this document placed at each of the following sites: (1) the Founders Library at Howard University in Washington, D.C.;[15] (2) the Howard University School of Law Library in Washington, D.C.;[16] (3) the Tomás Rivera Library at the University of California at Riverside;[17] (4) the School of Law Library at the University of California at Berkeley;[18] (5) the Bancroft Library at the University of California at Berkeley; (6) the Main Library in the city of Berkeley, California;[19] (7) the Claremont Branch Library in the city of Berkeley, California;[20] (8) the Doctors Bruce and Lee Foundation Library in Florence County, South Carolina;[21] (9) the Braswell Memorial Library in Rocky Mount, North Carolina;[22] (10) the Darlington County Historical Commission in Darlington, South Carolina;[23] and (11) the South Caroliniana Library at the University of South Carolina in Columbia, South Carolina.[24]

## · Notes ·

1. See "My Genealogy," to be published separately.
2. "My Genealogy."
3. "My Genealogy."
4. Or deoxyribonucleic acid.
5. Defined by the *Merriam-Webster Dictionary* as "a noninvasive diagnostic technique that produces computerized images of internal body tissues based on electromagnetically induced activity of atoms within the body."
6. Defined by the *Merriam-Webster Dictionary* as "an illuminated usu. fiber-optic instrument for visualizing the interior of a hollow organ or part (as the colon or esophagus)."
7. See "computed tomography" in the *Merriam-Webster Dictionary*: ". . . radiography in which a three-dimensional image of a body structure is constructed by computer from a series of plane cross-sectional images made along an axis."

8. I served in the U.S. Air Force during the Korean War but did not see combat.

9. NATO essentially consists of countries geographically located in Europe, plus the United States as a very important member.

10. I have excluded the 1991 invasion of Iraq, which I believe could be justified in terms of freeing Kuwait and of our country's need for Kuwaiti oil. Here, I refer to the 2003 invasion of Iraq under the direction of George W. Bush.

11. See the 2006 report titled *The State of Black America*, which is published annually by the National Urban League.

12. Al Gore, *An Inconvenient Truth* (New York: Rodale Books, 2006).

13. Lester R. Brown, *Plan B 2.0: Rescuing a Planet Under Stress and a Civilization in Trouble* (New York: W.W. Norton and Company, 2006).

14. William F. Pepper, *An Act of State: The Execution of Martin Luther King* (London and New York: Verso, 2003), p. 266. I do not commend or endorse this book as a meaningful treatment of the author's central thesis, namely that the killing of Martin Luther King Jr. on April 4, 1968, was a conspiratorial act carried out by various private and public (federal, state, and municipal) parties, including certain agencies of the United States government, e.g. the U.S. Army, FBI, and the CIA. I do, however, strongly urge you to read Chapter 10: A Vision Unto Death and a Truth Beyond the Grave, pp.163-180, as a meaningful source of insights regarding some of the important issues you will face as Americans and citizens of the world.

15. 500 Howard Place NW, Washington,. DC 20059. Visit the library's website at *www.howard.edu/library*.

16. Howard University School of Law, 2900 Van Ness Street NW, Washington, DC 20008; *www.law.howard.edu*.

17. 3401 Watkins Drive, Riverside, CA 92521. Also see Rivera Library, P.O. Box 5900, Riverside, CA 92521; *library.ucr.edu*.

18. School of Law Library, 225 Boalt Hall, University of California, Berkeley, CA 94720; *www.law.berkeley.edu/library*.

19. 2090 Kittredge Street, Berkeley, CA 94704.

20. 2940 Benvenue Avenue (at Ashby Avenue), Berkeley, CA 94705.

21. Florence County, South Carolina, Library System, 509 South Dargan Street, Florence, SC 25906.

22. 727 North Grace Street, Rocky Mount, NC 27804; *www.braswell-library.org*.

23. 204 Hewitt Street, Darlington, SC 29532-3214. Send an e-mail to DCHC1968@aol.com.

24. 910 Sumter Street (intersection of Sumter and College Streets), Columbia, SC 29208.

· *My Story* ·

[W]E SELECTIVELY COMB our past, targeting events and experiences that help us make sense of the present, which account for our path from then to now.[1]

—MARY WHITE STEWART

# 1

# 1934

I was born on January 22, 1934, at 728 North Mulberry Street, Florence, South Carolina, and was named HENRY RAMSEY JR.[2] My birth was not the only significant event in the United States during 1934. Indeed, one of the measures of its insignificance at the time is the fact that it was not reported in any national or regional newspaper, not even a newspaper in the city of Florence.

There were, however, many notable incidents and occasions during 1934. One of the first events reported in leading newspapers that year was Fiorello H. LaGuardia's being sworn in as mayor of New York City on January 1. On that same date, Columbia University upset Stanford University 7 to 0 in the Rose Bowl football game. On February 5, Henry Louis Aaron was born in Mobile, Alabama. I seriously doubt that "Hammerin' Hank" Aaron's birth was reported in the newspaper either. But he was destined to break "Babe" Ruth's several-decades-long record of 715 home runs in 1974 and to hit a total of 755 home runs during a 23-year career in major league baseball that ended in 1976 and won him a place in the Baseball Hall of Fame.

Willie Lewis Brown Jr. was born on March 20, 1934, in Minneola, Texas. His birth also was probably not noted in any newspaper. But Willie Lewis Brown Jr. was destined to have an extraordinary political career.[3] He became speaker of the California Assembly in 1980 and held that position for much longer than any other person in the history of the state (1980–1995). After term limits ended his service in the California Assembly, Willie was elected mayor of the city and county of San Francisco in December 1995 and served two consecutive four-year terms.[4]

On April 13, 1934, the *Chicago Tribune* reported that President Franklin D. Roosevelt had recently appointed Florence E. Allen as a judge of the U.S. Circuit Court of Appeal and that she was the "first woman ever appointed to a federal court of general jurisdiction."[5] In what may very well have been the sound bite of the year, if not decade, for the legal profession, New York's Mayor Fiorello H. LaGuardia was reported in the *Chicago Tribune* on April 26, 1934, as having said in a previous day's discussion, "Lawyers have done more to retard civilization than cancer and smallpox."[6]

The *Los Angeles Times* reported on May 6 that "because of the color ban put up by London hotels, the four Mills Brothers, popular [Afro] American singers at present earning $5,000 weekly, wandered about in the West End of London until 2 o'clock this morning. They were refused admission by more than 15 hotels."[7] A TWA Inc. mail plane set a new record when it flew on May 13, 1934, from Los Angeles, California, to Newark, New Jersey, in 11 hours and 30 minutes.[8]

On or about June 4, 1934, W.E.B. DuBois submitted his resignation to the Board of Directors of the National Association for the Advancement of Colored People (NAACP), both as a member of the NAACP and as the editor of *Crisis* magazine.[9] The acceptance of DuBois's resignation was reported in the *New York Amsterdam News* on Saturday, June 16. Italy won the World Cup on June 10, 1934, when it defeated Czechoslovakia in the final game, 2–1. Joe Louis became a professional boxer in June 1934 and retired in 1949 as an undefeated heavyweight champion. At the time of his death on Sunday, April 12, 1981, Louis had become one of the most revered sports figures in American history.[10]

On June 7, 1934, in Memphis, Tennessee, a white jury deliberated for only five minutes before finding Hilton Ammonds, a black man, guilty of shooting to death Joseph G. Harris, a white grocery clerk, and recommending that the defendant be sentenced to death in the electric chair.[11] Ammonds' trial was held just over two weeks after his arrest and lasted a mere two days.[12] During that same month, J.J. Simmons, a black man, declared his candidacy "for State Representative from the District No. 1 of Muskogee County," Oklahoma.[13] On June 21, 1934, Ms. Ruby H. Diggs became "the first Negro woman to graduate from the Brooklyn Law School of St. Lawrence University."[14]

The *New York Times* for Saturday, July 21, 1934, reported that three days of general strikes in San Francisco, Oakland, Alameda, and Berkeley, California, "had mounted to incalculable heights when they were called off."[15] The following day, the estimated cost of the three-day general strike in the San Francisco Bay Area was reported as $100 million.[16] John Dillinger, a notorious but celebrated bank robber of the 1930s, was shot and killed by federal agents in Chicago, Illinois, on Sunday, July 22, 1934.[17]

President Paul von Hindenburg of Germany died in Berlin on August 1, 1934,[18] and the next day, Chancellor Adolf Hitler had himself elected as president of Germany.[19] Hitler said he would not assume the title of president but would be known as Führer and Reichs Chancellor. Robert Bradford Moxon, a convicted bad-check writer, was installed during August as the first prisoner "in Uncle Sam's new penitentiary for incorrigibles on Alcatraz Island."[20]

It was front-page news in the *New York Times* on Sunday, September 16, 1934, that "the brilliant Ralph Metcalfe . . . equaled the world's record in the 100-meter dash" in Osaka, Japan. It was reported that "the Negro flash from Marquette University tied the mark of 0:10.3, "which had been set four years earlier in Toronto."[21] The *New York Times* reported on Thursday, September 18, 1934, that "Adolf Hitler . . . in his capacity as successor to the late President Paul von Hindenburg, at a reception today, disavowed the use of force as the determinant of nations' relations and reiterated that peace was his 'unswerving aim.' "[22] A widespread—and often violent—textile workers' strike occurred throughout New England and in several Southern states during much of September 1934.[23] In the same month, "the National Football League adopted an unofficial 'gentlemen's agreement' to ban black players in order to conserve jobs for whites during the Depression; the ban [lasted] for 12 years."[24]

The St. Louis Cardinals defeated the Detroit Tigers in a seven-game World Series (October 3–9) for the 1934 baseball championship. Charles "Pretty Boy" Floyd, another infamous American gangster of the 1930s, was shot and killed by FBI agents on a farm near East Liverpool, Ohio, on October 22, 1934.[25] The NAACP retained Charles Hamilton Houston in October 1934 as special counsel. Houston was charged with responsibility for directing the NAACP's legal campaign against racial segregation and for equal rights for Negroes, although he did not commence his full-time duties as special counsel until January 1935.[26]

The Mann Act conviction of Bishop Charles M. "Daddy" Grace was reversed by the U.S. Circuit Court of New York in November 1934.[27] In that same month, two Negroes were elected as justices of the peace in Durham, North Carolina. A newspaper article reporting their election noted, "No Negroes had been elected to a judicial post in Durham for fifty years."[28] On December 21, 1934, Governor Hill McAllister declared martial law and called out the National Guard to prevent a Shelbyville, Tennessee, mob of about 1,000 white men from taking and lynching a 22-year-old Negro male who was on trial for assaulting a 14-year-old white girl. Three members of the lynch mob were slain and 18 others were injured. During the course of the riot, "lawless bands of whites burned down the courthouse, a Negro hotel, and four militia trucks; terrorized the Negro community; and kidnapped the brother of the sheriff."[29] On December 22, 1934, it was announced that "Vassar College, exclusive women's institution at Poughkeepsie, N.Y., was 'now ready to admit Negro Students.'"[30]

In reading certain issues of the *New York Times* published during 1934, one notes a major interest in Adolf Hitler and implications for Europe and America from contemporary developments in Germany. There was also a great deal of discussion and concern about New Deal programs and policies, as well as major labor conflicts and violence in various parts of the nation.[31] Of particular interest during the first six months of the year were the exploits of and hunt for John Dillinger, the infamous bank robber.

Although political developments in Germany and economic issues in the United States were covered in the black press, a major focus of black newspapers was the effort to gain passage of a federal anti-lynching law as proposed to the U.S. Congress by the NAACP in January 1934.[32] There had been a sharp increase in the number of lynchings of blacks, from six in 1932 to 24 in 1933.[33] Also of common concern were the trials and legal appeals of the Scottsboro Boys, nine young black males accused of raping two white women in Alabama in 1931.[34] Despite extremely weak and conflicting evidence, all of the "boys" were convicted, and eight of the nine were condemned to death. After repeated trials and appeals, eight of the Scottsboro Boys were pardoned, freed, or paroled. The ninth escaped to Michigan.[35]

This time was also when the mayor of Jackson, Mississippi, could openly respond to a demand by "a committee of leading colored citizens . . . for a park, a playground, a swimming pool, a library, paved streets in the Negro section, two new grammar schools, extension of the sewerage system, and higher wages for Negro teachers" by publicly declaring that he "would not do a damn thing they asked and that if they didn't like the way things were being run in Jackson to get out of town."[36] The committee's requests were based on the fact that the federal government had given the city $380,000 "for public improvements and to aid unemployment, and since Negroes constituted 45 percent of the population and had none of the improvements requested, some of the money should be expended for their benefit."[37]

My birth was also in the middle of the Great Depression, when economic conditions were extremely difficult everywhere in the United States. The overall unemployment rate in 1934 was 21.7 percent.[38] But the unemployment rate for black Americans throughout the Great Depression was consistently twice that of white Americans.[39] Franklin Delano Roosevelt had been sworn in as the 32nd president of the

United States on March 4, 1933, and he and members of his administration were still struggling throughout 1934 to achieve an economic recovery. Prices were low, but the average American lacked the money for even inexpensive goods and services.

One could purchase a wool overcoat at Macy's in 1934 for $24.50,[40] more than a month's earnings for that average black worker. A new, five-passenger Studebaker sedan—fully equipped and delivered to your door in New York—cost $798.[41] New Cadillacs were advertised in the *New York Times* for $2,395. A new 1934 Ford V8 was advertised for $515 in the *Chicago Tribune* on Sunday, April 1, 1934, page 12. The *New York Times* newspaper was selling for 2 cents in New York City, 3 cents within 300 miles, and 4 cents elsewhere. The A&P Company[42] grocery stores advertised the following bargains in the *New York Times* on February 16, 1934: porterhouse steaks for 33 cents per pound, large eggs at 25 cents per dozen, sugar (cane granulated) at 5 pounds for 23 cents, and raisin bread (standard large loaf) for 8 cents.[43]

A Steinway grand piano could be purchased at the Aeolian Company in New York (Fifth Avenue and 54th Street) for $1,495.[44] Saks Fifth Avenue advertised boys' oxfords (for street, dress, and sportswear, sizes 1–6) for $3.95. Girls' shoes (strap pumps, step-in pumps, and oxfords, sizes 1–6) were also $3.95.[45] In Pittsburgh, the A&P was selling a pint box of strawberries for 19 cents, 3 pounds of prunes for 23 cents, a dozen California navel oranges for 35 cents, fresh tomatoes at 15 cents per pound, cauliflower at 15 cents for a large head, and Lifebuoy soap at 7 cents a cake.[46]

## BIOLOGICAL PARENTS

AT THE TIME OF MY BIRTH, HENRY RAMSEY and MARY LEE RAMSEY, *née* BRUNSON, my biological parents, lived in Florence, South Carolina.[47] Henry Ramsey and Mary Lee Brunson were married on August 5, 1933, in Florence, with the Rev. Bradley B. Brown officiating.[48] According to the Florence County Marriage Register, Henry Ramsey was

25 years of age when they married and Mary Lee Brunson was 19. This marriage was terminated by either death or divorce,[49] and I am the only child resulting from that relationship.

## BIOLOGICAL FATHER

HENRY RAMSEY WAS BORN in South Carolina, most likely in 1908. He died at age 43, on September 13, 1951, in Washington, D.C.[50] The age listed on his death certificate is consistent with his age as listed on my birth certificate and in the Florence County Marriage Register.[51] The age on these three official documents confirms that my biological father was born in 1908.

I know little else about Henry Ramsey. His occupation is listed as laborer on my birth certificate and also on his death certificate, which was filed 17 years after my birth. I do not know the town or county in South Carolina where he was born, the specific date of his birth, or where he may have worked as an adult. Henry Ramsey's mother's name is listed on his death certificate as VIOLA RAMSEY.[52] The informant for the personal history information on his death certificate is given as CHARLES RAMSEY, a brother. I do not know anything else about my biological father's parents, grandparents, or siblings, or if he even had any siblings other than Charles Ramsey. Finally, I do not know if any of his relatives are alive and, if so, where they now live or can be found. Henry Ramsey's address at the time of his death, according to the death certificate, was 107 D Street SW, Washington, D.C. His sole legacy to me was his family Bible and several World War II savings bonds that were payable to me in the event of his death.

## BIOLOGICAL MOTHER

I HAVE A LOT MORE information about Mary Lee Ramsey, *née* Brunson, and her family, because I have remained in contact with various members of her family. My biological mother was born on July 9, 1915, in

Florence, South Carolina,[53] and died, at age 81, on January 4, 1997, in Philadelphia, Pennsylvania.[54] The informant on her death certificate was SANDRA DIXON, née EVANS, her oldest daughter and second child. Mary Lee Brunson is buried near Philadelphia at Rolling Green Memorial Park in Westchester, Pennsylvania.

"Sister," as she was called,[55] married a second time, to Romus Evans. I have been unable to document the date or place of their marriage but it probably occurred in Philadelphia sometime during the late 1940s (an official record of their marriage is probably in Philadelphia but may be in Washington, D.C., or even South Carolina). Romus Evans[56] was born on August 8, 1910, in Fairforest, South Carolina,[57] and died, at age 74, on July 27, 1985, at Temple University Hospital in Philadelphia, Pennsylvania.[58]

Three children (my two half-sisters and my half-brother) were conceived during that relationship Sandra Lee Evans,[59] CHARLOTTE LORETTA EVANS,[60] and TONY EVANS.

I know almost nothing about Mary Lee Brunson's early life other than that she was born and reared in Florence, South Carolina. I do not think Sister had a great deal of formal education, and she probably was not a high school graduate.[61] For most if not all of her adult life, she worked as a housekeeper for white families in the District of Columbia and Philadelphia. She was never a "live-in" maid or housekeeper. Instead, she did what people where I grew up called "day work" or "domestic work." Each weekday, she would report for work early in the morning at the family home of her employer. I am certain Sister lived the great majority of her adult life in Philadelphia and probably began living there in late 1943 or early 1944.

According to MARY FRANCES CASLEY, née BRUNSON, her niece, and CHARLOTTE CALDWELL, née EVANS, her daughter, Mary Lee usually worked for one family for many years before changing her place of employment. LAURENE PORTER of Philadelphia was one of Mary Lee's closest friends. Mary and Laurene met shortly after Sister first came to Philadelphia; for a substantial period of time, they lived in the same apartment house at 762 South 18th Street in Philadelphia.[62] Ms. Porter confirmed in a telephone conversation on March 8, 2004, that Sister did domestic work during the time of their close friendship. My assumption is that Sister also did day work for white families during some of the years she lived in South Carolina, but that simply is a supposition on my part. For approximately the last 10 years of her working life, Mary Lee was employed by the housekeeping department at the Philadelphia College of Osteopathic Medicine, 4150 City Line Avenue, Philadelphia, Pennsylvania. She retired with benefits from that job several years before her death on January 4, 1997.

Notwithstanding her limited formal education and modest occupation, Sister was able to acquire ownership of two houses, where she lived during much of her time in Philadelphia. I find it interesting that in 1971, when Sister moved from 2133 West Stewart Street in North Philadelphia to 1819 South Alden Street in West Philadelphia, she was able to retain title to the West Stewart Street property and to rent it to tenants. In other words, she was able to purchase a home in West Philadelphia without having to sell the property she owned in North Philadelphia to acquire capital. Indeed, she still (essentially) owned both pieces of property at the time of her death.[63] Sister suffered from Alzheimer's disease and serious complications from diabetes during the final years of her life and lived with her two daughters during this period, alternating between their homes.

### · Notes ·

1. Mary White Stewart, *Silicone Spills, Breast Implants on Trial.* (Westport, CT: Praeger Publishers, 1998), 142.
2. Standard Certificate of Birth, State of South Carolina, Bureau of Vital Statistics, State Board of Health, Registration District No. 20-A, Registered No. 31, File No. 1083. Rose Anna Gibson, a midwife, attended my birth. My current address is 2955 Avalon Avenue, Berkeley, CA 94705. The telephone numbers are (510) 549-9033 and (510) 549-0582.
3. See Willie Brown, *Basic Brown: My Life and Our Times*, (New York. Simon & Schuster. 2008).

4. See James Richardson, *Willie Brown: A Biography* (Berkeley: University of California Press, 1996), especially pp. 1, 275, 390. The mayor of San Francisco, by law, can serve only two terms.

5. *Chicago Tribune*, April 13, 1934, p. 23.

6. *Chicago Tribune*, April 26, 1934, p. 7.

7. *Los Angeles Times*, May 6, 1934, p. 2.

8. *Los Angeles Times*, May 14, 1934, p. 1.

9. *New York Amsterdam News*, June 9, 1934, p. 1.

10. See, e.g., Chris Mead, *Champion. Joe Louis. Black Hero in White America*, (New York. Charles Schribner's Sons, 1985).

11. *Pittsburgh Courier*, June 9, 1934, p. 1

12. *Atlanta Daily World*, June 1, 1934, p. 1.

13. *Pittsburgh Courier*, June 30, 1934, p. 4 in first edition. This entry concerning J.J. Simmons will be meaningful for my children, but for the sake of other descendants: J.J. Simmons was the father of Kenneth H. Simmons, one of my very best friends. The article about Ken's father went on to state: "His entrance as a candidate is being watched with great interest by all voters—white and Negro—as Muskogee and Muskogee County have a considerable and unusually heavy Negro vote, despite the fact that Oklahoma is a Democratic state. Simmons is a product of Tuskegee Institute and has lived hereabouts his entire lifetime, having been born near Haskell, a small town in Muskogee County. Following his graduation Simmons entered the real estate business and made investments in oil." J.J. "Jake" Simmons' life is described in his biography titled *Staking a Claim, Jake Simmons Jr. and the Making of an African-American Oil Dynasty,* by Jonathan D. Greenberg (New York: Atheneum, Macmillan Publishing Co., 1999).

14. *New York Amsterdam News*, June 23, 1934, p. 8.

15. *New York Times*, "2,276,000 Days Lost by California Strikers," July 21, 1934, p. 1.

16. *New York Times*, "San Francisco Loss Put at $100,000,000," July 22, 1934, p. 2.

17. *Chicago Daily Tribune*, July 23, 1934, p. 1 in final edition. Also see the *New York Times*, "Dillinger Slain in Chicago," July 23, 1934, p. 1.

18. *San Francisco Chronicle*, "Von Hindenburg Expires!" Thursday, Aug. 2, 1934, p. 1.

19. *San Francisco Chronicle*, "All Military Pledge Fealty to Hitler as President," Aug. 3, 1934, p. 1.

20. *San Francisco Chronicle*, "Prisoner No. 1 Draws Cell on Alcatraz Island," Aug. 3, 1934, p. 1.

21. *New York Times*, "Metcalfe Equals World's 100-Meter Record as U.S. Team Gains Lead in Meet at Osaka," Sept. 16, 1934, p. 1 in section 3 (Sports).

22. *New York Times*, "Hitler Disavows the Use of Force," Sept. 18, 1934, p. 12.

23. See, for example, *New York Times*, "Textile Mills in South Plan to Reopen Today Under Guard of Troops," Sept. 17, 1934, p. 1.

24. Sharon Harley, *The Timetables of African-American History* (New York: Simon & Schuster, 1995), pp. 241, 243.

25. *New York Times*, "Pretty Boy Floyd Slain," Oct. 23, 1934, p. 1.

26. Genna Rae McNeil, *Groundwork: Charles Hamilton Houston and the Struggle for Civil Rights* (Philadelphia: University of Pennsylvania Press, 1983), pp. 116–18. The text includes the following:

    The selection of Charles Houston to direct the NAACP's legal campaign against racial discrimination was simultaneously an endorsement of his proposal to place major emphasis on educational inequalities and [to] fight racial discrimination by means of "a carefully planned [program] to secure decisions, rulings and public opinion on the broad principle instead of being devoted to merely miscellaneous cases." Equally important, the selection of Houston represented the adoption of his strategy and philosophy regarding the struggle of his people against racial discrimination and for equal rights. The NAACP would commit itself to the elimination of segregation through a protracted struggle. . . . That struggle would incorporate local communities' initiation of litigation, community political education, and participation with the guidance and assistance of the NAACP and the gradual evisceration of the separate but equal doctrine by means of test cases successively litigated. The direct constitutional challenge would follow such groundwork. . . ."

27. *New York Amsterdam News*, "Court Frees Daddy Grace," Nov. 17, 1934, p. 3.

28. *New York Amsterdam News*, "N.C. Gets Negro Democrats as Judges— St. Louis Ditto," Nov. 17, 1934, p. 5.

29. *New York Amsterdam News*, "3 Slain, 18 Shot in Mob," Dec. 22, 1934, p. 1. Also see *New York Amsterdam News*, "Lynch Mobs Seek 9 Victims, 2 White, in 3 Southern States," Dec. 29, 1934, p. 1.

30. New York Amsterdam News, "Vassar Will Take Negroes," Dec. 22, 1934, p. 2.

31. See, for example, *New York Times,* "The Nation Weighs the Great Labor Issues," July 22, 1934, p. 1 in section 8.

32. See, for example, *Pittsburgh Courier*, "Nation Rallies Behind N.A.A.C.P. Anti-Lynch Bill," Jan. 6, 1934, p. 2 in section 1, and *Pittsburgh Courier*, "Roosevelt Hits Mob Menace," Jan. 6, 1934, p. 1. Also see *Pittsburgh*

*Courier*, "Entire Nation Joins Fight for Nat'l Anti-Lynch Bill," March 3, 1934, p. 3 in Section 2.

33. See Schomburg Center for Research In Black Culture, The New York Public Library *African American Desk Reference* (A Sonesong Press Book, New York: John Wiley & Sons, Inc., 1999) at Table 12.1, Lynchings by Race and Year, 1882–1962, p. 316. The Tuskegee Institute also kept an ongoing record of lynchings during the 20th century. Their figures are more conservative than those provided by the NAACP because Tuskegee had a more stringent set of "parameters" for what the institute considered to be a lynching. For additional information, see Robert L. Zangrando's *NAACP Crusade Against Lynching, 1909–1950* (Philadelphia: Temple University Press, 1980), and Gunnar Myrdal's *American Dilemma* (New York: Pantheon, 1975), chap. 27. Also see *New York Amsterdam News*, "Lynch Mobs Seek 9 Victims, 2 White, in 3 Southern States," Dec. 29, 1934, p. 1, for a sense of the basis for this concern.

34. See, for example, "Ask President to Give Help to Nine Boys," *Atlanta Daily World*, Atlanta, GA, July 1, 1934; "French Citizens Appeal for Scottsboro Boys," *The Chicago Defender* (National Edition), Feb. 17, 1934, p. 16; "Alabama's Shame," *The Pittsburgh Courier*, May 5, 1934, p. A2; "Pardon The Scottsboro Boys," *The Chicago Defender*, p. 14; and "Sing Sing Inmates Donate Money to Aid Needy," *The New York Amsterdam News*, Dec. 29, 1934, p. 1. (Part of this donation by the "colored population of Sing Sing prison" was sent, in the words of the inmates, "to the Scottsboro boys who are under death sentences in Alabama" in an effort to "bring a bit of cheer and happiness at Christmas time to those more unfortunate than ourselves.")

35. See Leigh B. Bienen and Gilbert Geis, *Crimes of the Century: From Leopold and Loeb to O. J. Simpson* (Boston: Northeastern University Press, 1998), pp. 49–72.

36. *Pittsburgh Courier*, "'Not a Damn Thing for Negroes,' Says Mayor of Mississippi Town," Jan. 6, 1934, p. 2 in section 1.

37. *Pittsburgh Courier*, Jan. 6, 1934, p. 1.

38. Overall Unemployment Rate in the Civilian Labor Force, 1920–2006, www.infoplease.com/ipa/A0104719.html; U.S. Department of Labor, Bureau of Labor Statistics, stats.bis.gov.

39. William A. Sundstrom, "Last Hired, First Fired? Unemployment and Urban Black Workers During the Great Depression," *The Journal of Economic History*, Vol. 52, No. 2 (June 1992), pp. 415, 418.

40. *New York Times*, Jan. 2, 1934, p. 5L.

41. *New York Times*, Feb. 18, 1934, p. 8.

42. Atlantic & Pacific Tea Co.

43. *New York Times*, Feb. 16, 1934, p. 40.

44. *New York Times*, Feb. 21, 1934, p. 5.

45. *New York Times*, Feb. 23, 1934, p. 13L.

46. *Pittsburgh Courier*, Jan. 13, 1934, p. 7 in section 1.

47. I have reason to believe that my biological father's nickname was "Mutt" because that is what I was told by my biological, or birth, mother. Standard Certificate of Birth, State of South Carolina, Bureau of Vital Statistics, State Board of Health, Registration District No. 20-A, Registered No. 31, File No. 1083.

48. Florence County Probate Court, Florence County Marriage Register (Black), 1919–1929, File B4831. Also see South Carolina Department of Archives and History, Archives and History Center, 8301 Parkland Road, Columbia, SC 29223; phone: (803) 896-6100; fax: (803) 896-6198. It has the following record: Florence County Marriage Registry (Black), 1929–1936, Film Roll No. E1175, Frame No. 590, File No. B4831, Issue Date: Aug. 5, 1933.

49. I have been unable to document any divorce action between Henry Ramsey and Mary Ramsey, *née* Brunson. I have also been unable to document the subsequent marriage of Mary Ramsey, *née* Brunson, and Romus Evans.

50. Death Certificate, D.C. Health Department, Bureau of Vital Statistics, Certificate of Death: No. 509759, dated Sept. 13, 1951.

51. See Standard Certificate of Birth, State of South Carolina, Bureau of Vital Statistics, State Board of Health, Registration District No. 20-A, Registered No. 31, File No. 1083.

52. Death Certificate, D.C. Health Department, Bureau of Vital Statistics, Certificate of Death: No. 509759, dated Sept. 13, 1951.

53. See Standard Certificate of Birth, State of South Carolina, Bureau of Vital Statistics, State Board of Health, Registration District No. 20-A, Registered No. 2, File No. 23274. Mary Lee Brunson was actually given the name Beaular Brunson at birth. Her birth, which was attended by a midwife, was at 628 Mulberry Street, Florence, South Carolina. Her Social Security number was 578-26-5494, possibly 5484. Also see Application for Social Security Account No. 578-26-5494, dated March 18, 1942, which is in my personal files.

54. Certificate of Death, Commonwealth of Pennsylvania, Department of Health-Vital Records, No. 011184 and copy No. 2233839, filed Jan. 8, 1997.

55. Many, if not all, of her family members called Mary Lee Ramsey "Sister," and I grew up referring to her by that name. In fact, I always called her Sister when addressing her personally. It is possible that she required me

to call her Mother when I was 9 years old and living with her in 1943, but I have no recollection of that being the case or of my ever having called her "Mother."

56. His name is listed as "Romas Evans" on his Dec. 2, 1936, Application for Social Security Account No. 247-07-2458. However, I will refer to him as Romus because that is the spelling he used during the many years he was married to Mary Lee. For example, he is listed as Romus Evans on his daughter Sandra Evans's birth certificate and on his son Tony Evans's birth certificate. Also, his first name is listed as Romus on his death certificate.

57. On his application for a Social Security account, Romus Evans's birthdate is given as Aug. 8, 1910, and his birthplace is said to be Fairforest, South Carolina. See U.S. Social Security Act Application for Social Security Account No. 247-07-2458, dated Dec. 2, 1936. Romus Evans was 26 years old on that date and was likely to have known his own birthdate and birthplace. He listed his father's name as James Evans and his mother's name as Jamie Evans. But see Sandra Evans's birth certificate, Commonwealth of Pennsylvania, Department of Health, Vital Records, Certification of Birth, File No. 2094000-1947, filed on Oct. 22, 1947, and Tony Evans's birth certificate: Commonwealth of Pennsylvania, Department of Health, Vital Records, Certification of Birth, File No. 2136480-1953, filed on Dec. 4, 1953. In each instance, his birthplace is given as Spartanburg, South Carolina. I was told by Barbara Hart, one of the editors of this manuscript—who was born and reared in the city of Spartanburg—that the community of Fairforest is just outside the city and its records are maintained by Spartanburg County. Thus, the birthplace undoubtedly refers to Spartanburg County. Romus's age is listed as 35 on Sandra's birth certificate, and she was born in 1947. If Romus had, in fact, been born in 1910, then he would have been 37 when Sandra was born. Romus is listed as being 39 on Tony's birth certificate. If he were born in 1910, then he would have been 43 when Tony was born. Hence, the ages given for Romus on two of his children's birth certificates are not consistent with the birthdate on his Social Security application. It may simply have been that Romus wanted to be considered younger than he was.

58. Commonwealth of Pennsylvania, Department of Health, Vital Records, Certificate of Death, No. 2922991, State File No. 071627, Social Security No. 247-07-2458. My assumption is that the information on the birth certificates of Romus's children was provided by Sister and him and therefore was more reliable than information concerning his age provided years later by Sandra Lee Dixon as the informant for his death certificate.

59. Subsequent names through marriage: Sandra Lee Dixon, Sandra Lee Washington, and Sandra Lee Thompson.

60. Subsequent names through marriage: Charlotte Loretta Seville and Charlotte Loretta Caldwell.

61. Her daughter Charlotte Caldwell, *née* Evans, thinks she may have completed only the sixth grade.

62. Information about address provided by Laurene Porter.

63. Title to the West Stewart Street property was transferred to her daughter, Sandra, and title to the South Alden Street property was transferred to Sister and Sandra as co-owners, sometime well before Sister's death.

# 2

# Charles and Nellie Tillman
## "IN LOCO PARENTIS" [1]

According to NELLIE TILLMAN, *née* WATSON, the person I consider and honor as my mother,[2] I was "given to her" when I was about 3 months old, during a visit to Florence, South Carolina. She said that while in Florence in 1934 (it must have been during the early spring), she visited a house where Aunt HENRIETTA CASLEY, *née* WILLIAMS,[3] and some other women had two babies on a "pallet" (typically a blanket, quilt, or other cloth placed on the floor). She was told that I belonged to Sister and said that at some point she was told that the babies' mothers had left them to be cared for or raised by these women. My mother reported asking Aunt Henrietta and the other women to "give me one of these babies." She was told that they were going to keep the older baby–WILLARD CASLEY–but that Nellie could take me, the younger and smaller one.

Nellie Tillman was Sister's aunt by marriage[4] and therefore my great-aunt by marriage, as well as my mother by choice. My mother said she had a brief discussion about the matter with Sister later that day and immediately thereafter was permitted to take me to Rocky Mount, North Carolina. There I was given a new name–CHARLES ARTHUR TILLMAN JR.[5]–and was reared under that name as the child of Charles Arthur Tillman and Nellie Tillman. From the time of my earliest memory, I recall being told by my mother that I was not her natural child and that Sister was my "real" mother. However, I have no recollection of ever meeting Sister until I was 8 years old.

A question that has interested me for a long time is how Willard's life and my life might have differed had my mother taken him to Rocky Mount and left me in Florence. There was little chance of that happen-

NELLIE TILLMAN, *née* WATSON, *my mother.*

ing because, as my mother told me, she was advised in no uncertain terms that although I was available, Willard was not. One of the women in that group in Florence, probably the leader, was Aunt Henrietta. She was married to ROY CASLEY, and the two of them adopted and reared Willard Casley[6] from infancy.[7] Regardless, I do sometimes think about what would have happened had a different choice been made in 1934. As fate would have it, years later Willard Casley was to meet and marry my second cousin, MARY FRANCES "MICKEY" BRUNSON.[8] It was after Mickey and Willard were married that he and I met again. Mickey had been reared by Sister, my biological mother, and I first met her in that context. I had absolutely no contact with Willard between my leaving Florence as a baby and his and Mickey's marriage. Our reunion was purely a matter of chance, and it was through this connection that I was able to piece together much of Willard's and my common early background.

I have discussed with ANN BETH CASLEY, Willard's daughter, this "what if" question concerning a different selection between Willard and me, and she believes that it would not have made any difference had Willard been given to my mother instead of me. She is confident that our different paths are reflective of our different personalities. She notes that both Willard and I were reared by women and men who were not our biological parents. My mother was a strong and loving figure in my life, and she says that Willard felt the same about Aunt Henrietta's influence in his life. According to Ann Beth, Willard always said that his adoptive mother, Henrietta Casley, strongly encouraged him to "grow up to be somebody." That was also the advice and encouragement given me by my mother, Nellie Tillman.

Nevertheless, I sometimes find myself pondering the different paths that Willard and I took. He grew up in Florence and, like me, did not graduate from high school.[9] At some point fairly early in his life, Willard moved from South Carolina to New York and lived in Brooklyn.[10] He was never a member of the U.S. Air Force (as I was) or any other branch of the U.S. armed forces. He never attended college or acquired a GED high school equivalency diploma. While living in Brooklyn, he was introduced to my cousin Mickey Casley, *née* Brunson, by her brother. He and Mickey were married on November 6, 1955, and subsequently had three children—WILLARD LEROY "POOKEE" CASLEY JR., WILLIE ALFONSO CASLEY, and Ann Beth Casley. Willard held various jobs during his adult life: as a cook[11] at Horn and Hardart in Manhattan, as a sales clerk in a variety store, and as a chauffeur. As long as Ann Beth can remember, Willard always had a "hustle" on the side. In fact, Ann Beth stated to me that she believes the legitimate jobs were simply a cover for his hustles of selling illegal booze, selling illegal hard drugs, and gambling. He became a Jehovah's Witness in about 1974 or 1975 and consequently dramatically changed his behavior. After his religious conversion, he apologized to his wife and children for his past bad behavior and thereafter lived a moral and law-abiding life. He also sought out and found his biological mother sometime during the later years of his life. At the time, his biological mother was living in Newark, New Jersey.

Despite Ann Beth's belief that my life would not have been dramatically different had I been left in Florence, I strongly disagree. It is highly likely that my life would have turned out very differently and in a negative way. Although we were both reared in supportive communities, there were also differences in our development that I find important. My service in the Air Force and some of the people I met during my four-year tour of duty played a major role in how I turned out as a person. The same is true of the benefits I received as a result of attending college. Willard did not have that support or those advantages. Also, had I been left in South Carolina, there is a good chance that I would ultimately have been reared by Sister and subjected to her control and influence. Most likely, that arrangement would have been a disaster for me. As it was, I was reared by a caring and supportive mother and in an encouraging community.

Of course, neither Willard nor I had any excuse for the negative aspects of our lives that we caused ourselves. But I cannot share Ann

Beth's conviction that the different results reflected in our individual lives resulted simply from our different personalities. I am absolutely convinced that a major factor in the person I became as an adult was also the love shown me and the educational foundation I received from my father, Charles Arthur Tillman, discussed *infra*. I admit, however, that I do not know what the result would have been had my mother been given and exercised a different selection between the two babies— Willard and me.

The manner in which I was "adopted"[12] in 1934 was not unusual, particularly among black people, at that time in our nation's history and in the southern United States. And it should also be remembered that the event occurred during the Great Depression, when the arrival of a new mouth to feed often required poor and working-class families to confront difficult choices. Often an infant or young child would be given or entrusted to grandparents, or an aunt, or another close relative to rear to adulthood. As stated earlier, Nellie Tillman was Mary Lee Ramsey's aunt by marriage and, therefore, my great-aunt. She had previously been married to one of Sister's uncles, a brother of Sister's mother (CHARLOTTE BRUNSON, *née* WILLIAMS).

At the time Nellie Tillman brought me to Rocky Mount, she and her husband were living at 424 Raleigh Road in a colored neighborhood known as Little Raleigh.[13] The house that we lived in was essentially a duplex, consisting of a wood-frame house with a front porch that extended across the entire front of the house and two parallel front entrances. One set of steps provided access to the front porch. On each side of the "duplex" were four rooms: first was a front room (the living room), immediately behind the front room was a bedroom, behind that was a second bedroom, and behind that was the kitchen. The roof was tin and made a lot of noise whenever it rained hard. There was a toilet on the back porch, and steps led from the back porch down to a reasonably ample backyard.

Several years later, we moved to another Rocky Mount colored neighborhood known as Around the Y. There we lived at 108 Dunn

Street in a single-family dwelling. This house, like the one on Raleigh Road, was made of wood. The tin roof was painted red, and I think the house was painted gray. The house had no formal foundation but rested on brick pillars that were about two feet high and were placed at certain locations around the perimeter of the house and at a couple of locations under the middle of the house. The house in Little Raleigh had been similarly supported. We did not have a telephone at either site. In fact, I never lived in a house with a telephone at any time I lived in Rocky Mount. I presume my parents moved to Around the Y because my father's health was in serious decline and he could no longer work. My assumption is that they, therefore, could no longer afford the rent being charged for 424 Raleigh Road.

I remember our house on Dunn Street as having five rooms, a living room, three bedrooms, and a kitchen. A hallway led to the kitchen, between the side of the house with the living room and one bedroom, and the other side with two bedrooms. The toilet at the Dunn Street house was also on the back porch, just off the kitchen. The house was illuminated with coal oil (kerosene) lamps. I do not recall how the house on Raleigh Road was lighted, but I think it was the same. Although the Dunn Street house had more square footage than our previous home, it was in a much poorer neighborhood, very close (certainly no more than 25 yards) to the Atlantic Coast Line Railroad Company's railroad yards and maintenance shops. As best I can remember, like most other houses in our neighborhood, ours had a porch that extended across the entire front. I would often sleep on the porch on a pallet on hot nights in the summer and early fall.

Like many black Southerners, I had a nickname that was not directly related to my actual name, at least as far as I know.[14] Although my first name was Charles, I was never called "Chuck" or "Charlie." Nearly everyone called me "Bobby," as in "Bobby" Tillman. My schoolmates, those who did not live near me in Little Raleigh[15] (a relatively large geographic area) or in Around the Y[16] (a relatively small geographic area), tended to call me Charles or Charles Tillman. I have no idea why I was called "Bobby," or the source of that nickname, but that is the earliest name I remember.

For a period during my teenage years, I was also called "Straw." I was very skinny as a child and teenager. At some point during my early teenage years, someone remarked to me that I was so skinny that "if you stood behind a broom straw, no one would be able to see you." This comment was considered both apt and humorous and resulted in more than a few of my contemporaries calling me "Straw Tillman" for a number of years. Indeed, HENRY DAVIS and HENRY "SHORT" BARNES —two of my contemporaries in Rocky Mount—still do today.

## BIG BROTHER

MY MOTHER HAD A SON from a previous marriage who was already an adult when I came to live with her and my father. His name was JAMES WILLIAMS, and I grew up knowing him as my older brother. In fact, I called him "Big Brother" during my early years. He married QUEEN ROBERSON, *née* WELLS,[17] his second wife, on November 16, 1936, in Rocky Mount, Nash County, North Carolina.[18] I always called her "Aunt Queen." I do not know the specific year when James and Queen Williams ended their marriage. Big Brother left Rocky Mount and moved to Philadelphia sometime in the late 1930s or very early 1940s, and Aunt Queen remained in Rocky Mount. Thereafter, he would travel from Philadelphia to Rocky Mount on a regular basis to visit family and friends. He continued this practice until my mother moved to Philadelphia in 1955. I do not know if James and Aunt Queen ever got a formal divorce. I do know that Aunt Queen attended his funeral in Philadelphia in 1972 and so did his first wife, Alice Emily Laura Leva Lyde, who used Laura as her first name.

## · Notes ·

1. According to *Black's Law Dictionary,* fourth edition (1951), *in loco parentis* means "In the place of a parent; instead of a parent; charged, factitiously, with a parent's rights, duties, and responsibilities."

2. Whenever and wherever I use the word "mother" in this writing, unless specifically indicated otherwise, the reference is to Nellie Tillman.

3. Henrietta Casley, *née* Williams, was Sister's aunt (her mother's sister) and my great-aunt. She was also Nellie Tillman's former sister-in-law.

4. Her first husband had been one of Sister's maternal uncles.

5. I am certain that this change of name was without the use or benefit of legal process.

6. See discussion regarding Willard Casley and Mary Frances "Mickey" Casley in "My Genealogy," to be published separately.

7. There is also ugly family folklore insinuating that Willard was actually the result of a liaison between his biological mother and Aunt Henrietta's husband. I have absolutely no reason to believe there is any truth to that tale, but it is occasionally mentioned.

8. For a more detailed discussion of the marriage between Willard Casley and Mary Frances "Mickey" Casley, *née* Brunson, see "My Genealogy."

9. Ann Beth Casley, his daughter, was the initial and primary source of the information that Willard did not graduate from high school. Mickey Casley, his wife, later confirmed that Willard was not a high school graduate, as did Juliette Perry, Frizzell Harper's widow. Frizzell and Juliette were both schoolmates of Willard Casley in Florence. Not knowing that Frizzell had died about 10 days earlier, I called on December 10, 2004, to ask if he could confirm that Willard was a high school dropout. His wife told me that Frizzell had died but that she was a native of Florence and had attended high school with Willard, so she personally knew that he did not finish high school.

10. According to Mickey Casley and Ann Beth Casley, Willard most likely moved from Florence to Brooklyn in 1954, when he was 21 years old.

11. Family members and others refer to this position as "Chef Cook," although the word *Chef* necessarily implies cook.

12. One could describe it as an "informal adoption," but I know that any officially recognized or legally binding adoption requires state approval.

13. This home was in Nash County, Rocky Mount, North Carolina.

14. For example, I had contemporaries whose nicknames were "Boo Boo" (Irvin Jackson), "Boot" (Clifton Ingram), "Bro" (William Hobbs), "Cheetah" (Arthur Ingram), "Ham Bone" (Joseph Rollins), "Little Sugar" (Mary Shaw)," Jug" (Charlie Bullock), "Juke" (Isaac July), "Midget"

(Thelma Hobbs), "Peanut" (Jasper Gilmore), "Pig" (Virgie July), "Possum Pete" (Leroy Gibbs), and "Short" (Henry Barnes). Conventional nicknames would have been, in order, "Irv," "Cliff," "Bill," "Art," "Joe," "Chuck," "Ike," "Roy," and "Hank." Mary, Thelma, Jasper, and Virgie do not lend well to nicknames.

15. See discussion about this neighborhood in subsequent chapters.

16. More on this neighborhood in subsequent chapters.

17. See Nash County, North Carolina, Male Indexed Register of Marriages, from 1918 through 1937. Roberson was her last name from a previous marriage. Her maiden name was Wells.

18. This record is in Nash County. The marriage license was not available at the time of this writing because the paper that it is printed on is very fragile. It was anticipated that James and Queen's marriage license and certificate, along with all marriage certificates issued before 1953, would be scanned after October 2004, and thereafter paper copies of those documents would be available. The marriage index, which I was told by the Office of the Nash County Register of Deeds could not be copied, provides the name of the male being married as James Williams, age 33. It shows his father as Buster Williams and his mother as Nellie Williams Tillman. The name of the woman being married is given as Queen Roberson (Mrs.), age 26. Ruth B. Bunn, Justice of the Peace, performed the marriage, and it was witnessed by Eddie Dozier and William S. Bunn.

# 3

# New Family, New Home

Charles Arthur Tillman and Nellie Williams,[1] *née* Watson, were married on or about July 15, 1919, in Florence, South Carolina.[2] They were living in Rocky Mount, North Carolina, at the time of my birth. Nellie Tillman was born on December 3, 1894, in Marion, South Carolina,[3] and she died, at age 69, on February 22, 1964, in Philadelphia, Pennsylvania.[4] Although I know and accept the fact that Mary Lee Ramsey was my biological mother, it was Nellie Tillman who reared and nurtured me. Until the time of her death, she functioned as my mother in every positive meaning of that word. Therefore, I consider Nellie Tillman to be my mother and have always referred to her as such. She is buried at Eden Cemetery near Philadelphia, claimed to be the oldest public African American cemetery in the United States. The address is 1434 Springfield Road, Collingsdale (near Yeadon), Pennsylvania. Her burial plot number is Catto A, Lot 633, Grave #3.[5]

Charles Arthur Tillman,[6] whom I consider my father, was born on August 10, 1890,[7] at 208 Dixon Street (formerly East Dixon Street), in Marion, South Carolina,[8] and died, at age 52, on October 25, 1942, at 108 Dunn Street, Rocky Mount, North Carolina.[9] His body was buried in Unity Cemetery in Rocky Mount.[10]

I know that Charles Tillman lived in Florence for several years as an adult. When he and my mother were married in Florence in July 1919, he was not quite 29 and she was 25. I presume they were both living in Florence at that time. He was living there in 1925, according to the *1925 Florence City Directory*.[11] In all probability, my father and mother moved to Rocky Mount sometime between 1926 and 1929, and I would surmise that the actual year was 1928.

In the listing in the *1925 Florence City Directory*, Charles Tillman (colored) is described as married to Nellie, his occupation is said to be a fireman for the Atlantic Coast Line Railroad Company, and his address is given as 210 W. Sumter Street, Florence.[12] Charles Tillman and his wife, Nellie, are not listed in the *1928 Florence City Directory*. They are listed, however, in the *1930 Hill's Rocky Mount City Directory*. In that directory, Charles Tillman is listed as a fireman for the Atlantic Coast Line Railroad Company, his wife is listed as Nellie, and his address is given as 920 Red Row.[13] A fireman for the Atlantic Coast Line Railroad Company, almost always an African American during the steam-engine era, basically had the responsibility for shoveling coal and for maintaining the fire in the steam locomotive's firebox. That fire was the heat source that generated the steam that powered the engine, which pulled the train.

Six years later, in the *1936 Rocky Mount City Directory*,[14] my father is listed as a helper for the Atlantic Coast Line Railroad Company, with his address now being given as 424 Raleigh Road. My assumption is that he was basically a misclassified skilled laborer in 1936, but I do not know that. It was not unusual during his lifetime for black industrial workers to be classified and paid as unskilled or semiskilled workers, although they were actually performing skilled work. Because of racial discrimination, which was not then prohibited by local, state, or federal law, black skilled workers were not even permitted to join many of the American Federation of Labor (AFL) trade unions. This situation did not materially change until after 1955.[15]

In the *1938 Rocky Mount City Directory*, my father is listed as a silk worker at a local silk mill. My mother is listed as a cook at the Rocky Mount Sanitarium, which was a small private hospital.[16] Their address is still said to be 424 Raleigh Road. It was probably because of declining health that my father could no longer perform the physically demanding work required of either a fireman or a helper within the

Emerson maintenance shops of the Atlantic Coast Line Railroad Company. Only a few years later, he was bedridden with what people described as "heart trouble."

Because my mother took me to Rocky Mount in 1934 as an infant, I have no personal recollection of my father ever working as a fireman. I do recall his working in Little Raleigh at the silk mill, which was located near a neighborhood called Germantown, and my mother's working downtown as a cook at the Rocky Mount Sanitarium.

Whenever I read Paul Laurence Dunbar's "Little Brown Baby," I always think of my father and how I believe he felt about me:

> Little brown baby wif spa'klin' eyes,
> Come to yo' pappy an' set on his knee,
> What you been doin', suh—making san' pies?
> Look at dat bib—you's ez du'ty ez me.
> Look at dat mouf—dat's merlasses, I bet;
> Come hyeah, Maria, an' wipe off his han's.
> Bees gwine to ketch you an' eat you up yit,
> Bein' so sticky an' sweet—goodness lan's!
> Little brown baby wif spa'klin' eyes,
> Who's pappy's darlin' an' who's pappy's chile?
> Who is it all de day nevah once tries
> Fu' to be cross, er once loses dat smile?
> Whah did you git dem teef? My, you's a scamp!
> Whah did dat dimple come f'om in yo' chin?
> Pappy do' know you—I b'lieves you's a tramp;
> Mammy, dis hyeah's some ol' straggler got in!
> Let's th'ow him outen de do' in de san',
> We do' want stragglers a-layin' roun' hyeah;
> Let's gin him 'way to de big buggah-man;
> I know he's hidin' erroun' hyeah right neah.
> Buggah-man, buggah-man, come in de do',
> Hyeah's a bad boy you kin have fu' to eat.

Mammy an pappy do' want him no mo'
Swaller him down f'om his haid to his feet!
Dah, now, I t'ought dat you'd hug me up close.
Go back, ol' buggah, you sha'n't have dis boy.
He ain't no tramp, ner no straggler, of co'se;
He's pappy's pa'dner and playmate an' joy.
Come to you' pallet now—go to yo' res;
Wisht you could allus know ease an' cleah skies;
Wisht you could stay jes' a chile on my breas'—
Little brown baby wif spa'klin' eyes![17]

I have a strong memory of my relationship with my father. He often took me with him wherever he went in our neighborhood and around town, and he always expressed deep concern and affection for me. He taught me to read before I began school at age 5. Although I remember almost none of the details of those occasions, I do remember that my father took me to at least one minstrel show and also took me to the annual fair several years. I do not know whether it was a county or city fair, but there is a location in the city where the fair was held—the fairgrounds, on Fairgrounds Road. It was obvious to me and everyone around us that I was special in my father's eyes. He died in 1942 when I was only 8 years old, and I did not truly appreciate the depth of my loss until many years later. Still, I have no doubt that the too brief number of years we spent together contributed greatly to the person I have become and to all that I have achieved.

## Extended Family

Although Nellie Tillman essentially reared me, she was assisted in that effort by Elnora Ingram,[18] *née* Curry, who is my father's niece, my first cousin, and my children's second cousin. From my earliest memory, Elnora lived in Rocky Mount, either with or very near my family (my parents and, later, my mother and me). From the time I was a little boy, I always knew Elnora to be a kind, friendly, and gentle woman. At some point, when our own children were young, my wife Eleanor and I began to take a two-week trip abroad each year. For several of those years, Elnora flew out to California from North Carolina to stay with our children while we were away on vacation. I will always be grateful for the love and care she extended to my wife, my children, and me throughout her lifetime.

Indeed, my earliest memories of living with my parents at 424 Raleigh Road in Rocky Mount include Elnora Ingram living with her children at 813 Jackson Place, about a block and a half away.[19] Elnora's six children, in the order of their birth, were MEOLA INGRAM, MARION INGRAM, CHARLES INGRAM, ARTHUR INGRAM, CLIFTON INGRAM, and RAYMOND INGRAM. I was regularly at Elnora's house, and her children were often at mine. At that time, my father was the patriarch of both households. I do not know when ELWOOD INGRAM, Elnora's husband, essentially abandoned his family, but it was clear from very early in my life that he was an absentee father.[20]

I was essentially reared as an only child until about age 14 when my mother, now again a widow, married the Reverend JOHN ALEXANDER JULY. However, I was very much a part of a "family" that included Elnora's six children, because our two households were essentially one. We lived in the same neighborhoods and often as one family for most of my youth. We lived in the same house during several of those years, and even when not living under the same roof, we rarely lived more than two blocks apart. Besides the houses at 424 Raleigh Road and 813 Jackson Place in Little Raleigh, we were for a time at 108 Dunn Street and 1017 Red Row Street in Around the Y, about two blocks apart.

Elnora and her children lived for a time with us at 105 Ward Street in South Rocky Mount.[21] For the life of me, I do not see how all nine of us (my mother, Elnora, Meola, Marion, Charles, Arthur, Clifton, Raymond, and I) were able to live in various three-room or four-room houses. Three of the Ingram boys and I sometimes shared a regular-size bed—two at the foot, and two at the head. And while all of us recognized and expressed the familial relationship as cousins, our actual relationship was more like that of siblings. I have no genetic material in common with Elnora and her children, but no family relationship is closer than the one we share.

Elnora worked very hard as a single parent to support herself and her six children. At times in her early adult life, she was employed as a domestic worker or housekeeper, a laundry worker at the Quality Laundry, and a restaurant worker at the Pomi Inn. But she supported her children during their childhood primarily by working seasonally at the Lea W.B. Tobacco Factory. The city of Rocky Mount was—and is— the commercial center of Nash and Edgecombe counties, and it was then one of the nation's largest tobacco markets. The Chambers of Commerce of Rocky Mount and nearby Wilson, North Carolina, touted their cities as "The World's Largest Tobacco Market" and "America's Largest Tobacco Market,"[22] respectively.

In addition to warehouses where tobacco farmers brought their flue-cured[23] tobacco to be displayed and sold at auction, Rocky Mount had several tobacco factories that were owned by major tobacco companies. In those factories, the unprocessed tobacco that had been purchased at the tobacco auctions was cleaned, stemmed (the tough center stem removed from the leaf), cut, and otherwise prepared for storage and shipment. The processed tobacco would then be shipped to the tobacco companies in different tobacco manufacturing centers to be made into various tobacco products—cigarettes, cigars, snuff, chewing tobacco. Examples of those centers are Liggett & Myers Tobacco Co. in Durham, North Carolina; R.J. Reynolds in Winston-Salem, North Carolina; and Phillip Morris USA in Richmond, Virginia.[24]

The length of one's employ as a temporary worker at a given Rocky Mount tobacco factory was based strictly on seniority. The longer you had been working in the past, then the longer you would work in the new season. In other words, the more years you had been working for a specific tobacco factory or company, the earlier you would be hired by that factory and the longer you would be retained to work at the factory during a given season. At the Lea factory, the only tobacco factory where she ever worked, Elnora eventually gained sufficient seniority to be one of the first workers hired each season and among the last let go. Eventually, her seniority was such that she probably worked at the factory nine or 10 months each year.

As stated earlier, my father died when I was 8 years old, when we were living at 108 Dunn Street. Our family had probably moved from Little Raleigh to Around the Y a year or two earlier. Approximately a year after my father's death, I went to live with Mary Lee Ramsey, my biological mother. While the matter was never discussed with me, I have surmised that, after my father's death, my mother concluded that she could not continue to be responsible for me and somehow contacted Sister and asked her to come and get me.

Regardless of how the matter came about or what was the motivation, Sister appeared at our house on Dunn Street in Rocky Mount about a year after my father's death. I remember that—at some point soon after her arrival—Sister and my mother asked me if I wanted to take a trip to Washington, D.C. What 9-year-old child from little ole Rocky Mount wouldn't be excited at the prospect of going on the train to Washington, D.C., a major city and the nation's capital? I excitedly said, "Yes." I was not told that this trip would be one-way or permanent, but I now suspect that was their plan. Within a few days, or perhaps it was hours, Sister and I were on a train headed for Washington and what was to become, for me, the toughest and worst year of my life, before or since.

## · Notes ·

1. My mother's first marriage was to Buster Williams. I have not been able to find any official records concerning Buster Williams other than his name being listed as the groom's father on the marriage license of James Williams and Queen Roberson.

2. South Carolina Department of Archives and History, Archives and History Center, 8301 Parkland Road, Columbia, SC 29223; tel: (803) 896-6100; fax: (803) 896-6198. Florence County Marriage Registry

(Black), 1919-1929, Film Roll No. E1175, Frame No. 404, File No. A3512, Issue Date: July 15, 1919; Return Date: July 18, 1919. According to the Florence County Marriage Registry, Charles Arthur Tillman and Nellie Williams, *née* Watson, were married on July 15, 1919, in Florence, South Carolina, by the Rev. U. S. Rice. I have listed the specific date of the marriage as probable, in the text of this document, because the license was issued on July 15, 1919, and returned on July 18, 1919. Therefore, they may have been married on any day between July 15 and July 18. I doubt that they would have been married the same day as the license was issued, which was a Tuesday, and not return the marriage certificate until July 18 (the following Friday), although that very well may have happened.

3. Her Social Security number was 245-20-2076. Copy of original Application for Social Security No. 245-20-2076. Reference No. TAG: 4MESDR. Nellie Tillman's Certificate of Death, Commonwealth of Pennsylvania, Department of Health, Vital Records, No. 019006-64 and Copy No. 2233838, filed Feb. 27, 1964, lists her date of birth as December 23, 1899. The informant for the information on her death certificate was her son (and my brother) James Williams. I seriously doubt that James actually knew our mother's date of birth. I, therefore, accept the information provided by my mother on July 22, 1942, when she herself applied for a Social Security card, as much more likely to be correct.

4. Certificate of Death, Commonwealth of Pennsylvania, Department of Health, Vital Records, No. 019006-64 and copy No. 2233838, filed Feb. 27, 1964.

5. My brother, James Williams, is buried in the same plot.

6. In various records, the name "Tillman" is spelled in different ways: Tillman, Tilman, and Tillmon.

7. North Carolina State Board of Health, Bureau of Vital Statistics, Certificate of Death, Registration District No. 33-80, Certificate No. 59, dated Oct. 26, 1942.

8. This information about the place of his birth was provided by Dorothy Dixon, *née* Woodbury, a niece of Charles Tillman, in a conversation at her home on May 30, 2005. Her mother was Charles Tillman's sister. Dorothy Dixon currently resides in Jamaica, N.Y.

9. North Carolina State Board of Health, Bureau of Vital Statistics, Certificate of Death, Registration District No. 33-80, Certificate No. 59, dated Oct. 26, 1942 (Edgecombe County).

10. It is one of the cemeteries owned and operated by the city of Rocky Mount and is located at the termination of Scott and Holly streets. Both of those streets end at Unity Cemetery.

11. See *1925 Florence City Directory* at p. 321.

12. Ibid.

13. See *1930 Hill's Rocky Mount City Directory*, p. 305.

14. I have not been able to locate Rocky Mount city directories for 1931, 1932, 1933, 1934, or 1935.

15. The unions that composed the American Federation of Labor were autonomous unions and, therefore, left to manage their own internal affairs. Many of the unions prohibited Negroes from joining, while others organized Negro workers into separate locals. The AFL did not force these unions to stop practices of racial discrimination and segregation as a requirement for membership. Certainly, unions did agree to abide by AFL provisions (as they were decided by union delegates during national conventions), but eliminating racial segregation never became a stipulation for affiliation with the AFL. This practice did change after the AFL merged with the more progressive CIO in 1955. A. Philip Randolph was elected vice president of the AFL-CIO in 1955, and his presence did much to stamp out racial segregation within the unions affiliated with the AFL-CIO. But the evidence suggests that racial segregation was not officially stamped out until passage of the 1964 Civil Rights Act (Title 7).

16. See *1938 Rocky Mount City Directory*, p. 286, where Charles Tillman is listed as a "silk worker." My mother's occupation is listed on p. 287.

17. In Langston Hughes and Arna Bontemps, eds., *The Poetry of the Negro, 1746-1949* (Garden City, NY: Doubleday & Company, 1956), p. 37.

18. In some records, she is referred to as "Alora," and most of her children and some other family members pronounced Elnora as "Alora" (*A-low-rah*).

19. See *Hill's Rocky Mount (Edgecombe County, NC) City Directory, Vol. 1940,* 12 (Richmond, VA: Hill Directory Co. 1940), p. 180.

20. When Meola—Elnora and Elwood's daughter and oldest child—was about 20 years old, she learned or had reason to believe her father was in New York and undertook to find him. She succeeded in reestablishing contact between Elwood and Elnora (who had not divorced him) and each of his children. Indeed, after contact had been reestablished, periodically Elnora would go to New York to visit and live with Elwood, who was then a superintendent, or "super," in an apartment building in Harlem.

21. This was a three-room "shotgun" house.

22. Rocky Mount and Wilson are 18 miles apart. www.rockymounttravel.com; www.wilson-nc.com.

23. See Jerome E. Brooks, *Green Leaf and Gold, Tobacco in North Carolina* (Raleigh, NC: Division of Archives and History, North Carolina Division of Cultural Resources, 1997), p. 20, "Practical men, searching for a method of obtaining yellow tobacco through heat curing, were on the right track from the first quarter of the 1800s. The method depended on

flues, which brought heat from an outside furnace into a tightly closed curing barn. First to develop a fairly workable flue system was Dr. David G. Tuck, a resident of Halifax County, Virginia, around 1830."

24. The tobacco factories in Rocky Mount, when I lived there, were the China American Tobacco Co., Export Leaf Tobacco Co., Garrett G.R. Co., Imperial Tobacco of Great Britain and Ireland Ltd., Lea W.B. Tobacco Co., Liggett & Myers Tobacco Co., and Thorpe & Ricks Tobacco Co. The tobacco season at those seven factories typically started each year in the late fall; it was then that seasonal or temporary tobacco factory workers were usually hired.

· 4 ·

# *The Winter of 1943*

S ister and I resided in a small apartment in Washington, D.C., for
a very short while—probably two or three weeks. I was to remain
in D.C. for a five- or six-month period during the fall and winter
of 1943–1944. Throughout my adult life, I have referred to this period
as the winter of 1943, the worst period of my life. During only some of
that period did I live with my biological mother, and for a short time,
I lived with her second cousin, WILLIE MAE "GERTIE" WILSON, *née*
HICKSON. As I recall, it was not long after my arrival in D.C. that Sister
left me with Gertie and her family. But soon after that Sister came and
took me to southwest Washington to live with the Gordons, a family
that must have been friends of Sister.

For most of that fall and winter, I lived with the Gordons on
C Street SW, near Third Street. I can no longer recall the first names of
any members of the Gordon family, but I do recall a female member,
younger than I, whom everyone called Sweetie Pie. She had a severely
deformed ankle. A boy who was a member of the family and was about
two or three years my senior also lived there, as did a middle-aged man
whom everyone called Mr. Miles.[1]

The Gordons were a loving but extremely poor family. Their home
was part of an enormous slum in southwest Washington. Because it was
near and clearly visible from the U.S. Capitol building, this slum was
viewed nationally and internationally as a disgrace and the nation's
shame. Years later, the entire area was razed as part of a major redevelopment project.[2] I have no recollection of Sister ever coming to visit the
Gordons or me while I was in their home.

The Gordons told me I would not get any new clothes or gifts for Christmas because they did not have any money to purchase them. Indeed, they were so poor that they could not afford to purchase a supply of coal in advance of winter. They had a pushcart that the boy (his name may have been James Gordon) and I pushed each week to a coal yard near the Pennsylvania Railroad tracks in southwest D.C., where we would purchase about a week's supply of coal. I recall the winter of 1943 as being very cold; sometimes our bare hands would hurt something awful as we pushed the cart to and from the coal yard. (Although the Tillman family in Rocky Mount was decidedly poor,[3] we were not nearly as poor as the Gordons. When I lived with my mother in Rocky Mount, she would, in the fall of each year, order a ton of coal to be delivered to our house. I think she purchased the coal from the Yelverton Coal Company, which was on Arlington Street and near our neighborhood. A truck would deliver and dump the large pile of coal in our backyard. We used a bucket to bring coal into the house as needed. That coal heated our house from late fall until early spring. The stove used by my mother to cook our meals was also sometimes heated by coal, although it was most often fueled by wood. Before the time when coal-burning railroad engines were replaced by diesel engines, we supplemented our home supply of coal by walking along the Atlantic Coast Line railroad tracks with a bucket and collecting lumps of coal that had fallen from railroad coal tenders.[4] A significant amount of high-quality coal could be gathered in that way.)

Another memory from my time with the Gordons is of sleeping in a room where a large piece of fabric was used to cover something hanging on the wall. Because I didn't know what was under the cloth, my imagination took over. For quite a while, I went to sleep each night terribly frightened because I thought Mrs. Gordon was keeping her dead son's body under that cloth. I don't know why I didn't simply ask someone. At some point, however, I learned that it was just clothes hanging there. Needless to say, I was greatly relieved.

HENRY RAMSEY JR., AGE 9, *in Washington, D.C., winter of 1943.*

It was sometime during the fall or winter of 1943 that I met my biological father, I think shortly after I arrived in D.C. I do not recall seeing a lot of him. My vague recollection is that he was working at the time at a commercial food distribution warehouse somewhere in southwest D.C., and he once took me to see where he worked. I also remember that on one occasion he purchased a raspberry ice cream cone for me, a flavor I do not think I had tasted before. Beyond this brief period in my life, I have no memory of having met Henry Ramsey, my biological father.

Sometime around the beginning of the year, probably in January 1944, Sister appeared at the Gordons' house and took me to Arlington or Alexandria, Virginia. I do not know which, but it was one of the two. This was when I first met Romus Evans, whom Sister was later to marry. An instance of Sister's quick and sometimes violent temper was displayed during the two or three days I was with her in northern Virginia. She asked if I liked pancakes, and I said that I did. She then cooked and placed before me a large stack of pancakes. When I was unable to finish the stack, Sister became very angry. She said I had claimed to like pancakes, and she demanded that I finish what she had prepared. When I was unable to do so, she gave me a terrible beating.

## BACK TO FLORENCE, SOUTH CAROLINA

WITHIN A FEW DAYS OF retrieving me from the Gordons' home, Sister took me to Florence, South Carolina, where I was left with her sister, ELIZA HAWKINS, née WILLIAMS, whom everyone called Moses.[5] During the spring of 1944, I stayed at Aunt Moses's house, located at 717 Brunson Street.[6] I attended Wilson School, a racially segregated, combined elementary and high school for Negro students. Aunt Moses may have been a teacher at the school, but if so I was not in her class. At least two of Aunt Moses's sons, Isaac and Wilbur, also lived at her house while I was there.

During this stay in Florence I met "SON" BRUNSON, my maternal grandfather. At the time he seemed quite old and ill. He was in fact seriously ill, but he was only 62 years old. It is understandable that he would seem very old to a 10-year old. But this was also a time in our nation's history when most of the population, particularly African American males, did not live much beyond age 65.

Son Brunson was Sister's father and Aunt Moses's stepfather. It quickly became evident to me that Aunt Moses had no love for him, however. She would sometimes send me to his house to fan him, telling me that he was not a relative of hers but that he was my grandfather and therefore it was my responsibility to fan him. Sitting by his bed, I would use a paper fan until he fell asleep or some adult told me that I could stop. I recall a very unpleasant odor emanating from his person, which reinforced my idea of his being quite old. Fanning him was also highly unpleasant, but I had to do what I was told. He died on August 10 of that very year.[7]

Sometime in late May or early June 1944, about a year after Sister had taken me from Rocky Mount, Aunt Moses told me I was being sent to live with Sister in Philadelphia.[8] Shortly thereafter, I was taken at night to the train station in Florence, given a ticket, and put on the railroad train that was to take me to Philadelphia and Sister. I was still just 10 and would be traveling alone. Fortunately for me, as it turned out, this train, like all Atlantic Coast Line passenger trains traveling from Florida to Richmond, Virginia,[9] was to be serviced (refueled, restocked with food and water for the passengers, and to undergo a crew change) in Rocky Mount, North Carolina. I was unaware of that fact when I was put on the train in Florence, but when it was announced that the train was about to stop in Rocky Mount, I immediately reacted. I knew the train station in Rocky Mount; I had been in and about that station many, many times when I lived there. Indeed, Around the Y and my mother's house on Dunn Street were three-quarters of a mile at most from the station. At some point after the announcement that we would be stopping in Rocky Mount, I realized I was free from the dreadful experiences of the past year and was now home. I got off the train, remained on the platform until it left, and then walked to my neighborhood.

I believe the train I was traveling on was named the Champion. It stopped each night at Rocky Mount at about 1:00 or 1:30 a.m. So it was probably 2:00 or 2:30 in the morning when I arrived at Around the Y. I recall being unsure whether my mother still lived at 108 Dunn Street, because I knew we had rented and did not own that house. But I knew that Mr. NESBIT ROLLINS and his wife, CHERRY ROLLINS, owned their home at 905 Red Row and, therefore, would likely still be living at the same place. I went to Mr. Nesbit and "Fat" Cherry's[10] house, knocked on the door, and was admitted. They told me that my mother still lived at the same place on Dunn Street but that because of the lateness of the hour, I should spend the rest of the night at their house and go to my mother's in the morning.

When I awoke later that morning I left the Rollins's home and walked the two blocks to my mother's house at 108 Dunn Street. I knocked on the front door and announced who I was. Almost immediately I heard my mother loudly exclaiming over and over on her way to the door, "Thank you, Jesus! Thank you, Jesus!" That has always served as clear evidence in my mind that my mother had regretted sending me away with Sister and that she was overjoyed at my return. It was not long before a telegram came from Sister asking if I was at my mother's house and, if I was, requesting that my mother send her the unused portion of my railroad ticket.

· Notes ·

1. Mr. Miles may in fact have been elderly but probably was middle-aged; to a 9-year-old boy, a person who is 40 or 50 appears to be old.

2. Many privately owned structures (including private residences), plus buildings owned by the federal government, were constructed on that land pursuant to the redevelopment plan. I visited the area on March 4, 2004, for the specific purpose of noting the buildings, particularly those

constructed on land where I lived in the winter of 1943. I saw that the Gordons' home site was now covered by the Wilbur J. Cohen Federal Building. That building houses the Voice of America and certain agencies within the U.S. Department of Health and Human Services. On the south side of the street is the Mary E. Switzer Memorial Building at 330 C Street SW. It houses certain units within the U.S. Department of Education.

Also nearby is the Ford House Office Building; the Department of Health and Human Services, Public Health Service, and Food and Drug Administration at 200 C Street SW; the Hubert H. Humphrey Building, Department of Health and Human Services; the U.S. Small Business Administration at 409 Third Street SW; and the Department of Housing and Urban Development at Seventh and D Streets SW. The L'Enfant Plaza Hotel, construction of which was completed in 1973, is also in this area. See Wolf Von Eckardt, "In All Its Dead-End Glory," *Washington Post*, May 5, 1973, p. C1.

3. Our family would probably be characterized as "working poor" today, which is usually thought of as a family of four whose income falls below the federal poverty level. The Census Bureau does not use the term "working poor." However, the working poor have been characterized as individuals who are employed (often underemployed) but still fall within the category of poverty because their income does not enable them to participate fully and effectively in everyday life. Another view of the term is individuals who maintain full-time jobs but remain in relative poverty. Working poor may mean different things to different data users, according to the question they are trying to answer.

4. The coal tender was a specialized railroad car that was positioned immediately behind the engine and contained a large supply of coal, as well as water. The fireman used this coal as fuel for the fire in the engine. The railroad steam engine was essentially a huge boiler with a coal-burning firebox on wheels. The coal fire boiled the water in the boiler and converted it to steam. That steam provided the energy to turn the wheels of the engine and to pull the train's cars, whether they were for passengers or freight. It was black men who shoveled the coal and maintained the fire in the engine's firebox. In fact, I believe this job was the only one held by black men on trains during the era of the coal-burning engine, with the exception of the Pullman porters and dining room cooks. The engineers, brakemen, and conductors (ticket takers) were all white. With the advent of the diesel engine after World War II, even the fireman's position was limited to whites.

5. We probably traveled to Florence by train, but I do not remember the trip at all.

6. See *1942–1943 Florence South Carolina City Directory*.

7. See Certificate of Death, State of South Carolina Bureau of Vital Statistics, State Board of Health, Florence County, File No. 09703, Registration District No. 20-A, Registered No. 326.

8. While I do not remember the exact month, I do recall that it was not long after the end of the school year.

9. One of the two main railroad routes between New York and south Florida involved the train's being pulled by equipment and over rails owned by the Pennsylvania Railroad Co., between New York and Washington, D.C. (New York, Newark, Trenton, Philadelphia, Wilmington, Baltimore, and Washington, D.C.). Between Washington, D.C., and Richmond, Virginia, the train would be pulled by equipment and over rails owned by the Richmond, Fredericksburg, and Potomac Railroad Company. Between Richmond and Florida, on the route that passed through Rocky Mount and Florence, the equipment and rails used were owned by the Atlantic Coast Line Railroad Co. (The Atlantic Coast Line Railroad Co., with rail lines that extended several hundred miles, was actually owned by the Richmond, Fredericksburg, and Potomac Railroad Co., with railroad lines of only about 100 miles.)

10. When I was about 4 or 5 years old, my father had told me that her name was "Fat" Cherry, and I had always called her by that name. She was, in fact, skinny as a reed. I guess my father thought it was quite a joke to have me call her Fat Cherry, and that was what I called her—even into my adulthood.

# 5

# Elementary and High School

A t five years old in September 1939, I had been enrolled in the first grade at Annie W. Holland Elementary School in Rocky Mount, on Luper Street, at the southwest corner of Cleveland Street. BOYD L. ANCRUM was the principal for each of the years I was enrolled there. Most children at that time began first grade at age 6. Because I would not be 6 until January and therefore was not eligible to enter the first grade until the fall of 1940 when I would be almost 7, my father persuaded the school officials (probably just Mr. Ancrum) that I should be admitted in fall 1939. I suppose it did not hurt that my father had already taught me to read from a book he referred to as "The Blue Back Speller."[1] He was also very proud of the fact that he had taught me to recite the Twenty-Third Psalm.[2] I was the youngest person in my first-grade class, and RHETHA BRIDGES was the youngest girl.[3]

Annie W. Holland Elementary School was in the Little Raleigh neighborhood. Children attending the school lived in the black neighborhoods we knew as Little Raleigh, Germantown, Around the Y, South Rocky Mount, Joyner's Hill, and the Oil Mill Section.[4] My schoolmates and I walked to and from school as a group, which it occurs to me now must have been reassuring for our parents—"safety in numbers." The route was hazardous even without considering the potential danger of stray dogs, meanness from older white children as we crossed their areas, or just plain wandering off the route and getting lost.

When I lived in Little Raleigh and was in the first and second grades, the walk to school was about six or seven blocks. Our family moved to Around the Y while I was attending the third grade. Annie W. Holland was located several blocks west of the railroad tracks that passed immediately next to our new neighborhood. Elementary school students from Around the Y had to walk 10 or 12 blocks to get to school if we used the most direct route, which took us across several sets of railroad tracks. Those of us who lived Around the Y and those from the Oil Mill Section and Joyner's Hill (neighborhoods that were near Around the Y but even farther from Annie W. Holland) were told not to cross the railroad tracks at Dunn Street, which was the most direct route, but we often did. We were supposed to walk six or eight extra blocks to Bassett Street, which had railroad crossing gates that would afford us some protection in crossing the tracks. There were also fewer tracks to cross at Bassett Street than at Dunn Street, which ended in our neighborhood a few feet from the railroad tracks. But despite warnings by parents, other adults in the neighborhood, and school officials, we usually crossed the tracks at the end of Dunn Street. Incredibly, at least to my knowledge no child was ever killed or even injured by a train, notwithstanding the obvious danger.

Whether we took the long or short route from our neighborhood to Annie W. Holland, we also had to cross Church Street (U.S. Highway 301). This was a fairly wide and probably the busiest street in Rocky Mount, being a main transportation route from Richmond, Virginia, to Miami, Florida. We children reached Church Street after walking about two blocks from the forbidden railroad tracks that we had crossed when leaving Around the Y. I also do not recall any child being killed or injured crossing Highway 301.

Still, it was not lost on those of us living in Around the Y that one white elementary school—Bassett Elementary—was only two blocks from our neighborhood. But for segregation, we could have attended that school without ever having to cross the tracks and Highway 301. We actually passed another white elementary school on the other side of the railroad tracks several blocks before we arrived at Annie W. Holland. Black elementary school children who lived on Joyner's Hill and in the Oil Mill Section also passed two white elementary schools in getting to Annie W. Holland.

Annie W. Holland Elementary School opened in 1935 and was essentially a new building when I began the first grade there in 1939. The school's interior was attractive: clean, well-equipped with appropriate chalkboards, desks, and chairs, and well maintained. The principal had a private office, and each class had its own room. Although I am certain I never was inside any white school while living in Rocky Mount, Annie W. Holland appeared equal to what I could observe of the white elementary school buildings located near our neighborhood. I do not know the comparative square footage of the various schools and classrooms, their enrollment, or how the buildings were appointed. Perhaps the white schools had a lower student-teacher ratio, but I do not know that.

I do know that our school, like the white schools, was built of brick, and the playground and other grounds surrounding the building were landscaped and properly maintained. Lincoln and O.R. Pope, two other Rocky Mount elementary schools for Negro children, were also constructed of brick. The two high schools in Rocky Mount, Booker T. Washington High School for blacks and Rocky Mount High School for whites, were both brick, although Rocky Mount High School was larger and more attractive. (The two high schools were merged in 1969 as Rocky Mount High School.)

Still, the educational system, curriculum, and facilities to which my classmates and I were introduced in 1939 rested on an institutional base of nearly three-quarters of a century of separate and unequal education in North Carolina and elsewhere in the South. Our teachers were paid less than white teachers and, on average, had less formal education than teachers in white schools. Funds provided for our books, supplies, and equipment were significantly less than funds provided for white elementary school students. In fact, many of the "new" books provided for our use had previously been used by white students. Often the books we received would have several names already written in the spaces provided for that purpose on the inside of the front cover. I have been unable to determine the per capita expenditure for black elementary school students in Rocky Mount in 1939. However, Richard Kluger writes in his book *Simple Justice*:

> In 1945, the South was spending twice as much to educate each white child as it was per black child. It was investing four times as much in white school plants, paying white teachers salaries 30 percent higher, and virtually ignoring the critical logistics of transporting rural Negroes to their schoolhouses.
>
> In 1944, the seventeen segregating states spent a total of $42 million busing white children to their schools; on transporting colored children, they spent a little more than one million dollars.[5]

While statistics cited by Kluger were for 10 and 11 years after my birth, I seriously doubt that anyone would believe or claim that more money was being spent in 1934 on public education and transportation for black children than was being spent in 1944 and 1945, or that the disparity between what was being spent for white children and what was spent for black children was less in 1934 than it was in 1944 or 1945.

My contemporaries and I were taught the typical reading, writing, and arithmetic curriculum in elementary school. We were also taught social studies, which included geography and American and world history. The only material I recall being taught that might qualify as political history was limited to a description of the components of government—executive, legislative, judicial—but little, if anything, was taught about how those institutions of government functioned with regard to Negroes. The American history that we were taught had a very heavy bias in favor of the Southern view, with "separate but equal" being the order of the day.

I have absolutely no recollection of being taught in elementary school about the extreme difficulties and extraordinary suffering of black people in America, from the time of their first arrival in the American colonies in 1619 until the conclusion of World War II.[6] I don't recall any such instruction in the eighth or ninth grades either. That aspect of my education was gained outside school, from newspaper articles, the youth branch of the NAACP, black adults in my neighborhood, and personal observations and experiences as a child growing up in Jim Crow North Carolina.

We were taught that a good citizen was both religious (i.e., a good Christian) and patriotic. Those values were heavily emphasized. I do not recall religious instruction being an overt part of our school curriculum, but the overall tone in elementary school openly supported and respected a belief in Christianity. I often attended Sunday services at St. Mark's Methodist Church until my early teenage years. After we moved to Around the Y and my father died, I would sometimes participate in religious services conducted by the Rev. John A. July at what people in our neighborhood called the Clubhouse.

During recesses, we played various schoolyard games. Each May we participated in an event where we dressed in colorful clothing and wrapped the Maypole with long ribbons of colored crepe paper. At various times during the school year we children performed in recitals and plays. My favorite teacher in elementary school was Mrs. Lillian Pittman. She had a deserved reputation as a tough and demanding teacher. But she was also sensitive, caring, and very supportive and encouraging of me as an outstanding student in her class. I continued to visit her at her home well into my adulthood, on occasional trips to Rocky Mount. She was very proud of my going to college and becoming a lawyer. She said she always knew I would "make something" of myself.

Another aspect of our formal education—echoing what we heard at home—was that we should make every effort to be law-abiding, polite, and punctual and to emulate the language, dress, and decorum of educated white people. This lesson was not meant to imply that white people were superior to or better than black people. The implication was simply that if Negroes acquired an education and learned to speak (i.e., pronounce words) and dress like white people and to have the manners and education prevalent in the educated white community, then much—if not all—of the reasons offered in support of Jim Crow would be negated, and Negroes would gain their civil and political rights much more quickly. In other words, Negroes were being discriminated against because of *their* failure to dress right, speak appropriately, and acquire more formal education. To me, this reasoning was naïve and carried with it a strong dose of "blaming the victim." I don't think I can recall anyone ever claiming to seek social equality—for example, integrated housing or intermarriage—with white people.

We were in elementary school during much of World War II (all of 1942 through most of 1945), including my time away from Rocky Mount, and my classmates and I were directly involved in activities designed to support the war effort. We were encouraged to save coins toward the purchase of War Bonds and to collect tin cans to contribute to the supply of scarce scrap metals needed to fight the war. We were also urged to cultivate "Victory Gardens" at home as a means of conserving food needed by the federal government to feed the soldiers, sailors, and airmen fighting the war against Germany, Italy, and Japan.

Several of my first-grade classmates from Around the Y became life-long friends. Some moved back to Rocky Mount after retiring from jobs in northern cities. WILLIAM "BRO" HOBBS lived as an adult for many years in New York City, where he worked for the U.S. Internal Revenue Service. He and his wife, GARDENIA HOBBS, *née* BRASWELL, were living in Teaneck, New Jersey, when he decided to retire. They built a home in Rocky Mount and have lived there since 1988.[7] I almost always stay at their home when visiting Rocky Mount. MARY PERRY, *née* SHAW, another classmate who lived Around the Y, worked for many years as an administrative secretary for District 5 of the New York City Board of Education. She resigned from that position to return to Rocky Mount with her husband, John Perry, after his retirement as supervisor of material control for the New York City Third Rail Subway Department. JOSEPH ROLLINS retired from the U.S. Air Force after more than 20 years of service, and now he and his wife make their home in Rocky Mount. MILDRED BROWN lived with her husband away from Rocky Mount during his Air Force career, but they returned to Rocky Mount after his retirement from the Air Force in Alaska.

Rhetha Bridges never did leave Rocky Mount and still lives there after retiring as an employee of the local school district. ELLA "MISS GOLD" DOZIER[8] lives in Washington, D.C., but spends a great deal of time at her deceased mother's home in Rocky Mount. I always try to visit her when we are in Rocky Mount at the same time. In fact, I try to visit each of my elementary school classmates whenever I am in Rocky Mount.

There are other schoolmates who never moved from Rocky Mount and with whom I still have regular contact, although they were not in my Annie W. Holland class. For example, when I am in Rocky Mount, I always try to visit with HENRY "SHORT" BARNES and BERTHA "SIS" BARNES (both from Little Raleigh); ROSA MAE HARPER, *née* GARRETT (from Cross Town); and THELMA HOBBS (from Around the Y).

Members of my first-grade class have a reunion about every five years, to which I am always invited. They think of it as being for the Booker T. Washington Class of 1951. But because I did not graduate from Booker T. Washington High School, I think of it as a reunion of the Annie W. Holland Elementary School's entering first-grade class of 1939.[9]

Booker T. Washington High School was located at the intersection of East Virginia and Pennsylvania avenues in the Cross Town neighborhood, near Rocky Mount's northern city limits. Technically I attended Booker T. Washington for three years, but that statement is somewhat misleading. The first year, or eighth grade, was actually taught at the Booker T. Washington High School Annex, on Pennsylvania Avenue, about one block from the high school building on East Virginia Avenue—where the four years of actual high school—ninth, tenth, eleventh, and twelfth grades—would then be completed. Annie W. Holland Elementary School provided instruction through the seventh grade. The two other Rocky Mount black elementary schools—Abraham Lincoln, located in Happy Hill, and O.R. Pope, located in Cemetery Hill—offered instruction through the eighth grade. I do not know the reason for this difference.

I stopped attending high school either during or at the end of the tenth grade and have no memory of why I became a dropout. I was not a poor student and, in fact, always did well in my studies. And yet for reasons I do not recall, I dropped out. It clearly was not money or poverty, because my mother worked hard to provide for my basic needs, clothing, food, shelter, and school supplies. Although it was not unknown for students in my neighborhood to drop out of school, most of my contemporaries from Around the Y did not. Indeed, I was now a member of the July family, through my mother's marriage to Rev. John A. July, and most of the members of that family were high school graduates. Several were college graduates or in college.

All of my educational records from the Annie W. Holland Elementary School (fall 1939 through spring 1946), Booker T. Washington High School Annex[10] (fall 1946 through spring 1947), and Booker T. Washington High School (fall 1947 until sometime in 1949) should be recorded under the name Charles Arthur Tillman Jr. of 424 Raleigh Road (early elementary school) and 108 Dunn Street, Rocky Mount.[11]

· Notes ·

1. On August 4, 2003, thanks to Professor Ernest Allen Jr. of the W.E.B. DuBois Department of Afro-American Studies, University of Massachusetts, Amherst, I learned that the actual title of the book my father used to teach me to read was *The American Spelling Book: Containing the Rudiments of the English Language, for the Use of Schools in the United States,* by Noah Webster. It was commonly referred to as the Blue Back Speller because of its blue cover.

2. *The Master Study Bible*, Psalm 23, CornerStone Bible Publishers (1999):

> The Lord is my shepherd, I shall
> not want;
> He maketh me to lie down
> in green pastures.
> He leadeth me beside the still waters;
> he restoreth my soul:
> He leadeth me in the paths of righteousness
> for his name's sake.
> Yea, though I walk through the
> valley of the shadow of death,
> I will fear no evil;
> For thou art with me;
> Thy rod and thy staff they comfort me.

Thou preparest a table before me
in the presence of mine enemies;
thou anointest my head with oil;
my cup runneth over.
Surely goodness and mercy shall
follow me
all the days of my life,
and I shall dwell in the house of
the LORD forever.

3. Rhetha Farmer, *née* Bridges, confirmed her birth date as Oct. 14, 1933, in a telephone conversation with me on April 11, 2004.

4. I don't think any children from the nearby rural area attended Annie W. Holland School. I have no recollection of anyone from the country being in my classes there.

5. Richard Kluger, *Simple Justice* (New York: Alfred A. Knopf, 1976), p. 256.

6. See, for example, Leon F. Litwack, *Trouble in Mind: Black Southerners in the Age of Jim Crow* (New York: Alfred A. Knopf, 1998).

7. Although Hobbs actually moved into his new Rocky Mount home in September 1988 during the time he was on extended leave from his job with the IRS, he did not actually retire until November 1988, two months after he had moved back to Rocky Mount.

8. Ella Dozier's complexion or skin color was quite fair. Her mother began to call her "Miss Gold" in reference to her skin color. Before long, everyone in Rocky Mount who knew her also called her "Miss Gold."

9. Some members of the class of 1951 did not attend Annie W. Holland Elementary School but went to Abraham Lincoln and O.R. Pope elementary schools.

10. This was the name of the high school (including the Annex) for black students in Rocky Mount; it was located on East Virginia Avenue at the northeast corner of Pennsylvania Avenue.

11. Neither of these houses exists any longer, both having been demolished many years ago. I lived in three houses in Rocky Mount between the ages of 1 and 17—424 Raleigh Road (Little Raleigh), 108 Dunn Street (Around the Y), and 105 Ward Street (South Rocky Mount)—and none of them exists today. The entire neighborhood of Around the Y was demolished in the 1970s, as part of a redevelopment project, as was that part of South Rocky Mount in which 105 Ward Street was located. Much of what was the Around the Y neighborhood is now Thelonious Monk Park, named after the famous jazz pianist who was born and lived Around the Y on Red Row Street during his early childhood. Although the Little Raleigh neighborhood is still intact, the house where I lived was demolished and has been gone for many years.

# 6

# My Teenage Years

For five or six months after I dropped out of school (most likely in fall 1949), I lived with Sister at 2133 West Stewart Street in North Philadelphia. I have no recollection of how I arranged to live with her again, but somehow I did. I attended Philadelphia's Simon Gratz High School for a few months that fall before returning to Rocky Mount. Most of the boys my age living near me on West Stewart Street were interested in boxing as a career and spent a significant amount of time training at a local gym. I was not drawn to boxing, which was understandable given my frail build. Therefore, I spent no time in the boxing gym. I remember occasionally visiting the zoo and playing with friends in Fairmont Park, which was within fairly easy walking distance.

You might well ask why I decided to live with Sister after my experience in 1943–1944. The only answer I can give is that I had become a teenager and, then as now, teenagers are often foolhardy or at the least lack sound judgment. Apparently I was among that number. While I had no difficulty with Romus Evans, who was now Sister's husband, she and I simply did not get along. After a few months of quarreling, we found a way to avoid each other: I left.

Sister and a group of her friends had for some time had an informal card-playing club that met regularly to gamble, with the host gambling site being rotated among the various club members' homes. The game of choice was usually "Pitty Pat,"[1] a card game similar to gin rummy.[2] The person at whose house or apartment the game was being held was permitted to "cut" the game. That meant the person, known as "the house," was permitted to keep a "cut," or percentage, of the amount waged for each particular hand or "pot."[3] The cut was probably around 5 or 10 percent. Sister agreed to let me cut a game scheduled for her home as a means of getting bus fare back to Rocky Mount. After the game, I had the needed bus fare. My recollection is that the one-way fare from Philadelphia to Rocky Mount was around $7.00. I am certain Sister was as happy as I was on the day I got on that Trailways bus.

When I returned to Rocky Mount, my mother told me that I had a choice—either attend school or get a job. But because she worked from early in the morning—leaving home probably around 5:00 a.m.—until late in the afternoon, she couldn't monitor whether I was doing either. I told her that I was actively looking for work but simply was unable to get a job. I don't know whether she believed me, but she was not in a position to challenge my statement. The truth was that I spent many of my morning hours sleeping and many afternoons "hanging out," namely, engaged in largely unproductive activity, although this would not be true during the cotton and tobacco harvesting seasons in the fall.

After I dropped out of school, a typical weekday began with my sleeping until late in the morning, sometimes as late as noon. Once I had gotten up and dressed, I would eat lunch, which we called dinner. (The evening meal was called supper. Breakfast was breakfast.) It was not unusual for my dinner (lunch) to consist simply of what we called a "hobo" bun (a cinnamon-raisin pastry glazed with white icing) and a quart of whole milk. The hobo bun cost 5 cents. I do not recall the price of a quart of milk, but it was not very expensive. However, my choice of milk and a hobo bun was based on preference and not cost. It obviously wasn't based on nutrition. I truly enjoyed eating hobo buns and was also very fond of milk. Hobo buns were produced by local commercial bakeries and sold in grocery stores as well as other local neighborhood stores that typically carried canned goods, cigarettes and other tobacco products (snuff, chewing tobacco, and cigars), fresh milk, canned juices, soft drinks, and bakery products, but rarely sold produce or meats. Meats and fresh vegetables would usually be purchased in a grocery store.

After dinner, I would often go to Benny Cooper's neighborhood store on South Washington Street (unless I had purchased the milk from Folks' grocery store and the hobo bun from Benny, in which case, I would most likely have consumed my dinner onsite at Benny's). There I would play cards, usually bid whist, with the young adults and teenagers present until late afternoon or early evening. If I was not at Benny's store playing cards, I might actually be looking for work. At some point during my teenage years, I developed an interest in jigsaw puzzles and, over several years, spent a significant amount of time working on 500-, 1,000- and 1,500-piece puzzles.

By late afternoon my mother would be home from work, and I would return to our house for supper, which she prepared. Afterward I would spend the rest of the evening on the street corner or sitting on someone's porch talking until 10:00 or 11:00 at night, when I would normally return home and go to sleep.

But it is also true that when I was *not* hanging out, I would usually be involved during the day in some part-time income-producing activity—agricultural work, offering to shine shoes at the railroad station, general work around someone's house, washing dishes at a restaurant, collecting and selling scrap iron, and the like.

## Cotton, Tobacco and Ice

During some summers, I worked with an African American iceman who delivered ice to people's homes with a large horse-drawn wagon. I do not remember his name. Several 250-pound blocks of ice would be loaded on the wagon at the Colonial Ice and Coal Company, which was immediately north of our neighborhood and adjacent to the Atlantic Coast Line railroad tracks. This man, an employee of the ice company, would then deliver ice to various homes in Rocky Mount's black neighborhoods. It was a rare black home in Rocky Mount when I was growing up that had a refrigerator. That may also have been the case in white homes, but I did not have a clue as to what appliances were in white homes. Most perishable food in black houses was kept cold or chilled in an icebox, an insulated cabinet with separate compartments for ice and for food. The appliance was chilled by a 10-, 20-, or 50-pound block of ice that had been placed in its special compartment in the icebox. Before being loaded onto the wagon, the 250-pound blocks were scored into 10-, 20-, and 50-pound sections by a machine at the ice plant. This scoring allowed us to use an ice pick to fairly easily separate the individual, smaller pieces of ice from the large blocks on the wagon. We then used large ice tongs or ice hooks to carry the individual block of ice into people's homes and place it in the icebox. I also enjoyed driving the horse-powered wagon, when allowed. This ice delivery system probably existed in white neighborhoods as well, but the wagon on which I worked delivered ice only in black neighborhoods.

During the late summer and fall, I did seasonal work picking cotton, harvesting tobacco, and working at tobacco warehouses, where I helped other workers unload and fill baskets with cured tobacco that was to be sold at a tobacco auction. Every year at harvest time, cotton and tobacco farmers from the nearby rural areas would come to our neighborhood around 5:00 a.m. to solicit and select workers for the day.[4] Those farmers were invariably Caucasian. Early each weekday morning, men, women, and children (mostly teenagers) from our neighborhood who wanted to work would go to the area in front of the J.R. Folks Store[5] and, if lucky, would be chosen to work for the day. Those selected would get on the farmer's truck, usually a pickup, and be transported to the farm where the work was to be performed. I don't think we ever went more than 25 or 30 miles from Rocky Mount, usually less.

A song comes to mind:

> Remember if you can,
> When cotton was picked by hand,
> Down in Dixie,
> Under Southern skies,
> Working from sun to sun.[6]

Picking cotton was hot, hard, and sometimes painful work. The pain came mostly from the back strain that resulted from all day pulling a loaded cotton sack hung from one's shoulders. When we youngsters complained of back pain, the response from the adults would usually be "You don't have any back to hurt; you've just got gristle."[7] That meant, "gut it out." Pain was also often caused by a fairly hard and sharp thorn-like growth at the end of the mature cotton bolls from which the cotton was being extracted. This growth would prick the cuticles of your fingers and hurt something awful. Of course, the more adept you became at picking the cotton, the less harm your fingers suffered.

I do not recall the amount paid per pound picked, but I remember that it wasn't much. However, the money we did earn made the pain seem worthwhile. In any case, it would not have been possible for me to avoid the work because my mother knew when the farmers were hiring. Some of her friends in the neighborhood were picking cotton. Therefore, she got me up early in the morning before she left for work and made certain that I was in front of the J.R. Folks Store in "plenty of time." (The same was true when it was time to work in green tobacco, discussed hereafter.)

The farmer paid you at the end of the day for the total number of pounds of cotton you had picked. If you picked 150 pounds in a day, you were considered a good worker. But there were some men and women who picked 200 to 250 pounds of cotton in a day. I would always try to get on a farmer's truck with Mrs. Almeta Bullock, Walt Bullock's mother, so I could be in a cotton field with her.[8] If I was successful—and I usually was—I would position myself on a row of cotton plants next to the row that she was picking. If I could just keep up with the end of her cotton sack for most of the morning, I knew that I would have my 150 pounds at the end of the day. She would have more than 200 pounds, probably 250, but I would have 150. Why didn't I keep up with her for the whole day? It simply was not possible. As the morning wore on, Miss Almeta[9] would gradually pull away; by noon, she would certainly be one or two full rows ahead, and by the end of the day, five or six rows. She was, relatively speaking, a very small woman, but she must have been quite strong and had very nimble fingers. She died in Rocky Mount on January 20, 2003, at age 91.[10]

The tobacco harvesting process was referred to as "working in green tobacco" as distinct from working with "cured" tobacco, which was somewhat golden in color; the leaves of the tobacco plants we were working with had leaves that were dark to yellowish green. On tobacco farms, though, we were paid by the day, rather than by the pound. One started going to the tobacco fields at about 10 or 11 years old. A child could do what was called "handing tobacco," and boys that age were sometimes permitted to "drive truck." "Handing tobacco" was just what the name implies. The child would take an appropriate number of leaves from a sort of wooden table on which newly picked tobacco leaves had been placed and form them into a bunch. That bunch of leaves would then be handed to an older teenage girl or adult woman (always a female), who would very quickly tie the bundle of tobacco leaves securely to a long wooden stick (about 2 inches in diameter and 4 or 5 feet long) with white cotton twine.[11] This work was called "tying tobacco."

The stick the tobacco was tied to would be resting on and supported by a wooden frame called a "horse." The women tying the tobacco and the children with experience handing tobacco would teach a novice the appropriate-size bundle (number of leaves) to hand. As soon as the tobacco stick was full of bundles of green tobacco leaves, one of the children handing tobacco would remove it from the horse and place it in an adjacent wooden rack designed for that purpose. A new stick would then be placed on the horse and the process repeated all day long.

Older teenage boys and men (always males) harvested the tobacco leaves,[12] which were placed on the wooden table that was adjacent to the tobacco barn and used for the handing and tying process. Harvesting consisted of removing the mature leaves from the stalk of the tobacco plant in the field by hand. The work was physically demanding. The leaves first matured low on the 4- to 5-foot plants, and the larger and more desirable leaves were near the middle. Therefore, one typically had to bend at the waist for the full day.

Harvesters had to be able to appreciate when a given leaf was ready to be picked, which depended on how close it was to being somewhat yellowish green, as opposed to an immature dark green. Like the porridge in the tale of "Goldilocks and the Three Bears,"[13] which was not to be too hot or too cold but "just right," the harvested tobacco leaves could not be too green or too yellow. Therefore, one not only had to be old and strong enough to do the physical work but have sufficient experience to recognize ripeness or when the leaf coloring was just right. This knowledge would have been acquired while handing tobacco and driving truck.

In eastern North Carolina, picking tobacco leaves was called "priming tobacco,"[14] and this type of work commanded the highest daily wages. When a teenage boy became large enough and sufficiently experienced to be able to say at the morning call for workers that he knew how to "prime tobacco," he had arrived. A tobacco leaf makes a loud popping sound when manually picked from its stalk, somewhat like a sound that can be made with a bongo drum. The males priming tobacco would often use this sound to maintain a rhythm and cadence among themselves as they harvested the tobacco leaves during the course of the day.

As the leaves were individually picked in the field, the person picking them would collect and hold them under one arm while continuing to pick additional leaves with the other hand. When he had collected as many leaves as he could possibly carry in that fashion, the leaves would be placed in the nearest "truck," with that process being repeated throughout the day. The trucks were actually sled-like devices made of wood, with sides made from burlap sacks that had been nailed to wooden rails and could be lowered and raised. The trucks were pulled by mules driven by young boys between the field of tobacco plants, where the leaves were being primed, and the workstations at the tobacco barn, where women and children were tying the leaves on tobacco sticks. Two or three trucks were in constant use throughout the workday. When a truck was full of tobacco leaves, it would be driven from the field to the workstation to be unloaded. The tobacco leaves would be placed on the aforementioned table, and the now-empty mule-propelled truck would return to the field.

Toward the end of the workday, all of the day workers (primers, truck drivers, handers, and those who tied) plus the farmer and members of the farmer's family would come to the racks next to the tobacco barn, which were now packed full of sticks loaded with bundles of green tobacco. They would work together to put or hang the sticks in the barn to be flue-cured. This part of the process was called "putting in" the tobacco.

This type of day work in cotton and tobacco no longer exists in North Carolina and probably does not exist in any of the other major cotton- or tobacco-producing states. Cotton and tobacco have for a long time been harvested by machines. As a reminder of my time in the cotton and tobacco fields, a tobacco stick and a cotton scale, used to weigh the work product at the end of the day, are displayed in our home in Berkeley. My children certainly must have noticed those two objects over the door leading from my study to the guest room on the first floor, and now you have been told of their significance.

Besides work in cotton and tobacco I also worked for a while delivering newspapers—the *Norfolk Journal and Guide* and the *Baltimore African-American*—two major black weekly newspapers. I sold packages of vegetable and flower seeds door to door, and also some sort of salve—I think the name was Raleigh's. In the fall, I made yard brooms from the tall straw grass that grew in the nearby woods and tried to sell them. These brooms were effective in sweeping our yard, at least, since it had no grass or other groundcover. In December I would go to the woods and gather wild holly branches with red berries and try to sell them as Christmas decorations. When I lived on Ward Street, my friend Clifton Dozier was instrumental in getting me a job as a dishwasher at a new restaurant on Church Street in South Rocky Mount, not far from my house. The restaurant made delicious hotcakes, and as an employee I could eat all I wanted while on the job.

I even tried my hand at shining shoes. Following the example of a few others, I made a shoeshine box and went downtown to the train station, where I offered to shine the shoes of passersby. The Ricks Hotel, about a block from the train station, was the largest and most fancy (perhaps the only) hotel in Rocky Mount. Sometimes I would position myself in front of the train station and at other times in front of the Ricks Hotel, soliciting customers. I do not recall being particularly successful as a shoeshine boy.

None of my entrepreneurial activities were very profitable or long-lasting. My step-brother Isaac July and I would sometimes steal lengths of copper cable from the Atlantic Coast Line material yard. It was obvious to us that the wire was being stored for salvage and was not intended for further functional use. We would enter the material yard at night, take sections of the cable, and later start a fire to burn away the rubber covering from the copper wire cables. After pounding the wire into bundles we sold it to the junkyard at the N.C. Hide and Fur Company on South Washington Street. Although we intended no harm to the Coast Line, what we did was still wrong and unlawful, and I wish I had not engaged in that activity.

Some of the hard work that I did was fun. Rev. July, my mother's third husband, was what people referred to as a "truck farmer."[15] That term simply meant that, though he cultivated crops, Rev. July did not live on the land where the actual farming was done. Rev. owned two good-sized adjoining plots of land Around the Y, one facing on Washington Street and the other on Dunn Street. He grew vegetables on the two lots and also had a small shed on one, where he kept a mule and wagon. We boys played tackle football (without any protective equipment) on the larger of the two lots during the winter.

Rev. raised hogs in a pen on land just south of the Atlantic Coast Line property in South Rocky Mount. I estimate that land to have been about 2 miles directly south of Around the Y. Isaac and I would drive the mule and wagon through the neighborhood collecting food scraps (called "slop") from people's houses in a 55-gallon drum and then drive the mule and wagon with the slop to the hog pens, where we fed the hogs.

Isaac also knew how to plow, although I did not. In addition to owning the two lots Around the Y, Rev. July rented large sections of land outside town ("in the country"), where he planted corn, peanuts, and cotton. From time to time, Isaac would give me instruction on plowing, usually on the Around the Y lots. I enjoyed plowing, although I never did learn how to consistently plow a straight row.

From around age 11 to around age 17 I spent a significant part of my time simply walking in the woods. I could enter the woods near my neighborhood and not emerge until I had gotten well over to the other side of town, a distance of several miles. I enjoyed hiking from my house to out near the local airport, which was on the north side of town, and watching the planes take off and land.

Rev. July grew corn on a substantial plot of land near the airport, one of the several lots he leased outside town. Isaac and I liked to go to a large watermelon field also near the airport that was owned by one of the county sheriffs, either the Nash County or Edgecombe County sheriff. (The field was in Edgecombe County but very close to the Nash and Edgecombe county lines.) The sheriff grew wonderfully sweet watermelons, and Isaac and I would (without the sheriff's permission) eat our fill.

## CHILD'S PLAY

WHEN I WAS, SAY, BETWEEN the ages of 8 and 12, black kids in our town played the typical American children's games—dodge ball, marbles, pick-up-sticks, jacks, hopscotch, jump rope, and hide-and-seek.[16] Jacks, jump rope, and hopscotch were games typically played by girls, although boys would sometimes participate. Marbles, touch football, and baseball were boys' games, although it was not unknown for a girl to play.

Dodge ball was a game, however, that boys and girls usually played together. A group of children would position themselves in a rectangular area with agreed-upon sidelines. Two other children standing about 10 or 15 yards apart were at either end. The two children at the ends of this area would try to hit those in the middle with a rubber or tennis ball. Any person hit with the ball would be out and would have to cease playing. This process of elimination would continue until only one person remained, and that child would be the winner. Hide-and-seek and pick-up-sticks were other games that boys and girls often played together.

We were also involved in various school and church activities. As mentioned earlier, the May Day program was a major affair at school each spring. All children were involved in wrapping the May Pole with long ribbons of crepe paper. School plays and singing recitals took place during each school year and programs were held at church on Easter Sunday and at Christmas. There were also special Sundays, although I must confess that—beyond Easter Sunday—I do not remember what they were. Somehow First Sunday was special, but I don't recall why. I do know that it was on occasions like those that delicious food such as fried chicken, chopped collard greens, homemade ice cream, and homemade cakes would be served. Those were also times when we had lots of fun playing group games and simply enjoying being alive.

Immediately adjacent to our neighborhood was a somewhat hilly area (we called it "the Hill") where we boys often played baseball. The Hill was a fairly large triangular piece of land that was on Atlantic Coast Line property and was delineated by east-west railroad tracks from and to Norfolk, Virginia. When passing our neighborhood, these east-west tracks divided in a westerly direction to go north and south. The dividing tracks (one set going north and the other south) formed two sides of the triangle, and the base of the triangle was formed by another set of tracks going north and south and adjacent to the Atlantic Coast Line's material yard.

The Hill was a terrible place to play baseball because it had quite a few holes and ruts, many rocks, and lots of weeds. Also, the Coast Line used the land to store some wooden railroad ties at what was the base of the triangle and to store some iron rails on one of the sides. We placed home plate (usually a good-sized rock) near the apex of the triangle. A ball hit over the pile of railroad ties at the base of the triangle was a home run. A ball hit onto or over the tracks on either side of the triangle-shaped Hill was a foul ball. You can undoubtedly appreciate the difficulty of trying to catch a grounder under those conditions. But it was the only vacant site in or near our neighborhood that was large enough to accommodate a baseball game. The Young Men's Christian Association (YMCA) had a beautiful, well-groomed, formal baseball field for white children. It was located next to the railroad station, which was downtown and about one-half mile from our neighborhood, but use of that field was limited to white people. No YMCA facility or organization in Rocky Mount was available to black people.

During my early teenage years in Rocky Mount, I spent many weekends and long evenings in early summer playing sandlot baseball and—believe it or not, given how skinny I was—sandlot football. We played touch football on Dunn Street, which again was unpaved in our neighborhood, and on one of the Rev. July's two lots in the neighborhood. The Rev. usually planted string beans, cabbages, and collards each summer in one of the lots and sweet potatoes in the other. It was the sweet potato lot where we played tackle football.

At one point, I was a member of a baseball team composed of young teenagers from Around the Y. The team was organized and financed by a man named Willie Brooks Harrison. We did not have uniforms, but he provided all of the equipment we needed: gloves, balls, and bats. We played games against teams from other black neighborhoods in Rocky Mount and nearby small towns.[17] "Tater Bug," as everyone called Mr. Harrison, also provided the transportation for our baseball team to get to the other neighborhoods and nearby towns to play. Our home games were played at the Negro ball park across town, a welcome change from having to play on the Hill.

## Entertainment

Of COURSE, THE "MOVING PICTURE SHOW" and the radio were sources of entertainment and information. Movies were both popular and relatively inexpensive. I don't remember how much tickets cost, but they were cheap. Feature films at the Booker T. and later the Ritz changed just about every week. The Western films were morality plays about struggles between cowboys (good) and Indians (evil), or settlers and pioneers (good) and land grabbers, rustlers, or bank robbers (evil). Extremely popular, at least among us boys, were Western film stars like Wild Bill Hickok, Hopalong Cassidy, Bob Steele, and Gene Autry. Of course, many of us had favorite roles that we wanted "to be."

There were also the weekly serials at the theaters. These were special films that did not portray a complete story or account at any one showing but instead were presented in a series of weekly episodes. Each week's action would begin with the hero escaping from what had seemed an absolutely inescapable catastrophe at the end of the previous week's episode. Of course, the current week's episode would end with another breathtaking peril. Needless to say, we all were eager to attend the next week's feature to see how the hero would escape or avoid last week's disaster and to find out what new peril he would have to confront.

The radio was to our generation what television is to today's youth. We each had our favorite radio characters and programs. Important athletic events were broadcast over the radio. A Joe Louis heavyweight fight was mandatory listening, with the listener hanging on each word of popular announcer Don Dunphy's[18] verbal description of punches thrown, avoided, and landed. Sugar Ray Robinson's fights were also extremely popular. Weekly radio programs were religiously followed. We would gather around the radio to listen to programs such as "The Lone Ranger" (with his faithful companion Tonto), the "Green Hornet" (with Kato), "Amos 'n' Andy," "The Jack Benny Show" (with Rochester), and "The Shadow."

Some of those radio shows had parallel offerings on the movie screen. There were films that featured radio characters—for example, the Lone Ranger, Jack Benny, and the Green Hornet. Also, important events described or reported on the radio would soon be shown in the newsreels at the theaters. A Joe Louis knockout would fill the Booker T. when it was shown on that theater's newsreel. Indeed, the newsreel of that time was sort of like today's CNN (Cable News Network). Because no one had television, the only way to see a visual depiction of an event that was being broadcast on the radio or reported in the newspaper was to see the newsreel at the local movie theater.

My teenage peers and I attended high school athletic events (as did adults), particularly high school football and basketball games. Booker T. Washington High School's basketball games were played at the Community Center, located across town and about two blocks from Douglas Block. Booker T. Washington played its football games at Talbert Park, the black ballpark across town on Park Avenue near East Thomas Street. We teens would also attend games played by touring black baseball teams of the Negro major leagues when they came to town, usually by sneaking into the ballpark.

Occasionally we went to see the Rocky Mount Leafs play. The Leafs were the local white minor league baseball team. Again, we usually sneaked into the ballpark. The white stadium was immediately adjacent to the Little Raleigh neighborhood and had a special, small section in the bleachers set aside for Negro patrons. This arrangement was before Jackie Robinson integrated organized baseball in 1947.

## CIGARETTES

IT PROBABLY WAS also around this time that I began to smoke cigarettes. My recollection is that I began smoking at age 13, after having been introduced to the vile practice by Mary July, who later became my stepsister as a result of my mother's marriage to her father, the Rev. John A. July. I smoked various brands of cigarettes off and on—mostly on—for

22 years, beginning with Chesterfields, followed by Lucky Strikes, then Viceroys, and finally Marlboros. I occasionally smoked a pipe during some of that time and tried several times to quit smoking. There is a great deal of truth in the statement that it is quite easy to stop smoking—it is not starting up again that is the real difficulty. So there were several times when I was unable to "not start smoking again."

I did finally stop at age 35. At the time, a major antismoking campaign was being waged, especially on television. In one particular antismoking ad, a cartoon type character would begin smoking a cigarette, quickly become enveloped in smoke, and then begin coughing violently. His head would then come off and roll across the floor. The voiceover would say, "If you don't stop smoking, you will cough your fool head off."

My son Robert, who was then about 3 or 4 years old, took this antismoking ad literally. He believed that if one smoked, his head would actually come off. Whenever I lit a cigarette in his presence, he would try to get the cigarette from me and put it out, all the while crying frantically. I began to think that if my little son thought so much of my life, I should value it equally as much.

One day, I got into my automobile, took a cigarette out of a package, and—as I was about to light it—thought about Robert and his reaction to my smoking. I quickly put the package of cigarettes behind the sun visor above the steering wheel, pledging to myself that I would not smoke that day. It was not a pledge to quit permanently or even for a month or a week—just for that day. I did not smoke that day, and the next day I repeated the pledge. I continued this routine for several weeks, all the while keeping the original package of cigarettes behind the sun visor. After about six weeks, I threw away the package of cigarettes, now totally dried out, and resolved never to smoke again.

I am now 74 years old and have not smoked a single cigarette since making that commitment 39 years ago. There were times, especially during the first three years, when I would experience a powerful desire to smoke, usually when watching a character light up in a movie. But, fortunately, I never surrendered to the craving. I obviously owe my cessation of smoking cigarettes primarily to Robert's love and concern for me.

It was also during our early teenage years that the boys in our neighborhood began to "play the dozens."[19] This unfortunate activity typically involved telling "jokes" or making short, funny, and crude statements about sex with another person's female relative, typically his mother or sister. This form of entertainment was essentially limited to boys and some of my contemporaries were particularly good at it. They could easily make rhymes and give quick repartee to another person's comment. I do not recall hearing the dozens being played after my teenage years.

## RELIGIOUS INSTRUCTION

PARENTS AND OTHER ADULTS in our community devoted substantial attention to religion and to children's religious training. My mother attended St. Mark's African Methodist Episcopal (AME) Church, which was then located on Raleigh Road in Little Raleigh.[20] She continued this practice even after she had married Rev. July. He was an ordained Baptist minister, although he did not have a regular church pastorate. I regularly accompanied my mother to St. Mark's on Sundays until my teenage years.

However, my earliest recollection of attending any church is visiting a "holiness" or "sanctified" church that was two or three blocks down the street from our house at 424 Raleigh Road. I must have been around 6 at the time. I especially remember the tambourines and the people doing a lot of shouting—not yelling, but a form of energetic dance. I also remember thoroughly enjoying the music and being impressed by the energy of the service. I have tried to recall how I came to attend services at that church. My assumption is that a female friend of my mother must have taken me. Regardless of how I got there, I still remember attending. I do not know if I went more than once, but I have a sense that I probably attended several times.

Along with my mother, Aunt Sadie Hobbs and her children—Josephine, Thelma and William "Bro" Hobbs—were members of St. Mark's AME Church in Little Raleigh. All of the July children—Rev.'s and his son Melvin's—were devoted members of the St. James Baptist Church, which is still located in Crosstown on East Thomas Street. Every Around the Y family was decidedly affiliated with some church in Rocky Mount. Everyone was expected to be a Christian and to attend church regularly, but while middle-age and older women were probably devout Christians (although they could be horrible gossips) and attended church on most Sundays, I do not think that the great majority of young adult women were regular churchgoers. Certainly most young adult males were not.

In my judgment, the commitment of young adults—male and female—to the Christian faith was observed far more in words than by deeds. Young adults often engaged in adultery, cursing, fighting, promiscuity, stealing, and various other violations of the Ten Commandments. Indeed, a significant number of teenage girls had become pregnant well before their scheduled graduation from high school. Still, everyone I knew expressed a belief in and respect for God and Jesus Christ. Children were indoctrinated with Christian morality and were constantly exhorted to follow the principles embodied in the Commandments.

There was no church in Around the Y, and only one place that could be characterized as a religious facility. It was on Dunn Street and was called the Clubhouse. It was actually both sides of a fairly small duplex that had been remodeled as a meeting place. From the outside, the Clubhouse looked like the other residential duplexes in the neighborhood, with two adjoining three-room units.[21] It was diagonally, almost directly, across the street from my house. According to Norfleet July, another one of Rev. July's sons, a men's club named the Dunn Street Aid Club owned the house and held meetings there—hence, the name "Clubhouse." The purpose of the men's club was community service, community improvement, and youth development.

Community events were sometimes held in the Clubhouse, and the men's club allowed Rev. July to conduct his Sunday school program there on Sunday afternoons. Most people in this comparatively small neighborhood who attended formal services on Sunday went to churches located in one of the other black neighborhoods, usually South Rocky Mount, Little Raleigh, Happy Hill, or Crosstown. But a significant number of the Around the Y neighborhood children attended—or also attended—afternoon Sunday school services at the Clubhouse. In fact, both adults and children participated in those sessions, and Rev. July regularly attracted a fair-sized group. Now, we are not talking about large numbers. I would suppose there were 20 or 30 people; certainly 50 would have filled the place.

## An Old Friend

CLIFTON DOZIER WAS ONE of my earliest friends, and when I think about growing up in Rocky Mount, thoughts of him always come to mind. I had known Clifton since I was an infant. Mrs. Alma Dozier reared him, and I believe he was her nephew.[22] Alma Dozier lived on Jackson Place, one or two houses from my cousins, Elnora Ingram and her children. Clifton and I played together as young boys. I remember the two of us racing our tricycles down Raleigh Road when I was about 5 or 6 years old. That was when I lived in Little Raleigh on Raleigh Road and before our family moved to Around the Y.

Clifton and I were classmates in the first grade at Annie W. Holland Elementary School. I think he had entered school in 1938 and was in our class because he had not been promoted the previous year. In fact, he was not promoted with our class either. At some point, either at the end of or during elementary school, he ceased attending school altogether. Clifton wasn't retarded, but he wasn't very intellectually smart. I remember him as a good-hearted and generous person.

Unfortunately, Clifton Dozier was probably not the best influence when I became a teenager. The last year I attended high school was spent reading, playing bid whist and hanging out with Clifton and his close friend Raymond Lucky, another elementary school dropout. I already knew who Raymond was because Gladys Lucky, his younger sister, was a member of my elementary and high school class. My friendship with Clifton and Raymond strengthened after I also left school, and I suspect that our relationship contributed substantially to my becoming a fellow dropout.

Those of us who knew Clifton well were surprised at his being drafted into the U.S. Army during the Korean War because, while he was in excellent physical condition, none of us could fathom how he could possibly have met any intellectual requirement. Raymond was not drafted into the Army because his physical examination, required of all prospective draftees, disclosed that he had a serious heart condition. Raymond died at age 37, on October 23, 1967, in Rocky Mount. His death certificate states that his death was "probably due to coronary occlusion."[23] Clifton Dozier was apparently court-martialed while in Korea and sentenced to serve a prison term at Fort Leavenworth, Kansas. Someone told me that his court martial was for cowardice in the face of the enemy. If so, Clifton may very well have been one of the black Korean War soldiers on whose behalf Thurgood Marshall traveled to Korea to investigate the charge that their court-martial convictions for cowardice were without merit and racially motivated.[24]

In the fall of 1955, not long after I began my studies at Howard University, I went to visit my cousin Marion Johnson, *née* Ingram, who was then living in Baltimore, Maryland. When I arrived at her house, she told me that Clifton had died in Fort Leavenworth and that his funeral was scheduled for that very day in Rocky Mount. That was sad news. Although I had not seen him for several years, I was very fond of Clifton.

### · Notes ·

1. Pitty Pat is the national card game of Belize. It is played by from two to four players with a standard 52 card pack. Though it may not be apparent at first sight, Pitty Pat is essentially a rummy game with a similar mechanism to *conquian*, in which the objective is to make three pairs starting from a five card hand. This card game was very popular among

Negroes in the eastern United States when I was growing up. It may have been popular elsewhere in the U.S. as well but I knew it in North Carolina and Philadelphia. You should be able to get the details of this card game by going online and typing in Pitty Pat. It was mostly played as a form of gambling.

2. See David Parlett, *The Oxford Guide to Card Games* (New York: Oxford University Press, 1990) at pages 139–152, for a discussion and explanation of Gin Rummy and various variations of that game. Also see Peter Arnold, *The Book of Card Games* (Barnes & Noble Books, 1988) at pp. 129–134 and pages 229–233.

3. The total amount of money bet by the players for an individual hand of cards played.

4. I am confident that similar visits were made to other black neighborhoods. Today such workers are called day workers.

5. A relatively small, neighborhood grocery store owned and operated by a white male whose name was J. R. Folks. That grocery store was the only full-service one that was actually in my neighborhood.

6. "Henry," by Keb' Mo' and J. L. Parker, which is on the compact disc *Slow Down* (Okeh/550 Music, 1998).

7. "Gristle" is another word for cartilage.

8. Walt Bullock was a neighborhood friend and contemporary of mine. He was still living in Rocky Mount when I wrote this part of My Story (February 13, 2005), but he died suddenly in his home on April 12, 2005.

9. We typically called adults by their first name. Mrs. Marie Crawford was called Miss Marie, Mrs. Ida Brown was called Miss Ida, Mrs. Sadie Hobbs was called Miss Sadie, and Mrs. Nellie Tillman—my mother—was called Miss Nellie. A child would often call an adult in another family "Aunt" or "Uncle," where a very close relationship existed between the two families. Bro Hobbs's mother (Sadie) and my mother (Nellie) were very close friends. Bro, therefore, called my mother Aunt Nellie, and I called his mother Aunt Sadie. (Bro's name is William Maceo Hobbs, but his mother always called him "Brother." His sisters, Josephine and Thelma Hobbs, mostly called him "Brother." But, for reasons unknown, everyone else knew him as "Bro" or "Bro Hobbs.")

10. According to her son Walt Bullock, she was born on January 12, 1912.

11. I do not ever recall seeing a man doing this work.

12. I do not ever recall seeing a woman "priming" or picking tobacco.

13. See, for example, *Goldilocks and the Three Bears,* written by Hy Murdock and illustrated by Lunn N. Grundy, Ladybird Books, Ladybird Books, Ltd., Leicester, England.

14. See Jerome E. Brooks, *Green Leaf and Gold, Tobacco in North Carolina* (Raleigh, NC: Division of Archives and History, North Carolina Division of Cultural Resources, 1997), 35. "Flue-cured tobacco is 'primed,' that is, each leaf is pulled separately from the plant." I believe in New England this was called picking tobacco.

15. Such people are probably still today referred to as truck farmers.

16. I assume white children played the same or similar games, but because we had virtually no social contact after beginning elementary school, I really had no empirical knowledge of what games they played.

17. One of the boys we played against was Charlie E. Hinton Jr., who in later years became a major league ballplayer, and the only baseball player from Rocky Mount, N.C., to play in the majors. For most of his career, he played with the Cleveland Indians and the Washington Senators. We all knew him as "C" Hinton when he was playing baseball in Rocky Mount. He describes his baseball career in his autobiography, *My Time at Bat,* by Chuck Hinton, Christian Living Books, Inc. (Maryland, 2002). He briefly describes Rocky Mount, N.C., and the Crosstown neighborhood at pp. 8–9.

18. The sports announcer, at that time, of most championship fights.

19. See Roger D. Abrahams, *Deep Down in the Jungle: Negro Narrative Folklore from the Streets of Philadelphia* (Hatboro, PA: Folklore Associates, 1964), for an in-depth and scholarly description of this social practice or folklore called "playing the dozens."

20. St. Mark's AME Church was then located on Raleigh Road, about half a block west of Church Street, having been constructed on that site in 1896. The church moved in April 1954 to a new location in Little Raleigh on West Street. In September 2000, the church moved to its present location at 1150 Tarboro, across the street from what is now Buck Leonard Park, in the Crosstown neighborhood.

21. Not a three-bedroom, but a three-room house: front room (living room), bedroom, and kitchen. That was it, although typically there was also a front porch and sometimes a small back porch.

22. My cousin Marion Johnson, *née* Ingram, told me that Alma Dozier was Clifton Dozier's aunt. I know absolutely nothing about his biological parents.

23. North Carolina State Board of Health, Office of Vital Statistics, Certificate of Death, Registration District No. 33:90, Registrar's Certificate No. 318 (Edgecombe County).

24. See, for example, Carl T. Rowan, *Dream Makers, Dream Breakers: The World of Justice Thurgood Marshall* (Boston: Little, Brown and Company, 1993), Chap. 12, especially pp. 164–69.

# 7

# The Neighborhood

Around the Y, the neighborhood where I mostly lived between the ages of 7 or 8 and 15 or 16 years, was totally black, with the homes in that community occupying an area of roughly nine to 12 square city blocks. The Emerson maintenance shops and railroad tracks of the Atlantic Coast Line Railroad Company bounded the neighborhood on two sides, south and west. The north and east sides of our neighborhood were defined by the Colonial ice plant and coal yard, and two all-white neighborhoods. Those several racially segregated neighborhoods shared three streets—Arlington, Dunn, and South Washington. Each of the three was paved with asphalt in the white neighborhoods, but only South Washington and Arlington streets were paved in our black neighborhood. They led directly to entry gates of the Atlantic Coast Line's Emerson maintenance shops;[1] Dunn Street, on which I lived, did not provide direct access for motor vehicles to Atlantic Coast Line property and hence was not paved in the black neighborhood. The difference was dramatic: Dunn Street was fully paved everywhere within the white neighborhood until the precise point where the white-occupied homes ended and the black homes of our neighborhood began. From that point, which was about the middle of the block between Arlington and South Washington Streets, Dunn Street was unpaved until its termination at the Atlantic Coast Line tracks, a distance of about two and one-half blocks.

The primary black neighborhoods in Rocky Mount, while I lived there, were Cemetery Hill, Cross Town, Germantown, Happy Hill, Joyner's Hill, Little Raleigh, the Oil Mill Section, Around the Y, and

South Rocky Mount. I cannot tell you the origin of all those names, but a few are obvious. For example, the Oil Mill Section was adjacent to the Planters Oil Mill plant, and there were two or three cemeteries located in Cemetery Hill. Little Raleigh was traversed by Raleigh Road, a main road leading to Raleigh, the state capital of North Carolina, but I do not know if that is why it is called Little Raleigh. South Rocky Mount is just that—an area located in the southernmost part of the city.

Today, black people live throughout Rocky Mount, and there are probably a few blacks living in every neighborhood in the city. In fact, certain formerly all-white areas of the city are now mostly, if not exclusively, black, I assume because of white flight. Still, the overwhelming majority of Rocky Mount's black residents continue to live in the black neighborhoods that existed when I was there, with the exception of Around the Y, which was demolished in 1976.

There was also a significant black commercial area called "Douglas Block" that was a part of the Cross Town neighborhood and lay on the northern edge of Rocky Mount's downtown and the southern edge of Cross Town. It consisted essentially of two blocks on East Thomas Street. This commercial area contained black professional offices (a doctor and dentist), two pharmacies or drugstores (Armstrong Drug Store and Burnett Drug Store), two pool halls, two cafes, two movie theaters, and the offices of two colored taxi companies (United Cab Co. and the Pittman and Bullock Cab Co.). Originally there was just one theater, the Booker T. But sometime in the 1940s, a second and smaller black movie theater, the Ritz, was built.

The wealthiest Negro in Rocky Mount was probably C.C. Stokes.[2] Stokes Funeral Home was just off Douglas Block, on Albemarle Avenue at its intersection with East Thomas Street. Stokes had a virtual monopoly for many years on the Negro mortuary business in and around Rocky Mount.[3] I would not be surprised if he was among the wealthiest Negroes then in the state of North Carolina.

108 Dunn Street, *the house where I lived in Around the Y. This photograph and the ones on pages 100 and 113, all from the archives of the city of Rocky Mount, were taken when the Around the Y neighborhood was demolished for a redevelopment project in the 1970s. The site is now Thelonious Monk Park.*

## The June German

Several tobacco warehouses were located very close to Douglas Block. For many years, a major dance was held each June in one of two tobacco warehouses. Friends still live in Rocky Mount who attended and remember the dance, and they say that it was sometimes held in the Planters warehouse and at other times in the Cobb and Foxhall warehouse. This event was known as the "June German" and was very well attended.[4]

There were separate June Germans for whites and coloreds, but each was held in the same tobacco warehouse. The white dance was held first, always on a Friday night, with the colored dance being held the following Monday. I cannot speak for the white dance, but big-name Negro entertainers performed at the colored June German. It was common for musicians such as Cab Calloway, Louis Jordan, Fats Domino, Big Joe Turner, Ella Fitzgerald and the like to appear at the event, which was well known among Negroes along the East Coast, from New York to Florida.

The June German was also an occasion for Negroes who had moved from Rocky Mount to other cities (usually northern cities, such as New York, Philadelphia, Baltimore, or Washington, D.C.) to return home. They would spend several days visiting family and friends and also have a grand time at the June German dance, which was an opportunity to demonstrate with their cars, cash, and clothes how successful they had been "up north."

Being permitted to attend the June German was, for many teenagers, a rite of passage into adulthood. The dance and attendant entertainment lasted throughout the night and into the early morning hours. It was the first occasion for many young people when they could stay out all night. I remember having permission to stay out all night for my first June German at the age of 16 and am certain the same was true for many of my contemporaries. I also remember that Big Joe Turner and his band were the headline entertainers at the June German I attended.

As it turned out, that occasion was not only my first but also my only June German because I enlisted in the U.S. Air Force in January of the following year, after I turned 17. I was stationed in Texas by the time of the next dance and was never again in Rocky Mount for the June German. I do not know when the tradition ceased, but I am told that the black June German is no longer held. I have been told that the white dance is still held, but not in a tobacco warehouse.

## SEGREGATION

REAL ESTATE DISCRIMINATION meant that black professionals and other business owners could not rent, lease, purchase, or construct office space or shops in any of Rocky Mount's white commercial or residential areas. Most white-owned or white-operated commercial services (department stores, electricians, grocery stores, hardware stores, plumbers, service stations, and taxi companies) were willing to serve Negroes. Most white lawyers would accept Negroes as clients. However, other businesses, professions, and vocations would not serve Negroes.

There were three white theaters (the Cameo, Carolina, and Center) in Rocky Mount, all located downtown. Only the Center admitted Negroes, and that was through a separate entrance with stairs leading to a second floor or upper balcony in the rear of the theater where there were seats to which Negro patrons were restricted. For the most part, white restaurants would not provide any service to Negroes, although there were a few white cafes where Negroes could purchase food at the back door or at a specially constructed side window. I do not recall any customary or legal restrictions or limitations on whites being served in colored restaurants, although whites tended not to frequent them.

The great majority of white physicians and dentists, as well as white beauticians, did not serve Negroes. White morticians did not serve Negroes, and cemeteries were segregated. Consequently, as with C.C. Stokes, black health care providers, beauticians, and morticians had scant competition in providing those services to Negroes. With the

AUNT SADIE HOBBS' HOUSE *at 1022 S. Washington Street—a gathering place for me and my Around the Y teen-age contemporaries. This photograph and the ones on pages 97 and 113, all from the archives of the city of Rocky Mount, were taken when the Around the Y neighborhood was demolished for a redevelopment project in the 1970s. The site is now Thelonious Monk Park.*

exception of beauticians, most served their clients and customers in facilities on or very close to Douglas Block. Negro beauticians tended to serve their clients in their own homes or at alternate residential settings.

I suppose a great deal of the negative commercial change that has occurred throughout much of the South, particularly in black commercial centers, can be explained in significant measure by racial integration or the elimination of segregation. With the end of Jim Crow segregation, whites and blacks now have access to many services in both communities, and those providing such services compete for clients within all racial groups. This is particularly true for black merchants, trade workers, and professionals. However, that crossover does not appear to be the case among beauticians and funeral homes. C.C. Stokes has been deceased for some time now, but the Stokes Funeral Home is still at the same location and seems to be thriving. This appears to be the case in Northern cities as well, where blacks and whites tend to patronize beauty shops and funeral homes dedicated to serving their particular race.

Douglas Block still exists today, but it has little, if any, of the social energy and economic vitality of the 1940s, 1950s, and 1960s. Two pool halls are the remaining businesses. The two theaters are long gone, as are the two drugstores, and I understand that there are no longer any professional offices on Douglas Block. Of course, downtown Rocky Mount is also no longer anywhere near as vibrant or energetic as it was, having succumbed to the shopping malls located elsewhere in the city.

The Atlantic Coast Line was the 800-pound gorilla in our community and, indeed, in Rocky Mount. I have no doubt that the Atlantic Coast Line was Rocky Mount's largest employer of workers, both black and white. It certainly influenced every aspect of the lives of people living in our neighborhood. Most of the employed adult men in our neighborhood worked for the Atlantic Coast Line, albeit primarily in unskilled positions. A few black men probably worked in skilled positions but, if so, were probably denied the title and wages afforded white workers occupying the same or similar positions.

The women in our neighborhood mostly did "day work" for white families or seasonal work in the local tobacco industry. I do not think my mother ever was a day worker or worked in a tobacco factory while I lived with her. She always worked as a cook, primarily in white establishments, until after her marriage to the Rev. John A. July.[5] I recall her working as a cook at the Pomi Inn on Church Street when we lived in Little Raleigh, and at the Rocky Mount Sanitarium, then at a white café in South Rocky Mount that catered primarily to men working in the rail yards and maintenance shops of the Atlantic Coast Line Railroad. The last job I remember her having was at the Hunt's Motel cafe, which was located a few miles south of the city on Highway 301.

During the years before the diesel locomotive came into general use, people in our neighborhood were constantly bombarded by the loud noise and dingy smoke generated by coal-burning locomotives. Many, if not most, homes in the area—including the house where I lived—were located less than one city block from the tracks used by freight trains, but both freight and passenger trains passed our neighborhood constantly during the day and frequently during the night. We continued to be assailed by the noise even after the demise of the coal-burning steam engines that produced so much foul smoke. For many years, I have wondered about the illnesses and diseases people within our community may have contracted as a result of breathing smoke from those locomotives and the other toxic fumes from the railroad yards. Unfortunately, it would be almost impossible to make any determination in that regard today.

From the time my family moved to Around the Y until I was in about the eighth grade, my male peers and I regularly used the Atlantic Coast Line freight trains, Emerson maintenance shops, and rail yards adjacent to our neighborhood as a playground and, occasionally, as a public transit system. The boys in our neighborhood engaged in various made-up games, such as seeing who could walk the longest distance on a single railroad track without losing his balance and falling off. We would play hide-and-seek at night in the railroad material yard and among parked railroad freight cars. We challenged each other's courage by jumping from the top of railroad cars to the ground. Those games were a lot of fun, notwithstanding the danger. And we were essentially unaware of the danger anyway.

One of the events in my life that I feel most ashamed of took place when I was about 8 years old, and my father was very sick and bedridden. It must have been summer,[6] and my mother asked me to stay in the room with my father and fan him. He was in a front room of the house, and through the window I could see my friends playing in the nearby railroad material yard. I sneaked off from my task of fanning my father to join my friends, who were playing among the railroad cars. Even today I am ashamed of this behavior, though I was a young boy at the time. It affects my conscience, and I am still ashamed that I elected to play with my friends rather than care for my father when I had the ability and opportunity to do so. An occurrence like that can stay with you for the rest of your life.

Males in our neighborhood—typically teenagers, but also young adults—would often hitch a ride on an Atlantic Coast Line freight train as a means of getting downtown or simply within closer walking distance to the Cross Town and Happy Hill neighborhoods.[7] I engaged in the practice from the time I was about 12 or 13 years old until I left Rocky Mount at age 17. Freight trains moved fairly slowly when passing by Around the Y on the railroad tracks that were immediately adjacent to the southern edge (trains from Norfolk, Virginia) and western edge (trains from Alabama, Florida, Georgia, and South Carolina) of our neighborhood. They would not gain substantial velocity until they were passing through downtown Rocky Mount.

There is a metal step at both ends and on each side of all railroad freight cars. One can use this step to jump onto a slow-moving freight train as it passes. This practice was called "catching a freight." We would get onto this step and ride the "freight" until it approached downtown and began to gain significant speed. In fact, if you did not get off the train by the time it was near downtown, the chances were high that it would be going too fast for you to get off once it was passing through downtown Rocky Mount. No one I knew ever was trapped on a train, but it was always a possibility.

## Informal Education: Shanty Cars and Barbecues

Once my peers and I reached our teenage years—perhaps even as early as elementary school—our primary education no longer took place solely in school and church. Much of the life in our Around the Y community reflected the idea that "it takes a village to raise a child." Child rearing when I was a child and teenager was not just the responsibility of the adult women in our community; adult men also played a significant role in our development. There are several settings where I remember male influences as being important in my early teenage development and that of some of my peers.

As noted, most of the men in our neighborhood worked for the "Coast Line," so almost everyone had a husband, father, brother, or uncle working for the company. Some of the women worked as servants (cooks and housekeepers) in the homes of white people employed by the Coast Line, usually in some supervisory capacity. One woman from our neighborhood—Tut (rhymes with "put") Bethea—worked alongside men moving freight with a hand truck at the Atlantic Coast Line freight shed, which was located very close to our neighborhood.

Almost all of those railroad workers had come to Rocky Mount from the Pee Dee area of South Carolina, either as transferred or new Coast Line workers. In the late 1920s or early 1930s, much of the maintenance work being done in Atlantic Coast Line shops in Florence, South Carolina, was transferred to the Emerson shops in Rocky Mount. Men who were willing and able to move from South Carolina to North Carolina flocked to Rocky Mount either to preserve a job held in Florence or to obtain a new job with the Coast Line. The great majority of the workers were probably from Florence, Marion, and

Darlington counties in South Carolina. They and their families settled in as permanent residents of Rocky Mount.

Other railroad workers who lived Around the Y were also from South Carolina and Georgia. Those workers had usually come to Rocky Mount as members of "section gangs," which were composed of men the Coast Line hired to do the hard physical work of laying and maintaining the railroad tracks and road beds used by the passenger and freight trains. Those workers interacted socially with many of the people in our neighborhood, especially some of the young women. Many lived in converted railroad boxcars—called "shanty cars"—where they slept and kept their personal belongings. These shanty cars were parked on side railroad tracks[8] adjacent to our neighborhood.

The Atlantic Coast Line Railroad supplied section gang members with food, in addition to their shanty car housing. I don't know whether those expenses were deducted from their pay. A cook—who I assume was on the railroad company's payroll—purchased and prepared the men's food. After eating their supper, some of the shanty car workers would sit in front of their shanty car homes for several hours into the evening, playing musical instruments (usually a guitar, harmonica, or banjo), singing songs (typically the blues), and telling stories about different aspects of their lives. Those experiences may account for much of my own love of the blues.

Our parents and the other "decent" folk in our neighborhood generally opposed having any of us associate with railroad workers who lived in the shanty cars. Some people in our neighborhood saw shanty car workers as violent, dishonest, immoral, dangerous, and therefore, to be avoided. A few shanty workers probably deserved that reputation, but certainly nowhere near all. Some youngsters from my neighborhood—I was often among them—would sneak down to the railroad tracks in the evening to listen to the section gang workers. Their songs and stories were usually about athletics, women, work, race relations, and life in general. Even then my peers and I were convinced that a lot of their tales were exaggerations and, in many instances, simply untrue. But whether true or false or a mixture of both, the railroad workers' stories greatly influenced us youngsters as we formed our opinions about those subjects. While we did not have much to say to the shanty car people, we would later debate and discuss among ourselves what we had heard and how we planned to behave—or not behave—in light of what we had been told.

While the image of "a village raising a child" is usually perceived as something positive, in this instance that was not always the case. For example, most of the information those men shared with us about women was both wrong and outrageous—specifically, what women thought, how women behaved, whether women could be trusted by men, and how women deserved to be treated by men. As youngsters, given the times and the examples we sometimes actually saw of women being mistreated and abused, we were rarely in a position to challenge the relationship between men and women as described by those men. In their view, few if any women could or should be trusted with a man's heart or money. If a woman behaved inappropriately, such as cheating on her man or spending his earnings foolishly, then she deserved to be beaten. It was emphasized that the man was head of his household and should "wear the pants in the house." That pronouncement meant that important decisions had to be made by the man—or at least they required his approval or acquiescence before being implemented.

The men did, however, also offer much positive and helpful advice. For example, they emphasized the need to do a good job when working. We were always cautioned to be very careful when dealing with white people and not to take foolish risks. It was important to maintain your personal dignity, but reality meant that you should not get "out of your place." You had to appreciate the need to "curb ambitions, to contain feelings, and to weigh carefully every word, gesture, and movement when in the presence of whites."[9] Adult whites—and even older teenagers—were always to be addressed as Mr. and Mrs., never solely by their first name. You could say Mr. Bob or Mrs. Joan, but never Bob or Joan. That would be seen as "being uppity" or "getting out of your place," and adverse consequences could result—sometimes seriously adverse consequences, like losing your job, being arrested by the police on a trumped-up charge, or even losing your life.

Most of all we were told always to be careful to avoid getting into a position where we could be taken advantage of or where our rights could be trampled on. For this reason, these railroad workers (and other adults) admonished us to get as much education as possible (i.e., "get it in our heads"). We were also strongly admonished to avoid negative contacts with law enforcement officials and all unnecessary contacts with other white people.

When people in my neighborhood—and in other black communities in Rocky Mount—were talking about police officers or sheriff's deputies, the term used was "the law." It was atypical for police officers and sheriff's deputies to be referred to by their work title, such as police officer or deputy sheriff. If a police car was approaching, someone would say, "Here comes the law!" The tone, implication, and sense of the comment were literally that those white men (there were no black or women law enforcement officers) *were,* in fact, the law!

Indeed, the reality was—and we were being taught by Southern white tradition—that law enforcement officers *were the law,* when the matter involved Negroes. In theory, one could argue that statutes and written regulations—perhaps even the judge—were the law. But in our community, it was the law enforcement officers who, in general, knew the applicable legal rules and relevant facts that would be used to determine guilt or innocence. This knowledge provided them with the power to determine the facts—even if that meant lying about, mischaracterizing, or selectively reporting the actual facts.

Consequently, in every practical and societal sense of those words, those officers *were the law.* The outcome of any court hearing or trial would not necessarily be determined by *the truth,* but by what a judge *found to be* the truth. We were warned that, given a dispute between the testimony of a police officer and that of a black person, the testimony of the police officer or sheriff's deputy would always be believed. Even if the law enforcement officer's story was not credible, the judge or jury would still find it to be true and correct. So people knew the validity of what they spoke when uttering the words, "Here comes the law!'"

Another opportunity for boys to be heavily influenced by their male elders—outside of the church and home—was when a pig was being barbecued. A pit barbecue was a big deal everywhere in Rocky Mount. A pig was not roasted often Around the Y—perhaps only two or three times in a year, usually in connection with a very special event, such as a fund-raiser to help construct a new church or to improve an existing church structure, a Fourth of July celebration, or an affair being sponsored by an organization like the Masons[10] or the Eastern Star.[11]

When I was growing up in eastern North Carolina, people ate (they still do eat) what is called "chopped barbecue." In the case of a roasted pig, all of the meat is removed from the bones and all of the portions of the pig are chopped together—hams, shoulders, skin, loin, back, and so forth. Unlike barbecued ribs, this meat is finely chopped, with a cleaver, hatchet, and butcher knife. Then sandwiches are made or it is sold as a portion or serving of a dinner, usually with coleslaw, Brunswick stew, potato salad, and hush puppies (a small ball of deep-fried cornmeal batter).

The initial step in the barbecuing process was to dig a hole in the ground about 18 to 24 inches deep, 5 or 6 feet long, and 3 or 4 feet wide. A small fire was initially built in the hole to dry it out and, I guess, warm the pit's sides and bottom. The cooking process is somewhat different today with metal cookers and the like being widely used. Indeed, chopped barbecue is now readily available at fast-food joints throughout Rocky Mount and probably every city in eastern North Carolina. But, believe me, the quality is not the same as the pit barbecue that was prepared during my youth.

Metal rods would be placed at uniform intervals over the top of the pit to, essentially, create a grill. A pig, usually around 100 pounds in cleaned weight, would then be placed on the rods, skin side down. A substantial log fire would already have been built close by, using well-dried oak or hickory wood. Sometimes both types of wood were used together. This fire was used throughout the cooking process to produce red-hot embers that would be periodically spread in the pit and under the pig. Heat radiating from those hot cinders would cook the whole pig slowly and, at the same time, flavor it with the smoke that was generated by the oak and hickory embers. The pig, while being cooked, would also be basted frequently with a sauce consisting of vinegar, dried red peppers, salt, sometimes sugar, and other seasonings. Everyone in my immediate family knows how much I dislike the taste and smell of vinegar, and yet I developed a fondness for chopped barbecue, notwithstanding it being saturated with vinegar. Go figure!

Older and more experienced men from the neighborhood cooked the pig. It would not be unusual, however, for friends or co-workers who lived in nearby neighborhoods, such as South Rocky Mount, Joyner's Hill, and Little Raleigh, to stop by at various times during the evening hours to chat, comment on the process, offer suggestions, or just plain "signify."[12] I remember the cooking occurring over a period of many hours and mostly at night.

My young male friends and I would closely observe the process throughout the time the pig was being barbecued. But we were mainly interested in two events: the turning over of the pig and the chopping of the cooked meat. The cooks and their friends made it clear that turning the pig over was a critical event. After having been cooked over the hot embers skin side down for the appropriate number of hours, the pig had to be turned over, to be cooked skin side up.

The pig could not be turned over too soon in the process. It had to be at the appropriate degree of doneness, and not overcooked, when the turnover was attempted. There was almost always discussion—and sometimes debate—among the various cooks and commentators about whether the pig was ready to be turned over. If not cooked enough before the turnover was attempted, there was a serious risk that various parts of the pig would not have been uniformly cooked.

It was essential that the pig remain intact throughout the cooking process. If it was overcooked before being turned over, there was a significant risk that the major divisions of the pig would separate when people attempted to turn it over. I don't know precisely why it was so important that the pig remain intact throughout the cooking process, because the pig was to be chopped up anyway. However, the men made it clear that keeping the entire pig intact was essential.

The next big deal after cooking the pig was chopping it. Everything—from the snout to the tail—was finely chopped and combined into one large pile of pork or was placed in several containers. This event was particularly important to the children and teenagers because we would be given the bones after most of the meat had been removed to be chopped. Bits of meat, which we would immediately devour, would always be attached to the bones when we received them. Although it was the men who did most of the cooking and chopping, women would join the process during this event, primarily to help complete the seasoning of the barbecue. After the seasoning was complete would come the selling and eating of the barbecue sandwiches and dinners.

Throughout the many hours the barbecue process took to complete, the men—those cooking and those commenting on the cooking—would be talking and often arguing among themselves about personal histories, preferences, and problems. During the course of the evening, they might tell tales about local past events, as well as about matters that had occurred years earlier when they lived in South Carolina or Georgia. At various times there would be a sharing of views about segregation, Jim Crow laws and policies, "crackers,"[13] women, education, and work.

We youngsters would sit, watch, listen, and learn lessons about how barbecue was prepared and, more important, about life. As was the case with the shanty car workers, those men were an important part of our socialization and informal education. Community values were effectively transmitted and reinforced in those settings. On occasions like these we were given and eagerly received advice on how to deal with

AROUND THE Y NEIGHBORHOOD CHILDREN, *summer 1956 or 1957. In the upper right of the photograph is J.R. Folks' store.*

women and white people, how to obtain and keep a job, and how to live in society in general. Barbecues were not the only occasions for this kind of education, but they were important elements of our informal survival skills training and general socialization.

## NIGHTLIFE IN ROCKY MOUNT

THERE WERE SEVERAL "nightspots" in and around Rocky Mount, typically called "joints" or "juke joints," where people, including teenagers, could go for entertainment, usually to listen and dance to songs played on a juke box. I will not tell a lie: I had absolutely no skill at dancing, although I could slow dance. But who couldn't slow dance! Nightspots like these hosted many Negro entertainers who later went on to become famous. Performers such as Ruth Brown, Ray Charles, John Lee Hooker, B.B. King, Gladys Knight, and Lou Rawls spent substantial parts of their early careers playing in joints throughout the South on what was called the "chitt'lin' circuit."

If you were unable to hitch a ride with a friend who had a car, you could walk, take the city bus, or take a taxi to most joints within the city. But some of the popular joints were located in nearby rural areas, which we called "the country," and in not-too-distant towns, such as Sharpsburg (approximately 5 miles), Elm City (8 miles), Nashville (10 miles), Tarboro (16 miles), Wilson (18 miles), and Pinetops (18 miles). Young men with automobiles would transport their girlfriends and other friends to those town and country joints around Rocky Mount. I don't recall knowing any young woman who owned an automobile.

## SOUTHERN COOKING

OUR REGULAR DIET WAS distinctive—and much of it was also hazardous to our health. I now know that a lot of the meat we ate and the way it was prepared significantly increased our risk of an early grave from heart disease and stroke. I have no doubt but that an early death was the actual result in many cases.

Mrs. Ethel Grant's café and juke joint *on Dunn Street, looking essentially as it did in the 1950s. This photograph and the ones on pages 97 and 100, all from the archives of the city of Rocky Mount, were taken when the Around the Y neighborhood was demolished for a redevelopment project in the 1970s. The site is now Thelonious Monk Park.*

We ate every part of the pig, particularly the cheaper parts: "fat-back";[14] ham hocks; pig snout,[15] ears, feet, tail; back bone; neck bone; "streak of lean, streak of fat";[16] and most of the internal organs—heart, kidneys, liver, lungs, stomach, and even the intestines, which were called "chitt'lin's" or "chitterlings." My mother had a reputation for being able to prepare outstanding chitt'lin's and rice, but I truly disliked them. Although many contemporary blacks attempt to romanticize chitt'lin's, I have no fond memories of the dish.

Other food that we regularly consumed and that my mother and neighbors used to stretch the dollar included certain inexpensive chicken parts—specifically, the feet, necks, backs, and wings. My mother and I raised chickens at 108 Dunn Street for eating. I also raised rabbits for home consumption after we moved to 105 Ward Street in South Rocky Mount. But it was not always the cheap cuts that were served on our table; sometimes—certainly on special occasions, such as Easter Sunday, Christmas, and Thanksgiving, and even for Sunday supper—we would enjoy fried chicken legs, thighs, and breasts; slices of ham; pork chops; or occasionally steak. Those dishes were not usually served all at once, except at a holiday meal such as Christmas or Thanksgiving.

We often ate local freshwater fish—bass and catfish, for instance—and because we were not all that far from the Atlantic Ocean (about 100 miles), ocean fish (such as sea bass, spots, and croakers) were plentiful and frequently on the supper table. My mother sometimes fried oysters or made an absolutely delicious oyster stew. The women in our neighborhood also used canned salmon to make fried salmon croquettes, which I loved. Some of the men in our neighborhood were hunters, and my mother often purchased wild game from them. It was not unusual for us to have squirrel, wild rabbit, opossum (called "possum," and of which I was not particularly fond), and raccoon (called "coon") for supper. At one point, I acquired a BB rifle and would hunt birds, which my mother cooked into a bird pie.

But whether eating inexpensive fish, inexpensive poultry parts, inexpensive cuts of meat, canned salmon, or more expensive protein, we were putting our lives at risk in most instances. Most of the meat we ate had a great deal of fat on it. Even when it didn't, nine times out of 10 the meat we consumed (except ham, pig ears, pig feet, pig snout, back bones, neck bones, chicken necks, and chicken feet) would be fried—usually in lard. Although we ate those cheaper foods largely because of discrimination suffered by our race and our resultant poverty, the methods used to prepare our food were typical Southern "soul food" cooking.

On a more wholesome note, various fruits were both popular and plentiful in season. So not everything we ate was—or turned out decades later to be—unhealthy. We ate bananas, blackberries, blueberries, cantaloupe, cherries, grapes, honeydew melon, peaches, pears, plums, strawberries, and watermelon throughout the summer. Like many of the families in our neighborhood and town, we had a garden where we grew a variety of vegetables during the summer and fall. Most people in my neighborhood grew cabbage, carrots, collards, corn, cucumbers, kale, lima beans (called "butter beans"), okra, onions, peppers (hot and sweet), sweet potatoes, white potatoes, squash, string beans, and tomatoes. We also grew mustard greens and other greens that we referred to as "salad greens," although they were boiled and not eaten raw. I was particularly fond of the liquid from the cooking of those greens, which we called "pot liquor."

My mother also canned vegetables and fruits for our consumption during the winter. Those foods were typically preserved in pint- and quart-size clear glass Mason jars. The canning process involved cooking the particular food, sterilizing the glass jars in which the food would be preserved (by boiling them in hot water), filling the jars with the cooked food, and then sealing them with rubber seals and brass colored lids. The jars of food—peaches, tomatoes, green butter beans, corn, peppers, and string beans—were colorful and inviting when arranged on shelves in our kitchen.

Frozen foods were not yet generally available, at least not where I lived. We did eat dried pasta throughout the year, such as spaghetti with meat sauce and macaroni with cheese. I also remember a few times, in the Little Raleigh and Around the Y neighborhoods, when my mother had to resort to cooking the leaves of a plant called "poke salad" that grew wild in the area. I also remember strongly disliking its taste.

Some of the vegetables we ate were, unfortunately, boiled to death. I personally enjoyed eating certain vegetables raw—cabbage, carrot, cucumber, okra, sweet potato, rutabaga, turnip, and tomato. But often-times, cooked by our parents and neighbors, those vegetables were boiled until they were very, very, very well done. Sadly, most of the nutrients had thus been cooked out of the food. Fortunately for me, the pot liquor I liked so much was rich in nutrients. But our boiled vegetables were also almost always seasoned with fatback or "streak of lean, streak of fat." Our parents and neighbors were also liberal in their use of salt to season food, whether fried or boiled. As was the saying where I grew up, they "had a heavy salt hand."

We had a regular supply of desserts in the form of chocolate, coconut, pineapple, or pound cakes, homemade ice cream, pies (especially sweet potato pies), and another of my favorites—banana pudding. In the winter, whenever we had a particularly heavy snowfall, I would collect a large tub of snow that my mother would make into what she called "snow cream." Of course, there were also jams and jellies—many of them homemade—and preserved watermelon rinds.

Breakfast was probably the most harmful meal of all. We often had bacon or fried fatback; grits (seasoned with butter or grease from fried bacon, fatback, or pork sausages); eggs cooked in butter or lard; smoked sausage (containing a lot of fat, but also one of my favorite foods—we called it "smoke sausage"); or pork sausage patties and links. Not often but sometimes all of this food would be available at one meal. We also drank a great deal of tea, hot and cold, and thereby consumed a great deal of refined sugar. I note that today in the South when tea is offered in a restaurant or someone's home, you are usually asked if you want "sweet tea." When I grew up, the only kind of tea we knew was what is today called "sweet tea."

Also, probably until I became a young adult, I regularly consumed a significant amount of highly sweetened Kool-Aid and fresh lemonade. Probably until I left home for the U.S. Air Force, I also often drank "sugar water" during the summer: This was simply plain tap water sweetened with refined sugar and poured over cracked ice. My friends and I drank great quantities of soft drinks or soda pop—Orange Crush, Dr. Pepper, Nehi Grape, and Nehi Orange. Although I was not much of a cola fan, Coca-Cola, Pepsi-Cola, and Royal Crown Cola were also popular drinks among my contemporaries. With all of this sugar consumption and without a regular program of dental care, you can imagine the consequences for our teeth. Until I went into the Air Force, I think the only time anyone in my family visited the dentist was when we had a severe toothache or developed an obvious dental problem, a serious cavity or abscess, for instance.

## STRANGE FOOD

I SIMPLY MUST MENTION TWO gastronomic peculiarities of our community. I do not know about elsewhere in the state or nation, but in Rocky Mount's black neighborhoods, people consumed significant amounts of lump starch, normally used by housewives to help stiffen clothes during the ironing process. I myself ate quite a bit of starch as a youngster and, I must admit, enjoyed the taste.

We also ate clay. I do not know precisely where this particular type of clay soil was obtained, but the supply was plentiful. A few years ago (October 3–5, 2004), I visited the home of Rosa Mae Harper, *née* Garrett, a close friend who lives in Rocky Mount, and met a then 68-year-old woman who told me that people in her neighborhood of Happy Hill got clay from a local brickyard, where one of her uncles worked. People in our neighborhood called it "claydirt," pronounced as one word. I ate my fair share of both starch and claydirt. I do not know when I developed this habit, but I assume it was during my early teenage years. I have no recollection of eating either after leaving Rocky Mount for the Air Force.

It is my understanding that when people develop a taste for strange foods, it probably is in response to some nutritional deficiency that is being wholly or partially compensated for by the unusual food. I have often wondered if there was some nutritional deficiency that would explain why people in our neighborhood ate starch[17] and claydirt. After having said all of that about strange and unhealthy food, let me now mention certain foods I was particularly fond of and associate only with good memories.

## Favorite Foods

My all-around favorite vegetable dish was probably collard greens, which were boiled and typically seasoned with ham hocks, "streak of lean, streak of fat," or with plain fatback. In Rocky Mount, collard greens were finely chopped either before or after being cooked. When chopped after being cooked, they tended to be chopped quite fine. I found collards to be a fantastic dish when combined with plain white rice.

I liked both dried and fresh butter beans, especially green butter beans (lima beans). Other favorites were succotash, a dish combining green butter beans and fresh corn kernels cut from the cob; stewed tomatoes; fried okra, and just plain corn kernels that had been cut from the cob and stewed in a frying pan on the top of the stove. I was never very much a fan of biscuits or flour bread, but I loved corn bread in any form, whether boiled (dumplings), baked (muffins), or fried ("hoe cakes"). In my opinion, the hoe cakes prepared by Mrs. Lula Harrison, "Fat" Cherry's mother and Joe Rollins's grandmother, had to be the best in Rocky Mount. (I called Mrs. Lula "Grandma" although I don't know why or when I developed that practice. She was not my grand-mother. We were not related by genetics or marriage.)

As concerns meat and poultry, I would have to put fried chicken and fried pork chops on my list of favorites. I also ate as much as I could of chopped barbecue, and I liked pig ears and pig feet.

Like many youngsters, I had a sweet tooth. Mrs. Marie Crawford, who lived on Dunn Street about two houses from mine, made absolutely delicious cakes. My favorite was pineapple. I spent a lot of time at her house, especially during the winter, helping her in various ways. She enjoyed baking cakes, and often I was rewarded with the fruits of her exceptional baking skills.

My mother had a well-deserved reputation as an excellent cook but did not do a great deal of baking. She did however bake an excellent pound cake, which I enjoyed tremendously, as I did her banana pudding and gingerbread. Many of the women in our neighborhood baked outstanding sweet potato pies. Ethel Grant, who with her husband owned and operated a local combination juke joint and café that was diagonally across the street from our house, probably made her monthly profit solely on my purchases of her sweet potato jacks. (I'm exaggerating, but not that much.) The conventional name for pastries that we called "jacks" is "turnovers," as in apple turnovers. The jack was a flour pastry with a sweet potato filling very much like the filling of a sweet potato pie. The circular pastry was filled with the sweet potato filling, then folded over to form a semicircle. The edges were sealed and the pastry was fried. Those jacks were delicious and very popular.

I also favored vanilla ice cream (homemade or store bought) and liked Jell-O, almost any flavor, especially when made with fruit cocktail. My favorite candy bars were Baby Ruth, Milky Way, Mounds, and Almond Joy.

## CARE OF CLOTHES

ON LAUNDRY DAY EACH WEEK, women would boil the soiled clothes and linens in a large, three-legged iron pot, which was placed on three bricks over an open fire in the backyard. After being boiled, the items were washed in a tin tub using a scrub board (sometimes called a washboard —I have such a board on our back porch, just off the kitchen, at 2955

Avalon Avenue). Then they were rinsed in clear, cold water in a tin tub. The next step was to wring them out and hang them outside on a line to dry in the sun, secured with wooden clothes pins. The clothes would later be pressed on a wooden ironing board with a flatiron.[18] This pressing device was made of iron and heated on the top or side of a wood-burning stove.

The laundry soap was typically homemade and had been created in the same iron pot used to boil the soiled clothes. My mother made soap in our backyard two or three times each year. I never did know all the ingredients she used. I do know that she used animal fat (mostly pork) and lye. After the ingredients were cooked over a fire, they were allowed to cool and solidify. The soap would then be turned out onto a large piece of cardboard and cut into manageable-sized cakes before being allowed to harden completely. This strong and harsh soap—called lye soap—was sometimes even used for personal bathing.

## Liquor and White Lightning

Some of the people who lived Around the Y supplemented their legitimate income with illegal activities. Indeed, for a few, the primary, if not only, source of income was illegal activity.

To my knowledge, North Carolina did not permit the sale of hard liquor in privately owned establishments (nightclubs, cocktail lounges, bars). If you wanted to purchase hard liquor—whiskey, gin, bourbon, scotch, vodka—you had to go to the "State Store." The official name of the state-regulated but county-operated establishments was and still is the ABC Store, for Alcoholic Beverage Commission, a state regulatory agency. However, people in Rocky Mount tended to refer to those establishments as State Stores.

When I lived in Rocky Mount, the ABC Stores sold liquor only in half-pints, pints, and fifths. Therefore, a person who didn't want to buy a full bottle, or lacked sufficient funds to do so, was out of luck. You could not just buy a drink or "a shot." Hence, a cottage industry developed whereby liquor was sold in private homes, much like during Prohibition, when it was unlawful to sell any alcoholic beverages or "spirits" in any quantity anywhere in the United States.

An enterprising person in North Carolina could purchase a bottle of liquor or a variety of bottles from the ABC Store and resell the liquor as individual drinks in his or her home—and at a significantly inflated price. That person's living room or kitchen became a social setting, much like a small bar or cocktail lounge in states where it was legal to sell liquor by the glass or drink. Persons who could not afford a full bottle at ABC Store prices could converse with friends and neighbors while having one or a few drinks. Even at inflated prices, those small drinks were still affordable, although I am certain that some of the people who frequented the home establishments could, in fact, afford to purchase a bottle from the ABC Store but simply enjoyed the camaraderie found in the private home. This enterprise was, of course, illegal. Such places were at risk of being raided by the police, although I believe raids were infrequent.[19]

> Remember if you will,
> Lightnin' from a whiskey still,
> Blues in the breeze,
> The sweet Magnolia trees,
> A little church house up on the hill.[20]

Because my neighborhood was a poor one, some people still could not afford liquor from the ABC Store, even by the drink. It was here that bootleg liquor occupied a niche. Bootleg liquor, called "white lightning," "stump-hole" liquor, and "corn liquor"[21] where I lived, offered a significantly less expensive alternative to commercially produced "spirits" because it was untaxed and relatively inexpensive to produce. Some people simply preferred the taste and kick of stump hole over commercially produced liquor. Home brew[22] or homemade beer was also usually available.

One or two men in our neighborhood were wholesalers of white lightning or stump-hole liquor. They operated separately from the retailers who offered stump-hole for sale in their homes by the drink. The manufacturers and major distributors of stump-hole liquor were usually white males. My recollection is that the risk of arrest was much, much higher for being a wholesaler or manufacturer of stump-hole liquor than for reselling it—or ABC Store liquor—in one's home.

One of my earliest memories is of the police entering our home at 424 Raleigh Road in Little Raleigh at night and moving through it quickly. I was probably 3 or 4 years old, because I think it was before I began elementary school. One officer declared, "It's in the pea patch." My father was growing peas in our backyard, and a significant quantity of "stump-hole" liquor was found under the pea vines. Apparently someone had informed on my father. While I can remember the event, I have no memory of the details beyond police officers being in our house and the "pea patch" statement. I have no recollection of my father being taken away by the police, although I am certain he would have been arrested.

Stump-hole liquor was another source of danger to the health of the people in our community and town. I don't know personally of anyone in our neighborhood or elsewhere in Rocky Mount becoming ill or dying as a result of drinking white lightning, but plenty of newspaper and scientific journal articles have confirmed its hazards.[23]

## PLAYING THE NUMBERS

ANOTHER SOURCE OF supplemental income for two or three people in our neighborhood was the "numbers" racket.[24] In some areas of the country, this gamble was called "policy." Almost every adult I knew, including my mother, played the numbers. Unfortunately, my mother and our neighbors all seemed to have the notion that they had a reasonable chance of "hitting the number." If the number you played was the number announced for that day as "the number," it was said you had "hit the number."

The number played was a three-digit number. It could be played "straight" or in combination. If the number was played straight, then only the specific number played would count as a hit. For example, if you played 736, then only the number 736 would constitute a hit. If the number were played in combination, then any combination of the three digits would count as a hit: 736, 367, 673, etc. Thus, three different digits could be played as a six-way combination. Some numbers could be played only in a three-way combination. If two of the digits were the same (773, 737, 733), then the combination was considered a three-way combination. The odds of winning a three-way combination were lower than that of winning a six-way, but for that reason a hit for a three-way paid more than a hit for a six-way. A number that was played straight paid the highest return because the odds of hitting the number were lowest.

Different methods were used to determine the day's winning number. The particular method might very well differ according to the time of week, month, or year, as well as by geographical location. For example, the method used in New York City or Baltimore might be different from the one being used in Rocky Mount. As best I can determine, the two most popular means were the result of a given horse race and the commodities market. Somehow, the outcome of a particular horse race on the day in question generated the winning number. Certain formulas were used to determine the precise number for the day, which was called the "regular number."

I am told that the commodities market method was referred to as "butter and eggs" and would be determined by the closing price for certain commodities (butter and eggs, for instance) on that particular date. Obviously the precise time when the specific event that determined the day's number occurred was very important. There could not be any material time lapse between that event and the announcement of "the number." Otherwise, people would know the winning number in advance and play it. If a particular race was announced as the source for the day's number, for example, no bets would be accepted once that race was under way. Also, no bets could be placed after the commodities market had closed for the day.

People used various ways to decide what number or numbers to play. A certain amount of folklore was associated with numbers and particular events. For example, the birth of twins or triplets would be said to indicate that a certain number or numbers would soon hit. Some adults, particularly elderly people, claimed to know what numbers were portended by a divorce, marriage, or death in the family or neighborhood. "Dream Books" were commercially sold and listed a specific number or numbers that were said to be associated with a particular dream or event. For example, a dream about traveling to New York on a train would signify a certain number or numbers that you should play.

People were quite open about playing the numbers, and notwithstanding its illegality would yell to a neighbor down the street—or even to the numbers runner walking in the neighborhood—"What was the number today?"[25] People usually wagered small amounts, a nickel, a dime, a quarter, and even as little as a penny, but it was not unusual for someone to wager a dollar or more on a single number in a given instance. Some people had a standing order for a certain number or numbers to be played every day of the month or even all year. I think the numbers business was quite profitable for those involved, at least when measured by local financial standards. As with the unlawful selling of whiskey and other spirits, the police would from time to time arrest a numbers runner or others involved locally in the numbers business. We now know, however, that the Mafia was behind the numbers racket throughout the United States, and organized criminals were the people who really made "big bucks."

## VALUES LEARNED

Notwithstanding the obstacles and burdens, there were many positive aspects to my life while growing up in Rocky Mount. Neighbors were typically supportive of each other, and the idea of the village raising a child was certainly reflected in our community. It was as if every middle-age or older adult was your parent. Every neighbor's house was also, in most respects, *your* house. I cannot speak for life in the white neighborhoods in the city, because I essentially had no social contact with Caucasians.

My parents, neighbors, and teachers emphasized the value of work, but there was even greater emphasis on the importance of education, particularly as a means of alleviating or even escaping from the difficulties presented by Jim Crow laws and other forms of racial discrimination. Although many of us, including me, became high school dropouts, it was not because our parents, adult neighbors, educators, and others had stopped urging us to get as much formal education as possible. They never stopped. (Another feature of cotton and tobacco farming was the unfortunate fact that, on many of the small farms being cultivated by black owners and sharecroppers, it was not uncommon for their children not to attend school during the cotton harvest season, because their labor was needed in the fields. Much of cotton and tobacco harvesting occurred in the late fall after school commenced. This demand for their time had to have had an adverse effect on those children's intellectual, social, and career development.)

I am certain that most African Americans from my generation—whether from the North, South, East, Midwest, Southwest, or West—can remember being often told, "What you get in your head through education cannot be taken away from you by the white man, so get all you can." Money, property, and other possessions—all those could be wrongfully taken from you—but acquired knowledge could not.

## · Notes ·

1. These railroad shop and yard facilities were opened in South Rocky Mount by the Atlantic Coast Line Railroad Company in April 1893, according to William E. Bobbitt, *A Brief History of Rocky Mount, North Carolina*, Rocky Mount Chamber of Commerce, April 1, 1950.

2. C.C. Stokes's first name was Chauncey, but he strongly preferred C.C.

3. Hunter Funeral Home was another black funeral home, but Hunter had substantially less business than Stokes.

4. Other than the reference to the time of year I did not have a clue as to the origin of the name "June German," but an article on the website of the African American Heritage Foundation of Virginia attributes it to the popularity early in the 20th century of a group dance called the "german," perhaps after the polkas and similar dances that were arriving with new European immigrants (www.aaheritageva.org).

5. I say "primarily" because black workers may have been allowed to purchase food in the back of the restaurant, since that was the custom at that time.

6. He died in October 1942.

7. I don't think girls or women hitched rides on freight trains.

8. "Side tracks" were railroad tracks that were separate from the main railroad tracks carrying train traffic between the various towns and cities and were used for various purposes, including preparing maintenance vehicles, storing railroad cars, and the like. The tracks were typically off to the side of the main-line tracks, hence "side tracks."

9. Leon F. Litwack, *Trouble in Mind: Black Southerners in the Age of Jim Crow* (New York: Alfred A. Knopf, 1998), p. 7.

10. The Freemasons are the largest worldwide secret society. Members share a moral and metaphysical ideal, and they believe in a Supreme Being and in the immortality of the soul. Freemasons, though more open today, have long been criticized for their secrecy by religious and political groups with accusations of conspiracy theories. Prince Hall Freemasonry is a predominantly African American freemasonry organization. For more in-depth coverage of freemasonry, see Jasper Ridley, *The Freemason* (London: Constable, 1999).

11. The Order of the Eastern Star is a fraternal secret society that allows both male and female members. Its teachings are based around the lives of Biblical figures. The Order was originally intended as a vehicle for wives of Master Masons to acquaint themselves with each other, but it has developed into an esoteric organization that stresses the importance of virtues such as charity. For more in-depth coverage of the Order of the

Eastern Star, read Jean M'Kee, *History of the Order of the Eastern Star* (Bonesteel: The Torch Press, 1917), especially at pp. 17–52.

12. See *The American Heritage Dictionary of the English Language* (fourth edition), "Signify. Slang, To exchange humorous insults in a verbal game," and Jonathan Green, *The Cassell Dictionary of Slang* (London: Cassell, 1998): "signification n. (US Black) negative or hostile talk, criticism, ritualized abuse (cf. DOZENS). [SIGNIFY]"; "signify/sig: v. (US Black) 1. to cause trouble, to stir things up, often purely for fun, whatever the actual results. 2. a ritual game of testing a rival's emotional strength by insulting their relatives (cf. DOZENS). 3. to boast or to pretend to a greater sophistication than one actually possesses; signifying n. (US Black) boasting, insinuating. [SIGNIFY]."

13. There are several theories for the origin of this term. Black people in the South used the words "crackers" or "white crackers" as a derogatory name for white people. Blacks retained this term when they moved north; hence, it was used there as well. The most pejorative form of the term was "Georgia cracker," for a vicious white person. I suppose it could be said that, in one sense, cracker was to us as nigger was to white folk. But I think whites (and blacks) tend to use the term *nigger* to denote disdain, while blacks used the term *cracker* to denote meanness.

14. Fatback is the skin and the fairly thick layer of fat immediately under the skin, from the back of the hog. I assume this is the origin of the name "fatback." *Webster's Third New International Dictionary* (Unabridged, Springfield, MA, Merriam-Webster, 2002) says: "the strip of fat from the back of a hog carcass. Usually, cured by dry-salting."

15. The pig's nose.

16. This name refers to the skin and fairly thick layer of fat immediately under the skin and from the back, side, or belly of the hog that also had some of the muscle or lean meat immediately under that fat attached—hence it was called "streak of lean, streak of fat." This same cut of meat is preserved with salt and sold as salt pork. *Webster's Third New International Dictionary* (Unabridged, Springfield, MA, Merriam-Webster, 2002): "pork cured in salt or brine; *specif.*, cured pork from the belly, back, or side consisting largely of fat."

17. Dr. Gerald Whitehead Deas was commended by the U.S. Food and Drug Administration for "his successful struggle in the 1970s against the Argo Starch Company. . . . After discovering that laundry starch was being sold in grocery aisles as a snack, causing black women to become anemic, Dr. Deas forced Argo to repackage its product in powdered form and to add a warning label, 'Not Recommended for Food Use.'" See www. downstate.edu/giving/deas.html.

18. Defined as "a household device with a flat base that is heated and used for pressing cloth," in *The Merriam-Webster Dictionary (New Edition)* (Springfield, MA: Merriam-Webster, 2005).

19. Some would probably argue that bribery would explain the infrequency of police raids.

20. "Henry," by Keb' Mo' and J. L. Parker, on the compact disc *Slow Down* (Okeh/550 Music, 1998).

21. Although it was called "white lightning," "stump-hole liquor," and "corn liquor" where I lived, it was and is still better known nationally as "moonshine."

22. Defined in the *Webster's Third New International Dictionary* (Unabridged) as "an alcoholic beverage made at home or with homemade equipment usu. by trial-and-error methods."

23. For example, see Christopher P. Holstege et al., "Analysis of Moonshine for Contaminants," *Journal of Toxicology: Clinical Toxicology* 42, no. 5 (August 2004): 597.

24. Defined in *The American Heritage College Dictionary* (4th Ed., New York: Houghton Mifflin Company, 2002), as "a lottery in which bets are made on an unpredictable number, such as a daily stock quotation."

25. Interestingly, I found that people were much more circumspect in Philadelphia regarding the numbers.

# 8

# U.S. Air Force

I enlisted in the U.S. Air Force on May 15, 1951.[1] I was 17 years old[2] and was living at 105 Ward Street, Rocky Mount, North Carolina, at the time.[3] It was in connection with my enlistment that I discovered my birth name was HENRY RAMSEY JR. I had always known that my birth date was January 22, 1934, but, as already discussed, I believed my name was Charles Arthur Tillman Jr.

I had never been asked for—or even thought about—a birth certificate. But when I went to the Air Force recruiting office, located downtown in the basement of the U.S. Post Office building, I was told I would have to produce a copy of my birth certificate in order to establish my age. When I told my mother, she said we would have to "write to Florence." She must have done that, because soon after an envelope containing a copy of my birth certificate arrived. The birth date and the names of my biological mother and father I already knew, but my name was given as Henry Ramsey Jr. So at age 17, I learned for the first time the name given me at birth.

Roslyn Satchel, a friend of mine, once asked me why I joined the Air Force.[4] I told her I joined for the reasons offered on the enlistment posters positioned on the sidewalk outside the Post Office: "Travel and See the World" and "Learn a Trade." While that response was essentially true, another and probably more significant reason for my enlistment was an effort to escape poverty. For many poor young men[5] of my generation (and even today), the military was our "poverty program,"[6] a primary means by which poor young adult males—both black and white—could escape poverty. Not to be overlooked is that, in 1951, the military also offered blacks and other people of color a means to escape most of the direct effects of overt government-sanctioned racial segregation and to significantly reduce their exposure to racial discrimination, at least while on military bases.

On the morning of January 22, 1951, my 17th birthday and the day I became eligible—with parental consent—to enlist, I went downtown to visit the Air Force, Army, and Navy recruitment offices. Each military branch had its own separate office, but all were located in the basement of the Post Office building.

My first stop was the Navy recruiting office. I do not now recall why, but I probably thought travel opportunities would be greater in the Navy. Also, several men I knew, most of them living in my neighborhood, had served in the Navy during World War II. One was Mr. Nesbit Rollins ("Fat" Cherry's husband and James and Joseph Rollins's father), who lived on Red Row Street. Tony and "Fat" Maxwell, two brothers who lived on Dunn Street, were also Navy veterans from World War II, as was James Hines, husband of Mabel Hines (Rev. July's stepdaughter), although he lived in Crosstown and not Around the Y. One or more of those black Navy veterans had warned me that unless I specifically requested the seaman's branch, the Navy recruiting officer would enlist me in the steward mate branch. The steward mate branch, I was told, consisted almost totally of Negro sailors who served exclusively as cooks and other kitchen personnel, mess attendants (waiters), and stewards (essentially butlers and personal servants) for white officers. I know that Tony Maxwell was one of the persons who gave me this advice. He had experienced firsthand the Navy's discriminatory racial policies and practices during World War II. The role of a steward mate is clearly and succinctly described by Yvonne Latty in her book titled *We Were There*.[7] During World War II, she wrote, steward mates "washed dishes, served the officers their food, and did their laundry." Included in *We Were There* is an article about James Hairston, who served 22 years as a Navy steward mate from 1938 until 1960.[8]

Sure enough, when I went to the Navy recruiting office on that birthday Monday morning and cheerfully expressed my interest in joining the U.S. Navy, the recruiter on duty said that he could sign me up immediately. I told him I wanted to be in the seaman's branch, but he said matter-of-factly that my enlistment would be in the steward branch. I told him I was interested only in the seaman's branch and had no interest whatsoever in the steward branch.

Well, he said, if I was willing to accept enlistment in the steward mate branch, I could enlist right then. He made it sound as if there really was no significant difference between the two. But if I wanted to enlist in the seaman's branch, my name would have to be put on a waiting list because there were no current openings for the seaman's branch.[9] "Fine," I said. "Put my name on the waiting list."

While personal racism, Navy racist policy,[10] or both may have been the white Navy recruiter's motive, fairness requires me to mention that this incident occurred at the height of the Korean War and lots of draft-eligible young men—black and white—were volunteering for the Navy and Air Force in an effort to avoid being drafted into the Army and risking service as a combat infantryman in Korea. The Air Force, Navy, and Marine Corps were not drafting, but the Army was.

My next stop was the Air Force recruiting office. The Air Force required recruits to take an entrance examination, which I passed. I was told that there were no present openings for enlisted personnel in the Air Force and that my name would have to go on a waiting list. So my name was now on two waiting lists. I also went to the Army recruiting office but sought to condition my enlistment on being guaranteed that I would be in a tank. Fortunately for me, the Army was unable to offer such a guarantee. I say fortunately because some years later, I learned about armor-piercing shells and heard that tank crew members, at least at that time, had among the shortest combat life expectancies of any soldier in the Army, including members of the infantry.

In late April or early May 1951, I received a letter from the Air Force advising that there was an opening for me. If the letter had been from the Navy, then I most likely would have joined the Navy instead. The Air Force required a sworn affidavit from my mother (and possibly

HENRY RAMSEY JR., AGE 17, *newly enlisted in the U.S. Air Force.*

one or two other people–my recollection is fuzzy about who or how many) declaring that Charles Arthur Tillman Jr. and Henry Ramsey Jr. were the same person. Somehow the required affidavit was obtained, and on May 15, 1951, in Raleigh, North Carolina, I was sworn in as an enlisted member of the U.S. Air Force. I was not sworn in under the name Charles Arthur Tillman Jr. but as Henry Ramsey Jr. My serial number was AF 14409562.[11]

My first assignment as a new airman was to Lackland Air Force Base (AFB), San Antonio, Texas. The flight from Raleigh to San Antonio was my first airplane ride, and I found it exciting. I recall that the flight stopped in Charlotte, North Carolina, and New Orleans, Louisiana, before arriving in San Antonio. After about two weeks for initial processing and orientation at Lackland, I was sent north by bus from Lackland to Shepherd AFB in Wichita Falls, Texas, for basic training. After completing basic training, I was assigned and flown to Francis E. Warren AFB in Cheyenne, Wyoming, for training as a clerk-typist.

Originally I was assigned to wireman's school at Francis E. Warren AFB. (The workers you see on the poles and towers that carry power transmission lines were called wiremen in the Air Force.) I don't remember why or how it was that my assignment was changed from wireman to clerk-typist before I left Wichita Falls–but it probably was the proverbial "Air Force needs." I wonder what my civilian career path would have been had I actually been trained as a wireman instead of a clerk-typist.

I was in Cheyenne from August 1951 until February 1952 for clerk-typist school. I am certain that one of the most useful skills I have acquired during my life has been touch typing. Although I never worked as a clerk-typist in the Air Force, I have used my typing skill in college, in law school, and throughout my legal career. The winter of 1951–1952 in Wyoming was very cold and extremely windy. We clerk-typist students marched to and from school each weekday, past high snow drifts, and the sharply blown snow was piercing. We were in school the full day; it was usually dark when we returned to the barracks.

I went to Denver two or three times while stationed at Cheyenne, the two cities being only 100 miles apart. The area where blacks socialized in Denver was called "Five Points," because it was at the intersection of three streets, which created the five points. My first actual leave since joining the Air Force in May 1951 came during the Christmas season of that year. Everyone in our squadron was excited about going home. I was probably not the only one relieved to be getting away from the cold, the snow, and especially the harsh wind.

The two-day train ride home to Rocky Mount marked the first time I had traveled such a great distance at one time or eaten in a train's dining car. It was exhilarating to see—albeit essentially only from the train—Omaha, Nebraska; Chicago, Illinois; Pittsburgh, Pennsylvania; Washington, D.C.; and Richmond, Virginia. At the end of the journey, it was great to be home, to see and visit with family and friends, to eat my mother's cooking, and to show off my uniform. After Christmas, I returned to Wyoming by train and completed my clerk-typist training.

In February 1952 I was assigned to Ernest Harmon Air Force Base[12] at Stephenville, Newfoundland, Canada, for a two-year tour of duty. As fate would have it, my travel orders for this new assignment provided that I was to travel on a troop ship from the state of New Jersey to Newfoundland. A friend named Jesse Suggs and I were both ordered to report to Camp Kilmer outside Trenton, New Jersey, in February for processing before boarding the ship, which actually left from Newark. I think we were at Camp Kilmer for about two weeks, and during that brief period I came into possession of Henry Ramsey's Bible and some World War II savings bonds he had left me.

Mary Lee Ramsey,[13] my biological mother, had gotten my address from my mother and contacted me by mail to tell me that "Mutt," my biological father, had died. I was at Francis E. Warren AFB in Cheyenne at the time. She told me she had some war bonds that "Mutt" had left me and that I needed to come to Philadelphia to get them. I didn't know at the time that Sister had already tried to cash the bonds but was unable to do so because the face of each bond declared that it was "Payable on Death" to me.

"Mutt" must have been aware that I was alive, although he may not have known precisely where I was. Also, there had to have been some direct or indirect contact between him and Sister in order for his family members or friends to advise her that he had died and that he had personal property she needed to collect.

During the brief assignment to Camp Kilmer, I traveled to nearby Philadelphia to get the bonds from Sister, who was still living at 2133 West Stewart Street in North Philadelphia. She gave me the five or six bonds[14] sometime after I arrived at her home. She also gave me a large Bible, which she said "Mutt" wanted me to have. I thanked her, and the two of us went to a nearby bank where the bonds were negotiated. I gave "Sister" some of the money (I don't recall how much) as a sort of finder's fee.

My biological father had written in his own hand on the inside of the back cover of his Bible. Essentially, he wrote that he hoped I would get the Bible and read his comments, that he loved me although he did not really know me, and that he very much regretted that we had not had a meaningful father-son relationship. Sister asked me to leave the Bible with her for safekeeping. When I declined her offer, she snatched it out of my hands and ran to the kitchen on the first floor in the rear of her home.

There she took a wet cloth and erased what Mutt had written on the inside back cover. Unfortunately, he had not written in indelible ink; consequently, his words were easily erased. All that remains of his comments are a few single-letter fragments near the outer border of the Bible's back cover. This mean act by Sister was not unusual when she was displeased by the behavior of one of her children or by a position that the person had taken. I left Sister's home after forcibly taking the Bible from her; she tried to hold onto it as I pulled it from her hands. I still have "Mutt's" Bible at my home in Berkeley, more than 53 years after that unpleasant scene with "Sister."

There was (and probably still is) a procedure whereby people in the U.S. military were assigned to particular jobs and career tracks. But at least in my time that official procedure was trumped by a tradition

HENRY RAMSEY AND MARY LEE RAMSEY, *née* BRUNSON, *my biological parents, probably in the mid- or late 1930s.*

called "meeting Air Force needs." My job designation was changed to warehouseman shortly after my arrival at Harmon Field, probably because of Air Force needs. And that was the work I did throughout the remainder of my Air Force tour of duty. I have absolutely no recollection of any discussion with me before the change was made. I also do not recall challenging the change or making any inquiry about it. As a warehouseman, I was a member of the supply squadron and was responsible for receiving, storing, and issuing parts and materials (excluding foodstuffs) used in the Air Force. Such items would include, for example, parts and supplies ranging from aircraft ailerons to X-ray film.

I was also sent on temporary duty to Thule AFB, Greenland, during my stay at Harmon Field. I worked as a warehouseman in Thule for four months on a special project called Operation Blue Jay, mostly during the summer of 1952, and I don't recall the sun ever setting while I was there. It simply moved from horizon to horizon. Tiny wild flowers, some red and some blue, grew during the eight or 10 weeks of summer that I was in Greenland. But it was extremely cold during the final month of my stay. One could actually see an Eskimo village a few miles from the base, but we were prohibited from having any contact whatsoever with these indigenous villagers. I don't know the actual reason, but we were told it was because they had never been exposed to any of the serious diseases that we might be carrying, such as chickenpox, diphtheria, or even the common cold, and therefore had no immunity against or resistance to them.

Operation Blue Jay involved the construction of a distant early warning system of radar sites (DEW Line) around and within the Arctic Circle, intended to detect the presumed threat of Soviet bombers flying over the North Pole toward the United States. The radar installations would allow enemy bombers to be detected, challenged, and destroyed hours before they could reach American airspace.

Back at Harmon, I worked again as a warehouseman. There was little to do off base; in fact, other than work, there was not very much to do on base. I learned to play Ping-Pong and to shoot pool fairly well, although those skills faded decades ago. I tried ice-skating but was not very good at it. I also played a lot of pinochle and bid whist. Many of the airmen gambled, typically playing poker, blackjack, and dice. I ceased gambling–for life–after I lost all of my savings in a blackjack game in Greenland one evening. My total savings were $300 or $400 and I was devastated by the loss. Those were 1952 dollars; today that would be $2,000 or $3,000.

Airmen stationed at Harmon Field would occasionally go into the nearby town of Stephenville to drink alcoholic beverages. There were very few women–civilian or military–at Harmon, and I do not recall there being any black women. Consequently, black airmen went into town much less frequently than white airmen. I remember making only one trip to the not-too-far-away town of Corner Brook (about 60 miles from Harmon Field) during my entire 18-month stay in Newfoundland.

My next and final permanent Air Force assignment was to March AFB, a Strategic Air Command (SAC) post near Riverside, California. I think my return to the United States from Newfoundland was in mid-December 1953. I was home on leave until mid-January 1954 and then traveled by train to Riverside. My main job at March AFB, as it had been at Harmon Field, was as a warehouseman. It was basically an 8-to-5 job, five days a week. Except in special circumstances, we would have the weekend off and could leave the base at our own discretion.

Sometimes March AFB would be "on alert," and we would be restricted to the base. Alerts were essentially training exercises designed to prepare and keep us prepared for war. My special assignment during an alert was as a member of a JATO rocket team. The initials stood for jet-assisted take-off. In an actual alert–a notice that the United States had been or was about to be attacked, or was otherwise involved in hostilities–the base would go to a state of readiness for war.

The primary aircraft at March AFB in 1954–1955 was the B-47 medium jet bomber. In my case, I was assigned to a team whose job in an alert was first to assemble at a preassigned location, then go to a particular weapons storage bunker to get rockets that we would take to the flight line and quickly attach to the B-47s. In an actual alert, those warplanes had to get airborne as fast as possible to bomb an assigned target or to avoid being found vulnerable on the ground. The runways at March AFB apparently were insufficient in length to allow a B-47—carrying a full fuel and bomb load—to safely take off without assistance. The rockets that we attached to the planes would provide the additional thrust needed.

I took some United States Armed Forces Institute (USAFI) English grammar and English composition courses during my tour of duty at March AFB.[15] I also took some remedial mathematics classes at Riverside City Junior College. Those courses were of immense help to me in my later effort to gain admission to a four-year school. I am certain that I would not have been able to pass the entrance examination for Howard University without having taken such courses.

Jesse Suggs, who now lives in Sacramento, California, has been a close friend since we met in the fall of 1951, well over a half-century ago, at Francis E. Warren AFB in Cheyenne.[16] He played a critical role in my deciding to attend college—probably more than, and certainly as much as, anyone else in my life. Jesse is a native of Rocky Mount and had been an outstanding basketball player while a student at Booker T. Washington High School. We did not know each other in Rocky Mount, but we had acquaintances in common. I knew who he was because of his prominence as a high school basketball player.

Before the fall of 1951, neither of us knew or had any reason to know that the other had joined the Air Force, and we had not met during basic training. Jesse received his basic training at Lackland AFB in San Antonio, and I of course was at Sheppard AFB in Wichita Falls. But as fate would have it, both of us had been assigned to Francis E. Warren AFB for clerk-typist training. One day I was walking along a street at Francis E. Warren AFB when I spotted a person on the opposite side I thought I recognized. It was Jesse Suggs. I walked over and introduced myself as someone from Rocky Mount, and from that time forward, we have been close friends. Again, as fate would have it and as mentioned earlier, we were both assigned to Ernest Harmon AFB in Stephenville upon completion of our clerk-typist training.

Unlike me, Jesse was a high school graduate and planned to attend college after completing his four years in the Air Force. As a high school dropout, I wanted very much to complete high school but was not too clear about what I would do after that. I certainly had never thought about attending college, although I knew people who had. Norfleet July, who lived Around the Y when I did and later became my step-brother,[17] was a graduate of North Carolina A&T State University, and Josephine Hobbs (the daughter of one of my mother's very close friends), also from Around the Y, had attended or was then enrolled in Bennett College for Women. Both of those schools were in Greensboro, North Carolina.

Therefore, it was Jesse who was focused on attending college after the Air Force, and I was not. I don't think I had evaluated and rejected the idea; I simply had not yet considered it. As our friendship continued and deepened while we were in Newfoundland, we often discussed what our plans were for life after the Air Force. Jesse was definite that he was going to college. Through our friendship and discussions, I –perhaps I should say we–at some point decided that I too would attend college. But for our friendship, I might very well never have attended college or law school and never have enjoyed the enormous benefits of that education. I have always felt indebted to Jesse Suggs for the educational guidance he provided me more than 50 years ago.

Although Jesse and I both started our tour of duty at Harmon Field in April 1952, I returned to the United States in January 1954, about four months before he did. The regular tour of duty in Newfoundland was two years, but the Greenland tour of duty was one year. Therefore, time spent in Greenland was effectively credited at a rate of two days to one for service in Newfoundland, and my four-months' TDY in Greenland resulted in my returning to the United States 120 days earlier than I otherwise would have. When Jesse returned to the states, he was stationed at Hamilton AFB in Marin County, just north of San Francisco, and we stayed in contact by mail.

At March AFB I met one more person I must thank for my getting into college. Once I decided to attend college, I knew it would have to

JESSE SUGGS, *Air Force friend and "home boy," probably in the late 1940s or early 1950s.*

be financed with my G.I. Bill benefits. It was clear that if I returned to Rocky Mount or elsewhere—Philadelphia, for example, where my brother James Williams and my biological mother lived—to complete my high school education, I could easily exhaust my G.I. Bill benefits and not have money for college. So I sought advice from the base Information and Education (I&E) Office, where I was interviewed by a young officer whose name I do not remember. He told me that some colleges had a policy whereby as long as an applicant was 21 years old and could pass the college's entrance examination, he or she could be admitted without a high school diploma or a GED certificate. Armed with that information, I enrolled in the courses mentioned above at Riverside City Junior College in preparation for what I hoped would be some university's entrance examination. Again, who knows what my future would have been if that young Air Force officer had not provided me with that information?

I wrote to North Carolina A&T State University in Greensboro, North Carolina, to Howard University in Washington, D.C., and to Morgan State College in Baltimore, Maryland—three historically black colleges—inquiring about admission requirements. As I recall, Morgan State was willing to admit me without an entrance examination, whereas Howard required that I pass one. I don't recall what the situation was regarding North Carolina A&T. Regardless, I made arrangements by mail and telephone to take the Howard University entrance examination in late August 1955, as soon as I left the Air Force. Mr. R.D. Armstrong, then principal at Booker T. Washington High School in Rocky Mount, agreed to administer and monitor the examination.

When I was honorably discharged at March Field on August 1, 1955, my rank was A/2C—Airman Second Class. This was one time in my life when I can honestly say that I was ecstatic. As I passed through the main gate on my way to the train that would take me home, the more accurate word would actually be *euphoric*. Immediately after returning to Rocky Mount, I went to Booker T. Washington High

School to take the examination that Howard University had provided Mr. Armstrong. Not too long thereafter, I was advised that I had passed the entrance examination and was admitted to Howard University. It would be difficult for anyone to appreciate my elation at that moment. This was another occasion when I experienced euphoria.

A twist to this story about Jesse Suggs and me is that although we both enrolled in college in the fall of 1955, he at North Carolina A&T and I at Howard University, Jesse voluntarily withdrew from college, either during or at the end of his first semester, and re-enlisted in the Air Force. He retired from the Air Force in November 1971 as a technical sergeant (five stripes) after 20 years of service and soon went to work for the U.S. Postal Service in Sacramento. He retired from the Postal Service in 1993. We remain close friends, are in contact by telephone periodically, and occasionally see each other in person. However, Jesse never received the college degree that we envisioned as Air Force colleagues.

There are two other significant components to my story about how I came to be a college student. It is interesting how one's intuitive judgments can sometimes be so wrong and yet still work out so right. While stationed at March AFB, I became friends with members of a black family in San Bernardino (we usually called it "San Berdoo"). They lived off Waterman Avenue in a San Bernardino black neighborhood that was known as "the Valley." I came to know this family through a young San Bernardino woman I was dating, ALICE DIXON, *née* McDOWELL. WILLIE McKINLEY, a friend and fellow airman, was dating LILLY McDOWELL, Alice's sister, and it was Willie who introduced me to Alice.

Willie owned an automobile, and each weekend–sometimes even on a weekday–he, three other airmen from our squadron, and I would travel in Willie's car from the base outside Riverside to nearby San Berdoo, a distance of approximately 14 miles. There we would usually visit the two black nightclubs in San Berdoo–the American Legion Club and the Elks Club–and spend time with our girlfriends.

We almost always went the back way from Riverside to San Bernardino because it would get us to the Valley faster. This route involved our traveling about halfway to San Bernardino by freeway but then getting off the freeway and continuing the rest of the way to Waterman Avenue and the Valley on Riverside and San Bernardino county roads. Although most of the Valley was within the San Bernardino city limits, a significant portion was in an unincorporated area in San Bernardino County and not all that far from the Riverside County line.

As we traveled to San Bernardino the back way and off the freeway, we passed through two or three white neighborhoods composed of relatively new tract homes. I enviously considered those houses very attractive and was sure they afforded their owners a highly desirable lifestyle. I do not recall if I ever discussed the subject with my Air Force buddies, but I remember even now my intense interest in one day owning such a wonderful house. I suppose it was relevant that I had grown up in a neighborhood where, for some time, several of the occupied houses on my street had been posted with city signs that officially declared them "Not Fit for Human Habitation."

In thinking about those tract houses and what one would have to do to get one, I made an erroneous assumption that actually worked out for me. I assumed that the people who owned those houses were college graduates; therefore, if I wanted to own one, I would have to go to college. I am not so certain now that the people who owned those houses were college graduates. Probably most were skilled trade workers and people employed by the two Air Force bases in the area–March AFB, where I was stationed, and Norton AFB closer to San Bernardino. A more important factor is that they were also white people who had not been redlined or otherwise victimized by housing discrimination. But at that time I simply saw them as people who were college graduates and consequently had sufficient income to afford such houses. Even though I was probably wrong about their educational backgrounds, I was right about the worth and value of a college education.

Here, I am reminded of advice that I have often given to my children and to lots of other young people: "Saying it and doing it are two different things." It is always easy to declare that you will achieve a particular goal. But the declaration is meaningless unless and until you do what is necessary to make it a reality. Saying I was going to college was a lot different from taking the concrete action necessary to make it happen. As I look back, I am certain that the desire stimulated by those California tract houses played a significant role in my taking meaningful action to gain admission to college.

A third motivational factor for my taking specific steps to gain entrance to college was the black people I came to know in San Bernardino. Most of the people I knew in the black neighborhoods of Rocky Mount, North Carolina, were good, hard-working, and, for the most part, decent folks. But almost all of the adults in our neighborhood lacked significant formal education, and there was a significant element of violence, profanity, excessive drinking, gambling, fornication, and adultery, particularly Around the Y. I do not mean to suggest that this was the primary behavior of black people who lived Around the Y or elsewhere in Rocky Mount, for that would not be true. But that behavior was fairly common among my teenage contemporaries, many of the young adults I knew, and even some of the middle-aged folks who served as models for children and teenagers in my neighborhood. I certainly wasn't anyone's "goody two-shoes," but even as a youth I found such negative behavior inconsistent with the values taught in my home, school, and church and within most households in our community.

Life among most of my fellow black airmen at March AFB was not much different from that harmful element in Rocky Mount. It would be fair to say that was also true of Harmon Field in Newfoundland. I say black airmen because we rarely associated with our white colleagues outside of work. We lived together in the barracks, we performed Air Force tasks and missions together, but we rarely socialized together.

The primary difference between life at March AFB and life at Harmon AFB was that there were very few women at Harmon, and again I don't think there were any black women. There certainly were no black women off base. There were far fewer fights at Harmon Field than at March AFB probably because we spent substantially less time off base in Stephenville, Newfoundland, than in Riverside and San Bernardino. California. Otherwise, the culture of excessive drinking, crude language, and gambling was essentially the same.

Family life among the people whom I met in the Valley in "San Berdoo" was dramatically different. I saw little or no gambling, rarely heard even mild profanity, did not know of any adultery, and saw absolutely no fussing and fighting. (I would be surprised if their daily life was as pristine as I have described it. Every neighborhood and all families have at least some minor warts and flaws.) The Valley families frequently had cookouts and weekend gatherings where softball, volleyball, dominoes, and card games such as hearts, bid whist, and pinochle were played. I had become friends with the ARLET and CATHERINE GREEN family through Alice Dixon and her close friend, VERICE MURDOCK, who was Catherine Green's youngest sister.[18] I became a frequent visitor at Arlet and Catherine Green's home and would sometimes stay overnight there. Soon I was almost like a member of the family.

About this time another significant event occurred in my life. Although I was not much of a drinker before joining the Air Force, I had become a regular consumer of alcohol by the time I was assigned to March AFB, notwithstanding the fact that I was still not yet 21 years old. After my arrival at March AFB, there were weekends when I would be passed out on the grass in a park on 14th Street in Riverside, stone drunk. It was not unusual for me to have a terrible hangover in reporting to work on Monday morning. I had also developed a very profane mouth. Indeed, I used the "MF" phrase so often that my fellow black airmen called me "Mo-Tamper" as a nickname.

Three other black airmen from the supply squadron and I often drove to an off-base liquor store just outside the main gate to purchase a fifth of liquor, which we would typically consume by passing the bottle around as we traveled into town. One evening, just the four or five of us—no women—were going to a drive-in movie. I think we planned to go to San Berdoo after the movie. In any event, we stopped at the liquor store and purchased a fifth of Old Crow whiskey. The bottle was opened and passed around when we got to the drive-in theater. When it was my turn, for some reason I simply could not swallow the whiskey, try as I might. Declaring that because I had paid for my share of the liquor I was determined to drink it, I obtained a cup and poured a drink, but I was still unable to swallow. To this day I have no explanation for what happened. It was not until two or three years later, when I was a student at Howard University, that I consumed another drink of alcohol.

Once I had stopped drinking alcoholic beverages—and because the others had not—I became what we would today call the group's designated driver. As stated earlier, only one person in our regular group had a car, and that was Willie McKinley. I would drive Willie's car to San Bernardino and serve as the designated driver while we visited various nightspots. I would then drop each person off at his girlfriend's house late in the night and return the next morning to pick up each person in time for us to return to our jobs at March AFB.

Not long after this routine started, I began to critically observe the behavior of my airmen friends and others in the various clubs that we visited in San Berdoo and in Riverside and nearby Fontana. I soon saw how foolish and dangerous our behavior was, particularly the various fights we got into. It became clear, as I looked through sober eyes, that every fight was unnecessary and avoidable. Comments that intoxicated airmen and civilians perceived as unpardonable insults frequently led to fights that could easily have been avoided by a simple apology, by a reasonable explanation that no harm was intended, or by simply walking away from the confrontation. Behavior that had struck me as humorous and entertaining when I was drinking now seemed reckless and stupid.

Thus, not many months after I quit drinking, I stopped "hanging"[19] with the fellows altogether and started spending my free time either on the base or with the Green family and their friends in the Valley. I did not stop being friends or associating with my Air Force buddies, but I no longer served as their designated driver or went with them to the nightclubs.

## California Friends

In spending significant time with the Greens, the Murdocks, their relatives, and their friends, I came to respect the sensible behavior of those people and to participate in their lifestyle. I also soon recognized the merits of their way of life and wanted it for myself. While none of the people I met were college-educated or a member of a profession, they all lived what appeared to be an economically secure lifestyle and seemed reasonably happy. They took care of their children, were considerate of each other and their neighbors, and, in general, seemed to be basically honest, generous, courteous, hard-working, and understanding people. Even though none of them had been to college, I still felt that a college education was the best course to follow in trying to earn an income that would support the new way of life to which I aspired. I have always been grateful for the positive influence the folks from San Bernardino had in my life.

Arlet and Catherine Green; their son, DAVID GREEN; Catherine's sisters AMARITA MARTIN, CECELIA McDOWELL, and OPAL LEGARDY, and her brothers, WINFIELD MURDOCK and SHERMAN MURDOCK, have all been gone for several years now, but with the exception of Winfield and Sherman, we continued to be close friends for the remainder of their lives. Winfield, Sherman, and I did not cease being friends—we just did not have much contact after I graduated from the University of California at Riverside in 1960 and moved to Berkeley; perhaps it was because Sherman and Winfield remained in San Bernardino while all of their siblings and the other members of their families moved to Sacramento.

When I became acquainted with his family in 1954, Arlet Green was working as a jet engine mechanic at Norton AFB in San Bernardino.[20] The aircraft work that he was doing was discontinued at Norton in 1964, but he was able to secure a similar position at McClellan AFB in Sacramento that same year. His wife, Catherine, and DARWIN, their youngest child and youngest son, joined him in Sacramento the next year. The other three Green children–OLIVIA, ALVIN, and David–were now adults. Alvin was in the Marines, and David was in the Army. Olivia was working at Norton AFB in 1964, but she also moved to Sacramento in 1966.

Verice Jones, *née* Murdock, was now married to FREDDIE JONES, an Air Force sergeant. They moved to Northern California in 1965 when he was stationed at Beale AFB in Marysville. Verice and Freddie were divorced in 1974, and she moved to South Lake Tahoe, then to Sacramento permanently in 1977. Alvin, Darwin, and Olivia, Arlet and Catherine Green's surviving children, still reside in Sacramento. Verice lived in Sacramento until 2005 when she and her third husband, Benito Cruz, moved to Prescott Valley, Arizona. I continue to be close friends with all of them–Alvin, Darwin, Olivia, and Verice (now Verice Cruz)– and we are in regular contact.

General Curtis Lemay, then commander of the Strategic Air Command (SAC),[21] was the person responsible for my learning another valuable lifetime lesson. When I was assigned to March AFB, a SAC facility, I saw large banners in every hangar that declared, in the words of General Lemay: "When the Enemy Comes, Either You're Ready or You're Not!" In other words, half-measures are essentially worthless. When one is confronted by a significant challenge, there is no such thing as almost ready, virtually ready, practically ready, getting ready, just about ready, more or less ready, soon will be ready, or nearly ready–either you are ready or you're not! If I did not learn anything else in the U.S. Air Force except touch typing, how to tuck in my shirt-tails, and how to fold my underwear, I did learn "When the enemy comes, either you are ready or you're not!" That slogan has served me well during all of my life after the Air Force, and I could not commend it to you or anyone else more strongly.

· Notes ·

1. DD Form 214: Report of Separation from the Armed Forces of the United States, dated Aug. 16, 1955. A copy is in my files.

2. Because I was only 17, my mother had to give her written consent to my enlistment. I actually enlisted in Rocky Mount but received my physical examination and was sworn in as a member of the U.S. Air Force in Raleigh, North Carolina.

3. DD Form 214: Report of Separation from the Armed Forces of the United States, Aug. 16, 1955.

4. This conversation was during a May 15, 2003, visit at her home in Decatur, Georgia. Roslyn graduated from Howard University and was a student member of the Howard University delegation selected to observe the 1994 presidential elections in South Africa. After receiving her under-graduate degree from Howard's School of Communications in 1995, Roslyn completed a joint degree, in 2000, in law and religion from Emory University's School of Law and School of Religion in Atlanta.

5. Although women were eligible for service in the armed forces, most peo-ple who enlisted were male. The basic character and responsibilities of military service were not viewed as appropriate for women. Also, the posi-tions women could hold were extremely limited. They were restricted to working primarily as nurses or clerical personnel.

6. President Lyndon B. Johnson, in his 1964 State of the Union speech, pro-posed an "unconditional war on poverty in America." He envisioned a fu-ture "Great Society," where poverty in the United States, in both urban and rural areas, would be virtually eliminated. President Johnson and his administration guided legislation through the U.S. Congress that established the Office of Economic Opportunity (OEO), commonly called the "poverty program," which had primary responsibility for prosecuting the war on poverty.

7. Yvonne Latty, *We Were There* (New York: HarperCollins Publishers, 2004), p. xiii in Preface.

8. Latty, pp. 44–48.

9. See Sherie Mershon and Steven Schlossman, *Foxholes and Color Lines, Desegregating the U.S.Armed Forces* (Baltimore and London: The Johns Hopkins University Press, 1998) at p. 200: "According to the testimony of Lieutenant Dennis E. Nelson before the Fahy Committee, the Navy did not—and never had—possess any written policy specifying that only members of racial minority groups could serve as stewards. The present [1949] situation, Nelson explained, simply reflected the power of naval tradition. Committee discussions established that this tradition was in fact embodied in formal institutional structures and procedures that set the Steward's Branch apart from the rest of the Navy, steered blacks into it, and confined them there. The Navy had separate—and lower—entrance standards for stewards and targeted blacks for recruitment to this branch."

10. Yvonne Latty discusses in *We Were There,* particularly at pp. 140–141, the Navy's post-World War II policies concerning the recruitment of blacks. Also see Mershon and Schlossman at pp. 187–217.

11. See DD Form 214: Report of Separation from the Armed Forces of the United States, Aug. 16, 1955.

12. Many if not most Air Force bases were constructed when the Air Force was part of the U.S. Army and were known as air fields. Hence, while they officially were renamed Air Force bases after the Air Force became an independent branch of the U.S. Armed Forces, the facilities were still often referred to by airmen and locals as air fields, as in Harmon Field, or March Field.

13. By this time, her name may very well have been Mary Evans.

14. I do not remember the face value of the bonds, but my guess is that each was $100.

15. These were correspondence courses, and I recall them as being in English Composition and offered by the USAFI through the University of Oklahoma. See DD214, which is presently in my personal records.

16. His current address and telephone number in Sacramento are in my files.

17. See chapter 3, "New Family, New Home," *infra.*

18. Catherine Green's maiden name was Murdock, and she had four sisters: Amarita Martin, *née* Murdock; Opal Legardy, *née* Murdock; Cecelia McDowell, *née* Murdock; and Verice Murdock (today Cruz), and two brothers: Winfield Murdock and Sherman Murdock.

19. Short for "hanging out" or "hanging around."

20. Norton AFB was selected for closure by the Base Realignment and Closure Commission in 1988 and closed on March 31, 1994.

21. I later came to understand that he was a notorious right-winger. But the advice was sound.

HENRY RAMSEY JR. *as a student at Howard University in Washington, D.C., 1956.*

# 9

# University Life

In September 1955, I enrolled as a freshman in the College of Arts and Sciences at Howard University in Washington, D.C. Because my birth certificate, military records, and G.I. Bill benefits were in the name of Henry Ramsey Jr., I enrolled under that name and have used it to this day. Some of you may wonder why I did not take legal action to change my name from Henry Ramsey Jr. to Charles Arthur Tillman Jr. The answer is that, at the time I entered the Air Force in May 1951, I did not know one could change one's name. I had never heard of anyone else doing such a thing and had never thought of doing it myself. My mother, father, and other members of my family had very little formal education and certainly were uninformed and unsophisticated regarding legal matters. By the time I finished law school, I simply thought it too complicated and too late to make such a change.

I selected zoology as my major in college and declared that my career objective was to become a dentist. Zoology was one of the fields suggested for students considering careers in medicine and dentistry, and I thought that zoology would require significantly less mathematics than chemistry or physics, two other majors that were popular among premedical and pre-dental students.

I had first considered medicine as a career objective but believed medical students needed to know a lot of math, and be good at it, which I did not and was not. I naively assumed that dental students did not need to know much math. How I got that idea I do not know. Regardless, I soon learned that the undergraduate course of study for both disciplines was essentially the same and that medical and dental students actually studied the same curriculum during their first two years of professional school. I also assumed that doctors' incomes were significantly higher than dentists' earnings. Therefore, I declared after the first year of college that while my major would continue to be zoology, my career objective now was to become a physician.

I decided to pursue a career in medicine for the money, not because I was especially attracted to science or any particular health care field. The major reason I decided to attend college in the first place was that I thought a college education would permit me to earn a lot of money. In fact, I mistakenly thought that a college education was essential to earn a large income. I say mistakenly because, while a college degree substantially increases one's chances of becoming wealthy, a number of people have made fortunes without one. William "Bill" Gates,[1] Richard Grasso,[2] Kevin Garnett,[3] Michael Jackson,[4] William Powell Lear,[5] and Michael Moore[6] are examples of such people. Having said that, I still passionately encourage anyone seeking financial security to obtain a college degree and, if possible, a postgraduate degree. One's chances of being, for example, the next Bill Gates or Michael Jackson are extremely unlikely.

## Learning to Be a Student

As noted, I arrived at Howard University in 1955 with basically a tenth-grade education, although it had been supplemented by the courses I took while in the Air Force and by the military experience itself. I was housed in Cook Hall, a dormitory for male freshmen. I remember attending an orientation session held in Cook Hall for new students and feeling as out of place as a skunk at a picnic. My assumption was that everyone present except me was a high school graduate. And not just a high school graduate, but one who had worked hard in high school and had taken full advantage of the various educational opportunities typically available to a high school student. I felt intimidated by the college students with whom I was now associated and more than a little inadequate for the task I had undertaken. Still, I was determined to stick it out.

However, I started on the wrong foot. Early on, I made friends with Romie James, another first-year student, who owned an automobile and was also a military veteran. We began our college careers by spending a significant amount of time in various nightspots in D.C. and Baltimore looking for girls and a good time. Fortunately I flunked the first four examinations I took at Howard University, probably because of my night activities. I told my friend that we obviously were taking the wrong approach to our schoolwork and that I planned to quit the nightlife and concentrate on my studies.

There could be no doubt that I was poorly prepared for college work academically—incredibly so. I remember being tutored in grammar at Cook Hall by a couple of upper-division students, Dorval Carter and Frank DeCosta. In explaining the components of a simple sentence, they used as an example, "The man throws the ball," to show me that *man* was the subject, *throws* the verb, and *ball* the object. About as "simple" as a sentence can get, and obviously I still remember it. A Howard law school student named Leonard ("Len") Holt was also very helpful to me. He received free rent at Cook Hall as compensation for serving as a Student Resident Assistant—we called them "dorm daddies." He gave me advice and encouragement.

I needed academic support, but I was also very, very short of cash. Although I was eligible for the G.I. Bill, it turned out that I would not receive my first check from the government until well after the semester had begun.[7] In the business world, one would say that I had a serious cash-flow problem. "Sister" never gave me one nickel the entire time I was in college and law school. My mother, Nellie, was not in a position to provide me with any financial support. During that first winter I was in desperate need of a pair of shoes. Mine had holes all the way through the soles, and I was putting newspaper in them in an effort to protect my feet. But because of winter snow and rain, the paper soon wore out and afforded very little protection. I must have written my mother about the problem because she sent me a pair of previously owned shoes that she said she had purchased for me on Ridge Avenue in North Philadelphia. The shoes were much too small, and I could not use them. I assumed that she would not be able to return them, and never told her that I couldn't use them. I knew those shoes had been purchased by her at a great sacrifice.

In addition to giving me academic advice, Leonard Holt occasionally provided me with money to purchase food. In "loaning" me the money, Len would say, "I do not want you to pay me back. One day you'll meet someone who needs it as much as you do now. Give it to that person, and then you will have paid me back." I have never forgotten his kindness and believe I have kept the implied promise that I made by accepting his generosity. I have on quite a number of occasions extracted a similar promise from some needy student to whom I have provided financial support. Len Holt, after his graduation from the Howard University School of Law in June 1956, went on to become one of the most courageous civil rights lawyers that this country has ever known.

Notwithstanding my poor preparation and disastrous start, by the end of the first semester I had achieved a 2.6 grade point average. I thought that was a pretty good performance, given my lack of high school study and where I had been in my course work just a couple of months earlier. My friend Romie James did not follow my advice or apply a new approach in his studies and soon flunked out. My academic performance and grades improved markedly the next semester when I actually attended each scheduled class and conscientiously did my homework.

How, you might well ask, given my lack of high school preparation, was I able to achieve this? Was it that Howard University's liberal arts program was not challenging or that its teachers were not demanding? I don't think so. I believe the reason for my academic success at Howard was just the opposite. That is, the high quality of teaching available to

Howard students allows them to succeed, provided that they are willing to work hard and take advantage of the opportunity.

When I commenced my studies at Howard I was 21 years old and had the experience of four years of service in the U.S. Air Force. I was determined to do what was necessary to succeed. I attended the great majority of my classes, listened attentively to the lectures and classroom discussion, did my assigned homework, and, if there was something I did not understand or required clarification, asked questions of my teachers (in and outside class) and fellow students.

Also, I had the advantage of being a long-time reader. As mentioned earlier, I had been an avid reader since my early teenage years and was fortunate that I had good reading comprehension. This capacity was invaluable in my understanding and learning the academic material presented at Howard. I was also lucky enough to make friends with several other students who were disciplined, smart, and willing to help me.

During my tenure at Howard, I found a great many of its students to be disciplined, highly motivated, and exceptionally smart. Those students were as good as the best to be found at any of the nation's leading universities. Their outstanding performance when admitted to graduate and professional schools at leading historically white American private and public universities testifies to that fact. The performance and status of numerous Howard graduates in their chosen fields are also proof of the quality and value of a Howard University education.

The university itself had a kind of double status. On the one hand, Howard University enjoyed an excellent reputation among African Americans as an exceptional institution of higher education. Indeed, at that time, the great majority of black architects, doctors, dentists, lawyers, pharmacists, and other black professionals had been produced by Howard University. Howard and its graduates touted the university as the "capstone of Negro education." On the other hand, Howard also had a credible reputation as a party school. It was known among students at the nation's black colleges that you could arrive in Washington,

GEORGE W. COOK HALL, *the freshman dormitory at Howard University where I began my college career.*

D.C., at any time of day or night and easily find some Howard students having a party somewhere in the city. My experience and observations at Howard University confirmed that both reputations were deserved.

One incident shows how uninformed I was about college at the time. As school resumed for the spring semester of my first year, I was passing Douglas Hall (then the main administration building for the university) and noticed a long line of students extending from inside Douglas Hall out onto the public sidewalk. I was both puzzled and curious, so I asked someone why there was this line. I was shocked to hear that people in that line had flunked out and were meeting with the dean of students to petition for readmission. It had not occurred to me that any students—especially because I'd been convinced that everyone else was highly prepared—would flunk out.

I later came to know that far too many of those students had not taken advantage of the opportunities for learning afforded them in high school, nor had they developed in high school the academic discipline and study habits necessary for success in college. These were students who had matriculated from high school without having to work hard, and they believed that their high school study habits would be adequate for college work. Many were sadly mistaken.

A significant number of students at Howard while I was enrolled there were, in fact, overwhelmed by the considerable social life at the school. Some were disadvantaged by the silly view that if you had to study hard to get good grades, then you were not all that intelligent. In their minds, the truly smart individual was one who could master the subject matter without having to make an extraordinary effort. Such a person was said to be "heavy" (i.e., exceptionally intelligent). A person who was heavy could socialize, party, miss classes, and somehow still do well—indeed, exceptionally well—on the midterm and final examinations. Because they were heavy, they needed only to browse through the textbook and any distributed material the night before the examination. Some students—typically entering students—were actually taken in by that nonsense.

Upper-class males often directed this pitch toward first-year female students—particularly those who were quite young—seeing them as potential sources of sex. But both male and female students were among those who fell victim to the assumption that they were too smart to have to study hard. A sizable percentage of the men and women in that line outside Douglas Hall were such students.

## THE "GREEK WORLD" AT HOWARD

*I* JOINED THE ALPHA PHI ALPHA fraternity (the Alphas) during the spring semester of my first year. The Alphas at Howard were viewed as being mostly interested in academic excellence. Fraternity and sorority membership was also an obvious way to quickly gain friends and colleagues within the university's student community. Indeed, some of my lifelong friendships were established through my affiliation with Alpha Phi Alpha's Beta Chapter at Howard University. Ollie Duckett, Loretta Easton, and Loretta Argrett have been close friends for more than 50 years. Ollie Duckett is a fraternity brother, and Loretta Argrett was Queen of Beta Chapter the year that I became a member of the fraternity. Loretta Easton was a classmate who became the Alpha Queen about two years after I was admitted to the fraternity. Although Alpha Phi Alpha fraternity and Delta Sigma Theta sorority were not "brother and sister" organizations (Delta Sigma Theta was allied with Omega Psi Phi fraternity), a number of these longtime friends from Howard days were members of Delta Sigma Theta. Odessa Woods, *née* Crowder; Jacquelyn "Jackie" Davis, *née* Price; Sandra Cox, *née* Hicks; and Martha "Marty" Reynolds, *née* Scott, are Deltas from that time who remain close friends today.

I cannot speak for today, but Greek letter organizations were influential as well as popular when I was at Howard. All of the national black fraternities and sororities had chapters at Howard University: Alpha Kappa Alpha sorority and Alpha Phi Alpha fraternity (the AKAs and the Alphas), Delta Sigma Theta sorority (the Deltas), Kappa Alpha

SPHINX CLUB AT HOWARD UNIVERSITY, *spring semester 1956–Alpha Phi Alpha, Beta Chapter, pledges. From left: brothers Hillary Baker, Eddie Robinson, Nathaniel Murdock, Clarence Lang, Charles Ross, Alphonse Hart, Wendell Beane, Henry Ramsey Jr., and Willis Brown. We carried the books, symbolizing the fraternity's commitment to scholarship and academic achievement, throughout our "hell week" initiation.*

PYRAMID CLUB AT HOWARD UNIVERSITY, SPRING SEMESTER 1957—*Delta Sigma Theta sorority, Alpha Chapter, pledgees. From left: Shirley Vaughns, May Taylor, Shirley Ivy, Esther Blair, Dale Robertson, Inez Savage, Anne Eastman, and Miriam Adam. Thanks to longtime Alpha Chapter friends for the names.*

Psi fraternity (the Kappas), Omega Psi Phi fraternity (the Q's), Phi Beta
Sigma fraternity (the Sigmas), and Zeta Phi Beta (the Zetas). The heavy
hitters or most desirable and influential Greek letter organizations on
Howard's campus were the Alpha, Kappa, and Omega fraternities and
the AKA and Delta sororities.

There were negative aspects to fraternity and sorority membership
at Howard as well. Even if I do not recall this attitude as being extensive, I know that quite a few of the Greeks felt that they were superior
to so-called non-Greeks solely because of their membership in a Greek
letter organization. In fact, some believed that membership in a given
fraternity not only made them superior to non-Greeks but also made
them superior to members of other fraternities and sororities with
whom their organization was not affiliated.

As silly as it may seem today, there was also significant color discrimination or bias within the Howard University Greek world. Fair-
skinned men and women—particularly women—were seen as more
desirable prospective members than darker-skinned students. I do not
mean to imply that no dark-skinned students were welcome as members of Howard's fraternities and sororities, for that was not the case.
Some members of Beta Chapter were quite dark-skinned, including
myself. But it was also true that fair-skinned prospects were typically
much more sought after as members of fraternities and sororities than
dark-skinned students, particularly those who were very dark. This
prejudice was also practiced as concerns the women who were selected
as queen and as members of the queen's court of the several fraternities.
I must add, however, that this skin-color consciousness among fraternity and sorority members simply reflected the widespread skin-color
bias that existed within Howard University's general student body and,
for that matter, American society at large.[8]

There was also discrimination on the basis of wealth, whether
intended or unintended. Membership in a Greek letter organization
was somewhat expensive. Therefore, most students with limited finan-

cial means were excluded, even if they very much wanted to join. It was not unusual for students who really could not afford membership in a fraternity or sorority to spend their extremely limited financial resources on gaining and maintaining membership. I was able to pay my membership fees using my G.I. Bill benefits. I also had a part-time job working in the office of Armour J. Blackburn, then the dean of students at the University.

In addition to paying membership fees, some fraternity and sorority members felt that they had to spend money on fashionable clothes, trips, and other activities that they simply could not afford. My financial resources were also very limited but my ego was such that I saw no need to join a fashion race I could not afford. Because I subsequently left Howard at the end of my sophomore year, I was actively involved with Greek activities for only three semesters.

While for the most part I very much enjoyed my studies and stay at Howard University, I did miss California. Hence, I traveled by bus from Washington, D.C., back to San Bernardino in June 1957 to visit the Greens and my other friends. While there, I began to think about a permanent return to California and, in that regard, visited the Riverside campus of the University of California to explore the possibility of enrolling there. I liked what I saw and heard and decided that I would apply for admission.

## University of California at Riverside

I TRANSFERRED FROM HOWARD University to the University of California at Riverside (UCR) in September 1957 and graduated in June 1960 with a bachelor of arts degree in philosophy. My major was zoology when I transferred to UCR, but I changed it to philosophy after I had been there for a year.

On the many occasions when I passed the UCR campus while stationed at March AFB, it had never once occurred to me that I would study there one day, but I always noticed the University of California sign and I remembered it even after I began my college studies in Washington, D.C.

Once the transfer had actually been achieved, I initially lived in San Bernardino at the home of Amarita Martin, Catherine Green's sister, and hitchhiked to UCR each school day morning. It was not too long before Mel Kinder, a UCR student who owned an automobile, noticed me "thumbing" on Waterman Avenue and offered me a ride. Mel also commuted each day between San Bernardino and UCR and was willing to give me a ride regularly.

There were no dormitories at UCR at the time, but I was able to move into other student housing two or three months after my enrollment. UCR was mostly a commuter campus at that time, and the comparatively few students who did live on campus resided in two- or three-bedroom bungalows in an area called Canyon Crest. Those houses were owned by the university (read "low rent") and located immediately adjacent to the campus. Canyon Crest houses were conveniently within easy walking distance of the UCR library, recreational facilities, administrative offices, and classrooms. Two or three students lived in a unit, depending on the number of bedrooms. Canyon Crest had been constructed as housing for married U.S. Navy enlisted personnel during World War II and was subsequently acquired by the University of California as student housing. Dormitories would be built later (during my second year at UCR), and Canyon Crest would become housing for married students.

Life at UCR was dramatically different from what I had experienced at Howard University. The overall academic atmosphere was decidedly more somber at UCR than at Howard. Many of the Howard students were very serious about their studies, but a significant minority were not, while nearly all of the students at UCR were intent on their studies. The UCR student body was quite small for a university campus—about 850 students when I arrived there in the fall of 1957 and only about 1,260 students at the time of my graduation in June 1960.

Howard University's student body was much larger, and Howard had several graduate and professional programs.

Although the great majority of the students at Howard University were black, nearly all of the UCR students were white. My arrival at UCR in fall 1957 increased to exactly three the number of black students among the entire student body.[9] In fact, only 10 black students matriculated at UCR during the three years I was there.[10] Because the number was so small, I can still recall the names of the other nine: Zelma Ballard,[11] Edward Blakely,[12] Warren Blakely,[13] Carolyn Pippin (now Carolyn Morris),[14] Roy Overstreet,[15] Donald Spigner,[16] Carol Thomas (now Carol Smith),[17] Sari Wade,[18] and Lon B. Work (deceased).[19]

As I look back on college from today's perspective, I am struck by the fact that almost all of our teachers at UCR were male. Indeed, it very well may have been the case that males held all of the tenure-track faculty positions. Dr. Loda Mae Davis was assistant dean of students and dean of women,[20] both administrative positions, and was an assistant professor of psychology, an untenured position, although it was tenure track. Christina Lindborg taught dance, and Professor Francis Carney, a member of the Political Science Department and one of Christina Lindborg's contemporaries, says that her position was tenure track. I cannot recall even one other female teacher, although Professor Carney says that there was a female assistant professor who was on tenure track in the biology department, There had been several tenured or tenure-track female professors at Howard University. Eleanor, my wife, has just reminded me that this was a time when opportunities for women, even Caucasian women, were almost as limited in mainstream higher education as they were for blacks.[21]

I have searched my mind but can recall only one circumstance that might have indicated racial discrimination during my stay at UCR. The teachers and administrators were open, friendly, and very supportive. The Caucasian students I met and interacted with were—to a person—affable, approachable, and supportive. For example, the family of Sheila and Susan Pratt, twin sisters from Los Angeles, afforded me a place to stay in Los Angeles during vacation breaks when the dorms were closed, although I enjoyed some Thanksgiving, Christmas, and spring breaks with the Greens and Murdocks in San Bernardino as well. I certainly could not afford to go home to the East. Jeannette Warnken was a middle-aged philosophy student at UCR with whom I became friends. Her husband was an established local dentist and I was often invited to their home for dinner. They encouraged me and generously provided occasional financial assistance during my stay at UCR. It is possible that my personal experience at UC Riverside was unique, but I really do not think it was. Over the years, I have from time to time talked with black students who were then at Riverside, and they too recall their UCR experience in almost exclusively positive terms.

The one circumstance I personally know of that could support the proposition that black students were discriminated against while I was at UCR involved two social clubs. There were no fraternities and sororities at UCR until the fall of 1973. There were, however, three men's social clubs that functioned much as fraternities did at most other college campuses. The three clubs were Xanadu,[22] the Gaels,[23] and the Marquis.[24] As far as I know, at the time I graduated from UCR in 1960 no black person had ever been invited to be a member of Xanadu or the Gaels. Ed Blakely, Warren Blakely, and Don Spigner—all football players—were members of the Marquis. Don Spigner remembers the Marquis as being composed mostly of students from working-class families, a significant portion of them also athletes.[25] He remembers the other two organizations—the Gaels and Xanadu—as drawing most of their membership from students who came from middle-class and professional families. I never sought membership in either organization and do not know if any of the other black students did. I would be surprised to hear that Lon Work had sought membership. I do not know if membership in the Marquis made Ed Blakely, Warren Blakely, and Don Spigner ineligible for membership in the Gaels and Xanadu. All three have told me recently that they never received an invitation to become a member of either the Gaels or Xanadu.

Although each University of California campus is unique, UCR was special because of its size and position within the California Master Plan for Higher Education. The Riverside campus, as initially conceived under that plan, was to be a small liberal arts school with an undergraduate character but still a component of the general University of California system. UCR would essentially have no graduate programs or graduate students. It was intended to be the first of several small University of California undergraduate campuses that would be modeled after select private schools such as Oberlin College in Ohio, Reed College in Oregon, and Swarthmore College in Pennsylvania. While faculty members would be required to engage in research and to meet conventional university publication standards, the primary focus at Riverside would be on classroom teaching. UC Berkeley and the University of California at Los Angeles were to be populated primarily with large enrollments of graduate and professional students. The primary focus of those campuses would be research.

When I was at UCR, classes were for the most part very small, with the typical class having fewer than 30 students. The entire philosophy department had only eight philosophy majors, with Demetrios Agretelis and me being among those eight. I mention Demetrios because he and I later were schoolmates at Boalt Hall. We became close friends and served together for several years as judges on the Alameda County Superior Court. The only exception to the small class size was in the hard sciences, where basic or introductory courses in biology, chemistry, mathematics, physics, and zoology had large enrollments. But even there, I doubt if any introductory course had more than 75 students.

The central library was essentially open stack. In other words, you were free to browse in any part of the library or search for a particular book or document. I do not recall there being any restricted or private areas, although there must have been some.

On particularly pleasant days, when one might say it was "too nice to be inside," it was not at all unusual for a professor to conduct the class outdoors. We also had an honor system. Examinations were not monitored. In some instances, you could, for example, receive your examination paper in the classroom and then take it to another and more comfortable location, in or outside the building, to write your answers. I know that was true in some of the philosophy, political science, and upper-division English courses that I took. There was a particular tree near Watkins Hall that I sometimes sat under while writing my answers.

All of our classes were taught by people with Ph.D's, because there were no graduate students at Riverside to serve as teaching assistants.[26] We had the advantage of small classes and close contact with our professors, both in and outside class. Our teachers were readily accessible throughout most of each weekday. For the most part, our professors were quite young, although there were a few who were well into middle age. Probably because there was not all that great a difference between the ages of the younger professors and the ages of most of their students—and because class sizes were fairly small—a certain openness and collegiality existed between professors and students. It was not at all unusual for students to be invited to a professor's home or for a small group of students and a professor to share a beer at the lounge in the nearby bowling alley.

My change to a philosophy major after I transferred to UCR was a consequence of my taking a few introductory philosophy and political science courses. I truly enjoyed the class discussions in those courses and found them to be intellectually challenging and highly stimulating. While I enjoyed the intellectual rigors of the scientific method, I enjoyed even more the give-and-take of debate and discussions in my philosophy and political science courses. My performance in the science courses that I took also contributed to my decision to change majors. In my science courses—particularly the zoology courses—I usually earned one of the highest grades in the lecture component but among the lowest in the laboratory component.

Also, once I decided to pursue a legal career (a decision I will discuss in the next section), I concluded (wrongly, I might add) that philosophy and political science courses would provide a much better

MODEL UNITED NATIONS TEAM *from the University of California Riverside (representing Costa Rica), in Seattle, Washington, spring 1958. From left, Henry Ramsey Jr.; William Kraus, Redlands, Calif.; Carolyn Jones, San Diego; and Robert Melsh, Redlands.*

foundation for law study than courses in the hard sciences. I say wrongly because my later observations as a law student and law professor demonstrated to me that any college major that develops and sharpens the student's analytical and writing skills will provide an excellent base for law study. Some of the top students in my law school class at Boalt Hall had been undergraduate science majors. The basic principles that undergird the scientific method also provide excellent tools for developing sound legal analytical skills.

Not everything at UCR revolved around class attendance and scholarship. We had parties at our houses in Canyon Crest. Some of the students had cars and would occasionally drive to Balboa Park in San Diego (about 100 miles away) or to one of the beaches near Los Angeles (about 60 miles away). I was a member of the UCR debate team, the Judicial Council,[27] and the UCR baseball team (as a pitcher); a delegate (from Costa Rica) to the Model United Nations[28]; and a participant in various other extracurricular activities. I helped organize an NAACP chapter at UCR, and we established picket lines at Woolworth and Kress stores in Riverside to support efforts to desegregate and to eliminate hiring discrimination at branches of those stores in the South. Nonetheless, while my life at UCR was not all work and no play, it was mostly work.

Those of us who had the opportunity to attend the University of California at Riverside during the period 1955–1965 received an outstanding liberal arts education. It was at UCR that I came to realize that one could earn a comfortable living in almost any field. There I learned that one had the freedom and should have the confidence to select a field of study on the basis of intellectual interests and aptitude. The academic and intellectual confidence that I had first acquired at Howard University was substantially increased while I was at Riverside.

It has been said, "If something appears to be too good to be true, it probably is." Time has proven that the undergraduate liberal arts education I received at the University of California at Riverside was as good as it appeared to be at that time. But the notion of establishing small liberal arts colleges within the University of California statewide

UC Riverside baseball team, 1958-59; *author second from right, back row.*

Receiving my bachelor of arts degree, *UC Riverside, June 1960.*

system, while a wonderful idea, was simply too costly to be sustained. The per capita expense of educating an undergraduate student at UCR in 1960 was light-years beyond the cost of educating that same student at UC Berkeley or UCLA. And so a dream in 1955 of a campus with not more than 1,000 students has become in 2007 the reality of a campus with more than 17,000 students. I am confident that today's UCR undergraduate and graduate students are still being offered an outstanding education. But those of us who had the good fortune to attend UCR during the early years truly have been the beneficiaries of an extraordinary educational experience for which I will always be grateful.

· Notes ·

1. Bill Gates, founder and chairman of the board of Microsoft Corporation, is one of the world's richest persons—probably the richest. In 1973, Gates entered Harvard University as a freshman, but he never graduated from college. He left Harvard in his junior year to devote his energies to Microsoft, which he had founded in 1975.

2. Richard Grasso is not a college graduate but became chairman and chief executive of the New York Stock Exchange (NYSE). He began at the NYSE in 1968 making $80 a week. When he announced his resignation on September 17, 2003, he had been earning $50,000 *per working day* for the previous eight years. See Thor Valdmanis, "More Changes Ahead as Trouble Dogs NYSE," *USA Today*, Sept. 19, 2003, p. 6A.

3. Kevin Garnett did not attend college, but he was selected to play professional basketball out of high school by the Minnesota Timberwolves in the 1995 NBA draft. His earnings in 2003—the final year of a six-year contract for $126 million—were $28 million. He also signed a five-year extension of his Timberwolves contract in 2003 for another $100 million.

4. Pop music figure Michael Jackson never attended college, but he earned and is worth millions.

5. William Powell Lear, the inventor, aircraft manufacturer, and founder of Learjet, did not attend college and, indeed, had only eight years of formal education at the time of his death on May 14, 1978.

6. Michael Moore is not a college graduate but has made a fortune as a filmmaker and writer. His films include *Roger & Me, The Big One, Bowling for Columbine,* and *Fahrenheit 9/11.* He is the author of *Downsize This: Random Threats from an Unarmed American,* and *Stupid White Men.* On p. 92 of *Stupid White Men,* he writes, "Yes, I, Michael Moore, am a college dropout."

7. Sometime during the first year of college, I figured out that no G.I. Bill checks were disbursed until after the "drop date"—that is, the date after which you could not drop a course without academic penalty. Lots of veterans were not able to hold on until the first checks were received and had to drop out because of a lack of financial resources. Also, administrators tried to persuade professors to prohibit students who had not paid their tuition from attending their classes but, with few exceptions, professors refused to do so.

8. For an interesting and concise discussion of the role of skin color in African American and American society at the time I was growing up and in college, read Mary Beth Rogers, *Barbara Jordan: American Hero* (New York, NY, Bantam Books, 1998), pp. 3-5.

9. Roy Overstreet, Zelma Ballard, and I.

10. Some of the other African American students who were there at the time remember an 11th African American student being at UCR during this period. I have absolutely no recollection of this person.

11. Zelma Ballard graduated in 1959 with a degree in social science and went on to become an elementary school teacher. Her first job after college was as a recreational director for the U.S. Department of Defense at military bases in Germany. She later earned a teaching credential at the University of Redlands and retired in 1997 after 32 years as an elementary school teacher with the Colton, Calif., Unified School District.

12. Edward Blakely graduated in 1960 with a degree in political science and went on to become an urban planner and university professor (UC Berkeley, UCLA, the University of Sydney), and he is currently overseeing Hurricane Katrina reconstruction efforts in New Orleans, by appointment of Mayor Ray Nagin (www.npr.org). He is Warren Blakely's brother.

13. Warren Blakely graduated in 1961 with a degree in biology and went on to earn a degree in dentistry from Howard University and to become a dentist. He is Edward Blakely's brother.

14. Carolyn Pippin Morris graduated in 1963 as a social science divisional major (anthropology, psychology, and education). She became an elementary school teacher and ultimately retired in 1996 as director of Student Services for the San Diego, California, Unified School District.

15. Roy Overstreet graduated in 1958 with a degree in physics and went on to obtain a Ph.D and become a physical oceanographer.

16. Donald Spigner graduated in 1962 with a degree in biology and went on to earn a medical degree from the University of California at San Francisco and to become a physician.

17. Carol Thomas Smith attended UCR from September 1959 until June 1961. She transferred to UCLA in fall 1961 and subsequently to San

Francisco State where she received a bachelor of science degree in mathematics. She obtained a Ph.D from the University of Texas (Austin) in 1979 and is currently a professor of mathematics at California State Polytechnic University in Pomona, Calif.

18. Sari Wade transferred from UCR to the University of California at Berkeley in 1961. She graduated from UC Berkeley in 1962 with a bachelor's degree in Chinese history. She received a master's degree in social work from UC Berkeley in 1968 and went on to become a social worker with the City and County of San Francisco. She was an employee of the City and County of San Francisco for 35 years and, in 2005, retired as the acting manager of the San Francisco Department of Human Services Family and Children's Programs.

19. Lon Work graduated in 1961 with a degree in zoology and went on to earn a degree in medicine from Howard University and become a physician.

20. See 1958 UCR *Tartan*, p. 13.

21. As I write this particular material, it is 6:30 a.m., and Eleanor and I are both sitting in our bed at the Hanoi Hilton in Hanoi, Vietnam. She is editing an MTA proposal, and I am writing about my time at UCR. We are on a two-week People to People Ambassador Study Tour to Vietnam and Cambodia. I find this trip to be particularly interesting, given my remembrances of the war and relations between our countries from the early 1960s to the mid-1970s.

22. Described in the 1960 UCR *Tartan*, p. 100, as "the only strictly men's club on campus."

23. Described in the 1959 *Tartan*, p. 104, as a "social-service club."

24. Described in the 1960 UCR *Tartan*, p. 102, as a "social-service club."

25. Telephone conversation with Don Spigner on Feb. 22, 2004.

26. There were graduate students studying at the Citrus Experiment Station, which had been at Riverside since 1905, approximately 50 years before the UCR campus was established. However, although the Citrus Experiment Station was a part of UCR, its students had no role in teaching UCR undergraduates.

27. The UCR Judicial Council is described as follows in the 1960 UCR *Tartan*, p. 83: "The Student Judicial Council is nominated by the Associated Students and appointed by the chief administrative officer. This committee advises the [faculty] Committee on Student Conduct with reference to student views on disciplinary penalties and procedures. The committee also recommends the development of programs for creating conditions and attitudes in the student body conducive to high standards of conduct."

# 10

# *Boalt Hall*

My decision to apply to law school was based mostly on my interest in U.S. constitutional law, civil rights, and governmental issues, as well as personal experience with Jim Crow. Interest in those subjects had been stimulated and intensified by courses taken at Howard University and UCR. Once I had made a definite decision to pursue a career in law, the issue became how to finance my legal education.

I applied to three law schools for admission in fall 1960: the University of California at Berkeley School of Law (Boalt Hall), Hastings College of Law in San Francisco (Hastings), and the University of Pennsylvania's School of Law in Philadelphia (Penn). Although the two California state law schools–Boalt and Hastings–were tuition-free,[1] I would still have to pay living expenses, primarily room and board. In those days, the cost of tuition at a private school and room and board during the school year were about an equal amount. If I were admitted and enrolled at the University of Pennsylvania's School of Law, I would have to pay tuition, but my mother, Nellie July, could provide me with free food and housing. She was living at 1763 North Croskey Street in North Philadelphia, and I could have boarded with her. Thus I felt the best schools for me, when everything was considered, were Boalt, the University of Pennsylvania, and Hastings, in that order. I was fortunate enough to be accepted at all three and I decided to enroll at Boalt Hall. In addition to being tuition-free, Boalt awarded me a modest scholarship, the John Hay Whitney Opportunity Fellowship.

You may be wondering how and when my mother, Nellie, came to live in Philadelphia. Let me explain. When I was discharged from the

Air Force in August 1955 and returned home to Rocky Mount, I offered my mother a train trip to New York to visit some of her relatives and friends. She accepted the offer but became seriously ill on the train shortly before arriving at New York City. When the train arrived in New York, she was taken to a hospital by ambulance. She remained hospitalized for a couple of weeks.

While in the hospital in New York City, she was visited by my brother James Williams, who was then living in Philadelphia. I also traveled from Rocky Mount to New York to visit with her at the hospital. After she was released, it was agreed by all concerned that it would be best for her to stay in Philadelphia with James and not try to make the lengthy train trip from New York to North Carolina.

While she was in Philadelphia with James, she must have complained about her situation as the wife of the Rev. John A. July. I discuss elsewhere ("My Genealogy," to be published separately) how parsimonious Rev. July was. At the time I probably considered him cheap and stingy, but such a description could be unfair, given that Rev. had lived through the Great Depression as an adult. It has been my experience with such people that they are very cautious with their money—understandable given the hardships Americans, particularly black Americans, experienced during the Depression years. Regardless, James and primarily his adult son, James Jr., persuaded my mother to leave Rev. July and to move permanently to Philadelphia, where they said they would be better able to assist her.

I happened to be in Rocky Mount one weekend during my first semester at Howard University, walking on South Washington Street in Around the Y, when whom should I see but my mother. This was a surprise—I thought she was still in Philadelphia. She said that James Jr. had driven her to Rocky Mount to "get her stuff" and that she was "leaving Rev." She wanted to know what I thought she should do, and I replied that this was a judgment she should make and that I did not want to get involved. Although I did not say so to her, the truth is that I did not want to be blamed if she later regretted her decision, and I thought she very well might. Almost all of her close friends were in Rocky Mount, and I thought there was a good chance that she would soon become lonely in Philadelphia.

I also had serious doubts about the attention and support she would get from James Jr., not because I thought he didn't care about her, because I was sure that he did, but because I just didn't see him as having a lot of time to devote to his grandmother. Although I knew that he had visited us in Rocky Mount on two or three occasions during my lifetime, I had no reason to believe there had been frequent contact over the years. In any event, since I sincerely believed this was a decision that my mother should make without any pressure from others, I declined to express an opinion. Later that day, she and James Jr. departed Rocky Mount for Philadelphia. She had rented the house at 1763 North Croskey Street, and it was there that she lived—essentially alone—until the time of her death in February 1964. After her death, my brother James moved into that house and lived there until his death on January 21, 1972.

You may also wonder why I did not apply to UCLA, which, like Boalt and Hastings, offered free tuition.[2] Although UCLA was tuition-free, it also requested that a picture be sent with the application, and that requirement was a definite turn-off for me. My assumption was that the picture would be used as a device for discriminating on the basis of race. I now recognize that eliminating UCLA on the basis of that assumption was somewhat naïve. There were (and are) other means for determining race: graduation from or even attendance at a historically black school, a comment made in a letter of recommendation, a statement made in the personal essay.

I spent the summer of 1960 in Philadelphia with my mother. One day, as I was sitting on the steps in front of her house and she was talking with me from her open front-bedroom window, she asked me with all seriousness if I thought it was a good idea to attend law school and "get messed up in white people's business." I assured her that it would be OK, and she seemed to accept my word. Although my mother was proud of me and had great confidence in my intellectual abilities, I know she continued to be concerned about my personal safety as a result of my career choice. Her comments were illustrative of the unfortunate mindset and understandable fears of so many black adults of her and preceding generations who lived in or were from the South— namely, that affairs of law and governance were "white folks' business" and blacks would be wise to stay out of them.

I began my law studies at Boalt Hall on September 19, 1960, and graduated with a bachelor of laws (LL.B.) degree on June 6, 1963. If one characterizes American law schools as small (350-500 students), medium (500-900 students), and large (900-plus students), Boalt Hall was and is still a medium-size school with slightly more than 800 matriculates, including students enrolled in the graduate programs (LL.M. and S.J.D.).

My entering class of 268 students was divided alphabetically into two sections, approximately equal in size. Students in each section took all of their classes together and, for two years, essentially had no in-class contact with members of the other section. Although we were in a room with approximately 135 students, the design and acoustics of the room were such that there was a significant degree of intimacy among us all—teacher and students. Everyone could hear well, and verbal exchanges were easy.

Unlike law school these days, the curriculum for the first year and most of the second year was totally prescribed. Even one or two of the third-year courses were required. My first-year courses were Contracts,[3] Crimes,[4] Equity,[5] Pleading and Procedure in Civil Cases,[6] Property,[7] and Torts.[8] With the exception of Crimes and Equity, the classes were one-year (i.e., two-semester) courses.[9] The first-year curriculum also had an "Introduction to Law," or legal writing, component that met once each week for an hour and earned one unit for the first year. Today, at most if not all of the approximately 200 law schools approved by the American Bar Association (ABA), only the first semester is fully prescribed, with students usually being able to take at least one elective in the second semester of the first year; second- and third-year classes are completely elective.[10] I took Security Transactions during the summer immediately after my first year.[11]

The following courses were required during the second year:[12] Businesses Associations (one year);[13] Constitutional Law (one year);[14] Estates and Trusts (one year);[15] Income Taxation (one year);[16] and Marital Property.[17] We also were required to take The Legal Profession, a one-unit course given in the spring semester. Each second-year course, with one exception, earned two academic credits.[18] My elective courses in the second year were Modern Social Legislation, taught in the fall by Barbara N. Armstrong, and Administrative Law, which Frank Newman taught in the spring. (Frank Newman was appointed to the California Supreme Court in July 1977 by Governor Edmund G. Brown Jr.)

As noted, third-year courses were elective, with the exception of Evidence, a required one-year course. I remember my third-year courses being, in the fall: Conflict of Laws, taught by Albert Ehrenzweig; Evidence, taught by Ronan Degnan; Federal Jurisdiction, taught by Nicholas Johnson; State and Local Law, taught by Sho Sato; and Trial Practice Seminar, taught by Geoffrey Hazard and David Louisell. My third-year spring semester courses were Comparative Law, taught by Jerome A. Cohen; Evidence, taught by Ron Degnan; Constitutional Law Seminar, taught by Edward Barrett; and Family Law, taught by Herma Hill Schreter. David Rosenthal and I did a research project on police misconduct in Oakland, California, as students in Ed Barrett's Selected Problems in Constitutional Law Seminar. (Ed Barrett became the founding dean of the King Law Center at the University of California at Davis in 1964.[19])

As had been my experience with teachers at UCR, most of our first- and second-year law professors were relatively young. I doubt if the mean average age of professors at Boalt Hall teaching first- and second-year courses, if you exclude professors Ed Barrett, Rex Collins, William Laube, David Louisell, Bob McKay, and William L. Prosser, who was dean of the law school and also taught Torts,[20] was more than six or eight years greater than that of the law students they were teaching.

Again, as at UCR, I think this closeness in age helped establish an open and friendly academic atmosphere that afforded students easy access to faculty members and allowed for a remarkable closeness between teachers and students. Unfortunately, not too many years after our graduation this student-faculty relationship was to significantly change for the worse.[21]

My entering class was the first to reflect a decision by the University to significantly increase the incoming law school class size. My entering class had 268 students.[22] I have been unable to document a significant increase in the size of Boalt classes entering in 1958, 1959, and 1960. But the number of graduates in those classes is strong evidence of a substantial increase between the entering class in fall 1959 and the one in fall 1960. Students graduating in 1961 entered in 1958 and were 140 in number. The graduating class of 1962 had 142 members. The class of 1963, my class, had 202 graduates.

This significant increase in student body size necessitated an increase in the size of the faculty as well. In those days, full-time law teachers typically did not have substantial experience as practicing lawyers before joining a law faculty, as once had been the case. Instead, they were typically hired immediately after graduation from law school and completion of a judicial clerkship with a federal circuit or state supreme court judge.[23] At schools of the caliber of Boalt Hall, the judicial clerkship would typically have been with a justice of the U.S. Supreme Court. There were, however, several faculty members at Boalt during my days there as a student who had significant experience as practicing lawyers.[24]

In the two years before the arrival of our class in fall 1960, a number of young and intellectually gifted faculty members had been hired to teach at Boalt Hall:[25] Babette Barton,[26] Richard Buxbaum,[27] Geoffrey Hazard,[28] Ira Michael Heyman,[29] Ed Halbach,[30] John

Hetland,[31] Herma Hill Schreter,[32] Preble Stolz,[33] and Justin Sweet.[34] They constituted a clear majority of law faculty members who taught the class of 1963 during our first and second years.

The hiring of Herma Hill Schreter in 1960[35] and Babette Barton in 1965[36] as members of the full-time faculty reflected a 200 percent increase in the number of full-time, tenure-track female faculty members at Boalt Hall. That is to say, there was one female faculty member at Boalt before they arrived. Her name was Barbara Nachtrieb Armstrong, and she was the first female full-time faculty member, not just at Boalt Hall but at any major American law school.[37] Professor Sho Sato, a Japanese American,[38] was the only faculty member of color at Boalt while I was a student.[39] The first black law professor at Boalt Hall, John Wilkins, was hired in 1964.[40] He taught at Boalt until his death in 1976.[41] I became the second black professor at Boalt Hall when I was appointed to the faculty in 1971.

In 1960, at almost every law school approved by the ABA (and at some even today), the dean of the law school would ominously announce at the orientation assembly of entering students, "Look at the person immediately on your left and the person to your immediate right. Get to know them this year, because next year, one of you will no longer be here!" Dean Prosser issued that dire warning to our entering class at Boalt Hall, the clear implication being that approximately one-third of us would fail in the first year. The purpose of this at Boalt Hall was the same as elsewhere—namely, to get us to take our studies seriously.

I have a brochure with the name and picture of each of the 202 surviving members—including six women—of my third-year class (spring semester). I recall there being 12 women when we started. But not all the 66 departures would be because of academic deficiencies. Some did in fact flunk out, but a significant number of those who left after the first year did so because they found they did not like law school or the law and no longer wanted to pursue a legal career, or because of financial or health reasons or other personal considerations.

This is not to deny that Boalt was both demanding and difficult. Early in the first semester, I came to appreciate that my classmates were not only smart, but quick intellectually. That fact combined with the rigor of our first-year classes had me questioning my own ability. Then it occurred to me that there were thousands of Boalt Hall graduates and that I had to be as smart as some of those people! This comforting observation gave me confidence that all I needed to do to complete the course of study and graduate was to study hard and conscientiously attend my classes.

I had some sterling company as I set out to do exactly that. Thelton E. Henderson, a black second-year law student at Boalt Hall; John Jose Miller, a black graduate of the Howard University School of Law who was enrolled in the LL.M. program; Donald Warden (now Khalid Abdullah Tariq Al-Mansour), a black third-year law student at Boalt Hall,[42] and I, a black first-year law student at Boalt Hall, all lived in a rooming house at 2528 Benvenue Avenue in Berkeley during the 1960–61 academic year.[43] At that time, Don, Thelton, and I constituted 75 percent of the entire black LL.B. law student body at Boalt Hall, the other 25 percent being Eugene Swan, who was married and lived elsewhere. The other residents at 2528 Benvenue that year were Lowell Hughes, a black graduate of UC Berkeley[44] with an undergraduate degree in history, and Mae Eng, a Chinese American woman who was also a UC Berkeley undergraduate.

In *Berkeley Landmarks: An Illustrated Guide to Berkeley, California's Architectural Heritage*, author Susan Dinkelspiel Cerny says of 2528 Benvenue that the house ("Landmark #138, 1990") was designed by Arthur Ayers and constructed in 1899. Called the Arthur Ayers House, it is described as "a large brown shingle house . . . noteworthy for its complex composition and absence of superficial decoration. An excellent example of the shingle style imported from the Northeast coast, but uniquely used in Berkeley in an urban setting. . . . From the 1920s until 1989 the house was used as a rooming house, but [it] has been converted back to a single-family dwelling."[45] (I have provided this information about 2528 because it is now a landmark and may very well be still standing when you read this.)

Of the four ambitious young black lawyers-to-be who resided at 2528 Benvenue in 1960–61, Thelton E. Henderson became the first black lawyer hired in the Civil Rights Division of the U.S. Justice Department (1962-1963) and later served as an associate dean for student affairs at the Stanford University School of Law (1968–1976).[46] President Jimmy Carter appointed Thelton Henderson to the U.S. District Court for the Northern District of California on May 9, 1980. He was confirmed by the U.S. Senate on June 26, 1980, and received his commission two days later. At the time of this writing, he continues to serve with distinction on senior status.

Khalid Abdullah Tariq Al-Mansour became quite wealthy practicing law and representing various clients in the oil industry and international banking community. He also represented a member of the royal family of Saudi Arabia. He has continued to play a significant leadership role in African American affairs nationally and internationally. John J. Miller went on to have an illustrious political and judicial career, serving in the California Assembly for 11 years, followed by several years as an associate justice of the California Court of Appeal. I was number four among these future lawyers at 2528 Benvenue and will provide you with the details of my legal career in the following pages.

David Rosenthal, Jay Shafran, Paul Weiser, and I formed a study group fairly early on during the fall semester of our first year at Boalt. We met for two years at Paul Weiser's apartment in North Oakland, almost always on Sunday.[47] Our study group did very well academically, with Jay Shafran and Paul Weiser making law review.[48]

Several close friendships from my student days at Boalt Hall have lasted until this day. Demetrios Agretelis, Khalid Abdullah Tariq Al-Mansour,[49] Michael Ballachey, Professor Richard Buxbaum, Paul Halvonik, Professor Geoffrey Hazard, Thelton E. Henderson, Professor Ira Michael Heyman, Don Hopkins, Peter Korican,[50] David Larrouy, David Rosenthal, and Tom Silk immediately come to mind.

Law school graduates have long had a saying: "In the first year, they scare you to death; in the second year, they work you to death; in the third year, they bore you to death." There is some truth in that statement, although there is certainly no justification for third-year boredom today, when students can take clinical courses and can serve externships with judges and at public and private law offices. But there has always been an opportunity in the third year to take interesting courses that first- and second-year students are unable to take or even to take a course or two in other departments of the university.

While admittedly the first year of law school is demanding and frightening for nearly everyone—at least until after you have received your first-semester grades—there is breathing room in the second and third years. Indeed, during my first year of law school I met and courted EVELYN YVONNE LEWIS, a Berkeley undergraduate student. We first met on campus early during the fall semester.[51] On June 11, 1961, after completion of my first-year examinations, Evelyn Yvonne Lewis and I were married at Saint Dominic's Church in San Francisco, California. My oldest child and first son, CHARLES TILLMAN RAMSEY, was born on April 14, 1962, during the spring semester of my second year. At that time, we were living in an apartment at 2306A Dwight Way in Berkeley, and Charles was born at Herrick Memorial Hospital, a few blocks from our home.

I had two jobs during the summer between my first and second years, one of them as a "virtual janitor" for the university's Building and Grounds Department. Professor Geoffrey Hazard, who taught me civil procedure in my first year, had recommended me for a summer job to Arleigh Williams, who was then dean of men (later dean of students) for the College of Letters and Science.[52] Professor Hazard hired me to do some legal research for him that summer as well.

Dean Williams interviewed me in his office at Sproul Hall and referred me in turn to Building and Grounds, where I was assigned as a night janitor for a building on the north side of campus, one of the many "temporary"[53] buildings constructed during World War II at various sites throughout the United States. It was demolished years later.

It was a great schedule. I could attend Professor John Hetland's Securities Transactions class in the morning, do research for Professor Hazard in the afternoon, and work as a janitor at night. But it was a strange job. To my surprise, the building was not in use and was completely empty. While the matter was never explained to me, I later figured out for myself, at least to my satisfaction, why I got that particular non-job. First, Dean Arleigh Williams had been an All-American football player at UC Berkeley in the early 1930s, and it was he who referred me to Building and Grounds. Second, the supervisor at Building and Grounds saw that I was an African American when I showed up for the job and probably assumed I was a "jock" to be pampered. (In his eyes I would have to have been a basketball or baseball player. Given my physique–6-foot 1-inch and 160 pounds soaking wet– he couldn't possibly have thought that I was a football player.) It was a good thing while it lasted.

My usual routine was to check in at the Building and Grounds office each workday afternoon at about 5 p.m. and then go immediately to the building I had been assigned to clean. I tell you again that the building was totally empty–there was not a single chair, desk, stool, or floor lamp–and it was not then being used for any purpose. I would run a dust mop over the floor and then go to the law library at Boalt Hall to do research for Professor Hazard until about 10:00 p.m. At that time, I would return to the building, use the dust mop again, and wait until just before 11:00 p.m., when I would return to Building and Grounds to check out.

The "good thing" lasted for about six weeks. I guess at that point someone discovered that I was not an athlete. Revenge must have been intended, because I was assigned to work in the Life Sciences building, which can be described only as tough duty. The various offices were always crowded with desks, bookcases, chairs, and laboratory tables, making the overall job exceedingly difficult. In many rooms there were animal cages (for dogs, monkeys, or rats). The floor would usually have a layer of sawdust by the end of the day, and sometimes animal feces. Believe me, working in Life Sciences had to have been a janitor's worst nightmare.

But after about a month in Life Sciences someone must have had mercy on me, because I finished the summer working for a couple of weeks each in the Geology building and the Forestry building. I enjoyed the brief time I had living the life of a college jock, even though I had to pay the price later.

I was deeply involved in various political activities during my second and third years, both within and without the law school. While I did all right academically (top third of my class), I could and probably would have done better if l had been less active politically. But that is water over the dam or under the bridge, and I have no regrets about my political activism during law school. Indeed, I am proud of it.

I served as a member of the law school student council during my second year (1961–62) and was president of the campus-wide Graduate Students Association during the third year (1962–63). This was a time on the Berkeley campus of considerable student activism regarding American-Cuban relations, civil rights activities in the American South, U.S. military involvement in South Vietnam, and university attempts to control or even stifle student voices and activities on those matters. A new student political organization called SLATE had recently been formed at UC Berkeley, and its members were active on campus, as were political organizations such as Fair Play for Cuba and the Young People's Socialist League. I was not a member of any of those organizations, but I did spend many hours with various of their members and supporters, debating and discussing how students should address the political, economic, and foreign policy issues that we were intensely concerned about.

I was also an active member of the Berkeley Democratic Club, which met off campus. Some of us who were active in the Berkeley

Democratic Club did a survey of housing discrimination in Berkeley. Not only did we publish the results of our survey but also—to the consternation of Dean Frank Newman, who had succeeded William L. Prosser as dean of the law school at the end of our second year—we identified, by name, the discriminating real estate brokers and companies. Dean Newman was deeply concerned that Boalt or the university might be sued for libel or defamation.

During my last two years at Boalt, I was a very active member of the Afro-American Association. This organization of African American students at Berkeley was formed to help us prepare for community leadership after our graduation from the university. Donald Hopkins, one of only two black students in the Boalt class of 1965, was a founding member of the Afro-American Association and wrote the following explanation of the association and its purpose:

> Our discussion group was to become known simply as the Afro-American Association. If there was one idea that wed us all together, it was that we were not Negroes, but rather were American Blacks of African descent. Through our explorations we sought to come to an intellectual understanding of what this meant within the context of American life, and to come to a further understanding of what this meant in terms of our own political direction as future leaders of our people. Just as the sit-ins and related civil rights demonstrations were to confront the institutionalized aspects of American racism, our discussion groups and attendant political activity were to address the ideological aspects of racism—a role we felt more suited to northern Blacks who, after all, faced racism in a much more disguised and subtle form.[54]

It is clear to me that those early efforts of association members did indeed bear fruits of leadership and did result in substantial positive contributions to Afro-American people in particular, and American society in general. I know that those Sunday discussions of the Afro-

American Association, the extraordinary feast of intellectual and analytical challenges I discovered there, provided a foundation for—and one of the primary roots of—my commitment to excellence, intellectual integrity, and willingness to struggle on behalf of black and other oppressed people. A more comprehensive discussion of the Afro-American Association is included in the "Memorable Events" section of this manuscript.

Various intervals in my life have underscored for me my indebtedness to others for the professional success I have achieved and, indeed, for my personal survival as an undergraduate and graduate student. I experienced two such episodes during my law student days. Throughout my college career and continuing in law school, I had serious cash-flow problems, which frequently presented the serious predicament of my not having enough food to eat. This was especially so during my first year in law school. At Boalt Hall, I found an easy and convenient solution to the resulting missed-meals cramps.

Most of the fraternity and sorority houses—and some of the rooming houses serving UC Berkeley students—each year hired nonmember students to clear and wash dishes and to clean up the kitchen after the evening meal, with their own dinner as compensation. This job was called "hashing," and the dishwashers were called "hashers." Donald Warden, the third-year student at Boalt Hall during my first year who lived at the same rooming house I did, told me about this system. Don was a hasher at a rooming house for girls. Somehow early on in my first year, I learned that hashers were needed at the Pi Kappa Alpha fraternity house, located one block from Boalt Hall.[55] I immediately applied for and got the job.

The cook at the Pi Kappa Alpha house was an African American woman named Aldonia Richardson. She lived in east Oakland, and everyone called her Allie. She was an outstanding cook, and I truly enjoyed the meals she provided me as my compensation for hashing. Indeed, I thought she was such a great cook that I convinced David Rosenthal, then my classmate and years later my law partner, that he should come and hash at Pi Kappa Alpha so he, too, could enjoy Allie's cooking. David was from a well-to-do family in Detroit, Michigan. He did not have a financial need to hash. But after tasting Allie's cooking, he decided that hashing would be in his gastronomic interest. Plus, I had also convinced him that the hashing experience would teach us humility, a virtue I thought we both needed.

Quite a few members of Pi Kappa Alpha were jocks. Craig Morton, for example, a notable quarterback for UC Berkeley and later in the National Football League, was a member of Pi Kappa Alpha and lived at the fraternity house during the time I hashed there. It was also the case that many of the young residents of the house were rude and inconsiderate toward the hashers. It was not unusual for some of the members to declare a private meeting to be in session near the end of or immediately after dinner, and before we had an opportunity to clear tables. We would have to wait until their "meeting" was concluded before being admitted to the dining room to clear the dishes.

That inconsiderate practice was a considerable annoyance to David Rosenthal and me. David and I decided that we would teach the "frat boys" a lesson. We knew that it would be virtually impossible for them to hire anyone to hash during final examinations.

So we worked assiduously until a few days before the examination study period began and then quit without any advance notice. That meant the fraternity members would have to clear and wash their own dishes for two or three weeks. We advised the fraternity members of our reasons for quitting in our letter of resignation. I do not know whether our action changed their behavior, but I do know that it made David and me feel great.

For the next semester and, indeed, until I graduated from law school, I could go by the fraternity house to see Allie anytime during the school week that I was hungry. She would have me sit in a small private room just off the kitchen that the fraternity provided her as a rest area and bring me a generous and wonderful plate of food. Besides providing me with needed nutrition, she would also take my soiled clothes home, where her mother would wash and iron them. On occasional weekends I was invited to their home in east Oakland, where I had the opportunity to eat more of her delicious food and to relax with her family. I came to know Allie, her husband, and her children almost as family. Allie could not have been more proud on the day I graduated from law school than if I had been her own son. She and her husband were my first private clients when they hired me to draft their wills shortly after I was admitted to the California bar. My close friendship with Allie continued after my graduation from law school and lasted for 30 years until her death on December 2, 1993.

I also appreciated another source of food while I was in law school. Two African American women, Emma Coleman and her friend whose name has escaped me, worked in the restaurant at International House, almost directly across the street from Boalt Hall. I don't know how they got to know me or how they came to realize that I was frequently short of cash, but somehow they did.

Regardless, I would occasionally go into the I-House restaurant at lunchtime with just enough money to pay for a grilled cheese sandwich. I would order a grilled cheese sandwich from either of these women, and it would come back loaded with meat (usually baked ham), cheese, tomatoes and lettuce between the two slices of bread. On the side of the plate would be French fries. This plate was virtually a full meal. I would then pay the price of the grilled cheese sandwich I had ordered. This practice, probably unlawful but very helpful, continued for the entire time I was a student at Boalt Hall.

It was clear to me that Allie and these two women were proud of the fact that I, an African American, was enrolled at Boalt Hall and wanted to do all they could to help me make it through. I never forgot their acts of kindness and how they helped me complete law school. All three were present when I was sworn in as a member of the Berkeley City Council in 1973 and at my swearing-in as a Superior Court Judge in 1981, and I publicly acknowledged their exceptional and critical assistance while I was a student at Boalt.

The encouragement and reinforcement provided me by those three good women and by members of the Green family in San Bernardino are consistent with the support that black people have traditionally provided to those who seek to improve themselves. I am convinced that this tradition is practiced with the belief that the recipients of that assistance will then work to help improve the conditions of all black Americans. Many today call it "giving back." I am confident that most—and probably all—successful Afro-Americans from my era would be able to tell you stories about needed help that they received from black people as they struggled to achieve their life's goal or goals. So whether or not you—my children, grandchildren, great-grandchildren, and other progeny—have received such assistance directly, you should know that, through me, you are the beneficiaries of such support and, therefore, must recognize and accept your obligation to "give back," to "pass it on," to always help others.

The graduation ceremony for the University of California at Berkeley School of Law's class of 1963 was held at Boalt Hall on Thursday, June 6, 1963. That was another one of my euphoric days. My sister Martha Roberson, *née* July, came from Texas to attend the ceremony, a presence from my childhood in Rocky Mount. My only regret was that my mother could not be there. Neither she nor I had the money to bring her to California from Pennsylvania, but even if the money had been available her health would not have allowed her to make the trip by train, and I am absolutely certain she would not have been willing to travel by plane. Still, it was a great day.

My overall law school student experience was a very positive one. Nonetheless, I was the only black student in my class and, as mentioned earlier, was one of only four black students in the entire Boalt Hall student body. I believe I was the 13th black person to graduate from Boalt Hall since its founding in 1908, more than half a century earlier. The first black graduate of Boalt Hall was Walter A. Gordon, '22, who in 1955 was appointed by President Dwight David Eisenhower to be governor of the U.S. Virgin Islands.[56]

Other black graduates of Boalt Hall before my graduation in 1963 included George M. Johnson, '29,[57] who served for more than 10 years as dean of the Howard University School of Law; Annie Virginia Stephens Coker, '29, the first black woman lawyer in California[58] ; Justice Clinton Wayne White, '48, who was appointed to the Alameda County Superior Court in 1977 and appointed chief justice of the First District, California Court of Appeal, in 1978; the Honorable Allen Broussard, '53, who was appointed to the Alameda County Superior Court in 1975 and, in 1981, became the second person of color[59] to be appointed an associate justice of the California Supreme Court; Donald Warden, '61, who went on to become an exceptional transactional lawyer and entrepreneur;[60] the Honorable Thelton Eugene Henderson, '62, who in 1980 was appointed a U.S. District Court Judge, for the Northern District of California; and Eugene Swan, '62, who went on to hold several important positions as a lawyer: first black deputy district attorney in Contra Costa County, California; director of legal services for Contra Costa County (in 1972 declared the best Legal Aid Attorney in the United States), and director of the San Francisco Office of Citizen Complaints; and as a professor at various schools, including UC Berkeley (where he taught economics) and Napa Valley College (where he still teaches economics and business law).

## The California Bar Examination

I SPENT MOST OF THE SUMMER after my third year studying for the bar examination and participating in a summer program titled "Annual Workshop in International Legal Studies," which was directed by Professor Richard Buxbaum. He says this was the ninth program so held. The central topic at the 1963 workshop was Regional Political and Economic Integration. The program was funded by the Ford Foundation, and its primary emphasis was a comparison of the European Economic Community in Western Europe with that of the Eastern European bloc and the Soviet Union (Comecon[61]).

Paul Halvonik was also in that program, and he and I studied together to prepare for the bar examination. It was a convenient arrangement because we lived near each other in Albany Village, which consisted of married student housing owned by the university and rented to graduate and professional students. To be honest, Paul and I also foolishly spent some of our precious limited time that summer playing cards in the men's lounge at Boalt Hall.

Then as now, most law school graduates enrolled in a commercial bar preparation course. The popular course in California when I finished law school was referred to as "Wicks." It was composed of a series of lectures organized by a University of Southern California Law School professor named Richard Wicks. The approximately $300 course fee permitted you to (a) attend a series of lectures by various professionals on several of the subjects that would be on the bar examination and, most important, (b) receive two volumes of written bar preparation materials, called *Wicks' Outlines*.

Those written materials consisted of summaries of procedural and substantive law subjects likely to be covered on the bar exam. Wicks's contracts outline was excellent and would by itself have been worth the cost of the course. Anyway, David Rosenthal and I shared the expense. Neither of us was particularly interested in attending the lectures, but both of us wanted access to the outlines. I wouldn't have all that much time for the lectures anyway, because of the international legal studies summer program.

The week before the California bar examination, with terrible timing, I contracted the flu or a very bad cold, but a doctor prescribed some pills that suppressed my symptoms and allowed me to continue preparing. The first day of the examination was August 8, 1963.[62] We used manual typewriters because, for some reason unknown to me, electric typewriters were not permitted. I remember taking the last of the prescribed pills as I rode across the Bay Bridge on the morning of the third and final day of the exam.

I left the testing facility with mixed feelings that last day. It had been a challenging examination, but it was also quite similar to essay exams that I had experienced in three years of law school. It had helped to know that most Boalt Hall students taking it for the first time passed. As was the case when I began to have doubts in the first year about my ability to succeed in law school, I again assumed that I was at least as smart as the dumbest of those Boalt graduates who, in prior years, had taken and passed the bar exam on the first attempt. My successful results were mailed to my mother's house at 1763 North Croskey Street, Philadelphia, about 14 weeks later, in a letter dated and envelope postmarked December 13, 1963.

At that time, my then-wife, Evelyn, and I were visiting my mother. Evelyn was pregnant with our second son, GITHAIGA DANIEL RAMSEY, who was born New Year's Day 1964 at Women's Medical College Hospital in Philadelphia. We were advised by Evelyn's doctor to wait until three weeks after Githaiga's birth before undertaking the drive back to California. We left Philadelphia on January 21 and I was sworn in as a member of the California bar on January 29, 1964, in San Francisco.

## · Notes ·

1. And at that time, tuition-free meant exactly that: there was no tuition. The only charge I remember paying was $55 each semester as a student activity fee, or a total of $110 annually. (Non-residents paid an additional charge, but no tuition.)
2. The University of California at Davis did not then have a law school.
3. A one-year course, taught by Justin Sweet.
4. A one-semester course, taught by Ed Barrett.
5. A one-semester course, taught by Robert McKay, a visiting law professor from New York University.
6. A one-year course, taught by Geoffrey Hazard in the first semester and David Louisell in the second semester.
7. A one-year course, taught by Ira Michael Heyman, who years later would become chancellor of the University of California at Berkeley.
8. A one-year course, taught by William Prosser.
9. See Bulletin, University of California, Announcement of the School of Law, Berkeley, Fall and Spring Semester, 1960–1961, April 20, 1960, University of California at Berkeley, p. 25.
10. This statement, while true, can be misleading. Because almost all American law students plan to take a bar examination, their choice of

courses is still somewhat restricted by the need to take subjects or courses in law school that will be tested on the bar examination (e.g., courses such as Constitutional Law and Evidence).

11. Taught by John Hetland.

12. See Bulletin, University of California, Announcement of the School of Law, Berkeley, Fall and Spring Semester, 1961–1962, April 10, 1961, University of California, Berkeley, pp. 27–28.

13. The course basically covered corporations and partnerships. It was taught by Richard Buxbaum and Richard Jennings.

14. Taught by Ira Michael Heyman.

15. Taught by Ed Halbach.

16. Taught by Adrian Kragen (fall) and Babette Barton (spring).

17. Taught by Herma Hill Schreter.

18. The one exception was Business Associations, which earned three units each semester.

19. See Sandra P. Epstein, *Law at Berkeley: The History of Boalt Hall* (Berkeley, CA: Institute of Government Studies, University of California, 1997), p. 261.

20. William L. Prosser was dean of Boalt Hall from 1948 until 1961. See Epstein (1997, 243). It is an understatement to simply say that Prosser taught torts. William L. Prosser not only taught that subject but also was the author of *Prosser on Torts*, an authoritative and widely cited legal treatise on the topic.

21. See Epstein (1997, pp. 271–73).

22. According to Epstein (1997, p. 275), the entering class in 1960 was from a pool of 517 students who were admitted by the law school in 1960. (Admission is not the same as enrollment.) Also see Epstein (1997, pp. 222–23).

23. See Epstein (1997, p. 225.) "The common characteristics uniting the majority of these appointments continued to be experience in law review activity and in judicial clerkships, especially for the United States Supreme Court."

24. See Epstein (1997, pp. 223–24).

25. See Epstein (1997, p. 224).

26. Professor Babette Barton, who taught Tax, was initially hired in January 1961 to teach part-time but, according to Sandra P. Epstein, became a member of the full-time faculty in 1965. I spoke with Babette Barton by telephone on March 30, 2006, and she thinks it was later than 1965 when she became a member of the full-time faculty on a tenure track. She says she received tenure in 1969 or 1970.

27. Hired in 1961 and taught our class Business Associations (which included corporations), a second-year course.
28. Hired in 1958 and taught our class Civil Pleading and Procedure, a first-year course.
29. Hired in 1959 and taught our class Property in the first year and Constitutional Law in the second year.
30. Hired in 1958 and taught our class Estates and Trusts, a second-year course.
31. Hired in 1959 and taught Securities Transactions.
32. Hired in 1960 and taught our class Family Law during our second year.
33. Now deceased. He was hired in 1961.
34. Hired in 1960 and taught Contracts in our first year.
35. See Epstein (1997, p. 224).
36. See Epstein (1997, p. 255). Note my comments in note 26 regarding Babette Barton's recollection of when she became full-time and tenure track.
37. See Epstein (1997, p. 84).
38. Hired at Boalt in 1955 and was a Harvard Law School graduate.
39. Those years were 1960–61, 1961–62, and 1962–63.
40. See Epstein (1997, p. 255).
41. See Epstein (1997, p. 280).
42. He received his undergraduate degree in philosophy from Howard University.
43. Thomas Curtin was the Caucasian fellow who owned the rooming house.
44. We men then living at 2528 Benvenue Avenue, all of whom were black, typically referred to Lowell as "Natural," "Natural Business," or Lowell "Natural Business" Hughes. At that time, a common phrase used by many black men at and around UC Berkeley to refer to sexual intercourse was "taking care of natural business." Lowell was obsessed with his need to have sex with Caucasian females, particularly Scandinavian blonds. His model or ideal couple was Sammy Davis Jr. and Mae Britt. He was convinced that the children of such a couple would be exceptionally beautiful. Lowell constantly boasted about how often and how well he "took care of business." As a result, those of us in the house began to refer to him as "Natural" or "Natural Business." A comment might be "Is Natural in his room?" Or "Have you seen Natural Business today?"
45. Berkeley Architectural Heritage Association, Berkeley, CA, 2001, at p. 222 (Revised & Enlarged Edition).
46. See Jessie Carney Smith, *Black Firsts,* 2nd ed. (Detroit: Visible Ink Press, 2003), p. 307.

47. The apartment house was on 30th Street, just off Broadway, in Oakland.

48. In those days, one could make law review only on the basis of your first-year grades. There was no procedure whereby you could "write on" (i.e., write and submit a paper).

49. Then Donald Warden.

50. Peter died in 2004. Date as per Web site: www.sunnyridge.net/guestbook/history/tribute-peter.html

51. Evelyn was then living in Davidson Hall, a student dormitory. Her parents and most of her siblings were living at 1419 Scott Street in San Francisco. The family home was just off Geary and directly across the street from Benjamin Franklin Junior High School in the Filmore District. The specific area where they lived was completely redeveloped during the 1960s, and the family moved to a new home in the Haight-Ashbury neighborhood of San Francisco.

52. Arleigh Williams graduated from Berkeley in 1935 with honors in physical education and education. At 158 pounds, he starred as a "triple-threat" halfback and as captain of varsity football, played on the baseball team, and was active in the Order of the Golden Bear. In 1959, because of student, athletic, and career successes, he received the *Sports Illustrated* Silver Anniversary All-American award. Joining the administration at Berkeley in 1958, after more than a year as director of student activities for the Associated Students of the University of California, Arleigh was appointed Berkeley campus dean of men. He continued in that post until 1966, when he was advanced to dean of students. In 1970, he became assistant vice chancellor for student affairs and, in that capacity, also served briefly as acting director of athletics. On his retirement in 1976, he was named dean of students emeritus by the Board of Regents of the University and was awarded the Berkeley Citation by Chancellor Albert Bowker. For material on his life, see *Arleigh Williams* (Berkeley, CA: Regional Oral History Office, University of California at Berkeley, 1990).

53. I put quotation marks around the word "temporary" because throughout the United States the so-called temporary buildings constructed during World War II were so well built that many of them were still very much in use 20 years later and gave no evidence of deteriorating anytime in the near future. Indeed, it appeared that they could actually last into the next century.

54. Harriet Nathan and Stanley Scott, eds. *Experiment and Change in Berkeley: Essays on City Politics, 1950–1975* (Berkeley, CA: Berkeley Institute of Governmental Studies, 1978), p. 108.

55. The Pi Kappa Alpha fraternity house is located at 2324 Piedmont Avenue, Berkeley.

56. See Epstein (1997, p. 277). "[Walter A. Gordon] was an excellent scholar, as well as the University's heavyweight boxing champion and its first African American All-American football player. After receiving his law degree in 1922, Gordon went on to receive appointments to the California Board of Prison Terms and Paroles and to the California Adult Authority. After serving as governor of the Virgin Islands for three years," the Honorable Walter A. Gordon was appointed judge of the U.S. District Court for the Virgin Islands.

57. See Epstein (1997, p. 277). "[George M. Johnson] became tax counsel for the State Board of Equalization. In 1940, Johnson left California to join the Faculty of Law at Howard University and to serve from 1942 to 1945 as deputy chairman and general counsel of the U.S. Committee on Fair Employment Practice. From 1946 to 1958, Johnson was dean of the law school at Howard University."

58. *California Bar Journal*, February 2008.

59. Associate Justice Wiley Manuel, an African American graduate of the Hastings College of Law and a member of the Alameda County Superior Court, was the first person of color to be appointed to the California Supreme Court.

60. During the early part of his professional life, Donald Warden was an exceptional criminal and civil trial lawyer.

61. An economic organization from 1949 to 1991, linking the Soviet Union with Bulgaria, Czechoslovakia, Hungary, Poland, Romania, East Germany (1950-90), Mongolia (from 1962), Cuba (from 1972), and Vietnam (from 1978), with Yugoslavia as an associated member. Albania also belonged between 1949 and 1961. Its establishment was prompted by the Marshall Plan. Comecon was formally disbanded in June 1991.

62. See notice of the bar examination in my personal files.

# 11

# Professional Life

My first job after being admitted to the California bar was with the law firm of Bohn and Williams, located at 638½ First Street in Benicia, California. The partners of the firm were John A. Bohn, who had served for many years in the California Senate and was also city attorney for the city of Benicia, and Charlie Williams, who was at that time the city attorney for Pleasant Hill, California. Benicia had been the capital of California for all of a year—from February 1853 until February 1854. Evelyn and I and the boys were living in San Francisco with her mother and father, James and Evelyn Lewis, when I began working at Bohn and Williams. My daily roundtrip commute was approximately 72 miles.

Bohn and Williams had recently won a contract with the government of Guam to, among other things, write code comments to the version of the Uniform Commercial Code adopted by Guam, and I was hired to help with that project. While working in Benicia I learned that the Contra Costa County District Attorney's Office would be hiring several deputy district attorneys. The main office was in Martinez, the county seat, directly across the Carquinez Strait from Benicia.

I applied for one of the deputy DA positions and was hired during the spring of 1964. John A. Nejedly was the district attorney for the county, and I was the second black lawyer hired in that office. Eugene Swan, a schoolmate at Boalt Hall who graduated in 1962, had been the first. Eugene worked in the Martinez office, and I was assigned to the Richmond office, where I worked for almost two years.

Evelyn and I moved into a duplex apartment house at either 423 or 427 South 45th Street[1] in Richmond. We subsequently purchased a three-bedroom home in the same neighborhood, at 4710 Overend Avenue, about two blocks from the apartment where we had been living.

Only one black lawyer was then in private practice in the city of Richmond. He was George D. Carroll, who in 1964 became the first black mayor of Richmond and in 1965 was appointed to the Richmond Municipal Court by Governor Edmund G. Brown Sr.–a double first. George D. Carroll was not only the first black person appointed to the Richmond Municipal Court but the first black person appointed to any judicial office in Contra Costa County. I saw his appointment to the bench as an opportunity for me to leave the District Attorney's Office and enter private practice.

When George Carroll was appointed to the bench in 1965, both John Jose Miller (the Howard University Law School graduate who lived at the rooming house with me during my first year in law school) and I offered to buy his law practice. George decided to sell the practice to John. Fortunately for me, Allen Norris, a Jewish lawyer in Richmond, made me a generous offer of a furnished office in a building that he owned at 1016 Nevin Avenue[2] and where he had his own law office. He deferred all rent payments for the first six months (longer, if necessary). Because his practice was essentially civil, Allen said he would refer any criminal cases that came his way to me. It was an extremely kind and courageous act. I say courageous because, at that time, most white lawyers would not form a professional association with a black lawyer, let alone afford them the kind of support that Allen was offering me. Indeed, Allen Norris and I later became law partners.

It turned out that private practice was not John Miller's cup of tea, and although he got George Carroll's law practice, it was I who became the successful black lawyer in Richmond. John Miller did have a very successful career as a politician. A resident of Berkeley, he was appointed to the Berkeley Unified School Board in 1964 to replace the Rev. Roy C. Nichols, who, after being named pastor of the 4,600-member Salem United Methodist Church in New York City, had resigned as pastor of Oakland's Downs Memorial United Methodist Church[3] and also as president of the Berkeley Unified School Board. In

1965, John Miller successfully ran to complete the two years remaining on the Rev. Nichols's full term. He next ran for and was elected to the California Assembly in 1967, where he served for 11 years as representative of the 17th (1967-1974) and 13th (1975-1978) assembly districts.[4] In 1978, Governor Edmund G. Brown Jr. appointed John Miller to the California Court of Appeal (1st District), where he served as an associate justice until the time of his death on February 17, 1985, from diabetes-related complications[5].

I left law practice with Allen Norris in 1968 to form a partnership with David B. Rosenthal, my old law-school classmate and friend. We named our firm Ramsey and Rosenthal; our offices were at 145 Park Place in Point Richmond, California, in a building that had been the original firehouse and jail for the city of Richmond. We remodeled the building as a law office but retained many of the original features. For example, we kept some of the original metal doors from when the structure was a jail; the walls in my office, which was one of the original drunk tanks, still had graffiti that had been written by prisoners. My legal secretary during most of the time I was in private practice was the able and loyal Betty Cadwallader

The city of Richmond constitutes an important aspect of both my professional and personal development. Just as my student years at Howard University and the University of California at Riverside contributed greatly to my intellectual development and confidence as a student, my time and experiences in Richmond were of even greater significance for my professional and political development.

Going back for a moment, I acquired my basic skills as a trial lawyer while working for the Contra Costa County District Attorney's Office. I do not know the exact number of trials I tried during the essentially two years I was with the office, but the number was substantial. In those days, the office was relatively small, and new deputies were given responsibility for charging and trying cases fairly early in their careers.

District Attorney John Nejedly had an office policy that if you charged a case and it went to trial, then it was your responsibility to try that case. I don't know how long one had to be in the office before being assigned responsibility as the "charging deputy," but that responsibility rotated weekly among the deputy DAs in the office. The charging deputy had responsibility each morning for receiving and reviewing police reports. After reading a report, interviewing the police officer representing the police department, and reviewing any other relevant information available, the charging deputy then had to decide whether to issue a criminal complaint.[6]

In most instances, the matter would be fairly straightforward, and the deputy would issue the complaint. There were times, however, when additional investigation or facts were needed, and the police would be so advised. In rare instances, the charging deputy would decide that, although a criminal complaint was not warranted, the matter was sufficiently serious or hazardous that the parties involved needed to be talked to and warned regarding their conduct.

The criminal complaint process in those days was similar to that used today. Criminal complaints were typically made to the police, but sometimes a private citizen would request a criminal complaint directly from the DA's Office. In such instances, the charging deputy would usually refer the complainant to the appropriate police department, but occasionally the matter would already have been reported to the police, and the person's grievance actually was that the police had failed to respond or act.

DA John Nejedly's custom was to have his charging deputies in appropriate cases issue a citation, which would be in the form of a letter requesting that people who were the subject of a complaint come to the DA's Office for a "hearing." The person was told in the letter that he or she had been complained against and that a failure to cooperate could result in a criminal complaint being issued. Many of the complaints made directly to the District Attorney's Office by private citizens were resolved through these informal citation hearings— disturbing the peace,[7] assault,[8] or criminal trespass.[9] Disturbing the peace typically involved neighbors—

sometimes longtime friends—getting into a dispute and one or both cursing out or threatening to beat up the other. In some instances, each
would accuse the other of having disturbed the peace by threats of violence or profane language. Another typical cause of such disputes would
be "trespassing" animals—wandering dogs and cats. A dispute over where
a fence line was or should be could lead to such charges.

I was assigned minor misdemeanor cases to try almost immediately
after joining the office, and also early on I was assigned to work as a
charging deputy. Thus I quickly gained jury trial experience. I still
vividly remember—and it was more than 40 years ago—my first jury
trial. It was in the Richmond Municipal Court[10] and involved a charge
of making an illegal left turn. In those days—1964—defendants could
actually demand a jury trial in most, if not all, traffic cases.[11] The
Honorable David Calfee was the trial judge; Donald Warden, now
Khalid Abdullah Tariq Al-Mansour, was the defense attorney; and John
Fontenberry, commonly known in the Richmond black community as
"Big John," was the defendant. The jury's verdict was guilty.

My second jury trial was in the San Pablo Municipal Court,[12] and
the charge was battery. The trial judge must have been the Honorable
C. Wilson Locke, because he was the sole judge in that court. I am
pretty certain Coleman "Coley" Fannin was the defense attorney, but I
have no recollection of the victim's or defendant's names. This case
involved a husband who had badly beaten his wife and then had uri-
nated on her as she lay on the floor.

I issued the complaint for that case after advising the complainant,
the wife, that office policy was to prosecute such cases even in instances
when the victim later requests that the case be dismissed, not an
unusual occurrence in domestic violence situations. It was the practice
in our office to give this admonition to wife victims because the policy
differed then in other Bay Area counties, where if a wife requested that
a case be dismissed, it was usually dismissed. In the San Pablo case, the
wife did later ask that the complaint be dismissed, and we refused.

As the deputy who issued the complaint, it was my responsibility to try the case. The victim wife was subpoenaed to appear at the trial, and I called her as my first witness. She immediately asserted her Fifth Amendment right against self-incrimination and refused to testify. I advised Judge Locke that I had no additional witnesses and, on a motion by the defense, he dismissed the case for lack of sufficient evidence. While it is possible that I would have lost the case even if the wife had testified, it is clear to me that the case was actually lost because of my inexperience.

An experienced deputy DA would immediately have granted immunity to the wife-witness and thereby deprived her of any legitimate right to refuse to testify on the basis of the Fifth Amendment.[13] Even a slightly more experienced deputy would have known to ask for a brief continuance so that he or she could call the office and ask how to address this unanticipated situation. Instead, it became just the first of my several painful learning experiences as a beginning trial lawyer.

Samuel Mesnic was the supervising deputy of the Richmond office during my tenure in the District Attorney's Office. While Sam was not a great trial lawyer, he certainly knew what was required to present an effective case to a jury. The advice that he gave me and the other deputies in the office—and that I came to respect and appreciate for the rest of my career as a trial lawyer and judge—was that one should make the case as simple as possible. In other words, the more complicated the case you present to the jury, the more likely it will be that their verdict will be against you.[14]

I don't know how many jury cases I have tried as a lawyer and presided over as a trial judge, but the number has to be more than 100. That experience has confirmed over and over that Sam's advice—especially when coupled with thorough preparation—is the best formula for successful presentation of a sound jury case. I commend it to any of you who aspire to be first-rate trial lawyers. It certainly stood me in good stead.

Another key principle that I learned while in the District Attorney's Office was the significance of direct examination. I learned that lesson not from Sam Mesnic or other deputies in the office but from a very good defense attorney whom I had occasion to try two or three cases against. I cannot recall his name, but I do remember his telling me that, in putting a witness on the stand, one should not, in his words, "simply put on a piece of protoplasm." Instead, put on a person, a human being. His technique during the initial examination of a witness (a time when an objection was unlikely or would not be sustained even if made) was to offer the witness's background for consideration by the judge and jury. He asked for not just the witness's name, but also his or her occupation, neighborhood of residence, length of time living in the state and community, family status (for example, married with children), and any additional background information he thought he could get away with. That way, each member of the jury would see the witness as a person and not just as a "witness." A great deal of attention is paid to cross-examination, but the effectiveness of direct examination can also determine whether a trial will be won or lost. I am certain that some of the trials I won during my career as a trial lawyer were the result of effective direct examinations.

This is all by way of saying that when I left the District Attorney's Office and went into private practice, the trial skills I had developed stood me in good stead as a defense attorney and civil trial lawyer. And jury trials that I won early in private practice contributed to the development of a solid reputation as an effective trial lawyer.

My first criminal cases as a private attorney came through appointments as defense counsel for indigent criminal defendants. A public defender's office had not yet been established in Contra Costa County. Each of the various trial courts maintained a list of local lawyers who were willing to accept appointments by the court to represent indigent defendants. The names of lawyers recently admitted to the bar and those who had trial experience but were new to private practice would be put at the top of almost every court's list of names eligible for appointment. A newly listed lawyer would then receive the next one or two appointments in cases he or she was qualified to handle. That is, if you were new to the bar, then there was zero chance that your first assignment would be a murder case or other serious felony. If you were at the top of the list in several of the west Contra Costa County courts (El Cerrito, Richmond, Rodeo, San Pablo), you could fairly quickly have a reasonably profitable caseload.

In addition to the appointed cases, Allen Norris and several other people whom I knew referred criminal cases to me. Some of Allen's civil clients would from time to time be charged with a criminal matter, and he would refer the case to me. In fact, I represented Allen's brother in a significant criminal matter that I tried before a jury. His brother was acquitted—both because I was a good lawyer and because he was innocent.

Friends and other associates—particularly those in the East Bay—also referred civil cases to me, thereby helping my practice to grow. It did not hurt that, as a new attorney in private practice with a small caseload, I had plenty of time to devote to each case entrusted to me and could resolve matters fairly quickly. It was my hope that news of my efficiency and effectiveness would spread and that people would bring their cases to me because they thought I would handle them more efficiently than the more established lawyers. That strategy for building a practice apparently worked, and it was not long before I was much in demand and quite busy.

I was active in the local community, and soon I had developed a reputation—particularly in black neighborhoods—as a reliable, aggressive, and effective fighter against injustice. I was available to give community organizations free legal advice. Groups such as Welfare Rights, local NAACP branches, North Richmond Neighborhood House, and ADVANCE [15] were recipients of my pro bono services. While pro bono representation did not generate any immediate income, it was helpful in spreading my reputation and therefore in gaining me new clients. In that respect, it was an indirect source of income.

It was and continues to be my view that the people of Richmond, mostly the black people, and my experiences as a trial lawyer in that community made me free. Explanation: I came to appreciate that many of the black people of Richmond would retain and pay me to handle their legal problems regardless of what my political activities were, what important Richmond or Bay Area economic interests I challenged, or how I might be viewed by members of the white community—particularly those involved in business and politics. I knew that would be the case so long as I remained a strong and effective advocate for them in their search for fairness and justice. In other words, I was free, within reason, to live my life as I saw fit and to determine my own destiny. I shall always be indebted to the black people who lived in Richmond, California, when I practiced law there for having confidence in me, and for making me free.

I was involved as a trial lawyer in several complex civil and criminal matters while in private practice. One of the most interesting of those cases was a summer 1969 criminal trial in Detroit, Michigan, where I was a member of a trial team representing Kenneth Cockrel, an activist lawyer in Detroit. Kenneth had been charged with criminal contempt as a consequence of remarks he made immediately after a Detroit Recorders Court judge had improperly terminated a preliminary hearing in which Kenneth was participating as a defense attorney. He later served as a member of the Detroit City Council (January 1978 to December 1981). A "self-described Marxist," as the *New York Times* referred to him, Kenneth Cockrel "could talk a dog off a meat truck."[16]

This was a time of high racial tension between members of the Detroit police department and residents of Detroit's black community. On one occasion in 1969, there was a violent confrontation between a group of black people, members of the Republic of New Africa[17] who had taken shelter in the New Bethel AME Church, and some Detroit police officers. Police representatives later claimed that shots had been fired from the New Bethel church at the officers, killing one officer and seriously wounding another. Arrest warrants were later issued for several persons who were said to have been present in the church at that time. Later, upon learning that he was wanted, one of those persons voluntarily went to a police station in Detroit and surrendered. This was the person who was being represented by Kenneth Cockrel at the preliminary hearing.

The controversy involving Cockrel started when toward the end of the preliminary hearing and after the prosecution had rested its case, Judge Joseph Maher refused to hear testimony being presented by the defense, notwithstanding the fact that Michigan statutory law specifically permitted the defense to call witnesses and to offer evidence at a preliminary hearing. After holding the defendant to answer for the felony charge lodged against him, and as he was leaving the bench to return to his chambers, Judge Maher announced over his shoulder that he was doubling the defendant's bail.

Almost immediately after that, in a hallway outside the courtroom and beyond the judge's hearing, Kenneth Cockrel was asked by a reporter, "What just happened in [that courtroom]?" Cockrel replied (on television and, I might add, in living color) that Judge Maher had failed to comply with Michigan law in denying the defendant's offer of witnesses and that the bail increase was wrongful for three reasons: First, probably no one had requested that bail be increased; second, the amount imposed was excessive and, therefore, confiscatory; and third, it had been imposed without affording the defendant an opportunity to be heard on the matter.

In his response to the reporter's question, Kenneth Cockrel also referred to the judge as a "racist, honky dog fool; a pirate, bandit, and a thief, who calls himself a judge." He said the judge was acting like "a lackey of the district attorney's office." When asked what his position would be if the judge should take umbrage at his remarks and hold him in contempt, Kenneth said that if the judge could show that what he (the judge) had done was lawful, he (Cockrel) "would welcome being held in contempt." "In fact," he said, "I invite the judge to hold me in contempt." Not too many days later, Judge Maher in effect accepted Cockrel's invitation.

Several attorneys on Kenneth Cockrel's defense team enjoyed prominent reputations, local and national. Sheldon Otis was an excel-

K<small>ENNETH</small> C<small>OCKREL</small> *(left) and* H<small>ENRY</small> R<small>AMSEY</small> J<small>R</small>. *at a "People's Court" rally in Detroit, Mich., in 1969.*

lent and well-known Detroit lawyer who served as chief strategist for the team. Howard Moore of Atlanta, Georgia, who had represented Julian Bond in his litigation with the state of Georgia, was a member of the team. Harry Philo was a prominent Detroit personal injury and labor lawyer. Another team member was Arthur Kinoy, a U.S. Constitutional law expert from the Rutgers University School of Law in New Jersey.

What I found most interesting about the criminal contempt trial was the defense team's assertion of truth and the First Amendment of the U.S. Constitution as defenses. We asserted that the Constitution afforded Kenneth Cockrel a First Amendment right to criticize the judge's unlawful behavior. It was also our position that, in essence, the only limitations upon that right were that the criticism be made in good faith, be truthful, and not interfere with the administration of justice. Whether the criticism was in good or bad taste was irrelevant. We said that this was particularly true where, as here, the criticism was being made by a lawyer in an effort to inform the community about an injustice occurring in the courts. In this instance—when the offending words were spoken—Cockrel was neither speaking to the judge nor even in a courtroom, but rather was in a public hallway attempting to speak to the public through the media.

It was our position that in describing this injustice to members of the black community, particularly low-income people living in Detroit's inner city, Kenneth Cockrel was permitted—indeed obligated—to use words that persons within that community would understand. It was the defense team's position that, as a black lawyer, Kenneth not only had a right, but also, given what was happening at the time in Detroit, a professional responsibility to inform the people of Detroit—especially the members of the black community—about how the New Bethel defendants were being denied justice. So when the judge at the preliminary hearing wrongfully increased bail on this black defendant, one accurate way to describe his conduct was that he had acted like a "pirate, bandit, and a thief." When he refused to permit the defense to call witnesses as permitted by law, the judge was behaving like "a lackey of the district attorney's office."

The most difficult language to justify was "racist, honky dog fool." But we had an explanation even for that, plus prominent anthropologists and linguists who were willing to testify as to why—in describing the judge's conduct at the preliminary hearing to members of Detroit's inner city—that language was not only accurate and appropriate but indispensable.

The trial was held before Judge Joseph Sullivan of the Wayne County Circuit Court, a trial court of general jurisdiction. There was widespread interest in the case among people in Detroit, especially black residents. Unfortunately, seating in the courtroom was quite limited, and there was no television coverage of the trial. Therefore, each trial day at the end of court proceedings members of the trial team would go to nearby Kennedy Square and give a report to persons present, including members of the press, about what had occurred in court that day. These after-court sessions were well attended by hundreds of members of the public. Indeed, these sessions quickly came to be publicly known as "the people's court."

The resolution of this important litigation was achieved when the prosecution essentially "sued for peace." Justice Michael D. O'Hara, a former justice of the Michigan Supreme Court who was acting as the special prosecutor in the case, met with a small group of defense lawyers to discuss settlement. After extended discussion, Justice O'Hara said that if Kenneth Cockrel would apologize to Judge Maher, the charges would be dismissed.

Kenneth was disinclined to apologize, but after extended discussion, we defense lawyers prevailed in our more reasonable judgment that he should be willing to issue some sort of apology. Admittedly, the fact that the prosecution had approached us and asked if a way could be found to settle the case spoke volumes about the weakness of their case (or, perhaps, the strength of ours) and about the effectiveness of our presentation in Judge Sullivan's court (as well as in the people's court).

Still one can never be absolutely certain of success in any trial—court or jury. The potential consequences for Kenneth were substantial and grave—a sizable fine, possible imprisonment, and certainly disbarment. Given that all he was being asked to do was apologize, as compared to what was at risk, the choice was obvious to defense team members.

In the end, Judge Maher and Justice O'Hara accepted a written apology stating that while Kenneth did not think he had done anything wrong, if his words had been misinterpreted, then he expressed regret for that misinterpretation. And that was the end of the matter. Every member of the defense team was happy with that outcome and proud as well to have had the opportunity to participate in the trial and to work with the outstanding lawyers on the defense team. It was a very satisfied Henry Ramsey Jr. who returned to Richmond after the trial.

During the time I lived there, Richmond had a network of city-supported and highly effective neighborhood councils. The city provided a coordinator, who was on the city's payroll and whose office printed newsletters for the various neighborhood councils as well as notices of and agendas for their separate meetings. Just this limited support contributed greatly to the level of civic participation by the residents in the various neighborhoods.

I lived in the Plaza II neighborhood and was involved with the Plaza II Neighborhood Council. We had regular meetings where issues of neighborhood and citywide concern were discussed and action plans were developed. Richmond's neighborhood council program was an effective means for educating city residents about municipal affairs and projects. The program also showed them how to petition the city, county, state, and federal governments concerning proposals and grievances. It was a sad day and great loss for Richmond when the coordinator and other support for the neighborhood council program were eliminated because of budget cuts.

When the city of Richmond was founded in 1905, most residents lived in what is now called Point Richmond, and that continued to be the case until the United States entered World War II. On December

11, 1940, a year before the bombing of Pearl Harbor, the U.S. government contracted with Kaiser Industries to build ships—primarily transport vessels—in shipyards to be constructed in Richmond, with its natural deep-water port. In the next few years, with so many of the nation's male population being drafted into the armed forces, there was a great need for nontraditional workers—women, people of color, and older people—in the shipyards.

Kaiser Industries dispatched agents to the South and Southwest—primarily Alabama, Arkansas, Louisiana, Mississippi, Oklahoma, and Texas—to recruit workers. African American workers, perhaps for the first time since Reconstruction, were being offered an opportunity to work in significant numbers in the skilled trades. African American adults who had not been drafted into military service and were unlikely to be found eligible for the draft seized this opportunity for good jobs. Hundreds of thousands—if not millions—of African American men and women left their home states in the South for wartime job opportunities in the West (Arizona, California, Oregon, and Washington), the Midwest (Illinois, Indiana, Michigan, Ohio), and the Northeast (Massachusetts, New York, and Pennsylvania). Wartime jobs also existed in the South (in Norfolk, Virginia, and Charleston, South Carolina), but there was a great migration of black workers and black families out of the South and to the Northeast, Midwest, and West.

Many wartime workers who came to the San Francisco Bay Area obtained housing and work in Alameda, Oakland, Richmond, San Francisco, and Vallejo. They worked mostly at the Kaiser shipyards in Richmond, Hunter's Point Navy Yard in San Francisco, the Vallejo shipyards, Port Costa Naval Weapons Station, Todd Shipyard of Oakland, and the Alameda Naval Air Station. Richmond's population in the 1940 census was 23,600. In 1950, four years after World War II ended, it had increased to 99,545. (When Evelyn and I moved to Richmond in 1964, its population stood at approximately 75,000.) Temporary dwellings were constructed to house those needed new workers.

Many of those individuals were among the African American residents of Richmond whom I sought to represent when I initially rented office space from Allen Norris at 1016 Nevin Avenue and began the private practice of law. While I did not limit my law practice to the representation of African Americans, the socio-economic and racial realities of that time (and probably still today) meant that the overwhelming majority of my clients would, in fact, be African Americans.

## Activism

*I* QUICKLY BECAME IMMERSED IN local politics and community activism. "Bert" Coffey was a leader in the local Democratic Party and a close friend of Allen Norris. Bert's office was in the same building as Allen's at 1016 Nevin; in fact, Bert Coffey may have been part-owner of the building. It was through Bert that I became involved with the official Democratic Party apparatus in west Contra Costa County.

My instinctive support for civil and human rights and my fundamental antagonism against unfairness and belief in "the imperative of racial justice"[18] led to my becoming involved with many of Richmond's community activists. Quite a few young adult and middle-aged members of Richmond's black population were fighting hard to improve the lot of African Americans throughout western Contra Costa County, especially in Richmond. Most efforts were directed toward significantly increasing the percentage of African Americans within Richmond's civic and political leadership; providing better and increased job and housing opportunities for people of color; creating better schools; eliminating police brutality and other police misconduct; and substantially reducing, if not eliminating, racial discrimination in Richmond and nearby communities. I hasten to add that several Caucasian liberal activists were involved in the efforts.

I cannot recall all of the names of Richmond's community activists from that time, but I do remember several:[19] Booker T. Anderson,[20] Savannah Bello, Napoleon Britt, *Elton Brombacher,*[21] George D. Carroll,[22] *Lucretia Edwards,* Maxine Eason, Charlesetta Ford, Terry Hatter,[23] John

Haynes, Meadie Jackson, William "Bill" Lucy,[24] "Jim" McMillan,[25] *David Pierce*,[26] Dorothy Pitts, *Raymond Sawyer*, Jessie Smallwood, *Red Stevenson*,[27] and Larry Williams.[28]

I have already told you that I provided pro bono legal representation for several community groups in Richmond. In addition, I was appointed to the city of Richmond's Human Relations Commission. Later, on January 3, 1967, I was appointed a member of the Richmond Redevelopment Agency for a four-year term.[29] I served a term as chairman of each body.

## PERSONAL CHANGES

EVELYN YVONNE RAMSEY AND I were divorced in September 1967. Some of you may ask, "So what happened?" I cannot give you a definitive answer. I could tell you that sometimes marriages just don't work out, but if you are an adult, you already know that. My thoughts about why Evelyn and I divorced are not all that profound, but they are genuine. It is my view that neither one of us was mature enough to hold our marriage together when the inevitable stresses and strains within a marriage developed. After I left the DA's Office, most of my waking hours were devoted to building my law practice. That effort required more than simply meeting with clients and going to court. It also involved trying to get well known in the community, especially the black community, and to develop a sterling reputation for providing outstanding service. This effort involved (as I saw it, required) attending lots of community meetings, political events, some social events, and the like. Obviously and unfortunately, it also meant that I didn't spend a great deal of time at home with Evelyn and our boys. ROBERT ALLEN RAMSEY was born in 1965, a couple of years after we moved to Richmond, and Evelyn had what amounted to sole care of the three. It must have been frustrating for her that I was away from home so much of the time.

It is my present view that neither of us was mature enough to appreciate and understand each other's needs in that regard. I surmise that she saw my time away from home—particularly at night and on weekends—not so much as an effort to build a practice but as my being engaged in activities that were interesting, exciting, and fun. Her response was to frequently complain about the need for material things—not extravagant items like jewelry and expensive clothes but practical needs, such as a dishwasher, clothes dryer, or washing machine. But, in my judgment, as I look back on the matter, what she actually wanted and needed was for me to spend more time at home with her, particularly in the evenings. She wanted and needed for me to be home to help with our boys and also to pay attention and show affection for her. But she was not mature enough to understand and tell me that was what she needed and wanted. Instead, she complained to me about her need for *things*.

For my part, although I was now more than 30 years old, I was not mature or insightful enough to see that my wife and children needed me just as much I needed to devote time to building a law practice. Evelyn asked for things and I worked to provide them. So why wasn't she happy? This was a significant deficit on my part. I should have been able to recognize my wife's needs for attention, support, help with the boys, and reliable companionship. It was not things or the lack of things that was the issue. The issue was me. Unfortunately, I did not look beyond my own interests, needs, and wants.

Regardless of what either of us contributed to the strain on our marriage, the fact is that—40 years later—I cannot say with any certainty or confidence why we broke up. The fact is that we did divorce and go on with our lives. I don't know what Evelyn would say about the question, but what I am writing here is my honest appraisal of why our marriage failed. I recognize that such a complex issue is neither easy to understand nor as simple as I suggest here.

When Evelyn and I separated in late January 1967, neither of us knew that she was pregnant at the time. Our youngest son, ISMAIL JOMO RAMSEY, was born in San Francisco on October 3, 1967, shortly after our divorce in Contra Costa County on September 11, 1967.

Approximately two years later, on September 7, 1969, I married ELEANOR ANNE MASON, a graduate student at UC Berkeley. I asked her to marry me one evening as we sat next to Baisley Pond during a visit to her hometown of Jamaica, New York. Our wedding ceremony was held in the faculty glade on the UC Berkeley campus, between the faculty club building and the School of Music. Allen Broussard, then an Oakland municipal court judge, officiated. Eleanor's attendants were Dorothy Bropleh, Jacquelyn Fletcher, Priscilla Hilliard, and Lou Margaret Holland. Donald Warden was my best man. David Rosenthal, Marvin Smith, Harold Redic, and George W. Mason, one of Eleanor's brothers, served as ushers and as escorts for the bridesmaids.

A few days after our wedding, Eleanor and I left on a six-week honeymoon. Our first stop was in Jamaica, Queens, New York, for a couple of days. There we enjoyed a marriage reception—hosted by her father—for Eleanor's New York friends and for members of her family who had been unable to travel to California for our wedding. We then traveled, in order, to a number of capital cities: London, England; Paris, France; Rome, Italy; Cairo, Egypt; Addis Ababa, Ethiopia; Nairobi, Kenya; Dar es Salaam, Tanzania; Lagos, Nigeria; and Cotonou, Dahomey.[30] We were scheduled to fly also to Dakar, the capital of Senegal, as our last stop, but I was almost totally exhausted. When we got to the airport in Cotonou for the flight to Dakar, I noticed that the Air Afrique plane we were to take was actually a Pan American plane en route to New York, with a scheduled stop in Dakar.

To my later regret, I told Eleanor that I was staying on the plane until it reached New York. I was simply beat. I say the decision was to my later regret because I did get to Dakar a few years later and met Ami Sow, the friend of Eleanor's whom we had been scheduled to stay with. Ami and her family are lovely people, and we were shown a wonderful time. I very much regretted that I had not taken advantage of the opportunity to meet Ami and to visit Senegal during our honeymoon in September and October 1969. But on our return to the United States, I think I slept for three straight days.

THE WEDDING OF ELEANOR ANNE MASON *and* HENRY RAMSEY JR., *Faculty Glade, University of California Berkeley, September 7, 1969. From left, Walter Mason (partly hidden), Khalid Abdullah Tariq al-Mansour (then Donald Warden), and Harold Redic, with Allen Broussard (back to camera) officiating.*

ELEANOR ANNE MASON, *September 7, 1969.*

When Eleanor and I married, I was living in a two-bedroom house at 5012 State Avenue in Richmond that I had purchased in 1968. Several weeks after we returned from our honeymoon, Evelyn, my ex-wife, delivered the four boys to our house without notice. I shortly thereafter initiated court proceedings to get custody of our children. When my four young sons came to live with us that fateful morning in 1970, it was immediately obvious that we needed additional space. Eleanor and I purchased a four-bedroom home the following year at 2607 Woolsey Street in Berkeley. Her father loaned us a significant portion of the down payment. We decided to purchase a home in Berkeley primarily because of the quality of the schools, public and private.

### · Notes ·

1. I think it was 423 but am unsure. It was one of the two units that constituted the duplex, either 423 or 427. The fronts of the two units have been changed; from the street, one cannot see the front door of either apartment. The duplex is located on South 45th Street where it intersects with Cutting Boulevard, on the northwest corner of the intersection and diagonally across Cutting Boulevard from John F. Kennedy High School.
2. That address on Nevin no longer exists today, the building having been demolished as part of a redevelopment project. I think a Kaiser Hospital now covers that spot.
3. Located at 6026 Idaho Street in Oakland.
4. These assembly districts essentially covered the California cities of Albany and Berkeley, as well as north and west Oakland.
5. See "The Political Graveyard: Index to Politicians" at politicalgraveyard.com/bio/miller5.html.
6. Except in special cases—such as homicide, armed robbery, or certain particularly heinous felonies—there would typically be one or two detectives who had responsibility during a given period (e.g., several months) for presenting all of the matters from a given police department to the District Attorney's Office for a criminal complaint.
7. California Penal Code Sec. 415.
8. California Penal Code Sec. 242.
9. California Penal Code Sec. 602.
10. Located in Richmond, CA.

11. Several years later California changed the law to reclassify most traffic offenses as infractions instead of misdemeanors and thereby disallowed jury trials in traffic matters.

12. Located in San Pablo, CA.

13. A general grant of immunity would have deprived her, the witness, of any right to refuse to testify on the grounds of a right against self-incrimination. Giving her immunity for any offense associated with the current criminal charge would mean there would be no other charge for which her testimony could possibly incriminate her.

14. Oliver Wendell Holmes Jr. was essentially saying the same thing when he wrote, "I would not give a fig for the simplicity this side of complexity, but I would give my life for the simplicity on the other side of complexity."

15. This organization was started by Professor Harry Specht and the U.C. School of Social Work. Ms. Dorothy Pitts was the Executive Director. "Dudley Randall Rediscovered," by Kim D. Hunter, at www.solidarity-us.org.

16. *New York Times*, "Fights Break Up a Rally of Nazis in Detroit," Aug. 23, 1981 (on www.nytimes.com). The "meat truck" description is from "Dudley Randall Rediscovered," a book review by Kim D. Hunter on www.solidarity-us.org.

17. The Republic of New Afrika was a movement intent on establishing an independent homeland for black Americans within the continental United States. In 1968, Milton R. Henry, the leader of the "Black Government Conference" in Detroit announced that Mississippi, Louisiana, Alabama, Georgia, and South Carolina were to constitute this new country. See, for example, Molefi Kete Asante and Ama Mazama, eds., *Encyclopedia of Black Studies* (Thousand Oaks: Sage Publications, 2004) at pp. 416-417.

18. Mark V. Tushnet, *Making Civil Rights Law: Thurgood Marshall and the Supreme Court, 1936–1961* (New York: Oxford University Press, 1994), p. 138.

19. Names of Caucasians are in *italics*.

20. Booker T. Anderson was then the pastor of the Easter Hill Methodist Church.

21. Elton Brombacher owned a printing plant and was an activist in the Democratic Party, particularly in Contra Costa County.

22. George D. Carroll was then on the bench and hence could no longer be politically active.

23. Terry Hatter was then an assistant U.S. attorney in the San Francisco office and years later was appointed to the U.S. District Court for the Central District (Los Angeles) of California.

24. In 1972, Bill Lucy became the elected International Secretary-Treasurer, the second-highest ranking officer of the 1.3 million-member American Federation of State, County and Municipal Employees (AFSCME), and he has served in that position since then. He is also a founder and the first and only president of the Coalition of Black Trade Unionists (CBTU), which was formed in 1972.

25. Jim McMillan was then a local pharmacist. He was elected to the Richmond City Council years later and served three consecutive full terms.

26. David Pierce was then a member of the Richmond City Council. He was later elected mayor of the city of Richmond.

27. Red Stevenson was then Executive Director of North Richmond Neighborhood House. Neighborhood House of North Richmond is a private, nonprofit, multi-service agency with a community-based tradition of over 48 years of addressing neighborhood needs and supporting residents in their efforts to uplift their lives. Founded in 1954 by the American Friends Service Committee, a Quaker group, Neighborhood House has become a multi-service, social advocacy agency. Originally perceived as an African American voice for low-income families, the agency transformed itself into a refuge for Southeast Asians and Mexican immigrants during the urban migration of 1975. It has since evolved into a multi-faceted, multicultural hub for families of many ethnicities and races.

28. Larry Williams went on to become the director of personnel and subsequently Deputy General Manager for the Bay Area Rapid Transit District.

29. Resolution No. 9076 of the Council of the City of Richmond, dated January 3, 1967. A copy of the resolution is in my personal files.

30. The political capital city of what is now Benin, but the country was then named Dahomey.

# 12

# *Professor of Law*

I left Ramsey and Rosenthal and the private practice of law in 1971 to join the faculty at the UC Berkeley School of Law (Boalt Hall) as an associate professor of law. For 10 years, I taught first-year basic criminal law plus criminal procedure, an advanced course. I was granted tenure and became a full professor of law in 1979.

I very much enjoyed my tenure as a Boalt Hall faculty member. All of my faculty colleagues were friendly and supportive. Babette Barton, Richard Buxbaum, Albert Ehrenzweig, John Hetland, Richard Jennings, Herma Hill Kay,[1] Justin Sweet, and Preble Stolz were colleagues who had been members of the Boalt faculty when I was a law student. In academic year 1977–78, although still on the Boalt faculty, I taught as a visiting professor at the University of Colorado's Fleming Law Center in Boulder. I also taught criminal law at the University of Texas School of Law in Austin during the summer of 1977. In those 10 years, Eleanor and I were blessed with two daughters, Yetunde Olaniyi Ramsey, born February 12, 1973, and Abeni Baderinwa Ramsey, born October 23, 1974.

I drove across the country with my four sons toward the end of the summer of 1977, while Eleanor and the girls remained in Berkeley. The boys and I visited various state capital buildings during our trip— Austin, Texas; Baton Rouge, Louisiana; Montgomery, Alabama; Atlanta, Georgia; Raleigh, North Carolina; Richmond, Virginia; Harrisburg, Pennsylvania; Trenton, New Jersey; Boston, Massachusetts; Albany, New York; and Denver, Colorado. During the drive from California to Austin, Texas, we also visited Carlsbad Caverns and White Sands, New Mexico, and Juarez, Mexico. On the roundabout drive from Texas to Colorado, three of the boys—Githaiga, Robert, and

Ismail–and I visited the Basketball Hall of Fame in Springfield, Massachusetts; the Baseball Hall of Fame in Cooperstown, New York; and the Football Hall of Fame in Canton, Ohio.

Eleanor and the girls and the three boys and I were reunited in Boulder, Colorado, in September 1977. (Charles had returned to Richmond, California, with the assistance of his mother and lived with her during that year.) We lived in the Table Mesa neighborhood during our school year in Boulder. Githaiga attended Southern Hills Jr. High School and Robert and Ismail attended Bear Creek Elementary School. In June 1978 we returned to Berkeley, where I resumed teaching at Boalt and Eleanor–having earned her Ph.D. in anthropology from UC Berkeley–received a postdoctoral fellowship funded by the U.S. Department of Health and Human Services.

A significant amount of my time as a Boalt faculty member was devoted to counseling students. Faculty performance at the university level is typically judged by three standards–teaching, scholarship (research and publication), and service to the university (various committee assignments). Unfortunately, this meant that some of the faculty were not very accessible to students outside of the classroom, other than during scheduled office hours. This was especially significant for students of color, who, because they were a small minority among the student body, often felt less supported and appreciated.

I essentially had an open-door policy and because of my race, personality, and willingness to talk with them, students–especially black students–sought me out for counseling and advice. While their questions mostly concerned academic issues, they also asked for advice about personal matters and family problems. The topics might include career opportunities within the legal profession, academic performance, summer internships, judicial clerkships, marriage problems, romantic problems, concerns about a particular professor, financial difficulties, problems with or responsibility for family members, housing, transportation, and other matters. Although time-consuming, this aspect of my job was personally very rewarding.

I would also, from time to time, invite small groups of black students to my home (exactly 1 mile from Boalt Hall) for an evening meal and just to talk about being a law student. We would discuss how to succeed in law school and how to best prepare oneself for a career as a lawyer. Occasionally former students from my tenure as a faculty member at Boalt Hall express gratitude for the support I provided when they were in law school. I am always touched by and appreciative of their cards, e-mail messages, or verbal comments.

A significant number of Berkeley undergraduates—and a few from other schools—often sought my advice about the law schools they should consider attending. I was always willing to discuss and give general advice on this subject but would never tell a student what school I thought he or she should apply to. Besides my experience as a law teacher I also gained knowledge about legal education from serving for some years on the accreditation committee of the American Bar Association's Section on Legal Education and Admission to the Bar, but my comments to those students were mostly about the law school application process itself. We talked about factors relevant to that choice: location (urban, rural, or small town); student body and faculty size (large, medium, or small); means for financing one's legal education (grants, loans, employment, savings); curriculum; bar passage rate; diversity; and placement facilities.

I would tell law school applicants not to focus on a law school's national reputation or ranking—for example, the *U.S. News and World Report* rankings. I always told them that the question to be asked was "Do I want to attend law school?" and not "Do I want to attend Boalt Hall, or Harvard?" If you want to attend Boalt, Duke, Georgetown, Harvard, NYU, Michigan, Stanford, Virginia, or Yale, no matter how smart you are, the chances of being admitted are substantially against you. And there are several other of the 25 "top 10" law schools where the odds are against you. With from 7,000 to 9,000 applications being filed at each of the elite schools, there are simply not enough seats to admit even one-tenth of the students who apply. So, I told them, if you think only about the elite schools, then the chances are strongly against you.

It was and continues to be my view that students, after realistically evaluating their undergraduate grade point average and law school admission test scores, should try to identify two or three ideal or dream schools where they will apply, two or three other schools where their numbers (UGPA and LSAT score) make them competitive, and two additional schools where their numbers almost ensure admission.[2]

In 1968, after the assassination of Martin Luther King Jr., the Boalt Hall faculty had established an effective affirmative action program that continued until it was terminated October 1, 1996 as a result of Proposition 209.[3] Because of the controversy regarding affirmative action, many of the minority students were seriously affected—psychologically and emotionally—by implications that students admitted to law school through such programs, particularly black and Hispanic students, were unqualified or, at best, less qualified than many rejected white applicants. I had many lengthy conversations with individual Boalt minority students, or sometimes small groups of them, about those concerns.

My aim in those conversations was to help the students keep their confidence. In almost every instance, the minority student would be a good student but still would be anxious about surviving—or excelling—in law school. In other words, the student might not be concerned about completing law school but would be concerned that he or she was not in the top quarter or top half of the class. There would also be concerns about career opportunities.

Comments made by their white colleagues, insensitive comments in class by a professor, statements by politicians, negative articles about affirmative action in newspapers and academic journals—all of these took their toll, which was understandable, given the other pressures suffered by all law students regardless of skin color, gender, or ethnicity. The comments were typically to the effect that minority students, particularly black and Hispanic students, didn't belong in law school and

PROFESSOR HENRY RAMSEY JR. AND STUDENTS at Boalt Hall.

were likely to fail. In fact, black and Hispanic students were neither unqualified nor more likely to fail.[4] So, as a black faculty member, I accepted that my special responsibility was to help minority students through the difficulties of attending law school. The black and Hispanic students who were not admitted through affirmative action had their qualifications questioned just the same. This was less true for Asian students, especially Japanese, or for the very few Native Americans enrolled at Boalt (or any other ABA-approved law school) in any given year.

Also while on the Boalt faculty I handled several cases *pro bono*. As a matter of fact, I did not accept any cases for compensation during that period. I adopted a personal rule shortly after being appointed to the Boalt faculty that I would try always to be handling at least one case *pro bono*, and then I adopted a second personal rule: If I had gone for more than six months without handling a *pro bono* case, then I would accept the next request for *pro bono* representation that came through my door, no matter how complex or difficult it was, assuming I was competent to handle the matter. The following are three types of matters that I handled *pro bono* while teaching at Boalt Hall:

> Representation of a black male undergraduate student who had been in a fight with some intoxicated white UC Berkeley tennis team members at Larry Blake's[5] and was charged with the crime of battery. He was found not guilty.
>
> Representation of a white male UC criminology professor who had been arrested and charged with the crime of interfering with a police officer in the performance of his duties, during a demonstration at People's Park. The professor was acquitted of the charges.
>
> Representation of a law student who had been arrested and charged with the crime of burglary when he, being quite intoxicated at the time, broke into a house that he mistakenly thought was his own. I was able to get the charges dismissed.

Not all of my *pro bono* representation was in criminal cases. For example, I successfully represented a law student whose landlord was wrongfully trying to evict her.

I was usually in compliance with my self-imposed *pro bono* rule and can remember being "burned" only once. I had not represented a *pro bono* client for several months, and the next case that walked into my office was a federal criminal matter that was quite serious.[6] My client turned out to be an 18-year-old black male with no previous criminal or juvenile record. He and several older young adults had been observed engaging in target practice on a rifle range at Fort Ord in Salinas County, California.

This was a time when some African Americans as well as whites sought military-type training in anticipation of a racial conflict or race war. Some of the people who saw the young men engaged in target practice had called the military police because the weapons being used appeared to be military rifles, specifically M16s. My client and the other defendants were not dressed in military clothing, and the informants did not think they were soldiers. After their arrest, it was quickly determined that the rifles being used by the defendants were, in fact, stolen military property.

I was "burned" in that the case was highly political. The U.S. Attorney's Office took a very tough stance notwithstanding my client's age and lack of any prior criminal record, and the pretrial negotiations were tense, involved, and extended. I was ultimately able to achieve a reasonable result for my client because of his age and lack of criminal record. Nevertheless, the case required a great deal of time and effort on my part before it could be satisfactorily resolved.

While a member of the law faculty at UC Berkeley I campaigned for and was elected to the Berkeley City Council. I served one term, 1973–77. Those times were tumultuous for the council and I found the hours particularly difficult. It was not unusual for council meetings, which were scheduled to begin at 7:00 on most Tuesday nights, to last until after midnight. On one or two occasions, they lasted literally all night. The demands of the council position made it very difficult for me to meet my responsibilities as a law professor. For this reason I did not seek a second term. My experience as a member of the Berkeley City Council is discussed in greater detail in the "Memorable Events" section.

We had been living at 2607 Woolsey Street for about five years when Eleanor and I purchased our house on Avalon Avenue. We already had four children—Charles, Githaiga, Robert, and Ismail—when we purchased the three-bedroom house at 2607 Woolsey Street and moved to Berkeley in 1971. Because they were all boys, two could share a bedroom, and Eleanor and I could have our room. Eleanor was studying for her Ph.D. in anthropology at UC Berkeley, and I was teaching at the law school. Our house was in the Elmwood neighborhood on Berkeley's south side and about 1.5 miles from the UC Berkeley campus.

After Yetunde was born in February 1973 and Abeni in October 1974, we had six children, four boys and two girls, so three bedrooms became inadequate. The boys, particularly the older two, Charles and Githaiga, were now at the ages when conflicts between siblings often arose, and with their personalities the conflicts sometimes could be intense. In any case, it soon became clear to us that our family needed additional living space.

Eleanor discovered a house for sale on Avalon Avenue, not far from the Elmwood neighborhood and even closer to the university. It was particularly attractive to us because it theoretically had eight bedrooms. There clearly were seven bedrooms; therefore, each child could have his or her own room. The purchase price was substantial for that time, but it was affordable, given the equity we had gained in the Woolsey Street property and assuming we were prudent in managing our future income.

So on April 22, 1977, Eleanor and I purchased—for $140,000—our present home at 2955 Avalon Avenue in Berkeley's Claremont Court neighborhood.[7] We moved in shortly after. From then on, whenever there was a conflict or argument between any of the children, I could point out that each person had his or her own space to retire to and could easily avoid any further conflict.

We purchased the house from Gilbert Barron, M.D., and his wife, Mary Grace Barron. Gilbert Barron had recently announced his retirement as head of the surgery department at Alta Bates Hospital. Some history of our home: It was designed by architects George T. Plowman and John Hudson Thomas[8] and built in 1909 by Daily Pacific Builder at a cost of $7,700. The contractor was E.J. Squires of 2117 Rose Street, Berkeley, and the first owner was Richard C. Shaw, a mining engineer. The house was remodeled in 1913 by Walter H. Ratcliff Jr. at a cost of $2,000. A Berkeley Architectural Heritage Association brochure for a house tour in 1983 says, "Most of the houses Plowman and Thomas produced [in this period] fit comfortably and quietly into the Craftsman tradition of early twentieth century American architecture. Their Craftsman houses are not, like Maybeck's work of the same period, idiosyncratic and radical essays in this rustic style; they combine simple forms and natural materials to create perfect environments for the unfettered style of living which was idealized by their clients."[9]

At the time we purchased it in 1977, the house was 8,700 square feet, and we have not added to that. But Eleanor and I have made significant improvements. I suppose the major change is that we completely remodeled and modernized the kitchen. The bathroom adjoining the master bedroom has also been "taken down to the studs" and modernized. Another major project was landscaping the backyard and constructing a pergola. We also put in a modern lighting system that illuminates the artwork in our house and can be controlled from central panels on the first and second floors.

With the move we still had the advantages of Berkeley schools, and the house was convenient to my work at the law school. The Claremont Court neighborhood, one of Berkeley's finest, has very low crime statistics. Besides excellent neighborhood schools it has convenient neighborhood services—grocery stores, drugstores, hardware store, banks, butcher shops, a movie theater, gas stations, and dry cleaners. There are also several good restaurants within easy walking distance.

As mentioned, I spent the summer of 1977 teaching criminal law at the University of Texas at Austin and the 1977–78 academic year teaching criminal law and criminal procedure at the University of Colorado's Fleming Law Center. We leased our house in Berkeley for that academic year, spent the year in Boulder, and resumed living in Berkeley during the summer of 1978. I continued to serve as a member of the Boalt faculty from fall 1978 until fall 1981.

We gained an extended-family member during the late 1980s. Of all our children, Abeni presented the greatest challenge to her parents in getting her through high school and college. When Abeni was in high school, we met Maria Carmen Rodriguez, a young Mexican American woman who was working with minority students at Berkeley High School as part of an effort to motivate them to graduate from high school and prepare for college. Maria was working for a program called MESA (Math, Engineering, and Science Achievement),[10] a program jointly sponsored by the University of California at Berkeley and Berkeley High School.

When we first came to know Maria, she had just graduated from UC Berkeley with an undergraduate degree in mathematics, and Eleanor and I were looking for a tutor for Abeni, with an emphasis on mathematics. We heard about Maria from a teacher at Berkeley High and asked her if she would be willing to tutor Abeni. It was our hope that Maria—closer in age and cultural values to Abeni than we were—would become a mentor and role model for Abeni and help improve parent-teenager communication.

We quickly became very fond of Maria, and she liked us and all of our children. Within a relatively short time, Maria essentially became a part of our family. She never lived in our home but visited us often and spent substantial amounts of time at our house. Indeed, I think it would be fair to say she regarded our house as home. She interacted with our children like siblings, and our granddaughters all call her Auntie Marie. Maria calls me her Berkeley dad.

Maria Carmen Rodriguez was born on February 19, 1964, in Cueramaro, Guanajuato, Mexico. Her parents are Isidro and Maria Rodriguez. Our Maria attended Huntington Park High School in Los Angeles and graduated in June 1982. She earned her undergraduate degree in mathematics from UC Berkeley in 1987 and an M.B.A. degree from the University of Illinois in 1994.

Immediately after receiving her M.B.A., Maria began working for Hewlett Packard Corporation in Mountain View, California, as a financial analyst. She worked at HP during most of the next seven years as financial analyst, consultant, and pricing manager. After HP, she worked as a pricing director at several Silicon Valley software companies. Her last position in the United States was as senior pricing manager at Cisco Systems.

She married John Norris, a native of England, on August 30, 2003, and they have one child, a son named George Henry Norris, born on September 21, 2004, at Kaiser Santa Clara hospital in Santa Clara, California. George's middle name of "Henry" is after me. We are still in close and regular contact, although we do not see nearly as much of Maria as we did before John and she were married. They lived in Los Altos, California, about a 45-minute drive from Berkeley, until late last year—2007—when they moved to England. They now live in London, and Maria tells me that George Henry is beginning to develop an English accent.

## · Notes ·

1. Formerly Herma Hill Schreter.
2. Assuming it is still being published when you read this material, obtain and read: Official ABA, American Bar Association Guide to Approved Law Schools (most recent edition). See www.abanet.org/legaled. This book contains relevant information about ABA-approved law schools in a format that allows for easy comparison of such schools with regard to

factors such as type of school, faculty and administrators, enrollment and ethnicity, curriculum, GPA and LSAT scores, grants and scholarships, library resources, tuition and fees, placement, and bar passage rates.

3. Proposition 209 provided the following:

(a) The state shall not discriminate against, or grant preferential treatment to, any individual or group on the basis of race, sex, color, ethnicity, or national origin in the operation of public employment, public education, or public contracting.

(b) This section shall apply only to action taken after the section's effective date.

(c) Nothing in this section shall be interpreted as prohibiting bona fide qualifications based on sex that are reasonably necessary to the normal operation of public employment, public education, or public contracting.

(d) Nothing in this section shall be interpreted as invalidating any court order or consent decree that is in force as of the effective date of this section.

(e) Nothing in this section shall be interpreted as prohibiting action that must be taken to establish or maintain eligibility for any federal program, where ineligibility would result in a loss of federal funds to the state.

(f) For the purposes of this section, "state" shall include, but not necessarily be limited to, the state itself, any city, county, city and county, public university system, including the University of California, community college district, school district, special district, or any other political subdivision or governmental instrumentality of or within the state.

(g) The remedies available for violations of this section shall be the same, regardless of the injured party's race, sex, color, ethnicity, or national origin, as are otherwise available for violations of then-existing California antidiscrimination law.

(h) This section shall be self-executing. If any part or parts of this section are found to be in conflict with federal law or the United States Constitution, the section shall be implemented to the maximum extent that federal law and the United States Constitution permit. Any provision held invalid shall be severable from the remaining portions of this section.

4. See Linda A. Wightman, *LSAC National Longitudinal Bar Passage Study,* LSAC Research Report Series, 1998 Law School Admission Council, Historical Introduction, at page vii.

5. This combined local beer parlor, music venue, and restaurant, now called simply Blake's, is located near the campus at 2367 Telegraph Avenue.

6. As I write this, I am thinking about how serious such a case would be today, in the post 9/11 terrorism era.

7. The land is situated in the state of California, county of Alameda, city of Berkeley, and is described as follows: Lot 14, and the western 16 feet of Lot 13, Block F, Claremont Court, filed April 16, 1907, Map Book 22, page 78, Alameda County Records, A.P. No: 54-1702-83-1. Also see First American Title Guaranty Company, Title Insurance Policy No. 204175, Date of Policy: April 29, 1977, at 10:30 a.m., Name of Insured: Henry Ramsey Jr. and Eleanor Anne Ramsey. For a brief history of the Claremont Court neighborhood, see Susan Dinkelspiel Cerny, *Berkeley Landmarks, An Illustrated Guide to Berkeley, California's Architectural Heritage,* Berkeley, The Berkeley Architectural Heritage Association, 2001, at pp. 214–217.

8. See letter memorandum about 2955 Avalon Avenue by George Starr of the Department of English, University of California at Berkeley, where he wrote: "Between 1908 and 1910, John Hudson Thomas was junior partner—he was ten years younger—in the firm of Plowman and Thomas. In the absence of the firm's records, the respective roles of the two men in any given project are difficult to ascertain, except on stylistic grounds. For purposes of comparison, other Plowman and Thomas houses in the immediate neighborhood may be found at 2943 Avalon Avenue (March 1909; later remodeled by Ernest Coxhead), at 2826 and 2830 Garber Street, and at 2898 Oak Knoll Terrace." Copy of George Starr's letter is in my files.

9. Berkeley Architectural Heritage Association brochure, *1983 House Tour, Craftsman Houses by George T. Plowman and John Hudson Thomas.* For further information on George T. Plowman (b. 1869) and John Hudson Thomas (1878–1945) see Susan Dinkelspiel Cerny, *Berkeley Landmarks, An Illustrated Guide to Berkeley, California's Architectural Heritage,* Berkeley, The Berkeley Architectural Heritage Association, 2001, at pp. 282–284.

10. Since 1970, MESA's academic development program has supported educationally disadvantaged students so they can excel in math and science studies and can graduate with degrees in engineering, science, and technology. To the extent possible under California law, MESA emphasizes participation by students from groups with low eligibility rates for four-year institutions. MESA is administered by the University of California.

JUDGE HENRY RAMSEY JR., *January 1982.*

# 13

# Judge, Dean and Retiree

On September 18, 1981, Governor Edmund G. Brown Jr. appointed me to the California Superior Court, in and for the County of Alameda (thanks to the patronage and support of my close friend the Honorable Willie Lewis Brown Jr.).[1] I was able to responsibly leave my faculty position at Boalt Hall and to assume my position as a Superior Court judge on November 21, 1981. My initial Superior Court assignment was to a criminal trial department, where I handled mostly jury trials.

I had to stand for election on Tuesday, June 8, 1982, approximately eight months after assuming my position on the bench. The California Constitution provides that a judge appointed to the bench by the governor[2] must stand for election in the first general election occurring after his or her appointment.[3] Although each trial judge must stand for election, if no one files to oppose the trial judge, then that judge's name does not appear on the ballot, and he or she is deemed elected by operation of law. If someone does file in opposition, then the judge's name appears on the ballot and an actual election is held. In my case, I was challenged by Albert "Bud" Meloling, a senior prosecutor in the Alameda County District Attorney's Office. He asserted in support of his candidacy that I was a "lenient and defense-oriented judge" who needed "to be removed from the bench."[4]

The election for my judicial post was hotly contested, and both Meloling and I campaigned hard. I received widespread support from many people—including my wife and teenage children, Edith Austin,[5] Judith Briggs, Willie Lewis Brown,[6] Ernest Howard,[7] Helen Pulich,[8] Janet Roche, many judges and lawyers in the San Francisco Bay Area (particularly Alameda County), and a host of others—all of whom worked extremely hard to secure my election. I won the election and was very pleased by the outcome.

I was on the Alameda County Superior Court for roughly 10 years, the first three in a criminal jury trial department. In those 10 years, among other things, I served as the law and motion judge (under a Master Calendar system—1984 and 1985), presiding judge (1986 and 1987), a member of the Alameda County Superior Court Appellate Division (1982 and 1983), member of the California Judicial Council,[9] member of the California Blue Ribbon Commission on Inmate Population Management,[10] and as an assigned judge in the California Supreme Court case of *Aloy vs. Mash.*[11]

After my time as presiding judge, I was assigned to a civil jury trial department, first in Hayward and later in downtown Oakland. During almost all of my years on the court, Zenobia Mills was my court clerk and Karen Roberson was my court reporter. After Zenobia retired from the court in January 1989,[12] Cheryl McCarthy became my court clerk. Cheryl served in that capacity until my retirement in 1991. I was also well served by two bailiffs[13]—Steve Roderick and Trevor Redman—and two court attendants[14]—Zakiya Hooker and Andre Cober—during my judicial career. This aspect of my professional life is discussed in more detail in the next section, "Memorable Events."

## DEAN, HOWARD UNIVERSITY SCHOOL OF LAW

IN JANUARY 1991, I RETIRED from the Alameda County Superior Court to accept an appointment as dean of the Howard University School of Law, where I served until my retirement from that position effective December 21, 1996. I am particularly proud of quite a few accomplishments during my deanship—some projects undertaken by my administrative staff and certain faculty members, some projects of my own. Among them are establishment of the 500 Club for development funds, an essentially new clinical law program, the Dean's Lecture Series, the timely delivery of financial aid checks, a student computer center, individual student lockers, a Summer Abroad Program at the University of the Western Cape in South Africa, and nationally competitive faculty salaries. I discuss these and other matters in greater detail in the "Memorable Events" section.

During my nearly six-year tenure as dean of the Howard University School of Law, I lived in Washington, D.C., on Lamont Street NW, and Eleanor remained at our Berkeley home. It just was not practical for her to relocate to Washington and at the same time manage and maintain her consulting firm in Oakland. But throughout my stay in D.C., I typically traveled to Berkeley two weekends each month and Eleanor made the trip to D.C. one weekend. We continued to take our annual vacation together and usually got together during annual and midwinter meetings of the American Bar Association. I also went home to Berkeley during major holidays, such as Christmas and Thanksgiving.

When I left for Howard our four sons were either in university or living on their own after having graduated from college or law school. But another consideration for keeping our home in Berkeley was that Abeni, our younger daughter, had begun her junior year at Berkeley High School in the fall of 1990 and would not have wanted to change schools. After graduation in 1992, Abeni enrolled as a student at Howard. Yetunde, our older daughter, actually accelerated her graduation schedule from Berkeley High and completed all of her high school graduation requirements during the fall semester of academic year 1990–91. She then enrolled at Howard in January 1991 as a spring semester entering student in order to, in her words, live with and help me get settled in my new job. Yetunde had already been admitted to Williams College in Massachusetts for the class entering fall 1991.

## RETIREMENT

FOR THE PAST 12 YEARS, I HAVE kept busy, involved in a variety of activities. But a significant amount of this time has also been devoted to coping with cancer, specifically large cell/mantle cell lymphoma, which was first diagnosed in June 1997.

One evening during the spring of 1997, Eleanor and I were having dinner at our home with her brother George W. Mason, his wife, Tina, and a couple of friends, when I happened to feel a small growth on my neck. I had not noticed the bump before and asked my wife to look at it and tell me what she thought it was. One of the dinner courses that night was rock shrimp, and someone present said the swelling might be an allergic reaction. Tina commented that the growth looked to her like the hives. The dinner was on a weekend evening, but I telephoned my physician, John T. Jones, M.D., at his home and he told me to make an appointment to come into his office for an examination.

The following Monday I visited John at his office and, after examining my neck, he said we should watch the growth for a few days and see what happened. When it did not disappear after about a week, John referred me to Dr. Richard J. Kerbavaz, an ear, nose, and throat specialist in Berkeley, who performed what he called a thin needle aspiration. The results were inconclusive, and I was told that a biopsy would be required to determine the exact nature of the growth.

The biopsy was scheduled for a Friday afternoon, and Eleanor and I went to Alta Bates Hospital, where Dr. Kerbavaz performed the procedure. After the biopsy, we waited while the tissue sample was analyzed at one of the hospital's laboratories. Within a relatively short while, I heard the telephone ring in the next room. Dr. Kerbavaz picked up the phone, spoke to whoever was on the line, and hung up. He came into the room where Eleanor and I were waiting and said, "It's bad news." The biopsy disclosed that the growth was cancer, he said, specifically, non-Hodgkin's lymphoma. A short time later I spoke with Dr. Jones by telephone; he recommended that we see Dr. Gary Cecchi, an oncologist, at the Alta Bates Cancer Center in Berkeley.

I was able to reach Dr. Cecchi by telephone and made an appointment for early the following week. I will never forget that phone conversation. At one point I asked him what would happen if we simply did nothing. He replied, "Most likely you will be dead in six months." Then he added, "But you don't have to sell the boat. There are things we can do." That was just over 11 years ago.

Eleanor and I left Alta Bates on the day of the diagnosis and went straight home. We got into bed and remained there for at least 24 continuous hours. Neither of us ate any food during that entire period. We simply talked, held each other, and slept. A fair statement would be that we were both in shock. This covered Friday through Sunday morning. I often think back on that time and know that this was when, without saying it explicitly, we reaffirmed our unconditional love and support for each other. It was also a time when we jointly determined to fight the disease and to enjoy whatever life had to offer us that was positive for however long that might be.

We had reservations for dinner that Sunday at the French Laundry, an exceptional restaurant in the Napa Valley. Although neither of us had had any appetite from Friday evening through Saturday, we got up on Sunday and traveled to the Napa Valley that evening to have dinner at the French Laundry. I always view that weekend as a new beginning in our life together.

I can personally attest how important expressions of concern and support by friends are when one is experiencing a serious medical problem. I am confident that my ability to achieve remission of the lymphoma that I suffered from was in significant measure a result of the many expressions of support that I received from family and friends when I was undergoing chemotherapy and radiation treatments.

John Burris is a splendid example. I first met John when he was a student and I a professor at Boalt Hall. He worked on my city council campaign and we developed a friendship that has continued until the present. John Burris is a highly respected and nationally known civil rights lawyer. Notwithstanding his incredibly busy schedule, during the time of my treatments he called several times each week to ask how I was doing and to converse with me generally. Sometimes he would call from his car while going to work, or he might be at home after having just returned from his morning walk. Some of the calls were from his office during business hours. I appreciated each call and was all the more grateful because I knew how demanding John's schedule was and how little free time he had.

What did we talk about? Many things. A regular topic was our children. But somehow we always got around to the need for a trial lawyer to be ready for battle. No matter what is going on in a trial lawyer's personal life, or what was accomplished yesterday, last week, last month, or last year, one has to be prepared for a new fight today. So in that context, John would tell me about his expected negotiation or litigation struggle for today.

Regardless of the topic, I recognized that John's calls were intended to cheer me up and encourage me in the fight against the cancer. I will always be grateful for his support and that of other friends who provided physical and psychological support during what were tough times. I doubt if they can appreciate how important they were to my being alive today.

That I am still alive and can continue writing this paper in 2008 is thanks to the support I have received from my wife, Eleanor Mason Ramsey; medical care by my oncologist, Gary Cecchi, M.D.;[15] my primary care physician, John T. Jones, M.D.;[16] Bruce J. Rice, M.D.,[17] Otolaryngology–head and neck surgery; Grace S. Eng, M.D.,[18] specializing in diabetes and endocrinology; my friend and advisor, Ramona Tascoe, M.D.; my children; and other family members and friends. I was diagnosed on April 22, 2004, with congestive heart failure, which was most likely caused by one of the medicines used in chemotherapy. This is a "good news, bad news" situation. The diagnosis is the bad news. The good news is that the condition is in the early stages of development and, therefore, relatively mild and can be treated or managed with medicine (i.e., Coreg and Inspra), reasonable exercise, and a sensible diet and lifestyle. My cardiologist is George Horvath, M.D.[19] He is assisted in my care by Dies Birch, R.N., a nurse practitioner.[20] I had an echocardiogram on December 29, 2005, and the results were well within the normal range. My last echocardiogram was on September 10, 2008 and, again, the results were normal. The last stress test that I underwent produced results that were in the normal range.

My involvement with the law did not end with retirement as dean of the Howard Law School. Over these past 12 years I have worked abroad as a "rule of law" consultant regarding the elimination or substantial reduction of unnecessary delay in the processing of civil and criminal cases; served as chief of party during most of 2001 for a rule of law project in Nigeria funded by the U.S. Agency for International Development; sat as an assigned trial judge in various courts in the San Francisco Bay Area and elsewhere in California; served as a judge for the Alameda County Superior Court Mentor Diversion Program, as a co-Independent Assessor, with George Munoz, Esq., for the Dow Corning Breast Implant Settlement Trust, and as a member of the Infilaw Board of Advisors for the Charlotte School of Law in Charlotte, North Carolina. In addition, I was president and board member of the Center for Youth Development through Law, and chairperson and board member of the National Center for Human Rights Education.[21] I also enjoyed arranging for and supervising various home improvements at 2955 Avalon Avenue (for example, a new cedar gate, a home music system, renovation of the garage and construction of a new pergola, a new lighting system, installation of new French doors in the living room and dining room, and a new bathroom on the first level); and I supervised the refurbishment of a Victorian house that Eleanor and I own at 1820 Castro Street, Oakland, so that it could be leased. I have also found time to complete the general landscaping of our backyard and cultivate flowers (primarily azaleas, cymbidium orchids, irises, rhododendrons, and lots of roses) on Avalon. Eleanor and I have traveled abroad for pleasure and recreation; and, not least, I have written this "conversation" with you. As you can see, retirement is a relative term and mine has been a very active one.

· Notes ·

1. Willie Brown was then speaker of the California Assembly and later became mayor of the city and county of San Francisco (January 1996 to
   January 2004).
2. The law is somewhat different for appellate judges. The name of an
   appellate judge must appear on the ballot, essentially, in the first general
   election after his or her appointment to the appellate court. But appellate
   judges are considered in a *retention* election. Unlike in a contested election,
   there are no opposing candidates. The issue is not who will be elected,
   but, rather, whether the incumbent will be *retained* in office. If more than
   50 percent of the voters say yes, then the judge is retained in office for
   12 years. If more than 50 percent vote no, then the judge is out of office
   and the governor appoints his or her successor.
3. See California Constitution, Article 6, section 16.
4. See Candidate's Statement, Judge of the Superior Court, Office No. 5,
   County of Alameda, Sample Ballot & Voter Information Pamphlet, Direct
   Primary Election, Tuesday, June 8, 1982, page S5.
5. A close personal friend and long-time political ally.
6. Then Speaker of the Assembly and a close personal friend.
7. A close personal friend and long-time political ally.
8. Wife of then Superior Court Judge Martin Pulich.
9. The 28-member Judicial Council is the policymaking body of the
   California courts, the largest court system in the nation. Under the leadership of the Chief Justice and in accordance with the California
   Constitution, the council is responsible for ensuring the consistent, independent, impartial, and accessible administration of justice. The
   Administrative Office of the Courts serves as the council's staff agency.
   (This description of the Judicial Council was taken from the Judicial
   Council Fact Sheet. See www.courtinfo.ca.gov/reference/documents/pro-
   filejc.pdf.)
10. See the Blue Ribbon Commission on Inmate Population Management,
    Final Report, which was submitted January 1990. The report, in the
    Introduction on page 1, states that the commission was established in
    1987 "to examine prison and jail population projections, study options for
    criminal punishment, and make recommendations to the Governor and
    Legislature on the problems of prison overcrowding and escalating costs."
    The Final Report, submitted in January 1990 to George Deukmejian,
    governor of California; David A. Roberti, president pro tempore of the
    Senate; Robert Presley, member of the Senate; and Willie L. Brown,
    speaker of the Assembly, included "a comprehensive description of the

problem being experienced in California and elsewhere in the nation concerning jail and prison overcrowding; a discussion of public safety issues; a comprehensive review of proposed punishment options; and analysis, findings, and recommendations on how to approach, and hopefully resolve, problems in the specific categories of substance abuse, parole violators, sentencing, short-term new commitments, community corrections, and construction." See Report at p. 1.

11. *Aloy vs. Mash,* 38 Cal.3d 413; 212 Cal.Rptr. 162; 696 P.2d 656 (1985).

12. Although she left the court on leave in January 1989, her retirement was not actually effective until March of that year.

13. A deputy sheriff served as bailiff when I had a criminal assignment.

14. Alameda County Superior Court judges have civilian court attendants when sitting in a civil department.

15. Alta Bates Comprehensive Cancer Center, 2001 Dwight Way, Berkeley, CA 94704.

16. Dr. John T. Jones, 350 30th Street, Suite 320, Oakland, CA 94609.

17. 2316 Dwight Way, Berkeley, CA 94704. In 2001, Dr. Rice successfully performed surgery on a new cancerous growth of lymphoma in my throat. He has continued to monitor the site of the surgery since then.

18. Dr. Grace S. Eng, 350 30th Street, Suite 320, Oakland, CA 94609.

19. Dr. George Horvath, 2450 Ashby Avenue, Berkeley, CA 94705.

20. Berkeley Cardiovascular Medical Group, 2510 Webster St., Suite 200, Berkeley, CA 94705.

21. The National Center for Human Rights Education was formed in 1996 as a nonprofit organization. NCHRE focused on domestic human rights issues in the United States through the training of community leaders and student activists and by serving as a clearinghouse and technical assistance provider.

I WILL NEVER FORGET my dad pulling up to a hole in the ground in New Orleans where some people were digging. "Son, you see what's in that man's hand?"

And I said, "Yes, a shovel."

"That's not a shovel," he said. "It's an ignorant stick." Then he said, "If you don't stay in school and do something with your life, you will work the ignorant stick with that man."

I never forgot that, because that's what you do if you don't have an education.[1]

—CURTIS GRAVES

· 14 ·

# The Importance of Education

I have tried to impress on each of my children the importance of formal education. Knowledge is power, and education is the primary means for gaining knowledge. Knowledge is a resource that can be used to secure your future and the future of your children. You can also use it to help your children secure the future of their children. With knowledge, you and others of your generation can develop and demand adoption of policies and strategies to dramatically change the ugly circumstances of millions of Americans—regardless of race, gender, or nationality—who live in what is now the richest nation on Earth as members of an underclass mired in poverty and ignorance.

Life has taught me that a meaningful education for every child is the fundamental and principal answer to the problems faced by the poor in this country. It has to become the educational policy of each state and of the entire nation that every person is entitled to as much education as her or his talents will absorb and sustain. There is no greater investment that the United States of America could make for its future than to guarantee that each of its children is provided with the means for obtaining at least an undergraduate college degree.

I ask each of you, my descendants, to get all the education you can and to use that education to secure your personal future and that of your family and any children you may have. Please also use your education to help change the conditions of poverty that exist in America —indeed, that exist throughout the world. By the time you are a junior in high school, you should be able to do the research necessary to determine what changes, if any, have occurred with regard to any of the following:

- In 1968, 11 million American children were poor. In 2002, 12 million children were poor.
- Among black children, three of 10 black children are poor. Black children are more than twice as likely as white children to live in poverty.
- Overall infant mortality rates have declined, but they have declined faster for white children than for black. Black babies are about two and a half times more likely to die in the first year than white babies.
- Black women are about three times likelier than white women to die as a result of complications from pregnancy or childbirth.
- High school dropout rates have declined for black and white students, but black students remain almost twice as likely as whites to drop out—the same ratio as in 1963.
- If current trends continue, black males will be five times more likely than white males to be incarcerated. Almost one in every three black males will have spent some time in prison during his life.[2]

I strongly favor a liberal arts education as an important foundation for one's ultimate educational and occupational goals. Even if your undergraduate study is in a professional program such as engineering or architecture, there is still great value in establishing a strong educational base by also taking liberal arts courses. I have had this conviction since completing my undergraduate studies at the University of California at Riverside. Nothing I have experienced since then has changed my mind. Finally, the most important element of a liberal arts education is not just its breadth of knowledge and information—which is very important—but also its potential for developing a robust commitment to logical analysis and rational discourse.

Eleanor and I have both worked diligently to convince our children of the importance of graduating from high school and college and of earning an advanced degree. Eleanor frequently mentioned her father's admonition to her as a child that it was critical to "get a shingle" if she wanted to be independent and free. Both of us were told by our parents and their friends that it was vital for us to get an education because that is "the one thing the white man cannot take away from you."

Ignoring for a moment the question of race, I learned early that an 18-year-old high school graduate was qualified for a number of jobs. Then as now, you could enlist in the military. But you could also realistically aspire to be an automobile mechanic, clerk-typist, court clerk, firefighter, grocery clerk, internal revenue agent, legal secretary, mail carrier, police officer, real estate broker, Social Security employee, warehouseman—and on and on. These were not dead-end jobs but typically offered reasonably good wages and additional economic security in the form of health and retirement benefits.

Indeed, some well-regarded jobs were available in the building and mechanical trades for people who lacked even a high school diploma: automobile mechanics, carpenters, machinists, plumbers, and the like. That availability is no longer the case, and I am confident it will not be the case for the foreseeable future. Today, most careers that offer the opportunity for a meaningful income require a college degree, and many if not most of today's professions actually require a graduate or professional degree (for example, M.B.A., J.D., Ph.D., or M.D.) as a basic qualification for the position. This is not to denigrate the value of any honest work that contributes to the community good, including work with that shovel mentioned at the beginning of this chapter. It is merely to say that when you have an education it is you who will get to make the choice about what work you will do.

We have stressed the importance of education not only by personal example but also—early on and through their teenage years—by exposing our children to books (particularly about Afro-American history), special educational programs, travel, and cultural events such as plays, ballets, and other theatrical performances.

Eleanor and I and several of our black friends started and for several years operated a weekend educational program that we called

Black School. This was an effort to teach our children an unabridged and unvarnished history of African American people in and before their arrival in America. Our children were exposed to other educational programs, and the lives of several of our friends afforded models of the meaning and importance of education.

Finally, while you are in high school and in college, I strongly urge you to get involved in extra-curricular activities—whether political, athletic, musical, or community service—to develop and demonstrate your potential for leadership, your commitment to community, and the breadth of your personality and character.

## EDUCATIONAL COSTS

As you consider enrollment in an institution of higher education, you will of course want to take cost into account. That will be true of undergraduate school as well as any graduate or professional schools to which you may apply. When you select the schools to which you plan to apply, I urgently encourage you not to simply select schools you would like to attend. You should select the schools that you want to attend *from among the schools you can afford to attend.*

As of this writing, a very good undergraduate—or graduate, or professional—education can be had at dozens of American colleges and universities and in every geographical region of the United States. So please try to avoid being seduced by notions of "prestige." I beg you to first think about the kind of education and *educational experience* you want.

What is the course of study you think you want to pursue as an undergraduate? This is one of the earliest issues you should address. What is your intellectual or academic passion? What is the career you want to pursue? Or, at present, think you want to pursue. Anthropologist? Banker? Computer scientist? Engineer? Doctor, lawyer, schoolteacher? Explore the choices.

Next, ask your counselors, parents, teachers with whom you are close, and any friends who are already in college about what schools they think will offer a good education *for you.* Once you have your initial list of schools to consider, check their websites and write those schools for bulletins and other admissions material that they provide potential applicants. Be sure to ask about costs. You will want to know how much you will need to budget for an entire academic year—essentially, tuition, books and supplies, room and board, transportation (at school, and, if relevant, to and from school), health care, clothing, personal hygiene, and recreation. Always set aside about 10 percent of your budget for miscellaneous items—things that you don't anticipate but that somehow always "pop up."

After you have drawn up your budget, settle on what schools you can afford to attend on that budget. Again, remember *there are many schools in the United States where you can get an outstanding undergraduate education.* In deciding what school or schools you will apply to, think about in what area of the country you would like to live and study for four years, and whether in an urban or rural setting. Again, choices are many, from UC Berkeley to Harvard, University of Michigan to Florida A&M; you might also consider smaller colleges such as Morehouse, Pomona, Reed, Spellman, Swarthmore, or Williams.

Be certain to thoroughly investigate what financial aid opportunities —grants and loans, especially grants—are realistically available to you. Many books and websites offer guidance concerning available financial aid. Explore as many of those as you can. If you lack the funds or grades to go directly to a four-year college or university from high school, then enroll in a community college and do all you can to excel academically. Many outstanding college and university graduates have begun their college careers at a community college.

## Travel as Education

As a parent I hoped that travel would be a good instructional and educational stimulator. (See also the travel section that follows.) For example, when I was doing research in Lagos, Nigeria, during the summer of 1972, my four sons—Charles, Githaiga, Robert and Ismail—joined me there for a month. Eleanor was pregnant with Yetunde, and her gynecologist strongly advised against her traveling to Nigeria because of the inoculations she would have to take. The four boys lived with me in faculty housing on the University of Lagos campus. They visited other cities in Western Nigeria, including Ife and Ibadan, and traveled to the countries of Benin and Ghana.

Another example of educational travel was a roundabout trip with my four boys from Berkeley to Austin, Texas, and then on to Boulder, Colorado, in 1977 (chapter 12). The boys and I drove to some of the important sites of the 1960s civil rights struggles, such as Birmingham, Montgomery, and Selma, Alabama. We visited the District of Columbia, plus most of the capital cities of the various states we traveled through. We visited historically black colleges, including Prairie View in Texas, Grambling College in Louisiana, and Tuskegee Institute in Alabama. We also visited Harvard University in Cambridge, Massachusetts, where nine-year-old Ismail Jomo Ramsey posed in front of John Harvard's statue on the Harvard campus, saying he wanted to attend Harvard. Twelve years later, on the day in June 1989 that he received his undergraduate degree from Harvard, Ismail posed again with the founder's statute.

Eleanor and the two girls, Yetunde and Abeni, joined us in North Carolina, and we all traveled together until we reached New York City. The females then journeyed from New York to Boulder by plane. Thereafter, the remaining four of us—Githaiga, Robert, Ismail, and I—visited the Baseball Hall of Fame in Cooperstown, New York; the Basketball Hall of Fame in Springfield, Massachusetts; and the Football Hall of Fame in Canton, Ohio. Charles Tillman Ramsey, then 15 years old, had left us after Philadelphia to travel to Boulder, so he could be there in time for high school football practice. The plan, later changed, was for him to live with the football coach's family until we arrived in Boulder. I arranged for Charles to cross the country by bus because I thought it would be educational and interesting to see the country and its various geographical variations at eye level, rather than from 30,000 feet. I am still convinced that I was correct in that judgment, although Charles hated the bus trip.

When the two girls were about 14 (Yetunde) and 13 (Abeni), we took them to Italy (Rome, Florence, Pisa, Venice, and Milan), France (Paris), and Senegal (Dakar). They also had various opportunities to travel in the United States before graduating from high school. I made certain that all of my children visited Rocky Mount, North Carolina, where I grew up, as well as Jamaica, Queens, New York, where Eleanor grew up, so that they would have some sense of the physical circumstances of their parents' origins.

I expected that all those anthropological, cultural, geographical, historical, societal, and sociological experiences would help to stimulate my children's intellectual development and understanding. I saw those travels as an important element of their education and hoped that, by the time they achieved adulthood, they would as a consequence better appreciate the value of education as a means for improving their personal development, achieving personal satisfaction, and earning the personal wealth necessary to provide for themselves and any family they might have.

It is apparent that each of my children has internalized the importance of graduating from college and of obtaining a postgraduate degree as a means for earning a living and, where relevant, providing for a family. Charles has a law degree; Githaiga has a master's degree in public administration and a law degree; Robert completed medical school; Ismail has a law degree and an M.B.A.; Yetunde graduated from Williams College, Massachusetts, and then earned a degree from Institut des Hautes Etudes Economiques et Commerciales (INSEEC), a business school in Bordeaux, France; and as I write, Abeni is three courses short of receiving an undergraduate degree in International Relations from the University of California at Davis and has expressed an interest in seeking a postgraduate degree after she receives her undergraduate degree.

I know that each of my children understands and appreciates the value of education as a means of earning a living, gaining community respect and prestige, and making a meaningful contribution to society.

I earnestly want each of my grandchildren and subsequent descendants, if any, to understand that although education is extremely important for one's career development, ability to earn a meaningful income, and personal long-term financial security, the ultimate significance of education in one's life involves other factors. The overarching values of education—in my judgment—are in its capacity to generate curiosity; to stimulate our desire to know; and, most of all, to cause us to want to better understand our society and the world of which we are a part.

I genuinely hope that each of you will take advantage of every possible opportunity to gain as much education and knowledge as you can. I urge each of you to take every opportunity to read and to learn as much as you can and to do so for as long as you can. Please make every effort to develop logical analysis and rational thought as important components of your personality and life. Not only will you significantly increase your opportunity for financial security, but also—and most important—you will improve the quality and meaning of your life. You will then be in a position to meaningfully engage in the struggle to overcome the circumstances and policies that perpetuate poverty, injustice, and ignorance in our society.

· Notes ·

1. Curtis Graves, "Help From on High," in *My Soul Looks Back in Wonder: Voices of the Civil Rights Experience,* ed. Juan Williams (New York: AARP and Sterling Publishing, 2004), p. 148.
2. Marion Wright Edelman, "Where Do We Go From Here?" in *My Soul Looks Back in Wonder: Voices of the Civil Rights Experience,* p. 213.

# *Travel*

I want to discuss the matter of travel in more detail. During a trip to West Africa in the early 1970s, I had occasion to be in the Pan American Airways office in Accra, Ghana, and noticed a poster that I have never forgotten. The poster asked the question, "How can you change a world that you have never seen?" I was very impressed by that challenge. As a person interested in and seeing the need for us to change the world, I thought I should see as much of it as I could. And I have.

I had wanted to travel since I was a young boy. That fascination with travel probably began when I studied geography and history in elementary school. I remember reading and hearing about faraway places in the United States and abroad—Chicago, San Bernardino, and Los Angeles (from Nat King Cole's version of the song "Route 66"), Rio de Janeiro, Paris, and Athens, and wondering what those places were actually like, and wanting to visit them. I am certain that the African continent was not on my mind then. The United States was at war with Germany, Italy, and Japan, so it is unlikely that I would have thought about visiting those countries. But one of the reasons I joined the U.S. Air Force was that it offered an opportunity for travel. Once I entered college, I began to read more extensively about foreign countries and to meet people from other lands, which broadened my travel interests. It was then when I developed an interest in visiting African and Asian countries.

As I have accomplished my childhood travel dreams, I have found many places to be absolutely spectacular (as in "jaw dropping" spectacular). There surely are other equally impressive places that I have not visited, but among my wonderful travel experiences I have been greatly impressed by the following U.S. locales:

- the Grand Canyon and Painted Desert in Arizona
- Yosemite Valley (especially Yosemite Falls, hiking the mist trail to the top of Nevada Falls and backpacking in Little Yosemite Valley)
- the drive along Highway 1 from San Francisco to Carmel and through Big Sur
- watching the stars at night in Death Valley, California
- Carlsberg Caverns and the white sands in New Mexico
- New York City (especially Broadway plays)
- the Black Hills of South Dakota
- Yellowstone National Park in Wyoming.

Equally impressive outside the United States were these:

- Iguazu Falls on the border of Argentina and Brazil
- the Amalfi Coast (not far from Naples) in Central Italy, and Lake Como in Northern Italy (not far from Milan), especially the Grande Villa Serbelonni in Bellagio
- Paris, France
- the pyramids at Giza, the monuments on the Nile River at Abu Simba, and the royal tombs in the Valley of the Kings in Egypt
- a late night sail away on the *QE2*[1] (when Eleanor and I sat on deck at the stern of the ship looking at the countless beautiful lights in the Mexican hills surrounding Acapulco's crescent harbor, while drinking champagne and listening to wonderful Caribbean music being played by an excellent Haitian band, as the lights of the city slowly but ultimately faded into the darkness)
- Cape Point in South Africa (south of Cape Town), on the southern tip of the African continent—also the automobile drive from Cape Town to Cape Point
- Guilin, China, and a cruise on the Lijiang River.

Astoundingly stunning falls and mountain ranges around the world that I have viewed include Iguazu Falls (in Argentina and Brazil),[2] Niagara Falls in Canada and the state of New York,[3] and Yosemite Falls in California. Equally impressive are the Sierra Madre mountains in Northern California, the Rocky Mountains in Colorado, the Andes in Chile, and the Himalayas (especially Mt. Everest) in Nepal. I plan to visit Victoria Falls in Zambia next year (2009).

"How can you change a world you have never seen?" It is virtually impossible to see any detail of a place or even a country from 30,000 feet. Air travel is convenient and quick, but my advice is to develop and plan as many opportunities as you can to travel *at ground level.*

On the ground, you can see and experience who the people are, how they look, what they are wearing, what they eat, and what their lodgings are like. You will usually be in a position to observe remarkable differences between rural and city life. You will be able to see common modes of transportation (bicycles, boats, camels, donkey carts, trains, and various types of motor vehicles) and important architectural differences between and even within various countries, provinces, counties, and cities. There will usually be important topographical differences, and differences in animal and plant life. Most important, you can sometimes get insight into the thinking of the people–political, economic, educational and cultural.

If at all possible, it is particularly important to get outside of the capital and major cities of the United States and other countries. For example, I personally know that Abuja, Amsterdam, Asmara, Athens, Bangkok, Beijing, Berlin, Boston, Buenos Aires, Cairo, Cape Town, Chicago, Dakar, Hanoi, Hong Kong, London, Mexico City, Montreal, Moscow, Nairobi, Oslo, Rio de Janeiro, Rome, São Paulo, Santiago, Seattle, Shanghai, St. Petersburg, and Tokyo are all wonderful places to visit. In such cities you can learn a great deal about the culture, economy, history, politics, and vitality of the countries in which they are located. However, although I acknowledge that each has something different from the others, there is also an unfortunate sameness about such cities.

You develop a very different perspective when you get out of the city and into the less-developed and rural areas. You get a very different perspective of the United States from a few days spent backpacking in Yosemite Valley in California, or a few days in Yellowstone Park in Wyoming, or visiting Navajo land in Arizona. The white sands of New Mexico, the petrified forest and Grand Canyon in Arizona, and the Black Hills of South Dakota are amazing places. Try seeing the wheat fields of the Midwest, the various vineyards in Northern California, or the autumn changing of colors in a New England forest.

If you visit Cape Town and Johannesburg in South Africa but do not make an effort to see the various townships and squatters' camps outside those cities, then you will have missed much that one needs to know to understand the country, its history, its politics, and its people. A road or canal trip through the vineyards and villages of Bordeaux or Burgundy presents a view of France that is quite different from what one sees on the rue de Rivoli in Paris. A visit to Florence or Venice in Italy is exhilarating, educating, and engaging. Equally so—but in a dramatically different way—is Lake Como and the Amalfi Coast. Dakar, Senegal, offers views and insights that are quite different from what is available on the road trip from Dakar to Saint Louis.

During our marriage, Eleanor and I have taken several cruises that offer a dramatically different water level view of a place and country— again, dramatically different from what one can see from the air. We visited half a dozen Greek islands (Crete, Delos, Myconos, Patmos, Rhodes, and Santorini) and areas along the coast of Turkey during an August 1983 cruise on the MTS *Jupiter* (Epirotike Cruise Line) from Athens (Piraeus) to Istanbul and back. We traveled on the Nile River in Egypt in August 1985, and we saw and learned a great deal about Egyptian culture. We took most of our children and Maria Carmen Rodriguez on a 10-day Alaskan cruise in July 1994 that started in Vancouver, British Columbia, Canada.

GRANDDAUGHTERS ALIKE CHINASA PORTER, *11, and* ANAIS ANDRÉE-ELEANOR SCHUHMANN, *7, in Paris, France, June 2007.*

ELEANOR MASON RAMSEY *at Machu Picchu, Peru (2007).*

In March 1996 I took a bus trip alone across Turkey—from Istanbul to Antalya—so I could get a sense of the interior of that country. Eleanor and I toured Vietnam and Cambodia by land in January 2004 as part of a legal delegation to those two nations. In November 2004, we traveled 1,000 miles up the Amazon River in Brazil on the *Silver Wind*, a Silverseas Cruise Line ship. We took a 2-week cruise in January 2006 to Antarctica on the *Marco Polo*, an Orient Lines cruise ship, and observed incredible scenery.

One of the most interesting and educational trips I have ever taken was in 1972 when David Rosenthal, my former law partner, and I traveled by road for six weeks from Accra, Ghana, to Ouagadougou, Burkina Faso;[5] to Niamey, Niger; to Sokoto, Nigeria; and then to Lagos, Nigeria. Our modes of transportation were interstate buses, lorries (trucks), taxis (station wagons), and railroad passenger trains. We saw many people and visited many cities in addition to the ones already mentioned—Lome, Kumasi, Tamale, Bolgatanga, Kano, Kaduna, and Ibadon. But we also saw a lot of countryside where there was dramatically different architecture, different flora or the lack thereof, different native dress, and different daily lifestyles. Indeed, a lot of what we observed in the rural areas was the absence of much that we saw in the cities—namely, vehicular and human congestion, piles of rubbish and deferred maintenance of buildings, and beggars.

Eleanor and I have visited France annually (mostly Paris) for the past 26 years and almost always stay at the Hotel de Lutece, 65 rue Saint Louis-en-L'ile, Paris 75004. It is within easy walking distance of Notre Dame Cathedral and the Louvre. The most convenient subway stop is Pont Marie. I hope when my grandchildren and possibly their children get to Paris, the Hotel de Lutece is still there (perhaps you will stay where Taa-Ta and Bomba stayed during their many trips to the City of Light). During most of our visits to France throughout that 26-year period, we also stayed at a very nice hotel in Chagny that has our favorite restaurant in the entire world—Lameloise, which was (and I hope still is during your lifetime) located at 36, place d'Armes, Chagny 71150, France.[6]

So I hope that each of you—when you are financially able and can afford the time—will travel at ground level and take a close look at a world that is often beautiful, usually educational, and frequently enjoyable, a world you may very well have a part in changing or conserving.

Since leaving my hometown of Rocky Mount in May 1951, I have walked on each of the Earth's seven continents: Africa, Antarctica, Asia, Australia, Europe, North America, and South America. As of the date of this manuscript, I have visited as a tourist or worked (those in italics) in the following foreign countries:[7]

The *People's Democratic Republic of Algeria,* Antarctica,[8] the *Argentine Republic,* the Republic of Austria, the Commonwealth of Australia, the Commonwealth of the Bahamas, Barbados, the Kingdom of Belgium, the Republic of Benin,[9] Burkina Faso,[10] Bermuda, the *Republic of Belarus,* the Federative Republic of Brazil, the Kingdom of Cambodia, *Canada,*[11]the Republic of Chile, the *People's Republic of China,* the Republic of China (Taiwan), the Republic of Côte d'Ivoire (Ivory Coast), the Republic of Cuba, the *Czech Republic,*[12] the Kingdom of Denmark, the Arab Republic of Egypt, *Eritrea,* the Republic of Estonia, Ethiopia, the Republic of Finland, the French Republic (France), the *Republic of Georgia,* the *Federal Republic of Germany,* the Republic of Ghana, the Hellenic Republic (Greece), *Greenland,*[13] Hong Kong,[14] the *Republic of Hungary,* the *Republic of Indonesia,* the *Republic of India,* the *State of Israel,* the Italian Republic (Italy), Jamaica, *Japan,* the Republic of Kenya, the *United Kingdom* (England), the Republic of Latvia, the Republic of Lithuania, the Islamic Republic of Mauritania, the United Mexican States (Mexico), Monaco, Morocco, the *Kingdom of Nepal,* the Kingdom of the Netherlands (Holland), New Zealand, Niger, the *Federal Republic of Nigeria,* the Kingdom of Norway, the *Republic of Poland,* the Portuguese Republic (Portugal), the *Russian Federation (Russia),*

Scotland, the Republic of Senegal, the *Republic of Singapore*, the *Slovak Republic*,[15] the Republic of Korea (South Korea), the Kingdom of Spain, the *Republic of South Africa*, the Kingdom of Sweden, the Swiss Confederation (Switzerland), the *United Republic of Tanzania*, the Kingdom of Thailand, the Republic of Togo, the Republic of Tunisia, the Republic of Turkey, the *Republic of Uganda*, the Socialist Republic of Vietnam, and the *Federal Republic of Yugoslavia*.

I have also visited 44 of the 50 American states, the District of Columbia, a commonwealth associated with the United States, and two unincorporated U.S. territories (italics indicate those where I have worked):

Alabama, Alaska, Arizona, Arkansas, *California, Colorado*, Connecticut, Delaware, Florida, Georgia, Hawaii, Illinois, Indiana, Iowa, Kansas, Kentucky, Louisiana, Maine, Maryland, Massachusetts, *Michigan*, Minnesota, Mississippi, Missouri, Nevada, New Hampshire, New Jersey, *New Mexico*, New York, *North Carolina*, Ohio, Oklahoma, Oregon, *Pennsylvania*, South Carolina, South Dakota, Tennessee, *Texas*, Utah, Vermont, Virginia, Washington, West Virginia, and *Wyoming; the District of Columbia*, Guam, Puerto Rico, and the U.S. Virgin Islands.

### · Notes ·

1. The *QE2* (*Queen Elizabeth II*) is owned and operated by the Cunnard Cruise Line. This 2-week cruise was from New York City to Los Angeles through the Panama Canal.
2. Said to be the longest in the world, about 2.5 miles long or wide.
3. Said to have the greatest volume of water among the world's falls.
4. Said to be the highest in the world.
5. The name of the country at that time was Upper Volta.
6. Chagny is in Burgundy and is about 200 miles south of Paris and about 30 minutes from Dijon by automobile or 20 minutes by train.
7. Countries I visited simply as a tourist are not in italics. Countries in which I have worked *are in italics,* including countries I visited as a Site

Evaluator for the American Bar Association's Section of Legal Education and Admissions to the Bar, as a representative for the American Bar Association's CEELI (Central and Eastern European Law Initiative) Program, and on behalf of ABA-Africa.

8. I am aware that Antarctica is not a country or nation-state.

9. Formerly known as Dahomey.

10. Formerly known as Upper Volta.

11. I worked at Earnest Harmon Air Force Base, Newfoundland, as a member of the U.S. Air Force.

12. The Czech Republic was previously a part of the former Czechoslovakia.

13. I worked at Thule Air Force Base, Greenland, as a member of the U.S. Air Force.

14. Technically, Hong Kong is not now nor has it ever been a country or sovereign state.

15. The Slovak Republic was previously a part of the former Czechoslovakia.

· 16 ·

# *Diabetes*

Diabetes—a very dangerous, often harsh, and potentially fatal disease—regularly appears in my family. The common symptoms are: frequent urination, unusual thirst, fatigue (feeling tired) and unexplained weight loss. There are two types of diabetes: Type I, typically called juvenile diabetes, and Type II, commonly known as adult onset diabetes. It is Type II that frequently occurs in my family. Diabetes tends not to kill directly but significantly increases its victim's susceptibility to heart or liver disease, as well as kidney failure and stroke. It also can cause blindness through retinopathy (rupture or leaking of blood vessels inside the eyes); can compromise the circulatory system in the extremities, particularly the feet (often necessitating amputation of the feet and legs); and can compromise the body's ability to heal even minor cuts and bruises, which often develop into serious open sores that are extremely difficult to heal and that frequently serve as critical sources of serious infection. There are other problems but those should be enough to get and hold your attention.

What you have just read is the bad news. But there is also good news. While once seen by many as a death sentence, diabetes today is viewed as much less threatening. Diabetes, in many instances, may actually be preventable. In most, if not probably all cases, it is controllable. Let me repeat that for emphasis: *Diabetes in some instances is preventable and, in most if not all cases, can be controlled.* By control, I mean keeping one's fasting[1] blood glucose (blood sugar) readings within or close to normal limits. Today, July 4, 2008, that range is typically said to be a fasting blood sugar reading that is between 75 mg/dl and 110 mg/dl.[2]

A consistent program of regular physical exercise, sensible eating habits (i.e., well-balanced, low-calorie meals), and reasonable weight control will go a long way in helping one avoid diabetes. Even if you are unfortunate enough to be diagnosed with diabetes, a disciplined program of those three factors and consistent monitoring of your blood glucose levels will usually allow you to control and postpone, if not avoid altogether, the negative effects of the disease. I have found a diet of low-calorie vegetables and fish to be very effective in helping me keep my blood sugar under control.

I ask each of you to take this issue very seriously. As previously stated, adult-onset diabetes runs in *my* family. I have no reason to believe that it runs in Evelyn Yvonne Ramsey's family (Charles, Githaiga, Robert, and Ismail). Nor does it appear to run in Eleanor's family (Yetunde and Abeni). With one exception, Eleanor does not know of anyone in her family who suffers from the disease. The one exception is her oldest sibling, Robert P. Mason. I, however, know several people in my biological family who have or had diabetes. I have no information concerning my biological father and diabetes. I did not really know him, and his death certificate suggests that alcohol abuse was most likely the cause of his death.

But, on my maternal side are several relatives who have had to deal with diabetes. First, Mary Lee Ramsey, my biological mother, suffered terribly from diabetes, particularly for the last 10 years of her life. I was diagnosed with diabetes on October 25, 1984—when I was 50 years old—but have maintained good control during the past 24 years. My son, Charles Tillman Ramsey, was diagnosed with diabetes several years ago —probably at about age 40. My nephew, Tracey Caldwell—son of my half-sister Charlotte[3]—suffers terribly from diabetes and has serious kidney problems. Tracey presently undergoes dialysis several times each week. My half-sister Sandra[4] dropped dead from a sudden heart attack at age 53 on September 19, 2001.[5] Although she had not been diagnosed with diabetes, it is not all that unusual for a person to have diabetes and not know it,[6] which might very well have been the case with

Sandra. Wilbur Hawkins, my maternal first cousin (Aunt Moses's son), died on May 11, 2000, at age 69, of diabetes-related complications.[7]

I have observed firsthand the terrible consequences that can result from having diabetes. John Jose Miller, a friend of mine for many years —a former member of the Berkeley School Board and the California Assembly and, at the time of his death, a justice of the California Court of Appeal—went blind, lost almost all of his teeth, and died, at a relatively young age, as a result of diabetes. Edith Austin, another close friend, had her vision seriously compromised and died of a heart attack as a collateral consequence of diabetes. I have already mentioned the suffering of Mary Lee Evans, my biological mother, whose problems I personally observed. Marvin "Smitty the Cop" Smith, a friend of mine discussed in "Memorable Events," suffered a couple of heart attacks before his death and lost several of his toes because of diabetes. He died of a heart attack on January 29, 2006.

I served as probate judge for two years during my tenure as a member of the Alameda County Superior Court. One of my responsibilities as probate judge was to rule in cases concerning contested conservatorship petitions. Hearings were held in those matters on Thursday of each week. Most of the subjects of these conservatorship petitions were severely disabled and usually were completely unable to take care of themselves. Typically, the subject of the petition would have to appear in court as a witness, usually sitting in a wheel chair, when the matter was contested. Many of those people suffered from diabetes, and their circumstances were often horrific. This, for me, was a weekly demonstration of the gravity of diabetes.

Much has been learned about diabetes through medical research and clinical observations.[8] The cause of diabetes, however, is presently unknown. What is known about its cause—whatever that cause may be— is that it is related to one's genetic profile and is materially influenced by diet, weight, and exercise (or lack thereof). I am not a physician and what follows is not based on medical study or knowledge, but merely on what I have learned during the past 24 years as a diagnosed diabetic.

You cannot do anything about your genetics because that is a given. But you can control and influence the other three factors: diet, weight, and exercise. If you do not have diabetes, do all you can to follow a sensible diet, maintain proper weight control, and follow a regular program of recurrent physical exercise (including aerobic exercise). If you are unfortunate enough to develop diabetes, first find a competent physician to help you understand, manage, and control the disease. Second, independently read all you can to fully inform yourself about the disease. Third, it is very important that you *do all you can to follow a sensible, well-balanced diet; to maintain good weight control; and to engage in a program of regular physical exercise, including aerobic exercise. It is also critical that you conscientiously follow any regimen of prescribed medication and/or insulin injections.* Fourth, be aware of and sensitive to the presence of the classical signs of diabetes: frequent urination, unusual thirst, and unexplained weight loss. Of course, you can periodically check your blood sugar level when you visit your doctor for a general checkup. You can also check yourself with a home glucometer.

As I write this document, there is no vaccine or other medication existing that will provide immunity against diabetes, nor is there any cure (other than possibly a pancreatic transplant) for diabetes. By the time some of you read this document, there may very well be more effective medicines, medical procedures, or even a cure. But until that time comes, be careful and live your life recognizing that—if only because of your genetics—you are at risk for diabetes.

In this matter, youth is your strength and, at the same time, your weakness. It is your strength because you are probably a teenager or young adult and have time to develop the discipline and habits that can help you avoid or control diabetes. It may be your weakness because young people tend to take their good health for granted—thinking it will last for most, if not all of their lives; therefore, they have nothing to worry about at present.

As mentioned earlier, I was diagnosed with Type II diabetes (adult onset) at age 50, on October 25, 1984, and admitted to Alta Bates

Hospital in Berkeley, California, on that same day.[9] I was in the hospital for several days. The first thing I did on the day I was released from the hospital was to go to a medical supply company where I purchased a home glucometer. My second stop was home where I put on a pair of sneakers and started running. My initial goal was two miles—one mile from my house at 2955 Avalon Avenue, Berkeley, to a turnaround point at Boalt Hall (NW corner of Piedmont and Bancroft Way) and the return mile. I ran until I had to stop because of breathing difficulties (about two or, at the most, three blocks). I would then walk until I had recovered my breath and then repeat the same pattern. It was not too terribly long (probably two or three months) before I could run the full route without stopping.

Within a few months I had adopted a regular regimen of running at least three miles about three or four times each week. I ran for many years in the Bay to Breakers and the Bridge to Bridge annual runs in San Francisco. I would also run various 10K races in the various Bay Area counties. I was not at all competitive but enjoyed participating. When I went to Washington, D.C., in January 1991, to work at Howard University, I continued to run regularly in Rock Creek Park, which was only about three or four blocks from my home at 1812 Lamont Street NW. In fact, a major factor in deciding to purchase that particular house was its proximity to the park, where I could run every other day.

I ran until one day, when I was about 63, pain in my left knee told me that I should stop. I had truly come to enjoy running and really hated to have to give it up. I had developed a practice of running around places and things. For example, each spring when the cherry blossoms came out in Washington, D.C., I would run around the Tidal Basin at dawn. Fantastically beautiful! Another example is running around the exterior walls of the Forbidden City in Beijing, China; the Vatican City in Rome, Italy; the Kremlin in Moscow, Russia; the exterior perimeter of Central Park in New York City; several times around the Super Dome in New Orleans; and in the Bois du Bolonge in Paris. Once I stopped running, I started a regular program of walking for 30 minutes

HENRY RAMSEY JR. *(in a John Lee Hooker t-shirt from the John Lee Hooker café in Vienna, Austria), finishing the Bridge to Bridge 8-mile run in San Francisco, September 28, 1986.*

four days each week, which I still do, although at a significantly slower pace than when I first switched to walking several years ago.

Running helped me keep my blood sugar under control for many years—and without medication. Eventually, I had to take oral agents (Glucophage and Glyburide pills) to keep my blood sugar levels within normal limits. Once I stopped running and started walking, it became necessary to increase the dosage on my medications. The chemotherapy I underwent also had a very adverse effect on my blood sugar levels. In fact, during the time I was in chemotherapy, I had to take insulin from time to time.

In December 2005, my Glucophage medication was changed to Actos, out of concern for the potential harm Glucophage posed to my kidneys under certain circumstances. However, for some reason (unknown to me or my physician) the Actos had almost zero effect in controlling my blood sugar. Dr. Grace Eng, my endocrinologist, prescribed insulin instead, and I have been injecting myself with insulin daily since February 1, 2006. The insulin injections are quite effective; since I began taking insulin, my blood sugar readings are usually within or near normal limits.

· Notes ·

1. Definitions that you should find helpful:

FASTING The fasting period is defined as a time with no food intake for at least eight hours. Typically, you will only test fasting blood sugar levels first thing in the morning or at scheduled times as advised by your health care provider.

BEFORE MEAL The before-meal period is any time you test your blood sugar before you start to eat a meal or snack. Before-meal blood sugar levels will be higher than fasting levels because of the effect of carbohydrates from a prior meal or snack.

AFTER MEAL The after-meal period lasts for two hours from the time you take your first bite. The correct time frame to test after-meal blood sugar level is between one and two hours after your first bite. If you test before one full hour passes, your blood sugar may still be on the rise from the carbohydrates in the meal. Your reading may not show the full impact of the carbs in your last meal. If you wait longer than two hours after a meal, your reading may no longer show the effect of that meal on blood sugar.

Depending on the details of your personal diabetes management plan, you'll find it helpful to check before-meal and after-meal blood glucose levels occasionally throughout the day.

2. Source: Laboratory, Alta Bates Medical Center, Comprehensive Cancer Center, 2001 Dwight Way, Berkeley, CA 94704.

3. Charlotte and I share the same biological mother.

4. Sandra and I shared the same biological mother.

5. Commonwealth of Pennsylvania, Department of Health, Vital Records, Certificate of Death, No. 2957209, State File No. 089283. Social Security No. 193-40-1570.

6. *African Americans & Diabetes*, a 1999 brochure published by the American Diabetes Association, African American Program, states, "Almost 3 million African Americans have diabetes. One out of three people with diabetes doesn't know it."

7. See Standard Certificate of Death, State of South Carolina, File No. 00-012829.

8. An excellent source of information about diabetes (Type II) and its symptoms and consequences is David M. Nathan, M.D., "Initial Management of Glycemia in Type 2 Diabetes Mellitus," *New England Journal of Medicine* 347, no. 17 (October 24, 2002): 1342–49.

9. My blood sugar count was exceptionally high—595 *mg/dl*—on the day that Dr. John Jones diagnosed my diabetes. His office was then directly across the street from Alta Bates Hospital. Given my extremely high blood sugar reading, he immediately had me admitted to Alta Bates. My blood sugar level was fairly quickly lowered to normal through use of insulin, but I was kept in the hospital for several days. Once my blood sugar level had been lowered, there really was no medical need for me to remain in the hospital. But I was kept there while being educated about insulin, its role in controlling high blood sugars, how to inject myself, and diabetes in general. I sat in my hospital bed and watched videotapes about diabetes, self-injection, diet, and exercise. Obviously, this education could have been provided on an outpatient basis. It was done in the hospital because my medical insurance would pay for the service if I was a hospital patient but would not pay if it were provided to me as an outpatient. Talk about stupidity and waste of health resources.

# 17

# Religion

DATE: *September 3, 2008*
TO: *My Wife and Children*
FROM: *Henry Ramsey Jr.*
SUBJECT: *The Existence of God*

## INTRODUCTION

*Congress shall make no law respecting an establishment of religion or prohibiting the free exercise thereof. . . .*[1]

YOU LIVE IN A NATION, INDEED a world, where belief in a divine being, or "God," is considered an essential human value.[2] As is the case with several of the world's popular theologies, a monotheistic belief—a belief in one God—is a core component of North American religious philosophy. I am certain that the percentage of people in the United States (for example, Hindus) who believe in multiple gods is relatively miniscule.

On the one hand, I did not rear any of my children in a religious household or attempt to impose on or encourage any of you to adopt any particular religious orthodoxy or philosophy during your infancy, formative years, or teenage years, or at any other time in your lives. On the other hand, I never opposed any of you embracing a particular religious belief or philosophy. I know that Abeni has been active in preparing meals for poor children at a local church in South Berkeley, and she has also explored the Yoruba faith. Yetunde elected to have a Catholic wedding ceremony, and she had her daughter, Anais Andrée-Eleanor Schuhmann, baptized in a Catholic church. However, I am unaware of any of you being actively and openly involved in any religious denomination or formal religious practices.

Given the pressures in American society for people to embrace some form of monotheistic religious orthodoxy, you may at some point in your life have wondered why I neither introduced any of my children to a religious faith or philosophy nor encouraged any of you to adopt one. I did not attempt to impress a religious faith on you because I find no basis in history, logic, or reason that justifies a belief in God. I, therefore, did not try to impose on my children a belief system or theology that I find to be totally invalid.

While this writing is about religion in general, much of it will concern only Christianity because that is the dominant religion in the United States and the religion to which I, as an African American, have had the most exposure.

## BACKGROUND

> *When the old junk man Death*
> *Comes to gather up our bodies*
> *And toss them into the sack of oblivion*
> *I wonder if he will find*
> *The corpse of a white multi-millionaire*
> *Worth more pennies of eternity*
> *Than the black torso of*
> *A Negro cotton-picker?*[3]

WITH A FEW INTERRUPTIONS DETAILED in the early chapters of this book, I was reared in the small city of Rocky Mount, North Carolina, in the years from 1934 to 1951. As you know from those chapters, my immediate family—essentially for the first nine years of my life—consisted of my father, Charles Arthur Tillman, my mother, Nellie Tillman, and me. My mother attended the St. Mark African Methodist Episcopal (AME) Church in the Rocky Mount black neighborhood known as "Little Raleigh."[4] Until my teenage years, I regularly accompanied my mother to church on Sundays, although the first church I remember visiting. at about age six, was a "holiness" or "sanctified" church, where I remember greatly enjoying the music and being impressed by the energy of the services.

My father died when I was eight years old, and I know nothing of his religious values or beliefs. I think it safe to assume that he at least professed a belief in Christianity. I am certain I had never heard the words "atheist" or "agnostic" until sometime after I left Rocky Mount in May 1951. Indeed, I may not have heard those words until after I started college in 1955. In any case, I have absolutely no reason to believe that my father was an atheist or agnostic. If he was like his friends who survived him and whom I came to know during my teenage years, he probably expressed a belief in God and was a Protestant. He probably did not attend church with any particular regularity, nor was there anything distinctively religious about his character or personality. He was probably the "I do believe in God" type. My limited recollection of him is that of a kind, curious, and caring person. I deeply believe that he was a good father.

It may have been after my mother married my stepfather, Reverend July, that I began attending Sunday school services at what was called the Clubhouse (chapter 6). I was then about 14 years old. Regardless, I think Sunday school sessions at the Clubhouse were where I first began to openly question the religious doctrine being taught there. Indeed, it became a standard joke in our house that "Rev."[5] was greatly relieved when I stopped attending Sunday school sessions at the Clubhouse because the many questions I asked each week were often too difficult for him to answer and because I was so hard to persuade or convince of the correctness of many of the answers that he did offer. This situation was particularly true when his answers had their foundation in a literal interpretation of the Christian Bible. Although "skepticism" was not a word that I was familiar with at the time, reflection on those days makes it clear to me that I was a genuine skeptic of the religious doctrine being offered by the Rev. July and other adults at the Clubhouse.

However, it was years later in college–after I had served four years in the U.S. Air Force–when I first considered religious issues and my own personal religious beliefs (or lack thereof) in a serious and thoughtful way. My undergraduate liberal arts education helped me become more analytical and better informed about religious issues. It was in college–particularly in the context of my philosophy major–that I began to address, think about, and reflect on the issue of biblical or scriptural inerrancy and the several issues discussed later in this memorandum.

At some point during the latter stages of my college education, I began to describe myself as an agnostic. On reflection, I did so in part because I thought being an agnostic was more ingenious, and a lot more socially acceptable, than being an atheist. Also, I confess to being somewhat intimidated by the fact that I could not prove that "there is no God." After all, billions of people, many of them scientists and academic scholars, say they believe, or claim to believe, that there is a God. I suppose it was either during or not long after law school that I finally decided to accept the real truth that I actually did not believe in God. I guess I got around the "proving there is no God" problem by shifting the burden of proof to those asserting God's existence.

Having arrived at that position, I was still not willing to risk the social, political, and economic consequences of being an avowed or declared atheist. So I kept my atheism "in the closet." I confess that I used the fact that people in the United States tend to assume you are a Christian or, at least, that you believe in God. Thus, it has been quite easy to avoid the issue and controversy, by not talking about my personal religious beliefs and by providing truthful but not very helpful answers to inquiries about my religious beliefs. For example, if someone asks if I am Baptist, I simply say no. The questioner then assumes that I am a member of some other denomination. If people ask if I attend church and I say no, they will usually not press the issue and will assume that I am a person who believes in God but does not attend church. Often, people will extend an invitation for me to attend their church and I have often accepted such invitations. I could list several other examples of how one can avoid disclosing or making an issue of his or her atheism.

On those few occasions when I have been forced to address the question directly, I have been honest and said that I do not believe in God. For example, many of my family members are deeply religious and know that I am a non-believer. It truly disturbs some of them (particularly your Aunt Marguerite[6]) because they believe that if I am not "saved" before I die, I am doomed to spend eternity in hell.

Let me now turn my attention to a discussion of certain substantive issues regarding the existence or nonexistence of God.

## The First Cause

*Tibetans have the commonsense view that life is boundless, that we did not come out of nothing and cannot become nothing. We are both beginningless and endless.*[7]

MANY PEOPLE, IF NOT ALL, WHO believe in a monotheistic God anchor their belief in the notion that everything has been created and, therefore, must necessarily have a creator or a cause. It is their belief that God is the creator of humans and of all other living things—indeed, of all things, organic and inorganic. Humans had to have a creator because, again, "everything" must have a beginning and a creator. That approach leads to the assertion that not only did the Earth and each of its living occupants have a creator, but also there had to be a creator of the entire universe. The believers assert that God is that creator. In other words, God is the "first cause" of the universe and of everything that is.[8]

That assertion necessarily leads some of us to ask the question, "Who or what created God?" In other words, we see a problem with saying that everything must have a creator except God. If God exists and did not have a creator, then the statement that everything must have a creator is false. If God can exist without having been created, then, in my mind, why can't it be possible that the universe also did not have a creator? To say the universe had to have a creator because it is not God is unpersuasive because the statement is circular and merely tautological.

Thus, the flaw that I find in the first cause argument is its fundamental premise. It seems to me that the first cause argument is an infinite regression. If the universe had to have a creator, then why didn't that creator need a creator? And if that creator needed a creator, then why didn't its creator also need a creator? And so on *ad infinitum*. The response to this issue that I have heard most often is that God did not need a creator because that is what "God" means. In other words, by definition, God was either self-created, or God has always existed and will always exist. God "is, has always been, and forever will be." But if you reduce the idea of God to a simple definitional construct, doesn't that definition trivialize the concept of God? To my mind, such a concept would have no more meaning or significance than if one, like Benedict de Spinoza,[9] were to say that God is simply the totality of what is.[10]

I think the relevance of the notion of God for believers is that God is a being who is aware of, concerned about, and intervenes in human affairs. In other words, the God described in ancient and contemporary Christian, Islamic, and Jewish theology is not merely a definition or just a group of words, but a conscious being who is said to be concerned about and actively involved in the lives of humans.[11]

I simply accept the origin of the universe as just another mystery among the several mysteries or unknowns with which rational humans must contend and for which there appears to be no intellectually ascertainable or demonstrable explanation.[12] I do not say that my argument regarding the first cause disproves the existence of God, only that it negates the first cause argument as proof of the existence of God.

## Too Perfect to Have Happened by Chance

*We live in a world that manifests a generalized order. We speak,
somewhat longingly, of "the order of nature." The sun rises every
morning and sets every night, and the seasons change on schedule.
But hovering around the fringes of human existence is a barely
suppressed sense of impending doom: Illness, natural disasters,
economic distress, warfare, and an acute sense of alienation and
vulnerability.*[13]

Some believe the world is so perfectly ordered and balanced that it
could not have happened "by chance."[14] Those people believe that there
must have been a creator, planner, or designer who designed this perfect system. I, however, do not find the system to be perfect and, for
that reason and others, cannot accept this argument as proof of the existence of God.

It is true that the astronomical world appears to be very ordered and
balanced. I also readily acknowledge that numerous phenomena and
events occur in the world that can be viewed only as miraculous. But
the world is far from perfect. Out of many possible examples, let me
select two to illustrate my point that while the world is awesome and
phenomenal, it is less than perfect.

One example is the atmospheric shield that surrounds the planet
and protects us from the thousands, if not tens of thousands, of dangerous meteors that fall into our atmosphere each year. And yet this
protective shield is not perfect. Large and extremely dangerous objects
have penetrated our atmospheric shield in the past, and astronomers
predict that it will happen many times in the future. For instance, one
plausible theory for the disappearance of the dinosaurs is that they
became extinct as a consequence of a large meteor striking the Earth.[15]

Another pertinent example is the incredible reproductive systems of
many living things, particularly complex animals such as the large
mammals. While each is an incredibly wondrous and awe-inspiring

phenomenon, no reproductive system is perfect. The human and other reproductive systems often fail. I am willing to acknowledge that each normal human birth can be considered almost miraculous, but clearly the system is less than perfect. The fact that human children are sometimes born without an immune system, are stillborn, sometimes have incomplete organ systems, and may age prematurely[16] should conclusively demonstrate that the human reproductive system is not fail-safe. Where is the perfection in children being born with horrible physical and mental defects? For example, where is the perfection in Siamese twins?

Many other imperfections can be observed in this so-called God-created world. Where is the perfection in earthquakes, hurricanes and typhoons, tornadoes, or volcanic eruptions that randomly kill thousands, and sometimes tens of thousands, of people? Where is the perfection in innocent children being maimed or crippled by natural or manmade events? Where is the perfection and balance in wars of great or modest destruction? Where is the perfection in pandemic killer diseases such as AIDS, cholera, the Black Death, influenza, polio, and smallpox? Where is the perfection in the African slave trade, the Holocaust, the Inquisition, the Cherokee "Trail of Tears," the rape of Nanking, the explosion of atom bombs over Hiroshima and Nagasaki, the ethnic cleansing in the Balkans and Rwanda? How can a world with such horrific events and circumstances be viewed as perfect—or even orderly and balanced?

Why would a just and benevolent God, who has the capacity to design a perfect system, instead design one in which the creations often suffer horribly and needlessly because of flaws in their personal design or imperfections in nature?

## Free Will

*In much of the Bible, the main impediment to the full manifestation of God's power is human freedom. That God created human beings free even to rebel against God is never questioned. Adam and Eve were free to eat the forbidden fruit; Cain to kill his brother; the Israelites to build a golden calf. God had to live with the fruits of that freedom.*[17]

THE EXPLANATION I HAVE MOST OFTEN heard for wars and various acts of human cruelty is that God gave human beings free will[18] and, having done so, will not interfere with the exercise of that will. If God were to interfere or intervene, the will would not, in fact, be "free." First, I want to note that this theory does nothing to explain why a beneficent God would cause or allow horrible natural events such as pandemic disease, serious birth defects, avalanches, earthquakes, hurricanes, tornadoes, and floods that cause humans extraordinary pain, suffering, and death. These occurrences are not caused by, nor do they (except arguably in certain rare instances[19]) result from, any exercise of free will.

As concerns horrific events such as slavery, torture, and wars, which can be attributed to free will, my position is that if God knew in advance that these would be the consequences of giving humans free will, then why give it? Any omnipotent God could easily have created human beings with an instinctive loyalty and boundless love for peace, charity, and God. And from the human point of view—at least my point of view—if massive destruction and horrendous suffering by humans and other living things were to be the result of our having free will, who needs or would want it?

The idea that an omniscient, omnipresent, and benevolent God would create what is, in essence, a curious infant and, metaphorically speaking, then give that infant a box of non-safety matches in a room filled with buckets of gasoline is totally irrational and insane. In my mind, if wars, slavery, mass murder, mass torture, and the like are the results of God's giving humans free will, then both the notion of God and of free will make absolutely no sense. Obviously, the idea that God didn't know it would turn out this way is totally inconsistent with the idea of an omniscient God.

## The Devil Made Me Do It

Although I do not intend to spend much time discussing it, another argument offered is that Satan or the Devil is the cause and source of such catastrophic events and devastating disorders. Because the God I am discussing here is understood by believers to be omnipotent and completely benevolent, it seems sort of silly to spend time discussing and assuming the existence of a competing and powerful Satan who can limit the power of such a God. Rabbi Harvey Tattlebaum, rabbi emeritus at New York City's Temple Shaaray Tefila, says, "How can I, as a post-Holocaust Jew, accept that suffering of innocents is willed by God? If I acknowledge a God that gives commands then I am asked to accept the unspeakable, to accept that God wills evil."[20]

In other words, the God I am discussing is an omnipotent God and one that is completely beneficent. To assert the existence of Satan in a universe created solely by God is, to my thinking, totally inconsistent with this notion of an omnipotent and benevolent God.

What would be God's purpose in creating and releasing into the world this evil known as Satan or the Devil? How can evil come from that which is totally good? How could this evil constitute even the slightest limitation on an omnipotent God and God's protective beneficence? The whole idea of Satan's existence or of Satan's causing evil that God cannot prevent or must permit is totally incompatible with the notion of the loving, merciful, beneficent, omniscient, and omnipotent God that I am discussing here.

## MYTHS AND OTHER ANCIENT BELIEFS

MANY INTERESTING MYTHS AND ANCIENT beliefs antedate Christianity, Islam, and Judaism and can reasonably be seen as sources of many Christian, Islamic, and Jewish beliefs. A common Greco-Roman and Jewish myth that antedates the writing of much of the New Testament, particularly the Gospels, is one in which "a heavenly figure becomes incarnate as a man and the son of a deity, enters the world to perform saving acts, and then returns to heaven."[21]

Randel Helms begins his book, *Gospel Fictions,* as follows:

> In the first century of the Common Era, there appeared at the eastern end of the Mediterranean a remarkable religious leader who taught the worship of one true God and declared that religion meant not the sacrifice of beasts but the practice of charity and piety and the shunning of hatred and enmity. He was said to have worked miracles of goodness, casting out demons, healing the sick, raising the dead. His exemplary life led some of his followers to claim he was a son of God, though he called himself the son of a man. Accused of sedition against Rome, he was arrested. After his death, his disciples claimed he had raised from the dead, appeared to them alive, and then ascended to heaven. Who was this teacher and wonder-worker? His name was Apollonius of Tyania; he died about 98 A.D., and his story may be read in Flavious Philostratus's *Life of Apollonius.*[22]

Randel Helms asserts that the doctrine of the virgin birth "originated in the widespread pagan belief in the divine conception upon various virgins [of] a number of mythic heroes and famous persons in the ancient world, such as Plato, Alexander, Perseus, Asclepius, and the Dioscuri Diogenes."[23] He also writes that the source of the Lazarus miracle story[24] is the "Egyptian myth of the resurrection of Osiris by Horus." Helms writes, "The earliest written form of this myth stands inscribed upon the walls of the chambers and passages in the pyramids of kings of the Vth and VIth dynasties at Sakkhara, and hence [is] known as the 'pyramid texts.'"[25]

David Levinson, the author of *Religion: A Cross-Cultural Dictionary*, writes that:

> Founded in ancient Persia, Zoroastrianism heavily influenced the development of Judaism, Christianity, and Islam. Concepts such as heaven and hell, the resurrection of the body, the arrival of the Messiah, judgment at death, and the Armageddon battle at the end of this era are believed to originate from Zoroastrianism.[26]

According to Levinson, Zoroastrianism was founded during the seventh and sixth centuries B.C.E.[27]

## Other Analyses or Explanations

Many of today's scientific explanations for natural and medical phenomena were unknown at the time when many of today's religious concepts and philosophies were formed and embraced. For example, very little was known about astronomy, geology, or meteorology. Medical science was at a very primitive stage of development. Most people, if not all, believed that spirits or gods caused certain natural events such as eclipses and the appearance of comets. The causes of such astronomical events are scientifically understood today, and the events themselves can now be accurately and reliably predicted well before they occur.

Today, while still not very predictable, the causes of earthquakes, tornadoes, and volcanic eruptions can be rationally explained. We can now usually predict at least several days in advance—and with reasonable accuracy—where hurricanes and typhoons will strike. Again, remember that the ancients explained such now well-understood natural phenomena in terms of forces controlled and unleashed by spirits or gods.[28]

The causes of many of the diseases that killed significant percentages of various populations in the past are now understood. Many such diseases are now preventable or curable. In ancient and medieval times, pandemics were also believed to be caused by unusual natural phenomena or by God's wrath.[29]

Given the ignorance of ancient people, it is quite understandable why they sought comforting explanations for such fearsome events by looking toward the spirit world or among powerful and unseen gods. First, the forces involved are extraordinarily powerful, far beyond any power that humans[30] or even the largest animals possess. Second, the consequences of natural phenomena such as earthquakes, floods, lightning, tornadoes, avalanches, hurricanes, or volcanic eruptions can be quite devastating and terrifying. In addition, pandemic diseases often beset human beings. Therefore, the need or wish to control or avoid the consequences of such forces is both obvious and understandable.

Because the ancients had no actual observations or demonstrable explanations that would elucidate those phenomena, it is understandable that they would seek explanations in the invisible world—a world where spirits and gods were said and believed to reside. In an instance of what I view as classical egocentric thinking, those powerful and allegedly immortal spirits and gods were viewed as being concerned about, interacting with, and influencing human behavior in the known or physical world.[31]

Typically, such spirits and gods could be contacted only indirectly or through people endowed with or given special powers by the spirits or gods. It does not take a great deal of skepticism or research to view the early priests or shamans as people who simply took advantage of an opportunity to gain special status and power in their community, which usually led to personal security and wealth.

If it were true that the spirits or gods could be communicated with, usually through an intermediary, then it would follow that perhaps those spirits or gods could be persuaded or convinced to spare the people from the wrath of such powerful forces. If the gods were worshiped and treated with sufficient reverence and respect, they would protect the suppliants from the powerful and harmful events or the awful consequences of such events. Of course, the gods' human representatives would also have to be treated well.

I believe that is how it came to be that people developed the practice of praying to ancestral spirits and to specific gods as a means of avoiding calamity or of seeking favors. It is certainly possible that I am wrong, but that is what I believe.

## SPIRITS

*For the idols have spoken vanity, and the diviners have seen a lie, and have told false dreams: they comfort in vain.*[32]

SOME CONTEMPORARY MINISTERS OR PASTORS claim to have had a personal conversation with God. Indeed, some claim that they are still having such conversations. As a child (and even as an adult), I have heard some Christian preachers state that they had been living an extremely immoral and unethical life (usually involving excessive consumption of alcohol, illegal drug usage, gambling, womanizing, or a combination of those) when God spoke directly to them audibly and, in effect, told them "to get their act together." They then immediately changed their life for the better and ever since have enjoyed the rewards of a Christian life. The problem with this often-told tale is that the conversation with God is always verbal, private, and never in the presence of an independent witness. God never speaks out loud to the sinner at a time when others can hear, such as in a crowded bar or in the midst of an act of adultery or fornication. God, in modern times, seems incredibly shy in that He or She never makes an appearance that can be confirmed through independent witnesses.

Then there is the world of mediums or others who do not claim to speak directly with God but do claim to speak with spirits, usually a dead person. As concerns "spirits," I have neither seen nor communicated with one. People who claim to see and communicate with spirits have been unable to establish the existence of such beings to my satisfaction. Their reports regarding conversations with the dead are always imprecise and somewhat vague—indeed, often very vague. The validity of their reports of spirit contact always depends on confirmation and/or leads from the person to whom the report is made.

If you have the capacity to directly communicate with a spirit, then I see no reason why the spirit cannot give you precise and easily verifiable information. For example, "My name is John Doe, and I was born in Chicago, Illinois, on March 28, 1932. I worked continuously as an electrical engineer, or taxi driver, or carpenter, in Oakland, California, from June 1964 until August 1975."

Why does the medium always say something such as "I have a sense that this person worked with his hands," or "Did this person have a serious illness of some sort when he or she was young?" If you say, "Well, spirits can only communicate in limited ways," then my response is why? If spirits have the capacity to communicate, why is that ability limited so severely? I think the ability to communicate with spirits is presented in such a severely limited manner because such communication does not exist—the spirits do not exist in such a setting nor can they communicate. In other words, there are no spirits.

## Behavior Control

*So many gods, so many creeds,*
*So many paths that wind and wind,*
*While just the art of being kind*
*Is all the sad world needs.*[33]

Another reason sometimes given in support of a belief in God is that such a belief is an essential foundation for moral and ethical behavior. It is typically expressed as "If I did not believe in God, then I would have no reason to be moral or ethical."[34] Another way of expressing the same idea is "If there were no one to hold us accountable for our behavior, then what would limit our behavior?" If one believes that God is aware of our behavior and will one day hold us accountable for whether that behavior is bad or good, then we will behave properly in order to gain God's ultimate approval and blessing or to avoid ultimate disapproval and punishment by the Divine.

While many people find this philosophy to be an effective means for preventing themselves from engaging in antisocial behavior, such a belief does not prove or establish the existence of God. It only proves that, in some instances, a belief (whether well-grounded or not) can exert a powerful influence on human behavior. As noted by William James:

> All our attitudes, moral, practical or emotional, as well as religious, are due to the "objects" of our consciousness, the things which we believe to exist, whether really or ideally, along with ourselves. Such objects may be present to our senses, or they may be present only to our thought. In either case they elicit from us a *reaction*; and the reaction due to things of thought is notoriously in many cases as strong as that due to sensible presences. It may be even stronger.[35]

There are many examples of beliefs that influenced human behavior or that were thought for centuries but were later shown to be fallacious. Two obvious examples of such beliefs have been (1) that the Earth is the center of the universe and (2) that the Earth is flat. A strong case can be made for a fundamentalist concept of "creationism" being a third example. For centuries (and even today for some groups), most people have been taught that God created all animals and plants as they exist at present. However, today most, probably all, rational people accept the theory of evolution and the science of genetics as the correct explanation of how life has developed on Earth, and they reject as false the idea of all living things having been originally created by God essentially as they exist in their present form.

The most serious problem with such false ideas was that for so long they kept humankind from daring to see what was beyond the limits of most of our imaginations and the next horizon of our thought. The flat Earth theory kept us for centuries from traveling beyond a geographical horizon. Indeed, such a continued belief would have prevented today's interactions among the world's peoples. Problems presented by that theory are obvious and are, today, self-evident.

For centuries, people considered it sacrilegious, unnecessary, or impossible to challenge the theory of Earth as the center of the universe or to explore beyond that theory into the horizons of thought presented by astronomy, cosmology, and physics. Our ability to send probes to other planets and even outside our solar system would have been impossible had people continued to believe that Earth was the center of the universe. I do not see how global-positioning satellites and modern navigation could ever have been developed had such a narrow cosmic view of the universe not been abandoned.

Moreover, it is extremely unlikely that human beings would ever have explored beyond various biological horizons of thought if modern science had adhered to the notion of "creationism." Certain contemporary advances in medical science and agricultural production simply would not have been possible if today's leading scientists (biological, medical, and zoological) accepted the view that God originally created all living things—every type of animal and plant—independent of each other and as they exist today. It is highly unlikely, for example, that today's human genome research and the promise it offers for improved human health and longevity in the near future would have occurred under any system rooted in creationism. It is equally unlikely that the increase in quantity and the improvement in quality of the world's food supply that has resulted from our study and understanding of genetics could have occurred under any science or agricultural system based on creationism.

## Faith

WHEN ALL OTHER ARGUMENTS FOR God's existence fail—or perhaps this is actually the position that many, if not most, believers take at the beginning of their argument—the faithful base their belief in God on faith alone. I hear them saying, "God is, because I feel, believe and know He is! It is an article of Faith." Once one arrives at or is confronted with this position, the discussion really is over. There is nothing that I can require or demand to be proved beyond the fact of the believer's faith, and that the faith is genuine. I suppose fairness dictates that I acknowledge the believers' position that while they essentially and ultimately rest their belief in God on faith, that faith is, in turn, based on certain facts that they believe can be confirmed. Beyond that position, there are also those believers who assert that divine revelation is the source of their faith.

## Divine Revelation

I DO NOT WANT YOU TO THINK THAT I am ignoring the notion of divine revelation. I am fully aware that innumerable people hold the view that knowledge or truth can be acquired by observation, revelation, or both.[36] Indeed, many people believe that deeper knowledge and the more profound truths can be known only through divine revelation. Two classic accounts of divine revelation are the narration of the Qur'an to the Prophet Muhammad[37] and the change of Saul to Paul on the road to Damascus.[38]

My problem with this approach is that divine revelation cannot be tested. It cannot be subjected to the "scientific doctrine of falsification through observation."[39] What I find meaningful and persuasive about logic and reason is that one can use replication and prediction as a means of testing the validity of knowledge acquired through logic and reason. I find no comparable means for testing the "truth," or validity, of "revelations."

Further, nothing has ever been revealed to me personally. I understand that one can argue that I have never followed any of the rituals,
procedures, or techniques that are "necessary" for one to receive a
"revelation." But when I consider history and the obvious psychological
needs previously discussed under "Other Analyses or Explanations," I
have great doubt concerning such revelations. Indeed, I fail to see any
basis whatsoever for believing in divine revelation as a source of profound truths, and I see substantial reasons for not believing.

I know of no actual instances in which divine revelation has resulted
in any demonstrable diminution of human suffering or improvement of
the human or world condition. I know that some improvements in the
human condition are said or claimed to result from prayer—after the
fact. But I know of no instances in which anyone has been able to consistently predict such results before the fact.

## Mystery and Wonder

*To be spiritual is to accept that some things do not have answers.*[40]

I am also aware and can appreciate that it is probably inherent in the
monotheistic concept of God that the divine is, or involves, a reality
that is indescribable in human languages, inconceivable in human imagination, and transcendent of the ordinary or observable world. Karen
Armstrong stated this notion as follows:

> Throughout history, men and women have experienced a di-
> mension of the spirit that seems to transcend the mundane world.
> Indeed, it is an arresting characteristic of the human mind to be
> able to conceive concepts that go beyond it this way. However we
> choose to interpret it, this human experience of transcendence
> has been a fact of life.[41]

Still, I do not find it useful or meaningful to embrace such a philosophy or theology because I cannot disprove a negative (which is that

God does not exist). I find it much more productive, valid, and meaningful to rely on logic, reason, and the scientific method to conceive of and analyze the world within which I exist and function. I see no reason to accept on faith the notion of the existence of a God who created the cosmos and who is concerned about and interferes in human affairs.[42] That reasoning does nothing to solve or resolve several enigmatic concepts, imaginings, or issues that we find ourselves confronting when we contemplate questions of human origin, extinction, purpose, and meaning or contemplate the notions of immortality and the divine.

Our very existence is a mystery and a wonder. While I am unable to solve the conundrums presented by concepts such as immortality, creation, free will, infinity, or eternity, I have found no persuasive explanation or answer offered by any other person or persons for any of the questions that are presented by such ideas, notions, concepts, theories, and theologies. For those who offer God as an explanation or answer, I say, first prove that God exists! I certainly do not see any reason to accept the existence of God on faith. Acceptance on faith falls far short of the evidence or of any other form of concrete proof that I require to establish almost any fact, including the existence of God. As said by Corey S. Powell, "The discovery that the universe evolved from a hot, dense state does not prove a divine agent was responsible for establishing those initial conditions."[43]

## GENERAL OBSERVATIONS

CERTAIN OBSERVATIONS THAT I HAVE MADE during the course of my life provide me with substantial reasons for doubting the existence of either God or gods. Most of my skepticism is based on the premise that, by definition, the God described by monotheists during my lifetime is said to be an omniscient, omnipresent, and omnipotent being. In other words, there is nothing that God does not know or cannot do. There is also the assertion that God is benevolent, just, and rational.

If those assertions are true, then why are there wars? Why did—and do—we have slavery? Why are babies born with incredible physical and mental defects? Why do we have natural disasters like earthquakes, floods, hurricanes, avalanches, mudslides, tornadoes, and pandemics that cause numerous deaths and untold suffering? Why was there a Holocaust? Why did the September 11, 2001, cataclysmic attacks on the World Trade Center and Pentagon occur, or why did God allow it? Why do we still have instances of genocide in various areas of the world—Africa (Rwanda and Botswana) and Europe (the former Yugoslavia), as well as other mass killings (for example, Cambodia)? Why did human beings have to face the Black Death and now AIDS? I cannot conceive of a rational, let alone compassionate and caring, God allowing such horrific events, given that God is supposed to have the foresight and power to prevent all of them.

## God the Sports Fan

I am also amazed by certain behavior that in my mind trivializes the concept or notion of God. For example, a football player scores a touchdown, a basketball player makes the jump shot that wins the game, a soccer player scores a goal, or a baseball player hits a home run, and in each instance, the athlete immediately and publicly thanks God for allowing, permitting, facilitating, granting, or causing the exceptional performance or victory. What kind of divinity would be concerned with the outcome of something as trivial as an individual sports event? Why would God be concerned about the outcome of a horse race, a motorcar race, or a professional boxing match?

In a world beset with profound issues and problems, why would God be concerned with or devote precious time to such inconsequential and—in the overall scheme of human affairs—trivial matters? The idea that God would care whether the Yankees or the Giants win the World Series, whether one of the Williams sisters wins the U.S. Open, whether France or Brazil wins the World Cup, or whether Tiger Woods or David Duval wins the Master's or the British Open baffles my mind. I mean, assuming there is a God, shouldn't He or She be spending His or Her time concerned with and addressing fundamental tribulations such as disease, hatred, ignorance, poverty, and war?

## A Weak God

Rabbi Harold S. Kushner, in his insightful and intellectually provocative book titled *When Bad Things Happen to Good People*,[44] addresses the issue of whether God is responsible for what is bad in the world. His discussion concerns the book of Job[45] and how Job's suffering can be explained in a theological context. The rabbi writes:[46]

> To try to understand the book [of Job] and its answer, let us take note of three statements which everyone in the book, and most of the readers, would like to be able to believe:
> A. God is all-powerful and causes everything that happens in the world. Nothing happens without His willing it.
> B. God is just and fair, and stands for people getting what they deserve, so that the good prosper and the wicked are punished.
> C. Job is a good person.

Rabbi Kushner concludes that given the factual circumstances presented by the book of Job, only two of those propositions can be true. In other words, all three cannot be true. If A (God is all-powerful and nothing happens without His willing it) and C (Job is a good person) are true, then B is false. If A and B are true, then C cannot be true. But the facts given in the book of Job establish conclusively that Job is a good person. He may not be perfect, but he clearly is a good person. Rabbi Kushner, therefore, asserts that we must elect to believe in A or B, but we cannot believe in both. At least, we cannot believe in both and at the same time recognize the validity of C, that Job is a good person.

The Rabbi elects to believe B, that God is just and fair. He rejects A, the notion that God is all-powerful. According to Kushner, there is randomness in the universe that accounts for unfair and unjust results. God does not will or cause those events. Indeed, they occur despite God.[47] Kushner writes:[48]

Innocent people do suffer misfortunes in this life. Things happen to them far worse than they deserve—they lose their jobs, they get sick, their children suffer or make them suffer. But when it happens, it does not represent God punishing them for something they did wrong. The misfortunes do not come from God at all.

In my mind, what a great deal that is for God. If something happens that is good, God gets the credit and can take a pat on the back. If something happens that is bad, it is not God's fault, but the fault of randomness in the universe or, I suppose many Christians would say, the Devil or Satan. I do not think that those who assert or argue for the existence of an omnipotent and benevolent God can possibly claim that God is responsible only for the good. I would think that the most difficult issue for any theist is the question of how evil entered the world if not created by God. Kushner may describe how he thinks it (that is, evil) works, but he does not explain or account for its creation!

## A Petty God

*In studying the world's spiritual traditions and hearing the personal stories of people's search for God, it has become clear that the saying, "Different strokes for different folks," is as true for people's spirituality as it is for their diets and their love lives. Unfortunately, many of us have been taught that there is only one path to God and that those who don't follow it are either damned to Hell or doomed to lose their souls.*[49]

A major problem for me concerning Christianity is the belief held by many Christians, possibly the majority, that people who, at the time of their death, have not accepted Jesus Christ as their personal savior are consigned to eternal suffering in hell.[50] Why? Nothing about that result seems to me to be caring, fair, or rational. Clark H. Pinnock, a noted theologian, has put the issue well:

According to the larger picture, we are asked to believe that God endlessly tortures sinners by the millions, sinners who perish because the Father has decided not to elect them to salvation, though he could have done so, and whose torments are supposed to gladden the hearts of believers in heaven. The problems with this doctrine are both extensive and profound.[51]

For example, why would a loving and caring God consign to hell those innocent babies who die before reaching an age at which they have the mental capacity to appreciate, understand, and accept Christ as their "savior"? Keep in mind that "hell" is said to be a terrible place where one is subjected to indescribable suffering for eternity.[52] Why would a caring, fair, and rational God consign people to hell who are never exposed to Christian theology, but who live moral and ethical lives in non-Christian countries (for example, India, Saudi Arabia, Tibet, Iran and Indonesia) because they have not accepted Christ as their personal savior? [53]

What is rational or just about allowing a serial murderer—who on his or her deathbed sincerely accepts Christ as his or her personal savior—to gain the benefit of an eternal life in heaven, while another person who has lived a truly moral and ethical life (for example Mahatma Gandhi or Rabbi Abraham Heschel) is consigned to hell only because he or she never accepted Christ? Is it rational or just to assign to hell the devout Buddhist, Hindu, Jew, or Muslim who lives a completely moral and ethical life? I don't think so. Such a result is totally inconsistent with and completely negates any notion of rational or distributive justice. Albeit with other words and regarding a different issue, Rabbi Kushner expresses very well a view with which I totally agree. He wrote:

> Do I . . . really believe in a God who has the power to cure malignancies and influence the outcome of surgery, and will do that only if the right person recites the right words in the right language? And will God let the person die because a stranger, pray-

ing on her behalf, got some of the words wrong? Who among us could respect or worship a God whose implicit message was "I could have made your mother healthy again, but you didn't plead and grovel enough."[54]

## BELIEF AND BEHAVIOR

As a young person, probably beginning around age 12 or 13, I began to note and reflect on the fact that I did not observe any correlation between those who professed a religious faith and those evincing moral and ethical behavior. In other words, I observed that it was not unusual for a significant percentage of the people in my neighborhood who publicly claimed to be devout Christians to, at the same time, engage in the most atrocious conduct—lying, stealing, displaying other acts of dishonesty, and committing unjustifiable acts of violence. Some of those people were active members in local Baptist and Methodist churches.

Quite a few people in my neighborhood and hometown (especially Baptist, Pentecostal, and Methodist ministers and pastors) said that in their lifetimes they had been spoken to by—or had been engaged in one or more conversations with—God. Some claimed to converse with or be spoken to by God on a regular basis. Typically, God had given the person directions (about what or what not to do), a specific warning, a promise, or a prophecy. The implication and suggestion was that those conversations were verbal (that is, in a spoken language that was actually heard and understood by the reporter). I do not recall it being made clear whether God's voice was transmitted through the air with sound waves and heard using one's ear and olfactory nerves, or whether God's voice was perceived internally in the listener's brain (as usually happens, for example, when one is reading a book).

At or about the time I became a teenager, I began to note and found it significant that God had never spoken to me, that I had never heard God's voice. Also, whenever I prayed, I never had the sense that anyone was listening to me and there was never any verbal reply. It was as if one was trying to have a telephone conversation when no one was on the other end of the line.

On the basis of those two facts, I began to seriously doubt and question the credibility and truthfulness of the statements by others that they had conversed with God or heard God speak. In other words, I began to ask myself the question, "If God is speaking to all of these other people, why is it that God has never verbally, or otherwise, spoken to me?" My ultimate conclusion was that, at worst, people making such statements or claims were lying or, at best, they were hallucinating or dreaming. Otherwise, it was simply something they had imagined but honestly believed to be true.

Further, I did not perceive a correlation between those suffering hardships and living very difficult lives and those professing a devout belief in Christianity. In essence, I did not see those living Christian lives being rewarded and those living sinful lives being punished. A belief in Christianity or the acceptance of Jesus Christ did not seem to affect one's life either way.

Finally, I have been equally bothered—since at least my early teen years—by my perception of serious inconsistencies between professed Christian philosophy or theology and certain behavior of those claiming to be Christians. I have perceived that the central foundation of the Christian faith is love, charity, and forgiveness. And yet, in many instances during my life, I have found or observed people who claim to be devout Christians but who manifest little compassion or forgiveness in their relations with others. Indeed, as a youngster I often saw—and I see today—hatred, meanness, animosity, and ill-will instead of love, mercy, and kindness. While not limited to any one group or period in history, this anomaly was particularly true regarding slavery[55] and how blacks and other people of color were treated in the United States during the Jim Crow period.[56] Jim Crow or state-sanctioned segregation has been rightly described as "slavery's refined successor."[57]

How can an ardent and honest belief in Christianity be squared with certain conduct engaged in by countless numbers of Christians? At a general level, it was primarily people claiming to be Christians who carried out the Crusades, who perpetuated the African slave trade and American slavery, who almost annihilated the indigenous population of North America, who were responsible for the Holocaust, and who dropped atom bombs on Hiroshima and Nagasaki. Most, if not all, members of the Ku Klux Klan and the American Nazi Party claim to be Christians. I have no doubt that most people in the United States who support the death penalty are Christians. At a less notable level, in my hometown of Rocky Mount, North Carolina, during my youth, it was common practice for an unmarried young woman who became pregnant to be expelled from the Christian church.

None of this conduct can be viewed as consistent with Christian philosophy. Consequently, I seriously doubt the sincerity and validity of belief of many, if not most, Christians who purport or claim to believe in Christian faith and doctrine.

## Escape Clauses

*No man is an Iland, intire of it selfe; every man is a peece of the Continent, a part of the maine; if a Clod bee washed away by the Sea, Europe is the lesse, as well as if a Promontorie were, as well as if a Mannor of thy friends or of thine owne were; any mans death diminishes me, because I am involved in Mankinde; and therefore, never send to know for whom the bell tolls; It tolls for thee.*[58]

I HAVE ALSO BEEN BOTHERED FOR a very long time by the several broad "escape clauses" accepted as important tenets of the Christian faith. For example, as previously stated, there is the assertion that one can escape the detrimental consequences of an "un-Christian" or sinful life by accepting Christ as one's savior at any time before death.[59] The notion is that how you live your life is not all that important in the end, so long as you accept Christ as "your personal savior." According to that view, at the end of your life, what matters is not what you have done in life. Rather, what counts is what you ultimately believe. In other words, Hitler or a slavemaster can reside in the Christian heaven, but Mahatma

Gandhi and the moral and ethical Muslim are condemned to reside in hell for all eternity. Please, give me a break! I do not find it at all rational to judge the worth or value of a person's beliefs completely divorced from the person's conduct or behavior. To me, that view is absolute nonsense. As the film character Forrest Gump often stated, "Stupid is as stupid does."

Why would a rational God, who purports to hold people accountable for their behavior, establish a system where your behavior (that is, how you live your life) is essentially irrelevant[60] and where the only meaningful factor is your willingness to acknowledge Christ as your "savior"—sometime before your death? In responding to questions like this one, some Christians often give an answer that "God works in mysterious ways."[61] In other words, because God is immortal and all knowing, it is not possible for any human to comprehend or appreciate the reasons for or purpose of much of God's "work" or "conduct." Instead, one must simply have faith and accept that there is a sound reason for God's action or inaction.[62] In my mind, that is simply a cheap or easy way of trying to avoid having to confront or deal with the obvious inconsistencies between philosophy or theology and one's factual observations of daily life. I think the person asserting a proposition has the burden of proving or establishing the validity of that proposition. If one asserts that God has a good reason for a particular action or result, then it is incumbent on that person to demonstrate or confirm the reason.

Another "escape clause" that is often offered to explain this discrepancy between professed belief and conduct is that the believer is neither Jesus Christ nor perfect. The assertion is that only Jesus Christ (that is, one who is perfect) can achieve the standard of Christian conduct described in the Bible. Thus, when the believer is told that his or her conduct is inconsistent with Christian standards of conduct, the response is often that one cannot be condemned or criticized for such shortcomings because no one is perfect but Christ. Therefore, the level of conduct described by Jesus and his disciples is an ideal but is not to be expected of ordinary mortals. This position essentially rests on the biblical passage, "since all have sinned and fall short of the glory of God."[63]

Many friends and members of my family describe themselves as devout, God-fearing Christians. And yet, on those occasions when I point out the inconsistency between an unwillingness on their part to forgive a perceived slight or past hurt that they claim to have suffered and the Christian philosophy of forgiveness and love, it is not at all unusual for their response to be, "I am not Jesus Christ; I am not perfect!" The implication becomes, "It is acceptable for me to behave in a way that is inconsistent with my basic religious beliefs because, as a human being, I should be held to a lesser standard." Those alleged Christians seem to completely ignore their obligation to strive to meet biblical standards. Rather, because the standards of perfection cannot be completely achieved, they seem to feel that they are excused from even trying.

## OTHER GENERAL OBSERVATIONS

THE FOLLOWING ARE SOME ISSUES THAT, while not directly relevant to a discussion of the existence of God, are, in my mind, somewhat relevant to this discussion.

### Original Sin

> *When Adam and Eve disobeyed God, they opened the floodgates of sin so that forever after their offspring would be infected by the disease of sin.*[64]

I have no rational explanation for the Christian notion of original sin. For example, what is the "sin" of the infant who dies? As I understand it, God punished humans with the sanction of mortality[65] because they had violated God's admonition not to eat the fruit from the tree of knowledge. This concept makes absolutely no sense to me. The practice of imposing human suffering on each individual as a consequence of "original sin" is inhumane and cruel, because it is collective punishment being imposed over all human life and because that punishment is unrelated to any individual responsibility. And yet, this concept is supposed to be the judgment and acts of a benevolent and loving God? Again, give me a break!

I am aware that the Christian God is supposed to have shown mercy by sending Jesus Christ to die on the cross as a way of allowing humans to avoid the consequences of original sin, but only if they *accept Christ as their personal savior*.[66] Again, what about the infant who has absolutely no concept or possible chance of knowing Jesus Christ, let alone accepting Jesus as a personal savior? What about people who live in places where neither Christianity nor knowledge of Jesus Christ is taught in the home, in school, in the community, or in religious institutions? Are they still to be condemned to eternal damnation; if not, then why not?

Finally, what conceivable reason could a rational God with the capability of creating a perfect being—or at least one with any characteristics that God wanted the creature to have—create one that was flawed and then, incredibly, punish the creature for that flaw! And why would God design an absolutely horrible punishment to which the person would be subjected for all eternity! As stated earlier, any omnipotent God could easily have created human beings with an instinctive loyalty for and love of God.[67] Indeed, if God has the capacity and power to create a perfect world totally at peace with God at the end of days, then He or She obviously had that capacity and power at the time of the initial creation of the universe.

## Life After Death: The Resurrection

> According to the modern scientific worldview, the notion of survival of the soul after death is a nonoption. Once the brain waves cease functioning, life is over. No soul. No afterlife. No heaven. Dead is dead. It is this view of life and death that has become the predominant intellectual point of view in the twentieth century.[68]

Christians, Muslims, and some Jews all embrace the concept of a postmortem life or consciousness after bodily death.[69] For the Christians, there is the idea of "heaven," where one is rewarded for having lived a proper life, or "hell," where one is punished for having failed to live a proper life before death.[70] Muslims also believe in an afterlife where one is rewarded for having lived a good and proper life, and is punished for idolatry and for wicked or sinful behavior.[71] For Jews, as one might expect, the subject of an afterlife is somewhat complicated and by no means uniform. Still, traditional Judaism encompasses Gan Eden (paradise or heaven), Gehenna or Gahinnom (the realm of postmortem punishment or hell), and notions of resurrection at the end of days, as well as reincarnation or migration of souls.[72]

The Christian view is based on an acceptance of the Bible as the holy word of God. All extant popular versions of the Bible[73] describe the notion of a resurrection (that is, life after death).[74] The most famous biblical reference to the resurrection concept is the claimed resurrection of Jesus Christ[75] as described in Paul's first letter to the Corinthians[76] and in the four Gospels written by Matthew, Mark, Luke, and John.[77] Heaven[78] and hell[79] are both discussed in the New Testament in Matthew, Revelation, and other books.

The Muslim view is based on the Holy Qur'an. According to Islam, all who die are exposed to hell, where some will be condemned to remain for eternity, while others will continue on and be admitted into Paradise. "God keeps a tally of a person's good and bad actions in the Book of Deeds. On the Day of Judgment, the person's final destination—heaven or hell—is determined."[80]

> Man says: "What!
> When I am dead, shall I
> Then be raised up alive?"

> But does not man
> Call to mind that We
> Created him before
> Out of nothing?

> So, by thy Lord,
> Without doubt, We shall gather

MY STORY  ·  308

Them together, and (also)
The Evil Ones (with them);
Then shall We bring them
Forth on their knees
Round about Hell;

Then shall We certainly
Drag out from every sect
All those who were worst
In obstinate rebellion
Against (Allah) Most Gracious.

And certainly We know best
Those who are most worthy
Of being burned therein.

Not one of you but will
Pass over it: this is,
With thy Lord, a Decree
Which must be accomplished.

But We shall save those
Who guarded against evil,
And We shall leave
The wrongdoers therein,
(Humbled) to their knees."[81]

Since everyone is to be brought toward Hell on the Sirat, one has to prepare himself as of today before it is too late. One has to do all that he can to improve his qualities, his behavior, and his activities. He is to correct his intention as well. Above all, he has to do everything for the love of Allah.

While walking on the Sirat, one will be able to see and hear what is going on in Hell. The scene is horrible and the penalty is beyond imagination. Everyone is scared to see, to look, or even hear. Every person is worried about himself from being dumped into Hell.[82]

The eschatological issue is more complicated in Judaism:

> Just as Judaism and Jewish culture developed and changed repeatedly through contact with other world civilizations, so Jewish afterlife teachings evolved rapidly during the course of four millennia. In almost every era of history, we uncover many parallel and sometimes even conflicting [Jewish] ideas on life after death existing side by side.[83]

Most of today's North American Jews do not believe in an afterlife or the postmortem survival of the soul.[84] In seeking information about Jewish beliefs concerning the afterlife, I was totally surprised to hear several of my Jewish friends[85] tell me that Jews do not believe in an afterlife. I have subsequently discovered that there are, in fact, plenty of Jews who *do* believe in the resurrection and life after death. The following statement from the Internet probably expresses best the current topic of Judaism and the afterlife:

> Traditional Judaism firmly believes that death is not the end of human existence. However, because Judaism is primarily focused on life here and now rather than on the afterlife, Judaism does not have much dogma about the afterlife, and leaves a great deal of room for personal opinion. It is possible for an *Orthodox* Jew to believe that the souls of the righteous dead go to a place similar to the Christian heaven, or that they are reincarnated through many lifetimes, or that they simply wait until the coming of the *messiah*, when they will be resurrected. Likewise, Orthodox Jews can believe that the souls of the wicked are tormented by demons of their own creation, or that wicked souls are simply destroyed at death, ceasing to exist.[86]

Another helpful statement concerning Jewish eschatological thought is by Rabbi Neil Gillman, a noted Jewish theologian:

[C]entral to Jewish eschatology is the doctrine of an afterlife for each Jew. That doctrine, as it developed over time, taught that our death is not final, that at the end of days God will raise our bodies from the grave, reunite them with our souls, and reconstituted as we were during our lifespan on earth, that we will be brought before God to account for our lives and receive the appropriate reward or punishment.[87]

Of course, there are other religions in the world, for example Buddhism and Hinduism, that embrace notions of reincarnation, resurrection, and the afterlife. For example, the Buddhist view, or karma theory, "is that individuals mutate through life forms from life to life."[88] The following is a brief description of that process:

A subtle, mental level of life carries patterns developed in one life into the succeeding ones. Species develop and mutate in relation to their environments, and individuals also develop and mutate from species to species. This karmic evolution can be random, and beings can evolve into lower forms as well as higher ones. Once beings become conscious of the process, however, they can purposively affect their evolution through choices of actions and thoughts.[89]

Hinduism is the world's third most popular religion (after Christianity and Islam), and adherents to this faith are known as Hindus. They believe in a universal soul, reincarnation, and multiple gods. The primary gods are Brahman, who created the universe; Vishnu, the preserver of the universe; and Shiva, who destroys the universe. All other gods are viewed as expressions or manifestations of Brahman. Hindus believe that the soul passes through a cycle of successive lives and that its next incarnation always depends on how the previous life was lived.

The thought of death being the end of one's existence is understandably a terrifying notion for most people, regardless of their religious beliefs. Annihilation or extinction at the end of one's life is not a comforting thought, particularly where time is envisioned as infinite or without end. It is also easy to understand and appreciate that people will want to continue after death those relationships and actual contact with people whom they have known during life, particularly those whom they greatly respect or of whom they are fond.

Belief in an afterlife affords hope and tangible relief to those who cannot accept the notion that death will constitute their extinction. This notion also provides relief for those who want certain relationships to continue beyond the apparently impenetrable veil of death. Easy examples are husband and wife, parent and child, siblings, other family members, and close friends.

It is equally easy to understand why people who are presently living a miserable life would want an opportunity to live a much better life sometime and somewhere in the future—in this instance, after death. These are powerful and strong roots on which to develop an emotional desire or need. And it is a very short journey from the desire and need to belief and conviction. Belief in an afterlife also affords real hope to those whose lives are miserable by assuring them that this is not the only life they will ever experience—that the misery of this life is not their eternal fate. Of course, the assumption here is that the person will be deserving of a heavenly afterlife and not a hellish one.

Thus, the idea of a perfect place created by God—but not yet known or directly experienced—where one's relationships can be continued and a better life can be lived is very, very appealing. This wishful thinking is particularly attractive and plausible when its validity is certified by persons believed to have special powers that allow them to communicate with the spirits and gods.

While we cannot visit or see the place during this life, the priests or other intermediaries of the gods or spirits describe it for us and assure us of its existence. Their assurances become very appealing and plausible when we are convinced that those priests, pastors, monks, or "special people" have been endowed by gods or spirits with extraordinary powers that allow them to communicate directly with the gods or spirits.

## My Core Beliefs

*When my time comes, I will seek hope in the knowledge that insofar as possible I will not be allowed to suffer or be subjected to needless attempts to maintain life; I will seek it in the certainty that I will not be abandoned to die alone; I am seeking it now, in the way I try to live my life, so that those who value what I am will have profited by my time on earth and be left with comforting recollections of what we have meant to one another.[90]*

I have spent a lot of time telling you what I do not believe. Let me now share with you some of what I hold as my core beliefs. I profoundly believe the following:

- Education is the key that can most easily be used to unlock the cell doors and gates of the prison of poverty. I believe that local, state, and federal governments are morally and constitutionally[91] obligated to offer a free elementary and high school education—plus an affordable college or university education—to every resident of the United States. I also profoundly believe the government is morally obligated to provide concrete encouragement and meaningful inspiration that is designed to help every parent and child understand and appreciate the need for and the value of education. It is not enough to leave that responsibility solely to the parents (or to a single parent) who in far too many instances lack significant formal education themselves or the ability to properly guide their children in that regard.

- It is important that we help less fortunate people both financially and in person, particularly those who are the victims of poverty. I know that some people in the United States who are mired in poverty are responsible for their own economic condition, but I do not think that is true of the great majority of poor Americans. Indeed, for the great majority of poor people in the world, their personal poverty is not their own fault.

- Each group and individual should be held responsible for his or her actions and the consequences of those actions.
- Each of us should be self-reliant to the extent our circumstances allow.
- Each of us should live our lives in such a way that we make a positive contribution to our community and country, as well as to society in general.
- African Americans, given our history, have a special responsibility to reject and struggle against bigotry and intolerance.
- We should all be controlled by and subject to the rule of law.
- No person should be denied due process of law or the equal protection of the law.
- People should not hurt each other—physically or psychologically—whenever a rational alternative is available. I believe this same principle applies to human interaction with all living things because I am convinced that this approach is the best and most effective way for humans to function and survive. This core belief is the reason, for example, that I oppose the death penalty and do not support war except as an absolutely last resort.
- It is infinitely better to be caring, charitable, and compassionate than to be unkind, greedy, and selfish.
- Each of us should make every reasonable effort to be true and loyal to family and friends.
- All life and the conditions that support life are interrelated. For this reason, I believe it is critical for the well-being—or even survival—of humankind that we avoid unnecessary and preventable harm to people, other living things, and the environment.
- One's adult life—both personal and professional—should embrace and reflect the following words: analytical, charitable, collegial, compassionate, competent, committed, courageous, curious, dependable, determined, disciplined, empathetic, focused, forgiving, friendly, generous, gracious, honest, humble, industrious, kind, logical, loyal, loving, open-minded, peaceful, persistent, polite, rational, reliable, strong, thoughtful, and wise.

I hope that near or at the end of your lives, when people are asked to describe the type of person you are or were, those individuals in their response will be eager to use most—I hope all—of the words that I have listed immediately above.

I readily admit that there have been specific occasions and even periods in my juvenile and adult life when I did not adhere or conform to each of those principles and standards. I think, however, that for most of my life I have. Regardless, as I have grown older—and I hope wiser—I have come to appreciate and believe that one should fully adhere to those principles. I urge each of you to make the effort to do so for the rest of your lives.

## CONCLUSION

*Dear lovely Death*
*That taketh all things under wing?*
*Never to kill?*
*Only to change*
*Into some other thing*
*This suffering flesh,*
*To make it either more or less,*
*But not again the same?*
*Dear lovely Death,*
*Change is thy other name.*[92]

In sum and substance—according to what I have learned from United States and world history, from my personal history, and from learning, literature, logic, and rational analysis—I find no credible basis for a belief in God or an afterlife. Concurrently, those same intellectual, ethical, moral, and historical sources provide me with the necessary bases for an ethical and moral life. Neither God nor a belief in God is necessary for adherence to such ethical and moral principles or beliefs.

My view is that one does not (and should not) need to believe in an afterlife or in a God or gods in order to trust, interact with, rely on, and help others. I find those standards of behavior to be moral and ethical imperatives. God is not needed as the source of those insights and strengths. I find human experience, history, and consequent or acquired wisdom sufficient sources of those insights and strengths. I acknowledge that there are hundreds of millions, even billons of others who believe in and express a need for God in order to adhere to or embrace the values I have enumerated. Simply put, I do not have such a need.

With enduring care and love,
HENRY RAMSEY JR., husband and father

· Notes ·

1. First Amendment, U.S. Constitution.

2. According to Armstrong (1994, p. xxii): "Recent surveys have shown that 99 percent of Americans say that they believe in God." See also, Fineman (2002, pp. 23–24, especially the material on p. 24).

3. Rampersad and Roessel (1994, p. 24. "Question (1)" by Langston Hughes.

4. This was my mother's church until she left Rocky Mount in 1955 and went to live with my brother James in Philadelphia. According to St. Mark church history two structures were located on Raleigh Road. The original structure was on the north side of the street. In 1894 members began building a wooden structure across the street from the first site. This church was completed in 1896 and renovated in 1919. At that time, the church's street address was in the 200 block of Raleigh Road. A new site at 801 West End Street was purchased and a groundbreaking ceremony was held on July 13, 1952. The church building was completed on Sept. 1, 1954. On Friday, Sept. 15, 2000, a new church was acquired, located at 1150 Tarboro Street; the opening service was held on Sunday, Sept. 17, 2000.

5. Most everyone in our neighborhood called the Rev. John A. July simply Rev., although some called him Rev. July or Reverend July.

6. Marguerite W. Thompson is a stepdaughter of the Rev. John A. July. She is, in 2008, now 91 years old and has lived for many years in Rocky Mount, N.C.

7. See Thurman (1994, p. 19).

8. See Armstrong (2000, p. 19): "This God was the First Cause of all being, whose existence had been logically demonstrated by Aristotle." See also Armstrong (1994, p. 3): "In the beginning, human beings created a God who was the First Cause of all things and Ruler of heaven and earth."

9. See Elwes (1951, p. x3), "His separation from Judaism was marked by his substituting for his name Baruch the Latin equivalent Benedict. . . ."

10. See Craig (1998, p. 91), "What is distinctive of Spinoza's brand of rationalism, however, is that it allows no place for an inscrutable creator-God distinct from his creation, who acts according to hidden purposes. Instead, Spinoza boldly identifies God with nature, albeit with nature regarded as this necessary rational order rather than as the sum-total of particular things." See Armstrong (2000, p. 22), "[Spinoza] argued that 'God' was simply the totality of nature itself."

11. According to Gillman (2000, p. 31), "Religious supernaturalism teaches that religion originates through the initiative of a God Who is beyond the natural order, and Who intervenes in history to reveal a teaching to a specific community. But note the contemporary idea in certain scientific circles that, as expressed by Einstein, God is simply the 'rules of reality' and that humans can intellectually comprehend those rules." See also Powell (2002, p. 13).

12. See Armstrong (2000, p. 74): "Immanuel Kant . . . believed that it was impossible to prove God's existence, since the deity was beyond the reach of the senses and, therefore, inaccessible to the human mind. . . . The only comfort that Kant could offer was that it was, by the same token, impossible to disprove God's existence either."

13. See Gillman (2000, p. 24).

14. See Armstrong (2000, p. 68): "The British scientist Sir Isaac Newton (1642-1727) . . . posited the idea of gravity as a universal force that held the entire cosmos together and prevented the celestial bodies from colliding with one another. This system, he was convinced, proved the existence of God, the great 'Mechanick,' since the intricate design of the cosmos could not have come about by accident." But also see Armstrong (2000, p. 66), which notes that Martin Luther (1483–1556) believed that because "God was utterly mysterious and hidden, the world was empty of the divine. . . . In Luther's writings, God had begun to retreat from the physical world, which now had no religious significance at all." Again on page 71, Armstrong writes that for the philosopher René Descartes (1596–1650) "the universe was a lifeless machine, the physical world inert and dead. It could give us no information about the divine." Armstrong (2000, p. 67) also writes that the theologian John Calvin (1509-64) did not "subscribe to Luther's disenchantment of the natural world. He believed that it was possible to see God in his creation, and commended the study of astronomy, geography, and biology." See the discussion of this issue in Powell (2002, pp. 52–53). Also see the discussion in Thurman (1994, pp. 19, 27).

15. See Alvarez et al. (1980) in which Dr. Luis Alvarez and his UC Berkeley team published their K-T impact extinction theory. Also see Archibald (1966, pp. 13–14).

16. "Progeria" is also known as rapid aging.

17. See Gillman (2000, p. 253).

18. Apparently it is neither claimed nor asserted that other animals have free will, and as I see it they seem to behave quite well without it.

19. For example, disease can be spread and floods can be caused negligently or intentionally.

20. Hedges (December 2002, p. 38).

21. Helms (1988, p. 24).

22. Ibid., p. 9.

23. Ibid., p. 50.

24. See *The Holy Bible*, The New Revised Standard Version, John, 11:1–45 (text of 1989). All Scripture quotations contained herein are from the New Revised Standard Version Bible, (c) 1989 by the Division of Christian Education of the National Council of the Churches of Christ in the U.S.A. Used by permission.

25. Helms (1988, p. 96).

26. Levinson (1996, p. 261).

27. Ibid.

28. See, for example, Kushner (1981, p. 72): "The biblical mind saw the earthquake that overthrew Sodom and Gomorrah as God's way of punishing the people of those cities for their depravities. Some medieval and Victorian thinkers saw the eruption of Vesuvius and the destruction of Pompeii as a way of putting an end to that society's immorality. Even today, the earthquakes in California are interpreted by some as God's way of expressing His displeasure with the alleged homosexual excesses of San Francisco or the heterosexual ones of Los Angeles."

29. For example, Mark Derr (2001, p. D4) wrote: "Between 1347 and 1352, a mysterious disease ravaged Europe, killing an estimated 25 million people–30 percent to 50 percent of the population. At the time, people said the disease was caused by a peculiar conjunction of the planets, by a miasma stirred up by earthquakes in Central Asia, or by a conspiracy of Jews to undermine Christendom. Many called it the wrath of God and expected the end of the world."

30. Humans today do have such power (for example, the atomic and hydrogen bomb, as well as certain chemical and biological weapons such as nerve gas and weapons grade smallpox), but they lacked such power before the 20th century.

31. See, for example, Powell (2002, p. 15): "Greek philosophers had wrestled with many of the same questions two dozen centuries earlier. They looked past the popular mythologies of the day, which attributed the inexplicable vicissitudes of weather, crops, and disease to a cantankerous community of gods. Led by the libidinous Zeus and his volatile wife, Hera, . . . these immortals ruled the world in accord with their ever-shifting moods."
32. *The Holy Bible*, The New Revised Standard Version, Zechariah 10:2 (text of 1989).
33. See Wilcox in Bohle (1967, p. 218:14).
34. See Armstrong (2000, pp. 73–74): "Immanuel Kant (1724–1804) . . . believed that . . . the only rational grounds he could find for the deist God was the quite dubious argument that without such a deity and the possibility of an afterlife, it was hard to see why we should act morally."
35. James (1997, p. 59).
36. See, for example, Rahman (1979, p. 31): "The Qur'anic term for 'Revelation' is *wahy*, which is fairly close in its meaning to 'inspiration,' provided this latter is not supposed to exclude the verbal mode necessarily (by 'Word,' of course, we do not mean sound). The Qur'an says, 'God speaks to no human (i.e., through sound-words) except through *wahy* (i.e., through idea-word inspiration) or from behind the veil, or He may send a messenger (an angel) who speaks through *wahy*. . . . Even thus have We inspired you with a spirit of our Command. . . .'" (XL2, 51–52).
37. See Levinson (1996, p. 91), "Born in about C.E. 570 in Mecca, Muhammad led a relatively uneventful life as a member of the local Qurayish tribe and as a merchant and husband until 610 when God revealed himself to Muhammad in a cave outside Mecca. At first Muhammad was unsure about the revelations, but further messages from God, sometimes speaking through the angel Gabriel, convinced him and his family members that he had received the 'Revelation of the Words of Allah' and the 'Call to Prophecy.'"
38. *The Holy Bible*, The New Revised Standard Version, Acts 9:3–6 (text of 1989), "Now as he was going along and approaching Damascus, suddenly a light from heaven flashed around him. He fell to the ground and heard a voice saying to him, 'Saul, Saul, why do you persecute me?' He asked, 'Who are you, Lord?' The reply came, 'I am Jesus, whom you are persecuting. But get up and enter the city, and you will be told what you are to do.'"
39. Powell (2002, p. 37).
40. Hedges (December 2002, p. 38), quoting Rabbi Harvey Tattelbaum.
41. Armstrong (1994, p. xxi).

42. But see Raphael (1996, p. 33): "The post-World War II promise that science would fulfill all human needs has not materialized. Even with all kinds of profound technological innovations—satellites, computers, fax machines, and fiber optics, to name a few—the quality of life in the Western world continues to decline. Drugs have taken their toll on countless lives; families seem to be in jeopardy; fatal diseases like AIDS are spreading, not disappearing; the toxicity of the earth and its atmosphere is only now being understood. With all this going on, more and more people find themselves deeply questing for personal meaning. What's it really all about? The question is no longer 'Is God Dead?' but rather 'How can I, as an individual, personally access God in my own life and enhance the quality of life for myself and the people around me?'"

43. Powell (2002, p. 9).

44. Kushner (1981).

45. See *The Holy Bible*, The New Revised Standard Version, Job (text of 1989).

46. Kushner (1981, p. 51).

47. Also see the discussion in this document regarding free will.

48. Kushner (1981, p. 60).

49. See Borysenko (1997, p. xix).

50. See, for example, the statement by John F. Walvoord in Crockett (1992, pp. 80–81): "[T]he Bible makes plain that while God exercises grace to those who put their trust in Christ, there is no grace for anyone outside of Christ." Also note the statement by Borysenko (1997, p. xix): "Some of my relatives who are Jehovah's Witnesses sincerely anguish over my unwillingness to recognize their religion as the only true Way, since they believe that my soul will cease to exist after the Judgment, and I will be permanently lost to them."

51. See the chapter written by Pinnock in Crockett (1992, p. 136).

52. See, for example, Revelation 20:10, "And the devil who had deceived them was thrown into the lake of fire and sulfur, where the beast and the false prophet were, and they will be tormented day and night forever and ever." For a detailed discussion of the horror and torture of hell, read Crockett (1992).

53. Some contemporary religious scholars also have great problems with this conception of the Christian God. For example, see the statement of Pinnock in Crockett (1992, p. 38): "Second, Walvoord sidesteps a grotesque moral problem. He asks us to believe that the God who wills the salvation of the world plans to torture people endlessly in physical fire if they decline his offer of salvation. Questions leap to mind. Who would want to accept salvation from a God like that? . . . Is he not conscious of the sadism he is attributing to God's actions? I am baffled, knowing that

John [Walvoord] is a kindly man, how he can accept a view of God that makes [God] out to be morally worse than Hitler." Also see Crockett's statement (1992, p. 62): "Because the idea of a never-ending punishment is so harsh . . . a number of evangelicals have called for a reconsideration of the doctrine. In its place they have proposed that we embrace conditional immortality or, as it is often called, annihilationism. This view can be structured in many ways, but the essential point is that the wicked pass out of existence rather than endure eternal, conscious punishment in the next life." And, finally, see Wells (1996, p. 15): "I would not think much of a god who penalizes honest doubt, and I hope that a majority of Christians find such a god equally repulsive." For an interesting discussion of this subject, read Randy Klassen's *What Does The Bible Really Say About Hell* (2001).

54. See Kushner (1981, p.153).

55. As stated by Rev. Robert McNeill, "Consistency is the first virtue to die at the moment one man consents to enslave another." McNeill (1965, p. 35).

56. *God Wills Us Free* is a good book to read about this subject.

57. McNeill (1965, p. 80).

58. Woods (1980, p. 44), "For Whom the Bell Tolls," by John Donne.

59. Members of my family, particularly Marguerite Thompson, accept this position and base it on John 3:16, "For God so loved the world that he gave his only Son, so that everyone who believes in him may not perish but may have eternal life." In other words, as long as you believe in Christ at the time of your death, you are "saved" and nothing else is required. But see Revelation 20:12, "And I saw the dead, great and small, standing before the throne, and books were opened. Also another book was opened, the book of life. And the dead were judged *according to their works*, as recorded in the books." (Emphasis added)

60. Ephesians 2:8–9: "For by grace you have been saved through faith, and this is not your own doing; it is the gift of God–not the result of works, so that no one may boast." Galatians 2:21: "I do not nullify the grace of God; for if justification comes through the law, then Christ died for nothing."

61. See Cowper (1902, p. 96), "Light Shining Out of Darkness": "God moves in a mysterious way, His wonders to perform."

62. Ibid. "Blind unbelief is sure to err, And scan his work in vain; God is his own interpreter, And he will make it plain."

63. *The Holy Bible*, The New Revised Standard Version, Romans 3:23 (text of 1989).

64. See Crockett (1992, p. 124), William V. Crockett's response to Zachary J. Hayes.

65. See *The Holy Bible*, The New Revised Standard Version, Genesis 2:16–25 and Genesis 3 (text of 1989). Also see Romans 5. For a discussion of various historical conceptions regarding the origin of mortality, see Gillman (2000, pp. 37-38); for example, "This theme of a message that goes astray, or is garbled, or more generally of some primordial capricious mistake is one of the classical ways that the ancients explained the origins of death in the world. Another explanation understands death as punishment for the foolish action of some primordial human being, usually a woman."

66. See, for example, *The Holy Bible*, The New Revised Standard Version, John 14:6, "Jesus said to him, 'I am the way, and the truth, and the life. No one comes to the father except through me.'" Also see John 3:36, "Whoever believes in the Son has eternal life; whoever disobeys the Son will not see life, but must endure God's wrath." And John 3:17–18, "'Indeed, God did not send the Son into the world to condemn the world, but in order that the world might be saved through him. Those who believe in him are not condemned; but those who do not believe are condemned already, because they have not believed in the name of the only Son of God.'"

67. See the discussion titled "Free Will" in this document.

68. See Raphael (1996, p. 23).

69. Ibid., pp. 314–24.

70. "For almost two thousand years, eternal life, heaven, and hell have been the predominant themes of Christian doctrine. From the very beginning, Christianity promised eternal life and paradise to anyone who repented in the name of Jesus Christ. During the second to fifth centuries, Christianity evolved from a marginal Jewish sect to the dominant religious authority in the Roman world." Ibid., p. 27.

71. See Cornell at http://www/worldbookonline.com.

72. See, for example, in Raphael (1996), particularly p. 149, "Gan Eden and Beyond"; p. 160, "Gehenna–The Realm of Postmortem Punishment;" pp. 179–80; p. 156, "Resurrection of the Dead"; and p. 314, "Gilgul–The Kabbalistic Doctrine of Reincarnation."

73. There are several, including, for example, the *Living Bible, Modern Language Bible, King James Version, New King James Version, Amplified Bible, New American Standard, Revised Standard Version, New Revised Standard Version, Young's Literal Translation, Good News Bible* (Today's English Version, published by the American Bible Society of New York), and *New International Version.*

74. See, for example, Matthew 25:31–46, especially 25:46, "And these will go away into eternal punishment, but the righteous into eternal life." Also see Luke 14:14, John 11:25–26, Acts 2:31, Romans 6:5, and Revelation 19:20–21.

75. See, for example, Matthew 28:6–10, Mark 16:3–14, Luke 24:14–47, and John 20:6–18. See Helms (1988, chap. 7) for a detailed discussion and analysis of the origin and description of the resurrection of Jesus Christ, as described in the Gospels.

76. *The Holy Bible*, The New Revised Standard Version, I Corinthians (text of 1989).

77. See Helms (1988, pp. 129–30).

78. See, for example, Revelation 21:1–4, "Then I saw a new heaven and a new earth; for the first heaven and the first earth had passed away, and the sea was no more. And I saw the holy city, the new Jerusalem, coming down out of heaven from God, prepared as a bride adorned for her husband. And I heard a loud voice from the throne saying, 'See, the home of God is among mortals. He will dwell with them; they will be his peoples, and God himself will be with them; he will wipe every tear from their eyes. Death will be no more; mourning and crying and pain will be no more, for the first things have passed away.'"

79. See, for example, Revelation 20:10–15: "And the devil who had deceived them, was thrown into the lake of fire and sulfur, where the beast and the false prophet were, and they will be tormented day and night forever and ever. Then I saw a great white throne and the one who sat on it; the earth and the heaven fled from his presence, and no place was found for them. And I saw the dead, great and small, standing before the throne and books were opened. Also another book was opened, the book of life. And the dead were judged according to their works, as recorded in the books. And the sea gave up the dead that were in it, Death and Hades gave up the dead that were in them, and all were judged according to what they had done. Then Death and Hades were thrown into the lake of fire; and anyone whose name was not found written in the book of life was thrown into the lake of fire." Also see Revelation 21:8, 14:10–11; plus Matthew 13:42, 25:41, 22:13, and 25:30.

80. Levinson (1996, p. 94).

81. Surah 19:66–72.

82. See Sakr (1992, p. 108): "This is a long bridge over Hell which is sharper than [a] sword and more subtle than hair. He who treads on [a] straight and right path in this world will cross it easily and will get salvation. He who is misguided and saddled with sins will slip there from at the first step and will fall down into Jahannam (Hell). Below the Bridge, there is the fire of Hell."

83. Raphael (1996, p. 3).

84. See Raphael (1996, p. 29, especially Table 2-1).

85. For example, among others, I have spoken with Attorney David Rosenthal, Attorney Landra Rosenthal, Attorney Dennis Roberts, and Dean and Professor Sanford Kadish of Boalt Hall.
86. See Rich (2002). For an in-depth exploration of traditional and contemporary Jewish views on the afterlife, read Raphael (1996).
87. Gillman (2000, p. 34).
88. See Thurman (1994, p. 28).
89. Ibid.
90. Nuland (1994, p. 257).
91. I am fully aware of the U.S. Supreme Court opinion in *San Antonio Independent School District v. Rodriguez,* 411 U.S. 1 (1973) that the Equal Protection Clause of the U.S. Constitution does not obligate or require states to provide public education for their citizens. ("While education is one of the most important services performed by the state, it is not among the rights afforded explicit or implicit protection under the Federal Constitution." 411 U.S. 1, at p. 35.) I simply believe this 6 to 3 decision was wrongly decided.
92. Rampersad and Roessel (1994, p. 127), "Dear Lovely Death," by Langston Hughes.

## BIBLIOGRAPHY

• Alvarez, Luis; Alvarez, Walter; Asaro, Frank; and, Michel, Helen. "Extraterrestrial Cause for the Cretaceous-Tertiary Extinction." 1980. *Science Magazine*, vol. 208, pp. 1095–1108.

• Archibald, J. David. *Dinosaur Extinction and the End of an Era: What the Fossils Say.* New York: Columbia University Press, 1966.

• Armstrong, Karen. *A History of God: The 4000-Year Quest of Judaism, Christianity, and Islam.* New York: Alfred A. Knopf, 1994.

• Armstrong, Karen. *The Battle for God.* New York: Ballantine Books, 2000.

• *The Holy Bible*, The New Revised Standard Version, Iowa Falls, Iowa: World Bible Publishers, Inc., 1989.

• Bohle, Bruce, ed. *The Apollo Book of American Quotations.* New York: Dodd, Mead & Company, 1967. (See "The World's Need," by Ella Wheeler Wilcox, p. 218:14.)

- Borysenko, Joan. *7 Paths to God*. Carlsbad, Calif.: Hay House, 1997.
- Cornell, Vincent J. "Islam," *World Book Online* Americas Edition, http://www/worldbookonline.com. Accessed: 26 November 2002.
- Cowper, William. *Poetical Works*. New York: Macmillan & Company (1902).
- Craig, Edward, ed., *Routledge Encyclopedia of Philosophy*, New York. Routledge, 1998.
- Crockett, William, ed., *Four Views on Hell*. Grand Rapids, Mich.: Zondervan, 1992. (See chapters by William Crockett, Zachary J. Hayes, Clark Pinnock, and John F. Walvoord.)
- Derr, Mark. "New Theories Link Black Death to Ebola-Like Virus." *New York Times*, Oct. 2 , 2001, p. D4.
- Elwes, R.H.M.. *Chief Works of Benedict De Spinoza*. New York. Dover Publications, Inc. 1951.
- Fineman, Howard. "One Nation, under . . . Who?" *Newsweek*, July 8, 2002, pp. 23-24.
- Gillman, Neil. *The Death of Death*. Woodstock, Vt.: Jewish Lights Publishing, 2000.
- Hedges, Chris. "An Unending Journey Through Faith and Heartbreak." *New York Times,* Dec. 15, 2002, p. 38.
- Helms, Randel. *Gospel Fictions*. Amherst, N.Y.: Prometheus Books, 1988.
- James, William. *The Varieties of Religious Experience*. N.Y.: Simon & Schuster, 1997.
- Klassen, Randy. *What Does The Bible Really Say About Hell?* Telford, Pa.: Pandora Press U.S., 2001.
- Kushner, Harold S. *When Bad Things Happen to Good People*. New York: Schocken, 1981.

• Levinson, David. *Religion: A Cross-Cultural Dictionary*. New York: Oxford University Press, 1996.

• McNeill, Robert. *God Wills Us Free, The Ordeal of a Southern Minister*. New York: Hill and Wang, 1965.

• Murphy, Dean E. "Eagle Scout Faces Official Challenge over His Lack of Faith." *New York Times*, Nov. 3, 2002, p. 14.

• Nuland, Sherwin B. *How We Die*. New York: Alfred A. Knopf, 1994.

• Parker, Kathleen. "God, Country Gain Fragile New Toehold." *USA Today*, Oct. 1, 2001, Editorial/Opinion.

• Powell, Corey S. *God in the Equation*. New York: The Free Press, 2002.

• Rahman, Fazlur. *Islam*. 2d ed. Chicago: University of Chicago Press, 1979.

• Rampersad, Arnold and Roessel, David, eds., *The Collected Poems of Langston Hughes*, New York: Alfred A. Knopf, 1994.

• Raphael, Simcha Paull. *Jewish Views of the Afterlife*. Northvale, N.J.: Jason Aronson, 1996.

• Rich, Tracey R. *Olam Ha-Ba: The Afterlife*. http://www.jewfaq.org/olamhaba.htm. Accessed: 26 November 2002.

• Sakr, Ahmad H. *Life, Death, and the After Life*. Lombard, Ill.: Foundation for Islamic Knowledge, 1992.

• Thurman, Robert A.F., trans. *The Tibetan Book of the Dead*. New York: Bantam Books, 1994.

• Wells, G.A. *The Jesus Legend*. Peru, Ill.: Open Court Publishing, 1996.

• Woods, Ralph L., ed. *Golden Treasury of The Familiar*. New York: Macmillan Publishing Co., Inc. 1980.

I KNOW I am
The Negro Problem
Being wined and dined,
Answering the usual questions
That come to white mind
Which seeks demurely
To probe in polite way
The why and wherewithal
Of darkness U.S.A.–
Wondering how things got this way
In current democratic night,
Murmuring gently
Over *fraises du bois*,
"I'm so ashamed of being white."

The lobster is delicious,
The wine divine,
And center of attention
At the damask table, mine.
To be a Problem on
Park Avenue at eight
Is not so bad.
Solutions to the Problem,
Of course, wait.[1]

—LANGSTON HUGHES

# 18

# *Alike Porter, and Barack Obama*

SATURDAY, APRIL 19, 2003, 2:15 A.M.: ALIKE.

*I* AM WAKEFUL, SOMEWHAT SAD and troubled of mind. W.E.B. Dubois wrote in 1903—in *The Souls of Black Folk*—that the "problem of the twentieth century is the problem of the color-line—the relation of the darker to the lighter races of man in Asia and Africa, in America and the islands of the sea."[2] Some people have said that it will also be a problem throughout the 21st century. As much as I hope it won't, I am deeply concerned that it very well might be.

Last night, Eleanor and I attended a small 65th birthday party for David Rosenthal, my friend and former law partner, at his home in Berkeley. I didn't count but would estimate that there were 25 or 30 people at the party. Without taking the time to explain why, let me note that our 6-year-old granddaughter, Alike Akin Yele Chinasa Porter, accompanied us. We were at the party for only a short while because I am presently recovering from the effects of chemotherapy and was somewhat fatigued. Things in that regard, however, are going quite well, and I am probably only about three or four weeks from again being strong and vigorous. Regardless, we stayed only about an hour —from approximately 8:00 to 9:00—and, after apologizing for the early departure and saying our goodbyes, Alike, Eleanor, and I got into my car and started home.

We had been driving for no more than five minutes when Alike spontaneously announced to us from her child-safety seat in the rear of the automobile, "There were only white people at that party." It is possible that this was not the first time Alike had expressed the notion or concept of "white people" in my presence and that I merely had not heard or paid any attention to it. I certainly hope it is not something I simply have missed.

Eleanor responded from her position in the front passenger seat, "Uncle Githaiga[3] and Uncle Charles[4] were also at the party."

Alike replied, "They are members of our family." She added, "Those white people are not members of our family." The statement did not reflect or intimate any hostility or animus toward white people but was simply uttered as a statement of fact—sort of like saying "My teacher is not a member of our family" or "President Bush is not a member of our family." I do not know how sophisticated her thinking is yet, but she seemed to be saying, "Other than members of our family, only white people were at that party." Why was that significant for her? Why did she find that noteworthy?

It was obvious to me that she was also saying, "There were no black people at the party." Again, why was that important to her? Perhaps she was saying that there were no people of color at the party, but I did not question her in that regard. As an aside, she would have had her facts wrong, because a young Chinese woman was present, although I do not think she was there when we arrived.

Perhaps I am making too much out of Alike's comments. It could simply be that this is the life-point when children her age begin thinking about and trying to understand broad political, historical, economic, and social events, concepts, and notions. On our way to David's party, Alike had a dollar bill that she had received from the tooth fairy, and she asked who was depicted on the currency. We told her it was George Washington, the nation's first president. She then began a series of what I, at least, thought were difficult questions. Is President Bush a bad person? Does President Bush kill people? Would President Bush kill people if he came to Berkeley? Is George Washington dead? Was George Washington a good person?

Except for "Is George Washington dead?" and "Would President Bush kill people if he came to Berkeley?" I consider each of those questions to be difficult ones when asked by a 6-year-old. One does not want to confuse or mislead a young child with adult answers that use adult language and contain words or ideas that can really be understood only by a much older person or in an adult context. For example, how do you tell a 6-year-old that George Washington was a good or bad person given the existence and practice of slavery in the United States in the late 18th century and given Washington's ownership of slaves? Or given his failure to lead or join a fight for slavery's abolition?[5] Regardless, the point is that her age may simply be when children begin to think about things such as who is the president of the United States and what does that mean? What does the president do? Why does he do it? What is race? What do words like *power, fairness, poverty, rich,* and *justice* mean?

Nonetheless, I do not think I ever before heard Alike express an awareness of race as a concrete and socially relevant concept. What is my point, and why am I sad and troubled? Alike is only 6 years old, going on 7. Her next birthday will be on September 1, 2003. My point is that she already, at the age of—as children like to say—6 and a half, apparently has a full and fairly well-developed notion of, or appreciation for, race as a social concept that is used in our society to separate, divide, differentiate between, or classify people in the world in which she lives.

Why did she think only white people being at David's party was so significant or relevant that it should be noted and commented on? Is she demonstrating or proving that she and her 21st century contemporaries will not be able to avoid the race "problem of the 20th century"? That is why I am troubled, sad, and deeply concerned for my granddaughter.

## SUNDAY, MAY 11, 2003, 7 A.M.: ALIKE.

ALIKE HAS SPENT THE NIGHT with Eleanor and me at our house. Indeed, she has slept in our bed. Now she has been awakened, I think by the sound of our voices, and she asks if she may watch the Disney channel on television. I start to tell her that, although we will permit her to watch television on this occasion, she must not devote too much time to television, because when children spend too much time watching television, they neglect reading and other activities that are important for their educational development. This is a special problem for black people, I say, and I am quickly interrupted by Alike, who retorts that she is "not black." When I ask what she is, she replies, "I am brown." I accept this correction, and our conversation continues without further contention; I do not ask her why it is important that she be described as brown and not black. I also do not try to discuss with or explain to her the significance or importance of the issue. That is a conversation I will have with her in the future, perhaps soon.

This early in her life, whatever explicit and unconscious mechanisms exist in our society for developing or fostering the notion of race in our youngsters may already have done their work on Alike and probably on two of my other five granddaughters—Adrianne and Monica. (The other three girls are probably still too young to have been significantly influenced in that regard.) Having read this essay, Eleanor and our friend Gilda Feller[6] both think I may be putting unwarranted emphasis on Alike's statement that she is not black. They both think that more likely than not, Alike was simply making a factual correction and not a political or racial statement. I acknowledge their position as a possible or even probable explanation for Alike's comment, but I still have concerns. A child might very well not know or understand why but might have accepted—perhaps even unconsciously—the notion that black is not a good color or that it is not good to be black.

As I reflect on Alike's situation—and that of all the other 6-year-olds in America—I think back to an event that is deeply etched in my mind. My earliest recollection of being introduced to the concept of race as a negative limitation or restriction is from when I was at an inn where my mother was employed. Today, we would call such a place a "bed and breakfast." The establishment's name was the Pomi Inn, and it was

ELEANOR MASON RAMSEY *(center) and granddaughter* ALIKE CHINASA PORTER *with* WINNIE MANDELA *(left) at a Black Women Organized for Political Action (BWOPA) event in Oakland, Calif. Names of the other two women are not known.*

located at 602 South Church Street in Rocky Mount.[7] The Pomi Inn was owned by a family whose last name was Miller. My mother worked there as a cook. While I have almost no recollection of it, perhaps my mother often or occasionally took me to work with her. I do remember that one day when I was perhaps 4 or 5 years old and with my mother at her job site, for some reason I wanted to get Mrs. Miller's attention. Her back was turned to me, and I reached up and touched her in an effort to get her attention. I have a clear memory, not so much of the event itself, but of my mother telling me later that I should not have touched Mrs. Miller because "White people do not like being touched by colored people." I did not and do not have any sense of my mother being alarmed or particularly fearful—just that her child needed to be advised of one more of life's important rules: "Look both ways before crossing the street." "Eat all of the food on your plate." "Don't touch white people without their knowledge or permission." "Don't touch a hot stove."

I don't think it is inevitable that Alike and the other 6-year-olds in the United States will grow up to be racists, to hate white people, to hate black people, or to be hated because of their race. But I must confess that I am saddened and troubled to have it brought home to me that, apparently, race will continue to be an issue for them. Maybe I should not be surprised. Perhaps it should be obvious to any thinking person in America that race will continue as a problem in the United States for decades, if not centuries, to come. I merely hoped against hope that perhaps, just perhaps, circumstances had changed between when I was Alike's age—some 63 years ago—and now. I hoped that perhaps a 6-year-old today would not notice or find it significant that "There were only white people at that party'" or feel a need to declare, "I am not black.'"

I will, in the familiar phrase, "too soon be gone," but as a society, we must do all we can to make it possible to honestly write that race ceased to be a problem in America sometime in the early 21st century.

## Thursday, July 17, 2008: The Senator.

After five years of writing and research and revisions, I am finishing these chapters in mid-July 2008, a few weeks before Senator Barack Obama's scheduled nomination as the 2008 Democratic Party presidential candidate. His presidential campaign and potential election as the first African American president of the United States of America[8] is clearly one of the most important political events for Afro-Americans in my lifetime. Much of it has actually occurred while I have been writing to you. So why haven't I discussed and analyzed the election, you may ask. The answer is simple: because it will not have taken place before this manuscript becomes a book.

I am committed to having a published book by my 75th birthday, January 22, 2009, which means adhering to a strict production schedule. Therefore I will not be writing about the *results* of the contest between the Democratic candidate, Barack Obama (whose policies and views I support), and the Republican candidate, John McCain (whose policies and views I do not). But I do want to talk to you about the campaign.

Assuming that Barack Obama becomes the Democratic Party's 2008 presidential nominee (that is to say, that nothing unthinkable occurs before he is officially nominated at the party's convention), his nomination will be an event of extraordinary magnitude. His winning the Democratic primary contest over Senator Hillary Clinton and other Democratic candidates established a new milestone in the progress of black Americans and other people of color toward full equality and freedom within the United States. But his election as president would be a historic event of nearly unimaginable scale. In the words of today's young folk, "It will be huge."

The change in the United States of America as concerns racial matters during the 100 years between 1909[9] and 2009, the year in which Barack Hussein Obama may very well be inaugurated as the 44th president of the nation, could not have been credibly contemplated when I was born in 1934. Indeed, those of my generation, the generation immediately after mine, and those from the immediately preceding generation who are still living, are saying to themselves—over and over again—that none of us believed or ever even thought an Afro-American would be nominated by a major political party to be president of the United States in our lifetime, let alone actually be elected. And yet, maybe, just maybe, in 2008 . . .

Obama's nomination as the Democratic presidential candidate, whether or not he is elected (and I certainly hope he is), profoundly demonstrates for me the extraordinary generational change that has occurred in this country during the almost three-quarters of a century that I have been alive. Much remains to be done before economic security and economic equality, educational opportunity and educational equality, meaningful and affordable health care, affordable housing, and justice in the legal system will or can exist for all Americans everywhere in the United States. And obviously the election of an Afro-American, or any other person of color—or a woman for that matter, historic as that also would be—will not in and of itself make an immediate and meaningful change in the day-to-day lives of people of color and poor people in this country.

The United States of America is arguably the wealthiest nation on Earth in 2008, and yet poverty and its effect on millions of citizens is still a common reality of American life. In my judgment, the greatest problem facing American society at the end of the 20th century was, and continues to be today, the disparity between the haves and the have-nots. Yes, the serious issues of racial bias and discrimination continue to be of tremendous importance. But I am convinced that America's greatest domestic problem is not the racial divide or the color line, but the inequity between those who are poor and those who are not.

But that fact notwithstanding, I am now convinced that conditions today in the United States are more favorable than at any other time in American history for the achievement of economic security, political fairness, and justice for all. I also believe that if those goals are to be achieved, it is the generation born after the generation that followed mine who will take us there. The election of an African American as president of the United States of America will be a significant indicator that the American people are now on a political road that will ultimately lead to a society that is substantially more just and egalitarian. The election of a woman—when it occurs, and I am confident that it soon will—will also be such an omen. Why do I say this?

What I have written in this volume recognizes the tremendous cost —in lives and treasure—paid by those of my and preceding generations, particularly African Americans, in their struggle for full civil, economic, and political rights for all people. In that heroic marathon of more than 200 years, a great deal has been accomplished for human rights for everyone living in America. But I am convinced that until everyone of my generation—regardless of race, creed, or color—has passed on, there is little chance that the ultimate goal of securing and protecting the human rights of all residents of the United States will or can be achieved. If Barack Obama becomes president of the United States in 2009, I am confident that a substantial factor in his victory will have been the vote of a significant majority of white voters who are under 50 years of age, those born after *Brown v. Board of Education*, a case decided in 1954.

Those of my generation and the generations immediately preceding and following mine—white as well as black—bear the burden of having lived most if not all of our lives during the Jim Crow period of American history (arguably the 100 years between 1865 and 1965) and the decade immediately following. Many of us were victims of Jim Crow, many were perpetrators of the racial segregation and discrimination of that period, and there were others who probably saw themselves as or tried to be uninvolved bystanders. But regardless of our status or position in society during that terrible period of American history, each of us who lived through it carries scars and baggage from those times.

No matter how hard one might try or how sincere the effort, I am personally convinced that no one—whether black, brown, red, white, yellow, or polka dot—can escape the views and effects of prejudices that were forged during those times. That is why for a long time now I have believed that it is only after those of us who lived all or some of our lives during the Jim Crow period have died that those born after that period and essentially unencumbered by its evil legacy will be able to establish the "more perfect union" written about in the U.S. Declaration of Independence more than 200 years ago. Senator Barack H. Obama's nomination and Senator Hillary Rodham Clinton's accomplishments in the 2007–2008 Democratic primary campaign are powerful evidence for me that we are on the eve of such an era.

The task falls to your generation—Alike's generation—and subsequent generations of Americans—whether Afro-American, Asian American, European American, Hispanic American, or Native American—to make the flawed dream of 18th century America a meaningful reality of 21st century America. As Barack Obama is fond of saying, "This is your time!" I have no doubt but that the only reason a woman and a black man could be the "last persons standing" in the 2008 Democratic presidential primary is that the minds and views of those born after 1960 are now a powerful force within American political and economic life. I do not mean to denigrate or ignore the extraordinary sacrifices and struggles of those involved in the early anti-slavery movement and the civil rights crusade of the 20th century. Their achievements were extraordinary and of momentous value. But like Moses and Martin Luther King Jr., they did not reach the "promised land."

That attainment has been reserved for you and your progeny. You are the ones for whom we have worked and waited all these years. It is your leadership and commitment that I and other black men and women my age have embraced and now depend upon to validate our long-standing hopes and dreams of equality and justice. You and your progeny are the ones who now have the opportunity to join and work with other members of American society—regardless of race, religion, skin color, national origin, gender, disability, or sexual orientation—to actually establish a country in which everyone has a meaningful and realistic opportunity for "life, liberty, and the pursuit of happiness." I hope with all my heart that you will persevere and prevail in that endeavor.

## · Notes ·

1. Langston Hughes, "Dinner Guest: Me," in *The Collected Poems of Langston Hughes,* eds. Arnold Rampersad and David Roessel (New York: Alfred A. Knopf, 1994), p. 547.
2. W.E. Burghardt DuBois, "Chapter 2: Of the Dawn of Freedom," *The Souls of Black Folk* (New York: Dodd, Mead & Company, 1903).
3. Our second son.
4. Our oldest son and child.
5. Read, for example, Henry Wiencek, *An Imperfect God, George Washington, His Slaves, and the Creation of America* (New York: Farrar, Straus and Giroux, 2003), especially chapter 9, beginning at page 311.
6. Gilda is the widow of David Feller, a Boalt Hall faculty colleague who was a very close friend of mine until his death in February 2003. Gilda also served as a member of the Berkeley City Council, being elected in 1977, the year I chose not to seek re-election.
7. Located either at or very close to the southwest corner of the intersection of Church Street and Raleigh Road. Incidentally, U.S. Highway 301 (a main interstate route between New York City and southern Florida) was named Church Street within the city limits of Rocky Mount. See "Classified Business Directory, Hotels, Pomi Inn," *Hill's Rocky Mount (Edgecombe County, NC) City Directory,* Vol. 1940, XII (Richmond, VA: Hill Directory Co., Inc., Publishers).
8. Presidents Thomas Jefferson and William Jefferson Clinton notwithstanding. I mention President Bill Clinton because most adult Americans living today know that he is sometimes referred to as "the first black president," primarily because of his support for African American civil rights and appointment of African Americans to his cabinet and the federal judiciary. But he was initially referred to as the first black president by Nobel Prize-winning African American writer Toni Morrison, in an October 1998 *New Yorker* article ("Clinton as the first black president"). Her context for that label was different from its use in subsequent political conversations. Morrison wrote:

> African-American men seemed to understand it right away. Years ago, in the middle of the Whitewater investigation, one heard the first

murmurs: white skin notwithstanding, this is our first black President. Blacker than any actual black person who could ever be elected in our children's lifetime. After all, Clinton displays almost every trope of blackness: single-parent household, born poor, working-class, saxophone-playing, McDonald's-and-junk-food-loving boy from Arkansas. And when virtually all the African-American Clinton appointees began, one by one, to disappear, when the President's body, his privacy, his unpoliced sexuality became the focus of the persecution, when he was metaphorically seized and bodysearched, who could gainsay these black men who knew whereof they spoke? The message was clear: "No matter how smart you are, how hard you work, how much coin you earn for us, we will put you in your place or put you out of the place you have somehow, albeit with our permission, achieved. You will be fired from your job, sent away in disgrace, and–who knows?–maybe sentenced and jailed to boot.

Thomas Jefferson was called the "Negro President" during his time. But it was not because he was pro-Negro or sympathetic to the plight of Negroes. Rather, it was because slaves counted for three-fifths of a person in the determination of electoral votes, which won Jefferson the presidential election of 1800. After that election and because of that fact, many of his opponents referred to him as the "Negro President." See Garry Wills, *Negro President, Jefferson and the Slave Power* (Boston, New York, Houghton Mifflin Company, 2003).

9. The NAACP was founded in 1909, which was also the year that Sylvester Wesley Williams, my maternal great-grandfather, died.

339 · *Alike Porter, and Barack Obama*

Eleanor Mason Ramsey *and* Henry Ramsey Jr. *with granddaughters (from left) Adrianne Tillman Ramsey, Aisha Hunter Ramsey, Alike Akin Yele Chinasa Porter, Ade Mia Porter, Anais Andrée-Eleanor Schuhmann, and Monica Ruby Ramsey.*

· *Memorable Events* ·

WE WERE BOTTLED UP AND LABELED and set aside—sent to the Jim Crow car, the back of the bus, the side door of the theater, a side window of a restaurant. We came to know that whatever we had was always inferior. We came to understand that no matter how neat and clean, how law abiding, submissive, and polite, how studious in school, how churchgoing and moral, how scrupulous in paying our bills and taxes we were, it made no essential difference in our place.[1]

—PAULI MURRAY

HOW DO YOU CONVEY what it's like to live under threat and tyranny all the time, and to act in spite of it? To live in poverty and act out of generosity? To be part of something—building a better society for your kids—you're willing to risk your life for?[2]

—HEATHER TOBIS BOOTH

EVEN AS THEY LABORED IN THE FIELDS and kitchens, many black men and women dwelled on the thought that such labor was necessary if they were to release their children from the same compulsions. It was a way to sustain them as they performed their daily tasks, a way of making some sense out of their labor, particularly the amount of work they performed to enrich other people's lives.[3]

—LEON F. LITWACK

THE DOMINANT GROUP in a society is often shocked to find that subordinate groups remember the harms done to them, which often resurface as the primary basis of their attitudes and behaviors toward the dominant group.[4]

—RONALD W. WALTERS

# 19

# The NAACP Youth Branch, Rocky Mount, North Carolina

O ne of the more significant events in my life occurred during or just before my early teenage years, when Vivian Patterson, a young, black, female civil rights activist who lived on Henna Street in a nearby Rocky Mount black neighborhood that we called the "Oil Mill Section"[4a] asked me to become a member of the Youth Branch of the local NAACP chapter.[5] My NAACP Youth Branch experiences and Vivian Patterson's leadership contributed greatly to my personal development as a youth and, in fact, have continued to influence my life. Youth Branch members of my era knew about and were motivated by the important and courageous work being done by the NAACP for Negro[6] civil rights and personal dignity.[7]

I hope you can appreciate that this was a time when young black people my age were profoundly embarrassed by and ashamed of the submissive, obsequious, and sometimes cowardly behavior that some Negro adults in our neighborhood—and elsewhere in Rocky Mount—exhibited toward adult Caucasians and even toward some Caucasian youths.[8] This deferential behavior was not as extreme as that typically exhibited during slavery and during the seven or eight decades immediately following emancipation. Nonetheless, the inappropriate "yasshu," the grinning and shuffling, and the unnecessary scratching of the head were an embarrassment for us and a continuing acknowledgment and sign of white superiority and black inferiority.

Perhaps my contemporaries and I directed more emotion, more anger, toward those experiences than was warranted, but I doubt it. You must be sensitive to the social, political, and economic context in which the events were occurring. This was a time when almost every important element of American society had a propagandistic component that was designed to deny or undermine—if not destroy—black dignity, confidence, and power. I want to talk with you about that system, to help you understand why the attitudes imparted by our Youth Branch in Rocky Mount were and still are so influential in my life.

## PROPAGANDA DEPICTING IMAGES OF NEGROES

TWO EXAMPLES OF THIS EFFORT are the pictures used to advertise Uncle Ben's rice and Aunt Jemima's pancake mix. Because we knew there was no actual Uncle Ben or Aunt Jemima, what legitimate reason could the white people who owned those companies have for selecting *those particular invented images* of Negroes to market their product? The true reasons were obvious to us: first, the comfort and good feelings experienced by whites when seeing an image of a happy, servile, nonthreatening Negro and, second, further gratuitous deprecation of black people. Calling the images *Aunt* Jemima and *Uncle* Ben was absolutely consistent with the common and well-known practice of southern whites referring to obviously unrelated Negro adults as their aunts and uncles, that reference being a pretext to avoid calling them *Mr.* or *Mrs.* And although some Negroes purchased Ben's rice and Jemima's pancake mix, the products were primarily prepared for and marketed to the mainstream white population.

A major concern of mine is that it may not even be possible for my children and grandchildren—and particularly my great-grandchildren and their children—to fully understand or appreciate the comprehensive and totally overpowering nature of the various means and instruments used by the white majority to oppress and subjugate the black minority in America—particularly in the old Confederate South—during my childhood and the preceding six or seven decades. To have such an understanding should greatly help one, particularly a black person, understand and even forgive the shameful, deferential, and submissive behavior that some blacks continued to exhibit toward white people during my childhood. As an adult, I do understand.

The political and economic power that white people possessed and exercised over black Americans, particularly in the South after Reconstruction and during the Jim Crow period (1880 until the end of the 1950s), was used in a most brutal, cruel, and inhumane manner. And it must be recognized that this long period of unrestrained and extreme violence, brutality, and deceit was highly effective, both during and after Reconstruction, in restoring whites to a position of superiority over blacks and in forcing many blacks to assume submissive positions in interactions with whites. This apparent submission confirmed the belief of most white people that they were a superior race. At the same time, many black Americans believed that, in all their contacts with white people, it was critical for their very survival that they show deference, sycophancy, and docility.

Perhaps my contemporaries and I would have been less critical and had more sympathy for the black adults we viewed as Uncle Toms had we been better educated or informed about how our parents and their parents and grandparents suffered after emancipation. I think we had a fairly good idea of how horrible and cruel slavery must have been, but today, at this stage in my life, I see that we were almost totally ignorant of the details of the cruelties that our parents and grandparents had suffered under the Jim Crow system in existence during the last two decades of the 19th century and the first four decades of the 20th century.

For that reason, I now have a real concern—perhaps it is fear—as I look back on my 74 years of life, that too many of today's young people (black, other people of color, and white) lack a meaningful appreciation of the level or extent of humiliation, psychological cruelty, legal disadvantages, racial bigotry, and physical brutality endured by people of color—particularly black people—during the Jim Crow period of the 19th and 20th centuries, especially in the states of the former Confederate South. The horrific conditions known as Jim Crow were suffered by Negroes decades before the time of my birth in 1934. But

I was acutely conscious of Jim Crow and its effects. Indeed, in many instances, I directly observed and experienced those effects from my early childhood until I left North Carolina after joining the U.S. Air Force in May 1951. I strongly request that you read *Trouble in Mind*, by Leon F. Litwack,[9] to gain a better appreciation and understanding of black life and suffering during the Jim Crow period.

NAACP Youth Branch members were aware of the unjust treatment that Negroes typically experienced when involved with the legal system, of pervasive police misconduct and brutality (which we sometimes observed personally), and of the tolerance toward frequent lynchings[10] and other forms of brutal and outrageous violence by the Ku Klux Klan and other night riders throughout the South. I suppose what disturbed me most was the knowledge that, as a Negro, one could not rely on local, state, or federal government officials for protection, fairness, or justice, because in most disputes with a white person, you would be confronted by a Caucasian arbiter who was almost always strongly biased in favor of the white person, no matter how correct, valid, or legally sound the black person's position.

## LACK OF LEGAL STATUS

THE FOLLOWING AFRICAN AMERICAN folktale aptly describes the black man's position in southern courts—and arguably in courts almost everywhere else in the United States—during the Jim Crow period:

> One day Brother Fox caught Brother Goose and tied him to a tree.
>
> "I'm going to eat you, Br'er Goose," he said. "You've been stealing my meat."
>
> "But I don't even eat meat," Br'er Goose protested.
>
> "Tell that to the judge and jury," said Br'er Fox.
>
> "Who's gonna be the judge?" asked Br'er Goose.
>
> "A fox," answered Br'er Fox.
>
> "And who's gonna be the jury?" Br'er Goose inquired.

"They all gonna be foxes," said Br'er Fox, grinning so all his teeth showed.

"Guess my goose is cooked," sighed Br'er Goose.[11]

In matters traditionally left to a state's jurisdiction—for example, family matters and public safety—a black person simply had no judicial, legislative, or executive protection for constitutionally guaranteed rights of equal protection and due process of law.

My Negro contemporaries and I were deeply offended by and profoundly resentful of the racial bigotry we were forced to endure under North Carolina's Jim Crow laws, practices, customs, and traditions. Like everywhere else in the Confederate South, I and all other black people in Rocky Mount were personally confronted each day by invidious racial discrimination in various forms. Examples were lack of a public swimming pool for Negroes (constructed in later years but still segregated), although there was one for whites; want of Negro access to the one public library in the city; blatant job discrimination ("only whites need apply"); and, especially, denial of publicly funded jobs, such as work as police officers or firefighters or in other municipal posts— even at the federal post office.

There was segregated housing, and much of the housing for Negroes was substandard. For example, three or four houses on Dunn Street in our neighborhood (just west of South Washington Street, on the south side of the street), although occupied by families, bore prominent signs that had been posted by the city's Health Department and even then were severely weathered. The signs declared in large, albeit faded, letters: THIS HOUSE IS NOT FIT FOR HUMAN HABITATION. Financial institutions also practiced discriminatory lending policies, and there were segregated vehicles of public transportation; segregated waiting rooms in the interstate bus and train stations; segregated schools; segregated and obviously unequal water fountains and toilets in public department stores; segregated facilities of public accommodation, such as hotels, restaurants, and theaters; and many other gratuitous insults and forms of undeserved abuse.

Although racial discrimination in North Carolina was less extensive during my early life and teenage years than during earlier times, the pervasive and irrational violence that Negroes were subjected to during the Jim Crow years between 1880 and 1945 had a terribly crippling effect on our people. It would be difficult to overstate the lack of self-confidence, the self-hatred, and even the lack of hope that resulted from those terrible experiences.

That, in my mind, is the incredible emotional and psychological burden we were asked to bear. This burden was particularly harsh because the black victims of that denial of fundamental rights could everywhere see white people enjoying those rights, while the overwhelming majority of white people in the United States either denied or acquiesced in the denial of those rights to black people.[12]

I wish for the writing skills required to adequately describe the profound emotional effect that continuous exposure to segregation and bigotry had on my contemporaries and me. I suppose my sense of inability to put into words the sorrow and pain of enduring racial discrimination will always be a fact with which I must contend, because the intensity and actual emotional effect of a phenomenon like Jim Crow can never be fully understood or appreciated unless personally experienced.

The time and place of my upbringing was in a nation and world you have not experienced, and I hope with every fiber of my being that you never will. It would take too many pages for me to chronicle the various ways that American society undermined Negro self-confidence and caused far too many of us to seriously doubt our own worth. Nonetheless, I have devoted a few pages to this topic in an effort to help you understand and appreciate the cruelty, frustration, horror, madness, terror, and suffering of those days.

It was a world in which from your early childhood the general society bombarded you with the lie that you, and all persons who looked like you, were incompetent and inferior to every person of European ancestry. Every resource of acculturation was devoted to the task of reinforcing that lie and getting you and the rest of the nation to accept it as true. If a Negro exhibited exceptional merit or talent that could just not be denied by the general society, then, in the eyes of the white majority, the particular Negro was simply one of the few exceptions to the various inadequacies that were representative of his or her kind.[13]

## CARICATURES IN THE PUBLIC EYE

OF PARTICULAR IMPORTANCE FOR this widespread mission of deprecating blacks were the film industry, legislative bodies, news media, and various southern traditions. Hollywood, for example, was at the forefront of this propagandistic machine.[14] To obtain work as actors in television or film, movie and television personalities such as Stephen Fetchit,[15] Rochester on the "Jack Benny Show,"[16] and Man Tan Moreland[17] had to roll their eyes unnecessarily; display the whites of their eyes in a bizarre manner; scratch their heads frequently, as if bewildered or confused; speak broken English; and behave obsequiously toward white characters.

The several Tarzan films were also a major vehicle for perpetuating the propagandistic notion that Negroes were descendants of savages and, therefore, as ignorant and uncivilized as their African ancestors were said to have been.[18] Those films (and later pulp and comic books) portrayed Tarzan as of upper-class British origin and a virtual superman (intelligent, strong, clever, creative, honest, athletic, resourceful, and totally self-reliant) when compared with the Africans (cruel, ignorant, stupid, superstitious, savage, militarily weak, unimaginative, and somewhat dependent on Tarzan for guidance and protection) with whom he interacted. And this contrast existed notwithstanding that Tarzan was not reared in England but, from childhood, by apes in the rain forest, where somehow he learned to speak English and communicate with various animals, particularly his chimpanzee sidekick Cheetah, who was portrayed as being more intelligent than the African characters in the films!

This absurd and incredible film story was popular entertainment[19] in the United States, and it did much to reinforce white American opinion and thought about Negroes. The outrageous and insulting Tarzan movies provided moral support (whites were civilizing the African, saving Negro men, women, and children from the savagery of jungle life in Africa, and giving them the grace of Christianity) as well as political backing for policies and traditions that oppressed the Negro and continued our suffering in America, particularly in the former Confederate South.

We—and the entire nation—also had this mean view of the Negro reinforced by the highly popular "Amos 'n' Andy" radio comedy show that featured slow-witted, poorly educated, dishonest Negro characters (the actual roles being played by white actors), most of whom were portrayed as speaking broken English and being seriously challenged ethically and intellectually. When television replaced radio as the principal form of home entertainment for the American family, Negro actors were hired to play the "Amos 'n' Andy" roles[20] but still exhibited the exaggerated dimwittedness, dishonesty, ignorance, and unethical conduct that had characterized those roles when performed on the radio by white actors. Now the negative characteristics were no longer limited to being observed aurally but could be exacerbated by exaggerated and extremely demeaning facial and eye expressions of the Negro actors.

The film, radio, and television performances by or about Negroes certainly reinforced two malevolent views that were widely held in much of the country. One was that Negroes in America had to be civilized and educated in European values before they would deserve the civil, political, and economic rights enjoyed by Caucasian Americans—and even Caucasian noncitizen immigrants. The second was that because Negroes were descendants of ignorant savages, were intellectually inferior to white people, came from a land without culture or a meaningful history, and had only been fit to work as slaves for whites, teaching them European values would be exceptionally difficult and would take many decades, probably at least another century.

Until then, whites would have to lead and rule, and both Negroes and whites would have to be patient and accept that as the status quo until Negroes could demonstrate that they had caught up with, or had nearly caught up with and deserved the same rights as whites, because then the Negroes would have earned those rights. If Negroes would not wait and could not continue to accept the doctrine of separate but equal,[21] particularly in all matters social and most matters economic,[22] then violence as a means for keeping us in our place would simply have to be used and tolerated by the white majority.[23] This opinion was certainly true of views held in the Deep South—especially South Carolina, Georgia, Alabama, and Mississippi. Continued white supremacy in economic, business, political, and educational matters was considered vital to white and national well-being and even survival.

I beg you never to underestimate the power and influence of popular films and the news media, especially network and cable television. The media are a powerful determinant of many of the intellectual, physical, social, political, and economic standards that we use to judge others and ourselves. Indeed, I would say that it is probably impossible to overestimate the influence of the news media and film industry on American public opinion. No person is or can be a percipient witness to all the important events occurring in the world each day. Of necessity, we must rely on news reports presented on television and in the print media for information about those events. The news media are in a position to determine what will be published from among the numerous events that occur each day. The media can decide what "news" to focus on and how often to mention and discuss any particular news item, as well as choosing the days or weeks to highlight a particular subject or news item.

A given network, cable news station, newspaper, or news magazine can place a particular face on an individual, group, people, institution, corporation, or nation. I remember an occasion during spring semester 1994 when Connie Chung of CBS came to Howard University to interview students regarding whether Howard students were anti-white.[24]

It was obvious to me, and to many others at Howard, that she had limited her interviews to only a few students who held strongly anti-white views and then deliberately presented those views as proof of widespread anti-white sentiment among Howard students. She did not interview, nor was she interested in interviewing, students who did not hold anti-white views. Connie Chung's sensational treatment of this topic on her program—"Eye to Eye with Connie Chung"—was frequently cited by other representatives of the media as important and credible evidence of so-called reverse racism among black students in American institutions of higher education.

## Words and Language to Demean

In addition to economic and political deprivations imposed on Negroes during my childhood and youth (and during some of my adult years), numerous other cruel and mean-spirited traditions, practices, and policies were used to demean and oppress black people. For example, grown men were often referred to as "boy," instead of by their name. This language conveyed the notion that black adult males were to be considered as children and not as mature men. I have already made reference to the "aunt" and "uncle" ploy. There was common usage of the words *nigger, nigrah, monkey, apelike,* and *coon* to refer to and characterize Negroes as subhuman, animal-like, and as having significantly less merit than Caucasians (i.e., whites) and, indeed, all other humans.[24a]

I also think it significant that the word *black* itself was regularly associated with and attached to negative concepts in American society. For example, the majority of the definitions listed for black by *Webster's Third New International Dictionary* (unabridged)[25] are negative:

2a: *of human beings;* 2b: of, belonging to, consisting of, or connected with black, esp. Negroid, people [~Africa] [~races]; *esp:* having a large Negro population [a ~belt] . . . 4: soiled with dirt: dirty [how ~ your hands are] [the pot calls the kettle ~] . . .

6a: outrageously wicked: deserving unmitigated condemnation [a ~ deed] [a ~ heart] [a ~ villain]; *sometimes*: DISHONORABLE, DISCREDITABLE; b: expressing or indicating disgrace, dishonor, discredit, or guilt, sometimes through symbolic use of an object that is black in color [a ~ mark for tardiness] [with evidence so ~ against him −Charlotte Armstrong]; 7: connected with some baneful aspect of the supernatural, esp. the devil [a ~ curse] [~ magic] [the ~ art]; 8a: unrelievedly sad, gloomy, or calamitous [~ despair] [things are looking ~]; 9: expressing or characterized by menace or angry discontent : SULLEN, HOSTILE [he gave me a ~ look] [~ resentment filled his heart −Miriam James]; 10: being such to the greatest possible extent: EXTREME, UNQUALIFIED, UTTER [it was a ~ born fool I had for a son −J. M. Synge]; 11: constituting, committing, or connected with a violation of an official quota, price ceiling, rationing restriction, or other public regulation : ILLICIT, ILLEGAL [the ~ market] [~ gasoline]; . . . 15a: *of propaganda:* conducted so as to appear to originate within an enemy country and designed to weaken enemy morale−opposed to *white*; b: characterized by or connected with the use of black propaganda [~ psychological warfare] [~ radio].

Black art is sorcery and witchcraft. A blackball is a negative vote. A black book contains the names of people or organizations to be blacklisted.[26] (A blacklist is a list of people who are disapproved of or are to be punished or discriminated against.) A black bottle is one, according to folklore, from which a dose of poison is administered to unwanted patients in hospitals. A black cat crossing your path means you will soon experience bad luck. A black cloud on your reputation is extremely undesirable. To be black-hearted is to have a wicked disposition. Black magic is magic practiced for evil purposes.

Blackmail is extortion of money or anything of value by threats, especially by threatening to expose a criminal act or discreditable information.[27] Black market is the illegal business of buying or selling currency or goods. Black money is income, as from an illegal activity, that is not reported to the government for tax purposes. A blackout is a cut-off of electrical power. A black sheep is a member of a family or other group who stands in conspicuous and unfavorable contrast to the other members. Particularly in early popular western movies, the hero always wore a white hat and the villain always wore a black one.

Compare and contrast the treatment of the words *black* and *dark* in American society with the meanings and implications of the word *white*, at least in the context of race and racial relations. It is significant that the word *white* itself is regularly associated with and attached to positive concepts in American society. For example, the majority of the definitions listed for *white* by *Webster's Third New International Dictionary* (unabridged)[28] are positive:

> 2a: *of a human being* (1) *archaic:* having lightly pigmented skin, hair, and eyes: fair-complexioned: blonde; (2) *sometimes cap:* belonging to a racial group or subdivision of a racial group characterized by reduced skin pigmentation, typically represented by the European Caucasoids, and usu. specif. distinguished from persons belonging to groups marked by black, brown, yellow, or red skin coloration; (3): being of white ancestry either wholly unmixed with Negro blood or having an admixture of Negro blood less than that specified in various statutes of some states of the U.S.; 2b: of, relating to, or consisting of white and esp. Caucasoid people . . .; 2c: marked by upright fairness: straightforward and kindly: square-dealing . . .; 3: free from spot or blemish: as a: free from moral stain or impurity: outstandingly righteous: innocent . . .; c: not marked by or connected with malignant influences or intent: not intended to cause harm . . .; d: burnished or polished until shining bright and free from spot or mar . . .; e: notably pleasing or auspicious: favorable, fortunate.

This phenomenon is also succinctly described in *The Autobiography of Martin Luther King Jr.*, edited by Clayborne Carson:

The job of arousing manhood within a people that had been taught for so many centuries that they were nobody is not easy. Even semantics conspire to make that which is black seem ugly and degrading. In Roget's *Thesaurus* there are some 120 synonyms for "blackness" and at least 60 of them are offensive—such words as "blot," "soot," "grime," "devil," and "foul." There are some 134 synonyms for "whiteness," and all are favorable, expressed in such words as "purity," "cleanliness," "chastity," and "innocence." A white lie is better than a black lie. The most degenerate member of a family is the "black sheep," not the "white sheep."[29]

All of the preceding definitions, acts, or descriptions regarding *black* are bad and none are good; all are negative and none are positive. Even the word *dark* probably played a role in this effort, as in dark cloud, dark continent, dark days, dark mood, dark motives, dark thoughts, and dark times.[30] I am not a psychiatrist, psychologist, sociologist, or social anthropologist, and, therefore, I do not know with any academic or scientific authority what negative emotional and mental effect living in a society that uses such labels has on the psyche of people, particularly if that same society places such importance on skin color and if one's own skin color is associated with such negativity. But I am personally convinced that it must have had, and to some extent still has, a monstrous effect and incredibly injurious impact on the thinking of black Americans—an effect that not only seriously undermined our own sense of self-worth, but also determined in significant measure how white Americans viewed and believed they could treat us.

Laws requiring and supporting segregation in public and even private affairs (for example, miscegenation and restrictive covenants) were imposed by the legislature. Mr. or Mrs. would precede the names of white people printed in the newspaper but not Negro names. Crime stories in the newspaper identified Negro suspects or convicts by race but whites were not so identified. White social events (for example, engagements, weddings, and cotillions) and sports events received extensive coverage in the local white daily newspaper, but corresponding black events did not; indeed, they were usually not covered at all.

## Self-Hatred and Sense of Inferiority

Let me now turn to what I consider to have been the cruelest and most vicious deed by the white majority: planting the virulent seeds of self-doubt and self-hatred within even the strongest and most secure of us. Even black people who deny having ever been infected with this cruel disease know in their hearts that they too have been contaminated, however slight that contamination. White racism caused us to personally doubt the worth of our parents, relatives, friends, and neighbors. It infected most—probably all—of us with the deadly disease of self-hatred, a sickness that we and our descendants have had to contend with for our entire lives. It was an especially despicable act because the disease was not just hatred of self, but also hatred of all black people.

How was this deed achieved? It wasn't just the continual repetition over time of this vicious view in public discourse, in pseudoscientific commentary, in elementary and secondary schools, and in the news media, but also the constant reinforcement in so many other aspects of one's daily life. The economic world was permeated with support for this racist position. For example, professional services were, for the most part, provided by white people, except where racial tradition dictated otherwise.

Male Caucasians occupied every position of executive, legislative, and judicial power in our municipal, county,[31] state, and federal governments. So the model of competence and power in the political world was that of a white male. Our teachers in the South were black, but only because the schools were segregated. We had doctors, dentists, and undertakers who were black, but, in great measure, only because most Caucasians in those professions would not serve blacks.

The disease of self-hatred fed on and was exacerbated by the scarcity of strong black role models in the general society. Don't hire a black lawyer if a white one will handle your matter. If you can find any white doctor who will treat you, take that doctor over any black doctor, no matter how superior the black doctor's credentials. In a short, sad story my friend Ruby Burrows McZier often tells, a black person is asked why he always buys his ice from the white man and never from the black man who also sells ice. The black person answers by confidently declaring, "The white man's ice is colder." And so the perception was that the white plumber was competent, but the black plumber most likely was not; that the white carpenter was competent, but the black carpenter most likely was not; that the white electrician was competent, but the black electrician most likely was not.

To my mind, even greater significance for black economic development was the fact that the skilled trades were virtually reserved for whites. It was not until after the American Federation of Labor (AFL), the labor organization that represented almost all skilled trade unions (e.g., the Brotherhood of Boilermakers, Iron Ship Builders, Blacksmiths, Forgers and Helpers International; International Union of Operating Engineers; International Brotherhood of Electrical Workers; United Association of Journeymen and Apprentices of the Plumbing and Pipefitting Industry of the United States and Canada; and United Brotherhood of Carpenters and Joiners of America), merged with the Congress of Industrial Organizations (CIO) in December 1955 that a serious effort was made by organized labor to allow black skilled trade workers to apply for membership in AFL affiliated unions.[32] To its credit, the CIO did admit black workers as members, but most if not all skilled trade unions were affiliated with the AFL.

Unskilled positions and common labor were the occupations reserved for Negroes. Even when blacks were needed or allowed to work in the skilled trades, their worth was usually demeaned through denial of appropriate titles and comparable wages. In Rocky Mount, the highly skilled black carpenter was described as a carpenter's helper and paid accordingly. This selection of titles was true even when the black person (still classified as a helper) had actually trained the white worker through apprenticeship. Moreover, when the white person was no longer an apprentice and was classified as a skilled worker or journeyman, the black person remained a helper. And it was the same for the pipefitter, the plumber, and the mechanic. The white was the journeyman with the black as the helper, and there was typically a substantial pay differential between the two positions. I trust you to guess who enjoyed the higher salary. I do not have personal knowledge that those practices existed everywhere in the old Confederate South and in most, if not all, of the other states, but I am confident that they did.

For example, Negroes could not get city jobs as truck drivers in Rocky Mount.[33] They were not even permitted to drive the city's garbage trucks, although blacks did the physical act of handling and lifting the garbage cans. There was one exception, however: Negro men drove the truck used to collect human excrement from some of the houses in our neighborhood.[34] That was the one city-owned truck that Negroes were permitted to drive. (Needless to say, they also performed the physical act of actually collecting the feces and urine.) As children, we called the truck that came to our neighborhood to collect human feces and urine the "honey bucket." One man who drove such a truck was a friend of our family and known as "Bro' Johnny." I never knew his last name or any name but Bro' Johnny. He was a friendly man, who had a gold tooth and was always smiling, but he was very much a "natural Tom."

Not to be overlooked is the role played by the U.S. Armed Forces as an institution where young white males acquired training and experience in various skills that were denied to black men in civil society. "Blacks had participated in the Armed Forces and had fought in almost all of the nation's wars,"[35] but service in the armed forces throughout most of the 20th century was a means whereby hundreds of thousands of white American youth were, for example, trained as electricians, clerk-typists, operating engineers, machinists, automobile and aircraft mechanics, and medical technicians. And yet, during that same period, those same opportunities were blatantly denied to black American men.

The Rocky Mount and, in fact, North Carolina educational system available to Negroes—elementary, high school, and college—was obviously underfunded. Throughout Rocky Mount's black educational infrastructure, most physical plants suffered from neglect or deferred maintenance, and teachers were underpaid and sometimes inadequately trained. Books and equipment in Negro schools had usually been handed down after being used by white students, with the white students receiving new books and equipment at their school. Athletic programs at the Negro high school were limited (for example, typically no golf, gymnastics, swimming, or track and field).

It was also the case that American and world history being taught in schools at that time—in the South and the North—perpetuated the notion that blacks were inferior to white people in mind, body, and culture.[36] State-furnished textbooks, as far as I know, rarely if ever presented the role of blacks in American history in positive terms. Dr. George Washington Carver may have been an exception, but I doubt if even he was covered in most white schools.

If mentioned at all, the positive contributions of African Americans to the nation's development and well-being were typically seen as some form of musical or athletic entertainment. For example, the existence of numerous black troops in the Continental Army and their brave and important contributions to the defeat of Great Britain and to the establishment of the United States as a sovereign nation were never mentioned in the schoolbooks I studied in North Carolina. Indeed, I do not recall any significant coverage of that subject even in college.

Henry Wiencek, a Pulitzer Prize-winning historian, recently wrote that, as late as 1989, "Americans had to be informed that there was a black presence in the founding moment. Blacks had been so systematically overlooked or deliberately erased from the history texts that average Americans found it hard to imagine that blacks had played any role at all in creating the country."[37]

An example of this exclusion of achievements by blacks from U.S. history can be seen in the treatment of the leading role that Matthew

Henson played during the first recorded human travel to the geographic North Pole. Until recently, Henson, a black man, was hardly mentioned, and all of the credit for being the first to get to the North Pole was given to Admiral Robert Edwin Peary, a white man.[38] Another example is the role that Vivien T. Thomas, "the uniquely gifted laboratory technician and collaborator of Dr. Alfred Blalock at Vanderbilt and Johns Hopkins,"[39] played in the development of cardiac surgery. For his work, Thomas, a high school graduate, "was awarded an honorary doctorate by the Johns Hopkins University and was made a member of the medical school faculty in recognition of his contribution to the practice of cardiovascular surgery and to the education of young surgeons."[40] Yet, at the time of those achievements, sole credit for this work was attributed to Blalock; Thomas received no credit for his contributions to this groundbreaking cardiac research until much later in life. For a detailed account of Vivien Thomas's life and his contribution to medical science, read *Partners of the Heart: Vivien Thomas and His Work with Alfred Blalock.*

I recall that when I was in school, most mentions of blacks in history textbooks and other educational material had to do with the enslavement of the African, and even that was presented as if slavery, although morally wrong, was still a mostly benign institution. The point was not so subtly made in school that the primary contribution made to American development by the Africans forcibly brought to these shores—and even that of their descendants—was their labor, never their intellect.

Indeed, I believe the view held by most whites during my childhood (and it may still be the view of many today, if they were to express their opinion honestly) was that slavery was, in fact, beneficial for Africans because it introduced them to Christianity, to many of the constructive skills of the European world, and to civilized society. In their view, if the Africans had not been removed from "darkest Africa," albeit forcibly, they would still be savages struggling to survive in a jungle populated by wild and dangerous animals.[41] It is my opinion that this view also influenced and molded the history of black Americans taught in our public and private schools.

Fortunately for their students, black teachers in the South were for the most part dedicated and, using the words of Thurgood Marshall, "did the best they could with what they had."[42] Many of their students enrolled in college after graduation from high school and went on to have exceptional professional careers. Among those who did not seek additional or higher education, some enjoyed successful careers in the military or in the limited jobs that were open to high school graduates in the North, particularly city, state, and federal civil service jobs.

## BEAUTY IN THE EYE OF THE BEHOLDER

THE MEASURE OF BEAUTY FOR the great majority of Americans was the attractive Caucasian, and rarely could a Negro person come close to meeting a standard that obviously embraced only European characteristics. Beauty standards that are based on a Caucasian model and concern skin color, eye color, hair texture, and size and shape of one's lips obviously create standards that are impossible for the overwhelming majority of African Americans to meet.

Only a relatively few blacks had straight ("good") hair,[43] blue eyes, a thin nose, thin lips, or fair ("pretty") skin color. The white majority— especially the white media—disparaged as unattractive the basic physical characteristics that identified us as African: kinky hair (often called by us "bad" or "nappy" hair or "naps"[44]), flat nose, thick lips, and dark skin. With respect to physical beauty and the value to be attributed to personal characteristics commonly associated with physical beauty and societal acceptability, it is usually the media that "instruct us about what is 'average,' 'typical,' 'usual,' and 'normal,' often setting impossible standards and doing so through 'homogenized images' of perfect and perfectible" physical characteristics.[45]

As children, many if not all of us early on adopted the mean and warped values of North Carolina's white population and America's white majority. I recall a popular saying of my childhood, although usually said in jest, but with an undertone of real seriousness, "If you're white, you're all right; if you're brown, you can stick around; but if you're black, get back." Another example of our adopting those mean values at our own expense was the cruel taunts that Negro children sometimes directed toward other schoolmates whose skin complexion was very dark: "You are so black that you're purple—we should call you blurple!" or "You're so black that you're blue-black!" Such remarks were intended to hurt the recipient of the remark. I remember many of my elementary school classmates torturing a very dark-skinned girl, imposing on her the nickname "Tar Baby." I saw her in 2002 when visiting Rocky Mount, and what an attractive and beautiful woman she is!

I suppose the most important factor was skin color, followed by hair texture. It would not be inaccurate to say that we were obsessed with skin color, especially the idea that dark skin color or having a dark complexion was unattractive. It was the girls and boys who were fair of skin and whose hair had the fewest kinks who almost always got the "brass ring."[46] Because of the history of American miscegenation, mostly between Caucasian male slave owners and Negro slave women, there were and are significant numbers of Negroes with fair skin and relatively straight hair. For example, the town of Ahoskie in eastern North Carolina was and may still be known for its significant population of very fair-skinned or so-called white Negroes.

Fair-skinned Negro girls and boys were typically thought to be much better looking and more attractive than those with very dark skin.[47] Fair-skinned or "yella," "high-yella," "light-skin," and "red-bone" girls were said to be pretty. A phrase sometimes used as a positive description of such a person was that she was "light, bright,[48] and damn near white." Perhaps the lowest acceptable standard, or the "cut," for being fair of skin and, hence, pretty was to at least be "paper-sack tan." It would be unfair to say that no dark-skinned guy or girl would be considered handsome or pretty, but usually they were not. There was a very high probability, however, that a fair-skinned or light-complexioned person would be so viewed.

Indeed, a major component of the American cosmetic industry flourished during my youth, marketing bleaching cream to Negroes, particularly women determined to lighten their skin, usually their face. In July 1934, the year of my birth, an advertisement in the *New York Amsterdam News* touted the miracle-like benefits one could derive from using Dr. Fred Palmer's[49] Skin Whitener Soap, Skin Whitener Ointment, and Skin Whitener Powder. The ad declared:

> Just five minutes of your time and a few pennies a day is all it takes to make your skin shades lighter, white and free from ugly surface blemishes such as pimples and blackheads. Overnight, as you sleep, this delightful scientific method works with magic-like effect.[50]

Mme. C.J. Walker was then selling a product named Tan-Off Bleach Cream.[51] But the most popular bleaching cream product when I was growing up in Rocky Mount was Nadinola, which was advertised as "that sure way to get Whiter Skin!"[52] The Nadinola advertisement pledged:

> Just spread over face and neck at bedtime. While you sleep, it works wonders. Soon your skin grows whiter, shade by shade. Your friends find you more charming, more attractive than ever.

I recently called my 86-year-old sister Marguerite[53] to ask if she recalled Nadinola as a popular bleaching cream when she was young. She laughed and said that she did. "I put that stuff on my face trying to make myself pretty, but it didn't do any good," she said.

It is regrettable that, in considering the question of skin color, we did not embrace the wisdom of Langston Hughes, as expressed in his poem "Harlem Sweeties." But the simple fact is that most of us did not, probably because we had never even heard of the poem. I want to make certain that none of you make the same mistake:

Have you dug the spill
Of Sugar Hill?
Cast your gims
On this sepia thrill:
Brown sugar lassie,
Caramel treat,
Honey-gold baby
Sweet enough to eat.
Peach-skinned girlie,
Coffee and cream,
Chocolate darling
Out of a dream.
Walnut tinted
Or cocoa brown,
Pomegranate-lipped
Pride of the town.
Rich cream-colored
To plum-tinted black,
Feminine sweetness
In Harlem's no lack.
Glow of the quince
To blush of the rose.
Persimmon bronze
To cinnamon toes.
Blackberry cordial,
Virginia Dare wine—
All those sweet colors
Flavor Harlem of mine!
Walnut or cocoa,
Let me repeat:
Caramel, brown sugar,
A chocolate treat.
Molasses taffy,

Coffee and cream,
Licorice, clove, cinnamon
To a honey-brown dream.
Ginger, wine-gold,
Persimmon, blackberry,
All through the spectrum
Harlem girls vary—
So if you want to know beauty's
Rainbow-sweet thrill,
Stroll down luscious,
Delicious, *fine* Sugar Hill.[54]

As to hair: A Negro person with straight hair was said to have "good hair." Although an argument can be made that Negro women sometimes used the word good because straight hair is easier to manage than kinky hair, honesty should require us to admit that the primary use of the term *good hair* by Negroes had more to do with a standard for beauty and aesthetics than ease of care. And certainly, no one can convincingly argue that to describe men with straight hair as having good hair was a reference to ease of hair care.

In an obvious effort to straighten their hair and appear more attractive (i.e., have hair more like Caucasian men), great numbers of black men, particularly celebrities, applied a very caustic homemade chemical mixture, commonly called "conk" or "conkaline," to their hair, to straighten it. Conk was made of lye, white potato peelings, animal fat, and water. One's hair was said to have been processed after it was chemically straightened. William M. Hobbs, a lifelong friend of mine, remembers that one could at that time also purchase a commercial product called Silky Straight that was probably even more caustic than homemade conk.

While I never used conk or Silky Straight, my assumption is that using the homemade mixture was much more painful to the scalp and harsh to the hair than the chemicals used by beauticians to straighten or process the hair of celebrities like Sugar Ray Robinson, the boxer; Nat

"King" Cole, the singer; and Sammy Davis Jr., the entertainer. But I have no firsthand experience. Of course, now in 2008 many, if not most, black women (and I assume some black men) who achieve straight hair do so by having it "relaxed."[55]

## Athletics as an Exception

Let me now provide another and different example of how the notion of white superiority was promulgated and maintained. There were a few limited instances where merit could not be ignored—for example, on the athletic field. But perhaps with the exception of professional boxing, Negroes were simply excluded from the contest if direct competition might call white superiority into question. I suppose the argument would be that if whites were said to be inherently superior, they should not be required to compete against their inferiors, because that competition would seriously dilute the quality of the contest and make it a meaningless one. Thus, the Professional Golfers Association, major league baseball, and professional basketball, football, and tennis all had a "whites-only" policy for many years.

Consequently, Herman "Babe" Ruth could be the best home-run slugger in the world without ever having to face "Satchel" Paige[56] or compete against Joshua "Josh" Gibson, the legendary home-run hitter of the Homestead Grays.[57] Ty Cobb could be viewed as the best all-around baseball player in the world without ever having to officially compete against or be formally compared with black baseball players such as Walter "Buck" Leonard, first baseman for the Homestead Grays;[58] James Thomas Bell, known as "Cool Papa" Bell, who played center field for the Homestead Grays, Kansas City Monarchs, and other Negro League teams;[59] and William Julius Johnson, known as "Judy" Johnson, third baseman for the Homestead Grays, Pittsburgh Crawfords, and other black teams.[60]

Today the acceptance of black athletes as members of athletic teams at historically white colleges and in professional sports cannot be questioned. Still, the strength and longevity in the world of sports of the view that the Negro player was intellectually inadequate and inferior to the Caucasian player can be seen in the fact that it was not until late in the 20th century that blacks were generally accepted as being competent to play or to hold leadership or thinking positions in Division 1A college and professional sports.[61] As of January 2007, there were only three black head coaches among the 119 football head coaches at Division 1A schools.

James Harris, who played college football at Grambling State, became the first black person in the modern era to play as an established quarterback for a National Football League (NFL) team. He was drafted in 1969 by the Buffalo Bills in the eighth round and started at quarterback for the Buffalo Bills that same year.[62] Twenty years later Art Shell became the first black head coach in professional football when he was hired as the head coach of the Los Angeles Raiders. There were seven black head coaches in the NFL during the 2006–2007 football season,[63] an increase of two from fall 2005. A first: Both coaches in the 2007 Super Bowl were black.

The first black manager in major league baseball was Frank Robinson, who was hired by the Cleveland Indians in 1974. Currently,[64] only two black people hold the position of manager for any of the 30 major league baseball teams. The situation in professional basketball has for a long time been substantially better than in major league baseball or professional football. The first black head coach in the National Basketball Association (NBA) was Bill Russell, who served as both player and head coach for the Boston Celtics during the 1966–1969 seasons. In the 2006–2007 season, there were 12 black head coaches among the 30 NBA teams.[65]

## NOTABLE BLACK ROLE MODELS

THE PRIDE AND INSPIRATION THAT today's black youth derive from participation by black people in all aspects of mainstream American society were mostly denied black people of my time and of earlier generations. There was not–there could not have been–a Michael Anderson, for example;[66] or Dennis Archer;[67] or Rubin Blackwell, Helen Gay, and Lamont Wiggins;[68] Guion Bluford;[69] Lonnie Bristow;[70] Vincent Brooks;[71] Johnnie Cochran;[72] Benjamin O. Davis;[73] Harvey Gant;[74] Samuel L. Gravel;[75] Grant Hill;[76] Daniel (Chappie) James Jr.;[77] Mae Jemison;[78] Michael Jordan;[79] Thurgood Marshall;[80] Willie Mays and Barry Bonds;[81] Donovan McNabb;[82] Ronald McNair;[83] Steve McNair;[84] Barack Obama;[85] Frank E. Petersen Jr.;[86] Colin Powell;[87] J. Paul Reason;[88] Condoleezza Rice;[89] Michael Vick;[90] Togo Dennis West Jr.;[91] Douglas Wilder;[92] or Tiger Woods.[93] The list of activities, occupations and positions denied to black people that could have served as inspiration and models for the black youth of my time could go on and on.

This denial of opportunities for black Americans was probably of greater harm to the nation than it was to black Americans. Jim Crow racism denied America the many unknown talents and achievements that black Americans could have contributed to the nation's overall well-being. Even under Jim Crow, many black Americans contributed greatly to national development. But think how much greater that contribution would have been had equal opportunities existed during what we know today as the Jim Crow period, or for that matter during our entire stay in America. Who knows whether some black child denied educational opportunity in Georgia, Mississippi, or South Carolina would have discovered a cure for one or more of the various cancers from which we still suffer today. Who knows whether some black child denied a meaningful education in Alabama, Arkansas, or Louisiana would have been the very person to discover the key to cold fusion and the elimination of this nation's dependence on fossil fuels. Who knows?

I suppose one could argue that George Washington Carver, Benjamin O. Davis Jr., W.E.B. DuBois, Joe Louis,[94] Thurgood Marshall, Jesse Owens,[95] Jackie Robinson,[96] Booker T. Washington, and a handful of entertainers[97] were available as role models for black youth growing up during the 1930s, 1940s, and 1950s. But one would first have to confront the fact that during that time not a single black person was in a position of authority or leadership within any of America's mainstream corporate, educational, governmental, organized labor,[98] political, or social institutions. Therefore I do not see how such an argument could be seriously maintained or have any credibility. Indeed, to make such an argument would, in my judgment, be both insulting to all black people and ridiculous.

I hope that no person in the United States is ever again subjected to the extraordinary humiliation and personal devastation that our people suffered as a consequence of Jim Crow governmental policies and private racist traditions. Living under those conditions and circumstances made, in devilishly subtle ways, almost every black southerner feel inadequate—at least some part of every day—for his or her entire life.

It made our people feel impotent and powerless—every day. We had to submit to a system that denied our humanity, our value as a human being—every day. Even if I can describe those feelings, I cannot fully convey or transmit the consequential emotions that I and others of my generation experienced and suffered as a result of such an evil reality. I can describe, to my limited ability, but have no assurance that you can completely appreciate, understand, or actually sense the emotions and pain that we endured.

Perhaps the best analogy for what I am trying to convey is the difficulty you face when trying to describe to a physician or dentist the exact character or nature of a pain. The pain is not exactly sharp, not really dull, not cutting, not aching, and so forth. But you know that it hurts something awful and wish that somehow the physician or dentist could also *feel* what you *feel*, for then he or she would understand the character, quality, texture, intensity, and magnitude of your suffering and, you hope, know how to treat and relieve it.

## SUMMARY OF CIRCUMSTANCES THAT WERE OVERCOME

DURING JIM CROW, MANY OF our rights as American citizens were denied. Our rights to self-determination, to meaningful participation in the free selection of our elected representatives were denied. Our right to an equal opportunity to seek and hold an executive, judicial, or legislative office in the government was denied. Actually, in sum and substance, our human rights were denied. To have to submit to such a system on a daily basis was demeaning, was humiliating, and was actually a form of psychological torture.

I certainly do not want you or anyone else to have to actually know and suffer that experience, but at the same time, I fear that if people cannot appreciate the horror suffered by the victims of slavery and Jim Crow, there is a strong risk that such suffering will be forgotten and possibly be allowed to recur in our nation's future. As stated by the famous philosopher Santayana, "Those who cannot learn from the past are condemned to repeat it."[99] I sincerely and desperately hope that neither you nor anyone else in America—or indeed the world—will ever again have to experience such a life. Therefore, I say to you, never forget.

But we have survived. Not only did my generation and several before us survive Jim Crow, but also Africans survived the middle passage and slavery. How? How did our ancestors—including our grandparents and parents—manage to cope if, as a people, we were as cowardly, dumb, ignorant, uncivilized, and weak as the majority of white Americans claimed? How? The most correct, direct, and obvious answer to that question is that we were strong, not weak; brave, not cowardly; intelligent, not dumb; and neither ignorant nor uncivilized. It is true that our ancestors were not very knowledgeable about European technology and did not know any of the European languages when they were forcibly brought to the Americas. But they learned European technical skills in an incredibly short time. And certainly they mastered the ability to communicate in English, when it was unlawful in the Confederate South to educate Negroes, even to teach them to read.

## INFLUENCE OF RELIGION

But other factors also helped our ancestors to survive. It is obvious that religious faith and beliefs—especially Christianity—played a critical role in the survival of black people during slavery, Jim Crow, and even today. People were able to endure tremendous suffering because of their conviction that the horror of slavery or Jim Crow was merely temporary and not their ultimate lot. Most of those people passionately believed in eternal life and the Christian heaven, where they would be nurtured, would live an incredibly enjoyable life, and would be happy for all eternity.

The slave master encouraged this belief system and survival mechanism because it was in the slave master's interest. This fact is obvious to me. If the slaves could be convinced that this life was only a second of time when compared with eternity, that all pain and suffering would end in the afterlife and that thereafter they would know only joy and happiness, then they would be much more likely to be docile and far less likely to revolt against their oppressors because they would view their pain and suffering as temporary.

Also, to a significant degree, the Christian philosophy is fairly pacific in its focus. The commission to love others as you love yourself and to forgive your enemies is a powerful tool of absolution for trespasses suffered in this life. See, for example, Mark 11:25–26: "And when ye stand praying, forgive, if ye have aught against any: that your Father also which is in heaven may forgive your trespasses. But if ye do not forgive, neither will your Father which is in heaven forgive your trespasses."[100]

For me, the most noteworthy scriptures in this regard are to be found in Luke, where the following is written:[101]

> Then he looked up at his disciples and said:
> "Blessed are you who are poor, for yours is the kingdom of God.
> "Blessed are you who are hungry now, for you will be filled.
> "Blessed are you who weep now, for you will laugh.
> "Blessed are you when people hate you, and when they exclude you, revile you, and defame you on account of the Son of Man. Rejoice in that day and leap for joy, for surely your reward is great in heaven; for that is what their ancestors did to the prophets.

*But I say to you that listen, Love your enemies, do good to those who hate you, bless those who curse you, pray for those who abuse you. If anyone strikes you on the cheek, offer the other also; and from anyone who takes away your coat, do not withhold even your shirt. Give to everyone who begs from you; and if anyone takes away your goods, do not ask for them again. Do to others as you would have them do to you. . . . But love your enemies, do good, and lend, expecting nothing in return. Your reward will be great, and you will be children of the Most High; for he is kind to the ungrateful and the wicked. Be merciful, just as your Father is merciful. Do not judge, and you will not be judged; do not condemn, and you will not be condemned. Forgive, and you will be forgiven; give, and it will be given to you."* [Emphasis added.]

I cannot resist noting that many so-called Christian nations have dramatically ignored this element of Christian doctrine on many occasions, in terms of their national policies and actual declarations of war— England, France, Germany, Italy, Spain, and the United States being prime examples. I am willing to concede that there is a basis for believing that some individuals honestly embrace and act on this notion of forgiving one's abusers, but the numbers of those who do are few. For the most part, Christian individuals and countries tend to attack and make every effort to trounce, if not annihilate, those who grievously trespass against them. Forgiveness and absolution have not been the policy of those nations, nor do I see any reason to believe that they will be in the future.

The poem "Sister Lou" by Sterling A. Brown vividly captures the expectation of an afterlife when and where all suffering will end and only happiness and contentment will be known:[102]

Honey
When de man
Calls out de las' train
You're gonna ride,
Tell him howdy.

Gather up yo' basket
An' you' knittin' an' you' things,
An' go on up an' visit.
Wid fren' Jesus fo' a spell.

Show Marfa
How to make yo' greengrape jellies,
An' give po' Lazarus
A passel of them Golden Biscuits.

Scald some meal
Fo' some right down good spoonbread
Fo' li'l box-plunkin' David.

An' sit aroun'
An' tell them Hebrew Chillen
All yo' stories, . . .

Honey
Don't be feared of them pearly gates,
Don't go 'round to de back,
No mo' dataway
Not evah no mo'.

Let Michael tote yo' burden
An yo' pocket book an' evah thing.
'Cept yo' Bible,
While Gabriel blows somp'n
Solemn but loudsome
On dat horn of his'n.

Honey
Go straight on to de Big House,
An' speak to yo' God
Widout no fear an' tremblin'.

Then sit down
An' pass de time of day awhile.
Give a good talkin' to
To yo' favorite 'postle Peter,
An' rub the po' head
Of mixed-up Judas,
An' joke awhile wid Jonah.

Then, when you gits de chance,
Always rememberin' yo' raisin',
Let 'em know youse tired
Jest a mite tired

Jesus will find yo' bed fo' you
Won't no servant evah bother wid yo' room.
Jesus will lead you
To a room wid windows
Openin' on cherry trees an' plum trees
Bloomin' everlastin'.

An' dat will be yours
Fo' keeps.
Den take yo' time. . . .
Honey, take yo' bressed time.

However, equally important was the fact that the church services and other religious-based meetings provided a setting where rebellious planning and other prohibited interactions could occur. Religious services were used to conceal or mask discussions that were directed at survival and how to overcome, eliminate, or at least cope with racist laws, policies, practices, and traditions. One of today's popular phrases that could be applied to some of the subversive church activities of that time is "hidden in plain view."

It is well known that certain spirituals sung during the time of American slavery were used to transmit notices of antislavery activity and to support abolitionist plans and strategies. One of the most famous spirituals, "Swing Low,"[103] had verses that often provided notice that an Underground Railroad conductor was, or soon would be, available to help slaves escape to freedom:

> Swing low, sweet chariot,
> Coming for to carry me home,
> Swing low, sweet chariot,
> Coming for to carry me home.
> I looked over Jordan, and what did I see,
> Coming for to carry me home?
> A band of Angels coming after me,
> Coming for to carry me home.

Verses of "Steal Away to Jesus"[104] were used to achieve the same ends:

> Steal away, steal away, steal away to Jesus!
> Steal away, steal away home, I ain't got long to stay here.
> My Lord, he calls me, he calls me by the thunder;
> The trumpet sounds within my soul; I ain't got long to stay here.

Given the extremely small chance of any successful revolt during the period of American slavery, the Sunday sermon was also an obvious means for inspiring hope for a better tomorrow and for providing a foundation on which to base one's need to hold on and endure, no matter how "violent the storm" or "rough the road." The role that hope can play in finding the strength to bear one's difficulties and to struggle against great odds can never be overestimated.

The spiritual has continued to play an inspirational role, even in modern times. "Oh, Freedom,"[105] one of the most popular and inspirational spirituals sung by activists during the Jim Crow period and civil rights struggle, proclaims:

> Oh, Freedom! Oh, Freedom! Oh, Freedom over me!
> And before I'd be a slave,
> I'll be buried in my grave,
> And go home to my Lord and be free.

I believe that the black youth of our country are today profoundly more committed to the following view than the views held by African Americans during slavery and the Jim Crow period:

> Bitter was the day
> When . . .
> . . . only in the sorrow songs
> Belief was found—
> Yet no relief.
> But merely humble life and silent death
> Eased by a Name
> That hypnotized the pain away—
> O, precious Name of Jesus in that day!
>
> That day is past.
>
> I know full well now
> Jesus could not die for me—
> That only my own hands,
> Dark as the earth,
> Can make my earth-dark body free.
>
> I know that I am.[106]

## EDUCATION TO OVERCOME BARRIERS

WERE I A BETTING PERSON, AND I am not, I would wager that if today you asked any African American 60 years old or older—especially if that person were reared in the South—if he or she recalled being told by parents, other relatives, and neighbors to get as much education as possible, because knowledge "is something the white man cannot take from you," 99 if not 100 percent of those asked would say, "Yes."

In Rocky Mount, from the moment a black child entered elementary school until he or she graduated from high school, that child was constantly reminded that education offered the greatest opportunity and means to overcome the barriers of racial discrimination and segregation. Although not everyone listened or followed this wise admonition, many did and consequently were able to significantly improve their circumstances and to provide substantially better opportunities for their children. I am convinced that this constant promotion of education by our parents, grandparents, and neighbors was a critical factor for the survival of black people, particularly during the 1920s, 1930s, 1940s, and 1950s.

While material objects and positions could be taken away or denied, knowledge, once acquired, could not. A frequent model offered in that regard was Dr. George Washington Carver, the famous Tuskegee Institute scientist.[107] Even though he lived under the callous conditions and mean circumstances of Jim Crow, his knowledge of chemistry allowed him to achieve a great academic and scientific career and to make substantial contributions in the field of agriculture. Dr. Carver was highly respected and much admired by black Americans during the time of my youth. Indeed, he inspires that respect today.

Another role model my peers and I were offered during our youth was Booker T. Washington, the founder and president of Tuskegee Institute.[108] In the early 20th century, there was competition between the civil rights strategies offered by Booker T. Washington and the views of one of his contemporaries, the far more radical William Edward Burghardt DuBois. Today many, and probably most, black people embrace the uncompromising civil rights philosophy offered by W.E.B. DuBois and have little respect for the notion offered by Washington that Negroes should be willing to accept racial segregation as a way of life and function within that social construct. But my parents, their neighbors, our preachers, and our teachers admired and respected Booker T. Washington and used his life story to instruct my contemporaries and me about the value of determination and the importance of doing every job well, no matter how menial it was or how insignificant it appeared to be at the time.

We were often told the story of how, in working his way through Hampton Institute in Virginia, Booker T. Washington applied for a job as a handyman in a white family's home. As a test of whether he would get the job, he was told by the mistress of the house to clean a fairly dirty room. When the woman returned and inspected the room with a white handkerchief, no dirt could be detected, and he was awarded the job, which afforded him the financial means to complete his studies at Hampton. This story was hammered into us as proof that any job worth doing was worth doing well, that one should always do one's best and that one could overcome great adversity with resolve and fortitude. A particular point being made was that one should never underestimate the long-term significance of any task, no matter how unimportant it might seem at the moment.

## EQUALITY IN THE WORLD

As I HAVE TRAVELED AROUND the world, I have been impressed by the effect that principles articulated in the U.S. Declaration of Independence have had in various third-world countries where I have worked or visited. Most people in those nations admire and are inspired by the notions of freedom and liberation expressed by Thomas Jefferson:

> We hold these Truths to be self-evident, that all Men are created equal, that they are endowed by their Creator with certain unalienable Rights, that among these are Life, Liberty, and the Pursuit of Happiness—That to secure these Rights, Governments are instituted among Men, deriving their just Powers from the Consent of the Governed, that whenever any Form of Government becomes destructive of these Ends, it is the Right of the People to alter or to abolish it, and to institute new Government, laying its Foundation on such Principles, and organizing its Powers in such Form, as to them shall seem most likely to effect their Safety and Happiness. . . . But when a Train of Abuses and Usurpations, pursuing invariably the same Object, evinces a Design to reduce them under absolute Despotism, it is their Right, it is their Duty, to throw off such Government, and to provide new Guards for their future Security.[109]

I do not think such admiration was any less among the Africans in bondage in America. Those wretched souls also heard and were inspired by the words that all men are created equal and endowed with inalienable rights of life, liberty, and the pursuit of happiness. This inspiration was the case notwithstanding that even as Jefferson penned the above-quoted words, he was a slave owner[110] and an outright racist.[111]

The American Declaration of Independence is a powerful statement in support of freedom and human rights. I think a tragic victim of American foreign policy during the Cold War was the enormous goodwill that the United States could have enjoyed had our government not embraced a policy of supporting tyrants and dictators solely because they were, or declared themselves to be, anticommunist. In other words, we adopted as our national policy the position that "the enemy of my enemy is my friend," regardless of how inconsistent the internal political and human rights policies of the "friend" were with fundamental democratic principles. I believe it was no less so to the Africans in bondage in America.

## Concepts Begun in Rocky Mount

Vivian Patterson and other local leaders of the NAACP in Rocky Mount taught us that we were as good as, if not better than, those who were tormenting us. Certainly by any moral or ethical gauge, we were infinitely better. We were also taught that if we would be strong and courageous—that is to say, if, even when afraid, we would be brave, persevering, and industrious in all our undertakings—our future would be significantly better and brighter. It was critical that we be determined even as we suffered.

Most of all, those leaders rejected the notion that we should have to "earn" the right to equal treatment and enjoyment of rights that white citizens enjoyed simply because those rights were constitutionally conferred on them as a birthright. Vivian and other adults involved with the Youth Branch hammered into our minds that we deserved the same rights and privileges as every American and that Jim Crow and the denial of our rights were illegal, unjust, immoral, irrational, and indefensible.

As members of the Youth Branch, we were made acutely aware of the courageous and costly struggle being mounted by the NAACP and, later, the NAACP Legal Defense and Educational Fund[112] to fight Jim Crow and to eradicate the cancers of racial discrimination and state-mandated segregation from the American body politic. I believe the values then displayed by the NAACP are the same ones that form the foundation of my commitment to justice for black people, and indeed for all people throughout the world. It is also for this reason that I am an NAACP Diamond Level life member and purchased a life membership for my wife and junior life memberships for each of my children and grandchildren.

I trust that you will not forget—and that you will never permit anyone else in the United States to forget—this enormous debt owed by all Americans to the NAACP and the NAACP Legal Defense Fund, regardless or race, creed, color, or nationality. The escape of our people from the oppression of racial discrimination, from segregation and the horrific legacy of racial hatred that is rooted in slavery, is vivid testimony to our people's strength, courage and enduring commitment to the survival of their descendants and to all humanity.

· Notes ·

1. Pauli Murray, *Proud Shoes: The Story of an American Family* (Boston, Beacon Press, 1999) pp. 269–70, as quoted in Leon F. Litwack, *Trouble in Mind: Black Southerners in the Age of Jim Crow* (New York: Alfred A. Knopf, 1998), p. 217.
2. Heather Tobis Booth, "Hard-Wired for Freedom," in Juan Williams, ed., *My Soul Looks Back in Wonder: Voices of the Civil Rights Experience* (New York: AARP, Sterling Publishing, 2004), p. 146.
3. Leon F. Litwack, *Trouble in Mind: Black Southerners in the Age of Jim Crow* (New York: Alfred A. Knopf, 1998), p. 127.
4. Ronald W. Walters, *The Price of Racial Reconciliation* (University of Michigan Press, Ann Arbor, 2008), p. 5.

4a. The dominant physical feature of the Oil Mill Section was a mill that extracted oil from peanuts, cotton, and various other seeds. I believe it was owned by the Planters Peanut Company. One could smell from many blocks away the different odors produced by the process of extracting oil from assorted seeds, and my neighborhood was no more than four or five blocks distance from the oil mill. I am certain that the plant also ginned and baled cotton, with cottonseeds as a byproduct of that process.

5. A branch of the National Association for the Advancement of Colored People that was founded in Niagara Falls, NY, in 1906 and was specifically organized for and focused on youth.

6. I will usually refer to African Americans or black people as *Negroes* when discussing them and their situation during the period of my life between 1934 and, say, 1955, when I was honorably discharged from the U.S. Air Force. I do so because that is what we called ourselves, and, for the most part, it is what we were called by others. In discussing the period beginning around 1960, I will use the words *African American* or *black*. The period from 1955 to 1960 could be viewed as a transitional period, during which any of these terms might be used.

7. For a general review of this work by the NAACP, see Mark V. Tushnet, *Making Civil Rights Law: Thurgood Marshall and the Supreme Court, 1936–1961* (New York: Oxford University Press, 1994).

8. We called Negro males who displayed excessive deference to Caucasians "Uncle Toms" and said they were "dancing in the sandbox" for the entertainment of white people. In some instances, I suppose this deferential or obsequious conduct was actually a diversionary tactic—that is, they used it to divert the more powerful white person's attention from some conduct or activity the Negro did not want that person to notice. The reference to dancing in the sandbox flowed from the fact that an element of this obsequious conduct was a needless and pointless shuffling of the feet when speaking to or being spoken to by an adult white person. We, at least where I grew up, sometimes referred to women who exhibited such behavior as "Aunt Jemimas," after a corporate photographic logo that showed a black household cook who had a large satisfied smile on her face and wore a red bandana around her head. Most southern black people, if not all blacks, came to see Aunt Jemima and her pancake mix as a picture or caricature of a fat, grinning Negro woman, working in a white household, without a care in the world about segregation, discrimination, or what was happening to her and her people in the real world. "Uncle Ben" and his rice made an analogous picture that many of us also viewed as insulting and disparaging of Negroes.

9. Litwack, *Trouble in Mind.*

10. The following lynching statistics concerning blacks are from Schomburg Center for Research In Black Culture, *The New York Public Library African American Desk Reference* (A Stonesong Press Book, New York, John Wiley & Sons, Inc., 1999) at Table 12.1, Lynchings by Race and Year, 1882–1962, p. 316: 1930, 20 lynchings; 1931, 12; 1932, 6; 1933, 24; 1934, 15; 1935, 18; 1936, 8; 1937, 8; 1938, 6; 1939, 2; 1940, 4; 1941, 4; 1942, 6; 1943, 3; 1944, 2; 1945, 1; 1946, 6; 1947, 1; 1948, 1; 1949, 3; 1950, 1. This same data is available at *Historical Statistics of the United States Millennial Edition Online*, Table Ec251-253–Reported victims of lynching, by race: 1882–1964. http://hsus.cambridge.org/HSUSWeb/table/printTable. do?start. For a graphic history of lynching in the United States, see *Lynching in America: a history in documents,* edited by Christopher Waldrep (New York, New York University Press, 2006).

11. "His Goose Is Cooked," *Nolo News*, Summer 1985, p. 3, as quoted in Andrew Roth and Jonathan Roth, *Devil's Advocates: The Unnatural History of Lawyers* (Berkeley, CA: Nolo Press, 1989), p. 91.

12. See Sherie Mershon and Steven Schlossman, *Foxholes and Color Lines* (Baltimore and London: Johns Hopkins University Press, 1998), p. 5: "The turn-of-the-century hardening of racial attitudes was by no means confined to the southern states, however. Outside the South, most whites gradually ceased to regard race relations as a high-priority political issue. The support of northern and western whites for black equality–a support that had been limited and cautious even during Reconstruction–waned markedly as the passions of the Civil War era receded. Although whites in the North and the West rarely emulated the overtly discriminatory laws that the South adopted, they not only acquiesced in the South's actions but also tolerated and supported the behavior of local businesses, landlords, and government agencies that commonly practiced informal racial discrimination. Expressions of hostility toward blacks were national in scope, particularly after 1890 when virulent rhetoric that denigrated blacks and extolled white supremacy reached new heights of popularity in all sections of the country." But this was not a new phenomenon; the same circumstances extended back as far as the American Revolution and the adoption of the federal constitution. In that regard, read Henry Wiencek, *An Imperfect God: George Washington, His Slaves, and the Creation of America* (New York: Farrar, Straus and Giroux), particularly chapters 5–7.

13. "The Negro race, like all races, is going to be saved by its exceptional men. The problem of education, then, among Negroes must first of all deal with the Talented Tenth; it is the problem of developing the Best of this race that they may guide the Mass away from the contamination and death of the Worst, in their own and other races. Now the training of men is a difficult and intricate task. Its technique is a matter for educational

experts, but its object is for the vision of seers. If we make money the object of man-training, we shall develop money-makers but not necessarily men; if we make technical skill the object of education, we may possess artisans but not, in nature, men. Men we shall have only as we make manhood the object of the work of the schools— intelligence, broad sympathy, knowledge of the world that was and is, and of the relation of men to it— this is the curriculum of that Higher Education which must underlie true life. On this foundation we may build bread winning, skill of hand and quickness of brain, with never a fear lest the child and man mistake the means of living for the object of life.

"If this be true—and who can deny it—three tasks lay before me; first to show from the past that the Talented Tenth as they have risen among American Negroes have been worthy of leadership; secondly to show how these men may be educated and developed; and thirdly to show their relation to the Negro problem." *The Talented Tenth* by W.E.B. DuBois, September 1903, http://teachingamericanhistory.org/library/index. asp?documentprint=174.

14. For an interesting analysis of movies and their influence, see Colin McGinn, *The Power of Movies: How Screen and Mind Interact.* (New York: Pantheon Books, 2005).

15. Also known as Stepin Fetchit. Actual name: Lincoln Theodore Monroe Perry.

16. Actual name: Eddie Anderson. It was very little, if any, comfort to us that Rochester was often made to seem more clever than Jack Benny because we could see that Rochester was still being portrayed as a buffoon and we also believed that, comparatively, he was poorly paid.

17. Man Tan Moreland always claimed this was his given name, and there is no evidence to suggest otherwise.

18. Some historians attribute the broad dissemination of this notion among Americans, and even abroad, to Thomas Jefferson, who wrote in his widely published *Notes on the State of Virginia* (Baltimore: W. Pechin, 1800), p. 143, "but never yet could I find a black uttered a thought above the level of plain narration; never seen even an elementary trait of painting or sculpture." On p. 144, Jefferson continued, "Comparing them by their faculties of memory, reason, and imagination, it appears to me that in memory they are equal to whites; in reason much inferior, as I think one could scarcely be found capable of tracing and comprehending the inflections of Euclid; and that in imagination they are dull, tasteless, and anomalous," and on p. 147 he wrote, "I advance it therefore as a suspicion only, that the blacks, whether originally a distinct race, or made distinct by time and circumstance, are inferior to whites in the endowment both of body and mind."

19. Tarzan movies were to my generation what *Birth of a Nation* was to earlier generations.

20. The African American actors who portrayed those television roles were Alvin Childress as Amos Jones, Spencer Williams Jr. as Andy Brown, Tim More as George "Kingfish" Stevens, Ernestine Wade as Sapphire Stevens, Johnny Lee as Algonquin J. "Lawyer" Calhoun, and Horace "Nicodemus" Stewart as Lightnin' (the janitor). See Donald Bogle, *Blacks, Coons, Mullatoes, Mammies, and Bucks: An Interpretive History of Blacks in American Film* (New York: Garland, 1973).

21. "In *Plessy v. Ferguson* (1896), the U.S. Supreme Court decided that a Louisiana law mandating separate but equal accommodations for blacks and whites on intrastate railroads was constitutional. This decision provided the legal foundation to justify many other actions by state and local governments to socially separate blacks and whites. *Plessy v. Ferguson* was overturned in 1954 by *Brown v. Board of Education*." http://www.bgsu.edu/departments/acs/1890s/plessy/plessy.html (Bowling Green State University).

22. Booker T. Washington, in *Up from Slavery: An Autobiography* (New York: Doubleday, Page, 1902), pp. 221–22, wrote, "In all things that are purely social we can be as separate as fingers, yet one as the hand in all things essential to mutual progress."

23. See, for example, Litwack, *Trouble in Mind*, pp. 206–16.

24. The television program was shown as a part of the March 31, 1994, episode of the CBS news program *Eye to Eye with Connie Chung* and featured the views of some Howard University students. The date of this particular CBS show was researched by Jennifer McZier, who obtained the information from Rosemary Hanes, reference librarian, Moving Image Section, Library of Congress, 101 Independence Ave. SE, Washington, DC 20540; tel: (202) 707-8572; fax: (202) 707-8572.

24a. For an excellent article concerning the continued strength and current significance of this issue, see Brent Staples, Editorial Observer, "Barack Obama, John McCain and the Language of Race," *New York Times*, Editorials/Letters, Monday, September 22, 2008, page A28.

25. *Webster's Third New International Dictionary,* unabridged ed. (Springfield, MA: Merriam-Webster, 2002).

26. There was one good "black book": the address book with women's phone numbers that men used to rely on—"She's in my little black book."

27. *The American Heritage College Dictionary*, 4th ed. (Boston and New York: Houghton Mifflin, 2002).

28. *Webster's Third New International Dictionary.*

29. Martin Luther King Jr., *The Autobiography of Martin Luther King Jr.*, ed. Clayborne Carson (New York: Warner Books, 1998), p. 326.

30. For example, a dictionary definition of dark is "Gloomy; dismal; 7. Sullen or threatening; a dark scowl. 8. Difficult to understand; obscure. 9. Concealed or secret; mysterious. 10. Lacking enlightenment or culture; a dark age in history. 11. Exhibiting or stemming from evil characteristics; sinister. 12. Being or characterized by morbid or grimly satiric humor . . . —idiom: in the dark. 1. In a state of ignorance; uninformed. 2. In secret." See *The American Heritage College Dictionary*.

31. The city of Rocky Mount is actually in two North Carolina counties: Edgecombe and Nash. The county seat of Edgecombe County is the city of Tarboro (approximately 16 miles from Rocky Mount) and that of Nash County is the city of Nashville (approximately 10 miles from Rocky Mount). The political boundary between the two counties, or the county line, is the railroad tracks of the old Atlantic Coast Line Railroad Company (now used by Amtrak) that still runs through the middle of Rocky Mount's historic downtown.

32. See Herbert Hill, "Racism Within Organized Labor: A Report of Five Years of the AFL–CIO, 1955–1960," *The Journal of Negro Education*, Vol. 30, No. 2 (Spring, 1961), pp. 109–118.

33. The playwright August Wilson (April 27, 1945–Oct. 2, 2005) aptly portrays this sort of racial discrimination and times in his play *Fences* (New York: Penguin, 1986), especially at pp. 2–3 and 42–46.

34. A few of the houses in our neighborhood still had outdoor toilets and were not connected to the city's sewage system.

35. Mershon and Schlossman, *Foxholes and Color Lines*, p. 2. Also see Wiencek, *An Imperfect God*, particularly chapter 6, "So Sacred a War as This," pp. 189–249.

36. See, for example, Martin Luther King Jr., pp. 326–27.

37. Wiencek, *An Imperfect God*, p. 243.

38. See Matthew A. Henson, *A Black Explorer at the North Pole* (Lincoln: University of Nebraska Press, 1989).

39. Vivien Thomas, *Partners of the Heart: Vivien Thomas and His Work with Alfred Blalock* (Philadelphia: University of Pennsylvania Press, 1985), p. ix. The quotation is from the Foreword by Dr. Mark M. Ravitch.

40. Thomas, *Partners of the Heart*, back cover copy.

41. For a meaningful discussion of this issue, see John Hope Franklin, *Mirror to America* (New York: Farrar, Straus, and Giroux, 2005), at p. 304.

42. Thurgood Marshall was the first black associate justice of the United States Supreme Court (appointed by President Lyndon B. Johnson in 1967). After announcing his retirement from the Supreme Court, Marshall, who was obviously in poor health, was asked what he would want his epitaph to be. He quickly replied, "He did the best that he could with what he had."

43. For a contemporary and interesting comment on this "good hair" issue, see Erin Aubry Kaplan, "Racial Pride Is a Hairy Issue," *Oakland Tribune,* July 16, 2006, Metro section, p. 7.

44. What you observe when a person is at the very earliest stages of developing "dreds" was what we called "naps." Naps were viewed as undesirable and extremely unattractive.

45. Mary White Stewart, *Silicone Spills: Breast Implants on Trial* (Westport, CT: Praeger, 1998), p. 119.

46. That is to say, for example, those who were most sought after as prospective members of social clubs, favored by teachers, and chosen first for games. In other words, they were most likely to get "the prize."

47. For a contemporary perspective on this issue, see Tricia Capistrano, "Emil's Big Chance Leaves Me Uneasy," *Newsweek,* June 15, 2006, p. 14. "I do not want Filipino children who look like me to feel bad about themselves. When I was a kid, my grandmother would get upset whenever I told her that I'd be spending the afternoon swimming in my cousin's pool, because it meant that my skin would get darker than it already was. My mom, whose nose I acquired, has one of the widest among her brothers and sisters. She taught me to pinch the bridge daily so that the arch would be higher, like my cousins. Most of her girlfriends got blond highlights and nose jobs as soon as they received their first paychecks. . . ."

48. The word *bright* was not a reference to intellect.

49. Dr. Fred Palmer's Laboratories of Atlanta, Georgia.

50. See the *New York Amsterdam News,* July 21, 1934, p. 5.

51. I recently read, at the Schomburg Center for Research in Black Culture in New York, an advertisement in the *Pittsburg Courier* of Feb. 24, 1934, offering Tan-Off for 35 cents a box.

52. See the *New York Amsterdam News,* Nov. 10, 1934, p. 7.

53. Source: Telephone conversation of April 8, 2003. This was her age at the time of the telephone call.

54. Arnold Rampersad and David Roesse, eds., *The Collected Poems of Langston Hughes* (New York: Alfred A. Knopf, 1994), p. 245. "Harlem Sweeties" was first published in 1942 as a part of *Shakespeare in Harlem* (New York: Knopf, 1942); see *The Collected Poems of Langston Hughes,* pp. 611 and 645.

55. Relaxing is still a chemical process for straightening curly hair, but significantly less caustic than the lye-based conk. I am told that the chemicals used today to straighten or relax the hair of black men and women have a base of sodium chloride.

56. His actual name was Leroy Robert Paige, and he played in the Negro Leagues for several teams, including the Birmingham Black Barons, Kansas City Monarchs, and New York Black Yankees. In the major

leagues, he played for the Cleveland Indians. He was elected in 1971 by the Committee on Negro Leagues to the National Baseball Hall of Fame and Museum in Cooperstown, N.Y. See http://www.baseballhalloffame.org.

57. Gibson played catcher for the Pittsburgh Crawfords in addition to the Homestead Grays and, in 1972, was elected to the National Baseball Hall of Fame and Museum by the Committee on Negro Leagues. See http://www.baseballhalloffame.org.

58. Walter Fenner Leonard was a native of and, throughout his baseball career, a resident of Rocky Mount, N.C. He played first base for the Homestead Grays for 17 years and, in 1972, was elected to the National Baseball Hall of Fame and Museum by the Committee on Negro Leagues. See http://www.baseballhalloffame.org.

59. Bell was elected in 1974 to the National Baseball Hall of Fame and Museum by the Committee on Negro Leagues. See http://www.baseball-halloffame.org.

60. Johnson was elected in 1975 to the National Baseball Hall of Fame and Museum by the Committee on Negro Leagues. See http://www.baseball-halloffame.org.

61. One of the first black players—possibly the very first—in the starting quarterback or center position on any historically white college Division 1A college football team was Wilmeth Sidat-Singh at Syracuse University in the 1936 season.

62. He played quarterback for the Los Angeles Rams between 1974 and 1976.

63. Marvin Lewis, Cincinnati Bengals; Romeo Crennel, Cleveland Browns; Lovie Smith, Chicago Bears; Art Shell, Oakland Raiders (fired at end of regular season); Denis Green, Arizona Cardinals (fired at end of regular season); Herman Edwards, Kansas City Chiefs; and Tony Dungy, Indianapolis Colts.

64. This was written in January 2007. Dusty Baker retired as manager of the Chicago Cubs during October 2005.

65. Byron Scott, New Orleans/Oklahoma City Hornets; Avery Johnson, Dallas Mavericks; Eddie Jordan, Washington Wizards; Bernie Bickerstaff, Charlotte Bobcats; Mike Woodson, Atlanta Hawks; Maurice Cheeks, Philadelphia 76ers; Sam Mitchell, Toronto Raptors; Mike Brown, Cleveland Cavaliers; Dwane Casey, Minnesota Timberwolves; Isaiah Thomas, New York Knicks; Tony Brown, Boston Celtics; and Nate McMillan, Portland Trailblazers.

66. A black astronaut who died in the Feb. 1, 2003, space shuttle Columbia tragedy.

67. An associate justice of the Michigan Supreme Court (1985–1994), the mayor of Detroit (1994–2001), and the first black president of the

American Bar Association (2003–2004). The American Bar Association was founded Aug. 21, 1878.

68. Black members of the Rocky Mount, N.C., City Council in 2003.

69. The first black astronaut, who also became the first black astronaut in space on Aug. 30, 1983.

70. A physician and the first black president of the American Medical Association, 1995–1996. The American Medical Association was founded in 1847.

71. A U.S. Army major general, graduate of West Point, and prominent spokesperson for the U.S. Central Command of the 2003 Operation Iraqi Freedom campaign. A brief account of General Brooks's life can be found in Yvonne Latty, *We Were There* (New York: HarperCollins, 2004), p. 176. It was on July 26, 1948, that President Harry S. Truman issued "Executive Order 9981, which mandated the desegregation of the American armed forces—one of the most sweeping changes in the military's history." Material quoted from inside front jacket cover of Mershon and Schlossman, *Foxholes and Color Lines*. The book is an excellent history of racial segregation and desegregation in the U.S. Armed Forces.

72. A nationally prominent black lawyer.

73. A graduate of West Point (Class of 1936), Davis was appointed the first black U.S. Air Force general on Oct. 7, 1954. See *Jet* magazine, Nov. 5, 2001, p. 17.

74. The first black mayor of Charlotte, North Carolina, 1983–1987, Gant ran unsuccessfully for the U.S. Senate in 1990 and again in 1996.

75. On April 27, 1971, Gravely was appointed the first black admiral in the U.S. Navy. See *Jet* magazine, Nov. 5, 2001, p. 21.

76. An outstanding college basketball player who was at Duke University (a private school that did not admit black undergraduate students until September 1963 and admitted its first black student in 1961) and who later played in the NBA.

77. Named the first black four-star U.S. Air Force general on Aug. 29, 1975, James was assigned as commander-in-chief of the North American Air Defense Command. See *Jet* magazine, Nov. 5, 2001, p. 26.

78. The first black female astronaut in space, 1992.

79. An excellent University of North Carolina (Chapel Hill) basketball player, who was also a North Carolina native and arguably the best professional basketball player ever.

80. The first black associate justice of the U.S. Supreme Court (1967–1991) and a graduate of the Howard University School of Law.

81. Outstanding major league baseball players, both for the Giants.

82. Currently the starting quarterback for the Philadelphia Eagles.

83. A black astronaut reared in Lake City, S.C.; he died when the space shuttle Columbia exploded in January 1986.

84. Currently the starting quarterback for the Tennessee Titans.

85. U.S. senator (D) from Illinois and the Democratic party nominee for U.S. president in 2008. See chapter 17 in this book.

86. Petersen became the first black U.S. Marine Corps general on Feb. 23, 1979. See *Jet* magazine, Nov. 5, 2001, p. 27.

87. U.S. secretary of state under President George W. Bush and chairman of the Joint Chiefs of Staff during the 1991 Gulf War. Powell was the first black person to serve in either position. See Colin L. Powell, with Joseph E. Persico, *My American Journey* (New York: Random House, 1995).

88. Confirmed by the U.S. Senate on June 22, 1996, as the U.S. Navy's first black four-star admiral. See *Jet* magazine, Nov. 5, 2001, p. 40.

89. National security adviser to President George W. Bush (2001–04) and secretary of state during President Bush's second term (2005–present).

90. In 2004, the starting quarterback for the Atlanta Falcons.

91. Secretary of the Army (Nov. 1993 to May 1998) and secretary of veterans' affairs (May 1998 to July 2000) under President William J. Clinton. West was a 1968 graduate of the Howard University School of Law.

92. Lieutenant governor (1986–90) and governor (1990–94) of Virginia and also a 1959 graduate of the Howard University School of Law. He is currently mayor of Richmond, Va.

93. An Afro-Asian (black father and Asian mother) man who is clearly one of the greatest golfers of all time, and, as of 2008, was the No. 1 golfer in the world. The "one drop" rule would likely have precluded his participation in any Professional Golfers Association (PGA) tournament before 1961, the year when Charles "Charlie" Sifford became the first black person to gain membership in the PGA and the first black to play in a major PGA tournament in the South at Greensboro, N.C. See, for example, Jessie Carney Smith, *Black Firsts*, 2nd ed. (Detroit: Visible Ink Press, 2003), p. 688. The "one drop" rule held that, regardless of the source of other drops of your blood, if you had just one drop of black blood, then you were black. Althea Gibson was the first black woman to play on the Ladies Professional Golf Association tour. See Jessie Carney Smith, *Black Firsts*, p. 689.

94. A legendary heavyweight boxing champion.

95. A legendary Olympic sprinter, especially at the 1936 Olympics in Berlin, Germany.

96. Robinson, the first black person to integrate major league baseball, played with the Brooklyn Dodgers in 1947. According to *The New York Public*

*Library African American Desk Reference* (New York: Wiley & Sons, 1999), p. 520, "Though Jackie Robinson is properly credited with breaking the color line in modern major-league baseball by joining the Brooklyn Dodgers in 1947, he was not the first African American to play in the major leagues. That distinction belongs to Moses Fleetwood 'Fleet' Walker (1857–1924), a college-educated catcher who was a member of the Toledo, Ohio, team when it joined the American Association in 1884. . . . During the next few years, at least half a dozen more African Americans played in various professional baseball leagues. Resistance soon began to grow among white players and baseball officials, however. The African Americans were squeezed out during the 1890s, and from the beginning of the 20th century until Robinson's advent in 1947, an unofficial but ironclad policy of segregation reigned in the major leagues."

97. For example, Count Basie, Cab Calloway, Nat "King" Cole, Duke Ellington, Ella Fitzgerald, Billie Holliday, and Sarah Vaughn.

98. Although one could credibly argue that A. Philip Randolph's Brotherhood of Pullman Car Workers was an important labor organization, its potential influence in the world of organized labor on the American economy was relatively insignificant when compared with the power and influence of the AFL-CIO and its predecessor organizations.

99. John McCormick, *George Santayana: A Biography* (New Brunswick, NJ: Transaction Publishers, 2003), p. 173.

100. All biblical quotations contained herein are from the *The Holy Bible*, New Revised Standard Version, copyright 1989 by the Division of Christian Education of the National Council of the Churches of Christ in the U.S.A.

101. Luke 6:20–37.

102. The poem is published in Langston Hughes and Arna Bontemps, eds. *The Poetry of The Negro, 1746–1949*, (Garden City, NY: Doubleday, 1956), p. 92.

103. *The New National Baptist Hymnal* (Nashville, Tenn.: National Baptist Publishing Board, 1997), p. 486.

104. *The New National Baptist Hymnal* p. 497.

105. *The New National Baptist Hymnal* p. 504.

106. From "A New Song," by Langston Hughes, cited in Jean Wagner, *Black Poets of the United States* (Urbana, IL: University of Illinois Press, 1973).

107. See Rackham Holt, *George Washington Carver: An American Biography* (New York, Doubleday, 1965) or Linda McMurray, *George Washington Carver: Scientist and Symbol* (New York, Oxford University Press, 1981).

108. Booker T. Washington, *Up from Slavery, an autobiography* (New York, Doubleday, 1901).

109. Ralph L. Woods, ed., *Golden Treasury of the Familiar* (New York: Macmillan, 1980), p. 55.
110. For an excellent explication of Thomas Jefferson's support for and role in the maintenance of American slavery, see Garry Wills, *"Negro President": Jefferson and the Slave Power* (Boston and New York: Houghton Mifflin, 2003).
111. See Thomas Jefferson's *Notes on the State of Virginia* (Baltimore: W. Pechin, 1800).
112. See Tushnet, *Making Civil Rights Law*, p. 27, regarding the reason the NAACP Legal Defense and Education Fund was created, when it was created, and its function.

LONG HAVE I BEAT with timid hands

upon life's leaden door, Praying the patient,

futile prayer my fathers prayed before,

Yet I remain without the close, unheeded

and unheard, And never to my listening ear

is borne the waited word.


Soft o'er the threshold of the years there

comes this counsel cool; The strong demand,

contend, prevail; the beggar is a fool![1]


–GEORGIA DOUGLAS JOHNSON

# 20

# The Afro-American Association

S hortly after my arrival at the University of California's Boalt Hall[2] as a first-year law student in fall 1960, I had met most of the limited number of black students who were then enrolled at UC Berkeley. I estimate that there were around 40–no more than 50–black students among the almost 24,000 undergraduate and graduate students at UC Berkeley at that time.[3] It wasn't difficult to find each other.

I cannot remember everyone involved in the formation of the Afro-American Association at UC Berkeley, but the core group of early members certainly included Margot Dashiel,[4] Maurice Dawson, Donald Hopkins, Ann Cook,[5] Aubrey Labrie, Peter Labrie, James "Jim" Lacy, Mary Lewis, David Patterson, Evelyn Yvonne Ramsey, Belvie Rooks, Kenneth Harlan Simmons, Tamara Taylor, Toni Vincent, Donald Warden, and myself.

The only third-year black student at Boalt Hall during the academic year 1960–61 was Donald Warden, a 1958 graduate of Howard University with a bachelor's degree in philosophy.[6] Donald Warden changed his name to Khalid Abdullah Tariq Al-Mansour not long after graduating from Boalt Hall and being admitted to the California Bar Association. He was totally committed to achieving dignity, respect, and political, social and economic freedom for black people in America and, indeed, throughout the world.

I have never met anyone with greater capacity for analyzing economic, philosophical, political, or social issues than Donald Warden. He was the first person I knew who openly challenged the practice of black people in America calling themselves brown people, colored people, or Negroes. I may not have agreed in every instance with his proposed solutions, but it was a rare day when I disagreed with his analysis of a problem and assessment of what was required to address it. Everyone associated with the early period of the Afro-American Assóciation with whom I have spoken in connection with this chapter (and that is almost everybody) remembers Donald Warden as the intellectual and energetic force behind the association's formation and development.

Kenneth Harlan Simmons, a 1954 graduate of Harvard University with a bachelor of arts in biology,[7] was, in 1960, a graduate student in UC Berkeley's School of Architecture and Planning.[8] Ken was a member of the DuBois Club of San Francisco.[9] He was also a strong and influential San Francisco Bay Area voice for black economic empowerment. Like Warden, he was committed to unrestricted political and economic freedom for all black people and was willing to make any personal sacrifice necessary to achieve that end. I suppose my clearest memory of Ken Simmons from those days is his unconditional and total embrace of the need for mutual support and social equality among black people.

## Formation of the Association

There is disagreement among those involved in its formation about the exact origin of the Afro-American Student Historical Association, or Society (recollections differ on that final term), the precursor of the Afro-American Association. I do know that at some point early in the organizational process, I took the steps necessary to obtain UC Berkeley's recognition of this new group as an officially approved student organization with the name Afro-American Student Historical Society (or Association). I included the word *historical* because I thought doing so would make it easier to gain university recognition; we had to avoid the danger of recognition being denied on the grounds that we were a "political organization." At that time, the university's *Procedures for Recognition of Student Organizations*, under Standards for Recognition, provided that "[Student organizations] must have no partisan, political, or religious sectarian purposes or affiliations."[10]

Ken Simmons is now a permanent resident of South Africa and lives in Rosebank, a suburb of Johannesburg. He recalls the formation of the Afro-American Student Historical Association growing out of his acquaintance with brothers Aubrey and Peter Labrie, two other black UC Berkeley graduate students.[11] Ken says that the three of them were taking an upper-division political theory course in fall 1961 and, stimulated by several after-class discussions they had during the semester, came up with the idea of forming a book discussion group. He also said that after graduating from Harvard, he had spent a semester at Oklahoma State, where he was introduced to a book discussion group of Afro-American students, and that that experience also contributed to his suggesting the idea at Berkeley.

I spoke by telephone with Ann Cook, now named Tchaiko R. Kwayana, on December 25, 2003. Tchaiko's clear recollection is that, however the Afro-American Association started, it was Donald Warden who first decided that a study group should be formed. The various students participating in those discussions had diverse interests. Tchaiko was at that time most interested in the educational needs of African-American children, and even today—48 years later—the education of those children is still her primary intellectual and political interest.

Mary Lewis, like the rest of us, remembers the organization beginning as a book discussion group. It is her recollection that it was the important initial discussions on the terrace just outside the UC Berkeley Dining Commons that ultimately led to formation of a formal organization. She does not recall how long the original book discussion group was functional before it evolved into an activist organization.

Mary Lewis said different people had different reasons for getting involved and staying involved with the association. She was personally attracted by the activism of those who founded the association, especially "Warden's energy." She remembers that, in 1960 to 1961, "black students at UC Berkeley were experiencing a kind of alienation that fostered a need to come together." That period was one of "a collective identity crisis," she said, which was something we all shared. Once everyone got past the discussion stage and better understood who they were, there was no longer any need for just a book discussion group, and "it had to evolve into something else." Mary wishes she could remember the critical factors in the transition from the book discussion group to the more activist Afro-American Association, but she cannot.

## ESSAY ABOUT THE AFRO-AMERICAN ASSOCIATION

THE FOLLOWING ESSAY BY Donald Hopkins about his recollection of the founding accurately describes the purpose of the Afro-American Association:[12]

### The Afro-American Association and Black Student Nationalism: A Time for Ideological Assessment and a Prelude to Political Action

In September of 1960, a group of about 14 Blacks, all students at the University of California, met on the patio of the new student union at Berkeley to discuss our role in the historic events that began in Greensboro. This meeting was attended by a number of Blacks who are still prominent in different areas of public life in Berkeley and the Bay Area: Donald Warden, Henry Ramsey, Otho Green, Peter, Aubrey, and Gerald Labrie, Maurice Dawson, and Kenneth Simmons, to name a few. Henry Ramsey took the initiative of chartering an official organization on the Berkeley campus under the rubric of the Afro-American Historical Association. (The group rarely flew under this banner, so its name is mostly commemorative.) For some two years thereafter, we met, mostly in my Shattuck Avenue apartment, spending long hours in discussing the political, social, and economic ramifications of being Black in America. By 1963, this organization and its branches at San Francisco State University and Merritt College had touched the lives of hundreds of Black students in the Bay Area, and I think it fair to say that few lives that were touched by it were unchanged as a result.

Our discussion group was to become known simply as the Afro-American Association. If there was one idea that wed us all together, it was that we were not Negroes, but rather were American Blacks of African descent. Through our explorations we sought to come to an intellectual understanding of what this meant within the context of American life, and to come to a further understanding of what this meant in terms of our own political direction as future leaders of our people. Just as the sit-ins and related civil rights demonstrations were to confront the institutionalized aspects of American racism, our discussion groups and attendant political activity were to address the ideological aspects of racism–a role we felt more suited to northern Blacks who, after all, faced racism in a much more disguised and subtle form. . . .

I spoke with Khalid Abdullah Tariq Al-Mansour on February 6, 2004, at his home in San Antonio, Texas, about the Afro-American Association and its formation. He had a fairly detailed and expansive recollection of most if not all of the circumstances and general factors that were at play during the time the association was being established. Much of what follows is based on that February 2004 conversation. Khalid recalls that Ann Cook and Mary Lewis's apartment was not only convenient to the UC Berkeley campus but also sizable, with an ample living room that could easily accommodate quite a few people. Hence, many of the early discussions about civil rights and racial identity occurred at their place. It was from those discussions and from comparable discussions occurring at other venues at and around UC Berkeley that the Afro-American Association ultimately developed.

At the same time that we were forming the Afro-American Association, many of the black people in the Bay Area–students and non-students–were concerned about the struggle for civil rights that was occurring in the United States, particularly in the South, and about what the outcome of that struggle would ultimately mean for all black Americans.[13] Parallel to this interest in the civil rights struggle was an emerging interest by black students at the University of California and at other San Francisco Bay Area universities in discovering their own identity as individuals, as a race, as Americans, and as human beings.

## CRITICAL FACTORS

KHALID CITED SEVERAL ISSUES AS being critical to the formation and direction of the early Afro-American Association. The first, he said, was a profound concern with the question of racial identity. As he had reminded us during the time of the Association's formation, "The Irish came from Ireland, the Italians from Italy, the French from France, the Chinese from China, the Japanese from Japan, and we came from Africa." So he concluded that we should be Africans or, as some preferred, blacks. Thus, none of us would ever again refer to ourselves as Negroes. As Khalid was fond of saying, "There is no place called Negroland." There was absolutely no dissent among us on this issue.

A second factor, according to Khalid, was "the insistence by Don Hopkins and Henry Ramsey Jr.—from the very first meeting—that there be strict adherence to principles of logic and reason in considering any topic." Association discussions, conclusions, and decisions were to be based on logic, reason, and knowledge—never on emotion or wishful thinking.

With that settled, we confronted another racial identity question: whether we would be an all-black organization. This issue was pushed to the forefront because one of the founding members was a black woman whose husband was Caucasian. He was a graduate student at the University of California who was studying for a Ph.D. in history, with a concentration in U.S. history during the 19th century. He was also a militant advocate for and defender of Afro-American rights. We debated vigorously the question whether Caucasians, even one strongly sympathetic and supportive of black civil and political rights, should be permitted to attend and participate in Afro-American Association meetings. The decision of the group was that the association would be totally black.

Khalid remembers the most persuasive argument in favor of white exclusion being that there were plenty of opportunities for Afro-American Association members to talk and otherwise interact with white and other non-black students on and off campus. It was not asking too much to reserve one afternoon each week for black students to meet among themselves to discuss and analyze strategies for how they would determine their own destiny and what we needed to do to cope with bigotry and racism in America. We were not antiwhite, nor were we trying to discriminate against Caucasians. But we were clear and unyielding in our view that the weekly Afro-American Association meetings would be limited to black people.[14] This decision and all other important ones made by the association were arrived at by consensus, rather than by majority votes.

Khalid says that two additional important issues at that time were (a) whether and how to reach out to other black residents of the Bay Area in an effort to increase their consciousness and appreciation of the nationwide risks and difficulties blacks faced as a people, and (b) whether objectives and strategies of contemporary civil rights and other black organizations would be likely to solve the economic, political, and social problems of African Americans.

## INCLUSION OF STREET MEETINGS

KHALID RECALLED THE ASSOCIATION'S initial efforts to expand the organization as being mostly by word of mouth. But soon street meetings in West Oakland and San Francisco's Fillmore District were added. Members of the association—mostly Don Warden and I, plus a few others such as Herman Blake, who was then a graduate student in sociology—would stand on street corners in areas where there were significant numbers of black residents and speak to people passing by about civil rights issues.

Through those street encounters we attempted to convince passersby, primarily black people, that the problems being confronted by blacks in the South were not materially different from problems being encountered by blacks in the North. They were the same issues, just presented in different "garments" or a different form. The Oakland police took the position that we needed a permit to make such speeches. It was our view that our speech was constitutionally protected and that no

DR. J. HERMAN BLAKE *while a graduate student in sociology at UC Berkeley, speaking at an Afro-American Association street rally in Oakland, Calif., in 1961. Highlights of Dr. Blake's distinguished career appear on www.thehistorymakers.com/biography.*

HENRY RAMSEY JR. WHILE A LAW STUDENT *at UC Berkeley, speaking at the same rally in Oakland. For information on the racial tension in Monroe, N.C., at that time, see for instance* Freedom Riders, *by Raymond Arsenault (Oxford University Press, 2006).*

KHALID ABDULLAH TARIQ AL-MANSOUR *(then Donald Warden) while a law student at UC Berkeley, speaking at an Afro-American Association street rally in Oakland, Calif. in 1961 (see preceding pages).*

permit was required. However, beyond direct observation of those street speeches by uniformed (and probably plainclothes) officers, our right to speak was never challenged by the police in Oakland or San Francisco.

Khalid's view of the significance of the Afro-American Association and its influence on him and others is expressed in a letter he wrote to James L. Lacy, dated January 10, 2005:

> I prefer to remember those exciting, evolving times of the six-ties in the Bay Area as a rare if not predestined convergence of highly individualistic and complex personalities, who, left [to] their own devices might very well have withered on the vine. Fortunately for all, an emerging thirst for energized knowledge based upon our common African heritage created an internal explosion that became self-perpetuating. In the process, a sense of a constructive eternal reoccurrence became our joint mantra and legacy. I, for one, have continually drawn upon that legacy to pur-sue the mysteries of life within the one moment in time syndrome. There is little doubt in my mind but for that historic encounter my life would have had little sustaining meaning. Because of it, I would like to believe, I continue to expand. Because of it, I tend to measure my sought after evolution solely in spiritual, intellec-tual, and professional terms.

## My Personal Recollections

I do not remember being at the initial organizational meetings of the Afro-American Association. The first I recall is hearing from Khalid, as he and I were talking on the second floor main stair landing at Boalt Hall sometime during fall 1960, about plans to establish a book discus-sion group. Perhaps he was simply passing on the fruits of the earlier conversations that, by Ken Simmons' account, Khalid and Ken had had with Don Hopkins and Aubrey and Peter Labrie.

Regardless, I think it fair to say that three of us—Khalid, Ken, and I—constituted the initial leadership of the association. Khalid was the driving force at the University of California in stimulating black students' pride and dignity and in enhancing black students' awareness of our history and heritage. I was interested in that aspect of our development as black people, but my primary interest was political—specifically, civil rights and use of the law and legal system to eliminate racial discrimination and state-sanctioned segregation throughout the country. I wanted all people of color, but especially black people, to have the right to self-determination through free, full, and meaningful participation in every aspect of American government. Ken Simmons, as stated earlier, was most focused on communal cooperation among blacks and on meaningful business opportunities and economic development for black people.[15]

Another core notion shared by all of us was that, as black students at UC Berkeley, young adults, and future leaders within the black community—and probably within American society—we had an obligation to seriously prepare ourselves to undertake and implement that responsibility. Khalid suggested that we form a discussion group comprising black students who had shared objectives and who would read books and articles and hold weekly meetings. Each week, we would select a book to be read during the week. We would discuss that book at the meeting on Sunday and also analyze and discuss current events and issues that involved us directly in the civil rights struggle. The aim was that those discussions would allow us to address the current needs of black people in a meaningful way and would also prepare us for future leadership. I remember Khalid suggesting Melville J. Herskovits's *The Myth of the Negro Past* as the first book that we should read and discuss.[16] Khalid, in our conversation on February 6, 2004, remembers *Black Bourgeoisie* by E. Franklin Frazier as the second book,[17] with the third as *Black Moses: The Story of Marcus Garvey and the Universal National Negro Improvement Association,* by Edmund David Cronon.[18]

## Support for All Black Americans

I HAVE NO DOUBT BUT THAT EACH of us who were involved with the association genuinely wanted to contribute to the African American community and to help improve substantially the circumstances and conditions of black people in America and throughout the African diaspora. Looking at the subsequent history of those involved in the Afro-American Association, I am certain that we have made that contribution. It is clear to me that those early efforts did indeed bear fruits of leadership and result in substantial positive contributions to African American people in particular and to American society in general. I know that one of the anchors—one of the primary roots—of my commitment to excellence, intellectual integrity, and willingness to struggle on behalf of black and other oppressed people is those Sunday discussions of the Afro-American Association and the extraordinary feast of intellectual and analytical challenges I encountered during those discussions. I have interviewed, now some 48-plus years later, a number of the early members of the association and, to a person, they say that their involvement with the book discussion group and the Afro-American Association has had a comparable effect in their lives.

It is still very important in 21st-century America that black people never cease their struggle for self-awareness, self-esteem, confidence, self-reliance, and personal pride. The importance of their appreciating education as a means for achieving those values cannot be overstated. Within your households, your children's households, and their children's households, I hope that the values and message from the Afro-American Association of the early 1960s will never be lost or ignored. That message is simply to embrace the importance and value of education, preparation, courage, industry, integrity, community and—above all else—a belief in your self-worth as an individual and a confidence in your own ability. You should treasure those values as a means for success as a human being.

## · Notes ·

1. "The Suppliant," by Georgia Douglas Johnson, published in Langston Hughes and Arna Bontemps, eds., *The Poetry of The Negro, 1746–1949* (Garden City, NY: Doubleday, 1956), p. 58.

2. See Sandra P. Epstein, *Law at Berkeley: The History of Boalt Hall* (Berkeley, CA: Institute of Government Studies, University of California at Berkeley, 1997). As of 2008, Boalt Hall is now officially known as Berkeley Law.

3. According to the Office of the Vice President, Finance, *University of California Berkeley Statistical Summary 1960–1961: Students and Faculty*, p. 3, the total student enrollment at UC Berkeley for the 1960–61 academic year was 23,974 (16,227 undergraduates and 7,747 graduates).

4. Then a UC Berkeley undergraduate.

5. Many years ago Ann Cook changed her name to Tchaiko R. Kwayana.

6. There were only four black students then at the law school: Donald Warden, third year; Thelton Henderson and Eugene Swan, second year; and me, first year.

7. When Kenneth Simmons left his hometown in Muskogee, Oklahoma, to enroll in Harvard, he was uncertain whether he should become a physician or an architect. He says he was under the mistaken impression that the study of architecture required a solid background in mathematics, which he lacked. Therefore, he majored in biology with the intention of attending medical school after graduating from college. At about the time of his junior year, he discovered that architecture did not require a heavy math background. However, on the advice of his father, he continued studying biology. On completing his undergraduate degree in biology, Ken enrolled in the Harvard University Graduate School of Design, where he studied for two years. In 1960, he was admitted to the UC Berkeley School of Architecture and Planning, receiving credit for architecture courses he had taken at Harvard.

8. Today the name is the School of Environmental Design.

9. For a discussion of the WEB DuBois Club of San Francisco, see Young Communist League USA–History of Young Communist League Part II, by Tony Pecinovsky at www.yclusa.org/article:

> The fifties gave way to the sixties and youth, on campuses across the country, started demonstrating and protesting, calling for an end to the war being waged in Vietnam. This new movement became a turning point in the re-birth of a working class student movement.
>
> In 1964, out of this new radical upsurge, the WEB DuBois Clubs, USA were formed. The DuBois Clubs were named after W.E.B. DuBois,

the champion of African American liberation, who joined the CPUSA in 1961. The DuBois Clubs took an active role in opposing the U.S. war being waged on the people of Vietnam by publishing literature, holding campus educationals, demonstrating and working within the AFL-CIO to build working class opposition to the war. The first mass youth demonstrations against the war in Vietnam were organized by the DuBois Clubs. The DuBois Clubs also became an active participant and leader in the civil rights struggle. Young activists recognized that racist oppression was an experience shared by all African Americans and emphasized the nature of that oppression.

10. See Office of the Dean of Students, *Procedures for Recognition of Student Organizations* (Berkeley, CA, 1961), p. 1.

11. E-mail message from Kenneth Harlan Simmons dated April 6, 2003, in the author's files.

12. The essay is published in *Experiment and Change in Berkeley: Essays on City Politics, 1950–1975,* ed. Harriet Nathan and Stanley Scott (Berkeley, CA: Berkeley Institute of Governmental Studies), p. 108.

13. It is not my intent to suggest that student support for the civil rights struggle was limited to black students, for that would definitely be untrue.

14. Fortunately, we never had to face what can be a very difficult question of exactly who is a black person. No one looking white or mostly white but claiming to be black ever sought admission to any of the Afro-American Association meetings held in the early stages at Ann and Mary's apartment or at Don Hopkins' apartment.

15. The source of Ken Simmons' interest in and focus on business and black economic development becomes clearly understandable when one reads the history of his father and family as outlined in his father's biography: Jonathan D. Greenberg, *Staking a Claim: Jake Simmons and the Making of an African-American Oil Dynasty* (New York: Atheneum, 1990).

16. Melville J. Herskovits, *The Myth of the Negro Past* (New York: Harper Brothers, 1941).

17. E. Franklin Frazier, *Black Bourgeoisie* (New York: Free Press, 1965).

18. Edmund David Cronon, *Black Moses: The Story of Marcus Garvey and the Universal National Negro Improvement Association* (Madison: University of Wisconsin Press, 1960).

IGNORANCE, allied with power, is the most ferocious enemy justice can have.[1]

–JAMES BALDWIN

# 21

# Police-Youth Discussion Group

My involvement with troubled youth began not long after I became a deputy district attorney in the Contra Costa County, California, District Attorney's Office. Helping juveniles and young adults–particularly African American youth–avoid involvement in criminal conduct and imprisonment has long been a major concern for me. John A. Nejedly, then district attorney of Contra Costa County, operated an annual six-week summer camp for African American youth on land that he owned in the mountains of Sierra County, California, next to Hawley Lake and near the village of Johnsville. Nejedly generously paid all of the expenses associated with operation of the summer camp from his own personal funds.

## CAMP NEJEDLY

THE CAMP, UNDERSTANDABLY, WAS called "Camp Nejedly."[2] The program afforded African American youths from Richmond, California, and other areas of western Contra Costa County some exposure to outdoor life–very different from their experiences as inner-city youth. Nejedly also offered deputy DAs in his office an opportunity to work at the camp as unpaid volunteers. As soon as I learned about the summer camp I expressed an interest in participating. I very much appreciated what Nejedly was doing for the youngsters and his support for the African American community. I was selected as a counselor for the 1964 summer camp and was highly impressed by every aspect of the experience.

Camp Nejedly's objective was to significantly reduce the risk of the youngsters becoming serious juvenile offenders or adult criminals.

Emphasis was on managing anger, controlling impulsive behavior (thinking before acting), learning personal responsibility, developing life coping skills, developing positive aspirations and goals, becoming reliable and self-reliant, cooperating with and helping others, and becoming trustworthy.

## POLICE-YOUTH DISCUSSION GROUP (DYNAMIC YOUTH GROUP)

THE CAMP NEJEDLY EXPERIENCE helped me to recognize the tension that existed between the mostly low-income black youths in Richmond and members of the Richmond Police Department. It seemed to me that the serious and dangerous confrontations that too often occurred between those two factions were mostly avoidable. The consequences for the youngsters were often a trip to the hospital, followed by a trip to jail, criminal charges, and a criminal conviction—often for a felony offense.

As a member of the DA's office, I had close contact and reasonably good relations with many of the police officers who came into frequent contact with black youths in Richmond. In early 1965 I suggested setting up meetings between the youths and local police officers. I thought if they could talk to each other candidly and in a sheltered and neutral environment they might better understand each other's points of view, and unnecessary conflict could be significantly reduced, if not avoided altogether.

I spoke with then Police Chief Charles Brown, Captain Robert Murphy,[3] and Officer Ralph Rawson, then the Community Relations officer of the Richmond P.D., as well as with certain influential members of Richmond's Human Relations Commission, and asked for their support in establishing such a discussion group. I was at that time a member of the Human Relations Commission and chairman of the Commission's Youth Committee. The law enforcement and community leaders to whom I directed my appeal were receptive to the idea, and thus was formed what was initially known as the Police-Youth Discussion Group.[4]

I am deeply indebted to Rudolph "Rudy" Webbe,[5] who had the foresight to collect various newspaper articles, resolutions, and other materials concerning the Police-Youth Discussion Group and its successor organizations. Those materials were of immense help to me in reconstructing the formation and implementation of the Police-Youth Discussion Group, later named the Dynamic Youth Group.[6]

Initially, police and youth engaged in a series of 12 consecutive Monday evening meetings. The participants spent most of the first two or three meetings trading accusations and insults. The youths focused on charges of police insensitivity, unfairness, bias, brutality, and other misconduct. They also called the police "pigs." The police, for their part, noted that the youngsters typically made poor lifestyle choices, appeared to be living unproductive lives, and were frequently—some constantly—involved in property crimes and violent criminal activity. The police officers also called the youths "assholes." It was not a propitious beginning.

I insisted that the two factions continue to meet because I was convinced that people could hurl accusations and verbal insults at each other for only so long. You can call a person "pig" or "juvenile delinquent" or "asshole" only so many times before the tactic becomes boring and plainly ineffective. It also begins to sound stupid. I was correct, and by about the third meeting, the officers and youngsters had almost eliminated the name-calling and, instead, were raising and discussing substantive issues with each other.

Most of the youths came to appreciate that although certain socioeconomic circumstances might *explain* their behavior and lifestyles, those conditions did not *justify* criminal and other antisocial conduct. Such conduct was also obviously not in the youth's own interest. The police officers in the group soon came to a point where they could admit to the participating youngsters that some officers did engage in misconduct and even in behavior that could be fairly characterized as brutality.

The police officers and youth participating as members of the discussion group eventually came to understand that the deprecatory views most of them held about each other were based, in substantial measure, on ignorance and a lack of meaningful interaction. Most, if not all, of the participants came to see themselves and each other as individuals, each with his or her own strengths and weaknesses. The negative stereotypes expressed by both groups of participants at the beginning of the meetings had been candidly discussed. The two components came to better understand and appreciate each other's perspective and the result was a much-improved relationship. As reported in the *Oakland Tribune*:

> Now they [the youth] are willing to concede when the officers are doing their job. And the cops admit they used to think of the kids as hoods. Now they find they can reason with them. One officer, Marvin Smith, is extremely popular. The kids always want him to chaperone their parties.[7]

As a group, they had come to accept that name-calling and unfounded or thoughtless accusations did nothing to solve problems or to improve their respective circumstances.

I am proud of my leadership in the formation and development of the Police-Youth Discussion Group, and I continue to derive significant personal satisfaction from my involvement with Richmond's youth discussion group. A police officer[8] involved with the program went on record:

> Rawson gives most of the credit to Ramsey. "He's a Negro and an attorney, and they respect him," he says. "And he has an uncanny ability to reach kids."
>
> "I don't know of anyone his equal."
>
> "We don't know for sure and will never know how effective all this has been. But we can certainly be indebted to Henry for opening a door that I never thought would open."[9]

It soon became clear to nearly everyone involved, particularly the officers and the youngsters themselves, that continuing the discussions would benefit the entire Richmond community. The number of youth participants had increased from the initial 20 to 40. The Contra Costa County Probation Department and Richmond Police Department were exceedingly impressed by the positive results of the experiment.

None of the youngsters were in school when the sessions began, but all were enrolled at the end of the series of 12 meetings. There were few arrests by police of any youth involved in the first program; of those few, none of the arrests were for resistance, nor did they involve or result in a claim of police misconduct. Although everyone was elated about the positive results, it nevertheless had become clear to all of us that full-time staff support was needed if success was to continue.

About four months after the program began, a request was made to the Contra Costa County Probation Department for a full-time probation officer to be assigned to mentor and direct the group. The request was granted, and Deputy Probation Officer Rudy Webbe was assigned to be the first and, as it turned out, only director of the program during its existence. Under Webbe's leadership, the discussion group, soon renamed the Dynamic Youth Group (DYG), continued to provide meaningful service and support to Richmond's at-risk youth long after I left the Contra Costa County DA's Office and even after I moved to Alameda County in 1971.

Eventually a citywide advisory board was created—the Greater Richmond Youth Advisory Board—with a membership of community leaders from various professions: business owners, judges, police officers, lawyers in private practice, probation officers, school administrators, and teachers. The leaders "had all been interested in helping Richmond youths, and some had been very active in local youth organizations."[10] The DYG ultimately involved working with several different groups of youngsters, including one group that was for girls and another that was coeducational.

## DYG FINANCIAL SUPPORT

To RECAP, THE DYG PROGRAM initially received indirect financial support from the Richmond Police Department in the form of salaries paid to participating police officers, particularly Detective Ralph Rawson and Officer Marvin Smith. The next financial support was direct and from the Contra Costa County Probation Department when Rudy Webbe was appointed director of the program. His salary came from the Probation Department's budget. Two work-study students from the University of California at Berkeley's School of Criminology were assigned to work for the DYG program about 18 months after Webbe was appointed director. The cost of the work-study students was assumed by the university (90 percent) and the Contra Costa County Probation Department (10 percent).

Over the life of the program, funding also came from other sources. For example, ADVANCE (the Negro Council for Community Improvement) was able to provide two VISTA (Volunteers in Service to America) workers to DYG through a grant from the Office of Economic Opportunity, and Model Cities Block Grant funds were, at one point, also used to support the program. I think the overall significance of the DYG program was best captured by the following comment:

> What began as a program designed to improve communications between police and youth has gone far beyond this initial focus, has touched almost every problem the community faces, and has begun to bring varied community resources into focus through attempts at creative solutions to these problems.[11]

## · Notes ·

1. James Baldwin, *No Name in the Street* (New York: Dell, 1972).
2. I discussed this topic by telephone with John A. Nejedly—then 89 years old but still very mentally alert—on July 30, 2004.
3. Several years later, Murphy himself became Richmond's chief of police. See chapter 22 of this book.
4. For a newspaper account of the formation of the Police Youth Discussion Group, see Bud Wakeland, "Police 'Reach' Teens with Seminars," *Oakland Tribune*, Nov. 27, 1966, p. 4. Also see Resolution of the Assembly, California Legislature, 1967 Regular Session, Relative to Contra Costa Youth Delinquency Prevention, House Resolution 299, read and adopted unanimously May 11, 1967.
5. Rudolph N. Webbe currently lives in El Sobrante, Calif.
6. Rudy Webbe came to my home at 2955 Avalon Avenue, Berkeley, on Wednesday, April 14, 2004, for a discussion of our respective memories regarding the Dynamic Youth Group.
7. Ibid.
8. Officer Ralph Rawson was then the community relations officer of the Richmond Police Department.
9. Wakeland, "Police 'Reach' Teens with Seminars," p. 4.
10. Minutes of the first meeting of the Greater Richmond Youth Advisory Board. A copy of the minutes is in my possession.
11. Source: A brochure titled "The Community Responds to a Youth Group," published by the Contra Costa County Probation Department. A copy of the brochure is in my files.

NEGROES
Meek, humble, and kind:
Beware the day
They change their mind!

Wind
In the cotton fields,
gentle breeze:
Beware the hour
It uproots trees! [1]


–LANGSTON HUGHES

# 22

# Selma, Alabama, 1965

I n the fall of 1964, a determined effort to register black voters in Alabama, particularly in the counties of Montgomery, Lowndes, and Dallas, was initiated by the Student Nonviolent Coordinating Committee (SNCC)[2] and local civil rights activists. Later, in January 1965, Dr. Martin Luther King Jr.'s Southern Christian Leadership Council (SCLC) joined the endeavor.[3] The objective was to gain for eligible black voters fair access to voting booths where they could cast a secret ballot. In one sense, the effort culminated in the Selma march in the spring of 1965 (March 21-23), which ultimately resulted in passage of the Voting Rights Act of 1965, signed into law by President Lyndon B. Johnson on August 6 of that year.[4]

Under the guidance of the Rev. Martin Luther King Jr., SCLC announced a protest march from Selma, Alabama, to Montgomery, the state capital, a distance of approximately 50 miles, to demand that black citizens in Alabama be allowed to freely exercise their voting rights. The planned march was essentially motivated by the death of civil rights activist Jimmie Lee Jackson, who had died after being shot by police in nearby Marion, Alabama, the month before. George C. Wallace, then governor of Alabama, declared that the demonstration would not be permitted.

On the morning of Sunday, March 7, 1965, a group of approximately 650 protesters began what was intended to be a peaceful march from Selma to Montgomery.[5] After the protesters crossed the Edmund Pettus Bridge, just beyond the Selma southern city limits, armed state and local law enforcement officers—some on horseback—confronted the demonstrators and demanded that they turn back. Within minutes, the law enforcement officials, led by Sheriff James G. "Jim" Clark Jr. of Dallas County and Major James Cloud of the Alabama Highway Patrol, attacked the marchers, using billy clubs, tear gas, bullwhips, and horses. This cruel day in American history is now known as "Bloody Sunday."

I was a deputy DA in Contra Costa County, California, when the protest march from Selma to Montgomery was first attempted. Hosea Williams[6] of SCLC and John Lewis,[7] chairman of SNCC, were at the forefront of the march. Like most Americans and many people around the world, I was shocked and deeply angered when I saw the television coverage of Sheriff Jim Clark and his deputies, the sheriff's posse,[8] and Major John Cloud and dozens of highway patrolmen under his command violently and sadistically attack peaceful, nonviolent marchers, many of whom were women and children. The protesters' "offense" was to have peacefully assembled to petition the state and federal governments to protect African American voting rights in Alabama and to protect the lives of civil rights demonstrators and protesters.

I had previously participated in a few NAACP and Congress of Racial Equality (CORE) demonstrations, but I had never taken part in a SNCC or SCLC rally because I was not an adherent of the philosophy of nonviolence. I was by no means a proponent of violence—but it was certainly my view that, if attacked, I would and should strike back. But somehow, the attack on SNCC's John Lewis, SCLC's Hosea Williams, and other protesters at the Edmund Pettus Bridge got to me in a way that prior outrages had not. Something deep within me was touched by the awfulness of what I was seeing on television.

## THE BOMBING IN BIRMINGHAM

OF COURSE I HAD BEEN MOVED BY the September 16, 1963, church bombing in Birmingham, Alabama, in which four little girls were killed as they attended Sunday school: Addie Mae Collins, Denise McNair,

Carole Robertson, and Cynthia Wesley. That fall, almost immediately after I sat for the California Bar Examination, my then wife, our one-year-old son, Charles Tillman Ramsey, and I made a point of visiting Birmingham on a trip to see my mother in Philadelphia, Pennsylvania. We drove the southern route across the country and, after visiting my sister Martha Roberson *née* July in El Paso, Texas, stopped in Birmingham in October 1963 to visit the 16th Street Baptist Church, site of the bombing. I was fully conscious of and deeply abhorred the various indignities and physical harm being suffered by civil rights workers and just plain ordinary folk in the Deep South merely because they dared to demand full and equal civil rights.

Nevertheless, the events at the 1965 Selma march had an even more profound effect on me. Perhaps it was cumulative. But sitting at home in Richmond, California, on March 7, 1965, and seeing the violent conduct of those in Selma who were assaulting and seriously injuring nonviolent demonstrators, especially the women and children, was more than I could stand. I felt compelled to join the marchers as a nonviolent demonstrator. Indeed, I could not *not* join them. I had to do more than talk about my outrage at what was happening. I did not know what I would or could do, but I was going to Selma, and without delay.

## SELMA

$B$Y THIS TIME, MARCH 1965, my then wife Evelyn and I had two small children, Charles Tillman and Githaiga Daniel, for whom she would be the sole provider should something happen to me. We talked about my going, and while she did not advocate it, she was not openly opposed. The next morning I wrote and signed a letter of resignation to District Attorney John Nejedly. I told him it was not my intention to resign from the DA's Office, but because I had decided to go to Selma and did not know what would happen there or how controversial my presence there might become, I was giving him my resignation in case he should need or want it.

I do not remember where I got the money (probably a credit card), but later that day I went to the San Francisco airport and purchased a ticket for Montgomery, Alabama. Incredibly, now that I reflect on it, I traveled to the airport without knowing or having contacted anyone in Alabama. Equally amazing to me was the fact that there were others at the airport going to Selma on the same impulse as I had had. One of those people was the Rev. Ray Saunders, a white minister, also from Richmond. Ray and I became close friends as a result of being in Selma together, and we worked on various civil rights matters in Richmond after our return from Alabama. Another person from Richmond was the Rev. Booker T. Anderson. His trip most likely was not as impulsive as Ray Saunders's and mine, because Booker was already an associate of Dr. Martin Luther King Jr.

By the time the plane arrived in Montgomery, I was beginning to realize just how impulsive I had been. I had not made any arrangements for housing, food, local transportation, personal security, or anything else. I did not know a single soul in the entire state of Alabama, let alone Selma. Fortunately for me and for numerous others who had followed their convictions to Alabama, SNCC, SCLC,[9] and the Dallas County Improvement Association had planned well for our arrival and stay.

Few times in my life have I been as grateful as I was when we exited our plane and entered the Montgomery airport building and saw people with signs that read "Selma." After collecting my luggage, I went over to one of those people, introduced myself, and within minutes was in an automobile headed for Selma. I was placed with a family who lived in public housing near Brown Chapel African Methodist Episcopal (AME) Church, and I slept in that family's home throughout my three-week stay in Selma. We ate our meals at the First Baptist Church, located a couple of blocks from the housing project and Brown Chapel AME Church.

We spent most of our time listening to speeches and sermons at Brown Chapel, attending evening rallies at the church, and—when directed—marching to the Selma City Hall. A carefully choreographed exchange would take place there between the leaders of the demonstration and Wilson Baker, director of public safety for Selma. It was evident to me that an agreement—I assume it was informal and unwritten—had been reached with the police chief. The demonstrators would march from Brown Chapel AME Church, each time following the same route, to the steps of Selma City Hall. There one of the SCLC or local leaders—for example, Hosea Williams or the Rev. C.T. Vivian—would make a speech protesting the denial of constitutionally guaranteed voting rights to Negroes in Selma and elsewhere in the Deep South. The group of protesters and their leaders would then retrace their steps back to Brown Chapel AME Church. It was all very civil and polite—almost always nonviolent (see note 11).

Soon, however, I had the opportunity to observe firsthand the incredible courage of those mostly young freedom fighters. One afternoon, which became one of the most memorable occasions of my life, several of us were sitting in and around Brown Chapel AME Church. We and many other people had been urged to gather in the church's sanctuary to hear the Rev. James Bevel preach an important sermon. This was not unusual; Bevel and other ministers involved with SNCC and SCLC regularly gave what appeared to be spontaneous sermons on various topics relevant to the protest then going on in Selma. I went into the church along with the others to listen.

When a congregation of desired size had been assembled, James Bevel entered the pulpit and began his sermon. His basic theme was that in order for there to be salvation in one's life, the word of God had to become flesh or real. In other words, for meaningful salvation of sinners to occur, the word of God had to become flesh in the form of Jesus Christ, and Christ had to be crucified on the cross. Bevel pointed out that the white citizens of Selma knew no more about the civil rights demonstrations and protests occurring in their city than did citizens of Chicago, New York, or Los Angeles. All of them got their information about what was going on in Selma from the same sources: television, newspapers, radio, and news magazines. The demonstrations since the second march—namely the one Dr. Martin Luther King Jr. led from the church to the Edmund Pettus Bridge on March 9, 1965—had essentially been limited to the relatively mild round-trip protest marches between Brown Chapel AME Church and the Selma City Hall.

Bevel argued that this situation had to change if the demonstration was to be effective and result in positive change in Alabama and throughout the South. He said it was necessary "for the word to become flesh" by our—those of us at that moment sitting in Brown Chapel AME Church—getting into waiting cars and going to various white neighborhoods throughout Selma with picket signs. He said we were to march on sidewalks in those neighborhoods with our protest signs. That way, the white citizens of Selma would no longer be able to ignore the protest occurring in their city but would have to confront it directly. It was both a brilliant and a crazy idea. It was brilliant because it would substantially increase public interest in television coverage of the Selma protest throughout the United States and, indeed, the world. It was crazy because it put the picket sign carriers at great risk of physical harm from emotional, angry, and sometimes irrational whites in the various neighborhoods where the demonstrators would be dispersed.

The specific plan was for three or four people to get into one automobile with a driver, to be driven to a white neighborhood, to get out of the automobile (which would then drive away), and to begin picketing by walking on the public sidewalk with protest signs. There would not be one automobile in one neighborhood, but many different automobiles taking picketers to various areas within several different white neighborhoods. This tactic drove Public Safety Director Wilson Baker absolutely nuts. Baker was a sane, rational, and clever person who was doing all he could to prevent another public relations disaster for Selma like the one that had resulted from Sheriff Jim Clark and his posse's actions at the Edmund Pettus Bridge on Sunday, March 7, 1965.[10] Even if Baker was a racist and committed segregationist, he was no fool. The last thing he wanted to appear on the 6:00 p.m. network news was some white resident of Selma shooting a peaceful demonstrator or attacking one with a hammer or baseball bat.

The political and police leadership of Selma, probably Baker and Mayor Joseph Smitherman, made the decision to arrest the demonstrators for disturbing the peace and to hold them in protective custody. Those grounds for arrest were clearly a pretext that would deny the picketers their right to peacefully picket on a public sidewalk. However, if ever there was a circumstance in which demonstrators probably did need protection, this was it. Several people came from their houses armed with various instruments demanding that we, the demonstrators, "Get off of my sidewalk." Fortunately, none of the demonstrators were physically injured in any of the neighborhoods. City police officers drove around making arrests of the demonstrators, and after our arrest we were all taken to and held at a common place within the neighborhoods. The gathered demonstrators then began to lustily and joyfully sing freedom songs. The officer who arrested me chastised those in our group for singing so loud, telling us that there was a very sick woman in one of the nearby homes. People immediately stopped singing and became silent as Hosea Williams began praying for the sick woman. Concern for all people, even the oppressors, was typical of the Selma protesters.

Before long, a school bus that was being driven around Selma to collect the individual groups of demonstrators arrived at the spot where we were gathered, and we were herded aboard. Demonstrators on that bus and at least one other eventually arrived at the downtown jail to be booked. But the police had a problem: There was no more room in the county jail outside of town. It had for some time been filled beyond official capacity with other arrested civil rights demonstrators.

The people on our bus were initially taken into the downtown jail as if to be booked but, in fact, were quickly taken outside through a back door into somewhat of a courtyard behind the jail, which was formed by three brick buildings that formed a rectangle with one long side open. The long side of the "rectangle" was a laundry. The police building was at one end of the laundry building, and another building was at the other end. The long open side of this "courtyard" was a city street, and directly across the street from the courtyard were several Caucasian men with baseball bats, who were shouting threats and insults at us.

A major concern of those being held in the courtyard was that members of the press did not have a direct view of us. Media presence, in most circumstances, constitutes an important restraint on violence toward demonstrators. Certainly after the national and international press coverage of the March 7 attacks at the Edmund Pettus Bridge, the police had shown some restraint, but we did not see the few police officers present as being there to protect us. Rather, we perceived that their only assignment was to keep us in custody (i.e., to keep us from running away). I acknowledge that the March 8 attack on the Rev. James Reeb on a city street in Selma and the attack in February on Jimmie Lee Jackson (in nearby Marion) made it clear that there was a very real danger of violence, notwithstanding press coverage.[11]

Thus was it in this courtyard that I came to see firsthand the bravery displayed by those young activist freedom fighters.

We were arranged in a formation of three or four rows behind the laundry building, standing in what I have labeled the "courtyard," with each row comprising 15 or 20 people. People in rows two, three, and four were lined up directly behind those in the row immediately in front of them. I was in the last or next to last row and therefore in an excellent position to see almost everyone else in the formation.

We were a diverse group, men and women, black and white, younger and older. Every now and then, someone in our ranks would begin to tremble, cry, or otherwise evince extreme anxiety. When such a display occurred, a young man, perhaps 18 years old, would quietly ease from his position in the formation and work his way next to the person who was "about to lose it." I could see him quietly talking until the person had regained emotional control. Priests, ministers, and nuns were among those displaying such symptoms during the two or three

THE AUTHOR, *left, and a man whose identity is not known, about to set out on the third and successful march from Selma to Montgomery, Alabama, March 19, 1965.*

hours that we were kept standing in the courtyard. But in every instance, this young man was able to calm the person and help him or her regain both courage and dignity. I was highly impressed by his maturity, courage, and calm in the eye of the storm.

At some point, all of us were moved to a nearby recreation center, which I assume was owned and managed by the city of Selma. I think it was a black, as opposed to white, recreational center. Within a day or two of being placed in there, we were told that we were free to leave. Rather we were told that if we did not leave, the city would not provide us with food and would not allow any food to be provided to us by others.

We agreed among ourselves to refuse to vacate the recreation center until Mayor Joseph Smitherman and Director of Public Safety Wilson Baker apologized to all of us for our false arrest. The religious leaders within our group brought to our attention a passage from Acts 16, which we cited in our response to the city officials who were asking us to leave the recreation center:

> And when it was day, the magistrates sent the servants, saying, let those men go. And the keeper of the prison told this saying to Paul, "The magistrates have sent to let you go: now depart and go in peace."
>
> But Paul said unto them, "They have beaten us openly uncondemned, being Romans, and have cast us into prison; and now do they thrust us out privily? Nay verily; but let them come themselves and fetch us out." And the servants told these words unto the magistrates: and they feared, when they heard that they were Romans. And they came and besought them, and brought them out, and desired them to depart out of the city.[12]

The city officials never did apologize to us, but on March 18 we voluntarily left the building so that we could participate in the march that was now scheduled to begin the next day. Thus we were among the throng of marching and singing demonstrators who left

Selma on March 19 and crossed the Edmund Pettus Bridge bound for Montgomery.

There were many logistical and financial problems concerning the march that I was unaware of, but there were two that I did know about. One was that in Lowndes County the protest would be limited to 300 demonstrators.[13] I do not know how highway construction is funded in Alabama today, but in March 1965 it was my understanding that individual counties were totally or substantially responsible for such funding. For example, whether a highway was to be two or four lanes when it passed through a given county depended on that particular county's financial contribution to the cost of the highway.

U.S. Highway 80 between Selma and Montgomery was a four-lane divided highway (two lanes in each direction, with a landscaped median strip), except when it traversed Lowndes County, which was one of the poorest counties in the state. Lowndes County apparently could not afford or elected not to construct Highway 80 as a four-lane divided thoroughfare. Instead, the highway had only two lanes.

Judge Frank M. Johnson of the U.S. District Court for Alabama ruled on March 18, 1965, that the civil rights activist organizations—SNCC, SCLC, and the Dallas County Improvement Association—had a constitutional right to conduct a protest march from Selma to Montgomery, and he conditionally enjoined the state of Alabama from interfering with the march.[14] Where Highway 80 was a four-lane divided highway,[15] the marchers would be allowed to walk in the two westbound lanes, with vehicular traffic restricted to the two lanes that normally carried traffic only in the easterly direction.[16] That is, traffic was to be regulated in such a way that vehicles would move in both directions on two adjacent lanes of the divided highway, and the marchers (without any limitation being imposed on the number of demonstrators) would use the other two adjacent lanes. But because Highway 80 consisted of only two undivided lanes in Lowndes County, the scheme had to be modified for that part of the march. There, the marchers and vehicular traffic would have to share the two-lane highway. Judge Johnson approved the organizers' proposal to limit to 300 the number of marchers who could protest on the two-lane portion of the highway.[17]

The preliminary injunction issued by Judge Johnson stated, in pertinent part:

[I]t is:

> Ordered, adjudged, and decreed that, pending further order of this court, George C. Wallace, as Governor of the State of Alabama, Albert J. Lingo, as Director of Public Safety for the State of Alabama and James G. Clark, Jr., as Sheriff of Dallas County, Alabama, their successors in office, agents, representatives, employees, and other persons in active concert and participation with them be and each is hereby restrained and enjoined from:
>
> 1. Arresting, harassing, threatening, or in any way interfering with the efforts to march or walk, or the marching or walking, by the plaintiffs, members of their class, and others who may join with them, along U.S. Highway 80 from Selma, Alabama, to Montgomery, Alabama, said march, as presently approved by this Court, to commence in Selma, Alabama, not earlier than Friday, March 19, 1965, and not later than Monday, March 22, 1965, and to terminate in Montgomery, Alabama; and
> 2. Otherwise obstructing, impeding, or interfering with the peaceful, nonviolent efforts by said plaintiffs, members of their class, and others who may join with them, in protesting and demonstrating by assembling and by marching along U.S. 80 from Selma, Alabama, to Montgomery, Alabama, as said march is proposed in plaintiff's plan filed with this Court and served on the defendants on March 16, 1965, and to the extent that said plan is presently approved by this Court.[18]

Governor Wallace, who, ironically, was a law school friend and classmate of Judge Johnson, refused a request from President Lyndon B. Johnson[19] that the Alabama National Guard be used to provide protection for the marchers. President Johnson, therefore, on March 20, 1965, federalized the Alabama National Guard and ordered those troops to provide protection for the marchers along most of the 50-mile route between Selma and Montgomery, except in Lowndes County.[20] Protection for the marchers in Lowndes County was to be provided by regular Army troops of the 101st Army Airborne Division, known as the "Screaming Eagles" and stationed at Fort Campbell, Kentucky. It was this same 101st Army Airborne Division that President Dwight D. Eisenhower had on September 24, 1957, ordered to provide protection for the nine black students who integrated Central High School in Little Rock, Arkansas.

With many others, I had submitted my name as a volunteer to march the entire route of the demonstration, including in Lowndes County. I do not know nor was I ever told why I was selected to be one of the 300 who would be privileged to march through Lowndes County, but I was. My assumption is that I was chosen because of my status as a deputy district attorney. I hope you can appreciate that it was not common—indeed, it was extremely uncommon—for a member of law enforcement, particularly a deputy district attorney, to openly participate in a high-profile civil rights demonstration.

The organizers of the march also advised us "part-time demonstrators and protesters" about another problem. The march route and schedule was such that we would have to spend the night in Lowndes County, which was not only one of Alabama's poorest counties but also one of its most racist. The black population of Lowndes County at the time of the Selma march was 81 percent of the county's total population of 15,417, but according to the Lowndes County Registrar of Voters, none of the black adults in the county were registered to vote at that time.[21]

Thus, not only would the 300 marchers have to take care of their personal hygiene, be fed, and try to sleep in highly dangerous Lowndes

County, but also someone would have to be found who would allow his or her property to be used for those purposes. It was obviously highly unlikely that any Caucasian landowner would permit use of his or her property, no matter how much money was offered. There was also clearly a high probability that harmful economic and physical consequences would befall any black landowners or tenants who made their property available.

And yet Rosa Steele, a courageous black farmer who owned her land outright, allowed the marchers to spend the night on her farm in the county. Her courage was magnified by the fact that while she may have owned her land outright, nearly all farmers–black and white–live by credit. Each year farmers typically need credit from a bank or other financial institution to purchase seeds for planting, fertilizer, chemicals for weed control, and new equipment, or to pay for equipment repairs. Although Ms. Steele may have been financially independent and secure on the day of the march, her willingness to make her land available to the organizers of the march was an act of extraordinary heroism in light of the uncertainty of everyone's future.

Tents were erected on Ms. Steele's land, and we were fed and spent the night there. The soil was very damp because there had been a great deal of rain during recent weeks. But the sky was clear the next morning when we began our march out of Lowndes County. Indeed, I don't recall that it rained at all during the march.

There were no serious incidents during the march, despite the deaths of the Rev. James Reeb shortly before and Ms. Viola Liuzzo immediately after the march. As discussed earlier, Jimmie Lee Jackson, a black youth, was shot by a police officer in Marion, Alabama, on February 18, 1965, and died on February 26. His death was one of the main catalysts for the attempted march from Selma to Montgomery on March 7. However, incidents during the later march were comparatively mild. Nevertheless, in each town along the march route, both before and in Lowndes County, the streets were lined with white people

—mostly young and middle-aged adults—who made obscene and threatening remarks and gestures and displayed signs expressing comparable sentiments toward those of us who were marching.

I am proud to say that this crude behavior was in stark contrast to the behavior of those of us who were marching to Montgomery. Our signs spoke of freedom, liberty, love, and justice, not hatred. The air —as we passed through towns and down Highway 80—was frequently filled with the sound of our singing songs such as this one:

> I love everybody; I love everybody in my heart;
> I love Al Lingo; I love Al Lingo, in my heart,
> I love George Wallace; I love George Wallace, in my heart,
> I love Sheriff Clark; I love Sheriff Clark in my heart,
> I love everybody in my heart.[22]

I will always remember listening to the Rev. Andrew Young preach in Brown Chapel AME Church about how the people who were attacked at the Edmund Pettus Bridge on "Bloody Sunday" had fled from the beatings and tear gas to the sanctuary of the Chapel, where they huddled and, over and over, sang "I Love Everybody, I Love Everybody in My Heart."

Other songs lightened our steps on those 50 miles to Montgomery: "Ain't Gonna Let Nobody Turn Me 'Round," "This Little Light of Mine," "Come by Here, Lord, Come by Here," and "Keep Your Eyes on the Prize":

> Keep your eyes on the prize, hold on, hold on.
> I've never been to heaven, but I think I'm right,
> You won't find George Wallace anywhere in sight,
> Keep your eyes on the prize, hold on. . . .
> I know one thing we did right
> Was the day we started to fight.
> Keep your eyes on the prize, hold on, hold on.

But this simple refrain was, for me, the most moving and memorable:

I woke up this morning with my mind,
my mind it was set on freedom,
Woke up this morning with my mind,
my mind it was set on freedom,
Hallelu, hallelu, hallelu . . .

Through our signs and songs proclaiming our commitment to freedom, justice, and liberty for all people, we responded to the vulgar taunts and threats of violence by local whites as we passed through small Alabama towns on our way from Selma to Montgomery. I believe that the people who marched the entire 50-mile distance were courageous and deeply committed to full civil, political, and human rights for all Americans, without exception. But I believe that was also true of everyone who participated as a protester at any time in the march.

One of the people I met and became friends with during the Selma march was Harris Wofford. When we met—and even during most of the time we were on the march—I did not know (Harris did not mention it) that he had been a special assistant to President John F. Kennedy and was a colleague of Dr. Martin Luther King Jr. I also did not know that Harris had assisted in the formation of the Peace Corps and, since 1962, had served as associate director of the Corps under President Lyndon B. Johnson. To me, Harris was a regular guy who, like me, had simply traveled to Selma to provide support for the march.

Harris Wofford subsequently served, from 1966 to 1970, as president of the State University of New York, College at Old Westbury, and, from 1970 to 1978, as president of Bryn Mawr College. He was a U.S. senator from 1991 to 1994[23] and served as chief executive officer or chairman of the Corporation for National Service ("Americorps") from 1995 to 2000.

Somehow Harris and I became walking companions during the 1965 Selma march, and we have remained friends since, although it has now been several years since we have communicated. Harris is an alumnus of both the Howard University School of Law and Yale University School of Law, and he was very helpful to me during my tenure as dean of the Howard University School of Law. He was our leading supporter in the U.S. Senate for passage of the legislation that funded the Howard University Clinical Law Center. In later years, on a couple of occasions when we happened to be at the same event, Harris publicly commented that it was I who watched out for him and helped him survive the Selma march. I don't recall it that way. My recollection is that, while walking from Selma to Montgomery, we simply talked a lot about the civil rights movement, the need for change in the South and elsewhere in the United States, and the implications of the civil rights revolution for the future of American society.

March 25, 1965, is a day I vividly remember and hope I never forget—even more memorable for me than the next day when we finished the march at the state capitol building in Montgomery and speeches were delivered by Dr. Martin Luther King Jr. and others. March 25 is the day we marched from where we had spent the night in Lowndes County to the place where we would spend the night on the City of St. Jude Hospital grounds in Montgomery.[24] Keep in mind that we started out early that morning in Lowndes County on a two-lane highway with only 300 marchers.

There are many settings in which 300 people constitute an impressive crowd, but a highway is not usually such a venue. Our numbers appeared small when we started out in the morning in Lowndes County. But it was not long before we arrived at the Lowndes County-Montgomery County line and the resumption of the four-lane divided highway. A crowd was waiting there to join the march, and the number of demonstrators rapidly increased as we marched farther into Montgomery County. Automobiles would be driven on the opposite highway lanes until they were at a point even with the front of the demonstration. There the cars would stop, and passengers would get out, run across the median, and join us. Thousands of people joined the march in Montgomery County in that manner.

When we got to the place on the highway just outside the city of Montgomery where the roadway to and from the Montgomery Airport intersects with Highway 80, Dr. Martin Luther King Jr. and several other dignitaries joined the front of the demonstration. As the march continued into the city of Montgomery proper, we passed through black neighborhoods, and people rushed out to join us. It was as if the march was an enormous and powerful human magnet that, as it passed their homes and through their neighborhoods, literally pulled people who were observing the march from the sidewalk and from the steps and porches of their houses into the street to join the march. I hope and trust that I will never forget the feelings and sights I experienced as we entered Montgomery on that day.

In a speech the night before we left Selma, the Rev. Frederick Reese had expressed the hope that, when the demonstration reached the state capitol, like a description in Revelation, the multitude of demonstrators would be so great that they would constitute a "number that no man could number."[25] The Highway 80 roadway into Montgomery near the entrance to the Montgomery Airport presented a long, gradual, but substantial climb to the top of a relatively high hill. It may have been as much as a mile from the area of the airport until one reached the crest of that hill and Highway 80 became a city street, and one would then have a sense of actually being in the city itself. I can still remember reaching the crest of that hill and looking forward and backward at the marchers, who now filled the roadway from edge to edge and as far as the eye could see in both directions. At that moment I thought to myself, "Rev. Reese, your demonstration now truly involves a 'number that no man can number.'"[26] I was profoundly affected by that scene and even today am deeply moved by the memory of it.

The plan was for the marchers from outside the city to spend the night in Montgomery on the grounds of the City of St. Jude Hospital, then located at 2048 West Fairview Avenue. Big-name entertainers and civil-rights supporters, such as Joan Baez, Harry Belafonte, Sammy Davis Jr., Odetta, and Pete Seeger were to appear on a stage that had been set up on the hospital grounds. I recall being particularly impressed by Joan Baez's voice. I had never heard her in person before —nor since, for that matter. But I mostly recall that Harris Wofford, a few others, and I spent most of the evening sharing our impressions of the march and its significance.

The next morning, we awakened, dressed, ate, and joined those marching from the hospital grounds to the state capitol building, where speeches were to be made. Those of us who had been privileged to march the entire route from Selma to Montgomery were issued bright orange plastic vests to wear and were honored with positions very near the front of the marchers. The march to the state capitol building was exciting and dramatic. Still, for me, the march of the previous day is unsurpassed.

Dr. King's speech before the state capitol building was populist in tone and was well received. He declared:[27]

> The threat of the free exercise of the ballot by the Negro and the white masses alike resulted in the establishing of a segregated society. They segregated Southern money from the poor whites; they segregated Southern churches from Christianity; they segregated Southern minds from honest thinking; and they segregated the Negro from everything. . . .
>
> Let us therefore continue our triumph and march to the realization of the American dream. Let us march on segregated housing until every ghetto of social and economic depression dissolves and Negroes and whites live side by side in decent, safe, and sanitary housing.
>
> Let us march on segregated schools until every vestige of segregated and inferior education becomes a thing of the past and Negroes and whites study side by side in the socially healing context of the classroom.
>
> Let us march on poverty until no American parent has to skip a meal so that their children may eat. March on poverty until no

starved man walks the streets of our cities and towns in search of
jobs that do not exist.

Let us march on ballot boxes, march on ballot boxes until race
baiters disappear from the political arena. Let us march on ballot
boxes until the Wallaces of our nation tremble away in silence.

Let us march on ballot boxes until we send to our city councils,
state legislatures, and the United States Congress men who will
not fear to do justice, love mercy, and walk humbly with their
God. . . .

Our aim must never be to defeat or humiliate the white man
but to win his friendship and understanding. We must come to see
that the end we seek is a society at peace with itself, a society that
can live with its conscience. That will be a day not of the white
man, not of the black man. That will be the day of man as man.

After the final speech was given and the crowd began to disperse, I
was eager to get back to Selma and prepare for my return to California.
Fortunately, I was able to get a ride with someone driving the whole
way to Selma. As we rode down Highway 80 through Lowndes County,
I noticed an automobile stopped against a fence. Either someone had
accidentally driven off the road or it had been forced off the road. As
noted earlier, there had been a great deal of rain in that part of Alabama
in the days leading up to the march. One could see deep ruts that had
been made in the mud by the automobile's tires, from the roadway to
the rear of the automobile stopped against the fence several yards away.
We noticed the car as we passed and commented on its location and
appearance but did not stop because it seemed to be unoccupied.

Later that night we learned that Viola Liuzzo had been shot to death
in that automobile. I felt certain that Ms. Liuzzo's body and the sur-
vivors hiding in the car were there when we passed earlier that evening.
I still have profoundly etched in my memory, almost 50 years later, the
picture of those deep tire tracks leading to the rear of that automobile,
stopped against a fence beyond the shoulder of Highway 80.

I returned to Berkeley, now fortified and filled with inspiration for a renewed commitment to the civil rights struggle in America. I also had encountered new colleagues in the struggle–the Rev. Booker T. Anderson,[28] the Rev. Ray Sawyer,[29] the Rev. Cecil Williams[30]–and we maintained contact after our return to the Bay Area. While I acknowledge that nonviolence can be an appropriate tactic in certain circumstances, I still have grave doubts about it as a philosophy. Still, I look back on my 1965 Selma experience as one of the most inspirational and meaningful in my life.

· Notes ·

1. Langston Hughes, "Warning," in *The Collected Poems of Langston Hughes*, ed. Arnold Rampersad and David Roessel (New York: Alfred A. Knopf, 1994), p. 365.
2. Pronounced "snick" (rhymes with "nick").
3. For a detailed discussion of the 1964–65 Selma protest, see John Lewis with Michael D'Orso, *Walking with the Wind: A Memoir of the Movement* (New York: Harcourt Brace, 1999), pp. 300–62 (first published in 1998 by Simon and Schuster), and Juan Williams, *Eyes on the Prize: America's Civil Rights Years, 1954-1965* (New York: Viking, 1987), pp. 250–87.
4. The Voting Rights Act empowered the U.S. attorney general to replace local registrars with federal registrars in areas where prohibited discrimination was present. Fearing a flood of federal workers, local officials did everything they could to help blacks and other minorities register to vote. State literacy tests were also banned. Anyone over the age of 21 could legally register to vote. In 1966, poll taxes were also prohibited with ratification of the 24th Amendment.
5. See *Williams et al. v. Wallace et al.*, 240 Fed. Supp. 100, 104 (1965).
6. Williams was elected to the Georgia General Assembly in 1974 and served until 1984. He later served on the Atlanta City Council and the De Kalb County Commission. He retired from politics in 1994 and died on Nov. 16, 2000. See Daniel Lewis, "Hosea Williams, 74, Rights Crusader, Dies," *New York Times*, Nov. 17, 2000.
7. Years later, in 1981, John Lewis was elected to the Atlanta, Georgia, City Council. He was elected to the U.S. House of Representatives in 1986, where he still serves (2007). He tells his life story in John Lewis with Michael D'Orso, *Walking with the Wind*.

8. Sheriff Jim Clark organized a posse of volunteers mounted on horseback to attack Selma marchers. The posse members were further supported by about 50 Alabama state troopers. After the troopers fired tear gas at the marchers, Clark and his posse charged into the marchers and beat them with billy clubs. Sixty-five marchers were injured, giving the day the name "Bloody Sunday." See "What Became of Sheriff Clark?" *Journal of Blacks in Higher Education* 19 (Spring 1998): 17.

9. SCLC's local affiliate in Selma was the Dallas County Voters League.

10. See, for example, Williams, *Eyes on the Prize,* pp. 255–59.

11. Those acts of violence directed toward the Rev. Reeb and Mr. Jackson occurred at night and were not directly observed by the press. I suppose one could argue that Sheriff James Clark struck the Rev. C.T. Vivian on the Selma courthouse steps in broad daylight and in full view of the press. But that use of violence involved striking with the fist, did not involve the use of a deadly weapon, and appeared to be the result of an impulsive act by a hotheaded and not too bright sheriff. And it did bring more unwanted negative publicity about Selma.

12. Acts 16:35–39, *Master Study Bible, Containing the Authorized King James Version of the Old and New Testaments* (Nashville, TN: Cornerstone Bible Publishers, 2001), p. 802.

13. *Williams et al. v. Wallace et al.,* especially pp. 107 and 110.

14. *Williams et al. v. Wallace et al.*

15. That is, everywhere, except in Lowndes County.

16. *Walking with the Wind,* p. 356.

17. *Williams et al. v. Wallace et al.,* pp. 107 and 110.

18. *Williams et al. v. Wallace et al.*

19. Judge Frank M. Johnson and President Lyndon B. Johnson were not related.

20. See the executive order dated March 20, 1965, and signed by President Lyndon Baines Johnson, titled "Providing Federal Assistance in the State of Alabama." Section 3 reads, "I hereby authorize and direct the Secretary of Defense to call into the active military service of the United States, as he may deem appropriate to carry out the purposes of this order, any or all of the units or members of the Army National Guard and of the Air National Guard of the State of Alabama to serve in the active military service of the United States until relieved by appropriate orders. The Secretary of Defense is further authorized to recall any unit or member so relieved if he deems such recall appropriate to carry out the purposes of this order."

21. Source: Telephone call made to Lowndes County Registrar of Voters.

22. As a reminder of earlier references in text, Al Lingo was the head of the Alabama Highway Patrol, George Wallace was the governor of Alabama, and Jim Clark was the sheriff of Dallas County. All three were cruel, ruthless, and unsympathetic opponents of the civil rights movement in Alabama.

23. Harris Wofford was appointed to the U.S. Senate, as a Democrat, by the governor of Pennsylvania on May 8, 1991, to fill the vacancy caused by the death of Henry John Heinz III. He was elected to the remainder of the term in a November 1991 special election and served from May 9, 1991, to January 3, 1995. He was an unsuccessful candidate for reelection to the U.S. Senate in 1994.

24. The City of St. Jude Hospital was a Catholic medical complex that served the Montgomery black community. "Founded during the mid-1930s by Catholic priest Father Harold Purcell when segregation was the norm in the Southeast, the City of St. Jude Hospital pioneered nondiscriminatory health, education, and social service." The hospital closed in 1985; most of the campus has been converted to apartments for low-income families. See www.angelfire.com/me2/kulacoco/stjude.html.

25. *The Holy Bible*, New Revised Standard Version, Revelation 7: 9: "After this I looked, and there was a great multitude that no one could count, from every nation, from all tribes and peoples and languages, standing before the throne."

26. The Selma march demonstration before the state capitol building the next day was estimated to include 50,000 participants. See Alton Hornsby Jr., ed., *Chronology of African American History: From 1492 to the Present,* 2nd ed. (Detroit: Gale Research, 1997), p. 186.

27. King, *Autobiography*, p. 285.

28. Now deceased.

29. Now deceased.

30. Still pastor of Glide Memorial Church in San Francisco.

ON SOME POSITIONS, Cowardice asks the question, "Is it safe?" Expediency asks the question, "Is it politic?" And Vanity comes along and asks, "Is it popular?" But Conscience asks the question, "Is it right?" And there comes a time when one must take a position that is neither safe, nor politic, nor popular, but he must do it because Conscience tells him it is right.[1]

–MARTIN LUTHER KING JR.

# 23

# Black Police Officers
# of Richmond, California

$E$xcessive use of force by police officers has been a source of distress for the black community for well over a century. But rarely are police officers—black or white—willing to stand up and be counted by publicly naming fellow officers who engage in such improper and unlawful conduct.

As I began writing this section in 2003, a criminal trial known as the *Riders* case had just concluded in the Alameda County Superior Court.[2] It involved three Oakland police sergeants being tried "on criminal charges that they abused and framed suspected drug dealers in a conspiracy to obstruct justice."[3] The case was triggered when Keith Batt, a rookie Caucasian Oakland police officer, resigned from the department immediately after telling his police superiors that he had observed officers responsible for his training "[beat] people or [plant] drugs on them, then [fabricate] reports to cover their tracks."[4] An internal departmental investigation of Batt's allegations resulted in the accused officers being fired and subjected to criminal prosecution.

The *Riders* case ended in a mistrial after the jury, on Tuesday, September 30, 2003, returned verdicts of acquittal on eight of the 35 charges against the accused officers but were unable to agree on unanimous verdicts concerning the other 27 counts.[5] The case was then refiled, and a second criminal jury trial commenced on November 1, 2004.[6] That jury was unable to achieve a unanimous verdict on any of the counts, and the charges were later dismissed by the district attorney of Alameda County. At the least, however, rookie Keith Batt's courageous action brought the issue to public attention.

I cite the Riders case as backdrop for an even more extraordinary chain of events 35 years before. In 1968 nine black Richmond, California, police officers took the unprecedented action of telling then Police Chief Robert Murphy that a significant number of sworn officers within the Richmond Police Department were regularly engaging in unlawful acts including illegal detentions and arrests, beatings, and unjustified verbal abuse. These observed acts of police misconduct had been committed largely by white officers and directed primarily against black young adult males.

The nine informing black officers were Douglas L. Ellison, sergeant, age 44;[7] Ollie Sylvester Glover, patrolman, age 30;[8] Lee Arthur Johnson, patrolman, age 31;[9] Rudolph Johnson, patrolman, age 32;[10] Tecumseh "Danny" Nelson, patrolman, age 31;[11] Michael Nichols, patrolman, age 29;[12] Harold Redic, patrolman, age 29;[13] Marvin Richard Smith, patrolman, age 27;[14] and Otis Timmons Jr., patrolman, age 27.[15] Each of those officers had observed serious misconduct by other sworn officers (including sergeants) since being hired as members of the Richmond P.D. The officers who became informants had for some time been talking among themselves about their personal observations of police brutality and other forms of misconduct by Richmond police officers. They sincerely wanted to take concrete action to address this issue and to bring about positive change within the department.

At the time there were approximately 150 sworn officers in the department.[16] The nine black officers constituted 90 percent of the sworn black officers then on the force. Andrew Pringle, patrolman, was the one other black officer at that time, but he was a recent hire and was still on probation. The nine protesting black officers had permanent employment status and could be fired only for cause. They felt that Pringle should not risk almost certain loss of employment by making what would certainly be a controversial claim of police brutality against other officers within the department.[17] They might have also thought that his testimony wouldn't have been so valuable as to risk his career. He would only have been able to testify about what had happened in the months he had been there, whereas the other nine could testify that the behavior had been going on for years.

The black officers' first collective action after informing Police Chief Robert Murphy about their area of concern was to request a private, confidential meeting with Murphy and his captains for the purpose of providing specific and detailed information about their observations of police misconduct. The officers asked that the requested informal meeting with Chief Murphy be limited to just him and his four captains because they intended to name not only patrolmen but also lieutenants and sergeants, and to provide details about each named person's misconduct.

In retrospect, one can see that they—I suppose I should say we—were somewhat naive in thinking that a matter of such magnitude would be acknowledged by the chief and effectively addressed within the department. That would have been a tacit* admission by the chief and his command staff that sworn officers had been regularly engaging in unrestrained racist conduct without the police leadership having done anything meaningful to stop it. Naive or not, those mostly young black officers hoped that the matter could be resolved within the department.

Chief Murphy's response was that he would "not meet with a delegation of black officers." After receiving legal counsel, the officers then made a formal written request for a meeting with the chief and the four police captains, and a meeting was scheduled by the chief's office. The black officers thought that their request for a private meeting with only the chief and the four police captains had been granted and that it would be held in the chief's office at police headquarters.

But when the officers arrived for the meeting, they were for the first time told that the meeting would not be held in the chief's office but downstairs in the much larger Civil Defense Room. They were next advised that lieutenants and sergeants would also be present and would participate in the meeting. It was the black officers' unanimous view that they had been deceived and that the chief had broken his word. They remain convinced—even today—that Chief Murphy and his command officers believed that the nine black officers would be intimidated in this open and broader setting and would be afraid to provide specific information about the police brutality charges previously disclosed to the chief in private.

The curve thrown by the chief served only to unify and strengthen the group. In the downstairs meeting room, each black officer looked those present in the eye, named names, and candidly described specific acts of brutality and other misconduct he had observed since being hired as a member of the Richmond Police Department. The chief, captains, lieutenants, and sergeants were astonished that Sergeant Douglas Ellison was an active participant in this protest action.

One would have to know Doug Ellison to appreciate how unsettling it must have been for those white officers to hear and see him take what, by any measure then and now, was a strikingly militant stand. Doug had once been a very good prizefighter, but he was also a particularly quiet person and usually had very little to say. Until that occasion, he had always been moderate in his rarely expressed comments concerning race relations. One of the first black police officers hired in the city of Richmond, he was now a 44-year-old sergeant—indeed, the only black police officer in Contra Costa County above the rank of patrolman—and had been on the Richmond force long enough to qualify for his retirement pension. In other words, he had a great deal to lose in joining this protest with the eight other black officers.

Doug had to have been viewed by white people as a "good Negro," one who was not a "troublemaker" and who was not subject to influence from "outside agitators." White police officers who knew and worked with him probably assumed Doug would agree with them that race relations within the Richmond Police Department, while not perfect, were pretty good, and that substantial progress between blacks and whites in Richmond had been made since he had joined the force. They certainly would not have expected him to speak out about or accuse any of his fellow officers of any form of racist behavior. The other black officers at the meeting said the white officers were truly shocked when Sergeant Douglas Ellison spoke up, described specific incidents, and named names.

The primary catalyst for the brave actions of those black Richmond police officers was the June 25–July 2, 1968, riots in Richmond, California, that followed the assassination of Martin Luther King Jr. Dr. King was shot to death on April 4, 1968, while standing on the balcony of the Lorraine Motel in Memphis, Tennessee. Almost immediately, angry protests erupted in many cities throughout the United States. In California, riots were expected in Oakland as a consequence of Dr. King's assassination but did not occur there. Riots were not expected in nearby Richmond but did occur there. The Richmond riots were of such intensity and magnitude that mutual aid pacts with police departments in several nearby communities were invoked.[18] Unlike the Richmond Police Department, those departments were composed totally or almost totally of white personnel.

Several of the black officers shared with me various experiences that led to their taking action. Marvin Smith[19] told me that he was particularly offended by comments he heard from a white officer from the Walnut Creek Police Department. The officer said that shooting at and thumping[20] black suspects was his first opportunity "to do real police work." As already stated, Doug Ellison was one of Richmond's first black police officers and the first and only black sergeant. As Ollie Glover later recalled, Sergeant Ellison saw two white patrolmen engaging in unprofessional conduct while on patrol in Parchester Village–a black Richmond neighborhood–during the riots and ordered them to return to the police station. Glover reported, "The two white officers told Doug he could not tell them what to do."

Ollie also recalled for me an incident in which a black preacher from Marin City[21] was stopped by a squad of 16 officers (four police cars with four officers in each car) and told to get out of his car. The preacher was told that it was unlawful for him to be on the streets after curfew (declared because of the riots). He was thoroughly thumped[22] by some of the officers and told to get back in his automobile and get out of Richmond. I do not know if those specific incidents were shared with the chief and other white officers at the meeting held in the Civil Defense Room. I assume they were.

With the exception of Marvin Smith, all of Richmond's black officers were assigned to the patrol division at the time of those unlawful events. Nearly all enjoyed excellent relations with the community, especially the black community. Marvin Smith was the department's community relations officer and had especially good rapport with the black community. But it was the observations by all of the black officers of frequent inappropriate use of force by police officers during the 1968 riots that brought matters to a head. The black officers all decided that something beyond talk was required before the department would confront and eliminate the serious police misconduct they had observed in Richmond before and during the riot. They therefore decided to take the matter to the chief.

The black officers were intelligent and well educated. In 1968, the great majority of San Francisco Bay Area police officers were high school graduates, but—with the possible exception of the officers of the Berkeley P.D.—most had not earned any college credits. Those nine Richmond black officers not only were high school graduates but also had an average of at least two years of college. In addition, Marvin Smith had two and one-half years' experience as a military policeman in the U.S. Army when he joined the Richmond Police Department on August 1, 1962.

They all knew that disclosing their observations of police brutality by their white colleagues would be both controversial and divisive within the Richmond Police Department and the city. They knew—or at least believed—that every white officer, even the sergeants and command officers, would deny their charges and make a determined effort to have them removed from the force. They also knew there was a significant risk that some of the white officers would attempt to retaliate further against them and that they, the black officers, would be vulnerable to such retaliatory tactics. One obvious risk was that some white officers would fail to respond promptly to a black officer's call for desperately needed assistance. Another risk was that white supervisory officers–sergeants and lieutenants–would make unwarranted accusations of poor, cowardly, or incompetent performance by black officers.

A more immediate problem they had to face was that one of their own–one of the nine–had engaged in brutality. They knew that the obvious charge many white officers would make in response to their claims of white police officer brutality would be the old "pot calling the kettle black" claim. That accusation could cause confusion and might very well distract from any meaningful consideration of the real issue of police brutality within the department and how to eliminate it.

The other eight black officers knew that it was a big mistake for anyone, particularly a suspected criminal offender, to call Ollie Glover an Uncle Tom. When that happened, there was significant risk that Ollie would go ballistic and beat the hell out of the person. I gained personal knowledge of how Ollie would respond if called a Tom when I represented a defendant at a jury trial who was accused of resisting arrest and misdemeanor battery on a police officer.[23] The officer was Ollie Glover. The case was tried twice, before two different juries, with the first trial resulting in a hung jury and the second in conviction.

My client had been arrested outside Cutting Liquors, a popular liquor store on Cutting Boulevard in the city of Richmond, for disturbing the peace and being intoxicated in public. Ollie Glover initially responded to the call for police assistance. By all accounts, when he arrived at the scene and first spoke with my client, Glover had tried to be helpful and even offered to call a taxi so that my client could be safely transported to his home. My client, however, was highly intoxicated, belligerent, and verbally abusive. He ultimately made the grave mistake of calling Glover an Uncle Tom, and not only a Tom, but "a handkerchief-head Tom." My client later told me that at the time of the incident, his J&B[24] had told him that he "didn't have to do anything [he] didn't want to do."

Glover arrested my client, who was placed in another officer's patrol car for transport to the city jail. At the jail, my client, still very belligerent, was booked and then taken by Glover to his cell. My client testified at trial that Glover declined an offer from another officer to assist him in taking the prisoner to a cell because "the presence of a second officer might upset the prisoner." There, according to my client (and years later confirmed by Glover in a private admission to me), Glover beat my client badly. Privately, my client and I acknowledged that he had behaved terribly and, in the culture of the street, probably deserved a whipping. Nevertheless, Glover's conduct was illegal and constituted police brutality. In court, my client and I were adamant that the criminal charges of resisting arrest and battery on a police officer were false and totally unwarranted. The misdemeanor charges were simply a cover for the illegal beating administered by Officer Glover.[25]

Notwithstanding the probability that Ollie's personal history of misconduct would be disclosed and used by the departmental leadership and other white officers in an attempt to obfuscate the issues of generalized police misconduct, the black officers, with Glover's acquiescence, decided to proceed, a decision that was another measure of their extraordinary courage. The nine officers found that they now "were of one mind and had to do something beyond talk."

From the outset, the nine officers appreciated the gravity of the situation and concluded that they needed legal counsel. I was then in private practice in Richmond and had developed a reputation as a competent lawyer who was intensely committed to justice and fairness for everyone. I think I was also a member of the city of Richmond's Human Relations Commission. Hence, it was a logical choice for them to consider me for service as their legal adviser. (To tell the truth, I was probably their only choice in Contra Costa County, because the chance of getting another lawyer in the county to represent them was between slim and none.)

I had gotten to know Marvin Smith pretty well when I was in the Contra Costa County DA's Office and he was working as an evidence technician in the Patrol Division of the Richmond P.D. We had become acquaintants and lived in the same Richmond neighborhood (Plaza II). Marvin clearly was a leader among the nine black officers, and it was he who suggested to the others that I be asked to serve as legal adviser for the group. My involvement with the officers came well before their initial contacts with the chief's office. At first, I worked mostly behind the scenes, providing legal counsel and other advice concerning various strategies they were considering.

Later, when the officers' charges and their dispute with the police chief became public, my role became public as well. The officers have often said that they were successful in their effort to make public the police misconduct they had observed because, in significant measure, my advice and counsel was always "one and, sometimes, two steps ahead of the chief of police and his advisers." Whether or not that statement is true, I do know that representing those officers was one of my proudest achievements as a member of the legal profession. And if the statement is true, it is because I was committed to thorough preparation. As a lawyer, it was my experience that poor preparation was a certain formula for failure. While thorough preparation could not guarantee victory in litigation, it clearly was an essential element if victory was to be achieved.

Nothing significant happened in the department, nor was any meaningful action taken by the police chief, mayor, or city manager after the meeting between the black officers and the police chief, captains, lieutenants, and sergeants. As a consequence, the nine black officers decided to draft a protest document to be signed by each and presented to the chief of police and the Richmond City Council. Initially, Marvin Smith was to sign the document on behalf of the nine, but the black officers decided by consensus that all nine should sign. They were convinced that for the document to have a real effect each of them needed to sign it and that Doug's signature was especially vital.

On the occasion when they discussed among themselves the importance of Doug's signature, Doug himself reminisced that when he was hired as a police officer he was not specifically told that his authority was less than that of a white officer, particularly concerning arresting white people or patrolling in white neighborhoods, but that he "knew there was an understanding." The young officers reminded Doug that he had paved the way for each of them to become Richmond police officers. And while that path had been difficult for him and sometimes even demeaning, now times were different and he "did not have to take it anymore." It was a very dramatic and poignant moment when Doug declared in a forceful voice, "Hand me the board!"[26] and unhesitatingly signed his name.

The black officers held a press conference a day or two later at the local Holiday Inn to make their concerns public. I was also present. Captain Lourne Phelps later had a "speak freely discussion" within the department. A couple of the black officers' white colleagues said to them privately, "I appreciate what you are doing, although I cannot come out and support you publicly." Soon after receipt of the black officers' written complaint by the city, the matter was scheduled for an evening session of the Richmond City Council on Tuesday, February 3, 1969. At about 6:00 a.m. the day before the scheduled council meeting, each of the black officers was personally served at home by a Richmond police officer with a letter from Chief Robert Murphy. The chief's letter, on department letterhead, was concise and to the point. It was a written order not to appear before the city council, with the threat that an appearance at the city council meeting would constitute cause for discharge from the Richmond police force.

Eight of the nine black officers, dressed in civilian clothes, appeared in the council chambers the next evening at the time for the regularly scheduled meeting. The chambers were packed with citizens of Richmond, members of the press, and interested individuals from nearby communities. The black community was well represented by a substantial number of Richmond residents. I served as spokesperson for the Richmond Nine and introduced each officer individually to the assembled members of the city council.[27] Doug, the ninth officer, was not present because he was on duty. When advised of this, the mayor and council members directed the city manager to order Sergeant Ellison to report immediately to the council chambers from wherever he was at the time.[28]

It was a dramatic moment when, a very short time after the city manager had been directed to summon him, Sergeant Ellison proudly walked down the center aisle of the council chambers in full police uniform and joined the other protesting officers. As many of today's young black males would say, "The Black Nine was in the house." Each officer candidly described the problems about which he was concerned and the need for change in the department if those problems were to be corrected. When I advised the council of the threatening letter that each officer had received from the chief, we were told not to be concerned, because all nine were present at the meeting at the direction of the city manager and the council.

I wish I could report that meaningful and lasting positive change in the Richmond Police Department resulted from the courageous action of those black officers. Perhaps there was superficial change for a limited time. It may be that offending white officers curbed their behavior when a black officer was their partner or present at the detention or arrest of a black person. But it is now known that substantive and long-lasting positive change did not occur. Approximately 10 years later three lawsuits were filed in the U.S. District Court for the Northern District of California, alleging a practice and pattern of brutality directed at blacks by a group of Richmond police officers. The lead attorney in the three consolidated cases was Oliver Jones, Esq., a 1973 Boalt Hall graduate and, at the time of this litigation, counsel for the Western Division of the National Association for the Advancement of Colored People (NAACP) since 1976.[29] The offending officers were described in the press as "cowboys," an image intended to convey that the officers were wild and out of control. The behavior they were accused of was appallingly similar to that complained about years earlier by the Richmond Nine. The claims were that "the Richmond Police Department routinely harassed and beat black residents and then groundlessly charged the victims with offenses such as resisting arrest or interfering with the official lawful duties of an officer."[30] The NAACP played a significant role in the filing of these three cases.[31] The City of Richmond, on or about August 6, 1981, accepted a consent degree in the three cases and subsequently paid the plaintiffs an undisclosed amount to settle the federal police brutality lawsuits.[32]

Under the leadership of Ollie Glover, Art Johnson, and Hal Redic, black officers in the Richmond Police Department formed an association in 1972 named the Guardians of Justice. Its mission statement reads:

> We, the members of the Guardians of Justice Black Police Officer Association of the Richmond Police Department, are committed to professional law enforcement; to represent the association members in maintaining the health and welfare of its membership, address work related problems and morale issues; to promote fairness and justice and encourage the membership to work closely together in a spirit of mutual cooperation; to encourage and promote good citizenship in the youth of our community; and strive to enhance the quality of life in our community through support of various community events and organizations each year.
>
> We strive to assist the Richmond Police Department in continuing to provide the service that citizens of Richmond have come to expect.

In 1971, Ollie Glover traveled to Boston, Massachusetts, to attend a meeting of black police officers from all over the United States. This first meeting led to formation of the National Black Police Association, a membership organization, at a meeting the next year in St Louis, Missouri. Black police officer associations now exist in most major cities in the United States, along with Hispanic associations and a few Asian associations. In the early 1970s, there was extreme polarization between black and mainstream (mostly white) police associations, but, thanks in substantial measure to the efforts of black and other minority police associations, there is far less polarization now.

You may be wondering what happened to the nine black officers:

- DOUGLAS L. ELLISON, SERGEANT. Doug retired from the Richmond Police Department on January 30, 1973, and soon went to work as a police officer for Bay Area Rapid Transit (BART). He retired as a BART police sergeant in March 1983. He received two retired sergeant badges. Douglas L. Ellison died in Richmond on Saturday, May 6, 2006, at the age of 81.[33]

- OLLIE SYLVESTER GLOVER, SERGEANT. Ollie later became a helicopter pilot for the Richmond Police Department. He resigned from the department as a sergeant in December 1976 in order to pursue a Ph.D. in psychology, which he received from the Wright Institute, Berkeley, California, in April 1980. For the past 25 years, he has worked as a practicing clinical and forensic psychologist.

- LEE ARTHUR JOHNSON, CAPTAIN. Art continued as a member of the Richmond Police Department and retired as a captain of police in November 1992. Art was the first black captain for the Richmond Police Department.

- RUDOLPH JOHNSON, SERGEANT. Rudy took a lateral transfer from the Richmond Police Department to the BART Police Department in 1972. He retired as a BART police sergeant in 1988.

- TECUMSEH "DANNY" NELSON, CHIEF OF POLICE. Danny was the first black promoted to lieutenant in the history of the Richmond Police Department. Danny left the Richmond P.D. as a lieutenant in 1984, when he went to East Palo Alto, California, as that city's first chief of police. There he organized and staffed a totally new police department. When Danny arrived in East Palo Alto, the police department had no police cars and only one officer—him. Danny left the East Palo Alto Police Department in 1992, when he was appointed chief of police of Salinas, California, the position from which he retired in 1999.

- MICHAEL NICHOLS, PATROLMAN. Mike Nichols transferred to the San Jose Police Department and retired as a motorcycle patrolman with that department.

- Harold Redic, Sergeant. Hal Redic succeeded Marvin R. Smith in the Police Community Relations Unit of the Richmond Police Department. He left the Richmond P.D. in 1974 as a sergeant and went to work as a civil rights investigator at the San Francisco office of the U.S. Department of Housing and Urban Development (HUD). Hal retired from HUD in 1996. He is currently working with the Contra Costa County Probation Department as a probation counselor.

- Marvin Richard Smith, Patrolman. Marvin was an evidence technician in the Richmond Police Department when we first met in 1964. "Smitty," as he is called by his friends, was assigned to the Police Community Relations Unit, where he worked until resigning from the Richmond P.D. in early 1970 to accept a position with the San Francisco office of HUD as an investigator and conciliator. At the end of his first year with HUD, Marvin was appointed acting director of the Housing Opportunity Division. He later became director of the Fair Housing and Equal Opportunity Compliance Division of that office. Marvin left HUD in December 1977 to accept a position as the equal opportunity administrator for the Lawrence Livermore Laboratory. He retired from the "Lab" on February 1, 2001. Marvin Smith died on January 29, 2006, within days of his 65th birthday, in Oakland, California.

- Otis Timmons Jr., Patrolman. Otis left the Richmond Police Department in 1969 to accept a position with the New York Life Insurance Company as an insurance agent. One year later, he returned to police work as a sworn officer with the El Cerrito Police Department. He was seriously injured in 1981 in an on-duty automobile accident and subsequently resigned after receiving a settlement. He later opened Raphael's Shutter Café & Espresso Bar (serving breakfast and lunch) at 10064 San Pablo Avenue, El Cerrito, CA, 94530, a business that has been quite successful.

Today's popular notions in the United States of who is a hero or what is a heroic act tend to differ dramatically from my personal conception of heroism. It is not unusual for an athlete who demonstrates exceptional ability in professional sports to be characterized in the media as a "hero." People who are unfortunate victims of highly publicized events are sometimes described as heroes. I view people as heroes who are consciously aware of a clear, present, and significant risk of material harm to themselves or a loved one if they engage in conduct or behavior intended to assist or save another and who still act notwithstanding that known risk.

During the civil rights movement, ordinary people in the southern United States sought to vote when they *knew* that their behavior would put them at significant risk of being fired from their jobs, being denied a loan (which they may have needed to purchase a home, seeds for planting a crop, or essential farm equipment), being subjected to acceleration of a mortgage payment if just one payment was late, or even suffering grievous bodily harm or death. Their efforts to secure civil and political rights for others, as well as themselves, made them heroes in my estimation. The firefighters, police officers, and other emergency workers who voluntarily put themselves in harm's way by entering the burning Twin Towers in New York on "9/11"[34] in a brave effort to save others are also heroes.

In my mind, the nine young black Richmond police officers who took the extraordinary action of confirming the existence of significant police brutality by their white peers were heroes. They acted to help others notwithstanding their awareness of a clear, present, and substantial risk of significant harm to themselves. With one exception, these were not senior officers or people with established rights of retirement. At the time, except for Sergeant Douglas L. Ellison, none of the nine had been on the police force longer than six years. And yet they took this substantial risk in an effort to bring better police service to their community and to stop the unlawful abuse of black men, particularly black youth, who were the usual targets of unlawful police violence.

The courage of those young officers has inspired me when I have had to decide whether to act to help others, knowing that to do so would place me in serious economic or physical jeopardy. Many men and women have risked their economic and physical well-being for others, many times for people they didn't even know personally. Individuals such as Frederick Douglass, Charles Hamilton Houston, Robert "Bob" Carter, Fannie Lou Hamer, Medgar Evers, Robert "Bob" Moses, Leonard "Len" Holt, Constance Baker Motley, and Clinton Wayne White, to name just a few, have all served as role models for me in those circumstances. I place the nine black Richmond police officers in the same category as those other role models. Their conduct in 1968 was truly heroic.

· Notes ·

1. King, *Autobiography*, p. 342.
2. Superior Court of the State of California, in and for the County of Alameda, located at 1221 Oak Street, Oakland, Calif.
3. Glenn Chapman, "Mabanag Tells Jury Batt Wept, Then Resigned," *Oakland Tribune*, April 18, 2003, Local section, p. 1.
4. Henry K. Lee, "'Riders' Jury May Be Near a Verdict," *San Francisco Chronicle*, Aug. 31, 2003, section A, p. 25.
5. Glenn Chapman, "'Riders' Get off Hook, Retrial Likely," *Oakland Tribune*, Oct. 1, 2003, p. 1.
6. The case was retried and essentially resulted in another hung jury. "Judge Declares 'Riders' Mistrial," *Oakland Tribune*, May 20, 2005, p. 1, which states:

    The first Riders trial spanned more than a year and ended in September 2003 with acquittals on eight criminal counts and a polarized jury deadlocked on the remaining charges. The case was streamlined for the retrial that started Nov. 1, 2004. Two retrial jurors were replaced with alternates during a month of deliberations. The reconstituted panel spent 16 days deliberating before the trial ended [May 19, 2005].

7. Date of birth: Nov, 15, 1924.
8. Date of birth: July 3, 1938.
9. Date of birth: Dec. 11, 1937. The name on his birth certificate is probably Arthur Lee Johnson.
10. Date of birth: Feb. 10, 1936.

11. Date of birth: Jan. 22, 1937.
12. I have been unable to locate or speak with Mike Nichols to get his date of birth. However, Hal Redic told me on Feb. 6, 2006, at Marvin Smith's memorial service that Mike and he are the same age.
13. Date of birth: April 12, 1939.
14. Date of birth: Feb. 2, 1941.
15. Date of birth: Aug. 12, 1941.
16. A newspaper article entitled "Richmond Police Probe Promised," in the *Oakland Tribune,* Tues., Feb. 4, 1969, at page 35 stated that the 10 black Richmond police officers then on the force were part of a total force of 150 sworn officers. An article in the local newspaper, the Richmond *Independent,* Thursday, July 18, 1968, p. 1, entitled "Council to Add Nine Policemen," stated that the authorized strength of the department was 177 officers. The difference may very well have been the difference between "authorized strength" and the actual number of officers on the force.
17. On the one hand, I suppose Pringle would have had some limited con-stitutional protection in that, for example, he could not have been fired simply because of his race. On the other hand, I have no doubt but that joining the protest of the "Richmond Nine" would have led to his discharge by the department on some pretext.
18. In "Costs of Riots Here," July 30, 1968, p. 1, the *Independent* reported that police overtime for the city of Richmond alone was $33,477.
19. Many of Marvin's close friends, particularly those who knew him from the time when he was a police officer, call him "Smitty the Cop."
20. That is, beating the person with a police baton.
11. Marin City was then, and still is, a town in Marin County, California, consisting mostly of public and low-income housing that is occupied by low-income people of color, mostly black people. The per capita income of Marin County itself is among the highest in California and, indeed, the United States.
22. In other words, he was beaten.
23. *People v. Earl C. Smith,* Municipal Court of the Judicial District of the City of Richmond, County of Contra Costa, State of California, Action No. 133428, March 17–18, 1966.
24. J&B is a brand of Scotch liquor.
25. In this regard, I suggest that you read Paul Chevigny, *Police Power: Police Abuses in New York City* (New York: Pantheon Books, 1969).
26. The statement was attached to a clipboard.
27. See Minutes of the Regular Meeting of the Council of the City of Richmond, CA, Feb. 3, 1969, p. 118, available at the office of the City

Clerk of the City of Richmond. Also see the *Independent*, "City Council Hears Police Grievances," Tuesday, Feb. 4, 1969, at page 1.

28. See *Oakland Tribune*, "Richmond Police Probe Promised," Tues., Feb. 4, 1969, p. 35.

29. See *White v. City of Richmond*, 559 F. Supp. 127, 132 (1982).

30. *White v. City of Richmond* and *Bobby Darnell White v. City of Richmond, Henry L. Royal v. City of Richmond, & Anthony Evans v. City of Richmond*, 713 F.2d. 458 (1983); also see *Linda Roman v. City of Richmond*; *Wilbert Guillory v. City of Richmond*, 570 F. Supp. (1983), a case where a jury returned two separate verdicts of 1.5 million dollars against the City of Richmond and certain individual police officers for the killing of two black men in Richmond.

31. See Gerald Davis, "Reforms Part of Police Settlement," *Oakland Tribune*, Thursday, Aug. 6, 1981, p. C1.

32. "Reforms Part of Police Settlement." Also see *Bobby Darnell White v. City of Richmond, Henry L. Royal v. City of Richmond, & Anthony Evans v. City of Richmond*.

33. His obituary appeared in the *West County Times*, May 9, 2006, p. A10. Doug's wife, Tah-lee-tha, has survived him.

34. Sept. 11, 2001.

WELL, SON, I'll tell you:
Life for me ain't been no crystal stair.
It's had tacks in it,
And splinters,
And boards torn up,
And places with no carpet on the floor—
Bare.
But all the time
I'se been a-climbin' on,
And reachin' landin's,
And turnin' corners,
And sometimes goin's in the dark
Where there ain't been no light.
So, boy, don't you turn back.
Don't you set down on the steps
'Cause you finds it's kinder hard.
Don't you fall now—
For I'se still goin', honey,
I'se still climbin',
And life for me ain't been no crystal stair.[1]


−LANGSTON HUGHES

# 24

# Berkeley City Council

## THE DECISION TO RUN

THE BACKDROP FOR MY DECISION to seek a seat on the Berkeley City Council and my campaign for that office involved a number of factors and individuals. For several years, a small group of African Americans had been meeting occasionally to discuss the state of "black" politics in the San Francisco Bay Area, particularly in the East Bay. The group comprised Edith M. Austin, Willie Lewis Brown Jr., Ernest Howard, Jim McMillan, Warren Widener, and me. Not long after we began meeting, and at my suggestion, the group was named the "Watermelon Society."[2]

Members of the Watermelon Society had known each other for years and all were actively involved in Bay Area politics, although when we first began meeting most of us had never held elected public office. However, in 1972, when my running for the Berkeley City Council was first discussed at a Watermelon Society meeting, Willie Brown was a member of the California Assembly and, I think, chairman of the Ways and Means Committee. (He was elected Speaker of the Assembly in 1981.) Warren Widener was the new mayor of Berkeley.[3]

In 1970, Ron Dellums, then a member of the Berkeley City Council, had run for and won a seat in the U.S. House of Representatives and consequently resigned from the city council. Two African American male newcomers to Berkeley–D'Army Bailey and Ira Simmons–ran as a slate of "progressives" for the council in 1971. Surprisingly, they were both elected–notwithstanding each of them being very new to Berkeley. They had been endorsed and supported by Ron Dellums. As noted above, Warren Widener was elected mayor of Berkeley in that same election.

While not identified in Berkeley politics as a progressive, Warren was considered by Berkeley progressive and radical activists to be a friend and ally. That is, he was so considered until he refused to support a ballot measure intended to establish a police review commission in Berkeley that would have sole administrative jurisdiction over police misconduct cases in four distinct areas of the city. As a result, mayoral candidate Warren Widener came under increasing attacks in the progressive press. After his election as mayor, the criticism actually increased and was particularly aggressive and hostile during meetings of the city council.

Leading the challenge to Widener's effort to function as mayor of Berkeley were the two newly elected council members, D'Army Bailey and Ira Simmons. D'Army was particularly crude, disrespectful, and rude to Warren during council meetings. D'Army also often disrupted council sessions. For example, he would not wait to be recognized by Mayor Widener before speaking and would often interrupt other council members when they were speaking. D'Army frequently ignored rulings by Warren that held him out of order. He would often engage in a "filibuster" (i.e., speak for excessively extended periods of time), even after Warren had asked him to yield the microphone. In a nutshell, D'Army Bailey's behavior at council meetings and frequent disparaging comments to the media about Mayor Widener and some other council members made it extremely difficult for Warren to manage council sessions or to effectively perform his role as mayor of the city.

At one of our Watermelon Society meetings in San Francisco, the evening's primary topic was Warren's problem with D'Army Bailey at Berkeley City Council meetings. It was clear to all present that D'Army's mind worked faster than Warren's. Although Mayor Widener was as intelligent as D'Army, he just was not as mentally quick. D'Army easily bested Warren in public debate, especially given his willingness to use crude and impolite language. Warren was a very polite and civil person and simply would not sink to D'Army's level.

The Watermelon Society concluded that Warren needed an ally on the council to help him in his encounters with D'Army. But this person would have to be just as smart, intellectually quick, and tough as D'Army. The group decided that I was the person who should take on that responsibility. After some thought and discussion, I agreed to be a council candidate. A support team was formed, an announcement was made, and my campaign commenced. The primary supporters and advisers from the group were Edith Austin, Willie L. Brown, and Ernest Howard. Rosemary Towns was retained to serve as my campaign manager.

This particular campaign turned out to be a battle of slates. The election of D'Army Bailey and Ira Simmons in 1971 had demonstrated the effectiveness of candidates running as a slate in Berkeley. Now it was 1973, and the two contesting political groups from the 1971 city elections—the "April Coalition" ("progressives" or "radicals") and the Berkeley Democratic Club ("liberals" or "moderates") were geared up to fight for control of the Berkeley City Council. The progressive slate was named the April Coalition and the Berkeley Democratic Club slate was referred to as the "Berkeley 4."

The April Coalition was the first to select its slate of candidates: Peter Birdsall,[4] Margot Dashiell, Larry Goldberg, and Ying Lee Kelley. Members of the Berkeley Democratic Club decided to support its own slate of candidates, namely: Joe Garrett,[5] Susan Hone,[6] Henry Ramsey Jr., and Wilmont Sweeney.[7]

I first announced my candidacy as an independent, and, in fact, I maintained an independent campaign throughout the election. Nonetheless, I did seek the endorsement of the Berkeley Democratic Club and become a member of that slate. Therefore, I had the support of the Berkeley 4 campaign as well as the efforts of my own campaign.[8] In that election the Berkeley 4 slate won three (Susan Hone, Henry Ramsey Jr., and Wilmont Sweeney) of the four seats and the April Coalition won one (Ying Lee Kelley).

Besides the four candidates on each slate, there were several independent candidates in the race—I think about six. In my opinion, Harry

CANDIDATE HENRY RAMSEY JR. *addressing supporters at a Berkeley City Council campaign event in 1973.*

Overstreet, an independent, ran the best (i.e., most visible, exciting, appealing, energetic, and robust) campaign in the race. And yet, when all the votes were counted, he came in ninth, with each of the eight slate candidates coming in ahead of him in the race for four available seats. If I had run solely as an independent candidate, I would probably have fared about the same in the election as Harry Overstreet–probably worse.

Soon after I was sworn in and assumed my duties as a council member, I concluded that this position was not for me. But because I had run for the office and been elected, I felt an obligation to complete the four-year term. On the one hand, I enjoyed the work–thinking about and deciding how limited resources could best be used to address competing legitimate interests within the city. On the other hand, I was deeply disappointed by the failure of people, particularly political activists, to listen to and consider the positions of those they opposed. Compromise and concession were unacceptable to many of those then involved in Berkeley politics.

Also, one's worth as an elected official was too often judged not by what you did or the position you took concerning a given issue but by the "uniform" you wore (i.e., whether you were a liberal or a progressive). Much like today's Democrats and Republicans, people involved in Berkeley politics at the time thought your vote concerning many proposals should be based on whether it was offered or supported by progressives and their allies or by liberals and their allies. I really disliked that aspect of council service.

## SENIOR CITIZENS CENTERS

IF ANYONE REVIEWS THE POLITICAL and community activities with which I have been involved during my professional life, it should quickly become evident that I have a strong concern for the elderly and for underprivileged youth. My affection, respect, and concern for the elderly developed long before I myself became an elderly person. I am certain that this flows from my having been reared in North Carolina at a time when strong emphasis was placed by the people who reared me— and by people throughout my community—on respect and concern for the elderly.

I remember, when I was a young teenager, being told by Mrs. Marie Crawford,[9] a respected woman in my neighborhood whose house I often visited, that she had obtained a job as a cook at a convalescent home for white people. The home was near Sharpsburg, North Carolina, a community about five miles south of Rocky Mount on U.S. Highway 301.

I don't think I had ever heard the word convalescent before, and I asked her what a convalescent home was. She told me it was a place where old people who could no longer take care of themselves were put by their children. I was absolutely convinced—and told her so—that one should not seek or accept a job at a convalescent home because it offered no hope of continued employment. I simply could not conceive of anyone putting elderly and disabled parents in a convalescent home. How could one abandon the very people who had nurtured and protected them during infancy and childhood? How could one desert his or her parents at a time when they were helpless, frail, and most in need of assistance and support? I knew in my mind and heart that this practice would be limited to white people because, to my way of thinking, it certainly was not something any colored person or family members would do to their parents.

Today I am much older and more experienced. I also think our culture has changed to such an extent that I no longer see anything wrong with providing for one's parents and other relatives by placing them in a quality nursing facility or convalescent home. Indeed, I now recognize that, in many instances, placement in a nursing facility or convalescent home is very much in the best interests of all concerned.

With that as background, I received a telephone call in 1975 from Ms. Esther Gabriel, a woman I knew only slightly. She asked me in my role as a member of the Berkeley City Council to meet her at a church

467 · Berkeley City Council

in West Berkeley to discuss a problem at the West Berkeley Senior Citizens Center. Ms. Gabriel was at that time an articulate, thoughtful, and feisty 74-year-old black activist in Berkeley and a fighter for senior rights. I am writing this in 2007, and Ms. Gabriel is still feisty at age 97, but she lives in the Oakland Care Center,[10] a convalescent home owned and operated by the city of Oakland, which provides her with full-time care.

When I met Ms. Gabriel at the church in 1975, she told me that the city's Public Works Department was forcing the West Berkeley Senior Citizens Center to move out of its home in the Missionary Church of God and Christ at 1125 Allston Way (corner of Allston Way and Byron Street) in Berkeley and that the center had no other place to go. Ms. Gabriel reminded me that I was a Berkeley City Council member and asked what I was able and willing to do to help the seniors in West Berkeley keep their center operational and at the church.

I listened, but I needed more information. I soon learned that there were three city-funded senior citizen programs: the North Berkeley Senior Citizens Center, housed in the Lutheran Church of the Cross at 1744 University Avenue; the South Berkeley Senior Citizens Center, housed in the McGee Avenue Baptist Church at McGee and Stuart streets; and the West Berkeley Senior Citizens Center, housed in the aforementioned Missionary Church of God and Christ.[11] I also learned that the West Berkeley center was in a building that did not conform to current mandatory earthquake standards. There was and is an understandable concern in Berkeley (as well as throughout the entire San Francisco Bay Area and many other areas in California) about earthquake preparedness. After all, the infamous San Andreas Fault runs a few miles to the west of Berkeley under San Francisco. Parts of the lesser-known but probably (for Berkeley and Oakland) even more dangerous Hayward Fault run directly under the city of Berkeley.

Most professionals (e.g., accountants, dentists, doctors, engineers, lawyers) will never express a professional opinion as an absolute statement or prediction. Rather, they talk in terms of probabilities or chances. In this instance, however, the city engineers felt that this building was so shaky that, in the event of any serious earthquake, it would indeed collapse. They were not saying that there was a good chance the building would collapse but that it *would collapse*. The city could not fund and operate a program in a building that it knew was not earthquake safe, because of the substantial potential legal liability to which the city of Berkeley would be exposed.

(I know that hindsight is always "20/20," but I do find it notable that after the Loma Prieta earthquake on October 17, 1989, destroyed a substantial portion of the Cypress Freeway in Oakland, did serious damage to the Oakland City Hall and the state building located in downtown Oakland, collapsed one of the upper-deck sections of the cantilevered part of the Oakland-San Francisco Bay Bridge, and did significant damage to homes in the exclusive Marina area[12] of San Francisco, the Missionary Church of God and Christ *remained standing, essentially undamaged, and fully operational.* But, as I said, hindsight is always "20/20.")

Over the next week or two after my first meeting with Ms. Gabriel, I visited each of the above-mentioned senior centers and observed their principal inadequacies. Each of the churches was doing a great job in providing services to seniors, but the simple fact was that they all had serious space limitations that prevented them from fully addressing the needs of the seniors. For example, there was no space for any other activity to occur while meals were being served. At the McGee Avenue Baptist Church, the number of seniors exceeded the dining space, so tables and chairs had to be set up outside the building, with some of the seniors being served there. Fortunately, we live in Northern California, and most days are amenable to that arrangement. But even here, there are many wet and cold days in winter and early spring. So I saw the problems faced by the centers: not only too little space, but too little staff, and too few programs.

I was saddened by these circumstances. The churches were doing all they could to provide services for the seniors. I felt strongly that the elderly deserved better support and treatment from the residents of

Berkeley—that they were entitled to respect and the highest care we could afford to provide. This was in 1975, a time when the federal government was making large block grants to cities that could be used for a variety of municipal purposes, and it occurred to me that a good use for some of Berkeley's block grant money would be to provide quality centers for seniors.

This effort would require acquisition of land plus design and construction of three completely new centers. While the two centers in the mostly black areas of West and South Berkeley had been brought to my attention first, I knew about the North Berkeley center that served a mostly white population. To my thinking, every senior in Berkeley deserved to be treated well, without regard to neighborhood, ethnicity, nationality, race, or religion.

I also thought that these centers could actually function as multipurpose facilities and serve the immediate surrounding community, or for that matter the entire city, for meetings, wedding receptions, memorial services, dances, and other events. But I made it clear in all of my discussions with seniors, council colleagues, and other city residents that the centers should be built for the seniors and that the seniors were entitled to control their use. As with a brand-new, latest-model automobile that the owner does not want to entrust to anyone else until it has suffered a few scratches or dents, I was confident that after the newness had worn off, the seniors would be willing to allow non-seniors to use their facility for community events. It was my hope that the centers, if effectively used, would encourage intergenerational activities, which would provide an excellent side benefit for the seniors. I have no scientific evidence to support it, but I believe that older people live longer and healthier lives when they are able to interact with younger people. I am pleased to say that the centers did become a reality and that senior acceptance of appropriate use of the centers by many different groups has been the result.

In early discussions with the city manager and relevant members of the city staff, three potential sites were identified where centers could be built, assuming funds became available. I decided to use some of the annual allowance allotted each council member that I received to retain the San Francisco architectural firm of Hardison and Komatsu Associates[13] to provide advice and to develop conceptual drawings for the three proposed centers. Two architects at the firm were responsible for our project: Donald L. Hardison, FAIA, and George Ivelich, AIA. The firm charged me very modest fees—a total of $2,500. Indeed, their overall help in developing the proposal to build three senior centers was mostly free work on their part.

A committee of community people, mostly seniors, was formed, and we met regularly—often with the architects—at my house[14] or my council member office[15] to discuss what the seniors needed and wanted at each center. The seniors in West Berkeley, for example, wanted the design of their center to accommodate a vegetable garden. The committee also decided that the "Meals on Wheels" program would be implemented from the North Berkeley center. Those meetings were an exciting enterprise—community involvement in municipal affairs and grassroots city politics at their highest and best level.

But there was still a critical hurdle to be overcome—show me the money. The nine-member council was essentially split into two political camps—those who called themselves "liberals" (Warren Widener, Sue Hone, Shirley Dean, and Henry Ramsey Jr.)[16] and those who called themselves "progressives" (John H. Denton, Ilona Hancock, and Ying Lee Kelley).[17] There were also two independent council members who usually voted with us—Carole Davis, née Kennerly, and William "Billy" Rumford.[18]

I was able to garner support for the senior citizen proposal from my liberal colleagues on the council, and on the evening of March 15, 1977, we voted that the city should seek block grant funds from HUD for the specific purpose of building three senior centers in the city of Berkeley. A few city residents expressed modest opposition, primarily because they thought there were more pressing needs for the block grant monies. Those residents were not opposed to building senior centers but thought that two would be sufficient. I was of the view that convenient access was just as important as having senior centers and that the existing tradition of separate centers in West Berkeley, South Berkeley, and North Berkeley should continue and would be most convenient for the elderly residents of Berkeley.

The South Berkeley Senior Citizens Center was completed in January 1979, the North Berkeley Senior Citizens Center in April 1979, and the West Berkeley Senior Citizens Center in April 1981. All are still operational and are well used by the seniors across Berkeley. Each also functions as a multipurpose center, where various community meetings, weddings, and educational programs are held. Needless to say, I am very proud of my work in spearheading the effort to build the three centers in Berkeley.

I do have one regret. When they first opened, meals served at the three centers were cooked onsite and were consistently attractive, delicious, and nutritious. For nine continuous years from 1997, however, the meals were provided by the University of California, and starting in July 2005, meals have been provided by Project Open Hand. Perhaps the meals provided by the University of California were nutritious, but at least the few Open Hand meals I have eaten were neither delicious nor attractive. I haven't eaten at any of the centers for several years, but the last time I did the meal was lousy.

I am advised that this outsourcing of meal preparation saves the city money and is absolutely necessary, given the tough economic times with which local governments are confronted. One of my "if I were very rich" fantasies is to contribute funds to the city that would be sufficient to reestablish the home-cooked meals at the three centers. In my mind, those were a real aspect of the centers' "good ol' days."

## OTHER MATTERS

ALTHOUGH IT IS MY WORK REGARDING the three senior centers that I am most proud of, I also played a central role in other matters as a member of the Berkeley City Council. One was the council's approval for construction of a new library at the Graduate Theological Union;

another was acquisition of leasing rights from the city by Dock of the Bay Inc., a company established by A. Leroy Willis with Kenneth H. Simmons and a small group of other black investors. Willis, Simmons, and their group formed Dock of the Bay Inc. to design, construct, and operate a restaurant of that name at the Berkeley marina. Indeed, during its existence, Dock of the Bay was the first and only black-owned business at the marina.

I am also pleased to have been a leader in the successful effort to construct low-income senior citizen housing on the Clark Kerr campus of the University of California at Berkeley. The Clark Kerr campus, on a site two or three blocks from the then boundaries of the UC Berkeley campus, had held a state-owned and -operated elementary and secondary school for deaf and blind children. The school was located above the Hayward earthquake fault, and, under California law, had to be closed. A new school was built in Fremont, California, and the abandoned site of the old school was made available to the University of California.

The university wanted to use the property primarily for student housing and a conference center. The city could have competed for the land, but I proposed that the city agree to relinquish its claim if the university would agree, among other things, to include affordable housing for senior citizens on the site, along with the new student housing. Separately, I also supported Warren Widener's successful effort to have a lovely landscaped median constructed down the middle of Sacramento Street below University Avenue, which is one of the main streets through what historically had been Berkeley's black neighborhood.

During those four years on the council, my primary focus was bringing improvements and fairness to Berkeley's black community. Of course, my overall objective was the welfare of all residents. But I had a special interest in how the city treated its black residents, given the history of how black people had been treated in Berkeley, in California, and throughout the United States. Berkeley enjoys a reputation as an open, liberal, and tolerant city. It is not generally known that, until the

THE "BERKELEY 4" *with* MAYOR WARREN WIDENER *in 1973; from left: Henry Ramsey Jr., Joe Garrett, Mayor Widener, Councilwoman Susan Hone, and Vice Mayor Wilmont Sweeney.*

early 1960s, African Americans were actually openly discriminated against in Berkeley with regard to employment, housing, and public schools. Few blacks lived anywhere in Berkeley east of Grove Street (now Martin Luther King Jr. Way). As stated earlier, Wilmont Sweeney was the first black elected to the Berkeley City Council (1961), and Warren Widener was the city's first black mayor (1971).

I am confident that I was true to my objective. Working mostly with Warren, Wilmont, Sue Hone, Ed Kallgren, and our independent council colleagues, I know I helped improve city services for all Berkeley residents.

As concerns D'Army Bailey, I was able to help Warren maintain control at council meetings whenever D'Army acted up and tried to prevent Warren or the council from conducting business. My primary technique when D'Army interrupted Warren or refused to relinquish the microphone was simply to start speaking into my microphone at the same time. The result was that D'Army's comments could not be understood or, sometimes, even heard. He would then usually stop talking and relinquish the microphone.

Vice Mayor Wilmont Sweeney was also a frequent target of D'Army's ire. But because Wilmont rarely chaired council meetings, D'Army's attacks toward him were typically limited to name calling and other vile comments. For example, he would frequently call Wilmont an "Uncle Tom." In certain private council settings, he would attempt to insult Wilmont by calling Wilmont's wife a "drunk" and his son a "faggot." Wilmont was a large man, and D'Army was of average size. When D'Army would see that he was getting under Wilmont's skin, he would challenge Wilmont to hit him so that he, D'Army, could seek criminal charges and file a civil suit. Wilmont never did take the bait and strike or even attempt to hit D'Army. But the issue of D'Army's boorish conduct became moot two years after the 1973 elections.

Wilmont tolerated D'Army's derogatory remarks, usually without responding. But, at the same time, he was quietly organizing a group of Berkeley residents who, in 1975, mounted a recall campaign that resulted in D'Army's ouster from office. As Wilmont was fond of saying, "Revenge is best when served cold." This was the first and only recall in the history of the Berkeley City Council. After the recall election had been certified, Wilmont took the name plate from D'Army's council position home. Then, when one went to Wilmont's home and had to use the toilet, one would find, affixed to the underside of the toilet seat lid, D'Army's council chamber name plate–*Mr. Bailey.*[19]

· Notes ·

1. Langston Hughes, "Mother to Son," in *The Poetry of the Negro, 1746–1949,* ed. Langston Hughes and Arna Bontemps (New York: Doubleday, 1956), p. 104.

2. Years later, and well after Edith Austin's death, Elihu Harris, a former member of the California Assembly and former mayor of Oakland, became a member of the group.

3. Later, I was to be elected to the Berkeley City Council, serving one term. A few years after my service on the Berkeley City Council, Jim McMillan was elected to the Richmond City Council, where he served three terms.

4. An undergraduate student at UC Berkeley.

5. A graduate student at UC Berkeley.

6. An incumbent member of the city council, who had been appointed in 1971 to fill Warrren Widener's council position after he was elected mayor.

7. In 1961, Wilmont Sweeney was the first black person elected to the Berkeley City Council. In 1973, he was vice mayor and up for reelection to a third term on the council.

8. This meant, for example, that my campaign–separate from the Berkeley 4 campaign–put up its own posters, solicited and accepted separate campaign contributions, and sent out its own mailings.

9. I spent a lot of time at Mrs. Marie Crawford's home, only two houses from mine and on the corner of Dunn and Red Row streets. She was famous in our neighborhood for the quality of the cakes she baked, and I ate a lot of cake at her house–especially pineapple, which was my favorite. Her husband, Furman Crawford, was a member of a quartet that sang religious songs on the radio each Sunday morning.

10. Currently located at 3030 Webster Street, Oakland, CA 94609.

11. There was a fourth senior center that was (and still is) named the YMCA New Light Senior Center. It received some funds from the city of Berkeley but was not a city-operated center.

12. If it was not the most expensive and exclusive neighborhood in San Francisco, the Marina was certainly one of the top two.

13. The firm was then located at 522 Washington Street, San Francisco, CA 94111.

14. We were then living at 2607 Woolsey Street, Berkeley, CA 94705.

15. Councilmember Susan Hone and I shared council offices at 1915 Essex Street, Berkeley (near the east side of Adeline, a couple of blocks south of Ashby Avenue).

16. The progressives called the liberals "moderates." In certain areas of the country, such as in Orange County, California, or in South Carolina, the Berkeley liberals would have been called extremist liberals, if not outright communists.

17. The liberals called the progressives "radicals." Those folks, just like the so-called "moderates," were essentially liberal Americans; the progressives were simply more liberal. In other words, I am saying that both groups were liberals, but the progressives were considered more extreme. But even the less extreme "moderates" would have been considered extremist in conservative parts of the country.

18. It was a rare day when either of them voted with the progressives.

19. In fairness to D'Army, he returned to his hometown of Memphis, Tennessee, where he became an important civil rights activist. He was the primary force in the founding of the Civil Rights Museum. But, here again, his personality led to his subsequent ouster as chairman of that organization. He was later appointed to and became a well-respected judge of the Tennessee Superior Court in Memphis.

THE DEGREE OF CIVILIZATION in a society can be judged
by entering its prisons.[1]


NOTHING IS EASIER than to denounce the evildoer; nothing is
more difficult than to understand him.[2]


                                        −FYODOR DOSTOEVSKY (1821–1881)

# 25

# George Jackson's Death at San Quentin Prison

I have absolutely no present memory of how I got involved in this matter, but I do clearly recall the significance of the events and the excitement at the time. Even though I have struggled with every fiber of my being to recall its origins, I have been unable to do so. The primary backdrop for this memorable event and discussion is the death of George Lester Jackson, a Death Row inmate at San Quentin Prison in the San Francisco Bay Area who became internationally famous—some would say infamous. Jackson first gained fame as the author of *Soledad Brother*,[3] a collection of letters he had written to various family members, to Faye Stender, who was his appellate lawyer, and to other correspondents during five years of imprisonment.

George Jackson had been convicted of murdering a guard at Soledad Prison on January 16, 1970, for which he had been sentenced to death. He was thereafter transferred from Soledad to San Quentin and housed in the Adjustment Center.[4] He had been in prison for more than nine years when *Soledad Brother* was published and for almost 11 years at the time of his death.

On August 21, 1971, Jackson was shot to death at San Quentin by one or more prison guards. The official explanation for the shooting was that Jackson had escaped from the prison's Adjustment Center and, at the time he was killed, had made his way to one of the outside prison walls in an escape attempt. You should keep in mind that the Adjustment Center "is a prison's maximum security section that is reserved for the most difficult inmates."[5] San Quentin officials later asserted that Jackson was able to achieve the virtually impossible task of escaping from the

Adjustment Center by using a gun that Stephen Bingham, one of his lawyers, had provided during a private lawyer-client visit earlier on the day he was killed.[6] Two other inmates and three guards also died that day. A discussion of the controversy surrounding the claim that Stephen Bingham had provided Jackson with a gun, how Bingham could have gotten the gun into the Adjustment Center, and how Jackson could have gotten out of the Adjustment Center is beyond the intended scope of this manuscript but can be explored by reading *The Road to Hell: The True Story of George Jackson, Stephen Bingham, and the San Quentin Massacre*, by Paul Liberatore, and other material about the case.[7]

Notwithstanding the debate about how George L. Jackson came to be outside the Adjustment Center and my present lack of a clear memory of how I got involved in the aftermath of that chain of events, there can be no dispute concerning the fact that California Department of Corrections and San Quentin Prison officials imposed a total lockdown of the San Quentin population almost immediately after Jackson was shot.[8] The lockdown was so extreme that no visits with prisoners were permitted, except by prison personnel and other Department of Corrections officials. Prisoners were not permitted visits by lawyers, family members, members of the press, private doctors, or spiritual advisers.[9]

Exclusion of the press and of the prisoners' lawyers essentially blinded public officials, including members of the state legislature and federal Congress, regarding what had happened and was happening with inmates at San Quentin. The only sources of information were the prison guards and Department of Corrections officials. One can readily appreciate how this inability to communicate distressed family members of San Quentin prisoners and, in turn, intensified their demands to their political representatives in the local, state, and federal governments for relief.

Civil rights activists and organizations such as the American Civil Liberties Union (ACLU) and the NAACP, family members, lawyers, and the media all expressed outrage at the lockdown, particularly the extraordinary extent of the restrictions. They were concerned not just about the denial of legal counsel and visits by family members, but even more so about the prisoners' physical and psychological well-being. For example, had the prisoners been beaten, or tortured? The warden at San Quentin and Ray Procunier, director of the Department of Corrections, took a hard line and refused all requests to lift the lock-down or to modify its terms.

At the time of this incident, I was a brand-new law teacher at Boalt Hall. But I had for several years also been well-known as a member of the activist legal community who was concerned about protecting the civil rights and civil liberties of all people, including prison inmates. I don't know who contacted me and asked that I help gain access to the prisoners so their families and the public at large could know whether they were being treated properly. I do remember that once I was asked, I had an epiphany. My strategy was to demand access to the prison and prisoners by a group comprised of a member of the California legislature, a member of the U.S. Congress, a member of the press, and a representative of the religious community. (I did not seek to be included as one of those who would actually interview prisoners.) Although the prison officials could deny access to members of the general public—even family members—I knew (at least strongly believed and, as it turned out, correctly perceived) that such a position could not be sustained with regard to important state and federal officials.

I asked Willie Lewis Brown Jr., a personal friend and, at that time, a member of the California Assembly and chairman of the Ways and Means Committee, to participate.[10] I knew that the director of the Department of Corrections would not want to insult or alienate Willie Brown by denying him access to the prison, if only because the budget of the Department of Corrections was subject to Willie's review when it was considered by Ways and Means. Willie Brown was also an exceptional lawyer—one with substantial criminal law experience—who could bring that perspective to his questions and observations as a member of the group. At my request, Willie Lewis Brown Jr. agreed to be a member of the group demanding access.

I also contacted Ronald V. Dellums, another friend, who was then a member of the U.S. House of Representatives. His constituency included residents of certain areas of Alameda County, mostly Albany, Berkeley, and Oakland. My view was that the federal government provided substantial funds to the state of California, which supported various correctional activities. Ron Dellums, as a member of the U.S. Congress, had a legitimate interest in seeing that those funds were being properly used. Also, a significant number of the San Quentin prisoners were from his district in Alameda County; therefore, he had a responsibility to the prisoners and their families to determine if they were being abused and whether their federal constitutional rights were being denied. If they were being abused, then it would be proper and necessary for him to introduce new federal legislation to address that issue. At my request, Ronald V. Dellums said he would be a member of the group.

Dr. Carlton Goodlett, another friend, was a prominent practicing physician, newspaper publisher, and political activist in the San Francisco Bay Area. Dr. Goodlett was known throughout California, and even nationally, for his commitment to civil and human rights for all people. As the owner and publisher of the *Sun-Reporter*, Carlton was highly influential both in the San Francisco Bay Area and in California statewide politics. His newspaper was based in San Francisco, but it also had substantial circulation in black neighborhoods throughout the East Bay. Carlton would make an ideal member of the group not only because he was a publisher of a newspaper and, therefore, a member of the press, but also because, as a practicing physician, he could randomly examine prisoners to determine whether there was any evidence of torture or other physical abuse. At my request, Carlton Goodlett agreed to join the team.

The fourth and final member of the group that would seek direct contact with the prisoners at San Quentin was the Rev. Cecil Williams, pastor of San Francisco's Glide Memorial Methodist Church. I had met and become friends with Cecil when we were in Selma, Alabama, for the 1965 voting rights protest march from Selma to Montgomery.[11] As a highly respected Bay Area minister, Cecil could confirm and would bring needed credibility to any comments made by the group concerning whether prisoners had been mistreated—as the family members and lawyers of the prisoners feared might be the case—or whether such general mistreatment had not taken place, as prison officials asserted. He could also provide spiritual counseling to the prisoners at a time when there was very high anxiety among both guards and inmates at San Quentin. At my request, Cecil Williams agreed to join the group.

Warden Louis S. Nelson and Director Ray Procunier were advised that a delegation consisting of Assemblyman Willie L. Brown Jr., Congressman Ronald V. Dellums, Dr. Carlton Goodlett, and the Rev. Cecil Williams, accompanied by a few others, would present itself at the East Gate of San Quentin on Friday, August 27, 1971, for the specific purpose of being admitted to the prison and afforded reasonable access to the prisoners so that the delegation could observe, question, and physically examine them.

For some time a crowd of several thousand people had been assembling immediately in front of the East Gate, demanding that lawyers, family members, and media representatives be allowed access to all prisoners in San Quentin. The mood of the crowd was obvious: They believed that the lockdown was no less than an attempt to cover up police brutality suffered by the inmates of San Quentin. There were even expressions of concern that George Jackson was not the only prisoner who had been killed and that prison officials were covering up that truth.

On the morning of August 27, 1971, I had spoken to the thousands of protesters and asked them to remain resolute but calm. We had a constitutional right to appear at the prison, I told them, to protest the lockdown and the denial of access to the prisoners by their lawyers. But I said that nothing would please the armed guards standing just behind the initial gates at San Quentin more than for us to charge the gates. Even if our numbers were many, such an action would not be successful,

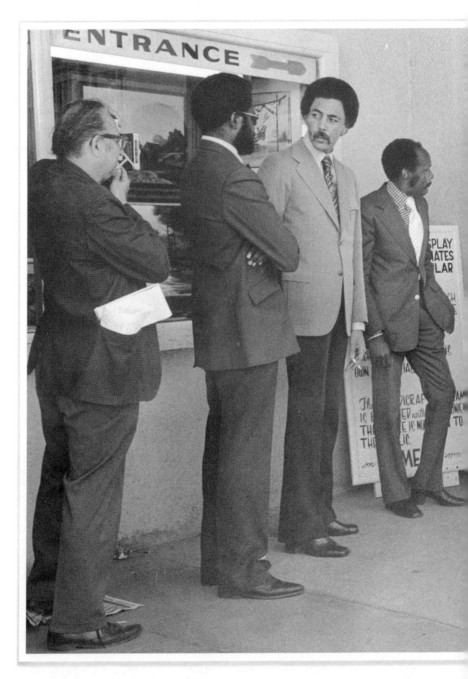

OUTSIDE THE MAIN ENTRANCE TO SAN QUENTIN PRISON, *August 27, 1971. From left: unidentified newspaper reporter, Henry Ramsey Jr., Congressman Ronald V. Dellums, and Assemblyman Willie Lewis Brown Jr.*

would be suicidal for some, and would, in fact, ensure the failure of our efforts to gain access to the prisoners by responsible representatives of government and the community.

When our group arrived at the prison's East Gate later that day and requested admittance, the guards put us in contact with Ray Procunier by telephone. He listened as I again explained who the members of our delegation were and our purpose for being there. (At least two other people had accompanied us; one was Ernest G. Howard, and I cannot remember who the other was.) Ray Procunier's initial position was that he would not agree to a face-to-face meeting but that we should wait at the gate and he would soon get back to us. We did not know it at the time, but Ray Procunier was in a heated debate with the leadership of the Prison Guards Association about whether we should even be admitted to the warden's office, let alone the areas of the prison where inmates were locked down.

After a wait of some time, probably less than an hour, the telephone rang at the guard's post where people were normally checked into the prison. We were told that we would be permitted to enter the prison and have a conversation with Ray Procunier in the warden's office but that there would be absolutely no visits with the prisoners. At that point, the guards at the entrance booth started the process of granting us access to the prison grounds, which they said involved a search of our persons.

Their insistence on a search led to somewhat of a delay when Congressman Dellums stated that he would not submit to a search of his person. He considered it demeaning and said it would be a personal insult to him as a human being and as a member of the Congress of the United States. The rest of us were willing to be searched but said we would not attend the meeting at the warden's office without Congressman Dellums. This development led to a telephone consultation between the guards and officials in the warden's office. The officials yielded, and our delegation was permitted to enter the prison grounds without Ron Dellums being searched. At that moment, Ron Dellums stood eight feet tall in my eyes.

We quickly covered the 200 or so yards from the gate to the building that housed the warden's office. We were greeted and admitted by Ray Procunier and a few other prison officials. After introductions, we—I think it was I—explained yet again to Ray Procunier why we were there and that we were not seeking access to the prisoners by the entire delegation. The four specific persons we wanted admitted were California Assemblyman Willie Brown Jr., U.S. Congressman Ronald Dellums, Carlton Goodlett, M.D., and the Rev. Cecil Williams, pastor of Glide Memorial Church. If allowed access to the prisoners, the four men could then provide the prisoners' families, members of the legislature, and the public with an accurate and honest account of the prisoners' personal condition, as well as the circumstances of their confinement.

In our discussion with correctional and prison officials in the warden's office, we also indicated that an immediate public safety issue needed to be addressed. We emphasized that matters could quickly get out of hand and that the consequences could potentially be tragic. Many people in the crowd outside the gate were family members of prisoners. There were also many political activists in the crowd who were far less reasonable or restrained than we were. I also again emphasized that we were only requesting access to the prisoners in the actual prison (for technically, being in the warden's office, we were already in the prison) by the four men already named.[12]

We debated the wisdom and potential danger (for the guards and inmates) of allowing the four people to randomly interview inmates. We wanted the interviews to be semiprivate. That is to say, access to the inmates would be such that, while the guards could see everything being done physically, they would probably not be able to hear what the inmates or the interviewers were saying.

Ray Procunier was the primary negotiator for the correctional officials. At some point in the negotiations, Ron Dellums commented that any person in a leadership position had to decide if he or she was a leader or not. I think Ron used the metaphor of a person being face to face with a bullet and having the willingness to stare it down unblinkingly. Shortly after that statement by Dellums, Procunier "blinked." The positions of power and influence held by the persons seeking admission to the prison were surely not lost on him. In fairness, he was a progressive and forward-thinking prison administrator, whose correctional philosophy was quite enlightened.[13] He went to a telephone in the office where we were meeting, and we heard him say to whoever was on the other end of the line, "I am going to let them in."

After that call Procunier told us that he had been speaking to the prison guard leadership and that the guards were extremely unhappy with his decision. But as a leader, he said, this was a time when he had "to face the bullet." However, he said, before he could authorize the group of four to enter the prison he had to make one more telephone call. To my personal embarrassment as a black man and, in my view, to the everlasting shame of the person to whom he placed the call, Procunier called the late John J. Miller,[14] who at that time was a member of the California Assembly and represented the 17th Assembly District, which included Albany, Berkeley, and a substantial part of Oakland. We could not hear what Miller was saying, but we could hear Procunier.

Procunier apologized for breaking his promise to Miller that he would not let us in after having refused to allow Miller to have access to the prisoners. Although Willie Brown was from San Francisco, the protest had been organized and was primarily led by people from Alameda County, particularly within Miller's district. I never spoke to Miller about the incident, but I assume that his ego was such that he was unable to accept others exercising leadership and succeeding in an effort that he probably saw as his responsibility. Whatever the reason, I never forgave John Miller for his gutless and treacherous conduct.

The four community leaders were then admitted to the prison and allowed to interview prisoners semiprivately and at random. Later that day, they appeared before the crowd outside the prison gates and reported that the prisoners did not appear to have been brutalized, that they were being fed, and that there was no evidence of any prisoners other than George Jackson and two others having been killed. The four had also gotten agreement from Ray Procunier on five points:

- Visits by family members would be resumed immediately.
- Inmates would be given writing materials.
- The entire prison population would be given two hot meals each day.
- Prisoners would be reissued shoes as quickly as possible, and,
- The Marin County Grand Jury would be permitted access to the prison and prisoners.

The crowd dispersed and the immediate crisis presented by the lockdown was resolved.

## · Notes ·

1. Attributed to Fyodor Dostoevsky (1821–1881).
2. Attributed to Fyodor Dostoevsky (1821–1881).
3. See George Lester Jackson, *Soledad Brother: The Prison Letters of George Jackson* (New York: Bantam Books, 1970). Also see "Book Review," *Stanford Law Review* 24 (May 1972): p. 965. You may also want to read Paul Liberatore, *The Road to Hell: The True Story of George Jackson, Stephen Bingham, and the San Quentin Massacre* (New York: Atlantic Monthly Press, 1996).
4. The Adjustment Center consisted of 6- by 10-foot cells in which prisoners were placed for 23 to 24 hours each day for extended numbers of days. Inmates were thrown in the cells for punishment or for "institutional convenience." They experienced total sensory deprivation and sometimes abuse at the hands of the guards. The Adjustment Center was commonly referred to as "the hole." See Lynne S. Hollander, "The Adjustment Center: California's Prison within a Prison," *Black Law Journal* 1 (Summer 1971): 153–55.
5. "Book Review," *Stanford Law Review* 24 (May 1972), p. 965.
6. See *San Francisco Examiner*, Sunday, August 22, 1971, "3 Guards, 3 Cons Slain in Quentin Break Try," p. 1, and *Oakland Sunday Tribune*, August 22, 1971, "6 Slain in San Quentin Escape Try," p. 1.

7. New York: Atlantic Monthly Press, 1996. Also see *New York Times*, Thursday, July 3, 1986, "Bingham Case: Trial Yields No Answers," p. A18.

8. See *Oakland Tribune*, Tuesday, Aug. 24, 1971, "New Facts Revealed In Quentin Slaughter," p. 1.

9. See *San Francisco Chronicle*, Saturday, Aug. 28, 1971, "Blacks Visit Quentin Scene," p. 2.

10. Willie L. Brown Jr. would in later years become Speaker of the California Assembly and thereafter a two-term mayor of San Francisco.

11. See chapter 21, "Selma, Alabama, 1965," *infra*.

12. The primary public entrance to San Quentin involves a gate, with an entrance booth, where visitors present and identify themselves. Before being allowed entry, they are searched for weapons and contraband. Beyond this initial gate and entrance booth is a roadway that is lined by a fire station and various administrative offices. Beyond those structures, maybe another 50 or 60 yards, another set of fences guards access to the areas of the prison where the inmates are housed and, for the most part, where they work.

13. For information about Ray Procunier, read John J. Dilulio Jr., *Governing Prisons: A Comparative Study of Correctional Management* (New York: Free Press, 1987), pp. 117–18, 223–25.

14. John J. Miller, an African American, was a graduate student at Boalt Hall when I was enrolled there as a first-year student and was one of my housemates and friends at 2528 Benvenue Avenue in Berkeley.

A LAWYER, as a member of the legal profession, is a representative of clients, an officer of the legal system and a public citizen having special responsibility for the quality of justice.[1]

—PREAMBLE, AMERICAN BAR ASSOCIATION
MODEL RULES OF PROFESSIONAL CONDUCT
(2008)

# 26

# Boalt Hall Faculty Member

I was appointed a full-time faculty member of the law school at the University of California at Berkeley, generally known as Boalt Hall, effective July 1, 1971. My faculty rank at the time of my initial appointment was associate professor of law. I was appointed professor of law and granted tenure in 1979. The primary courses I taught were criminal law and criminal procedure. My faculty colleagues could not have been more gracious or supportive during my stay at Boalt as a faculty member, and I formed several relationships and enduring friendships during my tenure: Dick Buxbaum, Jesse Choper, David Feller, Sandy Kadish, and Larry Sullivan immediately come to mind. I resigned from the faculty in 1981 after my appointment as a judge of the California Superior Court, in and for the county of Alameda.

My most enjoyable experiences as a law teacher were my interactions with students, particularly students of color. Many law students, regardless of race, ethnicity, or gender, needed and appreciated faculty encouragement and support. Boalt students were among the brightest law students in the country. Almost all of them had always been in the top 5 or 10 percent of any class in which they had been enrolled—elementary school, high school, and college. Now—for the first time in their lives—half of them would no longer be in the top 5 or 10 percent of the class, but, instead, in the bottom 50 percent. For many of the students, even some of the Caucasians and Asians, this repositioning created serious issues concerning personal confidence. It was a major problem for many, if not most, African American students.

Rigorous classroom discussions (verbal exchanges between teacher and student or student and student) could easily undermine a student's personal confidence. Some of the students had other problems—family, financial, health, and sometimes even academic concerns—and needed someone in whom to confide, someone to give them counsel. I saw my responsibility as a faculty member to be particularly responsive to those needs and interests.

My office policy was "open door" for any student who wanted to talk with me about any subject. Any student could drop by my office for a sympathetic ear and supportive advice. The kinds of advice that students needed typically involved course selections, career choices and objectives, financial difficulties, family pressures, and the like. Of course, there were many requests for letters of recommendation. Each year, I would occasionally invite black students to my family's home for dinner and open-ended conversation. I developed several lasting friendships as a result of student visits to my home and office.

I would also occasionally provide representation for UC Berkeley students with legal difficulties, mostly law students. In some instances, the students needed representation in criminal cases—valid and invalid—and sometimes in civil matters. In most criminal cases, I was able to either avoid a criminal charge even being filed or, if not, still get a dismissal or acquittal. Any lawyer can appreciate the importance of this representation for a law student. But I assume that not all of my descendants will be lawyers. I hope you recognize the problem that a criminal conviction—especially one that is recent—presents in trying to gain entrance to the legal profession. Those students tended to have little or no money with which to hire a lawyer, and a criminal conviction while in law school would have made admission to the bar almost impossible. I often see two prominent Bay Area lawyers whom I represented when they were students at Boalt Hall. I successfully represented one of the students in an unlawful eviction matter and the other in a burglary case.[2] Those are two examples of the sorts of supportive legal representation I provided Boalt students, usually African Americans.

Over the years since my retirement from the Boalt Hall faculty in 1981, I have had many former students—African American, Asian, Caucasian, male and female—comment about the importance of my accessibility, advice, and personal support during their three-year stay at Boalt. Their recollections rank among my own most satisfying memories of my days as a law professor.

### · Notes ·

1. Preamble, American Bar Association Model Rules of Professional Conduct (2008).
2. For those of you who are curious, the student was not guilty of burglary or any other criminal offense.

UNDER OUR CONSTITUTIONAL SYSTEM, courts stand against any winds that blow as havens of refuge for those who might otherwise suffer because they are helpless, weak, outnumbered, or because they are the non-conforming victims of prejudice and public excitement.[1]

— *Chambers v. Florida*

# 27

# Alameda County Superior Court

G overnor Edmund G. Brown Jr. appointed me to the Superior Court of the state of California, in and for the county of Alameda, on September 18, 1980, and I was sworn in as a Superior Court judge on November 21, 1980.[2] I had initially sought an appointment as a U.S. District Court judge for the Northern District of California but was unsuccessful in that effort. On May 9, 1980, President Jimmy Carter nominated Thelton E. Henderson—my former schoolmate at Boalt Hall and 1960–61 housemate at 2528 Benvenue in Berkeley—for the position I had sought. The U.S. Senate confirmed Thelton's nomination on June 26, 1980.

I cannot say that but for two factors I would have gotten the federal appointment and Thelton would not. However, I do know that there were two specific issues that played an important role in Senator Alan Cranston's decision not to recommend me to President Carter for the appointment. A digression is in order—you deserve an explanation.

The first factor was that sometime during the late summer of 1954,[3] I was arrested at March Air Force Base, Riverside, California, for attempting to steal three phonograph albums from the Base Exchange (BX).[4] I had intentionally taken the albums and left the store without paying for them. Unbeknownst to me, an Air Force officer who was an employee of the BX had observed my taking the albums. He followed and caught up with me about a block from the BX. The Air Police were called, and I was taken into custody on a charge of petty theft.

Within a few weeks, I was brought before a Special Court-Martial Board, where I admitted the truth of the charges. Needless to say, I was convicted of the offense. At the time, I was 19 years old and had no prior juvenile or criminal record. My sentence was reduction in rank from airman second class to airman basic, confinement in the base stockade for six months, and forfeiture of two-thirds pay during the period of confinement. I have no explanation for the offense except youth, stupidity, and, at the time, an inadequate appreciation of the immorality of such behavior when directed toward commercial entities. By this I mean that in the community where I was reared, it was made pretty clear that one should not steal from any individual, but taking certain things from a company (e.g., lumber or coal from the Atlantic Coast Line Railroad Company) was a different matter. I do not offer this as an excuse or justification for my criminal behavior because there is none. I simply offer it as an explanation for my conduct at the time.

Life within the stockade was in some respects the same as life outside the stockade. But work performed by prisoners was mostly limited to unpleasant tasks, and there was the obvious issue that one's freedom of movement and opportunity to interact with the civilian world were highly restricted. For example, my work as a free airman outside of the stockade was as a warehouseman. As a prisoner in the stockade, I worked for a while on a garbage truck, collecting garbage at various locations on the base.

When not working outside the base stockade, prisoners were almost always confined to the relatively small area within a fence that surrounded the stockade. I would estimate the total area to be about one square city block. As prisoners, we slept and, during off hours, lived in barracks that were in every respect like the typical Air Force and Army barracks of that day. We marched in formation three times each day from the stockade to a mess hall in a nearby squadron, where we received our meals. Family members were permitted to visit prisoners each Sunday afternoon at the stockade.

I had a disconcerting—to say the least—experience soon after my arrival at the stockade. There were at least two prisoners who cut other prisoners' hair, and this particular incident occurred as I was waiting my turn for one of them. Although it was a time of day when prisoners were expected to be at work on their assigned jobs, some prisoners were in the process of having their hair cut, and a couple of others, like me, were waiting. I had been in the stockade for only one or two days and had not yet received a job assignment, nor was I familiar with stockade routine.

In any event, an officer entered the room, observed us sitting there and talking, and said in a loud, authoritative, hostile voice, and with an obvious southern accent, that we boys should get out of the room immediately and go clean up the latrine.[5] I resented his reference to us as boys and challenged him on it.

Speaking in an annoyed voice, I said to him that he could call me airman, he could call me Ramsey, and he could call me prisoner, but that he had absolutely no right to call me "boy" and he should never do so again. He responded by saying, still authoritatively, "Okay, airman, get in there and clean up the latrine."

That evening, when it was time for all of the prisoners to assemble and march to the nearby mess hall for the evening meal, I was told by a member of the staff that I should remain at the stockade. Later that evening, I was put in solitary confinement ("the hole") for two weeks as disciplinary punishment for insubordination. As it turns out, the officer I had told off was the base provost marshal.

The hole was a windowless room at the end of one of the barracks where prisoners were housed. I had to sleep on a wooden platform about six inches off the floor, without a mattress and with a single blanket for cover. Although the room was fairly dark even during the daytime, there was an opening at the top of one of the walls—I assume for ventilation—that permitted modest light to enter during most of the daylight hours. The only reading material permitted was the Bible. Apparently, Air Force regulations mandated that prisoners be allowed access to a holy book. I therefore spent a significant amount of my time during the day reading the Bible. My assumption is that this regulation also applied to the Koran and Torah, but I do not know that. I am confident that it would today (2006) but am not so certain about 1954.

The diet of a prisoner in the hole was essentially restricted to a very limited number of calories each day. I do not remember the exact number but I know it wasn't many. Indeed, an inmate in the hole was to be visited and examined by a doctor at least once each week. I have told you elsewhere that I had always been skinny and was still so at that time—6'1" and 160 pounds. I also have never been particularly strong physically, and the restricted diet quickly began to take its toll on me. My weight loss was fairly dramatic, notwithstanding that other prisoners smuggled me food. A prisoner in the hole was permitted (probably required) to take a shower late each night after the other prisoners in the barracks were in their beds and presumably asleep. The prisoner was permitted to take this shower in private. Word had been gotten to me that I should look in the air vent in the shower room, where I should expect to find a meat sandwich secreted. I did, and it was. I placed the sandwich in my briefs before being taken back to the hole. Security was fairly lax in the sense that you were not thoroughly searched before being taken to the shower or when you returned.

Notwithstanding the dietary supplement provided by this smuggled food, I was still losing weight. The solitude, extended darkness, and boredom didn't help, but I managed somewhat by taking every available opportunity to read the Bible. The experience was difficult and unpleasant, but not long after the first week, the doctor said that my health dictated that I be released from the hole, and I was.

After working on the garbage truck for a few weeks, I was assigned to work in the stockade's administrative office as a clerk-typist. For the life of me, I cannot remember how I got that job. Perhaps someone noticed in my personnel file that I had been to clerk-typist school, or perhaps I had some conversations with the prison guards or administrators that caused them to think that I could fill this position for which they needed help. I seriously doubt if there were other prisoners with competent clerical skills in the base stockade. Regardless of how it came to be, I did get assigned to work in the stockade administrative office, and fortunately for me, I was an efficient and competent filing clerk and typist. Consequently, my supervisors liked me and appreciated my work.

Each year a limited number of stockade prisoners who had performed exceptionally well during their incarceration and who would still be in the stockade during the Christmas holidays were released early by the stockade commander as an act of Christmas clemency. This early release was always extended a few days before Christmas, hence it was actually labeled "Christmas clemency." I was pleasantly surprised to be told that I was on the list for Christmas clemency in 1954 after having served 94 days of confinement. I was reassigned to the 807th Supply Squadron, still at March Air Force Base, California, and resumed my job as a warehouseman.

I completed my Air Force enlistment, regained the two stripes I had lost as a result of my court-martial, and was honorably discharged on August 16, 1955. I was one very happy young man on the day of my discharge. Although not familiar with the word at the time, I now know that the word for what I felt is *euphoria*.

In one sense, my court-martial can be viewed as having been beneficial.[6] Who knows what my rank would have been in 1955 when I completed my tour of duty had I not been reduced in rank as punishment for the theft? I might very well have achieved the rank of staff sergeant or at least airman first class and, like Jesse Suggs, reenlisted. That may very well have resulted in no college, no law school, and no legal career. Who can say?

The second serious factor that most likely kept me from an appointment to the federal bench involved a 1968 altercation with my first wife, Evelyn. As a result of that incident, I was charged with and subsequently pled *nolo contendere*[7] in the Richmond Municipal Court[8] to the misdemeanor charge of malicious mischief. The matter arose from a dispute Evelyn and I had concerning our four minor children (Charles, Githaiga, Robert, and Ismail) and the manner in which she was exercising her custody rights.

On several different occasions before the day of the incident, Evelyn had failed to return the children at the time specified in our custody arrangement. I do not mean to imply that she would keep the children for days beyond the time specified for their return, but it could involve her being one or more hours late. We had agreed between ourselves to share custody of the boys.

Evelyn was very late in returning the children on the day in question, and I became concerned and annoyed. Fearing that something untoward had happened to them I had been trying desperately to locate her and the children by telephoning and visiting various places where they might logically be. Incidentally, my house at 5012 State Avenue in Richmond was only about four blocks from her house at 4710 Overend Avenue, also in Richmond. As I look back on the matter from my present perspective and level of maturity, I recognize that, while I had reason to be annoyed, there really was no rational reason to be angry or even alarmed.

My former wife showed up with the children at my home after I had been searching for approximately two hours. I told her that in the future she should either return the children as provided in the court order or, if unable to do so, must inform me that she would be late. I am certain that I did not utter those words in the most polite tone or manner. She responded by dismissing my complaint with a crude gesture, namely, giving me the "finger." I immediately rushed into my house where I grabbed a Ruger .22 caliber rifle that I used for target shooting, returned to the street, placed the muzzle of the barrel in turn against two of the tires of my former wife's automobile (then still parked in front of my house) and punctured both tires by firing the rifle.

I cannot and will not try to justify my actions. My behavior was outrageous and indefensible. I am certain that Evelyn and my children were extremely frightened and distressed by my conduct. Although I should have done so at or near the time of the event and did not, years later I did call Evelyn Ramsey to apologize for my conduct on that day. This incident, while wrong and without justification, did ultimately serve to make me much more aware of the psychological limitations within which all of us function. I learned the importance and wisdom of withdrawing from situations involving extreme stress before they become explosive or uncontrollable.

The two matters I have just discussed also serve as clear reminders that serious mistakes made early in life can have negative consequences for the rest of one's life. I must acknowledge that the incident involving Evelyn Ramsey did not occur extremely early in my life but when I was 34 years old. Regardless, I have long been both ashamed and burdened by those two events. They have continued to exist as a self-created barrier to career development that I have had to address and overcome in my personal life. And as noted, I have no doubt that they kept me from receiving serious consideration for appointment to the U.S. District Court.

I have also had to disclose this embarrassing and shameful personal history each time I have sought high office—when I applied for admission to the bar;[9] sought appointment to the Boalt Hall faculty; ran for the Berkeley City Council; applied for appointment to the Superior Court of the state of California, in and for the county of Alameda; was being considered for the position of dean of the Howard University School of Law; and when I applied for a position on the Board of Regents of the University of California. I hope each of you will always do everything you can to avoid placing yourself in such a situation.

To return to the topic of my appointment to the Alameda County Superior Court: After failing to get an appointment to the U.S. District Court, I applied for an appointment in the state judicial system because I still wanted to be a judge. Willie L. Brown Jr. was then Speaker of the California Assembly and was just as supportive of my application for the state bench as he had been of my application for the federal appointment. I am certain his support was critical for the decision by Tony Kline, then appointments secretary to the governor, to recommend to Governor Edmund G. "Jerry" Brown Jr. that I be appointed a Superior Court judge.

Allen Broussard was completing his term as presiding judge of the Alameda County Superior Court at the time. In those days, new appointees to the Alameda County Superior Court were almost always assigned to handle criminal matters, and so it was that Allen assigned me to a criminal jury trial department. (As an aside, I note that as a municipal court judge Allen had presided at the ceremony when Eleanor and I were married on September 7, 1969.) Not too many years after my appointment to the court, Allen was named an associate justice of the California Supreme Court, the second black so honored in the history of that court. Wiley Manuel, the first black California Supreme Court justice, was also an Alameda County Superior Court judge when he was appointed to the Supreme Court.

On April 10, 1981, just over four months after my appointment to the bench, I made a ruling in a criminal case that received significant local publicity.[10] A jury had found a defendant guilty of second-degree murder in a trial over which I presided. In deciding various post-trial motions made by the defense,[11] I made a ruling that reduced the defendant's conviction from second-degree murder to voluntary manslaughter. My ruling was that while the evidence admitted in the case was sufficient to support a verdict of voluntary manslaughter, as a matter of law, it was insufficient to support a verdict of murder. There was substantial local publicity concerning that ruling[12] and harsh criticism of my decision by the deputy district attorney who had tried the case, as well as by some newspapers and quite a few members of the public. Indeed, the decision even received limited national attention. All of the publicity—local and national—was negative.

The California Constitution requires each person whom the governor appoints as a trial or appellate court judge to stand for election in the first general election occurring after appointment.[13] Trial judges in California run unopposed unless someone files a specific challenge to their retention or reelection. In my case, I was challenged when I was required to stand for election in 1982.

Two other Alameda County Superior Court judges were required to run in that election—Richard "Dick" Hodge and Benjamin "Ben" Travis. Albert "Bud" Meloling was a senior prosecutor in the Alameda County DA's office who for several years had unsuccessfully sought an appointment to the Superior Court. He decided in 1982 to run against a sitting judge. So, as the filing date approached, the only question was whom he would challenge—Hodge, Ramsey, or Travis. Meloling named me as his target shortly before the date by which the law required him to declare the specific judge's seat he would contest.

There were few women and even fewer blacks and Hispanics sitting as judges in California when Jerry Brown was elected governor. California judicial positions were staffed mostly by white males, and a significant percentage of those white males were former prosecutors. Jerry Brown's election changed all that. He took a courageous stand early after assuming office that he would significantly integrate the California judiciary—with minorities and women. And he did so forthrightly. A consequence of his action was that the appointment of more white males to the California judiciary was for the most part put somewhat on hold for a while. That change caused great resentment among many of the white male lawyers, whose predecessors had previously enjoyed an almost exclusive privilege of serving as new California judges. Some of the white male lawyers adopted the tactic of filing against trial judges who had been appointed by Jerry Brown whenever those judges had to stand for election. Most judges being challenged were black, Hispanic, or female—sometimes with more than one of those attributes. Historically, California judges were rarely challenged, and then it usually was only when the judge had become senile, had suffered from alcoholism, or had been convicted of a crime.

But now challenges became commonplace, and in almost every instance, the challenger's claim was that the Brown appointee was unqualified to be a judge because he or she lacked significant trial experience, was soft on crime, or lacked judicial temperament. In some instances, all three deficits would be asserted. It was also not unusual for the challenger to assert or imply that the incumbent's appointment to the bench had been political (i.e., that the only reason for the appointment was race, gender, or both).

The Ramsey versus Meloling campaign was spirited and hotly contested. My opponent claimed I was a "lenient and defense-oriented

Judge Henry Ramsey Jr.

judge who needed to be removed from the bench."[14] In other words, he charged me with being soft on crime. His campaign literature emphasized his "30 years experience as a trial attorney, the last 20 of them as a prosecutor."[15] Meloling was endorsed by almost every police association in Alameda County and by at least eight Alameda County mayors.

I received widespread support from many people—including my wife and children. Edith Austin,[16] Judith Briggs, Willie Lewis Brown Jr.,[17] Ernest Howard,[18] Helen Pulich,[19] and Janet Roche all worked hard on my behalf. Several California appellate justices, numerous trial court judges, and many lawyers in the San Francisco Bay Area, particularly Alameda County, endorsed and worked on my campaign. I was also endorsed by several local bar associations and various labor unions, whose members, along with a host of other people, worked extremely hard to secure my election. When the votes had been counted on the evening of Tuesday, June 8, 1982, I had won the election. I cannot overstate how pleased and happy I was to retain my judgeship.

Of course, I would have preferred not to be challenged or required to participate in a contested election. I was not angry with Meloling for filing against me. He had the same right as every other lawyer who wanted to be a judge to file for the office. If he wanted to be a judge, then challenging an incumbent was a perfectly legitimate route to take. I did think he had made a big mistake in deciding that I was the judge he would file against. I had been very active in local politics (and he had not). I had campaigned before for elective office (and he had not). I also had important political friends—including Willie Lewis Brown Jr. (and, except for a few mayors, he did not).

I did, however, regret and resent the time I had to take away from my family and devote to the campaign. I worked full time on the bench throughout the election and campaigned every night and each weekend. One of my campaign strategies was to undermine Meloling's confidence in the outcome of the election. I thought that if my opponent saw me or heard that I was on the bench each day—knowing that I would still be out each evening on the campaign trail—it would shake his confidence and thereby lessen his ability to be an effective campaigner.

Unfortunately, this strategy also had its down side. Specifically, it resulted in my seeing very little of my family throughout the entire campaign. I had almost no time for my wife and children. I usually left home around 8:00 a.m. each day. After working at the courthouse all day, I would then attend one or more campaign functions each week-night and also on the weekend. I kept this pace up until election night and, therefore, was almost never at home except when sleeping. I missed being with my family very, very much. A few days after the election, I was at lunch and complaining about having had to neglect my family during the campaign. My friend Judge Martin N. Pulich brought a touch of reality to the situation when he responded dryly, "Henry, I can understand a sore loser, but I will never understand a sore winner!"

A few highlights of my tenure on the court: Among other things, I served as a member of the Alameda County Superior Court Appellate Division (1982 and 1983); as a law and motion judge (under a master calendar system—1984 and 1985); as presiding judge (1986 and 1987); as a member of the Judicial Council of California;[20] as a member of the California Blue Ribbon Commission on Inmate Population Management;[21] as an assigned judge in the California Supreme Court case of *Aloy v. Mash*;[22] and as an assigned judge in the Santa Clara County Superior Court jail overcrowding case of *Beck v. County of Santa Clara*[23] and the companion Santa Clara County case of *Branson v. Winter*.[24] I also worked closely with plaintiff and defense lawyers in trying to resolve a serious backlog of asbestos cases filed in the Alameda County Superior Court.

One of the professional achievements that I am most proud of is the significant reduction in the Alameda County Superior Court's civil and criminal case backlog that existed when I became presiding judge. Soon after my election by the judges of the Alameda County Superior Court, I held a series of meetings with various Alameda County lawyers and asked their advice on how the court's obvious calendar management problems might be effectively addressed. At that time, the court had for several years been experiencing a serious backlog of criminal cases, mostly those involving homicide, as well as a backlog of civil cases, especially asbestos cases. I was determined that during my tenure as presiding judge we would bring the trial calendar essentially into conformance with American Bar Association (ABA) standards for the processing of civil and criminal trial cases.[25]

In 1984, the ABA adopted time standards recommending that the average time from arrest to trial in a felony criminal case should be no longer than one year. The ABA recommended that all general civil cases should be disposed of within 24 months.[26] When I became presiding judge in 1986, the average time for resolving felony cases in the Alameda County Superior Court, from initial arraignment until commencement of the criminal trial, did not come anywhere near to meeting ABA time standards. In civil matters, it often took five years from the filing of the complaint to get to trial. Most matters did not take that long to be resolved because the overwhelming majority of cases—civil and criminal—were (and still are) resolved by settlement (civil) or plea (criminal). But there still were a substantial number of cases that required a trial for resolution of the civil dispute or a determination of guilt or innocence in criminal matters.

It was, and still is, my view that one of a trial judge's highest priorities should be the elimination of all unnecessary delay in the processing of civil and criminal cases. For several obvious reasons, a person accused of a crime who is awaiting trial and is in custody is seriously disadvantaged when compared with the defendant who is at liberty (released on bail or on his or her own recognizance). A pretrial detainee is unable to maintain employment, is physically separated from family and friends, typically has significant difficulty in consulting and maintaining contact with defense counsel, is seriously disadvantaged in finding witnesses, and is also disadvantaged in locating evidence that is relevant to his or her defense.

Pretrial detainees are particularly at a disadvantage with regard to financial resources needed to pay legal fees, retain an investigator, retain defense experts, and in many cases to financially support a spouse and children. Those factors alone place great pressure on even an innocent defendant who is in custody to accept a plea bargain and to plead guilty. But what was highly significant for me was that an accused person who was innocent of the charged offense deserved to be free of the accusation and its stigma and, most important, ought to be at liberty. Instead, an innocent person could languish in jail for several years before going to trial. That is not justice.

On the other side of criminal matters are the interests of both society and the victims in a prompt resolution of the criminal case. By prompt, I mean without any unnecessary delay in the processing of the matter. There is typically some necessary delay in a criminal case. A laboratory report, for example, may not be available for several weeks. An important witness may be unavailable because of illness or some other compelling reason. Certain appropriate and necessary pretrial motions typically will be made and have to be considered. Delay for reasons such as those do not occur in every case but are not at all unusual in the processing of criminal cases, as well as in some civil cases.

Society has a profound and crucial interest in a correct, just, and timely determination of whether a criminal act has occurred and, if so, who is responsible for it. Victims and their families want responsibility established so that they can get on with their lives. In some cases, victims can receive compensation once criminal responsibility has been established. Society and the victims also have an interest in seeing an appropriate sentence promptly imposed on a guilty offender, usually to achieve one, two, or each of three objectives: punishment and rehabilitation of the offender, protection of society from future harm through isolation of the offender, and deterrence of other prospective offenders.

In civil matters, the plaintiff should not have to unnecessarily wait one extra day to receive deserved relief requested in a civil complaint that has been filed and served. Likewise, the civil defendant should not have to suffer continuing consequences from an unfounded claim or the uncertainty of a civil trial's outcome one day longer than is absolutely necessary. So whether the matter is civil or criminal, it is the responsibility of the judicial system to achieve expeditious resolution of the case.

I soon discovered that the primary source of unnecessary delay—in both civil and criminal cases—was the frequent request by lawyers for gratuitous continuances and the frequent irresponsible granting of those requests by trial judges. A continuance is an order extending into the future—in other words, "continuing"—the date on which a particular event is scheduled to occur.

Under the master calendar system, the pretrial management of cases is the responsibility of the presiding judge or some other trial judge assigned that role. A request for a continuance of a trial date or a pretrial matter under this system is typically made to and ruled on by the presiding judge. Under the direct case management system, each trial judge is responsible for the pretrial management and the trial of all cases on his or her calendar or docket. A request for a continuance under this system is made to and decided by the individual trial judge.

The Alameda County Superior Court followed a master calendar system. Soon after assuming the position of presiding judge, I instituted a policy of denying all requests for continuances of a trial date unless the lawyer or lawyers involved could establish that a continuance was absolutely necessary and unavoidable. I implemented this policy in all cases—criminal and civil. The initial responses of lawyers were mostly negative and hostile. But within a fairly short period of time, this new policy was accepted by the great majority of civil trial lawyers and enthusiastically embraced by many. Quite a few members of the civil trial bar were pleased by the certainty and reliability of trial dates that this new policy engendered.

In criminal cases, particularly murder cases, the response was a wholesale "pulling of time waivers,"[27] mostly by public defenders. My response in each instance was to immediately set a new trial date within statutory requirements. What I absolutely refused to do was negotiate whether or how much of a continuance should be granted. If it was necessary to assign the case to a civil judge for trial, I did so.[28] Also, once a criminal defendant and his or her counsel "pulled time," I refused to accept a new "time waiver." In other words, even if the defendant and defense counsel later, in effect, wanted to admit that the withdrawal of a time waiver had been a bluff, I would not allow the filing of a new time waiver. Pull your time waiver, and you could safely bet that you would get a trial date within the time limits imposed by law—and have to live with that new date.

In fact, most of the lawyers who pulled time were not really interested in a speedy trial. Their main interest was to force me to end my new policy of denying requests for continuances unless the lawyer could present a compelling reason in support of the request. It was not long before defense lawyers abandoned the ploy of pulling time as a strategy to get me to return to the old continuance policy.

Twelve months after I initiated the new continuance policy, the number of felony criminal cases awaiting trial in the Alameda County Superior Court had been reduced from 715 (including 208 non-murder cases that were more than six months old) when I assumed the position of presiding judge to a total of 453 cases (with only 15 non-murder cases on the calendar that had been pending more than six months).[29]

A short time thereafter, the court's criminal calendar had fewer than 400 cases pending. The average time between arraignment and commencement of trial in criminal cases had also been substantially reduced. The effect of the new policy was also dramatic as concerned the backlog of cases on the civil calendar. Those positive changes did not result from my actions alone. Ms. Joanne Lederman, who was then the court executive; many members of her staff; a significant majority of the Alameda County Superior Court judges; and some lawyers also contributed substantially to achieving those improvements in court and calendar management.

I had already learned (in seminars offered by the California Judicial Council and the National Center for State Courts) two lessons or principles that I found to be rational, prudent, effective, fair, and wise. One, already mentioned, was that a request for a continuance should never be granted without a compelling reason for doing so. Another, and better, way of stating this rule is that *events should occur when scheduled to occur.* I am absolutely confident that this simple rule, if conscientiously followed, will always keep criminal and civil calendars under control. The second principle is that a judge should not allow any pretrial court appearance to conclude without having established a date, time, and purpose for the next appearance.

My years of judicial service, experience, and training have shown me that control and management of cases—civil and criminal—and court calendars will not be a problem if judges have the courage and wisdom to faithfully adhere to those two principles. That conclusion is based on my experience as a judge of the Alameda County Superior Court, as well as on my personal observation with respect to courts I have visited elsewhere in the United States and abroad.

## CALIFORNIA JUDICIAL COUNCIL

THE JUDICIAL BRANCH OF OUR state government has responsibility for deciding cases and interpreting the laws of the state of California. It has responsibility for the orderly resolution of civil disputes between parties in controversy, for the determination of guilt or innocence of those accused of violating laws, and for the protection of rights of individuals. The California court system is the nation's largest and serves more than 34 million people with more than 2,000 judicial officers and 21,000 court employees. The chief justice of California is the head of the state's judicial branch.

The California Judicial Council is the policymaking and rulemaking body for the California judicial system. One of my most satisfying experiences as a California Superior Court judge was my service on the California Judicial Council. Chief Justice of California Malcolm Lucas appointed me to the California Judicial Council on October 5, 1988, and I served for three years. Staff support for the California Judicial Council is provided by the Administrative Office of the Courts, which serves as the council's staff agency.

Much of my work as a member of the Judicial Council concerned the development of proposed legislation that would help reduce criminal and civil case backlogs, wherever the problem existed in the state. First, policies were developed, adopted, and published as California Rules of Court. The new rules encouraged the various trial courts to expedite the processing of cases and to significantly improve the management of caseloads.

Second, in February 1986, a bill–Assembly Bill 3300–was introduced in the California Assembly which, when enacted into law, set standards for the efficient processing of cases in California trial courts.[30]

There was a potential conflict between the pretrial procedural rules being considered by the California legislature in Assembly Bill 3300 and the pretrial procedural rules that had already been adopted by the Judicial Council and published as California Rules of Court. This situation created a significant risk of a constitutional separation-of-powers conflict between the legislature and the judiciary. A wise approach to avoiding this potentially controversial and politically explosive issue was found when the chairman of the Assembly Judiciary Committee, the chairman of the Senate Judiciary Committee, and the chief justice of California–in his role as both chief justice of California and chairman of the California Judicial Council–agreed to form a joint committee to resolve differences between the legislature and judiciary regarding the various procedural provisions to be included in Assembly Bill 3300.

I was appointed by Chief Justice Lucas to serve as one of the several judicial council representatives on this joint legislative-judicial committee. Phil Isenberg, then chairman of the Assembly Judiciary Committee, was also a member of the joint committee. Also, the State Bar of California appointed practicing lawyers to represent the interests of both plaintiff and defense lawyers.

After several meetings, the joint committee arrived at a consensus regarding recommendations that we thought would resolve the procedural differences between some of the California Rules of Court and certain rules proposed in Assembly Bill 3300, the Trial Court Delay

Reduction Act. Our recommendations were accepted, and the proposed legislation—Assembly Bill 3300—was adopted by the legislature on a pilot basis[31] in 1987 as Government Code sections 68600 *et seq.* and was signed into law by the governor. The act was extended to all civil cases in the early 1990s.[32] The enactment of Assembly Bill 3300 did much to improve the performance of California trial courts—particularly the civil trial courts—and to reduce court backlogs in Los Angeles County and the several other counties where trial delay had for many years been a particularly serious problem.[33]

I am very proud of my involvement in and contribution to the development of Assembly Bill 3300. I later served as a facilitator in several of the many seminars sponsored throughout California by the Administrative Office of the Courts and the National Judicial College in Reno, Nevada, to train trial judges concerning the provisions of the act and how best to effectively implement those provisions.

## NATIONAL COMMISSION ON TRIAL COURT PERFORMANCE STANDARDS

THE NATIONAL CENTER FOR STATE COURTS received a grant in 1987 from the Bureau of Justice Assistance (BJA) to develop performance standards for trial courts. The purpose of the grant was "to increase the capacity of the Nation's trial courts to provide fair and efficient adjudication and disposition of cases. The program's goals included the development of a set of standards and an accompanying measurement system that would define and measure effective trial court performance."[34] The anticipated standards were envisioned as (a) a conceptual framework for understanding and improving court performance and (b) a means for court self-assessment, self-improvement, and accountability to the public.

I was among the 12 original members of the National Commission on Trial Court Performance Standards when it was established by the National Center for State Courts in September 1987. Other initial members were the Honorable Robert C. Murphy, chair, chief judge, Court of Appeals of Maryland;[35] Robert N. Baldwin, state court administrator, Virginia; Carl F. Bianchi, administrative director of the court, Idaho; the Honorable Robert C. Broomfield, judge, U.S. District Court, Arizona; John A. Clarke, trial court administrator, Superior Court, Hudson County, initially, and then Essex County, New Jersey; Judith A. Cramer, court administrator, Court of Common Pleas, Montgomery County, Ohio; Robert D. Lipscher, administrative director of the courts, New Jersey; Doris Marie Provine, professor of law and political science, Syracuse University, New York; Whitfield Smith, clerk of court, Superior Court for DeKalb County, Georgia; the Honorable Leo M. Spellacy, presiding and administrative judge, Court of Common Pleas, Cuyahoga County, Ohio; and the Honorable Fred B. Ugast, chief judge, Superior Court of the District of Columbia, as well as Edward B. McConnell (ex officio), president emeritus, National Center for State Courts.

Three years later—after many meetings—the commission adopted a set of Trial Court Performance Standards,[36] identifying five performance areas that encompassed "the fundamental purposes and responsibilities . . . that may be considered a court's mission:"[37]

- Access to justice.
- Expedition and timeliness.
- Equality, fairness, and integrity.
- Independence and accountability.
- Public trust and confidence.

The commission developed specific performance standards in each area. For example:

- Ensuring that court facilities are safe, accessible, and convenient to use (Standard 1.2).
- Establishing and complying with recognized guidelines for timely case processing, while keeping current with incoming caseloads (Standard 2.1).

- Taking appropriate responsibility for the enforcement of court orders (Standard 3.5).
- Anticipating new conditions or emergent events, and adjusting court operations as necessary (Standard 4.5).
- Ensuring that the trial court is perceived to be both independent (i.e., not unduly influenced by other components of government) and accountable (Standard 5.3).

The U.S. Department of Justice, via its Office of Justice Programs, states in the Bureau of Justice Assistance Fact Sheet (November 1995), "Trial Court Performance Standards and Measurement System":

> The creation of [the Trial Court Performance Standards (TCPS)] is one of the most significant events in judicial administration in the last 10 years. Bringing attention to trial court performance, self-assessment, and consumer orientation, TCPS has provided a new framework for understanding the practical effectiveness of trial courts and their unique local legal cultures. The improved court performance that can result ensures a more responsive justice system in a variety of ways, including [the following]:
>
> - Helping victims get through the system as expeditiously as possible, while ensuring that they are treated with dignity and respect.
> - Ensuring that child support orders are enforced.
> - Encouraging interagency communication and coordination in cases involving drugs, domestic violence, and mental illness.

I expect that my pride and satisfaction at having served as a member of the National Commission on TCPS is evident. I learned a great deal about trial court management, responsibility, and accountability, and I feel that my participation in the commission's work made a significant contribution to improvement of the nation's judiciary.

## · Notes ·

1. *Chambers v. Florida*, 309 U.S. 227, 241 (1940).

2. "In 1998 California voters passed a constitutional amendment that provided for voluntary unification of the superior and municipal courts in each county into a single, countywide trial court system. By January 2001, all 58 California counties had voted to unify their municipal and superior court operations." See Administrative Office of the Courts, "Fact Sheet," February 2005, Trial Court Unification. Trial court unification eliminated the administrative, salary, and titular differences between municipal and superior court judges in California.

3. I do not remember the exact month or date.

4. The BX is a relatively modest-sized department store on the base where items can be purchased at significantly lower prices than at civilian stores. Comparable establishments on Army posts were referred to as the Post Exchange, or PX.

5. Toilets are called latrines in the U.S. Air Force.

6. Bruce Bohle, ed., *The Apollo Book of American Quotations* (New York: Dood, Mead 1967), p. 86. An updated version is "every cloud has a silver lining but it is sometimes a little difficult to get it to the mint." (From Don Marquis, "certain maxims of archy," from *archy and mehitabel*.)

7. No contest, or, essentially, "I do not contest or deny the charges."

8. City of Richmond, Contra Costa County, California.

9. The U.S. Air Force court-martial.

10. The case was *People of the State of California vs. Jimmy Harold Springer*, Alameda County Superior Court, Action No. 70993. The Information in the case was filed on Oct. 15, 1980, and charged Mr. Springer with the crime of "Murder, a violation of Section 187 of the Penal Code of California," and alleged Use of a Deadly Weapon and Great Bodily Injury, as enhancements. My decision in reducing the defendant's conviction from second-degree murder to voluntary manslaughter was affirmed in an unpublished opinion of the Court of Appeal of the State of California, First Appellate District, Division Four, Action No. A011438/1 Crim. 22727, filed June 22, 1983.

11. A detailed discussion regarding the motion and my ruling on it would be too legalistic for the purposes of this book.

12. See, e.g., Lance Williams, "Judge lessens murder ruling, raises furor," *Oakland Tribune*, Saturday, April 11, 1981, p. 1.

13. See California Constitution, article 6, section 16(c,) which provides as follows: "c) Terms of judges of superior courts are six years beginning the Monday after January 1 following their election. A vacancy shall be filled

by election to a full term at the next general election after the second January 1 following the vacancy, but the Governor shall appoint a person to fill the vacancy temporarily until the elected judge's term begins."

14. See Candidate's Statement, Judge of the Superior Court, Office No. 5, County of Alameda, Sample Ballot and Voter Information Pamphlet, Direct Primary Election, Tuesday, June 8, 1982, p. S5.

15. Meloling campaign literature.

16. A close personal friend and long-time political ally.

17. Then-Speaker of the Assembly and a close personal friend.

18. A close personal friend and long-time political ally.

19. Wife of then-Superior Court Judge Martin Pulich.

20. The 28-member Judicial Council is the policymaking body of the California courts. Under the leadership of the chief justice, the council is responsible for ensuring the consistent, independent, impartial, and accessible administration of justice. (This description of the Judicial Council was taken from the California Judicial Council Fact Sheet.)

21. See the Blue Ribbon Commission on Inmate Population Management, *Final Report*, submitted in January 1990. The introduction to the report states on p. 1 that the commission was established in 1987 "to examine prison and jail population projections, study options for criminal punishment, and make recommendations to the Governor and Legislature on the problems of prison overcrowding and escalating costs." The *Final Report* was submitted in January 1990 to George Deukmejian, governor of California; David A. Roberti, president pro tempore of the Senate; Robert Presley, member of the Senate; and Willie L. Brown, Speaker of the Assembly. It included "a comprehensive description of the problem being experienced in California and elsewhere in the nation concerning jail and prison overcrowding; a discussion of public safety issues; a comprehensive review of proposed punishment options; and analysis, findings, and recommendations on how to approach, and hopefully resolve, problems in the specific categories of substance abuse, parole violators, sentencing, short-term new commitments, community corrections, and construction." See *Final Report*, p. 1.

22. *Aloy v. Mash*, 38 Cal. 3d 413; 212 Cal.Rptr. 162; 696 P.2d 656 (1985).

23. *Beck v. County of Santa Clara*, 204 Cal. App. 3d. 789 (1988). Each judge on the Santa Clara Superior Court had recused him or herself in the case.

24. *Branson v. Winter*, Santa Clara County Superior Court, Action no. 78807.

25. These standards can be found at the National Center for State Courts website: http://www.ncsconline.org/D_Research/TCPS/Measures/me_2.1.1.htm.

26. Ibid.

27. Under California law, a felony defendant must ordinarily be brought to trial within 60 days after arraignment, unless the defendant waives that right. See California Penal Code section 1048. For certain felony offenses specifically noted in section 1048, the defendant must be brought to trial within 30 days after arraignment, unless good cause is shown for a continuance. If the right is waived, the defendant still has a right to withdraw the waiver at any time before trial. See Penal Code section 1382. This practice is commonly called "pulling one's time waiver" or "pulling time." If a time waiver is withdrawn, then the defendant's trial must commence within 10 days after the withdrawal. See Penal Code section 1382(a)(2)(A). If the case is not brought to trial within the statutory time limit, then the case must be dismissed. See Penal Code section 1382(a).

28. As stated earlier, each Alameda County Superior Court judge was assigned to a specific civil or criminal trial department. Judges in civil departments, absent an emergency situation, handled only civil matters. Criminal judges handled only criminal matters. The authority to make those assignments rested with the presiding judge, and each assignment was for one year. In November of each year, all of the Alameda County Superior Court judges would meet and—in order of seniority—request their assignment for the following year. The presiding judge always honored those requests. Judges with high seniority almost always requested a civil assignment, although a couple of them preferred criminal. Judges did not request specialized assignments (e.g. law and motion, presiding judge-juvenile, or felony arraignment) during those sessions, because specialized assignments were in the sole discretion of the presiding judge.

29. See Shannon Hickey, "Ramsey Takes Another Hot Seat," *Recorder*, Aug. 1, 1990, p. 11.

30. Assembly Bill 3300 (The Trial Court Delay Reduction Act of 1986) was carried by Assemblyman Willie Brown and ultimately enacted by the legislature and signed into law by the governor as California Government Code sections 68600 *et seq.* The 1986 Trial Court Delay Reduction Act was repealed in 1990 by AB 3820.

31. Government Code section 68605 reads, "The Judicial Council shall designate the four superior courts with 18 or more judicial positions which, as of June 30, 1986, had the highest ratio per judicial position of at-issue civil cases pending more than one year, and the five superior courts with more than eight judicial positions, not otherwise designated, with the highest such ratio. In each such court, an exemplary delay reduction program shall be established."

32. See Judicial Council of California, Administrative Office of the Courts, "New Civil Delay Reduction Rules Adopted for California Trial Courts," News Release 71, Oct. 21, 2003.

33. Ibid., which states, "As a result of the delay reduction program, the time from filing to disposition of civil cases has been significantly reduced. By fiscal year 2001-2002, 65 percent of cases over $25,000 and 85 percent of cases under $25,000 were disposed of within one year."

34. See Bureau of Justice Assistance Fact Sheet, "Trial Court Performance Standards and Measurement System," November 1995, p. 1.

35. Maryland's highest state court, named the Supreme Court in most states.

36. The Measurement System was later developed and approved.

37. See Bureau of Justice Assistance Fact Sheet, "Trial Court Performance Standards and Measurement System," November 1995, p. 1.

ON THE DOMESTIC FRONT, this dogma [of aggressive militarism] expands police power, augments the prison-industrial complex, and legitimates unchecked male power (and violence) at home and in the workplace. It views crime as a monstrous enemy to crush (targeting poor people) rather than as an ugly behavior to change (by addressing the conditions that often encourage such behavior). [1]

—CORNELL WEST

# 28

# Mentor Diversion, Alameda County

I cannot remember the exact year I became concerned about the issue of overly harsh and lengthy sanctions in narcotics cases, but it was sometime after my appointment to the California Superior Court and probably after my appointment as a member of the state of California's Blue Ribbon Commission on Inmate Population Management.[2] I developed a deep concern about California's newly but rapidly developing policy of imprisoning adults (California criminal law defines as an adult anyone who has reached the age of 18) who had been convicted of illegally selling narcotics—regardless of their age or personal history.

In fact, the 1980s were a time when many Californians were becoming alarmed about criminal behavior in general and were discarding longstanding notions of rehabilitation and individualized punishment. A new and strident call was being made by politicians and members of the general public for much more aggressive law enforcement and considerably harsher sentences, especially for crimes involving violence, sex offenses, and sales of illegal drugs (crimes involving "dope dealers"). Punishment rather than rehabilitation became the purpose of imprisonment,[3] and the effect of these harsh new policies fell disproportionately on the poor, particularly those who were members of minority groups.

Provisions incorporating this new approach to sentencing were supported by then Governor Jerry Brown and were established by the state legislature, which virtually eliminated indeterminate sentencing by trial judges and replaced it with a scheme of predetermined sentences.[4] In essence, the sentencing discretion of trial judges was significantly reduced, and the role of the prosecutor in determining criminal sentences was significantly enhanced. Factors that a trial judge could consider in granting probation were statutorily mandated, and in several instances, the prosecutor could limit or expand the judge's sentencing discretion as a function of the charges made in the case.

An obvious illustration is when the prosecutor decides whether or not to ask for the death penalty in a murder case. If the prosecutorial decision is not to charge special circumstances, then there can be no consideration of the death penalty by the jury or judge, no matter how horrific the offense or how extensive and grave the offender's criminal history. If the prosecutor decides to charge special circumstances[5]—and proves the special circumstances by legally sufficient evidence—the judge and jury will have the discretion to impose the ultimate sanction of death.

But other examples are less obvious and less well known: whether to charge forcible rape (a felony) or simple battery (a misdemeanor), whether or not to charge use of a firearm in the commission of a robbery, whether to charge petty theft with a prior (a felony) or simple petty theft (a misdemeanor), whether to charge unlawful possession of a controlled substance as a misdemeanor or felony. In each of these examples, the prosecutor's charging decision either limits or expands the trial judge's sentencing options.

With regard to the sale of illegal drugs, legislative policy was fairly draconian, particularly for the dealers. The problem, as many others and I saw it, was that the new criminal policy and sentencing scheme essentially abandoned the notion of individualized punishment. Sanctions became tailored to a class of offenders, much more so than to the facts of the specific offense. The new policy also severely limited a judge's discretion to take into account an offender's age or personal history and the circumstances surrounding the offense when determining sentences in individual cases. This could be particularly harsh when an adult offender without a significant criminal record was convicted of selling illegal narcotics—and even more so when the offender was a young adult, say between the ages of 18 and 26.

The illegal sale of narcotics was and is typically a felony under California law, even for first offenders. A person so convicted, while eligible for felony probation, would still be a felon and have to receive a prison sentence. Plea-bargaining in such cases was possible but with a twist. As part of a plea bargain, the convicted individual would usually receive a prison sentence, with that sentence being suspended and the offender placed on probation. It would typically be a condition of probation that the offender be incarcerated for a relatively short term in the county jail. If the offender had been in custody before his or her conviction, the county jail sentence would often be jail time served while awaiting trial.

The offender would usually be willing to plead guilty with the promise of a plea bargain that projected a suspended prison sentence and probation, as an alternative to trial and a substantial risk of conviction, in which case he or she would usually immediately be sent to prison. This avenue was especially attractive to an accused person who was in custody and could not afford bail or was ineligible for release on his or her own recognizance.

People involved in the case—the police officers, prosecutor, defense attorney, the judge—were aware that the defendant would very likely soon commit some new offense and thereby violate the terms of his or her probation—even if the new matter was only a nonviolent minor misdemeanor.

The plea bargain was attractive to prosecutors because it allowed them to gain a conviction via a guilty plea while avoiding the uncertainty of a jury trial. And any new offense would now support two new charges—for the new offense and for a probation violation. The prosecution then got to decide whether to pursue one or both of those charges. Most often, if the new charge was a misdemeanor, the probation violation would be the focus.

A charge for the new criminal offense—whether a felony or misdemeanor—would entitle the defendant to a jury trial and have to be proved beyond a reasonable doubt. However, a person charged in

California with a violation of probation is *not entitled to a jury trial* and the prosecution's burden of proof is not *beyond a reasonable doubt*, but the materially lesser evidentiary standard of *more likely than not*. The prosecutor is required only to prove the probation violation charge before a judge (i.e., in a court trial). Also, the prosecutor is required only to prove that the probation violation charge is more likely to be true than not, rather than having to meet the more difficult evidentiary standard of beyond a reasonable doubt. The prosecutor thereby avoids much of the evidentiary difficulty involved in achieving a felony conviction.

On a finding that the individual has violated his or her terms of felony probation, a judge will almost always sentence the defendant to prison on the original or underlying felony charge, and therein is the twist. The offender, at the time of sentencing, will essentially have been convicted of a felony and sentenced to prison on the basis of charges and facts that were never submitted to a jury or proved beyond a reasonable doubt.

I was very concerned that such harsh sentences were being imposed with little or no regard for the offender's age, his or her personal history, or the circumstances of the particular case. I concluded that—in too many instances—we were imprisoning for substantial periods of time, and disabling probably for life, what I saw as much of "our future." The young people who were being arrested, being convicted as dealers, and thereby being declared felons would most likely never have the opportunity to make a meaningful contribution to society. Most of the youngsters were African American; a significant percentage were Hispanic. The financial costs to our society to prosecute and imprison the young offenders were (and still are) enormous. I thought that this practice should not be permitted to occur without our making an effort to avoid it.

At that time, I was presiding judge of the Alameda County Superior Court. I discussed the matter with Richard "Dick" Iglehart, then chief assistant district attorney of Alameda County, and he was interested in helping me find a solution. We came up with the idea that young adult offenders who had little or no criminal history and who were arrested for selling an insubstantial amount of a controlled substance could be diverted from the criminal justice system for two years. The person would be required, during that two-year period, to meet certain conditions, and if he or she was successful in that effort, then the suspended criminal charge would be dismissed.

I took the lead in discussing the idea with other stakeholders in the matter: Don Perata, then chairman of the Alameda County Board of Supervisors;[6] Wilmont Sweeney, presiding judge of the Alameda County Juvenile Court and the person to whom the county's probation officer reported;[7] James R. Jenner, Alameda County Public Defender, and Jack Mehan, district attorney of Alameda County. The discussions and negotiations soon resulted in a formal memorandum of understanding that was signed by the Alameda County district attorney, Alameda County Probation Department, Alameda County public defender, and presiding judge of the Alameda County Superior Court.

One of the special things about this program, beyond the class of offenders it was designed to help, was that there was no statutory authority for it. A statutory provision (Penal Code section 6000) authorized diversion in criminal cases in which possession of a controlled substance *for personal use* was alleged. But there was no specific statutory authority for diversion if the charge was the *sale*, *attempt to sell*, or *possession for sale*, of a controlled substance.

Those of us who established the mentor diversion program did not doubt that doing so was clearly within the authority of the DA's office and of individual judges. We had given serious consideration to the issue of how we could legally achieve our objective of avoiding felony convictions in cases involving the sale of illegal drugs where the offender was a young adult who had little or no significant criminal record and where the amount of drugs involved was not great. We concluded that we had the authority to create the program that we ultimately designed.

Central to the program's purpose and utility was the district attorney's agreement that his deputies would ask the court to suspend further consideration of the criminal charges, provided the defendant voluntarily agreed to participate in the mentor diversion program and meet all program conditions. At the end of the two-year period—provided the defendant had met program conditions—the charges would be dismissed and records of the arrest and criminal charges sealed.[8] The Alameda County mentor diversion program was established in 1989 and has existed ever since.

The essential components of the program today (2007) are essentially the same as when the program was established almost 20 years ago. The district attorney has final say as to whether a defendant is eligible for the program. Only accused people who have no significant prior criminal or juvenile history,[9] have no history of significant violence, and are between the ages of 18 and 26 years are eligible to participate. Once the DA's office determines that a defendant is eligible for the program because of the described factors, that defendant is interviewed by a probation officer, who—using his or her education, training, and experience—determines whether the defendant is suitable for the program. That is, is the person under consideration likely to comply with program requirements and successfully complete the required two years? Assuming a person is found by the DA's office to be *eligible* and by the probation officers to be *suitable*, a motion is then made in open court that the person be considered for the program. I do not know of any instance in which that motion has been denied.

Once admitted to the program, the mentee is obligated, among other things, to (a) essentially remain drug-free throughout the two years of the program;[10] (b) attend meetings—first weekly and later monthly—at which, among other things, the mentee is tested for narcotics; (c) be employed or actively seeking employment; and (d) obey all laws. Most mentees do not have a high school diploma. The program requires those people to complete high school.[11] If ineligible (e.g., because the person is too old to reenroll in high school), then he or she must obtain a GED (General Educational Development) certificate. High school graduates are required to enroll in college. Sometimes the mentee is already enrolled in college and, in those instances, he or she is required to continue that enrollment. The Mentor Diversion program is currently under the able leadership of veteran probation officers Aleshia Odom and Charles Wright.

Those of us involved with the mentor diversion program believe that a fairly high percentage of defendants admitted into the program succeed. In other words, they remain drug-free while participating in the two-year program, they attend school, and most either remain in school or become employed during the two-year period. But that view is based on our anecdotal impressions. In 2005, we began a program of collecting statistics that should provide solid data to answer the question of how successful our program is in meeting its immediate two-year objectives. Unfortunately, we lack the resources or authority to follow our mentees for a significant period after they complete the program to see if they remain crime free. But I am personally convinced that our mentees and our community benefit greatly from the program.

· Notes ·

1. Cornell West, *Democracy Matters: Winning the Fight against Imperialism* (New York: Penguin Books, 2005), p. 5.
2. I was appointed by the Honorable Willie Lewis Brown Jr., then Speaker of the California Assembly.
3. California Penal Code Section 1170.
4. California Penal Code Section 1170.
5. California Penal Code Section 190.2.
6. Today (2007) Don Perata is president pro tempore of the California State Senate.
7. Judge Wilmont Sweeney retired from the Alameda County Superior Court on May 31, 1996, and died on April 24, 1999, in Oakland, California.
8. See California Penal Code section 851.90.(a)(1). The adoption of this Penal Code section cured a serious failing in our program. Before its adoption, there actually was no statutory authority allowing a court to

seal arrest or court records of persons successfully completing our program. There had for some time been a program that allowed the sealing of records of people convicted of simple *possession* of narcotics, but there was not a provision in cases of conviction involving the sale or possession for sale of narcotics.

9. The overwhelming majority of program participants are, and in the past have been, people with no material criminal record.

10. A person is allowed 30 days for his or her system to eliminate any trace of prohibited drugs used before admission into the program.

11. Some high schools will not permit students over a certain age to reenroll. These students may be eligible to attend an "adult high school" or a community college.

No STUDENT LEFT HOWARD during [Charles] Houston's tenure without considerable understanding of the workings of the government with respect to race and justice. And why? There was a social engineering job which they could not avoid. Not for a moment did Houston equivocate. "A lawyer's either a social engineer or he's a parasite on society," he told all students.

"What is a social engineer?" was a question that was answered before any could ask. A social engineer was a highly skilled, perceptive, sensitive lawyer who understood the Constitution of the United States and knew how to explore its uses in the solving of "problems of . . . local communities" and in "bettering conditions of the underprivileged citizens." [1]

—GENNA RAE MCNEIL

# 29

# Dean of the Howard University School of Law

I became an active member of the American Bar Association's Section of Legal Education and Admission to the Bar in July 1977. By 1990, through my active and long-term participation in the Section of Legal Education's law school accreditation process, I had developed a national reputation as a person who was quite knowledgeable about American law schools and legal education in general. Sometime that year I was at my office in Department 22 of the Alameda County Superior Court in Oakland, California, when I received a call from Loretta Argrett, *née* Collins.

Loretta Collins[2] was an undergraduate schoolmate of mine at Howard University and had been queen of Beta Chapter of the Alpha Phi Alpha fraternity when I became a member of that organization during the 1956 spring semester. When we were in college together, she was also the girlfriend of James Argrett, who was dean of pledges when I pledged for the Alpha Phi Alpha fraternity. So I knew her quite well, although, as of 1990, I had neither seen nor spoken to her for more than three decades—probably not since 1957.

After graduating from Howard University with an undergraduate degree in chemistry, Loretta worked for several years as a chemist, mostly at various agencies of the U.S. government: the National Institutes of Health, the U.S. Food and Drug Administration, and the Walter Reed Army Institute of Research. But in 1973, she decided to change her career and applied for admission to law school. When she called me at the court in 1990, she had graduated from Harvard Law School and had for several years been a member of the full-time faculty at the Howard University School of Law.

At the time of her call, Loretta was a member of a search committee for a dean for Howard University School of Law. Loretta told me that the committee had decided that they needed to look for a dean who would be respected within legal education and enhance the law school's standing nationally. After some brief introductory "What have you been doing?" chitchat—remember, we had not spoken to each other for probably 30 years—she said she was going to ask me a question and that I could not say no: Was I willing to allow Howard University to consider me as a candidate for the position of dean of the Howard University School of Law? I told Loretta I would not object to being considered a candidate.

Although that was my decision, I do not mean to imply that it was a simple one. On the one hand, when Loretta called, I already knew that the programmatic situation at the Howard law school was not good. I was a personal friend of Daniel Bernstine, the interim dean, and therefore knew the school did not have a permanent dean. More important, I knew that according to the Accreditation Committee of the ABA Section of Legal Education and Admission to the Bar, the Howard University School of Law was having trouble complying with certain provisions of the ABA Standards for the Approval of Law Schools. Hence, I knew that the school's status as an ABA-approved law school was actually somewhat at risk. On the other hand, I did not have a clue about the quality of the faculty, the internecine faculty politics at the law school, or the commitment of university resources to the law school, all factors that would later prove to be extremely important.

To resign or retire from the court, leave my family,[3] and relocate to Washington, D.C., would require great personal and financial sacrifice. I truly enjoyed my position as a California Superior Court judge. It was then—and still is, in my mind—the best job I ever had, and I was not eager to leave. Additionally, the California judicial retirement system at the time I was appointed to the court was very generous if the retiring judge had served 20 years, and certainly not fewer than 12, at the time of retirement. I had served only 10 years.

If I retired with only 10 years' service, my retirement pay would be 37 percent of the salary of a sitting Superior Court judge. If I served 12 years it would be 45 percent, and it would be 75 percent if I served 20 years. So again, the move would be a great financial sacrifice. At the same time, I felt a deep sense of obligation to the Howard University School of Law. I was very much aware of the contributions made by several Howard law professors, several of the school's deans, and many of its graduates in the struggle for civil, political, and economic rights of black Americans.[4] I had personally benefited from that struggle.

I had separate, private discussions about Loretta's call with Eleanor, my wife, and with three colleagues and friends whom I highly respected: the Honorable Willie Lewis Brown Jr., who was then Speaker of the California Assembly; the Honorable Allen E. Broussard, who was then an associate justice of the California Supreme Court;[5] and the Honorable Clinton Wayne White, who was then chief judge, Division One, California First District Court of Appeal. In each instance, we fully discussed the sacrifices I would be making (leaving my family, interrupting if not abandoning my judicial career, and reducing my potential retirement pay), as well as the Howard law school's needs and what I could likely contribute–if I were offered and accepted the position. My wife and each of my colleagues advised me to accept the position if it were offered.

Not long after my conversation with Loretta, I was formally invited to visit the law school to meet and be interviewed by members of the law school community (administrators and selected alumni, faculty members, and students), by Dr. Joyce Ladner, who was then the university's vice president for academic affairs, and by Dr. Franklyn Jenifer, university president.

Of those interviews, the final one was with Dr. Jenifer. At the end of our discussion, he informally offered me the position as dean of the Howard University School of Law. After further discussion concerning compensation, I indicated that I would accept the offer if it were formally made. In a letter to me dated July 16, 1990, Dr. Jenifer confirmed his offer to appoint me dean of the Howard University School of Law, effective November 26, 1990. I accepted the offer in a letter dated July 17, 1990.

During the time we were both at Howard, I found Frank Jenifer to be intelligent, competent, and reasonably devoted to the university. In my judgment, however, he was not all that supportive or insightful concerning the law school. Joyce Ladner, on the other hand, was an exceptional administrator during her tenure as vice president for academic affairs and, later, as interim president of Howard. I found her to be extremely bright, energetic, accessible, committed, insightful, and supportive of the law school and of me as dean.

Many of the changes needed at the Howard University School of Law probably simply reflected a 15- or 20-year history of having deans who had had little or no previous law school administrative experience. Daniel Bernstine (the interim dean who served between Wiley Branton and me) did achieve certain positive changes at the law school with the help of associate deans Alice Gresham Bullock and Michael deHaven Newsom. The three were somewhat hampered in their efforts by the fact that everyone knew Bernstine was an interim dean and a permanent dean was being sought.

Nonetheless, Bernstine had seen to the retirement of two senior faculty members who had for many years been major barriers to law school progress. He and his associate deans had also managed to bring in five new faculty members, all good teachers, productive scholars, and good law school citizens: Andrew Gavil, Steven Jamar, George R. Johnson, Adam Kurland, and Andrew Taslitz. Bernstine and the associate deans also persuaded the law school faculty, the university president, and the Board of Trustees to reduce the entering class size from 150 to 100 students, thereby significantly lowering the school's student-faculty ratio, and to significantly strengthen the standards being used to admit students, especially the numerical predictors (undergraduate grade point averages and Law School Aptitude Test, or LSAT, scores).

Also—and of particular importance—during the deanship of J. Clay Smith, Howard University began making substantial financial aid funds available for law students, which allowed the School of Law to better compete with other ABA-approved law schools for African American applicants with strong numerical predictors. This financial support, the Merit Fellowship and Scholarship Program, provides substantial financial aid (up to $15,000 each year) for three years, as long as the student maintains a certain minimum academic average for each of those years.

I too had no previous law school administrative experience when I was appointed dean of the Howard law school, but I did have nearly 14 years of experience in law school accreditation as a member of the Accreditation Committee (one term as chairperson) and of the Council (one term as chairperson) of the ABA Section of Legal Education and Admission to the Bar, and as a site evaluator at several ABA-approved and Association of American Law Schools member institutions.[6] The Accreditation Committee was and is responsible for monitoring compliance with the ABA Standards for the Approval of American Law Schools,[7] which address, among other things, all material aspects of law school administration. Although less relevant, I had also been a member of the Boalt Hall full-time faculty for 10 years.

A few weeks before my permanent physical arrival at the law school in January 1991,[8] I wrote for myself a personal list of objectives for the first five years of my tenure:

## HOWARD UNIVERSITY SCHOOL OF LAW

13 December 1990

Some thoughts regarding what should indicate my success [or lack thereof] as Dean of the Howard University School of Law five years from now. . . . Henry Ramsey Jr.

### A. General

I.  Fund-raising:
1. Law school endowment:
   a. Obtain $200,000.00 match for endowed Chair in constitutional law.

b. Establish Club 500: contributions during calendar year 1991 of $1,000.00 each from at least 500 Howard law graduates and other friends of the Howard University School of Law. Money to be used to provide (1) match for endowed Chair in Constitutional Law, (2) endowment support for the alumni publication (*The Jurist*), (3) the Clyde C. Ferguson Lecture, and (4) the Moot Court Team.

c. Develop sufficient endowment for need-based financial aid (e.g., $10,000,000.00) such that, when coupled with available loan and grant monies, no first-year student will have to work during an academic term to pay for tuition, books and supplies, transportation, and living expenses. Also obtain endowment to support Moot Court Program

Second- and third-year students will not work more than 20 hours per week. There will be sufficient *law-related* jobs available so that second- and third-year students do not have to accept non-law-related jobs during academic terms.

d. "Veterans' Day." A major annual or bi-annual event (dinner) in Washington, D.C., to (1) raise significant monies for need-based financial aid and support of the Howard University School of Law public service effort, and (2) honor two Howard-trained lawyers for significant contributions to the civil rights movement and the achievement of freedom by black people—the William Hastie Award and the Thurgood Marshall Award.

e. Establish a Howard University School of Law Foundation to solicit, manage, and control law school endowment.

II. General personnel:

1. Computer Specialist on law school staff.

2. Administrative Officer position filled [Done Deal: March 1991]

3. Dean's support staff that is appropriate in size, organization, efficiency, and effectiveness.

III. Library:

[Talk with acting librarian about library staff, collection, and building needs.]

1. Substantial improvement of library services for students and faculty.
   a. Improve competence of professional and nonprofessional staff:
      (i) Professionalism
      (ii) Civility
      (iii) Helpfulness
   b. Improve library facility:
      (i) Access to collection
      (ii) Study space: carrels and reading room
   c. Enhance collection.

IV. Clinical programs:

1. Improve and expand existing clinics [criminal law, civil, equal employment, and labor law] to involve more students. [Talk with current Director of Clinical Programs, Dean Bullock, and Dan Bernstine re quality and scope of existing Clinical Program.]
2. Provide clinical legal services to D.C. poor:
   a. Juveniles
   b. Elderly [probate, landlord/tenant, and consumer protection] [(1) Talk with Chief Judge Fred Ugast about clinic offerings and relationship with D.C. Superior Court. (2) Talk with D.C. officials and Directors of Law Students in Court Program about legal services to D.C. poor. Will need "green light" from Vice President for Academic Affairs Ladner and President Jenifer. Clinical programs are costly when done right.]

V. Bar passage rate:
[If this isn't achieved, then I should resign as dean of the law school.] *Major improvement in bar passage rate in all states where Howard Law School graduates sit for the bar examination,* especially California, District of Columbia, Maryland, New York, Pennsylvania, and Virginia. GOAL: Howard law graduates taking the bar examination for the first time should do at least as well on any particular administration of the bar examination as the overall state average for first-time takers of that bar examination.

Develop programs and gain cooperation and support of students and faculty to achieve an excellent bar passage rate. The "How" must be developed in detail. This will be a major undertaking. We should be able to build on what has been done to date. Initial thoughts:

1. Students with stronger admission credentials
2. Stronger faculty
   a. Improved teaching
   b. More supportive of students
   c. Available to students on an individual and small group basis
3. Comprehensive academic support programs
4. Financial support while studying for the bar examination (first attempt only and within first year after graduation from law school)
5. Loan forgiveness for passing bar examination on first attempt [source of funds?]

VI. Faculty:

1. Support students:
   a. Teach well [always prepared, on time, and present for all classes].
   b. Be available for students immediately after class, during scheduled office hours, and at other appropriate times during the law school day.
   c. Take and display an interest in students who need more attention and additional academic support.
   d. Encourage students to do their best; instill confidence. Don't put students down. Be positive.

VI. Alumni:

1. Improve alumni relations overall.
2. Publish alumni magazine [*The Jurist*] three times each year –i.e., Fall (October–primary emphasis: Students), Winter (January–primary emphasis: Faculty), and Spring (May–primary emphasis: Alumni).

3. Alumni giving above the 40% level.

4. Alumni office.

VII.   Public interest emphasis:

1. Clinical externships

2. Independent study

3. Placement:
   a.  Summer clerkships
   b.  Permanent employment

4. Loan forgiveness for public interest and public service employment. [source of funds?]

VIII.   International programs:

1. Foreign-based instructional programs (e.g., summer abroad). [source of funds?]

2. Foreign visitors
   a.  Academics
   b.  Professionals
   c.  Exchange students

IX.   Plans for new Law School Building on or adjacent to main campus. [President Jenifer must be primary force here.]

## B. Law School Mission

The mission of the Howard University School of Law is:

To *train lawyers*, especially minority lawyers. Beyond their "legal" training, Howard law graduates should also be well informed about the struggle for civil rights in the United States. Additionally, they should recognize and appreciate the contributions of Howard law graduates to the civil rights movement.

To increase the annual number of *well-trained minority law graduates* who gain entry to the legal profession in the United States (i.e., pass the bar examination).

To significantly increase the number of *well-trained minority lawyers* serving the poor and involved in public service.

To provide an *opportunity for law study* to qualified college graduates, especially economically disadvantaged members of racial and ethnic minority groups.

*C. Questions:*

1. What is the Howard University School of Law *doing well?*
2. What is the Howard University School of Law *doing poorly or not doing at all, and therefore should*
   a. Stop doing.
   b. Start doing.
   c. Do differently.

My views regarding Howard law school's most immediate and urgent needs were based on my general knowledge of legal education at ABA-approved law schools, visits I had made to the Howard University School of Law, and discussions with various Howard law school administrators and faculty members since my appointment as dean. I had also had conversations with students and alumni.

On the one hand, some of the goals were unrealistic for a school with Howard's limited resources. An obvious example of an unrealistic goal was loan forgiveness. On the other hand, several changes were obviously needed and could be easily made. For example,

*Long-Distance Telephone Calls.* Members of the full-time faculty could not make long-distance telephone calls from their offices. One of the important needs of a law professor is to be able to confer easily with colleagues at other law schools in the United States and sometimes even in foreign countries. When I arrived at Howard as dean, to make a long-distance telephone call a faculty member had to go to the dean's office and request permission from the dean to make the call. If permission was granted, the faculty member would then give one of the secretaries in the dean's office the number to be called, and she would attempt to place the call. If the call went through, the faculty member would be directed to a small, closet-sized room adjacent to the dean's office to conduct the long-distance telephone conversation. This process, in my judgment, was inefficient, awkward, unnecessary, and—equally important—demeaning to every member of the full-time law faculty.

I was advised that this procedure was part of a mandatory university-wide policy intended to reduce costs. I quickly made an appointment with Ms. Wanda Gibson, who was then the director of information technology, and explained why I thought the policy was not in the best interest of the law school or the university. She was a very smart person and, after some discussion, agreed to permit law professors to make job-related long-distance calls from their offices without prior approval of the law school dean or anyone else.

*Student Personal Mailboxes.* If a professor, an administrator, another student, or a family member had an urgent need to contact a particular student, the only available means were using the regular mail; sending someone to a class where the student was scheduled to appear; posting a notice on a bulletin board (and hoping it would be seen); or asking a teacher, friend, or acquaintance of the student to give him or her a message, if and when that person saw the student. Notices of last-minute class changes and special programs had to rely mostly on "hit-or-miss" bulletin board postings.

Most if not all ABA-approved law schools provide each of their students with a personal "mailbox" (typically a small but reasonable-sized "cubby" space) that is conveniently located and can easily be checked throughout the day for letters and messages. Soon after my arrival at Howard, I used funds in the law school budget to have mailboxes installed in the student lounge, so that each Howard law student would have a personal mailbox.

*Individual Student Lockers.* The Howard University School of Law was and is still essentially an urban commuter campus. Although both the law school and the university campuses are in northwest Washington, D.C., the law school campus is at 2900 Van Ness Street NW, approximately three miles from the main campus at 2400 Sixth Street NW. Most Howard law students live a significant distance from the law school campus.[9] Therefore, students must bring their textbooks and other needed materials to school each day from home. At school, they had either to keep their books in the trunk of a parked automobile, assuming they had one (on-campus parking was limited, and even when parking was available, driving a car to school was especially daunting during inclement weather), or to store their books in one of a limited number of shared lockers.

A lottery was held each year to determine which students would be assigned space in a locker. And even with this sharing arrangement, more than a third of the law student body did not have access to a locker. Students who did not have an automobile or a shared locker had to carry their heavy law books around throughout the day. Thus, additional lockers were desperately needed.

I convinced the university administration that lockers were essential for our students and should be provided for in the next law school budget. Funds were allocated for that purpose, and sufficient lockers were purchased and installed in Holy Cross Hall to provide each law student with a personal locker. Floor space in Holy Cross Hall was specifically rearranged to accommodate the new lockers. There no longer would be any need for sharing.

Other problems were equally obvious, but their solutions were much more difficult and would take significantly more time to resolve:

*Financial Aid.* A critical issue at the law school when I arrived was the dreadfully late distribution of financial aid checks each semester. As is the case at many, if not most, American law schools, almost all Howard law students relied on government-guaranteed student loans as the principal means for financing their legal education. In some instances financial aid was the sole source of funds for tuition, room and board, and law books and other educational materials.

For several years, many of the Howard law students who were dependent on financial aid did not receive their *first* financial aid check until two or three months after the beginning of the fall semester. As difficult as it may be to believe, it was not at all unusual for some of those students to receive their *first* financial aid check for the fall semester as late as the middle of *the spring semester*, and there were confirmed cases of students not receiving their first financial aid check until April or May of the academic year. The negative effect of late financial aid checks on student morale and oftentimes academic performance cannot be overstated.

It quickly became clear to me that our monstrous financial aid problem stemmed from the simple fact that we did not have a financial aid officer. Dr. Ladner, vice president for academic affairs, and Dr. Jenifer, university president, agreed with my analysis, and a formal request that the university fund a new administrative position at the law school was quickly granted. The new position was advertised, applications were received, and interviews were conducted. Ms. Cathy Geier was hired in July 1991 as Howard law school's first financial aid officer.

The financial aid position was extremely demanding and soon was also subject to frequent criticism. Almost all of that criticism was totally unwarranted. Students who failed to conform to each of the various banking, government, and university regulations or requirements in submitting their student loan applications were generally reluctant to accept personal responsibility for their own fiascos and were quick to blame the financial aid officer. If a student was disqualified from receiving requested financial aid because of a particular rule or regulation, too often, in the student's mind, it was the financial aid officer's fault. Ms. Geier handled this difficult position competently and with aplomb. It was a terrible loss for Howard law school when she resigned her position in February 1996 to accept a position as associate director of financial aid at the American University School of Law, also in Washington, D.C.

When the spring 1991 semester opened I publicly made a promise to the Howard law school student body that every Howard law student who submitted a timely and properly completed financial aid application would receive his or her financial aid check during the first week of the 1992 spring semester, or I would resign as dean of the law school. This statement was neither a false promise nor an idle threat. I meant every word. Shortly after Ms. Geier reported for work at Howard we met in my office to discuss the financial aid crisis and, among other things, my expectations concerning her performance as the financial aid officer. I told her that I knew of no valid reason that past financial aid checks had not been distributed to Howard law students within one week of the commencement of the fall semester, as was typical at most, if not all, other ABA-approved law schools. I told her about my promise to the student body, and I told her that if she did not fulfill my promise of timely delivery of financial aid checks, my last act before submitting my resignation would be to fire her.

Cathy Geier did a great job as the law school's financial aid officer, and the checks for the 1992 spring semester—and for each semester thereafter—were delivered to law students receiving financial aid within the first week of each semester. My promise and threat had nothing to do with Ms. Geier's outstanding performance. She was a highly competent and dedicated professional, and we were very lucky to get her as our financial aid officer.

*Admission Application Material.* Information distributed by the Howard University School of Law in 1991 to prospective applicants for admission was decidedly unprofessional in appearance—merely a few mimeographed sheets of paper without any color print or graphics. The new material that Barbara Powell[10] (hired as administrative assistant to the dean), other members of my administration, and I developed was professionally designed and printed, with relevant pictures of student life at the law school, including classroom snapshots with faculty members, photos of administrators at work, and scenic pictures of the campus buildings and grounds. The cover of the new application packet was a rich dark blue and on quality stock.

Inside, along with detailed information about law school admission requirements and curricular offerings, were open letters from the university president and the law school dean warmly welcoming applications from prospective students. The new packet was a dramatic change from what the law school had previously provided, and I am convinced that it contributed materially to an increase in applications for admission received by the law school.

In addition to mailing the new material to prospective applicants who had requested application forms, we distributed the packet at the various law school admission forums held around the country. Black staff members from admissions offices at several historically white law schools congratulated me on the new materials. They told me that, as black people, they had for several years been personally embarrassed for Howard by the previous application materials. Just as Notre Dame is a source of pride for most Catholics, whether or not they have ever attended the school, so is Howard University a source of pride for most black Americans (and, indeed, many black foreigners), whether or not they have ever attended the university. The comments from black admissions officers and staff members at other universities should be understood in that context.

The Jurist. Before I was appointed dean, the law school had published two or three one-issue editions of a magazine named *The Jurist*. I think the very first issue was published during J. Clay Smith's tenure as dean. I thought the idea for an alumni magazine was a good one, but the quality of the previous issues left a great deal to be desired. Also, there was no regular publication schedule. I assigned to Dr. Barbara Powell responsibility for serving as editor of *The Jurist* and materially improving its quality. The results of her effort were spectacular and much appreciated by alumni, and by students and faculty as well.

Barbara produced at least three editions of *The Jurist* each academic year. It was basically a one-woman operation, although she did have the assistance of Wayne Rainey, an experienced graphics designer whom we retained as a consultant, and of Barbara Hart and her editorial services company, Publications Professionals. *The Jurist* now had a four-color cover, and the inside pages were printed on 80-pound matte Vintage Velvet paper. I suggested a new feature that Barbara liked and incorporated as a standard element of the magazine, namely having various alumni write an article—for each issue—about a former law school dean who made an outstanding contribution to civil rights or enhanced the reputation of the school for academic quality. She named this piece "Building the Legacy."

Another feature in each issue of the magazine was "Continuing the Legacy," about outstanding alumni and faculty members. Among the Howard law school graduates highlighted during my term as dean were Mahala Ashley Dickerson, Vernon E. Jordan Jr., Gabrielle Kirk McDonald, and Frank Wu, who was a member of the clinical faculty although not a Howard graduate. Two other popular sections were "Scenes from Howard Law," a photographic journal of various events at the law school, and the "Hearsay" section, which allowed alumni an opportunity to share with each other significant events in their lives since their law school graduation.

*Law School Bookstore.* When I arrived at Howard in January 1991, I was surprised to learn that there was not a bookstore at the law school and that law books were not even sold at the bookstore on the Howard University main campus. Howard law students had for many years purchased their books and other educational materials at Lerner's Bookstore, which was across the street from the Georgetown Law School campus—but approximately five miles from the Howard University School of Law. Needless to say, this trip was inconvenient for Howard law students. It also represented a substantial loss of revenue for the Howard University Bookstore. To have a bookstore at the law school seemed to me a win-win solution for the law school and the university bookstore. The bookstore manager soon agreed to stock and staff a law bookstore at the law school, provided space could be found for that purpose.

Holy Cross Hall was already being renovated pursuant to a plan developed under the leadership of the immediately preceding law school administration of Interim Dean Daniel Bernstine and associate deans Alice Bullock and Michael Newsom. Because I had already requested that plans be modified to accommodate the new student lockers we had ordered, it was a fairly simple matter to further alter those plans to provide space for a modest bookstore. In September 1992, renovations were complete, the store was stocked with law and other appropriate books, and a law bookstore staff was on duty.

The value of a bookstore to the law school community was obvious and generally much appreciated. Besides the immediate convenience of not having to travel five miles to purchase books, our law students would now be able to purchase Howard University and Howard law school memorabilia (T-shirts, jackets, mugs, book covers, pennants), just as students at other D.C. law schools were able to do at their campus bookstores. Howard material had not been available at Lerner's. Finally, there was simply the increased pride that Howard law school students, faculty, and administrative personnel took in having a bookstore of their own.

*The 500 Club.* In January or February 1991 I was invited to a meeting of the District of Columbia branch of the Howard University School of Law Alumni Association, where some officers of the law school's Moot Court Team delivered a presentation that saddened and embarrassed me.

We were told that, while the Howard Moot Court Team was a strong one and very competitive, it was seriously disadvantaged because it had no funds with which to travel to moot court tournaments outside of the Washington, D.C., metropolitan area. Even when the team members were themselves able and willing to pay the expense of attending an out-of-town tournament, there were no funds for the coach to attend.

As dean of the law school I was embarrassed that the students had to publicly beg for funds to support their team—and there was no way to describe their presentation other than as begging. I made some inquiries upon returning to the law school and learned that the students had not exaggerated the high quality of the team, the desperate need for financial support, or the material disadvantage caused by the lack of financial support from the law school or university. My inquiries also revealed that other important law school extracurricular activities were suffering because the law school and university provided either no or inadequate financial support.

I found it both appalling and incredible that the law school would sponsor programs such as the C. Clyde Ferguson Annual Lectures[11] and the Moot Court Team but would fail to provide sufficient funds for their support. Another shock came in learning that Howard University was one of three universities awarded a $200,000 matching grant from the U.S. Congress to endow a constitutional law chair at its law school but was the only one at risk of losing the grant because it had not raised any of the required matching funds.

Thus was put into practice my idea for a capital campaign to get 500 graduates and friends of the Howard University School of Law to contribute $1,000 or more each, thereby providing at least half a million dollars. The funds would be used to provide (a) the $200,000 in matching funds needed for the constitutional law chair, (b) a $240,000 endowment for the Moot Court Team, and (c) a $140,000 endowment to provide a speaking fee to each year's C. Clyde Ferguson lecturer.

It took two years to raise the $500,000, but we did it. Each contributor of $1,000 or more was promised that her or his name would be etched on a wooden block to be prominently displayed at the law school. On Sunday, May 13, 1994, a new section of a wall in the foyer of Charles H. Houston Hall was unveiled.[12] It held 409 etched wooden blocks with the name of each 500 Club member.[13]

The 500 Club funds were used as promised: to provide matching funds for the constitutional law chair, to establish an endowment dedicated to partially funding the Moot Court Team, and to provide funds for a fee to be paid each year's C. Clyde Ferguson lecturer.

*The Law School Budget.* In every proposal seeking increases in the law school budget for needed improvements, I included a plan explaining how the university would be able to afford what was proposed. Either the money was to be raised from outside sources or to be saved through modification of the existing budget—typically through elimination of an existing position or reorganization of an existing administrative component.

*Lack of Respect or Concern for Students by Certain Faculty Members.* A situation that I had no knowledge of when I was appointed dean of the law school—and, frankly, that I had not anticipated when considering the job—was what I can only describe as a mind-boggling lack of respect or concern for our students by several of the law school's senior faculty members. Those particular faculty members behaved as if the students should be grateful for being allowed to be in their presence or to breathe the same air as those self-anointed "great" men (and they were all men).

One example of this attitude involved the previously discussed new bookstore on the law school campus. Not long after the bookstore was established, the store manager came to see me. One of our senior faculty members had refused to give the manager the names and authors of books that the professor planned to use in his courses for the coming semester. He told the bookstore manager that he would continue to list his books with Lerner's Bookstore, notwithstanding the five-mile trek his students would have to make to shop at Lerner's. I went to see the faculty member, who unashamedly told me that because no one had asked him whether a bookstore should be established at the law school, he would continue to list his books at Lerner's.

I could not believe my ears. I made it clear that his position would not be tolerated. After some argument, he finally agreed to provide the Howard law school bookstore with the needed information.

But his attitude reflected a more general problem that was also implied by the conduct of several other senior faculty members. Consistently, their behavior implied that students weren't all that important in the scheme of things and that what mattered was how much deference students and administrators paid to faculty members, especially senior faculty members.

This lack of concern for students was also reflected in several problems that I have previously discussed: financial aid, the absence of student mailboxes at the law school, and the totally inadequate number of student lockers at a law school whose entire student body lived off campus. The absence of those facilities, to my mind, reflected the lack of concern for overall student welfare displayed by many of the Howard law school faculty members and administrators. They should have seen the needs and been at the forefront of an effort to address them. There may have been other explanations for such circumstances that did not reflect negatively on law school faculty members and administrators. But to my mind, the explanation I have offered is the correct one.

*Admission to Law School and the Bar.* There was a dramatic downturn in the overall numerical predictors of students admitted to Howard between the early 1970s and the early to mid-1980s. I am convinced, on the basis of my personal knowledge of the circumstances at Howard well before Dan Bernstine or I arrived, that this downturn stemmed primarily from a flawed understanding of the law school's mission by senior faculty members and, probably, by some of the administrators who were responsible for determining and implementing the admission policies of the law school.

An important, if not the only, mission of the Howard University School of Law during the period of Jim Crow and overt racial discrimination in legal education was to provide an educational opportunity for students denied admission by white law schools—primarily state-funded law schools in the South—because of their race. Many outstanding black students who were denied admission to public and private law schools in their home state or region solely because of their race received their legal education at the Howard University School of Law and went on to have outstanding legal careers. I suppose the most famous example from that period was U.S. Supreme Court Associate Justice Thurgood Marshall, a resident of Maryland who was admitted to and attended Howard law school after being denied admission to the University of Maryland Law School because he was black.

So it was the case that for many years Howard had the good fortune to have its pick of exceptional black students interested in law, simply because there was little competition for those students by the nation's predominantly white law schools, especially those located in the old Confederate South. Howard University correctly and fortunately saw its mission and responsibility as providing an opportunity for a first-rate legal education to those hundreds of young black men and women who were being wrongfully denied a legal education by many, if not most, of the nation's predominantly white law schools. At that time in our nation's history, those institutions included *all* of the nation's white law schools in what had been the Confederate South.

In 1969, after the assassination of Martin Luther King Jr. in 1968 and well after the 1954 U.S. Supreme Court decision in *Brown v. Board of Education*,[14] many of the nation's public and private exclusively or predominantly white law schools adopted affirmative action admission programs. These schools began to aggressively recruit black students, particularly those with strong academic records and solid LSAT scores. In many cases, black and other law school applicants of color were recruited with offers of substantial grants and loans.

In this changed context, a new and different class of black students would be denied admission to many of the same white schools where other black students had been denied admission before affirmative action. But now many of the black students were being denied admission not explicitly because of race but because of noncompetitive numerical predictors–primarily their LSAT scores but also their undergraduate grade point averages, their weak transcripts, and the perceived quality of the college they had attended.

I am convinced that key faculty members at the Howard University School of Law honestly believed that the school should continue to offer admission to black students who were being denied admission to historically white law schools regardless of the changed circumstances.[15]

Moreover, many law professors showed a reluctance to fail such students after they had been admitted to the Howard law school. This reluctance, in my judgment, resulted in a substantial increase in the percentage of Howard law school graduates failing the bar examination in whatever jurisdictions they took it. Howard is a national law school with students from throughout the country, and its graduates may take the bar examination in any number of jurisdictions, including California, the District of Columbia, Florida, Illinois, Maryland, New York, Pennsylvania, Texas, and Virginia.

On May 10, 1991, after I had physically been at the law school as dean for about five months, I submitted a draft mission statement to the faculty for their consideration and, I hoped, adoption, at a scheduled faculty retreat. The following was my proposed mission statement (with some minor edits):

MISSION OF THE HOWARD UNIVERSITY SCHOOL OF LAW

*A.*

The mission of the Howard University School of Law, like that of any American law school, includes more than one purpose or objective. Any meaningful discussion of the law school's "mission" must of necessity involve consideration of several objectives. Any mission statement of the Howard University School of Law should list [the following] as principal goals:

1. Teaching Howard University law students to be competent lawyers.
2. Significantly increasing the number of well-trained black and other minority members of the legal profession.
3. Providing an opportunity for law study to qualified college graduates who otherwise would not have that opportunity, especially disadvantaged members of minority groups that have been discriminated against historically because of their race or skin color.
4. Significantly increasing the number of well-trained lawyers serving the poor and otherwise involved in public service.

The importance and vitality of such objectives cannot be clearly seen if they are merely viewed in the abstract. The mission of the law school has meaning only to the exact degree that the dean and faculty understand and embrace it. When one asks what is the mission of the Howard University law school, the inquiry is really about the responsibilities and duties of the dean and faculty: What must the dean and faculty do in order to achieve the objectives of the law school? To what goals must they be committed? And with what purpose or purposes must their conduct and programs be consistent?

*B.*

The primary objective of the Howard University School of Law is to teach its students to be competent lawyers. In the law school bulletin and other materials provided for prospective applicants and newly admitted students, it is implicitly if not explicitly promised that those who elect to study law at Howard University will receive a sound legal education which fully prepares them to pass the bar examination and enter the legal profession. Fulfillment of that pledge has to be the school's highest priority.

Even if the law school's primary mission were to be characterized as producing *black or minority* lawyers, that objective still could not be achieved unless our graduates pass the bar examination. Simply put, one cannot become an American lawyer until he or she passes a bar examination.

## C.

A second part of the law school's mission is to increase the number of well-trained black and other minority lawyers and judges. The need and desire of black and other minority students to gain a legal education is just as great in 1991 as it was in 1951, 1941, and 1931. Howard University has a long and distinguished tradition of affording all black men and women of exceptional ability an opportunity to receive a first-rate legal education and to gain entry to the legal profession. It is critical that the law school continue to embrace this moral trust and to deeply commit itself to advancing this tradition.

There are two major needs within American society that provide extraordinary opportunities for Howard law graduates. One need is for lawyers who are prepared to aid in community development and in the political and economic empowerment of black and other people of color. The other is the continuing need for new, exemplary, and courageous leadership in the struggle for political, social, and economic justice for all Americans. I believe it is a responsibility of the Howard law school to prepare its students to take advantage of those opportunities for both professional success and public service.

On the one hand, the business opportunities and legal service needs of minority entrepreneurs and professionals have increased dramatically since 1954, when *Brown v. Board of Education of Topeka et al.* was decided.[16] It is the well-trained Howard lawyer who should be providing legal counsel to the many small businesses that are now being formed and succeeding within the American economy. The Howard lawyer should be in the vanguard of those providing legal services to individuals and companies trying to do business abroad, especially in the Caribbean and black Africa. Howard should also be the primary source of exceptionally well-trained lawyers to meet the demand for black lawyers in private law firms, public law offices, corporate legal departments, and on American law faculties.

Although many of the "Jim Crow" conditions, circumstances, and evils with which Charles Hamilton Houston, William Hastie,

Oliver W. Hill, Thurgood Marshall, and Althea Simmons had to contend have in great measure been overcome, racism is still alive and well in America. The "form" may have materially changed and, to a certain extent, the substance also, but black Americans still daily bear the disabling effects of more than three centuries of racial hostility and neglect of people of color.

Both American society and the minority communities have a profound need for minority lawyers and judges. This law school must now, as it has in the past, continue to assume responsibility for producing first-rate minority lawyers to provide the leadership and creativity necessary to challenge the existing racial climate in the United States and to change it for the better. The Howard University School of Law should provide an academic environment and curricular offerings that expose every law student at Howard to the significance of civil rights for all Americans, especially for members of minority groups.

At the same time that the black middle class is growing in absolute numbers and as a force within the American political economy, there has been an even more dramatic increase in the number of black people—individuals and families—living in poverty.

Thanks in great measure to the vision and effort of Charles Hamilton Houston, Howard law school graduates have always been—and continue to be—in the front ranks of those providing leadership in the continuing struggle for social, economic, and political justice in every corner of American society. Today that leadership is no longer limited to a counsel table in the courtroom and to community meetings, but it actually sits in a governor's chair, in the United States Senate, on the United States Supreme Court, and on the supreme courts of several states, as well as in the State Attorney General's chair and that of the United States Attorney. It must be the mission of the Howard law school to continue and expand those models of leadership.

It is important to note that the leadership that Howard law graduates have provided and can still provide the nation is not limited to serving the interests of black people. The courage and efforts of Howard-trained lawyers have resulted in increased civil and political rights, increased access to higher education, and increased economic opportunities for all Americans. Among the many civil rights cases that were fought on behalf of and by black Americans and that laid the foundation stone for civil rights of others are *UAW v. Johnson Controls*, 11 S. Ct. 1196 (1991), and *Hishon v. King and Spalding*, 467 U.S. 69 (1984) [employment opportunities for women]; *Int'l. Ass'n. of Firefighters v. City of Cleveland*, 478 U.S. 501 (1982) [employment opportunities for Hispanics]; *Plyler v. Doe*, 457 U.S. 202 (1982) [educational opportunities for non-citizens]; *Mississippi University for Women v. Hogan*, 417 U.S 718 (1982) [educational opportunities for white males]; and *Ted W. Brown, et al. v. Socialist Workers '74 Campaign Committee (Ohio) et al.*, 459 U.S. 87 (1982) [rights of members of political parties].

Accomplishing this mission of increasing the number of well-trained black and other minority lawyers and judges, of course, will require the education and training of law graduates who are capable of passing the bar examination. But I believe it is implicit in this second objective that Howard University will aggressively recruit and admit not only those who will be so capable, but also the best and brightest of those black and other minority applicants who apply for admission to law school. If one of our objectives is to train leaders, then we must seek to enroll those who we believe can achieve leadership.

## D.

Of equal importance is the responsibility of the Howard University School of Law to provide an opportunity for law study to qualified college graduates, especially economically disadvantaged members of racial and ethnic minority groups who have been the victims of discrimination based upon race and skin color. Although it is important that only students with a realistic chance of benefiting from a Howard University legal education be admitted, it is also important that we develop admission criteria that can reliably identify minority students who have low numerical predictors but are still quite capable of successful law study.

Howard University presently receives approximately 64 percent of its budget from the United States Congress. This federal patronage has to be premised upon the notion that it is justified and still needed as a special means for providing access to higher education for a subgroup within our society that continues to suffer from the consequences of centuries of racial discrimination that was sanctioned by law and custom. It is, therefore, incumbent upon the Howard University School of Law, as a beneficiary of that federal support, to adopt and implement an admission policy that affords the broadest possible opportunity for law study to members of the endangered class.

### E.

It is also the mission of the Howard law school to significantly increase the number of well-trained minority lawyers who serve the poor and are otherwise involved in public service. For an institution founded to serve a great public need, it would be ironic indeed if, at a time when majority institutions are emphasizing preparation of their graduates for public service, the Howard University School of Law should neglect or even ignore this important responsibility of the profession.

A strong case can also be made in support of the proposition that the need for lawyers committed to public service is even greater in the minority community. It is commonly known that racial and ethnic minority groups are much more likely to suffer consumer fraud, landlord-tenant problems, employment discrimination, denial of constitutional, statutory, and regulatory rights, and the like than their majority counterparts. Howard University is identified with defending the oppressed and is known for service to the needy. It is this reputation that distinguishes Howard from many other American universities. Our mission should reflect that trust and tradition.

### F.

Finally, while the focus of the above discussion is on black and other minority students, it should always be remembered that Howard University, although it was "particularly established with funds from the federal government to aid in the higher education of freed and free blacks,"[17] has been open from its beginning to all qualified people regardless of race or gender. Therefore, consistent with the sound educational principle of maintaining a diverse student body, its admission policy should rest upon the ethic of offering a quality legal education to all persons whose enrollment will serve to meet the goals of the institution.

The faculty did not adopt my proposed mission statement at the retreat, nor was it ever adopted. But I still think it reflects what should have been and even today should be the mission of the Howard University School of Law.

My deepest regret concerning my tenure as dean of the Howard University School of Law is that I and my administrative team were unable to increase the first-time bar passage rate of our graduates to a level where it was comparable to the leading law schools in our immediate area, schools such as American University, Catholic University, Georgetown, and George Washington. Significant progress was made in raising the passage rate above the lows that were being experienced before my arrival. But our graduates never achieved a first-time bar passage rate higher than 71 percent of those taking the examination at any time during my tenure as dean. That percentage was for the summer 1994 bar examinations. In all other years, the percentage was less than 70 percent, and in a couple of years, it was slightly below 60 percent.

This failure to achieve an acceptable first-time bar passage rate was certainly not for lack of effort. At each year's orientation for entering students, I would emphasize in my remarks to them the importance of passing the bar examination, the fact that each of them could pass a bar examination, and that they could do so on the first try. I would tell them that with hard work, especially during the first and second years, each person could be confident that he or she would pass the bar on the first attempt.

I was, and still am, firmly of the view that bar passage has little if anything to do with race. To successfully pass the bar examination requires adequate bar preparation, diligent study throughout one's law school years, and the academic support provided by the law school. I readily acknowledge that students admitted with low numerical predictors need additional and special resources. In that regard, each year we invited the executive director of the Committee of Bar Examiners for the state of Maryland to talk with our students about subjects covered on the Maryland bar examination, the structure of the examination, and how it was scored.

We also established a six-week bar support program in the spring of 1992 that was offered to all graduating students during the summer of that year and before they were to take the bar examination. Dean Denise Spriggs[18] was responsible for implementing this program. A modest fee of $35 was charged to cover the cost of written materials distributed during the course. Our bar support program was based on Minority Legal Education Resources Inc. (MLER) of Chicago, a program established in 1978 by Professor Ronald Kennedy at Chicago's Northwestern Law School[19] in response to historically low bar passage rates among African Americans and other minority candidates for the Illinois bar. Like that program, our Howard University Bar Support Program (HUBSP) focused on (a) improvement of study habits, (b) effective time management, (c) examination-taking techniques, (d) essay-writing skills, (e) stress management, and (f) development of self-confidence. Our course was intended as a supplement to the standard commercial bar preparation courses, like the BAR/BRI courses,[20] that the students were obligated to take concurrently with our bar support program. The HUBSP, as structured during my tenure as dean, is no longer being offered by the Howard law school. I am still at a loss as to why the HUBSP did not have a greater effect on our student bar passage rate.

The list of improvements that did occur on my decanal watch included the following:

*Construction of New Classrooms.* One law school classroom (Classroom 3) had been designed and constructed in such a way that load-bearing posts obstructed the view of many students sitting in the rear of the room. They had difficulty seeing the professor, other students seated toward the front of the room, and the blackboard. The posts also obstructed the professor's view of many students in the back half of the classroom. That design certainly did not conform to ABA accreditation standards.[21]

Some renovations at the law school had been designed, approved, funded, and begun even before I was hired as dean, but they did not address the problem of Classroom 3. After consulting with associate deans Alice Bullock and Michael Newsom and the university engineer responsible for monitoring the renovations then under way (the new dean's suite, which included a new bathroom, as well as the renovation of Notre Dame Hall), I requested that Classroom 3 be demolished and that two new and larger classrooms be constructed as an addition to Notre Dame Hall.

The engineer and the building contractor were both confident that the footprint of Classroom 3 could easily accommodate two new rooms. This proposed change was approved by the law school and supported by Dr. Joyce Ladner, vice president for academic affairs. President Franklyn Jenifer and the Howard University Board of Trustees ultimately approved the change, and the two new large classrooms were constructed.

*Larger Entering Class.* I also suggested at that time that the size of each year's entering class be increased by 50 students (50 percent). The resulting increase in tuition would generate sufficient additional income to more than pay for the two new classrooms. This suggestion was approved by the law school faculty and the university administration, and the increase in class size resulted in an additional $1.5 million income to the university annually.

*Increases in Faculty Salaries.* At my insistence, a substantial increase in faculty salaries was achieved in 1995. This brought faculty salaries at the Howard law school in line with faculty salaries at other law schools in the metropolitan area of the District of Columbia and brought us into conformance with the ABA accreditation standard that required ABA-approved law schools to hire and retain a highly competent faculty.[22] The support of then Acting President Joyce Ladner was critical. Both Dr. Ladner and Wayman Smith, who was then chairman of the Board of Trustees, promised the ABA Section of Legal Education and Admission to the Bar that faculty salaries would be significantly increased and that a new law school library would be constructed. Faculty salaries were soon increased. The new law library was built after I left, but preparations for its design had commenced before I left.

*New Faculty Furniture.* The furniture in faculty offices was old, well worn, and inconsistent in style, age, size, and type among the various offices. For a more professional setting, new desks, credenzas, and office chairs were purchased for each faculty office, except for those of two senior faculty members who said they were perfectly happy with the furniture they had and would not accept new furniture.

*Administrative Reorganization.* When I arrived at Howard as the law school dean, there was no professional admissions officer. Two people shared the position of associate dean (without specific portfolio); another person served as assistant dean of student affairs. One of the two associate deans was primarily concerned with academic matters and the other with student affairs. It seemed to me that this arrangement involved a serious duplication of effort, in that there was also an assistant dean for student affairs. Therefore, I proposed that the existing budget position of dean of students be eliminated and the position of associate dean be formally divided, one of the individuals sharing the position to become associate dean for academic affairs (faculty and curriculum), and the other to become associate dean for student affairs. Two other assistants to the dean were responsible for preparing and monitoring the budget and for procurement of supplies and materials. I saw no reason that one person could not perform both functions; hence, one position was eliminated.

Those and other staffing changes freed up funds that could be used to significantly increase the efficiency and professionalism of the law school's administrative services, without requiring any additional funds from the university. A new position of assistant dean for admissions was created. A new position of registrar was created and assigned responsibility for the maintenance and security of academic records.

Before this reorganization, the law school administrative structure was as follows:

- Associate dean for academic affairs
- *Associate dean for student affairs*
- Assistant dean for student affairs[23]
- *Two administrative assistants to the dean*[24]
- *Admissions coordinator*
- *Records coordinator*
- Director of placement and alumni affairs

The reorganization eliminated five positions, in italics above,[25] and significantly increased the number of professional[26] administrative staff members. The reorganized administrative staff was comprised of the following positions (with new and previously unfilled positions in italics):

- Associate dean for academic affairs
- *Assistant dean for student affairs and records*
- *Records specialist*
- One administrative assistant to the dean
- *Administrative officer*
- *Assistant dean and director of admissions*
- *Admissions specialist*
- *Financial aid officer*
- Director of career services[27]
- *Systems manager*[28]

This administrative reorganization freed up significant money that was used to hire professionals to fill certain of those positions—new and old.

*Clinical Law Program.* Reorganization of Howard's clinical law program is one of my proudest accomplishments as dean of the Howard law school. When I arrived in January 1991, the clinical law program at Howard University was not very well organized or supported financially. In fact, in my judgment the clinical program at that time was unworthy of its name. Only one full-time faculty member—Donald Golden—was assigned to the clinic, and he was not devoting much attention or energy to it. There were also two adjunct clinical law teachers, but they were also full-time practicing lawyers with their own private practices.

Shortly after my arrival at the law school, clinical program students began streaming into my office, complaining about the lack of faculty supervision of their work and the two adjunct professors' lack of professionalism. One of the first projects I assigned to Dr. Barbara Powell after hiring her was to interview all students enrolled in the law school who were taking or had taken the clinic. She was asked to get the students' confidential comments about their experiences as clinical students and their assessments of the program and its faculty. I also personally interviewed many of the students about their clinical experiences. Clinical student comments to Dr. Powell and to me were mostly negative.

I suspended the clinical law program for spring semester 1992 and embarked on a reorganization plan. I had learned that the U.S. Congress had funded clinical programs at three ABA-approved law schools. It was the intent of the Congress that those federally funded clinical law programs serve as models for other American law schools for establishing or improving clinical programs at their schools. I sought approval from Dr. Joyce Ladner, by then acting president of Howard University, to explore the possibility of the

Howard University School of Law becoming a federally funded clinical law center. Dr. Ladner promised her support, so we began our campaign for congressional approval of a clinical law center at the Howard University School of Law.

Our effort was successful, and the U.S. Congress passed legislation providing $5.5 million for Howard University (a) to establish a clinical law center and (b) to use $4.5 million of the appropriation as an endowment to provide permanent support for three full-time, tenure-track, clinical faculty positions. Because one full-time clinical position was already authorized in the law school budget, we would now be in a position to fund four full-time clinical faculty positions.

Several members of the Howard University and Howard law school community contributed substantially to the success of our effort. It would be impossible to overstate the support, guidance, and insights provided by Dr. Hassan Minor, then vice president for government relations and Howard's primary liaison with the U.S. Congress regarding budgetary matters. Dr. Minor was absolutely brilliant in conceptualizing, organizing, and successfully executing our campaign strategy for the law school to be designated a federally funded clinical law center.

William A. "Buddy" Blakey, a 1968 graduate of the Howard University School of Law and a prominent and respected District of Columbia lobbyist, was also of invaluable assistance. Buddy gave us great advice and provided significant guidance as we worked with certain members of the U.S. Congress and their staffs. His assistance was especially valuable with regard to the House. I should mention that Buddy Blakey was also supportive of my other efforts at the law school throughout my tenure as dean. For that support, I was and remain very appreciative.

Joyce Ladner, in her capacity as acting president of the university, was tireless in her support of our endeavor to establish the clinical law center. Congressman Neal Smith (D-Iowa) provided essential congressional leadership in the House Education and

Labor Committee. He was also a member of the Committee on Appropriations and an acting chairman of the Subcommittee on Labor, Health and Human Service, and Education. The help of Congressman Louis Stokes (D-Ohio), a member of the Committee on Appropriations, and Congresswoman Eleanor Holmes Norton (D-D.C.) was essential. Our effort also received meaningful support from Congressman Barney Frank (D-Massachusetts).

Ms. Joyce Clements-Smith, who worked in Dr. Minor's office; Professor George Johnson Jr., who was then the law school's associate dean for academic affairs; Dr. Barbara Powell, the executive assistant to the law school dean; and Alice Gresham Bullock, the former associate dean for academic affairs at the law school,[29] all worked exceptionally hard to gain federal funding for and establish the new clinical law program at Howard University School of Law.

After passage of the legislation and the university's receipt of the funds needed to establish the clinical law center, I proposed—and the law faculty, university president, and university Board of Trustees approved—the establishment of such a center at the Howard University School of Law. A search was conducted for a director, and Professor Homer C. LaRue[30] was appointed—effective January 1, 1995—as the first director of the Howard University Clinical Law Center. Besides Professor LaRue, the first tenure-track clinical faculty members of the new and reformed clinic were Peter A. Krauthamer, assistant professor, and Sharon Styles-Anderson and Frank Wu, associate professors.

The first of the newly organized clinics of the center covered criminal justice litigation (12 credits) and a civil law of the elderly clinic (six credits). We also participated in a program called D.C. Law Students in Court. It was my expectation that when all of the faculty positions were filled, we would also offer clinical instruction in the areas of equal employment law and labor law. In addition, we established a public justice institute, which placed students in internships.

*Howard South Africa Summer Abroad Program.* Nelson Mandela was freed in February 1989, after more than 27 years' imprisonment. About five years later, on April 26-28, 1994, the first free and fair elections were held in South Africa. Those events and the struggle leading up to them caused many people throughout the United States, especially many African Americans, to develop a keen interest in South Africa. Many wanted to and did visit South Africa after the elimination of apartheid. Indeed, Kenneth Harlan Simmons, one of my very best friends, actually emigrated to South Africa in 1995 and became a permanent resident in 2000. He now teaches part-time in the School of Architecture and Planning at the University of Witwatersrand in Johannesburg.

Associate Professor Ziyad Motala, a native of South Africa who teaches at the Howard University law school, had been personally involved in the struggle against apartheid in his country. Ziyad Motala first came to Howard in 1992 as a visiting professor from Chicago Kent School of Law, at the invitation of then Associate Dean George Johnson Jr. He became a full-time, tenure-track faculty member at the Howard law school in August 1994.

Professor Motala received a bachelor of arts degree in November 1983 and a bachelor of laws degree (LL.B.) in November 1985, both from the University of Natal in Durban, South Africa. He has a master's degree in law (LL.M), granted in August 1987, and a doctoral degree in law (S.J.D.), granted in 1991, both from Northwestern School of Law.

Professor Motala has an extensive network of professional colleagues throughout South Africa—within the African National Congress, the South African court system, and the South African parliament, as well as among progressive legal educators and practicing lawyers. He has taught courses on American constitutional law, international business transactions, comparative law, international law, comparative race relations in the United States and South Africa, and international moot court.

George Johnson Jr., Denise Mitchell,[3i] Ziyad Motala, and I traveled to South Africa in December 1994 to try to persuade the Honorable Dullah Omar, who was the South African minister of justice, and the local office of the U.S. Agency for International Development to contract with the Howard law school to provide judicial training for South African trial judges. The proposed training was to cover delay reduction and trial management (my area of expertise) and constitutional litigation (Ziyad and George's area of expertise). We included the constitutional litigation component in our proposal because all South African judges then sitting had been trained and performed their judicial services under apartheid. For them to function under the new South African Constitution—which now contained provisions that focused on individual liberty, human rights, civil rights, and political rights—it was critical that the judges be educated about such topics.

During this trip to South Africa, George and I were able to observe the legal education structure in the Western Cape, the facilities and faculty structure at the University of the Western Cape, and the local housing stock. Ziyad was already familiar with this infrastructure. On our return to the United States, we revived a discussion we had had two years earlier regarding the possibility of establishing a summer abroad law program in South Africa.

As a longtime member of the Council and of the Accreditation Committee of the American Bar Association's Section of Legal Education and Admission to the Bar, I knew that many ABA-approved law schools had summer abroad programs in various foreign countries. In fact, I had served as an ABA site evaluator of several separate summer abroad programs offered in Argentina, China, England, Germany, Hungary, Japan, and Singapore.

Because Ziyad was now a full-time faculty member and no longer a visitor, I authorized him to proceed with developing his original idea for a summer abroad program in South Africa. The proposal developed by Ziyad, in consultation with George Johnson

Jr. and me, was submitted to and unanimously adopted by the full-time law faculty at a faculty meeting on October 5, 1995. George, Ziyad, and I later met with Howard University President Patrick Swygert and received his enthusiastic support for the proposal.

I made a subsequent trip to South Africa, February 11–20, 1996,[32] where I again scrutinized the facilities and other university support that would be available for students and faculty members of the summer abroad program. While there, I negotiated a draft memorandum of understanding between the University of the Western Cape and Howard University, to establish (a) a Howard University summer abroad law school program at the University of the Western Cape, (b) a limited faculty exchange program between the two schools, and (c) a student exchange program between the schools. The memorandum of understanding was signed by leading administrators of the University of the Western Cape while I was there: P.C. Smit, dean of the University of the Western Cape faculty of law, and C.A. Abrahams, rector of the University of the Western Cape. On my return to the United States, after the document had been approved by the Howard law school faculty, I presented it to President Patrick Swygert, who signed the document on behalf of Howard University on April 15, 1996.

I do not think the faculty exchange or student exchange programs described in the memorandum of understanding were ever fully implemented. ABA approval of the summer abroad program, however, was applied for and received during the spring semester of 1996. Ziyad Motala organized and implemented the first Howard University summer abroad program in South Africa at the University of the Western Cape, Cape Town, South Africa, and it was held from June 22-August 1, 1996.

Dean Harry E. Groves, professor emeritus of the School of Law of the University of North Carolina and a highly experienced ABA site evaluator, conducted a comprehensive site visit during July 8-10 of that summer on behalf of the ABA Section of Legal Education and Admission to the Bar. Dean Groves made the following comments in his report to the Accreditation Committee and Council of the ABA Section of Legal Education and Admission to the Bar:[33]

> The program was not only operating effectively at the time of my visit, it was the most effectively administered of a number of programs I have visited over a span of years. . . .
> The summary word for this program is that it was excellent. I have at no other program encountered such universally pleased students. I really do not know how the program could have been improved. It was well conceived, well planned, and brilliantly executed. The use of the director's and one of the professors' remarkable contacts with the highest levels of government and with the University [of the Western Cape] gave the program a richness no student could have anticipated and for which every student to whom I spoke expressed profound gratitude.

The Howard University summer abroad program was held each summer thereafter during my tenure as dean. The program was fully subscribed by students, and a small profit was made during each summer of its existence. In other words, the program never experienced a financial loss.

Professor Motala announced in May 2003 that he was resigning as director of the summer abroad program, effective August 2004. He told me that one reason for his resignation was that various administrative offices at Howard were not providing the support required to maintain an efficient and effective program, notwithstanding the fact that the summer abroad program had been successful in every respect during each year of its existence. No program was held in 2004, but in August 2004, Kurt Schmoke, the new law school dean, persuaded Professor Motala to resuscitate the program for summer 2005. The program has been operational each summer since.

Not all of my time at Howard was devoted to solving serious problems or even to dealing with the day-to-day grunt work required for competent management of a law school (or any other institution or unit of higher education). During my stay I had several challenging, exhilarating, and personally gratifying opportunities to engage in creative and meaningful undertakings. These brought me a great deal of personal satisfaction because they substantially enhanced the overall importance and value of the Howard law school and its educational program.

They included, for example, these efforts:

*Student Dinners.* Each year I would personally cook a series of dinners for groups of 10 of the Howard first-year and third-year law students. The first-year dinners gave the new students and me an opportunity to get to know each other in an informal setting. "Dinner with the Dean" was held at my house, at Barbara Powell's[34] house, or at the home of one of the first-year law teachers (which also allowed the students to meet informally with one of their teachers). I cooked either pasta (usually fettuccine or spaghetti) with my "secret" sauce or chicken lo mein.

Initially, the dinners were for first-year students in the fall semester and for third-year students in the spring semester. After the first year of "Dinner with the Dean," I reversed the order. The idea was to get to know the students and to learn what they were thinking about the law school at the beginning of their careers as law students (first-year) and at the end of law school (third-year). It also afforded me an opportunity to discuss with them their responsibility to act professionally—to begin to act like lawyers—and to discuss their right to hold the faculty and me accountable for providing them with a quality legal education. The discussions were open-ended and unrestricted. The students were asked to speak candidly and tell me what they liked about the school and what they did not like.

*Lecture Series.* The Dean's Lecture Series is a program of which I am still very proud. The basic idea was that we should take advantage of the law school's location in the nation's capital and bring to the campus prominent and influential members of the bar and bench to interact with, stimulate, and motivate our students. Each year, several members of the legal profession were invited to the law school to talk with students about their personal history, their professional career, and their thoughts about how today's law students (especially African Americans) could make a difference in the legal profession and could contribute positively to our community and country.

The Howard University School of Law's annual admission brochure announced and provided a brief biography of each person who had been invited to lecture that academic year. The following statement—published in the 1995-1996 admission brochure—is typical of the one I wrote for each year's brochure:

> The Dean's Lecture Series is designed to provide a unique opportunity for students at Howard University School of Law to hear, in an informal setting, presentations from some of the nation's most prominent lawyers, academics, judges, and political figures. Those people are making a difference in our society. Speakers in this series conduct wide-ranging discussions on legal and political issues and frequently provide personal recollections about some of the landmark cases or issues in which they played significant roles.

I wish my core idea of providing students contact with major figures in the legal profession had been an original one, but it was not. My idea for a Dean's Lecture Series at the Howard law school actually came from a program that was held at the University of California at Riverside when I was an undergraduate there. Prominent writers, philosophers, and the like were from time to time invited to the UC Riverside campus, where they simply sat in a seminar room or small lecture hall for a specified period of time, and students could stop by and talk with them. I am certain that they had other interactions with the academic community while on campus, but it was those open sessions with students that I remember. For example, I will always remember a session where I had the opportunity to discuss with Eric Hoffer the philosophical views that he had published in *The True Believer*.[35]

The lectures held at Howard were always delivered in the law school's moot courtroom,[36] and most were well attended. Time was always reserved for student questions. An impressive group of people accepted our invitation to be Dean's Lecturer at the Howard law school and to interact with our students. Among the lecturers during my tenure as dean were the following:

- The Honorable ROLAND W. BURRIS, Class of '63, attorney general of the state of Illinois
- The Honorable DREW S. DAYS III, U.S. solicitor general
- The Honorable RUTH BADER GINSBURG, associate justice of the U.S. Supreme Court
- JACK GREENBERG, Esq., civil rights lawyer, former director general of the NAACP Legal Defense and Educational Fund, and Columbia University Law School professor
- CONRAD HARPER, Esq., legal adviser at the U.S. Department of State
- WADE J. HENDERSON, Esq., director of the Washington Bureau of the NAACP
- OLIVER W. HILL, Esq., Class of '33, civil rights lawyer
- The Honorable EARL F. HILLIARD, Class of '67, member of the U.S. House of Representatives
- ERIC H. HOLDER JR., Esq., U.S. attorney for the District of Columbia and, later, U.S. deputy attorney general
- The Honorable ELEANOR HOLMES-NORTON, member of the U.S. House of Representatives and former Georgetown University law professor
- ELAINE JONES, Esq., director-counsel of the NAACP Legal Defense and Educational Fund
- The Honorable SHARON PRATT KELLY, Class of '68, former mayor of the District of Columbia

- The Honorable ANTHONY M. KENNEDY, associate justice of the U.S. Supreme Court
- RUBY BURROWS MCZIER, Esq., Class of '65, attorney at law[37]
- The Honorable CONSTANCE BAKER MOTLEY, U.S. district judge of the Southern District of New York
- The Honorable SANDRA DAY O'CONNOR, associate justice of the U.S. Supreme Court
- CHARLES J. OGLETREE, Harvard University law professor
- PAULINE SCHNEIDER, Esq., president of the District of Columbia Bar Association
- The Honorable FRANKLIN A. SONN, ambassador of South Africa to the United States of America
- The Honorable CLARENCE THOMAS, associate justice of the U.S. Supreme Court
- The Honorable MAXINE WATERS, member of the U.S. House of Representatives
- The Honorable HARRIS WOFFORD, Class of '54, U.S. senator
- MARILYN YARBOROUGH, then dean of the University of Tennessee School of Law.

*Student Computer Center.* The first student computer center at the Howard law school was established with a $65,000 grant from the late Bernard E. Witkin of California. Witkin was a Berkeley, California, resident and a successful author of books about California law, such as *Witkin on Evidence, Witkin on Criminal Law, Witkin on Criminal Procedure,* and the multi-volume *Witkin on California Law.* He was a wealthy man and a staunch supporter of legal education.

Witkin was also a personal friend of mine. We had become friends when we were both members of the Judicial Council of California.[38] "Bernie" readily agreed when I asked him to provide funds that would be used to establish a student computer center at the Howard University School of Law.[39] He imposed only one condition—that we name the computer center after the late George M.

Johnson, who had been his friend. Bernie had worked many years before with George, who was a graduate of Boalt Hall, Class of '29, and a past dean of the Howard University School of Law (1946–1958). The George M. Johnson Student Computer Center was a much-needed and warmly welcomed addition to our law library. It was enthusiastically received and regularly used by our students.

*40th Anniversary of* Brown v. Board of Education. Great credit must be given to Ruby Burrows McZier, Class of '65, for the idea that the Howard University School of Law sponsor a celebration of the 40th anniversary of the U.S. Supreme Court decision in *Brown v. Board of Education*[40] and for her vigorous support of its implementation. A commemorative reception was held at the U.S. Supreme Court Building on Thursday afternoon, May 12, 1994, from 4 to 6 p.m. Invitations to the reception were issued in the name of Associate Justice Anthony M. Kennedy, Dean Henry Ramsey Jr., and the Howard University School of Law. The affair was funded by equal dollar contributions from 30 Howard law school graduates and the law school dean.

The event was both elegant and poignant. Associate Justice Kennedy made remarks in which he said that *Brown v. Board of Education* served the national interest by correcting a longstanding and evident wrong done by the U.S. Supreme Court in 1896 when it decided the case of *Plessy v. Ferguson*.[41] In *Plessy*, the court had ruled that state-mandated segregation did not violate the U.S. Constitution. The court reversed that ruling in 1954, when it held in *Brown v. Board of Education* that segregation mandated or financed by federal, state, or local governments violated the equal protection and due process clauses of the U.S. Constitution. Justice Kennedy's comments were followed by two beautiful songs, sung by the student choir of Eastern High School.[42]

I was next to comment on the *Brown* case, the significance of its holding that "separate but equal" was unconstitutional, and the historic struggle required to get the case considered by the U.S. Supreme Court. I also named and commended those Howard law school graduates, professors, and deans who served as lawyers in the case. Prominent among them were George E.C. Hayes, William R. Ming Jr., James M. Nabrit Jr., Robert L. Carter, Oliver W. Hill, Thurgood Marshall, and Spottswood W. Robinson III. We were fortunate that Cecilia Marshall, wife of Thurgood Marshall; James M. Nabrit Jr.; and Judge Spottswood Robinson were among those present at the reception. The Honorable L. Douglas Wilder, the first and, as of now, only black governor of Virginia was also present. Governor Wilder graduated from the Howard law school in 1959 and served as governor of Virginia from 1990 until 1994.

It did not appear that the significance, purpose, and location of the reception were lost on anyone present. Particularly significant for me was that the young high school students, who represented the intended beneficiaries of the *Brown v. Board of Education* and *Bolling v. Sharpe*[43] decisions, were that evening celebrating receipt of those benefits in the very building where the cases had been argued and won. I wondered to myself how anyone could ever have been so cruel and malicious as to try to deprive children such as these of the opportunity to receive a first-rate education. The very thought almost brought tears to my eyes. And so, I felt extremely proud that on this day they were celebrating with us the 40th anniversary of the *Brown* victory. The interactions between the veteran civil rights lawyers in attendance and the young beneficiaries of their work gave added meaning to the occasion. It felt especially appropriate and right to bring them together.

Much of the credit for the successes during my tenure as dean of the Howard University School of Law must be shared with a core of strong and gutsy faculty members. Those professors supported my proposals and offered positive proposals themselves. They will always have my respect and appreciation for their courageous assistance. That important core of faculty members included Loretta Argrett, Alice Bullock,

Lisa Crooms, Andrew Gavil, Steven Jamar, George Johnson, Adam Kurland, Homer LaRue, Isaiah Leggett, Richard Leiter, Ziyad Motala, Laurence Nolan, Sherman Rogers, Reggie Robinson, Warren Rosmarin, Sharon Styles, Andrew Taslitz, Patricia Worthy, and Frank Wu.

I am equally appreciative of the hard work and loyalty of my administrative staff, particularly Delphine Bruner, LuEllen Conti, Cathy Geier, Roberta Herbert, Tedd Miller, Denise Purdie (now Denise Spriggs), Barbara Powell-Smith (now Barbara Powell-White), Maria Tracey, Virginia Williams, and Jesse Wimbish.

My departure from Howard University was not quite as I had planned. When I assumed the position of dean of the law school, I expected to remain at Howard for about 10 years. After graduating from law school and being admitted to the California bar, I was first a trial lawyer for almost 10 years, then a law professor for 10 years, followed by 10 years as a state trial court judge. So there was a certain career symmetry that I saw in a 10-year term as dean of the law school (which would have been significantly longer than the four-year term that was typically being served at the time by law school deans at ABA-approved law schools).

I had served nearly six years as dean when I submitted a letter of resignation to President Patrick H. Swygert in September 1996. In that letter, I said my resignation, as dean, was effective June 30, 1997, nearly seven years after my appointment. That would allow adequate time for the law school faculty and university administration to conduct an effective search for a new dean.

President Swygert responded to my letter by saying that he would not wait until June 30, 1997, for me to conclude my duties as dean but instead was removing me effective December 31, 1996. He advised the law school faculty that he intended to appoint an interim dean, who would serve until a permanent dean could be selected. Like other deans at the university, I served at the pleasure of the university president. Therefore, Swygert had full authority to advance my resignation date.

CLINICAL LAW PROGRAM FACULTY AND STAFF *at the Howard University School of Law with Dean Henry Ramsey Jr. (seated). From left: secretary Marilyn Toran, associate professors Frank Wu and Sharon Styles-Anderson, professor Homer C. LaRue, and assistant professor Peter A. Krauthamer. The newly constituted Clinical Law Program began operations in 1995.*

But President Swygert's action, in my judgment, significantly compromised the usual procedure used at ABA-approved law schools for selecting a new dean. Law school faculty members and the university typically have from 10 to 12 months to conduct a national search for a new dean. However, Alice Gresham Bullock, the person selected as my replacement, was a well-experienced law school administrator who, in my judgment, did an excellent job as dean. Alice came to the position with many years experience as an associate dean under Dan Bernstine (the interim dean who preceded me) and as my associate dean for academic affairs. She had also served for two years at the Association of American Law Schools as deputy director.

The question that will probably come to your mind is why the university president responded so vindictively to my letter of resignation. The answer lies in our mutual history. It was clear to me soon after Patrick H. Swygert arrived at Howard in his capacity as university president that I was not "his cup of tea." Swygert would have to give you his explanation for his view of me as a person and dean of the law school. He and I never had a discussion of that topic.

But I do have a postulation for the objectionable attitude that he sometimes exhibited toward me after his arrival at Howard. Not always, but often enough, he made the point that our relationship was not a close one and that was the way he wanted it.

When the Howard University Board of Trustees elected him to be president of the university, Swygert's salary and all the other aspects of his compensation had not been negotiated. Swygert had a lawyer who he said would represent him in those negotiations with the university. At that time, I was serving as acting general counsel for the university and was designated by the Board of Trustees to represent the university.

The process went along fairly amiably except with regard to two or three issues where the negotiations were quite difficult. Certain income tax issues and language concerning what would constitute cause for the Board of Trustees to discharge the president were particularly contentious. I never took the disagreements personally. I simply saw them as differences of opinion between the parties that would have to be resolved through hard negotiations. But I am convinced that Swygert held against me certain positions that I took during the course of the negotiations. I have no doubt that the positions I took—and stood by— were in the interest of the university, the university's Board of Trustees, and, indeed, Patrick H. Swygert himself.

In representing the university in negotiations with Swygert's lawyer, I retained a competent lawyer at a well-respected Washington, D.C., law firm to advise me regarding certain contested matters. The lawyer had provided legal services to the Board of Trustees before I became acting general counsel. That law firm's advice seemed sound to me, when I compared it with the specific opposing positions being offered by Swygert's lawyer. As concerns other contentious matters—for example, what would be grounds for discharge of the president in the event he was convicted of a crime—I relied on consultations with board members and my own legal education, experience, and analysis.

I believe that Swygert held against me some of the positions I took during those negotiations, after he moved into the president's office and I was no longer serving as acting general counsel. He manifested a certain coolness toward me in most of our discussions and other interactions. He also severely restricted my direct access to him by instructing that all of my communications with him be made through the vice president for academic affairs. Although as dean of the law school I had always submitted written proposals to the president through the vice president for academic affairs, I had also always enjoyed free access to the president to discuss ideas and proposals before submitting anything formally.

There were also certain petty matters that led to my decision to resign as dean and return to my family, friends, and home in California. One of the things Swygert did after taking office and after I had returned to the law school was to have the new general counsel demand that the lawyer who had advised me on certain special issues concerning his employment agreement with the university significantly reduce her fee. The general counsel refused to authorize payment of the lawyer's original bill, notwithstanding documentation of the work performed and the reasonableness of the fee charged. While this action did not affect me directly, it was an example of Swygert's vindictiveness and his resentment regarding the contract negotiations.

I suppose that the "last straw" involved my submission of a request to the university president—through the interim vice president for academic affairs—for approval of a trip to South Africa. I thought I should be present when our summer abroad program in South Africa was inspected by the American Bar Association Section of Legal Education and Admission to the Bar in July 1996. There were adequate funds in the summer program budget for me to travel to Cape Town, and no expenses would have had to be paid from university general funds. Also, it was my experience as an ABA site evaluator and as a member of the Accreditation Committee that the law school dean was often present during such site visits—not always, but often, and almost always during the first visit.

I submitted the required written request for the president's approval on April 15, 1996, nearly three months before the time scheduled for the ABA site visit. A couple of weeks before the date I was scheduled to travel, I still had not received approval or any other communication from the university president about the matter. I contacted Harry Robinson, vice president for academic affairs, and reminded him of my plans to travel to South Africa and the outstanding request for presidential approval. A few days before my scheduled departure, Harry called me to report that the president would not approve my trip. When I asked why, Harry said Swygert thought that I "traveled too much."

There are other examples of actions by Swygert to which I was subjected, but this is not a legal brief. It is simply an attempt to give you my view of what led to my early resignation as dean. I also wanted to be honest and accurate with you concerning the actual circumstances of my departure.

· Notes ·

1. Genna Rae McNeil, *Groundwork: Charles Hamilton Houston and the Struggle for Civil Rights* (Philadelphia: University of Pennsylvania Press, 1983), p. 84.
2. Loretta Collins changed her last name to Argrett when she married James Argrett.
3. As discussed in chapter 13 of "My Story," it just was not practical or realistic for the family to make the move with me.
4. Read, for example, Tushnet, *Making Civil Rights Law*. The book demonstrates that many of the important lawyers litigating civil rights cases were either graduates of the Howard University School of Law or had worked there as a dean or faculty member. Examples are Robert Carter, Oliver Hill, Charles H. Houston, Thurgood Marshall, Robert Ming, and Spottswood Robinson.
5. Allen Broussard was the presiding judge of the Alameda County Superior Court when I was appointed to that court in 1981, and we served together as Superior Court judges until he assumed his position as associate justice of the California Supreme Court in July 1981. Allen, as a municipal court judge, had performed the ceremony when Eleanor and I were married on Sept. 7, 1969.
6. In chapter 30 I list the law schools I visited as an ABA site team member.
7. See American Bar Association Standards for Approval of Law Schools, The American Bar Association's Role in the Law School Accreditation Process.
8. I was actively involved by telephone and fax with management of the law school prior to moving to Washington, D.C., in January 1991.
9. A small percentage of the law student body lived in a few private upscale apartment units within one block of the law school campus.
10. At that time she was married, and her name was Dr. Barbara Powell-Smith.
11. The following description is from the Howard University School of Law website: Clarence Clyde Ferguson Jr. (1924–1983) was a professor of law and a United States Ambassador to Uganda. In 1969, he served as the U.S. ambassador-at-large•and coordinator for civilian relief in the Nigerian civil war and negotiated the Protocol on Relief to Nigerian Civilian Victims of the Civil War. He served as ambassador to Uganda in 1970 and as deputy assistant secretary of state for African affairs in 1973. From 1973 to 1975 he was the U.S. representative to the United Nations Economic and Social Council. Ferguson held a professorship at Rutgers University and served as dean of the Howard University School of Law

from 1963 to 1969. He joined the faculty of Harvard Law School in 1976 and worked there until his death. The C. Clyde Ferguson Annual Lecture at Howard Law School is named after him, as is the Clyde Ferguson Award presented by the Association of American Law Schools.

12. See *The Jurist* 7 (Summer 1994), p. 19.

13. A significant number of the 409 contributors gave more than $1,000, which allowed us to achieve our goal of $500,000 with fewer than 500 contributors.

14. *Brown v. Board of Education of Topeka et al.*, 347 U.S. 483 (1954).

15. I am aware of the view that use of numerical predictors, particularly the LSAT score, simply reinforces the racial, ethnic, and class bias believed to be within the LSAT.

16. *Brown v. Board of Education of Topeka et al.*, 347 U.S. 483 (1954).

17. McNeil, *Groundwork*.

18. At that time, her name was Denise Wright Purdie.

19. See Doris A. Hightower and Raymond S. McGaugh, *The MLER Supplementary Bar Preparation Program* (St. Louis, Missouri: Saint Louis University Public Law Review, 1991), p. 71, for a detailed history and description of Minority Legal Education Resource Inc. (MLER) of Chicago.

20. For more than 40 years, BAR/BRI has provided the most experienced, personalized, and up-to-date bar review course. BAR/BRI combines comprehensive yet concise outlines, dynamic law school professors, and the most complete Multistate and Essay Testing programs. (As described on the BAR/BRI website.)

21. See Standard 705 of the ABA Standards for the Approval of Law Schools.

22. See Standard 405(a) of the ABA Standards for the Approval of Law Schools.

23. This title was changed to assistant dean for student affairs and records.

24. One of the two positions was eliminated.

25. The fifth position eliminated is not in this list but was the placement secretary.

26. I use professional to designate people who are qualified for the position by virtue of education, specialized training and experience and who are active in the field in which they work.

27. The title of director of placement and alumni affairs was changed to director of career services.

28. This position was the in-house computer or information technology person—that is, computer systems manager.

29. Professor Alice Gresham Bullock took a two-year leave of absence to serve as deputy director of the Association of American Law Schools. She made an important contribution to the effort to gain funding for and establish the clinical law center before leaving to join the association.

30. Professor Homer LaRue, at the time of his hiring as director of the Howard University Clinical Law Center, was a clinical law professor at the University of Maryland School of Law.

31. Denise Mitchell was a graduate of the Howard law school and a person we contemplated hiring as a staff member should we be successful in getting approval for the judicial training proposal.

32. Eleanor Mason Ramsey, my wife, accompanied me on this trip.

33. See Harry E. Groves, Report of Howard University School of Law Foreign Summer Program, Cape Town, South Africa, June 22–August 1, 1996, submitted to the Accreditation Committee and Council of the ABA Section of Legal Education and Admission to the Bar, p. 7.

34. Then known as Barbara Powell-Smith.

35. Eric Hoffer, *The True Believer: Thoughts on the Nature of Mass Movements* (New York: Harper & Row, 1951).

36. The moot courtroom was our largest classroom and was often used as the school's auditorium.

37. Also former special assistant to Assistant Secretary Samuel Jackson when he was with HUD.

38. Witkin was a permanent fixture on the council; I was appointed for a fixed term by the chief justice.

39. The funds for the computer center were actually provided by the Bernard E. Witkin Foundation, which at the time was solely funded and controlled by Bernard E. Witkin.

40. *Brown v. Board of Education of Topeka et al.* 347 U.S. 483, 74 S.Ct. 686 (1954).

41. *Plessy v. Ferguson*, 163 U.S. 537, 16 S.Ct. 1138 (1896).

42. A public high school in the District of Columbia.

43. *Bolling v. Sharpe*, 347 U.S. 497 (1954).

HENRY RAMSEY JR., *chief of party, and* AISHA M. BELLO, *program coordinator, at a Nigerian Rule of Law Assistance Project meeting in Abuja, Nigeria, in 2001. "To most outsiders, the very name Nigeria conjures up images of chaos and confusion, military coups, repression, drug trafficking, and business fraud," wrote Karl Maier in* THIS HOUSE HAS FALLEN. *"It remains a mystery to all but a handful of academics and diplomats. ..."* [1]

# Nigerian Rule of Law Project

O n November 14, 2000, I signed an agreement with the National Center for State Courts (NCSC) to provide international consultant services in Nigeria for approximately 14 months. My specific position was to serve as chief of party for a Nigerian Rule of Law Project funded by the U.S. Agency for International Development (USAID) and to be managed by NCSC. What I write here about this memorable event is based on, and quotes extensively from, a report concerning project objectives and activities that I submitted to Dr. Heike Gramckow, project executive director and my immediate superior, near the end of my tenure as chief of party.

I arrived in Lagos, Nigeria, five days after signing the agreement with NCSC and immediately assumed my duties, with overall responsibility for Project activities in Nigeria and primary responsibility for day-to-day management of the Rule of Law Project. The basic objective was to achieve substantial improvement in the performance of the Nigerian high courts and high court judges by strengthening the independence of the Nigerian judiciary and working toward the elimination of judicial corruption.

Our headquarters was established in Abuja, the capital city of Nigeria. The Project was to be implemented in three pilot jurisdictions—the High Court of Kaduna State, located in the city of Kaduna; High Court of Lagos State, in the city of Lagos; and High Court of Justice of the Federal Capital Territory, in the city of Abuja. Justice R.H. Cudjoe was the chief judge of the Kaduna High Court, Justice C.O. Segun was chief judge of the Lagos High Court, and Justice M.D. Saleh was chief judge of the High Court of Justice of the Federal Capital Territory. The idea was that if the Project was successful in the pilot courts, then comparable activities would be extended to high courts throughout Nigeria.

As chief of party, I worked closely with high officials in each branch of the government—judicial, legislative, and executive. Among them were the chief justice of the Federation of Nigeria[2] (the Honorable Chief Justice Mohammadu L. Uwais); the chief registrar of the Supreme Court of Nigeria (the Honorable M.M. Dodo); the presiding justice of the Court of Appeal, Abuja Division (the Honorable Justice Umaru Abdullahi); the attorney general and minister of justice of the Republic of Nigeria (the Honorable Bola Ige[3]); the chairman of the Independent Corrupt Practices and Other Related Offences Commission[4] (the Honorable Justice M.M.A. Akambi); the chairman of the Senate Committee on the Judiciary (the Honorable Mike Ajegbo); the chairman of the House Committee on Judiciary, Human Rights, and Legal Matters (the Honorable Chief Obeten O. Obeten); the chairman of the House Committee on Justice, Human Rights, and Legal Matters (the Honorable Ibrahim Zailani); and the state attorneys general and chief judges of the high courts in the three pilot jurisdictions.

Nine fundamental tasks had been identified as Project objectives and were scheduled to be accomplished during my tenure:

1. *Training for Budget Officers*—to provide judicial budget officers with information about preparing annual budgets and to suggest strategies for presenting budgets to the funding authority and for monitoring budgets for fiscal accountability.

2. *Legislative and Judicial Study Tour*—to provide 15 Nigerian legislators and judicial officers who had responsibilities in the judicial budgeting process with an opportunity to travel to the United States to learn about U.S. court budgeting.

3. *Three-Branch Meeting on the Judiciary*—to provide important representatives of the three branches of government opportunities to develop a mutual understanding of the requirements of judicial independence. A particular focus would be on the

budget process and its effect on the judiciary's ability to fulfill its responsibilities and function as an independent branch.

4. *Alternatives to the "Written Note"*–to study the existing court recording system and look for opportunities to more effectively record court proceedings and publish judicial decisions.

5. *Case Management and Judicial Management Technical Assistance*–to improve court administration and processing of cases at the national and individual court levels and to identify alternatives that offered less complex procedures (e.g., through diversion and alternative dispute resolution).

6. *Backlog and Case-Tracking Studies*–to conduct such studies and recommend improvements to ensure that court cases were processed in the most effective manner.

7. *Civil Society Assistance: Nigerian Stakeholder Process*–to assist Nigerian nongovernmental organizations (NGOs) and civil society organizations (CSOs) in their efforts to formulate an agenda to contribute to rule of law and legal reform.

8. *Judicial Ethics and Professional Responsibility Study Group*–to assist the Nigerian judiciary in fostering ethical conduct and compliance with judicial standards of professionalism.

9. *Library Development Assistance*–to help the Nigerian courts improve legal research capabilities.

David Anderson,[5] who had traveled with me to Nigeria, and I set about finding office space and a place for me to live in Abuja. We also interviewed candidates for the positions of Project coordinator and staff assistant. But as noted in my initial report to Dr. Gramckow at NCSC headquarters in Arlington, Virginia, my first 10 days or so were spent mostly meeting people directly or indirectly related to the Project. These were key players at USAID-Lagos, various persons at the U.S. Embassy in Abuja, representatives of the Nigerian federal government (e.g., the Chief Justice and several other members of the Nigerian Supreme Court, the President of the Court of Appeal, the Attorney

General and Minister of Justice of Nigeria, the Chair of the Senate Judiciary Committee and Chair of the National Assembly's Justice Committee), representatives of England's Department for International Development (DFID), key officials at USAID's Office of Transition Initiative (OTI), representatives of the Nigerian Institute for Advanced Legal Studies (NIAL), the Chief Judge and several other judges of the Kudana High Court, and representatives of various NGOs in Lagos and Abuja.

The first meeting of Stakeholders was organized and held as scheduled on November 30, 2000, at the Nicon Hilton Hotel in Abuja. It was my impression that USAID and the Nigerian Stakeholders were pleased with what transpired at the meeting. The Nigerians in attendance confirmed their essential acceptance of all material aspects of the Nigerian Rule of Law Project as outlined in the NCSC proposal. I wrote to Dr. Gramckow that "while I (and the others) expected and would have appreciated better attendance, I was quite satisfied with the meeting and its outcome."

The first monthly meeting of a Project Advisory Committee was scheduled for December 11, 2000, but its membership had not been determined by the time of my initial report and it seemed likely that the first meeting would therefore have to be rescheduled. I hoped to keep Advisory Committee membership to a maximum of 15 people; at the same time we wanted to assure adequate representation from the various constituencies of Nigeria's judiciary and justice system. Toward that end, in an early memo to Dr. Gramckow I wrote:

> Obviously, there will have to be at least one representative from the Office of the Chief Justice, the Attorney General's Office, the Court of Appeal, and each house of the national legislature. It would probably be wise to have someone on the committee from the Ministry of Finance. I suggest that we have two representatives from each of the pilot courts and perhaps two representatives from the CSO/NGO community. Finally, I suggest that we have one academic. This would give us a committee membership of 15,

which would be manageable, based on an expectation that we will have full attendance at each meeting.

It is my suggestion that—in addition to active members of the Advisory Committee—the Chief Justice of the Supreme Court, the Attorney General of Nigeria, the Attorneys General of the two pilot states, the Chief Judges of the High Court in the two pilot states and the Federal High Court for Abuja, and the Chairpersons of the two legislative committees concerned with the judiciary be listed as *ex officio* members. *Ex officio* members could, but would not be expected to, attend committee meetings. This would simply be another public expression of their support for the Project. . . .

Melissa Brown of USAID[6] and I agreed that it was important for the Project to have some early "successes." I recommended the following six items as having that potential:

a. Successful budget training in Nigeria (Task 1).

b. Successful budget training in the United States (Task 1).

c. Introduction of electronic recording (Task 4).

d. Implementation of an ADR (alternative disputes resolution) program (Task 5).

e. Implementation of a limited grant program (Task 7).

f. Providing a one-year subscription to the *Supreme Court Reporter* and *Weekly Reporter* for the three Federal Court libraries in Lagos, Kaduna, and Abuja.

In a memo to Heike Gramckow, I noted that we had emphasized to the Nigerian leadership and other Nigerian Project participants that "it is Nigerians who have defined these issues as having priority and reflecting serious problems within the Nigerian judicial system." I underscored that it was, therefore, their responsibility to lead the efforts required to implement this Project and its nine tasks.

At the same time, I also stressed the importance of our meeting the goals we in NCSC had set for ourselves. As regards Task 1 (budget officer training), for instance, I felt I could not overstate the need to keep to the current training schedule "if Project credibility is to be maintained with the Nigerians. Both Melissa Brown and I, in various conversations with Nigerian judicial leaders, have emphasized to them that the last 12 months have been spent talking and now is the time for action. The Project will then look pretty foolish if *our* first 'action' is to delay implementation of one of the Project's most critical tasks."

In my final report to NCSC headquarters, I undertook to discuss the various task objectives and what had been accomplished during my tenure in Nigeria. Regarding Task 4 (alternatives to the "written note"), I wrote that the aim was to find a practical replacement for the system under which judges were responsible for writing down, virtually verbatim, all testimonial evidence and oral presentations by counsel. "Indeed," I said in my report, "the judges are eager for a practical alternative. It was brought to my attention during my visit with judges in Kaduna that not only does this practice of the 'written note' seriously delay the pace of trials, but it also is physically burdensome and can become quite painful as the day progresses." However, what might seem obvious alternatives were not easily put into place.

> The expense and time required to train and equip certified court reporters makes implementation of that option impractical, at least for the near future. This conclusion is without regard to the complex problems that would be associated with any consideration of computer-aided transcription equipment and the operation and maintenance of that equipment.
>
> Video recording equipment has not been found to be all that practical even in the technologically advanced United States. I seriously doubt if video recording offers any realistic alternative to the "written note" for the courts of Nigeria. Plus, the cost that would be associated with any effort to adopt video recording at this point in Nigeria's technological development makes that option impossible. The same is true respecting needed staff to operate and maintain the equipment.

That basically leaves one option: electronic recording using multitrack tape recorders. While judges in Nigeria might be receptive to operating such equipment, my suggestion is that Electronic Recording Monitors be hired and trained to operate the equipment. Unlike certified court reporters, monitors could be trained in a reasonably short period of time to operate the equipment and keep a log of number positions on the tape, key words and names, etc., that would be required to quickly find specific testimony or oral argument. Further, persons with a sound high school education could handle the job. The cost of the Electronic Recording Monitor position would, therefore, not be a significant barrier to implementation of electronic recording in the pilot courts.

The judges that I have discussed this issue with are very positive in their response to the suggestion that electronic recording machines and Electronic Recording Monitors be used as an alternative to the "written note." . . .

An important issue raised by the judges in Kaduna is what legal authority is there for an electronic recording, or transcript typed from an electronic recording, to serve as the official record of any proceeding? At present, the judge's "written notes" are the official record. It may require a statutory amendment or a change in the Rules of Court for any other form of recording to also be considered "an official record" of the proceedings.

I appreciate the complexity of this topic and the several issues that will have to be addressed and resolved, particularly in the Nigerian context. Still, I hope that we can adopt as our goal to have an alternative recording system up and running in the pilot courts by July 1, 2001.

I did not see any serious problems regarding case management (Task 5). The judges all acknowledged a serious problem of court delay and congestion and wanted to do something about it. I suggested that NCSC/Nigeria prepare a memorandum regarding what was known already within the pilot courts and among the judicial leadership of Nigeria about case management, timelines, and the like. "In the main," I wrote, "we are not dealing with people who are uninformed or who 'do not have a clue.' It will be important for the consultants to understand this as they prepare for their visit and any training that they plan to provide."

Task 8 (Judicial Ethics and Professional Responsibility Study Group) could have been limited to the issue of corruption, but I felt that it was in the Project's interest to approach the topic in the broader context stated in the title. "There is ready acknowledgement of deep corruption within the judiciary," I wrote. "The conventional view is that corruption is much more pervasive in the lower courts. Persons I have spoken with are convinced that there is little, if any, corruption at the higher levels of the judiciary, e.g., the Supreme Court. As an aside, it is interesting that the 'written note' by trial judges is one area that presents an opportunity or temptation for corruption. This is because the 'written note' determines what is or is not in the record."

During the eight months following my arrival in Nigeria, I mostly worked seven days each week on the Project. When I left Nigeria in late August 2001, seven of the nine tasks had been successfully completed: Task 1 (training of budget officers), Task 2 (legislative study tour to the United States), Task 3 (three-branch meeting on the judiciary), Task 5 (case management/judicial management training and technical assistance), Task 6 (backlog and case tracking study), Task 7 (civil society assistance–Nigerian stakeholder process), and Task 8 (judicial ethics and professional responsibility study group).

As concerns Task 4 (the "written note"), William Hewitt of the NCSC staff and I wrote separate reports for consideration by the three pilot courts. None of the recommendations from those reports were ever implemented during my tenure as chief of party. As far as I know, none have been implemented as of the date of this manuscript. Technical and training difficulties were responsible for this failure to effectively address the written note problems.

Task 9 (library development assistance), the other remaining assignment, was not completed primarily because the Supreme Court organization and staff structure of the Supreme Court library were still far from completed and it would have been premature to ship books—or even to try to identify library materials to be provided for use by justices and staff of the Supreme Court—until that work had been completed.

During my time in Nigeria in 2000 and 2001, much progress was made with regard to the implementation of the various tasks, and there was significant improvement in the understanding of the various judges and staff at the pilot courts regarding court and calendar management. But I do not know what progress, if any, has been made since my departure. I have not been back to Nigeria, nor have I had any continued contact with the NCSC staff since my return to the United States in 2001.

· Notes ·

1. Karl Maier, *This House Has Fallen: Midnight in Nigeria* (New York: PBS Publications, 2000), p. xviii.
2. Chief Justice of the Nigerian Supreme Court.
3. The Honorable Bola Ige was assassinated within three months after my permanent return to the United States.
4. Commonly called "the Anti-Corruption Commission."
5. David Anderson was the employee at NCSC headquarters responsible for financial matters concerning the project.
6. Melissa Brown was the USAID official in Nigeria with primary responsibility for the Rule of Law Project when I arrived in the country.

YOU WILL STUDY the wisdom of the past, for in a wilderness of conflicting counsels, a trail has there been blazed. You will study the life of mankind, for this is the life you must order, and, to order with wisdom, must know. You will study the precepts of justice, for these are the truths that through you shall come to their hour of triumph. Here is the high emprise, the fine endeavor, the splendid possibility of achievement, to which I summon you and bid you welcome.[1]

–BENJAMIN N. CARDOZA

# ABA Section of Legal Education and Admission to the Bar

I t was in 1977 that I became involved with the American Bar Association's Section of Legal Education and Admission to the Bar.[2] I had not joined the ABA before then, probably because of the organization's history of excluding black lawyers from membership, although the ABA House of Delegates voted in 1943 to accept black lawyers as members.

I am most proud of my work as a member of the Section of Legal Education and Admission to the Bar concerning ABA law school accreditation.[3] I am certain that my energy and intellect made significant contributions to the quality of regulations and the regulatory process adopted by the ABA in accrediting American law schools. I hope my contributions in that regard have helped to materially improve "the quality of American legal education and, in turn, the quality of legal services provided to the public."[4]

In 1978 I was appointed to the Accreditation Committee. I served on that committee until May 1983, including a term as chairperson, August 1980–August 1981. I was later elected a member of the Council of the Section for the years 1982 until 1993, and served as chairperson from August 1991 until August 1992 and Council secretary from August 1995 until 1997.

I have also had the privilege of serving on a number of ABA site-visit teams, both in the United States and abroad. Two of us– Ms. Kathleen Ritter and I–were the first site evaluators sent abroad under new ABA regulations requiring that ABA-approved law school foreign summer programs be visited by ABA site evaluators.[5] We spent six weeks during the summer of 1986 visiting programs in Tokyo, Singapore, Hong Kong, Guangzhou,[6] Shanghai, and Beijing, in that order. Later foreign site visits were usually conducted by one site evaluator, involved no more than two summer programs, and lasted no more than two weeks.

Accreditation site visits to full-time and part-time law programs in the United States and Puerto Rico typically involved a site-visit team of five to seven members, with each team having among its members one law school administrator (usually a dean or former dean), one law librarian, and one clinician. I have served as a member of ABA site-visit teams for the following law schools, with teams that I chaired in italics:

- *Regular Site Visits.* Antioch School of Law;[7] Boston College School of Law; International School of Law;[8] Thomas M. Cooley Law School;[9] Georgetown University School of Law; *New York School of Law*; *Hofstra University School of Law*;[10] University of Houston School of Law; *University of Oregon School of Law*; *Texas Southern University, Thurgood Marshall School of Law*;[11] *Florida Coastal School of Law*;[12] *Vermont School of Law*; University of Nevada at Las Vegas, William S. Boyd School of Law; West Virginia University College of Law; and *Barry University School of Law*.[13]

- *Special Site Visits.* Boston University School of Law and Thomas M. Cooley Law School.

- *Foreign Summer Program Visits.* University of Florida: England; Tulane University: Germany; Santa Clara University: China, Hong Kong, Hungary, Japan, and Singapore; Southwestern Law School: Argentina and China; Columbia University School of Law: Amsterdam; and New York University School of Law: Amsterdam.

Another area that I am proud of concerns affirmative action in legal education. I exercised leadership and worked hard with other colleagues to get the American Bar Association to adopt Standard 211,[14] which provides as follows:

Consistent with sound legal education policy and the Standards, a law school shall demonstrate, or have carried out and maintained, by concrete action, a commitment to providing full opportunities for the study of law and entry into the profession by qualified members of groups, notably racial and ethnic minorities, which have been victims of discrimination in various forms. This commitment typically includes a special concern for determining the potential of these applicants through the admission process, special recruitment efforts, and a program that assists in meeting the unusual financial needs of many of these students, but a law school is not obligated to apply standards for the award of financial assistance different from those applied to other students.

I also served as the American Bar Association's representative to the Council of Legal Education Opportunity (CLEO) and twice served as chairperson of CLEO, from July 1975 until July 1981 and again from 1989 until August 1992. CLEO's purpose was (and is) to expand legal education opportunities for members of underrepresented groups in the legal profession. CLEO did (and does) this by providing pre-law recruitment, counseling, admission assistance, and training to low-income, minority, and economically disadvantaged college students and graduates seeking to attend law school.

The centerpiece when I was involved with CLEO was the organization's summer institutes, held each year since 1968 and serving three purposes: (a) to introduce students to the rigors and expectations of law school, (b) to permit CLEO representatives to evaluate students' potential for success at law school, and (c) to permit admission officers at a given law school to evaluate a particular student's potential for success at that institution. With regard to this last purpose, some law schools would admit one or more students on condition that they successfully complete a CLEO institute.

In 30 years of ABA membership I have also served on several other Section of Legal Education committees and commissions: the

Affirmative Action Committee;[15] the Standards Review Committee; as chair of the Special Committee to Study the Law School Approval Process (known as the Ramsey Committee);[16] the Commission to Review the Substance and Process of the ABA's Accreditation of American Law Schools (known as the Wahl Commission);[17] the Central European and Eurasian Law Initiative Sister Law School Consortium Committee; and, after Jim White announced his retirement as consultant in August 1999,[18] the Ad Hoc Committee to Recommend a New ABA Consultant on Legal Education. Jim White had served continuously for 26 years as the ABA consultant on legal education.

· Notes ·

1. "The Game of the Law and Its Prizes," address at the Seventy-Fourth Commencement of the Albany Law School, June 10, 1925. Found in Cardoza, B.N. (Benjamin Nathan), *Selected Writings*, ed. by Margaret E. Hall, with a foreword by Edwin W. Patterson, New York, Fallon Publications (1947). This quotation also appears on the west wall of Boalt Hall, where it has been etched in stone tablets.

2. For a history of the Section of Legal Education and Admission to the Bar, see Susan K. Boyd, *The ABA's First Section: Assuring a Qualified Bar,* American Bar Association, printed by West Publishing Company in the United States of America (1993).

3. See Henry Ramsey Jr., "The History, Organization, and Accomplishments of the American Bar Association Accreditation Process," *Wake Forest Law Review* 30 (1995): 267.

4. James P. White, "The American Bar Association Law School Approval Process: A Century Plus of Public Service," *Wake Forest Law Review* 30 (1995): 283.

5. See American Bar Association (ABA) Standards for the Approval of Law Schools, Standards 307 and 23; Rules of Procedure For Approval of Law Schools, and Criteria For Approval of Foreign Summer Programs.

6. Formerly known as Canton.

7. I was on three different site teams that visited the Antioch School of Law.

8. The school was located in Northern Virginia and was the predecessor of the George Mason University Law School.

9. In Lansing, Michigan.

10. In the state of New York.

11. I was on two different teams that visited Texas Southern.

12. In Jacksonville, Florida.

13. In Orlando, Florida.

14. See Standard 211 of the Standards and Rules of Procedure for Approval of Law School. When originally adopted, this statement was numbered Standard 212.

15. During the period from 1981 through 1985–86.

16. See Report of the Special Committee to Study the Law School Approval Process, to the Council of the Section of Legal Education and Admissions to the Bar of the American Bar Association, dated July 26, 1990. It is known as the Ramsey Committee because I was chairperson.

17. It is known as the Wahl Commission because Justice Rosalie Wahl, an Associate Justice of the Minnesota Supreme Court, was chairperson.

18. Jim announced his resignation in August 1999, with the effective date of resignation being Sept. 30, 2000.

# LAW SCHOOL ADMISSION COUNCIL

## RESOLUTION OF APPRECIATION

WHEREAS, he has shown an extraordinary commitment to the betterment of American legal education and the American legal system, and

WHEREAS, he has demonstrated a deep and life-long concern for the welfare of disadvantaged persons in the United States, and

WHEREAS, his belief in truth and truth-seeking created in him an irrepressible desire for facts about the experiences and progress of minority law students and bar applicants, and

WHEREAS, he had the vision to conceptualize a precedent-setting, national, longitudinal study of the pathways leading to a legal career, and

WHEREAS, he had the energy, tenacity, persistence, and sheer force of personality to transform his vision into reality,

## FOR ALL THESE REASONS, BE IT RESOLVED

That the Board of Trustees of the Law School Admission Council expresses its sincere and abiding appreciation and admiration for HENRY RAMSEY, JR. on the occasion of the publication of the LSAC National Longitudinal Bar Passage Study.

MAY 29, 1998

[T]HE EQUAL PROTECTION CLAUSE does not prohibit the law school's narrowly tailored use of race in admissions decisions to further a compelling interest in obtaining the educational benefits that flow from a diverse student body.[1]

*—Grutter v. Bollinger,*
539 U.S. 306, 343 (2003)

# 32

# LSAC Bar Passage Study

I n 1989, the Law School Admission Council (LSAC) funded a longitudinal study of bar passage rates in the United States. A statement of the reasons for the study was set forth in the first paragraph of the Executive Summary:

> The LSAC National Longitudinal Bar Passage Study was undertaken primarily in response to rumors and anecdotal reports suggesting that bar passage rates were so low among examinees of color that potential applicants were questioning the wisdom of investing the time and resources necessary to obtain a legal education. There were no reliable sources of national empirical data to support or refute those claims. When the LSAC committed to conducting this study, it was done with the conviction that the information was vital to legal education regardless of the outcome. If the dismal failure rates being reported in whispers were accurate, legal education would need to rethink both its admission and educational policy and practice. If they were false, they needed to be replaced with accurate information.[2]

Dr. Linda F. Wightman, then LSAC's vice president for test development and research, was appointed principal investigator of the bar passage study. As I wrote in the Historical Introduction to the study, an "eight-member Bar Passage Study Work Group was formed to give advice to Dr. Wightman in developing the study. Professor David Hill of the University of Colorado School of Law, then chairperson of the [LSAC] Minority Affairs Committee, appointed me chairperson of the work group, which included state Supreme Court justices, law school professors, and former bar examiners."[3]

An initial barrier to achieving the study objectives was the reluctance of the majority of state boards of bar examiners to share bar passage data with anyone other then their own officials and staff members. I met personally with the chair and chief administrative or executive officer of a majority of the boards of bar examiners in the United States and asked them to cooperate with the study. In nearly every instance, we were successful in securing their cooperation.

In her introduction to the study, Dr. Wightman was most gracious about my contributions:

> Most importantly, I am indebted to Judge Henry Ramsey Jr., whose vision for this research was the impetus for initiating funding for this study, whose commitment to the publication of the findings whatever they might be was a major reason for my involvement in the endeavor, and whose tireless work and dogged determination to enlist the participation and support of every law school and state board of bar examiners are the foundation on which the success of the effort was built.[4]

The bar passage study was of full-time students who had commenced their first-year law study at an ABA-approved law school in the fall of 1991, had graduated from law school, and had taken one or more bar examinations. The study involved a six-year data collection effort. The work group met regularly from inception of the study until its publication in 1998.

I viewed the primary and most important purpose of the study as being to test the validity of the assertions then being made by some politicians, legal educators, university administrators, and white students—the "rumors" referred to above—that affirmative action programs at American law schools were a waste of public and private resources and that most minority law school graduates—particularly blacks and

Hispanics—do not ever pass the bar examination and gain admission to the profession.

For those of us active in working to maintain affirmative action programs and to gain resources with which to support existing programs, there was real concern that views such as those would cause a significant reduction in such programs at ABA-approved law schools. I did not believe the negative statements were true and felt strongly that we needed to somehow determine the facts.

The findings of the study included the following:

- The eventual passage rate for all study participants of color was 84.7 percent (2,950 of 3,482).
- The eventual passage rates for racial and ethnic groups were as follows: American Indian, 82.2 percent (88 of 107); Asian American, 91.9 percent (883 of 961); black, 77.6 percent (1,062 of 1,368); Mexican American, 88.4 percent (352 of 398); Puerto Rican, 79.7 percent (102 of 128); Hispanic, 89.0 percent (463 of 520); white, 96.7 percent (18,664 of 19,285); and other, 91.5 percent (292 of 319).
- Among those examinees of color who eventually passed, between 94 and 97 percent did so after one or two attempts, and 99 percent passed by the third attempt.
- As measured by undergraduate GPA and LSAT scores, students of color entered law school with academic credentials significantly lower than those of white students, but their eventual bar passage rates justified admission practices that look beyond those measures.

I was very happy that the study provided solid data to refute the claims, rumors, and gossip permeating legal education and American politics about affirmative action programs at American law schools, and I consider my work on the bar passage study to be among the most important and rewarding of my legal career.

## · Notes ·

1. *Grutter v. Bollinger*, 539 U.S. 306, 343 (2003).
2. Linda F. Wightman, *LSAC National Longitudinal Bar Passage Study* (Newtown, PA: Law School Admissions Council, 1998), p. viii.
3. Henry Ramsey Jr., "Historical Introduction," in Linda F. Wightman, *LSAC National Longitudinal Bar Passage Study*, (Newtown, PA: Law School Admissions Council, 1998), p. vi.
4. Wightman, *LSAC National Longitudinal Bar Passage Study*, p. 1fn.

IF THERE IS NO STRUGGLE, THERE IS NO PROGRESS. Those who profess to favor freedom, and yet deprecate agitation, are those who want crops without plowing the ground; they want rain without thunder and lightning; they want the ocean without the awful roar of its many waters. This struggle may be a moral one, or it may be a physical one, and it may be both moral and physical, but it must be a struggle. Power concedes nothing without a demand. It never did, and it never will.[1]

—FREDERICK A. DOUGLASS

# 33

# First Free Elections In South Africa

I was honored and privileged to serve as a member of the Howard
University South Africa Observer Delegation that helped monitor
the South African elections of April 26–28, 1994, the first free and
fair democratic elections ever held in South Africa.[2] Our delegation was
in South Africa from April 17 until May 3, 1994. The 14-member How-
ard University delegation also included Ms. Portia Bruner,[3] Mr. Derrick
Cogburn,[4] Dr. Robert "Bob" Cummings,[5] Ms. Adrienne Shahnaaz
Davidson,[6] Mr. Henry Joseph,[7] Dr. Mae King,[8] Mr. Yohance Maqubela,[9]
Mr. Oronde Miller,[10] Ms. Cynthia Ross,[11] Ms. Roslyn Monise Satchel,[12]
Dr. Alvin Thorton,[13] Mr. Anthony Venuto,[14] and Ms. Anita Womack.[15]

Several Howard University faculty and administrative staff members
served on the Committee on South Africa, which planned and provided
important support for the Howard University South Africa Observer
Delegation but did not travel with us to South Africa. In this group
were Dr. Frances Stubbs, then the executive assistant to the vice president for institutional advancement; Dr. Shirley A. Friar, then an associate professor in the Accounting Department; Mr. James A. Fletcher II,
then the vice president for business and fiscal affairs; Dr. Robert R.
Edgar, then a professor in the Department of African Studies; and
Ms. Thelma Austin, then a program officer in the Office of Institutional
Advancement.

According to Dr. Stubbs, Dr. Friar "crunched the numbers, did the
budgets, figured out daily stipends, lodging, meals, etc., for all the participants and was one of the people on the front-end of the logistics."[16]
Vice President Fletcher identified Howard University funds that could
be used to support the delegation. Dr. Stubbs and Mr. Robert Hagans,

then an assistant vice president for business and fiscal affairs as well as a member of the committee, traveled to Nigeria to secure a $25,000 pledge from S. Dike Odogwu, a Nigerian chief. This generous donation was to help finance the delegation's travel to South Africa, and it actually made the project a reality.

Our group traveled from Washington, D.C., to New York's John F. Kennedy (JFK) Airport by bus on Saturday, April 16, 1994. At 6:30 that evening we departed JFK for Johannesburg, South Africa, on South African Airlines Flight 202, with a scheduled arrival at 4:25 p.m. on Sunday, April 17, at the Jan Smuts (now OR Tambo) Airport. We were transported to our living quarters outside Johannesburg by bus.

During a three-day orientation program at Wittswatersrand University ("Witts") in "Jo'berg," we were housed with other observer delegations at the Karos Indaba Hotel (Sartbeespoortdam Road, Wiktoppen) on the outskirts of the city. Each day, all delegation members were transported by bus from the Karos Indaba Hotel to Witts. An Independent Electoral Commission (IEC) had been established to confirm whether the election was free and fair. Most members of the IEC were from South Africa; Ms. Gaye McDougal, an African American, was the sole representative on the IEC from the United States. It was the IEC that had arranged the orientation program for outside election observers from Canada, various European countries, the United States, and elsewhere.

We were informed that the election would commence on Tuesday, April 26, 1994, and would last for three consecutive days. The first day would be a special voting day for people who could not physically go to the polls, such as incarcerated criminal offenders and patients in hospitals. The next two days would be for people who did not have such limitations and were able and free to travel to the polling places. We were also told what our role would and would not be. We were simply to observe and, where appropriate, to report our observations. We were not to give advice or orders to anyone. We were not to assist anyone in voting. If we observed inappropriate conduct by election officials, police officers, or anyone else that would compromise the free and fair character of the election, then we were to report it to the appropriate on-site representative of the IEC.

Each delegation of observers was assigned to a specific electoral area within South Africa. Potential violence during the election was a matter of significant concern. The Inkatha Freedom Party (IFP), after initially declining to take part, had at the last moment registered to participate in the election. But earlier, when IFP had declined to register, Chief Mangosuthu Buthelezi had "threatened that war would result from the election being contested without the participation" of the IFP.[17] Because of political strife between African National Congress (ANC) members and the IFP members, there was a high expectation of violence in Natal Province, particularly within the KwaZulu homeland, which was controlled by the IFP.

There was also concern about possible violence in the Eastern Cape, where the majority of the population was Afrikaner and the National Party was strong. Because the Howard University delegation had mostly student members (several of them were minors[18]) and because the probability of violence in the Western Cape was not high, we were assigned as observers in the Mitchell's Plain area of the Western Cape, which is near Cape Town.

The delegation was housed in Cape Town at the Breakwater Lodge, which was originally a 19th-century prison but had been completely renovated. It is now a hotel owned and operated by the Business School of the University of Cape Town as part of its program in hotel management. Still, the thick walls and design of the structure leave no doubt as to its original purpose. The Breakwater Lodge is in a great location, near the shore and within easy walking distance of Cape Town's beautifully developed Victoria and Albert waterfront, and looks a great deal like the waterfront development of Baltimore, Maryland. I have heard that it was modeled after Baltimore's Inner Harbor development.

You should know and understand that the people of South Africa were not voting for an individual but for a political party, such as the

African National Congress, the Keep It Straight and Simple (KISS) Party, the Federal Party (FP), the Inkatha Freedom Party, or the African Democratic Movement (ADM). The ballot used in the election was particularly impressive. Because many of the voters would be illiterate or would not be able to read English or Afrikaans, the ballot was designed with five separate ways the voters could determine and indicate the party for which they were voting among the 19 parties listed:

1. The name of each party was written on the ballot in English and, in some instances, in a second language (e.g., African National Congress or National Party, or Nasionale Party).

2. The party's initials were printed separately on the ballot (for example, AMCP for African Moderates Congress Party, NP for National Party, and ANC for African National Congress).

3. The party's position on the ballot was another indicator. For example, the 5th position from the top on every ballot (14th, when counting from the bottom) was occupied by the Women's Rights Peace Party. The Africa Muslim Party (AMP) occupied the 8th position from the top (11th position, when counting from the bottom) on every ballot.

4. Each party could be identified by its unique logo and particular colors.

5. There was a picture of the party's leader (for example, a picture of Nelson Mandela for the ANC and a picture of F.W. deKlerk for the National Party).

I was impressed by the courage and commitment of the voters who participated in the election. On the second day of voting, it was raining hard and steadily in the Mitchell's Plain area during the morning hours. And yet for hours before the polls were scheduled to open, orderly lines of people waiting to vote stretched for at least half a mile. These included many who were elderly and some who were infirm. Even

AFRICAN NATIONAL CONGRESS POSTER *from the 1994 South African election campaign.*

when it was announced that the opening of the polls was to be significantly delayed because the ballots would be delivered late, those waiting to vote remained in the lines, and the lines remained orderly.

A great deal of the pre-election publicity focused on the fact that voters would be casting a secret ballot—only the voter would know his or her vote. Certain election officials were designated to assist people who requested help in casting their ballots; the voter might, for example, be blind or illiterate. When a voter requested such assistance, an election observer would usually also be present as the ballot was being cast. This procedure was intended to prevent voter fraud and undue influence by the election official. Bob Cummings reported a poignant experience in this regard to the members of our delegation.

Many of those voting at the polling place where Bob was assigned were workers from various farms in that area of the Western Cape; most had been transported in large groups to the polling place by farmers for whom they worked. Bob said that an elderly black woman went into a voting booth after requesting assistance, and Bob was the election observer in the booth. When he entered, the woman asked for his and the election official's assurance that their conversation could not be overheard, that her vote would be absolutely secret, and that her employer would not know how she had voted.

After being assured several times that her ballot would be secret, she untied a knot in the end of the shawl she was wearing and displayed a piece of paper with a picture on it. "They told me to vote for the bald-head man," she said, "but this is the man I want to vote for." The "bald-head man" was deKlerk. The picture she was showing the election official and Bob was of Nelson Mandela.

I saw a man who carried his child in his arms throughout the voting process, obviously wanting to impress on his son the importance of this event. Adding to the solemnity—and media coverage—at Mitchell's Plain, Bishop Desmond Tutu voted at that polling place.

I have maintained close contact with two of the student members of our delegation, Portia Washington *née* Bruner and Roslyn Satchel, and they have shared personal remembrances of the trip. Portia says it was when she met Dr. Ben Carson, a famous physician from Baltimore, Maryland, during the fuel stop at the Cape Verde Islands on our way to Johannesburg that she suddenly began to appreciate how important this election was. She also came to better accept her status as an American. She had an appreciation of being on the African continent but did not feel at home. I believe the students were deeply shocked at the disunity or absence of unity among black people (including "coloreds") in South Africa. What bothered Portia most were the various color classifications.[19] She saw herself as a black African, but her friend Roslyn would have been classified as colored. We are both American, she said. Portia remembers talking with "colored" South African citizens in the Western Cape who told her that they would never vote for "a criminal," specifically, Nelson Mandela. Roslyn remembers crying often, because she felt so impotent. She says the trip focused her thinking on the need to work against injustice in the United States.

A side observation: The name "coon" applied to an African American in the United States is a pejorative term. The coloreds of the Western Cape each year conduct a parade in Cape Town that is named the Coon Parade. Participants apply minstrel-type face paint to themselves—white faces, red lips, and the like—and march along a lengthy prescribed parade route. The Coon Parade can be compared in character and appearance with the annual Mummers Parade in Philadelphia. I found even the idea of such a parade to be insulting.

Among the highlights of our visit for student members of the Howard delegation had to have been the opportunity to meet with Bishop Desmond Tutu. The students also met with the Rev. Jesse Jackson (accompanied by Howard University Professor Ron Walters and others), who was the official representative of President William Jefferson "Bill" Clinton as an observer of the elections process. After our return to the United States, the student delegation members attended a reception at which President Clinton appeared (I was not present at the reception).

The 1994 South African national election ended apartheid and was a first for many elements of South African politics. It was the first free and fair election in the nation's history, the first election in which all people of South Africa were permitted to participate, the election of the first black president of South Africa, and the election of the first black people to serve in the national legislature. I will always be proud of my participation in that election as a member of the Howard University observer delegation.

· Notes ·

1. Frederick A. Douglass, "West India Emancipation," speech delivered at Canandaigua, New York, on August 4, 1857.
2. Much of the information in this chapter is based on conversations I had over May 15–17 and May 23–24, 2003, in Atlanta, Georgia, with Portia Washington *née* Bruner and with Roslyn Satchel, and on pictures and written material that Portia has from and about the trip. Dr. Frances Stubbs also provided helpful information about those who helped organize and obtain funding for the delegation.
3. A junior in the Howard University School of Communications. She is now Ms. Portia Washington and lives in Atlanta, Georgia.
4. A political science graduate student who planned to do postgraduate work in international affairs and spend time in South Africa.
5. Professor and chairman of the Department of African Studies and head of our Howard University South Africa Observer Delegation. Bob had played a major role in the work of the committee that organized, obtained funding for, and selected members of the delegation.
6. A junior in the Howard University School of Communications.
7. A film instructor in the Howard University School of Communications who planned to do a documentary on the delegation.
8. Professor of political science.
9. A junior in the Howard University Department of Economics. Mr. Maqubela was formerly named Yohance Gregory and is the son of Dick Gregory, the famous comedian and civil rights activist.
10. A junior in the Howard University Department of Education.
11. A third-year Howard law student.
12. A junior in the Howard University School of Communications.
13. Professor of political science.

14. Production assistant for Henry Joseph, a film instructor in the Howard University School of Communications.

15. Staff member of the Howard University Office of Communications (typically called the Public Relations Office at most college campuses).

16. According to a July 22, 2005, e-mail to the author from Dr. Frances Stubbs.

17. Southern Africa Project, "Focus on the Violence in Natal," *South Africa: The Countdown to Elections.* 9 (March 25, 1994): 1.

18. Under 21 years of age.

19. In the United States, African Americans of various shades of skin color are still classified as African American, or black, but in South Africa, under apartheid, people of color were placed into various classifications and had different political rights based on that classification. A significant percentage of the South African population is of Indian and Malay heritage and was classified as Indian and Malay; black South Africans were classified as colored (typically "light skinned") and as "African" (typically "dark skinned"). While classified as "colored" and "African" in South Africa, in the United States all the people in these two categories would have been viewed simply as African American or black.

# Conclusion

The preceding 15 assignments and roles, somewhat arbitrarily chosen, are among the most memorable in my professional life. There are other significant experiences that I could have written about. I also found it exciting, educational, and socially meaningful to serve (1988–1989) as a member of California's Blue Ribbon Commission on Inmate Population Management; as a director (1994–99) of the Fibreboard Asbestos Compensation Trust, which was charged with responsibility for determining settlement policies for a $2.5 billion trust; as a special consultant (1997–98) to Daniel Glickman, secretary of the U.S. Department of Agriculture, concerning elimination of a substantial backlog of civil rights complaints within the department's civil rights division; as a member (1997–2002) of the American Bar Association's (ABA) Ethics 2000 Commission, which was formed in 1997 to review the ABA Model Rules of Professional Conduct, and as a director (2000– present) of the Center for Youth Development Through Law, a fellowship program that provides disadvantaged high school students with academic and life skills classes designed to help them pursue higher education and career goals.

In February and March 2000 I spent a month in Eritrea with Dr. Kebreab Habte Michael, a law professor at the University of Asmara, assessing that nation's judicial needs (e.g., additional judges, law clerks, staff personnel, supplies and equipment, law books, and new courthouses).[1] I have also been privileged to serve as a director (1999– present; chairperson 2008–09) of the Rosenberg Foundation, an independent grant-making organization based in San Francisco that is charged with responsibility for helping to set policy and manage a plus-$670 million charitable trust, with present primary funding priorities in the areas of justice and public safety, immigrant rights, and immigrant integration.

Here I will close. I hope that what I have written about my life illustrates for you the importance of education as a practical and effective means for escaping the shackles of poverty. Even more I hope it will help you appreciate how interrelated are our needs and values as human beings, and the importance of working together and cooperating with and caring for each other. The memorable events I have chosen to discuss are intended to give you a view of the contributions I have sought to make to my profession, community, and society.

Most of all, I hope that what I have written has resulted in a meaningful conversation with my descendants about my life and my hopes for being a positive influence in theirs.

## SUGGESTED READINGS

- Burris, John, with Catherine Whitney. *Blue vs. Black*. New York: St. Martin's Press, 1999.

- Chevigny, Paul. *Police Power: Police Abuses in New York City*. New York: Pantheon Books, 1969.

- Collins, Jim. *Good to Great*. New York: HarperCollins, 2001.

- DuBois, W.E.B. *The Souls of Black Folk*. Unabridged edition. New York: Dodd, Mead, 1961.

- Fisher, Roger, and William Ury. *Getting to Yes*. Boston and New York: Houghton Mifflin, 1981.

- Kluger, Richard. *Simple Justice*. New York: Alfred A. Knopf, 1976.

- Kozol, Jonathan. *Savage Inequalities: Children in America's Schools*. New York: Crown Publishers, 1991.

- Mandela, Nelson. *Long Walk To Freedom, The Autobiography of Nelson Mandela*, Little, Brown and Company, New York, 1994

- Maynard, Robert C., with Dori J. Maynard. *Letters to My Children.* Kansas City, Missouri: Andrews and McMeel, 1995.

- McNeil, Genna Rae. *Groundwork: Charles Hamilton Houston and the Struggle for Civil Rights.* Philadelphia: University of Pennsylvania Press, 1983.

- Mebane, Mary E. *Mary,* The Viking Press, New York, 1981

- Mershon, Sherie, and Steven Schlossman. *Foxholes and Color Lines.* Baltimore and London: Johns Hopkins University Press, 1998.

- Nuland, Sherwin B. *How We Die: Reflections on Life's Final Chapter.* New York: Alfred A. Knopf, 1994.

- Skolnick, Jerome H. *Justice Without Trial, Law Enforcement in Democratic Society,* John Wiley & Sons, Inc., New York, 1967

- Woodward, C. Vann. *The Strange Career of Jim Crow* (Third Revised Edition), Oxford University Press, New York, 1974

· Notes ·

1. Our report was titled *An Assessment of the Eritrean Judicial System— March 2000,* dated Nov. 17, 2000, and submitted to the United Nations Development Program, Asmara, Eritrea, and Ms. Roswitha Newels, Head Governance Unit, United Nations Office of Project Services, on Nov. 18, 2000. The project number was ERI/94/006.

# INDEX

**Boldface** numbers indicate photographs.

Casley, Ann Beth, on Willard Casley,
37–39
Casley, Henrietta Williams, 35
Casley, Mary Frances Brunson (Mickey),
26, 37
Casley, Willard, 35, 37–39
Casley, Willard Leroy Jr. (Pookie), 38
Casley, Willie Alfonso, 38
Caucasians. *see* whites
Cecchi, Gary, 244–246
Center for Youth Development Through
Law, 247, 620
Central High School, Little Rock, AR,
429
Cerny, Susan Dinkelspiel, *Berkeley
Landmarks: An Illustrated Guide to
Berkeley, California's Architectural
Heritage*, 186
chance, universe unlikely to have hap-
pened by, as argument for existence
of God, 283–284
charging deputy duties, District Attorney's
Office, Contra Costa Cty., 205–209
Charlotte School of Law, Infilaw Board of
Advisors, 247
chitt'lin' circuit, 112
Choper, Jesse, 493
Christianity. *see also* religion
history & origins, 277–278, 287–288
religious instruction, 67, 88–90
and slavery, 350, 360, 371–376
Christmas clemency, 501
Chung, Connie, 351–352
church & state, U.S. Constitutional separation, 277
church bombing, Birmingham, AL,
418–419
churches, housing Berkeley senior centers,
468–471
cigarettes, 86–88
citizenship & deportment, 67, 106–107,
112. *see also* conduct, influence of
religion; whites, behavior around

City of St. Jude Hospital, 434
civil rights. *see also* discrimination, racial;
justice & equality, in society; segregation
Afro-American Assoc., UC Berkeley,
191–192, 393–405, **400, 401, 402**
blacks to learn European values before
achieving, 350–351
Holt, Leonard (Len), 156
and Howard U. School of Law, 535,
538, 541, 556–558, 576–577
NAACP Youth Branch, 67, 343–380
Selma, AL (1965), 417–437
spirituals, role in sustaining black
Americans, 375–376
United States, 10, 12, 67, 335–337
voter registration, Alabama, 417–437,
455
Clark, James G. Jr. (Jim), 418, 422, 428,
431
Clark Kerr campus, UC Berkeley, 472
Clarke, John A., 516
class membership & description, Boalt
Hall, UC Berkeley, 172, 182, 184
class size, increase in entering class,
Howard U. School of Law, 562
classroom construction, Howard U.
School of Law, 561–562
Clements-Smith, Joyce, 567
clerk-typist, HR, U.S. Air Force, 133–134,
139, 500
Clinical Law Center, Howard U. School
of Law, 433, 539, 565–567, **579**
Clinton, Pres. William Jefferson (Bill), 617
Cloud, James, 418
The Clubhouse, 67, 89–90, 279
coal heat, 56
Cobb, Ty, 366
Cober, Andre, 242
Cockrel, Kenneth, 211–216, **213**
Coffey, Bert, 218
Cogburn, Derrick, 611
Cohen, Jerome A., 183

# ACKNOWLEDGEMENTS

I am grateful to a number of early readers of this manuscript. Barbara B. Hart (Publications Professionals, Fairfax, Virginia) was my first editor and has my first thanks. Loretta Argrett, Ann Casley, Gilda Feller, William M. Hobbs, George Johnson Jr., Ziyad Motala, Zenira H. Oden, Barbara Powell Smith, Abeni B. Ramsey, Eleanor Mason Ramsey, and Ismail J. Ramsey generously read and commented on portions of various drafts. Roman J. Rezanowicz, Ann Casley, and Jennifer McZier have been willing and able researchers.

At Hardscratch Press, editor Jackie Pels and designer David R. Johnson have turned these chapters into a book I am proud to leave for my children's children's children.

H.R. Jr.

*The Life Story of Henry Ramsey Jr.: An autobiography*

Project coordinator and editor: JACKIE PELS
Book design and production: DAVID R. JOHNSON
Typography and composition: DICKIE MAGIDOFF, Burney, Calif.

Index by ANDREA AVNI, Vashon Island WordWrights, Vashon Island, Wash.
Proofreaders: VICTORIA C. ELLIOTT (manuscript) and LEAH H. PELS (index)
Permissions consultant: LEWIS DOLINSKY, Berkeley, Calif.

Unless otherwise noted, photographs are from the Ramsey family collection.
The back-cover photos (clockwise from upper left) are of the author newly
enlisted in the U.S. Air Force, 1951; as a student at Howard University, 1956;
on a trip to Antarctica in 2006; and as a professor of law at the University of
California, Berkeley, mid-1970s.

Printed and bound at McNaughton & Gunn, Saline, Mich.
Alkaline pH paper (Natural Offset)

Hardscratch Press
2358 Banbury Place
Walnut Creek, CA 94598-2347
Phone/fax 925/935-3422

[HARDSCRATCH]
www.hardscratchpress.com